Theory and Practice in Policy Analysis

Many books instruct readers on how to use the tools of policy analysis. This book is different. Its primary focus is on helping readers to look critically at the strengths, limitations, and the underlying assumptions analysts make when they use standard tools or problem framings. Using examples, many of which involve issues in science and technology, the book exposes readers to some of the critical issues of taste, professional responsibility, ethics, and values that are associated with policy analysis and research. Topics covered include policy problems formulated in terms of utility maximization such as benefit-cost, decision, and multi-attribute analysis, issues in the valuation of intangibles, uncertainty in policy analysis, selected topics in risk analysis and communication, limitations and alternatives to the paradigm of utility maximization, issues in behavioral decision theory, issues related to organizations and multiple agents, and selected topics in policy advice and policy analysis for government.

M. Granger Morgan is the Hamerschlag University Professor of Engineering at Carnegie Mellon University where he was the founding Head of the Department of Engineering and Public Policy. He also holds appointments in Electrical and Computer Engineering and in the H. John Heinz III College of Public Policy and Management. He has worked extensively on policy problems that involve issues in science and technology. Much of his work has focused on the characterization and treatment of uncertainty, especially as applied to environmental issues, that involve energy and electric power, and many aspects of the problem of climate change. Morgan's formal academic training is in applied physics. He is a member of the U.S. National Academy of Sciences and of the American Academy of Arts and Sciences. He is the author of many papers and five books, including two with Cambridge University Press: *Uncertainty: A Guide to Dealing with Uncertainty in Quantitative Risk and Policy Analysis* and *Risk Communication: A Mental Models Approach*.

Theory and Practice in Policy Analysis

Including Applications in Science and Technology

M. GRANGER MORGAN

Carnegie Mellon University

CAMBRIDGE
UNIVERSITY PRESS

University Printing House, Cambridge CB2 8BS, United Kingdom

One Liberty Plaza, 20th Floor, New York, NY 10006, USA

477 Williamstown Road, Port Melbourne, VIC 3207, Australia

4843/24, 2nd Floor, Ansari Road, Daryaganj, Delhi – 110002, India

79 Anson Road, #06-04/06, Singapore 079906

Cambridge University Press is part of the University of Cambridge.

It furthers the University's mission by disseminating knowledge in the pursuit of education, learning, and research at the highest international levels of excellence.

www.cambridge.org
Information on this title: www.cambridge.org/9781107184893
DOI: 10.1017/9781316882665

First published 2017
Printed in the United States of America by Sheridan Books, Inc.

A catalogue record for this publication is available from the British Library.

ISBN 978-1-107-18489-3 Hardback
ISBN 978-1-316-63620-6 Paperback

Contents

Preface

As the title indicates, this is a book about the theory and practice of policy analysis. It is not a book designed to make readers expert in the use of specific analytical tools. That is something that can be gained through more specialized books, courses, and practice. Rather, this is a book designed to help readers to develop their own independent understanding and critical assessment of the strengths, limitations, and underlying assumptions of key policy research and analysis tools and problem framings. Hence my focus is on:

- the underlying assumptions and implications of various analytical techniques;
- the strengths and limitations of these techniques;
- the role and objective of policy-related studies, especially those that involve technology and public policy;
- the behavioral, institutional, organizational, political, and historical contexts in which issues of technology and public policy play out and the role of analysis in the broader process of policy development and implementation.

The book grew out of a course that I have taught for many years as one of the core courses in the Ph.D. program in the Department of Engineering and Public Policy at Carnegie Mellon University. That course has revolved around intensive classroom discussion of a large number of readings. In writing this book I have faced the problem of trying to figure out how to preserve at least some elements of the process of self-discovery and learning that has occurred through those classroom discussions.

Because I believe it is important for readers to be exposed to some of the more important writings in the primary literature, I have used more direct quotations from the literature than are found in many books, and in many sections I have included recommended readings and a number of discussion questions. I have tried to limit my summary of many of the readings, since the point of this book is not to supply Granger Morgan's "CliffsNotes" but rather to help readers to develop and refine their own views. This is of course an explicitly normative process.

While I have not been reluctant to express my views about specific methods or literatures, I have tried to do so in a way that encourages readers to consider, and perhaps disagree with, those views. When I have taught the course at Carnegie Mellon, it has always been most successful when students in the class were prepared to disagree vigorously with some of the views I expressed.

In order to avoid the awkward use of "his or her" in sentences such as "the decision maker must consider his or her preferences," I have sometimes adopted the (grammatically incorrect) phrasing, "the decision maker must consider their preferences." In discussing decision making, I have also sometimes adopted the convention, widely used in the decision analysis literature, of referring to "your" decision.

While the book should be accessible to readers from a wide variety of backgrounds, most of the examples I have used involve issues in science and technology. A significant number are drawn from the domain of climate change because policy analysis in this domain often stretches the boundaries of conventional tools and analysis strategies – and because I have been fortunate to help lead three large NSF-supported centers that have focused on a variety of decision-making issues related to climate change. However, in most cases, the issues being illustrated with these climate examples generalize to a variety of other problems in technology and public policy.

During the first week of the course from which this book has grown, I include a brief discussion of some topics in the philosophy of science. Our faculty in Engineering and Public Policy asked me to add this material when it became apparent that a number of our Ph.D. students could not state a "falsifiable proposition." Because I think it is valuable for practitioners in science, technology, and public policy to have some familiarity with the ideas of philosophers such as Popper and Kuhn, I have included a brief discussion in Appendix 1.

There are many important topics related to science, technology, and public policy that this book does *not* address. Two especially important excluded topics are issues related to technological innovation and R&D policy, and issues that are often termed science and technology studies. A few suggested readings on these topics can be found in Appendix 2 and Appendix 3.

Acknowledgments

Carnegie Mellon and the Department of Engineering and Public Policy (EPP) have provided me, and my graduate students, with a uniquely supportive interdisciplinary environment in which to tackle problems in science, technology, and public policy. Indeed, there is no other more attractive academic setting anywhere in the world in which to address such problems. Many people have been responsible for creating the environment that has made EPP possible. Especially notable among them have been Dick Cyert, Herb Simon, Herb Toor, and Bob Dunlap, all of whom are sadly now gone.

Over the course of more than forty years of teaching, doing research, and making practical applications of the ideas that are the focus of this book, I have benefited from associations with many wonderful graduate students and colleagues. None have been more important to my intellectual development than Baruch Fischhoff, Max Henrion, and Lester Lave. I have also benefited greatly from years of collaboration with Jay Apt, Inês Azevedo, Ann Bostrom, Liz Casman, Hadi Dowlatabadi, Greg Fischer, Keith Florig, David Keith, Sam Morris, Indira Nair, Ed Rubin, and Henry Willis. Jerry Cohon made valuable suggestions on my treatment of utility in Chapter 2 and then kindly co-authored Chapter 6 on multiobjective methods.

Additional thanks for assistance, collaboration, critiques, and ideas go to Ahmed Abdulla, Peter Adams, Myles Allen, Deborah Amaral, V.S. Arunachalam, Cindy Atman, Jesse Ausubel, Barbara Barkovich, João Barros, Anshu Bharadwaj, Wändi Bruine de Bruin, Bill Clark, Aimee Curtright, Mike DeKay, Michael Dworkin, Kerry Emanuel, Scott Farrow, Paul Fischbeck, Lauren Fleishman, Marie-Valentine Florin, David Frame, Erica Fuchs, John Graham, Mike Griffin, Iris Grossmann, Ümit Güvenc, Bob Hahn, Manuel Heitor, Gordon Hester, Alex Hills, Paul Hines, David Hounshell, Harald Ibrekk, Paulina Jaramillo, Karen Jenni, Milind Kandlikar, Doug King, Kelly Klima, David Lincoln, Ragnar Löfstedt, Scott Matthews, Sean McCoy, Tim McDaniels,

Fran McMichael, Alan Meier, Kara Morgan, Anu Narayanan, Bob Nordhaus, Warner North, Claire Palmgren, Paul Parfomak, Elisabeth Paté-Cornell, Dalia Patiño-Echeverri, Jon Peha, Lou Pitelka, Stefan Rahmstorf, Anand Rao, Daniel Read, Ortwin Renn, Kate Ricke, Bill Rish, Emilie Roth, Costa Samaras, Steve Schneider, Vanessa Schweizer, Debra Shenk, Elena Shevliakova, Kyle Siler-Evans, Marvin Sirbu, Paul Slovic, Bill Strauss, Jun Suzuki, Sarosh Talukdar, Parth Vaishnav, Francisco Veloso, David Victor, Charlie Wiecha, Elizabeth Wilson, Xue Lan, Kirsten Zickfeld, and many others. Debbie Scappatura assisted in securing figure approvals and helping with the index. Jenni Miller, a remarkably careful proofreader, provided valuable editorial assistance.

My views on many of the topics discussed in this book have been shaped by the research I have done with my students and colleagues with support from many agencies and foundations. I am especially thankful for many years of generous support from the National Science Foundation. Thanks, too, for support from Carnegie Mellon University, the Doris Duke Charitable Foundation, the Department of Energy, the Electric Power Research Institute, the Exxon Education Foundation, the International Risk Governance Council, the MacArthur Foundation, the R.K. Mellon Foundation, the Sloan Foundation, and others.

My original training was in experimental applied physics. Ken Bowles, Henry Booker, and my father, Millett Morgan, imbued me with a set of perspectives on research and professional activity that have been central to all of my subsequent work.

Much of this book was written during stays in the family home in which I grew up, located on 120 acres of New Hampshire countryside five miles east of Hanover, New Hampshire. Interspersing work on the book with work on the house and the land has been an enjoyable way to pass many days.

In my professional life, I have been fortunate to have 37 years of outstanding support from my assistant and very good friend, Patti Steranchak.

In my private life, my best friend, biggest critic, and the love of my life for over fifty years has been my wife, Betty. To her go my greatest thanks of all.

1

Policy Analysis: An Overview

This chapter addresses five questions:

1. What is public policy?
2. What is policy analysis?
3. What is good policy analysis and what should be its objective?
4. How is doing policy analysis different from doing science?
5. What role does analysis play in making and implementing policy?

The questions are deceptively simple. My objective in writing this book is to help you develop your own answers to these and similar questions. Too many people who work in performing, assessing, and using policy analysis do so with little or no critical reflection on the assumptions that underlie the analysis they are doing or the methods they are using. Just as when people use powerful computer-based statistical packages without really knowing any statistics, performing and using policy analysis without a deep understanding of the ideas and assumptions that underlie the methods being used can often lead to results that are muddled, incomplete, or sometimes even dangerously misleading.

1.1 WHAT IS PUBLIC POLICY?

Bauer (1968) has observed that:

> Various labels are applied to decisions and actions we take, depending in general on the breadth of their implications. If they are trivial and repetitive, and demand little cognition, they may be called routine actions. If they are somewhat more complex, we may refer to them as tactical decisions. For those that have the widest ramifications, and the longest time perspective, and which generally require the most information and contemplation, we tend to reserve the word *policy* ...

> It is true that one man's policy may be another man's tactics inasmuch as the level of organization is critical. The superintendent of a factory may pass along a directive to his foremen, which then becomes policy for them, that is, it forms the general framework of principles within which the foremen make their own "tactical" decisions, which in turn become policy for their subordinates ...

The process of policy formation, especially when it occurs in the public sector, is typically highly complex, involving large numbers of actors, interacting over extended periods of time, and often involving several different levels and parts of government. Today, much policy formation also involves complex technical issues about which different parties hold different views, sometimes because of genuine disagreement about the underlying science and technology, sometimes because the parties hold or represent very different values and interests (Sabatier, 2007).

Much intellectual effort by academics has gone into trying to develop theories of the policy process. Sabatier (2007) has invested significant effort in organizing and publishing summaries of the current state of theorizing about policy processes. He identifies five different theoretical traditions:

1. The *stages heuristic* that consists of agenda setting, policy formulation and legitimation, implementation, and evaluation. This is less a theoretical framework than a simple descriptive ordering.
2. *Institutional rational choice* that explores how participants motivated by material self-interest operate within a set of institutional rules and constraints (see the discussion of Graham Allison's models in Chapter 15).
3. *Multiple-streams* in which a set of different actors and processes operate largely independently until they occasionally come together through "policy windows" (see the discussion of the Kingdon model in Chapter 16).
4. *Punctuated-Equilibrium*, which adopts the perspective that policy processes are "characterized by long periods of incremental change punctuated by brief periods of major policy change ... when opponents manage to fashion new 'policy images' and exploit the multiple policy venues characteristic of the United States."
5. *Advocacy Coalition Framework*, which, as the name implies, "focuses on the interaction of advocacy coalitions – each consisting of actors from a variety of institutions who share a set of policy beliefs – within a political subsystem."

Sabatier (2007) provides a bibliography of the literature on each of these and also summarizes several other theoretical traditions whose formulation and application have largely been limited to the United States. Readers interested in learning more about these different theoretical strands can find details in the individual chapters of Sabatier's edited collection, which summarize and discuss each one.

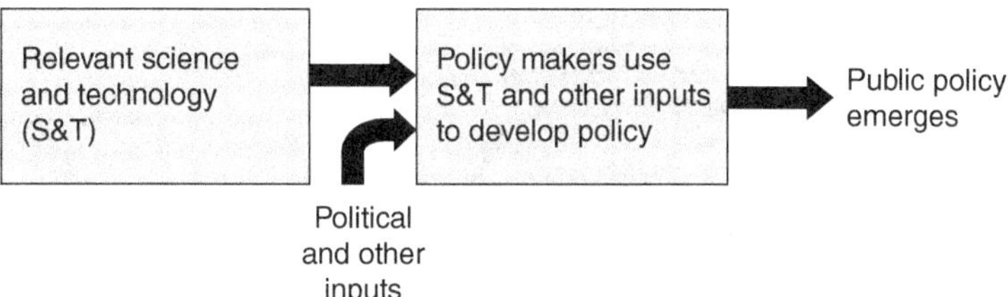

FIGURE 1.1. A classic "technocratic" vision of the way in which scientific and technological knowledge contribute to the development of public policy.

1.2 WHAT IS POLICY ANALYSIS?

While this is a book about the tools and practice of policy analysis, my more specific focus is on policy problems in which scientific and technical details are of central importance – that is, on problems where ignoring those details is likely to lead to dumb or silly answers. For many years, and indeed in some circles even today, the model adopted of how science and technology contributes to the development of public policy has been the "technocratic model" shown in Figure 1.1. In this model, insights from science and technology feed directly into the policy processes where they are combined with political and other considerations to shape public policy.

Beginning in the late 1960s, Arthur Kantrowitz (1913–2008), who was then president and CEO of Avco-Everett Research Lab (AERL), began to promote the idea of science courts (Kantrowitz, 1976, 1995). His idea was to convene a jury of accomplished scientific experts in an area that was of importance to a pending policy decision. This group would take testimony, deliberate, assess the present state of science, and then pass the results along for use by the policy community.[1] Kantrowitz (1976) argued that such a science court should "be concerned solely with questions of scientific fact. It ... [should] leave social value questions – the ultimate policy decisions – to the normal decision-making apparatus of our society, namely, the executive, legislative, and judicial branches of government as well as popular referenda."

I believe that Kantrowitz had two objectives in promoting the use of science courts. He was clearly interested in devising a mechanism to get the best available science into the hands of the policy community. I may be doing him an injustice, but in conversations I had with him in the 1970s it seemed clear to me that his second objective was to protect and isolate the clean and objective

[1] While somewhat different, the IPCC process for assessing climate change, its likely impacts, and strategies that might be used for mitigation and adaptation, has some similarities to the process Kantrowitz envisioned, although some aspects of the work of Working Group III have probably gone further than a strict interpretation of the science court model. Note, too, that while Kantrowitz was only concerned with natural science, the same model could be applied to empirical social science, as Working Group III has also done in a limited way.

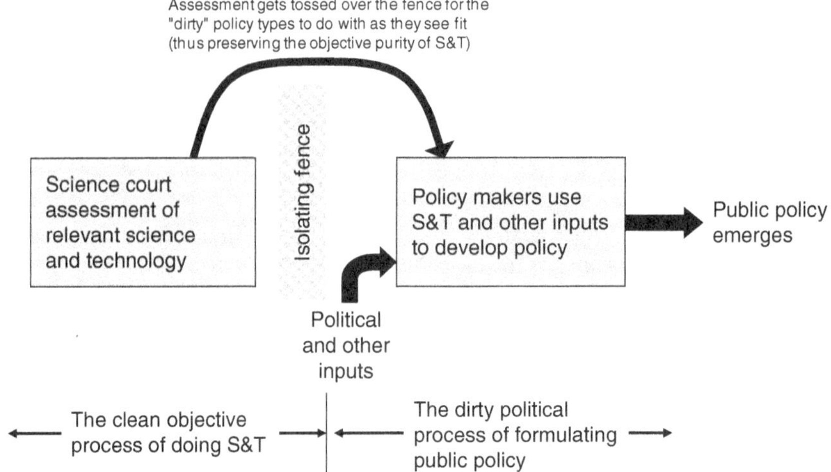

FIGURE 1.2. A "science court" strategy in which the science and technology are assessed by a jury of technical experts in a clean and objective way and then that assessment is tossed over the fence to be used by the "dirty" political policy process. This figure may be an exaggeration of what some of the proponents of science courts had in mind, but it is clear that a motivation of at least some of them was to isolate science from the policy process.

work of science and technology from the "dirty" and inherently political work of policy development and implementation. To the extent that this reading is correct, the model is shown in Figure 1.2.

A key problem with either of these two models is that the raw results that come out of research in science and technology are rarely in a form in which they can be directly applied to the development of public policy. The key role of policy analysis and policy-focused research is to determine the needs of the policy-making process and then frame, interpret, and, as needed, extend available scientific and technological knowledge to place it into a form that is relevant to, and addresses the questions faced by, the policy community.[2] This model is displayed in Figure 1.3.

Most of the players in government policy processes are generalists, often lawyers or liberal arts graduates. The best ones are quick studies, able to master a wide range of new issues. However, analysts who are performing policy

[2] While I often use the phrase "policy analysis" in this book to refer *both* to policy analysis and to policy-focused research, the two concepts are different. In its narrow sense, policy analysis is undertaken in direct support of decision makers who face a specific policy choice. Policy-focused research is a more general concept involving analysis that is informed by, and intended to inform, the present or likely future needs of the policy community. For an elaboration of these ideas, see pp. 16–18 in Morgan and Henrion (1990).

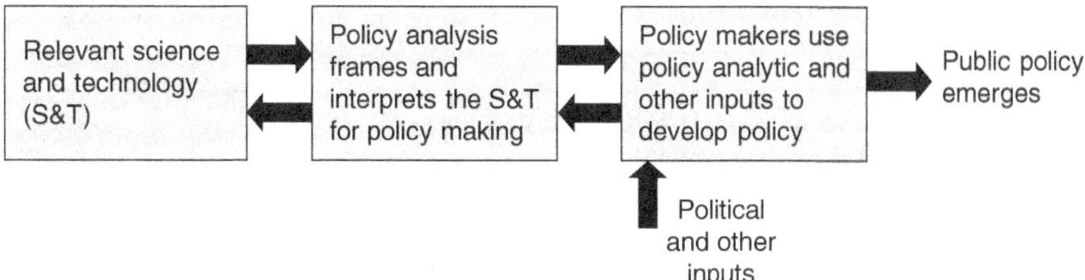

FIGURE 1.3. Policy analysis plays an essential role by framing, interpreting, and, as needed, extending available scientific and technological knowledge to place it into a form that is relevant to, and addresses the questions faced by, the policy community.

analysis on scientifically and technically substantive issues need to have a strong domain expertise.

1.3 WHAT IS GOOD POLICY ANALYSIS AND WHAT SHOULD BE ITS OBJECTIVE?

The word "good" implies a normative (i.e., value) judgment. People commission policy analysis for a variety of reasons, so what is a "good" piece of analysis might be expected to depend on the motivation of those who commission it. Morgan and Henrion (1990) list a variety of motivations that people have for engaging in analysis. While these include "substance-focused" analysis that is designed to develop insight or understanding about a specific or general class of problems, they also include: "position-focused" analysis that is designed to produce results to substantiate and provide support for the preferences and views of a participant in an adversarial setting; "process-focused" motivations that result from institutional or legal mandates that require analysis; and "analyst-focused" motivations related to the professional and personal interests of those performing that analysis.

Given this wide range of motivations, it might be tempting to conclude that producing a general set of attributes of "good" policy analysis is a hopeless task. However, Morgan and Henrion (1990) argue that while:

> people and organizations undertake research and analysis with a wide range of motivations, if it is to serve its purpose, analysis must be able to pass, at least to a minimal extent, as having been undertaken with a substance-focused motivation. For example, for a piece of analysis with a position-focused motivation to be effective, others must be prepared to treat it as substance-focused. If one can readily demonstrate that the inputs for the analysis were artfully chosen to get the desired answer, the effectiveness of the analysis as an adversarial tool is greatly diminished.

Morgan and Henrion (1990) conclude that while one can "identify a wide variety of motivations for commissioning or performing policy research and

TABLE 1.1. *"Ten commandments" of good policy analysis from Morgan and Henrion (1990).*[3]

1.	Do your homework with literature, experts, and users
2.	Let the problem drive the analysis
3.	Make the analysis as simple as possible, but no simpler
4.	Identify all significant assumptions
5.	Be explicit about decision criteria and policy strategies
6.	Be explicit about uncertainties
7.	Perform systematic sensitivity and uncertainty analysis
8.	Iteratively refine the problem statement and the analysis
9.	Document clearly and completely
10.	Expose the work to peer review

analysis ... if it is to be effective all such work must meet some minimal standards as successful substance-focused work." Table 1.1 summarizes the attributes they argue such work should display. An elaboration of each attribute can be found on pp. 36–43 of Morgan and Henrion (1990).

Item 8 in Table 1.1 deserves special notice. Figure 1.4 contrasts the sort of linear approach to policy analysis that is adopted by many, especially inexperienced analysts, with the approach of iteratively refining both the problem statement and the analysis.

I first produced my own answer to the question "What is good policy analysis and what should be its objective?" in an editorial I wrote in the journal *Science* in 1978. I believe it is still a pretty good answer:

Good policy analysis recognizes that physical truth may be poorly or incompletely known. Its objective is to evaluate, order, and structure incomplete knowledge so as to allow decisions to be made with as complete an understanding as possible of the current state of knowledge, its limitations, and its implications. Like good science, good policy analysis does not draw hard conclusions unless they are warranted by unambiguous data or well-founded theoretical insight. Unlike good science, good policy analysis must deal with opinions, preferences, and values, but it does so in ways that are open and explicit and that allow different people, with different opinions and values, to use the same analysis as an aid in making their own decisions. (Morgan, 1978)

[3] In using the phrase "ten commandments" Morgan and Henrion (1990) write: "We know of no analysis, including any of our own, that satisfactorily meets all of these commandments. Some may object that if the commandments are unachievable, they should be abandoned. We disagree. Most Christians consider a life without sin unachievable. Nevertheless they have found it to be a useful guiding objective. The point is to try to get as close to the ideal as possible." Morgan and Henrion argue that the commandments they list should play a similar role.

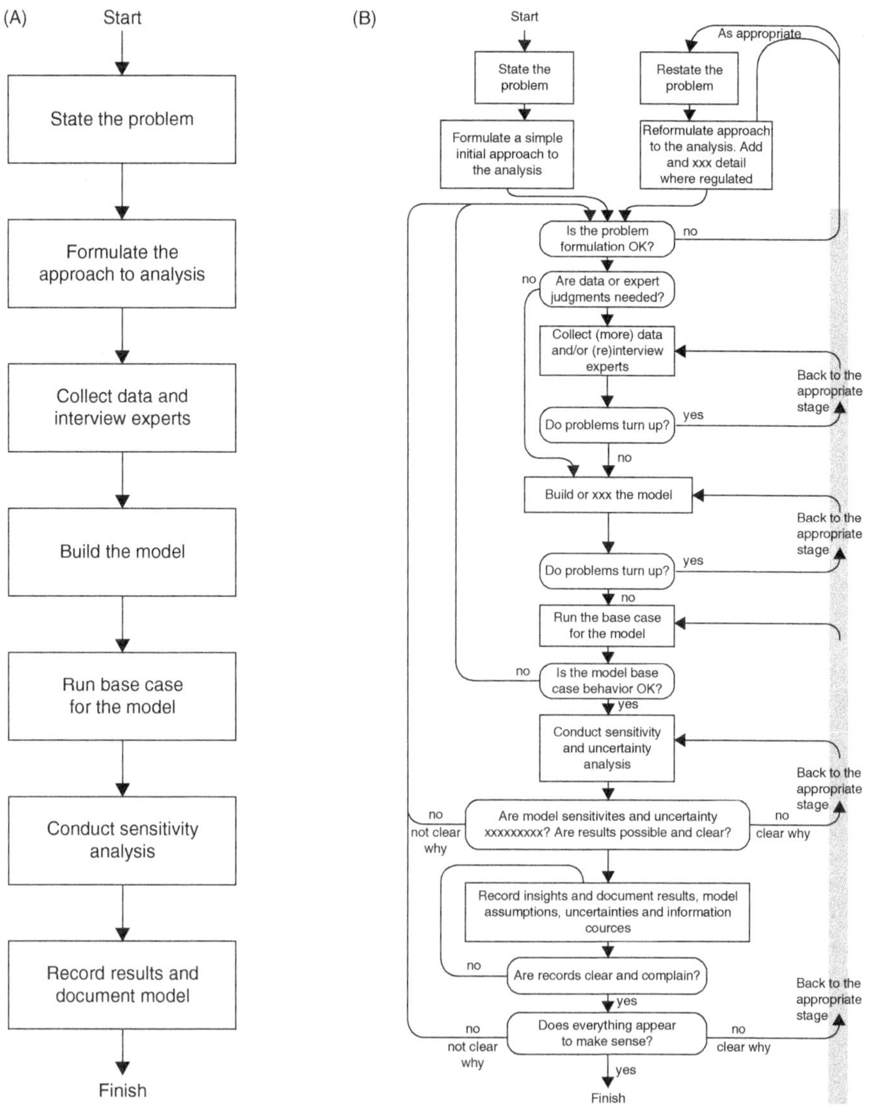

FIGURE 1.4. **A.** Example of the linear approach to analysis adopted by many, especially inexperienced analysts, as contrasted with **B.** the approach of iteratively refining both the problem statement in the analysis that characterizes good policy analysis. Figure modified from Morgan and Henrion (1990).

READING 1.1

Sections 3.3–3.7 (pp. 23–36) of "Chapter 3: An Overview of Quantitative Policy Analysis," in M. Granger Morgan and Max Henrion, *Uncertainty: A Guide to Dealing with Uncertainty in Quantitative Risk and Policy Analysis*, Cambridge University Press, 332pp., 1990.

DISCUSSION QUESTIONS FOR READING 1.1

- Why does James March argue that goal development and choice are *not* independent? In doing policy analysis, when might that matter and when does it probably not matter?
- Table 3.2 in Morgan and Henrion lists a number of different decision criteria for policy analysis for risk management. Are they all equally feasible? Can you describe situations in which one might choose to use: cost effectiveness; approval/compensation; best available technology?
- Are you persuaded by the argument that, whatever the analyst's motivation for performing an analysis, to serve its purpose, policy analysis must be able to pass, at least to some extent, as having been undertaken with a substance-focused motivation? Why or why not?

1.4 HOW IS DOING POLICY ANALYSIS DIFFERENT FROM DOING SCIENCE?

Section 3.2 in Morgan and Henrion (1990) addresses the difference between how policy-focused research and analysis is typically performed and the process of doing science. An updated summary is reproduced in Table 1.2.

We argued that empirical testing was typically far more feasible in many branches of science than it is in the domain of policy. That remains the case, although small-scale policy experiments are sometimes possible. Unfortunately, such experiments are too rarely tried.[4]

Both policy analysis and empirical science should document work with care so that others can understand what assumptions were made and reproduce the results obtained. This is standard practice in science, aided by the fact that in many fields standard laboratory and analytic procedures have been adopted that can be referenced in a way that all readers in that field can

[4] The fact that the United States has 50 states offers an opportunity to use the policy initiatives of one or a few states as a "laboratory" to assess new policy ideas. Of course, that requires that these "experiments" be well instrumented, which too rarely happens. It is also possible to simulate or "red team" policies before they are put into practice – again a strategy that is too rarely adopted. For example, if some of the policies that were put into place in the restructuring of the U.S. electric power system had been subjected to such assessments, a number of problems might have been anticipated and avoided.

TABLE 1.2. *A comparison of the process of doing science with the process of doing policy analysis as made by Morgan and Henrion c.1990 and updated 25 years later.*

Features of science	Common practice in policy analysis *c.*1990	Common practice in policy analysis *c.*2016
Empirical testing	Testing often impractical	Testing often impractical
Full documentation	Documentation typically inadequate	Documentation slightly better but still often inadequate
Reporting of uncertainty	Uncertainty usually incomplete or missing	Uncertainty frequently addressed but with uneven quality
Peer review	Review not standard and in some cases arduous	Review much more common especially in some agencies like EPA and in peer-review publications
Open debate	Debate hindered by above problems	Debate still hindered by some of the above problems

understand what was done. While progress has been made in recent decades, adequate documentation is still insufficiently practiced in policy analysis.

Another standard practice in science is the routine reporting of uncertainty in all results. To quote Carl Sagan (1995), "Every time a scientific paper presents a bit of data, it's accompanied by an error bar – a quiet but instant reminder that no knowledge is complete or perfect." At the time Morgan and Henrion was published, the treatment of uncertainty in policy analysis was relatively rare. Today, in part because of that book as well as the work of many others, most analyses, especially for agencies such as EPA, include a discussion and treatment of uncertainty, although quality remains uneven.

Peer review is the norm in science, but is still too rarely practiced in policy analysis. However, here too, in recent decades, the emergence of outlets for peer-reviewed publication of policy-focused research has begun to change the situation.[5]

Debate is the norm in science. It occurs in policy analysis as well, but to the extent that the four previous problems remain unresolved, informed debate can be difficult.

In 1972, the nuclear physicist Alvin Weinberg (1915–2006), who had long served as director of Oak Ridge National Laboratory, addressed the role

[5] One of the first leading journals to introduce a separate peer-reviewed section for policy analysis was *Environmental Science and Technology*, under the editorial leadership William H. Glaze. Mitchell J. Small of Carnegie Mellon served as the first area editor, and was instrumental in establishing the high standards that continue to characterize that section.

of science in the public policy process in a thoughtful essay titled "Science and Trans-Science" (Weinberg, 1972). Weinberg observed that, with increasing frequency, questions in public policy "hang on the answers to questions which can be asked of science and yet *can not be answered by science.*" He proposed the term "trans-scientific" for these questions since "though they are epistemologically speaking, questions of fact and can be stated in the language of science, they are unanswerable by science; they transcend science."

As examples of such questions, Weinberg identifies the biological effects of exposure to very low levels of ionizing radiation and the probability that an extremely improbable event will occur, such as a catastrophic accident in a new reactor design. The first is trans-scientific because one simply cannot design a large enough case-control experiment to obtain meaningful answers; the second is trans-scientific because, even employing all the modern tools of failure mode and effect analysis (see Chapter 10), there is still no way to be confident that one has captured all accident paths, or assigned appropriate probabilities to the various event trees.

Weinberg noted too that many activities in engineering, especially in fields that are developing rapidly, have the attributes of trans-science:

> The engineer works against rigid time schedules and with a well-defined budget. He can not afford the luxury of examining every question to the degree to which scientific rigor would demand. Indeed "engineering judgment" connotes this ability, as well as necessity, to come to good decisions with whatever scientific data are at hand ...
>
> Uncertainty is in a sense inherent in engineering: unless one is willing to build a full-scale prototype, and test it under the precise conditions which will be encountered in practice, there is always the uncertainty of extrapolating to new and untried circumstances.

Clearly, trans-scientific questions are not limited to natural science and engineering. While Weinberg's treatment displays the perspective of a twentieth-century physicist when he discusses the social sciences,[6] he provides several relevant examples.

The one topic on which I think Weinberg was misguided is his inclusion of questions about establishing priorities in science and about criteria for scientific choice. Since such questions are inherently normative (i.e., requiring value judgments), unlike his other examples, they do not have a unique, value-free answer. If by "questions that can be posed to science" one means questions that could be answered experimentally if one had a large enough sample size, an appropriate observing platform, and a long enough observing time, I would not call this final set of questions trans-scientific.

[6] While Weinberg was much better in this respect than most of his generation, and some physicists have become much more broad-minded, it is still the case that too many physicists believe there is nothing in the social sciences that a good physicist couldn't invent during a weekend cocktail party. For those of you who (like me) have backgrounds in physics, I hope that this book, especially Part III, will disabuse you of this view.

READING 1.2

Alvin M. Weinberg, "Science and Trans-Science," *Minerva*, pp. 209–222, April 1972.

EXERCISE 1.1

Excluding the category of normative questions such as establishing priorities in science, write down three questions that are clearly trans-scientific and three that are clearly scientific. Explain why you classify each in the way that you do.

1.5 WHAT ROLE DOES ANALYSIS PLAY IN MAKING AND IMPLEMENTING POLICY?

For those who are new to thinking about how policy is developed and implemented, it is easy to exaggerate the role that is played by, or even *can* be played by, rational objective analysis. Almost all of the conventional tools of policy analysis are based on the assumption that people and organizations know what they want and that the purpose of analysis is to show them how to meet their objectives. Occasionally, especially in simpler private decision settings, that may actually be true, but usually the situation is far more complex. Policy analysis, and policy-focused research, *can* make a difference in the way people frame and think about an issue, and in how they choose to act, but the process by which analysis influences policy is often rather incremental and convoluted.

Frequently people and organizations are not very clear about what they want. In all but the most routine situations they could use help in structuring and thinking about what they care about. Even when they think they know, they often find that determining their preferences is a process of iterating and learning. Further, different parties may have different preferences and objectives, and may prefer a particular policy for different reasons.

The process of making decisions is cognitively challenging. This is especially true when there is uncertainty about the future, which of course is virtually always the case. Our brains do not come hard-wired with reliable statistical processors. While we don't realize we are doing it, when we make such decisions in the face of uncertainty we generally rely on a set of simplifying "cognitive heuristics," or mental rules of thumb. Sometimes these subconscious mental short cuts serve us well enough. However, in many cases they can lead us to conclusions that are different from those we would reach if we were fully "rational decision makers" who made choices so as to maximize some well-defined desired outcome.

In short, the reality of how people make decisions can be quite different from the assumptions that underlie most of the analytical tools of policy analysis. Simply applying those tools and telling a decision maker what actions they should take rarely leads them to declare, "Oh yes, now I see, thanks for straightening me out!"

While some decisions are actually discretely "made" by individuals, in the policy domain, and in organizations, they are often not so much "made" as they are the emergent consequence of a set of complex processes within and among different participants. Individuals in organizations, and stakeholders, play a variety of different roles and exert varying degrees of influence on the resulting "decision."

Developing and promulgating policy is typically only part of the story. Implementing policy, especially in public domains or in all but the smallest or most hierarchical organizations, involves yet another wide set of behavioral, social, legal, and other interactions and challenges. Nor is policy formulated and implemented in a vacuum. Rather the history and evolution of the settings in which it evolves and is adopted are critically important to shaping the choices that are made and how they play out.

Analysis *does* matter, but only rarely in the form that a specific piece of serious analysis leads in a simple linear way to the adoption of some new policy. More often analysis is just one part of a far more complex and iterative process. Frequently, it takes years of policy-focused research and analysis before an idea becomes widely shared and conditions develop in a way that make its adoption possible.

As I explained in the Preface, this book has grown out of a graduate core course I have long taught to Ph.D. students in the Department of Engineering and Public Policy at Carnegie Mellon. These students have excellent technical backgrounds, and take very comfortably to the more formal analytical aspects of policy analysis. In helping them to develop a sophisticated understanding of policy making, and the role of analysis in the policy process, I have found it best to start with those formal tools and explore their assumptions and the limitations. Then I have gradually widened the discussion to include all the more messy elements I've outlined in the paragraphs above.

A senior colleague, who is very accomplished in the art of policy analysis, has suggested that I should have started this book with the material in Part IV on the processes of policy formulation and the historical and institutional settings in which policy is developed and implemented, then I should have moved to Part III on how individuals and organizations *actually* make decisions, before finally taking a critical look at the tools of formal analysis. Indeed, some readers may wish to read the book in that order.

However, if you are new to the domain of policy-focused research and analysis, or if you are most familiar and comfortable with the formal analytical tools of the field, my advice is to work through the material in the order I have laid it out. Even before moving on to the messier reality of the policy process in the later sections, readers may be surprised by the implicit assumptions and associated limitations of widely used tools that many of us took for granted when we first learned about them and began to put them to use.

REFERENCES

Bauer, R.A. (1968). "Chapter 1: The Study of Policy Formation: An Introduction," in R.A. Bauer and K.J. Gergen (eds.), *The Study of Policy Formation*, The Free Press, pp. 1–26.
Kantrowitz, A. (1976). "The Science Court Experiment," *Jurimetrics Journal*, *17*, pp. 332–341.
(1995). "The Separation of Facts and Values," *Risk*, 6, pp. 105–110.
Morgan, M.G. (1978). "Bad Science and Good Policy Analysis," *Science*, *201*, p. 971.
Morgan, M.G. and M. Henrion with M. Small (1990). *Uncertainty: A Guide to Dealing with Uncertainty in Quantitative Risk and Policy Analysis*, Cambridge University Press, 332pp.
Sabatier, P.A. (ed.) (2007). *Theories of the Policy Process*, Westview Press, 344pp.
Sagan, C. (1995). *The Demon-Haunted World: Science as a Candle in the Dark*, Random House, 457pp.
Weinberg, A.M. (1972). "Science and Trans-Science," *Minerva*, April, pp. 209–222.

PART I

MAKING DECISIONS THAT MAXIMIZE UTILITY

Many argue that the way people *should* make decisions – either for themselves or when formulating public policy – is to maximize (expected) utility.

Indeed, most of the standard tools used in quantitative policy analysis are based on the idea of maximizing utility for some decision maker who is a rational actor. Chapter 2 explores the question "What is this thing called utility that folks say we should maximize?" The answer turns out to be rather more complicated than one might think. Then, having reflected in Chapter 2 on what it is that should be maximized, Chapters 3 and 4 introduce and discuss a number of the strengths and limitations of two widely used analytical tools: benefit–cost analysis and decision analysis.

These and similar methods work best when it is possible to quantify the value of outcomes of interest. However, not all the things that matter in decision making are easily quantified. Chapter 5 discusses and critiques a number of the standard ways in which analysts assess values for intangible outcomes such as lives lost or saved, or impacts on the health of ecosystems.

Multi-attribute utility functions provide a strategy to avoid converting all values into some single metric such as money. Methods in multi-attribute utility theory and multi-criteria decision making are discussed in Chapter 6.

Finally, many decisions involve outcomes that occur at different moments in time, in different locations, and in and across different societies and cultures. Chapter 7 first discusses well-established and widely accepted methods to address such issues when the values of outcomes, and the times across which they occur, are not enormous, and when the people involved share a similar culture and similar values. Things get far more complicated when these conditions do not apply, as, for example, in the case of making decisions today to address likely future climate change.

2

Preferences and the Idea of Utility

The objective of a great deal of policy analysis is to "maximize utility." Before spending a lot of time studying various methods for doing that, it is important first to step back and ask, what is utility, and is maximizing it a sensible objective for policy analysis? Unlike mass or charge, which are inherent properties of physical objects, utility is *not* an inherent property of a good, service, or system state. Rather, it describes a relation between any of these things and some person or group of like-minded people. Their utility provides an indication of their choice preference, desire, or valuation.

In chapter 3 of his classic, *The Wealth of Nations*, Adam Smith (1776) wrote:

> The word VALUE, it is observed, has two different meanings, and sometimes expresses the utility of some particular object, and sometimes the power of purchasing other goods which the position of that object conveys. The one may be called "value in use;" the other "value in exchange." The things that have the greatest value in use have frequently little or no value in exchange; and on the contrary, those which have the greatest value in exchange have frequently little or no value in use. Nothing is more useful than water; but it will purchase scarce anything; scarce anything can be had in exchange for it. A diamond, on the contrary, has scarce any value in use; but a very great quantity of other goods may frequently be had in exchange for it.[1]

Kahneman et al. (1997) draw another distinction that is more relevant for our needs. They write:

> The concept of utility has carried two quite different meanings in its long history. As Bentham ... used it, utility refers to pleasure and pain ... This usage was retained in the economic writings of the 19th-century, but it was gradually replaced by a different interpretation ... in current economics and in decision theory the utility of outcomes

[1] While much quoted, George Stigler (1950a) complains that "the fame of this passage rivals its ambiguity" because Smith had no concept of marginal utility and hence "no basis ... on which he could compare such heterogeneous quantities."

FIGURE 2.1. **A.** Adam Smith (1723–1790), who first drew the distinction between "value in use" and "value in exchange." **B.** Jeremy Bentham (1748–1832), who is generally credited as the "father" of modern utilitarian philosophy. **C.** John Stuart Mill (1806–1873), who elaborated Bentham's views, differentiating various qualities of pleasure. **D.** Jules Dupuit (1804–1866), a French engineer and economist who was the first to articulate the idea of marginal utility. Figures are from Wikipedia.

> and attributes refers to their weight in decisions: utility is inferred from observed choices and is in turn used to explain these choices. To distinguish the two notions, we shall refer to Bentham's concept as *experienced utility* and to the modern usage as *decision utility*. With few exceptions ... experienced utility is essentially ignored in modern economic discourse.

In Chapter 5 we will explore yet other meanings of the word "value," including aesthetic and other judgments as articulated by Sagoff (2004).

2.1 HISTORICAL DEVELOPMENT OF THE IDEA OF UTILITY

The "utilitarian" philosophical perspective has a long history. The first recorded instances of "hedonic" philosophical theories date to Aristippus in the fifth century BPE and Epicurus in the fourth century BPE.[2]

Modern Western ideas about utility began to enter the thinking of philosophers in Britain beginning in the 1600s. In his book *An Introduction to the Principles of Morals and Legislation,* Jeremy Bentham (1780) defined utility as "that property in an object whereby it tends to produce pleasure, good or happiness, or to prevent the happening of mischief, pain, evil or unhappiness to the party whose interest is concerned."

Bentham argued that legislation should promote the "greatest good for the greatest number." He believed that each person cares only about increasing their own pleasure and decreasing their pain. He also suggested that pleasure can be exactly measured via a hedonic calculus, in which Utility was defined as the net value of the sum of all pleasure minus the sum of all pain.[3]

[2] Hedonic *adj.* characterizing or pertaining to pleasure.

[3] Ackerman (1997a) notes that Utilitarianism was "inconsistent with other ... [nineteenth-century] expressions of individualism and equality. Both the Declaration of Independence of

Bentham's views were subsequently elaborated by John Stuart Mill (1806–1873) who, among other things, differentiated various qualities of pleasure, identifying some as intrinsically more preferable (i.e., morally superior) to others. While Mill was concerned with the ethical dimensions of economic choices, he argued that many acts do not constitute moral choices. Acts should be classified as morally right or wrong only if their consequences are of such significance that a person would wish to see the agent compelled to act in the preferred manner.

While Bentham and Mill's philosophical views have been modified by subsequent utilitarian philosophers, and while the basic premise of utilitarians has been rejected by many later philosophers, they had some very tangible impacts on their own society in the form of reforms in courts of law, which began to do a better job of promoting the good of all.

The Utilitarian perspective stands in contrast to:

- Philosophical traditions based on "natural rights."
- Egoism that argues for individuals to pursue their own self-interest even at the expense of others.
- Any theory that views some acts as right or wrong independent of consequences (some forms of utilitarianism do advance general rules, e.g., about lying).
- Theories that make rightness or wrongness dependent on the motivations of actors.

2.2 UTILITY IN MODERN MICROECONOMICS

As microeconomics was developed, the general concept of utility began to take on a more specialized meaning. It was used to describe individual preferences and explain how they are aggregated into a market demand curve, which, along with a supply curve, sets the prices of goods and services in a competitive economy.

Original attempts by economists, such as Adam Smith and David Ricardo, to develop price theory focused on costs. As elaborated in Section 3.1, the French engineer Jules Dupuit appears to have been the first to systematically articulate the idea of marginal utility.[4] Stigler (1950a) notes that "he distinguishes total and marginal utility with great clarity" and discovered "une espèce de bénéfice" that we now call consumer's surplus.

the American Revolution and the Declaration of the Rights of Man of the French Revolution received a contemptuous dismissal from Bentham since both documents spoke of natural rights, not just happiness."

[4] For details on Dupuit's development of the idea of consumer surplus, see Section 3.1. For an account of how similar ideas were being explored by mathematicians more than a century earlier, see Szpiro (2013).

Analysis of demand was made possible by the work of the German economist H.H. Gossen (1810–1858), who, in 1854, formulated three statements that are now often termed Gossen's laws.[5] These are:

1. The utility to a person of an additional unit of a given good (or service) is inversely proportional to the number of units a person already has (this concept is now termed the law of diminishing marginal utility). See Figure 2.2.
2. When goods have multiple uses, for maximum utility a person must equalize the marginal utility of the good in all its possible uses.
3. A good has value only when the demand for it exceeds supply.

Figure 2.3 shows a typical indifference curve between two substitutable goods A and B. In the figure, they are not perfect substitutes because when consumption of A is cut in half, because of decreasing marginal utility it takes a bit more than double the consumption of B for this consumer to remain indifferent between the two options (i.e., maintain the same level of utility). Figure 2.4 shows examples of perfect substitutes and perfect complements for several different levels of utility.

If these goods are available for sale, then based on their prices we can add a "budget line" that reflects the consumer's available resources for purchase of A and B. This is shown in Figure 2.5. The point at which this line is tangent to an indifference curve yields the combination (A1,B1) that is optimal for this consumer. If the price of Good B falls, then the consumer could afford to purchase more of it, so the budget line rotates to the right as shown in Figure 2.6.

From here it is relatively straightforward to complete the standard microeconomic derivation of the demand curve for Good B. In Figure 2.7, we replace Good A on the vertical axis with M, the bundle of all other possible consumption. Then, if we vary the price of B, we can extract the amount consumed at each value. The resulting family of intercepts with the indifference curves can then be plotted to yield the demand curve for Good B.

Ackerman (1997b) suggests that there have been two crucial episodes in the evolution of neoclassical economic theory:

> First, the marginalist revolution ... introduced the assumption that consumers seek to maximize utility, just as firms seek to maximize profits ... [Second], the ordinalist revolution of the 1930s, declared that it was neither necessary nor possible to make interpersonal comparisons of utility, nor even to assign cardinal numbers to utility. All that was needed for economic theory was an ordinal ranking expressing each consumer's preferences.[6]

[5] Gossen's contributions were largely overlooked by later generations until they were reintroduced by economist Jevons in 1878. Stigler (1950a) writes "Heinrich Gossen is one of the most tragic figures in the history of economics. He was a profound, original and untrained thinker who hid his thoughts behind painfully complex exercises ... He displayed every trait of a crank ... [except that] history has so far believed he was right."

[6] As elaborated in Section 2.4, an ordinal scale simply places things in order (e.g., from most to least preferred) without saying anything quantitative about the value attached to the things being ordered. In contrast, a cardinal scale not only assigns an order but also provides a quantitative indication of the relative or absolute magnitude of that order.

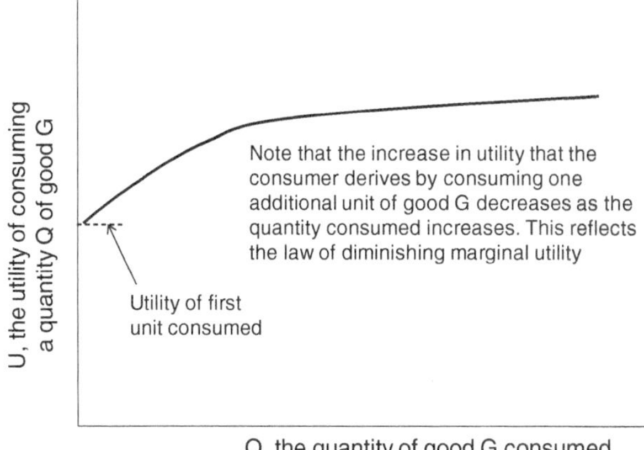

FIGURE 2.2. Illustration of the change in utility U derived by a consumer who consumes various quantities of a good G. Note that as more of good G is consumed, the amount of additional utility (i.e., the marginal change) decreases. This reflects Gossen's first law, now termed the law of diminishing marginal utility.

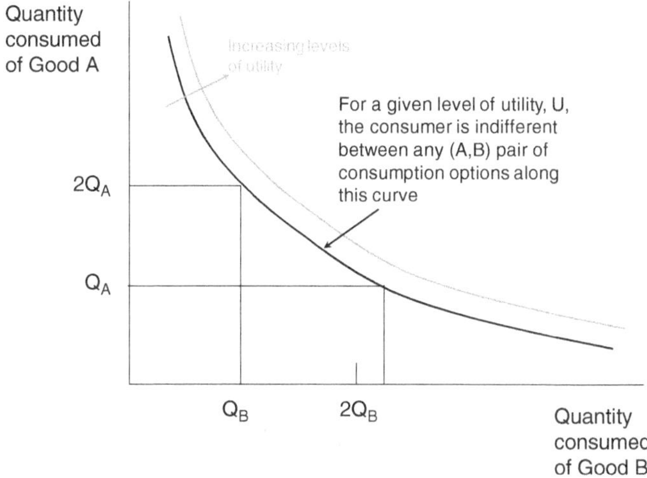

FIGURE 2.3. The dark line shows a typical indifference curve between two imperfectly substitutable goods A and B. The consumer derives the same amount of utility from (i.e., is equally satisfied with) any (A,B) pair of consumption options that lie along the curve. Because the two goods are not perfect substitutions, when halving the consumption of Good A (i.e., moving from amount $2Q_A$ to Q_A) the consumer requires more than a doubling of consumption in Good B. A second indifference curve, shown by the light gray curve, achieves a higher utility.

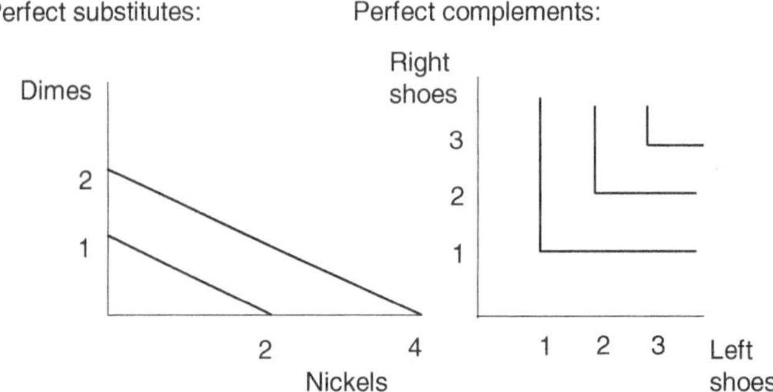

FIGURE 2.4. Most people are prepared to accept 2 nickels in place of 1 dime or 4 nickels in place of 2 dimes. Thus, at least in small quantities (before weight becomes an issue), nickels and dimes are perfect substitutes. In contrast, left and right shoes are perfect complements.

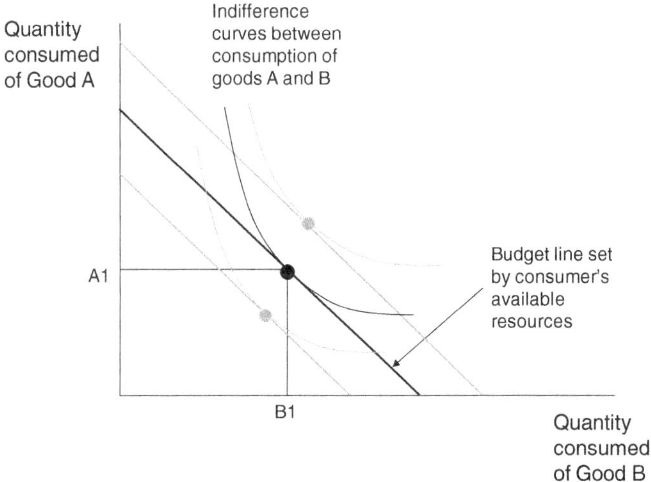

FIGURE 2.5. For a rational consumer who wants to maximize their utility, the amount of A and B purchased is determined by finding the point at which their budget line falls tangent to one of their indifference curves (black dot) resulting in the consumption bundle (A1,B1). If their budget increases or decreases, the budget line moves up or down (gray curves), resulting in an increase or decrease in the consumption bundle (gray dots).

The history of how the concept of marginal utility entered the mainstream of economics is very complex. Blaug (1985) writes, "marginal utility was independently discovered over and over again in different countries between 1834 and 1874." While arguing that it is unclear how the concept of marginal utility came suddenly to be widely adopted by neoclassical economists after it had been repeatedly discovered, and ignored, Ackerman (1997a) notes that:

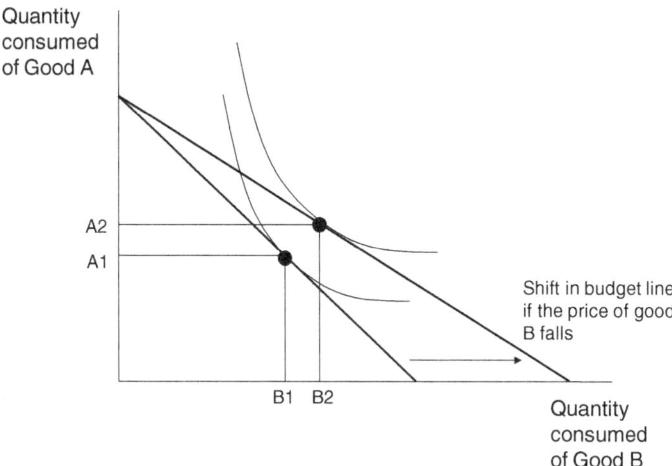

FIGURE 2.6. If the price of Good B falls, the budget line rotates to the right, and the consumption bundle moves from (A1,B1) to (A2,B2).

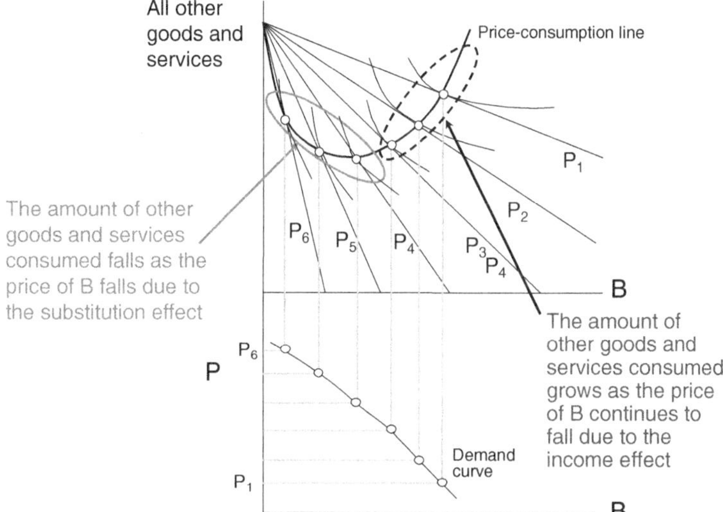

FIGURE 2.7. Derivation of the demand curve for Good B. In the upper figure, the vertical axis is the quantity of all other goods and services. As the price of B falls, in this example the quantity of all other goods and services also falls due to the substitution of cheaper B for other consumption. As the price of B continues to fall, the marginal utility of more B falls and enough income is freed up so that, with these additional resources, the consumer begins to purchase other goods and services. The lower figure displays how the demand curve for Good B can be derived.

By the 1880s the neoclassicals had come to dominate British economics; their descendants continue to define economic theory today. The key to the new approach was the notion of declining marginal utility. This explained Adam Smith's famous paradox of water and diamonds: water is essential for life, yet its price is little or nothing compared to inessential but expensive diamonds. The explanation was that, despite the vastly greater total utility of water, so much of it is consumed that the last unit has little marginal utility. Diamonds have little utility in total, but so few are purchased that an additional one still has substantial value at the margin.

These ideas of marginal utility and the indifference curve remain the basis for constructing each consumer's demand curve in modern microeconomics. The basic formulation is hedonic, that is, it is based on each individual satisfying their own wants and needs. All major results are derived by assuming that people only care about their own consumption and that their individual utility does not depend on that of anyone else. Interpreted narrowly, this means that in developing an individual's utility function, issues such as equity do not matter. Clearly in most cases, especially in public policy, that does not reflect reality.

SUGGESTED RESOURCES TO LEARN MORE ABOUT THE HISTORICAL EVOLUTION OF ECONOMIC THOUGHT ON UTILITY AND WELFARE

For a concise historical summary and critique, see:

- Frank Ackerman, "Utility and Welfare I: The History of Economic Thought," pp. 49–57 and "Utility and Welfare II: Modern Economic Alternatives," pp. 81–92 in Frank Ackerman, David Kiron, Neva R. Goodwin, Jonathan M. Harris, and Kevin Gallagher (eds.), *Human Well-being and Economic Goals*, Island Press, 1997.

For a detailed history of the development of utility theory through the eyes of contemporary economics, see:

- George J. Stigler, "The Development of Utility Theory I," *Journal of Political Economy*, *58*(4), pp. 307–327 and "The Development of Utility Theory II," *Journal of Political Economy*, *58*(5), pp. 373–396.

2.3 IS UTILITY THE SAME THING AS HAPPINESS?

When I took introductory undergraduate economics, the instructor went on and on about consumers making choices to achieve "satisfaction." As Nettle (2005) has noted, the fact that (economists have asserted that) there is no "practical way of measuring happiness or utility meant that, over time, economists took the utility of an outcome to mean the propensity of people to choose it." However, he argues that just because someone chooses a car over a boat does not necessarily mean that they derive more pleasure from the car. They may simply require a car to get to work, independent of whether they find it pleasurable to use. Thus, Nettle notes, "the greater utility of cars cannot explain why people choose them, since the greater utility of cars is defined as the propensity of people to choose them. The concept is therefore merely a device for predicting people's behavior when allocating scarce resources." In much the same vein, Frey and Stutzer (2002) note that:

> The classical economists were convinced that utility has content that can be measured. The well-being of persons was seen to consist of subjective happiness. The new welfare economics – which was new in the 1930s – changed this view in a revolutionary way: Utility was deprived of all content and was reduced to a preference index reflecting revealed behavior. There was no way [it was claimed] to scientifically measure cardinal utility. Moreover, ordinal utility suffices to derive the relevant theorems of economic theory.[7]

In much the same spirit, Ackerman (1997a) has observed that "Those who succeed in penetrating the mathematical armor cannot fail to notice the narrowness at the heart of modern economics. Contemporary theory takes for granted a one-dimensional understanding of human goals, restricted to the maximization of satisfaction of existing, unchanging desires for ever more private consumption." Until recently, psychologists devoted far more attention to the determinants of human unhappiness than to human well-being. Thanks in large part to the work of psychologist Ed Diener, that situation has changed and there is now a considerable amount of empirical literature on well-being and happiness (see, for example, Strack et al., 1991 and Eid and Larson, 2008). Eid and Larson (2008) summarize: "what turns out to be the best predictor of global subjective well-being, in terms of affective experience, is the frequency of positive to negative states in a person's life over time."

Nettle (2005) argues that the idea of "happiness" can be classified into at least three different "levels" (Figure 2.8).[8] He argues that "the most immediate and direct sense of happiness involves an emotion or feeling." How people answer general questions about their overall happiness may be influenced by whether the questions are framed so as to bring to mind a consideration of the respondent's "level one" state of happiness. For example, Kahneman (1999) describes two studies with German students. In the first, respondents received two questions:

[7] The concepts of ordinal (i.e., only ranked with no strength of preference) and cardinal utility (i.e., with some quantitative strength of preference) are discussed below in Section 2.4.

[8] A report by the NRC (2013) makes a slightly different distinction between *experienced well-being*, which is defined as people's emotional states (arguing that "The term 'hedonic' is typically used to denote the narrower, emotional component of" experienced well-being); *evaluative well-being*, which is defined as judgments about how satisfying one's life is; and *eudaimonic well-being*, which "refers to a person's perceptions of meaningfulness, sense of purpose, and the value of his or her life." The NRC (2013) report is primarily concerned with the measurement of experienced well-being.

How happy are you these days?

And then:

How many dates did you have last month?

He reports that virtually no correlation was found between the two answers. However, when the order of the two questions was reversed, "the correlation between the number of dates and reported happiness was about as high as correlations between psychological measures can get."

Nettle (2005) argues, "when people say they are happy with their lives, they do not usually mean they are literally joyful, or experiencing pleasure, all the time." Rather, with the exception of framing effects of the sort just mentioned, he argues that people generally understand and answer in terms of what he has called "level two" happiness. He argues that it was this level of happiness that Bentham had in mind when he talked about the greatest happiness for the greatest number.

Finally, Nettle (2005) notes that:

there are yet broader senses of happiness. Aristotle's ideal of the good life, *eudaimonia*, is sometimes translated as "happiness." However, what is meant by *eudaimonia* is a life in which the person flourishes, or fulfills their true potential. Though such a life *could* include many positive emotional experiences [it need not] ... Note that "level three" happiness is not an emotional state. There is no single thing that it feels like to achieve *eudaimonia*, since everyone's potential is different.

In what follows, we will explore what is involved in increasing "level two" happiness.

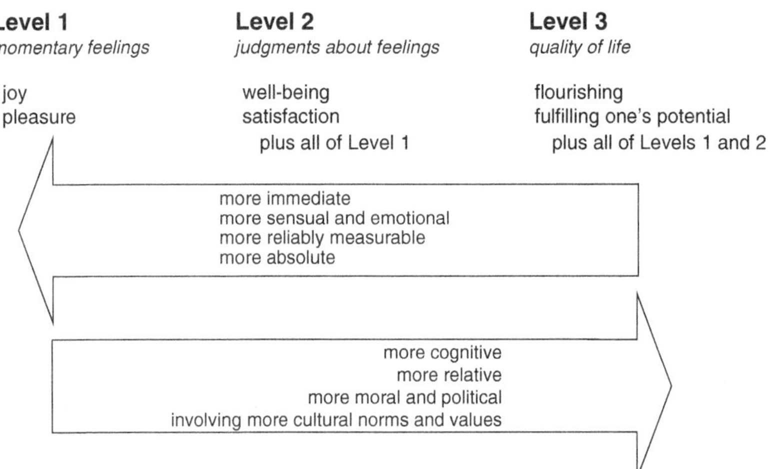

FIGURE 2.8. The taxonomy of three different levels of happiness proposed by Nettle (2005).

Psychologists note four processes that play a role in determining happiness. Frey and Stutzer (2002) summarize them as follows:

a. *Adaptation.* People get used to new circumstances and accordingly adjust their subjective level of well-being. Hedonic adaptation thus reduces individuals' responsiveness to continued stimulus.[9]
b. *Aspiration.* People evaluate their situation with regard to an aspirational level that is formed by their hopes and expectations.
c. *Social comparison.* There is no absolute measuring stick with respect to subjective happiness. People compare their positions with those of relevant other persons.
d. *Coping.* People have a strong capacity to overcome unfortunate events. Perhaps the most striking example is paraplegics. Initially they suffer a huge drop in subjective well-being. But over time, many of them are able to actively adapt to their misfortune. After some time, they indicate a not-much-lower level of personal happiness than before the accident.

One of the earliest empirical studies to look at people's assessment of their overall well-being was conducted by Cantril (1965). He devised a ten-step "ladder" and then asked respondents to define the top and bottom rungs in terms of "what really matters in your life." After having respondents define the attributes and their levels for the top and bottom rungs, he then asked them to locate themselves at present, "five years ago," and what they expected "five years from now." These studies were conducted in 14 developed and developing countries. Results were reported both in terms of ladder positions as well as lists of the specific concerns of respondents (health, income, etc.). From this work, Cantril drew a variety of broad conclusions about "the demands human beings everywhere impose on any society or political culture" and explored how these varied across factors such as level of economic development.

Building on Cantril's methods and results from polls conducted by the National Opinion Research Center (NORC) and the American Institute of Public Opinion (AIPO), Easterlin (1974) wrote an extended review. He concluded that within a single society at any given time, self-reported happiness showed a correlation with income. However, across societies that had different average levels of income and within a single society in which average levels of income have increased over time, the level of happiness shows little association with income. In a subsequent paper, Easterlin (1995) summarized additional data, concluding:

Today, as in the past, within a country at a given time those with higher income are, on average, happier. However, raising the income of all does not increase the happiness

[9] The fact that people are highly adaptive (i.e., have preferences that are labile) has given rise to arguments that we are on a "hedonic tread mill" (i.e., that we adapt to any improvement so there is no net improvement in affect) or perhaps more weakly a "satisfaction treadmill" (i.e., with changing life experiences we modify the standards we use to judge happiness). For a concise summary of these ideas, see Kahneman (1999).

of all. This is because the material norms on which judgments of well being are based increase in the same proportion as the actual income of the society.

The evidence for this conclusion continues to get stronger. Reaching much the same conclusion, in a commentary Knight (2012) has observed that:

> Subsequent literature has provided much evidence (based on increasingly rich microdata but mainly for developed economies) that is consistent with the original findings ... Relative income is important for happiness, and although happiness always rises with income in the cross-section, it often fails to do so in the time series. It is true that a thorough investigation of many countries found a positive effect of income growth on happiness when imposing the same coefficient on income across countries ... However, an analysis of the same data without that restriction found that the average value of the country coefficients was not positive.

Easterlin and colleagues (2012) have conducted a set of studies exploring the relationship of happiness in China over the course of that nation's very rapid changes in GDP. They summarize:

> Despite its unprecedented growth in output per capita in the last two decades, China has essentially followed the life satisfaction trajectory of the central and eastern European transition countries[10] – a U-shaped swing and a nil or declining trend [see Figure 2.9]. There is no evidence of an increase in life satisfaction of the magnitude that might have been expected to result from the fourfold improvement in the level of per capita consumption that has occurred. As in the European countries, in China, the trend and U-shaped pattern appear to be related to a pronounced rise in unemployment followed by a mild decline, and an accompanying dissolution of the social safety net along with growing income inequality. The burden of worsening life satisfaction in China has fallen chiefly on the lowest socioeconomic groups. An initially highly egalitarian distribution of life satisfaction has been replaced by an increasingly unequal one, with decreasing life satisfaction in persons in the bottom third of the income distribution and increasing life satisfaction in those in the top third.

In summary, the literature suggests that once an individual's income has exceeded the level required to meet basic needs in their society, happiness is only weakly correlated with the absolute level of income or consumption.[11] Comparisons of one's situation with others in terms of income, social status, and similar factors show a larger effect, with people who find themselves coming out lower in these comparisons feeling less happy. Being married and having strong family and social connections increases happiness. There is only limited evidence of a dependence on age, sex,[12] or ethnicity. Personality traits such as liking one's

[10] See Easterlin (2009) for a discussion of the U-shaped swing of life satisfaction in Eastern European countries that made the transition to capitalism after the break-up of the Soviet Union.

[11] For an extended discussion of the economic effects of happiness, see part II in Frey and Stutzer (2002).

[12] Easterlin (2010) reports that "women start adult life happier than men but end up less happy ... an important reason ... is that women form unions – married or cohabiting – at an earlier age than men; at older ages, however, they are less likely than men ... to have a partner."

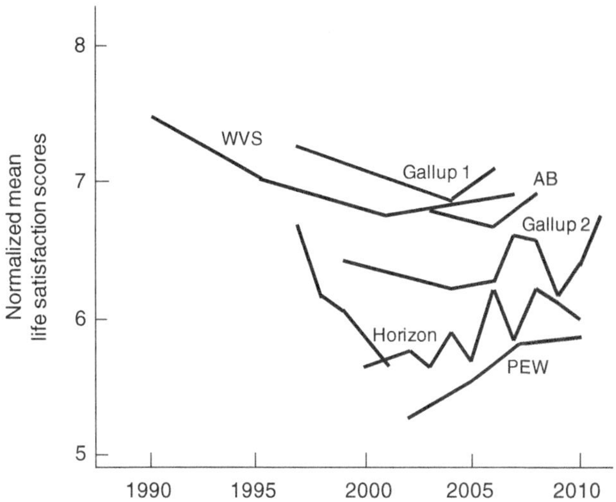

FIGURE 2.9. Mean life satisfaction scores obtained in a variety of different surveys conducted in the United States. The figure is redrawn, simplified, and renormalized from the original plot in Easterlin et al. (2012) that reports results in terms of a variety of Likert scales of different length. While it conveys the proper general impression, before citing any values, readers should consult the original figure and SI details in Easterlin et al. (2012).

self, having a sense of being personally in control, being optimistic, and being extroverted are all positively correlated with happiness (Myers and Diener, 1995, 1996; Nettle, 2005), although the causal direction is not clear.

Recently, conducting large cross-national studies of happiness has become a popular pastime (White, 2007; Helliwell et al., 2012).[13] Results from these studies take the form of large arrays of bar graphs reporting the relative happiness of citizens in different nations. A number of Scandinavian countries generally rank at the very top – countries and regions such as Armenia, Burundi, Congo, Iraq, Palestine, Togo, and Zimbabwe at the bottom.

SUGGESTED RESOURCES TO LEARN MORE ABOUT HAPPINESS AND WELL-BEING

For a very readable non-technical treatment, see:

- Daniel Nettle, *Happiness: The Science behind Your Smile*, Oxford University Press, 216pp., 2005.

[13] See also: http://en.wikipedia.org/wiki/Satisfaction_with_Life_Index.

For a more detailed review of the relevant empirical studies, see:

- Daniel Kahneman, Ed Diener, and Norbert Schwarz, *Well-being: The Foundations of Hedonic Psychology*, The Russell Sage Foundation, 593pp., 1999.
- Fritz Strack, Michael Argyle, and Norbert Schwarz (eds.), *Subjective Well-Being: An Interdisciplinary Perspective*, Pergamon, 291pp., 1991.
- Michael Eid and Randy J. Larsen (eds.), *The Science of Subjective Well-Being*, Guilford Press, 546pp., 2008. Chapter 1 of this book has a review of the "prescient and groundbreaking work of Ed Diener, who has devoted his scientific life over the last 25 years [to the empirical scientific study of happiness]."

For an assessment of issues in measuring well-being, see:

- National Research Council (NRC), *Subjective Well-Being: Measuring Happiness, Suffering, and Other Dimensions of Experience,* National Academy Press, 204pp., 2013.

READING 2.1

David G. Myers and Ed Diener, "The Pursuit of Happiness," *Scientific American*, pp. 70–72, May 1996.

DISCUSSION QUESTIONS FOR READING 2.1

- Myers and Diener argue that, with the exception of *very* poor societies, there is not a strong correlation between income and happiness. How would you qualify that statement in light of the findings by Frey and Stutzer (2002) about the importance of social comparisons?
- What are the four characteristics of happy people according to Myers and Diener?
- Correlation does not necessarily imply causation. To what extent might this be an issue in some of the literature on happiness?

2.4 MEASUREMENT SCALES FOR UTILITY (AND OTHER THINGS)[14]

While utility may not be the same thing as happiness, there is a variety of scales that can be used in measuring both, as well as a variety of other quantities of interest. Stevens (1946) observed that "measurement, in the broadest sense, is defined as the assignment of numerals to objects or events according to rules.

[14] I thank psychologists Michael L. DeKay and Wändi Bruine de Bruin for their contributions for the material in this section. For readers unfamiliar with the statistical tests discussed, see Gelman and Hill (2006).

The fact that numerals can be assigned under different rules leads to different kinds of scales and different kinds of measurements." He argued that

> the problem of what is and is not measurement then reduces to the simple question: "What are the rules if any, under which numerals are assigned?" If we can point to a consistent set of rules, we are obviously concerned with measurement of some sort, and we can then proceed to the more interesting question of what kind of measurement it is.

Stevens proposed a taxonomy of measurement scales that he termed: nominal, ordinal, interval, and ratio.

A *nominal scale* simply sorts things into mutually exclusive categories (male or female; French, German, Spanish, Italian; spicy or bland). However, in contrast to the other scales we consider, there is no apparent order to the items in a nominal scale. Any transformation performed on such a scale should preserve a one-to-one mapping (e.g., male or female maps to boy or girl). Statistics that can appropriately be computed on a nominal scale include counts, mode, and contingency correlation.

The next more complex scale is an *ordinal scale*. Items are assigned numbers that only represent the ordering of the items. However, the distances between these values is meaningless. For example, I might rank candy bars as follows:

Cadbury with almonds $>$ Baby Ruth $>$ Kit Kat

This says I prefer Cadbury to Baby Ruth which I prefer to Kit Kat, but it does *not* say how much more I prefer one over another. Such ordinal rankings form the basis of utility theory in modern microeconomics.

Transformations performed on ordinal scales should preserve rank order. Permissible statistics include counts, mode and contingency correlation, plus median, percentiles, Spearman rank order correlation, and nonparametric statistics.

In an *interval scale*, items are assigned numbers such that equal differences between numbers represent equal differences between items *but* the zero point is arbitrary. The Fahrenheit temperature scale is an example of an interval scale. 70°F is as much warmer than 50°F as 45°F is than 25°F. But, it makes no sense to say that 50°F is twice as warm as 25°F, because in this scale the zero point is arbitrary. Transformations should preserve ratios of differences. Permissible statistics include all of those articulated above, plus mean, variance, standard deviation, Pearson correlation, regression, ANOVA, and t-test.

Finally, in a *ratio scale* there *is* a meaningful zero. In this scale, items are assigned numbers so that ratios between items are preserved. Measure of mass and the Kelvin temperature scale are examples of a ratio scale. In this case, it is meaningful to say that 10g is twice the mass of 5g or that 150K is half as warm as 300K. In a ratio scale, all transformations are allowed, including multiplication and division. All of the statistics discussed above are allowed as well as the geometric mean and coefficient of variation.

As noted in Figure 2.10, interval and ratio scales are called *cardinal scales*. Classical microeconomics uses an *ordinal* scale in constructing utility functions, because it argues that inter-personal comparisons cannot be made. As noted below in Section 2.6, not all fields or experts share this view.

Table 2.1 lists these scale types along with a summary of the traditional view of what transformations and statistical computations are "permissible" for each. This formulation, together with the associated rules for analysis, has become widely adopted. For example, Velleman and Wilkinson (1993) observe that textbook authors quickly adopted these ideas, "perhaps because they appear to provide simple guidance and protect naïve data analysts from errors in applying statistics." Indeed, some statistical packages require the user to specify what scale is associated with the data being analyzed and then will only perform the "permissible" statistical computations. Velleman and Wilkinson (1993) recount a history of disagreement within the statistics and other communities about the appropriateness of adopting such strict rules. They note:

> Many of the discussions of scale types, and virtually all of the mathematical results, treat them as absolute categories. Data are expected to fit into one or another of the categories. A failure to attain one level of measurement is taken as a demotion to the next level. However, real data do not follow the requirements of many scale types ...
>
> [Furthermore,] the scale type of data may be determined in part by the question we ask of the data or the purposes for which we intend it ...
>
> Good data analysis rarely follows the formal paradigm of hypothesis testing. It is a general search for patterns in data that is open to discovering unanticipated relationships.[15] Such analyses are, of course, impossible if the data are asserted to have a scale type that forbids even considering some patterns – but such an approach is clearly unscientific. A scientist must be open to *any* interesting pattern.

In course materials developed at Carnegie Mellon, Michael DeKay and Wändi Bruine de Bruin have summarized a number of problems with traditional scale types and the associated recommendations for statistical procedures, especially as they apply to social science data. Their advice follows:

- The scale type is not inherent in the data; the scale also depends on how the data are used. For example, the number a runner wears may be nominal if it is only associated with their names – to identify who they are, but it may also be ordinal if it reflects their national ranking based on performance in previous competitions. To put it bluntly, "The numbers don't know where they came from."
- Most statistical packages do not distinguish between interval and ratio scales. For most analyses you will use, interval scale measures are sufficient, so the distinction will not matter. Norms differ between disciplines. When in doubt, conduct analyses both ways.

[15] For a discussion of such methods, see Tukey (1977).

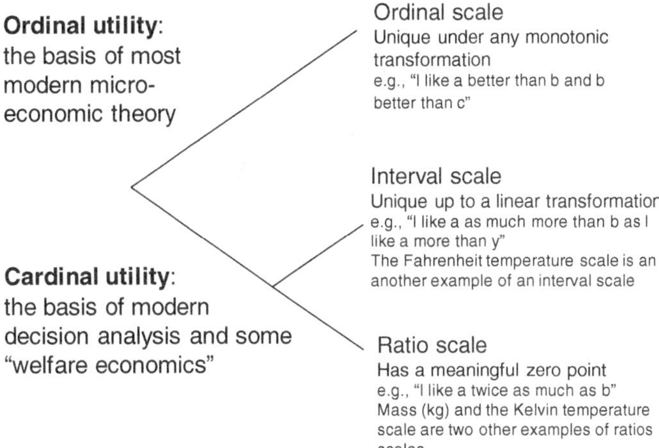

FIGURE 2.10. Taxonomy of different types of utility and the scales that are used to measure them. Modern welfare economics is built on ordinal utility because the argument is made that it is not possible to compare the value that different people attach to a good or service. However, modern decision analysis, and some welfare economics, does make such comparisons and thus employs a cardinal scale in constructing utility. A fifth scale type, not shown because it carries no normative implication, is a nominal scale such as "red, green, blue" or "freshman, sophomore, junior."

- It is often quite useful and informative to calculate "forbidden" statistics, such as when computing means from ordinal data. For example, we regularly convert ordinal letter grades (A, B, C, etc.) to numbers (4, 3, 2, etc.) in order to compute grade-point averages. Similarly, it is often useful to compute Pearson correlations (which "require" interval data) between questions answered on 7-point response scales. Some argue that such response scales lie between ordinal and interval scales. Others argue that if you learn something useful, the computation is clearly permissible. And, because you never know when you might learn something, you should not treat statistical procedures as forbidden based on the scale type of the data. For example, powerful scaling techniques have been developed for deriving interval scales (in one or more dimensions) from ordinal data.
- Overemphasis on scale types often leads researchers to use less powerful nonparametric statistics, all of which are based on a rather severe monotonic transformation (ranking). In many instances, ranking the data throws away lots of potentially useful information.
- Overemphasis on scale types often leads researchers to avoid applying transformations (e.g., log transformation for response time or income, logit or arcsine transformations for fractions) that would greatly improve the quality of the data analysis by solving other more important problems (e.g., distributions with thick tails that contain outliers, constrained variance).

TABLE 2.1. *The traditional view of scale types (adapted from Stevens (1946) by Michael DeKay and Wändi Bruine de Bruin).*

Scale type	Description	Examples	Permissible transformations (i.e., those that preserve "meaning")	Permissible statistics
Nominal	Items are assigned to mutually exclusive categories, but there is no apparent rank-order to the categories	Name, gender, social security numbers, electricity provider	Any one-to-one mapping	Frequencies, mode, chi-square
Ordinal	Items are assigned numbers in order (1 to n), but the distances are meaningless	Top ten rankings in competition, ranked preferences, ordinal utility	Any monotonic transformation that preserves the rank order: $s(i) > s(j) \Rightarrow f[s(i)] > f[s(j)]$	All of the above, plus median, percentiles, Spearman correlation, nonparametric statistics
Interval	Items are assigned numbers with equal differences but zero point is arbitrary	Time stamp, Fahrenheit or Celsius temperature, von Neumann and Morgenstern's utility	Any linear transformation that preserves *ratios of differences*: $f[s(i)] = a[s(i)] + b$, where a is positive. Note that ratios of differences are maintained: $[s(i) - s(j)]/[s(k) - s(l)] = \{f[s(i)] - f[s(j)]\}/\{f[s(k)] - f[s(l)]\}$	All of the above, plus mean, variance, standard deviation, Pearson correlation, regression, ANOVA, t, F, parametric statistics (if assumptions are met)
Ratio	Items are assigned numbers so that ratios between items are preserved. The zero point is not arbitrary	Income, willingness to pay, age, Kelvin temperature, length or distance	Because *ratios* are meaningful, multiplication and division can be used	All of the above, plus geometric mean coefficient of variation

- The scale also depends on the level of knowledge about the phenomenon in question. For example, the scale for temperature has changed from ordinal to interval to ratio as knowledge has progressed. Is it possible that we might discover absolute zeros for space, time, or utility?
- The scale that appears correct depends on framing. For example, we say that time in number of minutes is measured on a ratio scale, but this reflects just the difference between the start and end time. As there is no non-arbitrary zero for time itself (at least with our current state of knowledge), timestamp is measured using an interval scale (at best).
- Not all possible data types are represented. For example, where would counted fractions (for which no transformations leave the scale unchanged) fit in the traditional scheme? Measurement theorists have also defined and used other scale types, including absolute, difference, hyperordinal, and log interval scales.

2.5 THE UTILITY OF CHANCE OUTCOMES

Many things that are not certain also have value. For example, what would you be willing to pay to play a game where I flip a fair coin and if it comes up heads I give you \$100 and if it comes up tails I give you \$0? Presumably, you'd be willing to pay something for the opportunity to play such a game. The fact that you are willing to pay something to play means that you view the chance outcome as having some value.

Keeney and Raiffa (1976) note that when the distribution describing the outcome from one choice stochastically dominates the distribution describing the outcome from another (Figure 2.11), then the full paraphernalia of utility theory is not needed because B is unambiguously preferred to A. There may also be cases when choosing on the basis of the expected values of uncertain outcomes would be sufficient without going through the assignment of utilities, but they note that most of us would probably not be indifferent between the following four options, each of which has an expected value of \$100,000:

- Receive \$100,000 for sure.
- Receive \$200,000 or \$0, each with probability 0.5.
- Receive \$1,000,000 with probability 0.1, or \$0 with probability 0.9.
- Receive \$200,000 with probability 0.9, or lose \$800,000 with probability 0.1.

It is precisely because almost all of us are not indifferent among chance outcomes, such as the ones shown above, that utility functions were introduced in decision-making problems.

John von Neumann and Oscar Morgenstern (1944) formalized the idea that not only do sure things have value but that gambles can also have value. This insight was used to form the basis of cardinal utility as now used in modern

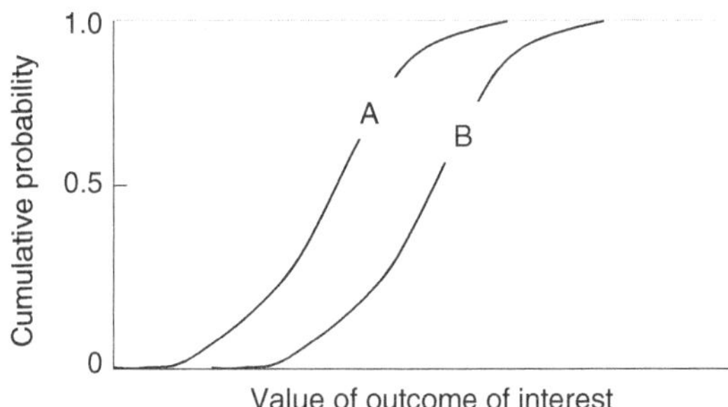

FIGURE 2.11. The cumulative distribution function B is stochastically dominant to the cumulative distribution function A. As Keeney and Raiffa (1976) note, in a case such as this, one can simply choose the option that leads to B over the one that leads to A without resorting to the full paraphernalia of utility theory.

FIGURE 2.12. Mathematician John von Neumann (1903–1957) and economist Oscar Morgenstern (1902–1977) who, in their book *Theory of Games and Economic Behavior*, laid the foundations for modern expected utility theory. Figure reproduced with permission: Dorothy Morgenstern Thomas, photographer. From Shelby White and Leon Levy Archives Center, Institute for Advanced Study, Princeton, NJ, USA.

decision theory. The utility-based theory of choice was subsequently axiomatized by L.J. Savage (1954) (see Chapter 4).

In a later edition of their book, von Neumann and Morgenstern (1953) explain their reasoning as follows:

> [We assume that someone has a] system of preferences that is all-embracing and complete ... [and that] for any two alterative events which are put before him as possibilities ... [he is able] to tell which of the two he prefers.
>
> It is a very natural extension of this picture to permit such an individual to compare not only events, but even combinations of events with stated probabilities ...
>
> By a combination of events we mean this: Let two events be denoted by B and C and use, for the sake of simplicity, the probability 50%–50%. Then the "combination" is the prospect of seeing B occur with probability 50% and (if B does not occur) C with the (remaining) probability of 50%. We stress that the two alternatives are mutually exclusive so that no possibility of complementarity and the like exists. Also, that an absolute certainty of either B or C exists ...
>
> We expect the individual under consideration to possess a clear intuition whether he prefers the event A to the 50–50 combination of B or C, or conversely. It is clear that if he prefers A to B and also to C, then he will prefer it to the above combination as well; similarly, if he prefers B as well as C to A, then he will prefer the combination too. But, should he prefer A to, say B, but at the same time C to A, then any assertion about his preferences of A against the combination contains fundamentally new information. Specifically: If he now prefers A to the 50–50 combination, this provides a plausible base for the numerical estimate that his preference for A over B is in excess of his preference C over A ...
>
> [This logic provides] a criterion with which to compare the preference of C over A with the preference of A over B ... thereby utilities – or rather differences of utilities – become numerically measurable.

Decision analysis and many psychologists now routinely use this basic insight to elicit cardinal utility functions.

The most concise mathematical elaboration of these ideas that I have found is provided by Keeney and Raiffa (1976, pp. 132–136). Here I paraphrase their explanation. Suppose that we have a set of possible outcomes, call them x_1, x_2, ... x_n. Suppose further that your preference ordering among these outcomes is:

$$x_1 \prec x_2, \prec x_3 \ldots \prec x_n$$

where the symbol $\prec$ means that the outcome on the right is preferred to that on the left. Suppose that instead of being offered these outcomes for sure, you are asked to express your preferences between a pair of acts a' and a'' where a' leads to x_i with probability p'_i for i = 1,2...n ($p'_i \geq 0$ and $\sum_i p'_i = 1$) and act a'' leads to consequence x_i with probability p''_i for i = 1,2...n (again, $p''_i \geq 0$ and $\sum_i p''_i = 1$). There is, of course, an infinite number of possible probability distributions across this finite set of consequences.

Keeney and Raiffa (1976) then posit that a decision maker is indifferent between:

receiving x_i with certainty

or

receiving the best outcome (x_n) with probability π_i and the worst outcome (x_1) with probability $1-\pi_i$

And the sequence $\pi_1 < \pi_2, < \pi_3 \ldots < \pi_n$ can be viewed as a numerical scaling of the sequence $x_1 \prec x_2, \prec x_3 \ldots \prec x_n$. The reasoning is that a relatively high chance of obtaining the best outcome (i.e., the highest value of π_I) implies a preference for that x_i compared to an outcome with a lower chance of the best outcome.

Keeney and Raiffa (1976) continue:

The fundamental result of utility theory is that the *expected value* of the π's can also be used to scale the probability distributions over the x's. To illustrate this reasoning, let us reconsider the choice between act a' (which results in x_i with probability p'_i) and act a'' (which results in x_i with probability p''_i). If we associate to each x_i its scaled π_i value, then the expected π scores for acts a' and a'', which we label $\overline{\pi'}$ and $\overline{\pi''}$, are

$$\overline{\pi'} = \sum_i p'_i \pi_i$$

and

$$\overline{\pi''} = \sum_i p''_i \pi_i$$

There are compelling reasons for the decision maker to rank order act a' and a'' in terms of the magnitude of $\overline{\pi'}$ and $\overline{\pi''}$.

Their argument goes as follows: if the decision maker chooses a', then with probability p'_i the result will be x_i. However, the decision maker has indicated that they are indifferent between x_i and a π_i chance of getting outcome x_n and a $1-\pi_i$ chance of getting x_1. That means that choosing a' is effectively the same thing as giving the decision maker a $\overline{\pi'}$ chance of ending up with x_n and a $1-\overline{\pi'}$ chance of ending up with x_1. In the same way, choosing a'' results in a $\overline{\pi''}$ chance of ending up with x_n and a $1-\overline{\pi''}$ chance of ending up with x_1.

Obviously, this argument rests on the decision maker being willing for each x_i, to substitute the option of obtaining x_i with certainty for risky option "receive the best outcome (x_n) with probability π_i and the worst outcome (x_1) with probability $1-\pi_i$." We also assume that we can interpret the π_i's as values of the utility function defined over an interval scale with arbitrate end points, though we generally set $u(x_1) = 0$ and $u(x_n) = 1$.

When someone has a choice between receiving some sure outcome or some gamble between two possible larger or smaller outcomes, his or her associated utility curve can take a number of forms. If there is a linear relationship, the individual is said to be risk neutral (i.e., will give up the option for its expected value). If the utility curve is concave (i.e., bowed upward), the individual is said to be risk averse (i.e., they will give up the option provided by the gamble for a payment that is smaller than the expected value of the gamble). If the utility curve is convex (i.e., bowed downward), the individual is said to be risk seeking (i.e., they will only give up the option provided by the gamble for a payment that is larger than the expected value of the gamble). See Figure 2.13.

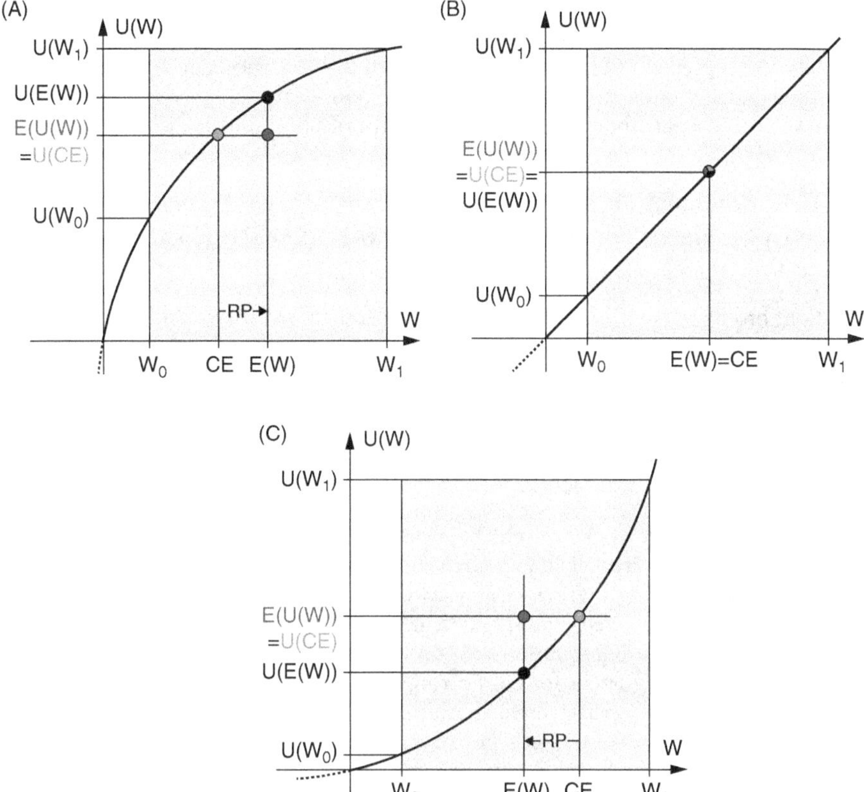

FIGURE 2.13. Examples of utility functions for (**A**) a risk-averse individual, (**B**) a risk neutral individual, and (**C**) a risk-seeking individual. In these plots CE = Certainty equivalent; E(U(W)) = Expected value of the utility (expected utility) of the uncertain payment; E(W) = Expected value of the uncertain payment; U(CE) = Utility of the certainty equivalent; U(E(W)) = Utility of the expected value of the uncertain payment; $U(W_0)$ = Utility of the minimal payment; $U(W_1)$ = Utility of the maximal payment; W_0 = Minimal payment; W_1 = Maximal payment; RP = Risk premium. Figure adapted from Wikipedia.

2.6 CAN DIFFERENT PEOPLE'S UTILITIES BE COMPARED?

Most modern microeconomics adopts the view that utility can only be measured on an ordinal scale, so that the utilities of different individuals cannot be compared. On the other hand, it is not uncommon in welfare economics to adopt a cardinal measure of utility and then assume that some strategy can be found to combine the utilities of separate individuals to assess an overall social utility. Psychologists and decision analysts are typically also much more willing to view utility in terms of a cardinal scale.

For example, after explaining ordinal judgments about preferences, the psychologists von Winterfeldt and Edwards (1986) observe:

> Some theorists and practitioners will stop at ... [an ordinal scale]. Others, mainly those with backgrounds in psychology, go further. They argue that people can communicate not only about preference, but also about strength of preference. Such communication, if possible, greatly enriches the vocabulary of responses available to us in discovering utilities and consequently makes the measurement of utility much easier. We take this view ourselves.

Similarly, Adler and Posner (2006) support the idea that it is sometimes useful and possible to compare the utilities of different individuals. As they summarize:

> intuition, ordinary practice, and the widespread use of interpersonal comparisons in moral theorizing all undercut the view that these comparisons are impossible. Overall welfare is a meaningful concept. We have very strong reasons to think that Pareto-noncomparable states (or at least some of them) can be compared in light of overall welfare.[16]

Finally, Kahneman et al. (1997) write:

> The view that hedonic states cannot be measured because they are private events is widely held but not correct. The measurement of subjective experiences and the determination of the functions that relate subjective variables to features of present and past stimuli are topics in the well-established field of psychophysical research ... The loudness of a noise and the felt temperature of a limb are no less subjective than pleasure and pain. The main argument for considering these experiences measurable is that the functions that relate subjective intensity to physical variables are qualitatively similar for different people. For example, reported subjective intensity is often a power function of physical magnitude, with an exponent that varies for different sensory dimensions. Pleasure and distress have the same status: psychological functions that govern the pleasure of drinking sugar solutions and the pain of electric shock are orderly and interpersonally similar ... Verbal or numerical reports of hedonic values can be

[16] The idea of "Pareto optimality" is discussed in Section 3.2. A Pareto optimal choice or policy is one that makes at least one person better off without leaving anyone else worse off. Comparing among two or more Pareto optimal states requires explicit or implicit interpersonal comparisons (see, for example, Little, 1952).

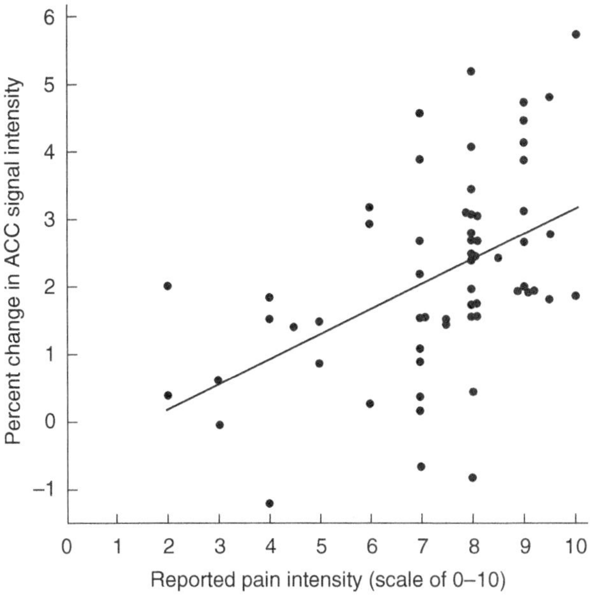

FIGURE 2.14. Comparison of pain rating (scale of 0–10) with percentage change in ACC excitation observed via functional MRI. Figure redrawn from Davis et al. (1997).

> supplemented by physiological indicators of emotional quality and intensity, including objective measures of subtle facial expressions ... Although the correlations among these measures are imperfect, the variance they share can serve to operationalize the concept of instant experienced utility.[17]

If you have ever been in a hospital, you know that it is common practice for the nursing staff to ask you to assess your pain on a scale of 1 to 10. Of course, different people have different levels of tolerance for pain but, in the context of interpersonal comparisons, an obvious question is how these numerical ratings compare with the degree of excitation of pain-related regions in the anterior cingulate cortex (ACC) of normal human subjects as measured via functional MRI. Figure 2.14 reports the results of such an experiment conducted by Davis et al. (1997) for ten volunteer subjects subjected to various levels of pain via electrical stimulation of the right median nerve. While there is considerable scatter, and Davis et al. (1997) unfortunately do not associate specific individuals with specific points, it is clear that pain assessments by different subjects show somewhat similar patterns.

[17] Note that this statement applies to "instant experienced utility." See Kahneman et al. (1997) for a discussion of how this relates to remembered and total experienced utility.

READING 2.2

Detlof von Winterfeldt and Ward Edwards, *Decision Analysis and Behavioral Research*, Cambridge University Press, 604pp., 1986. Read pp. 205–241.

Optional readings: If you are interested in seeing more details on methods of eliciting utility functions, you might also skim or read pp. 241–258 of von Winterfeldt and Edwards. If you would like to gain a better understanding of the theory of value and utility measurement, you might also skim or read pp. 314–325.

2.7 COMBINING INDIVIDUAL UTILITIES AND THE CONCEPT OF A SOCIAL WELFARE FUNCTION

In the late nineteenth and early twentieth centuries, "welfare economics" adopted the idea that social decision making could be guided by a social welfare function that is constructed as some combination of individual utility functions. In 1950, Arrow confounded this simple formulation by showing that, under a deceptively simple and apparently sensible set of basic principles, no voting system can be devised that is guaranteed to yield a unique preference ordering when three or more voters have more than three distinct alternatives among which to choose (Arrow, 1950). This finding dramatically complicated the assumption that it is possible to produce a meaningful social welfare function. Ackerman (1997b) summarizes:

> After ordinalism, both Abram Bergson and Paul Samuelson separately proposed that some unspecified method of aggregation of individuals' (ordinal, noncomparable) preferences could still lead to a function expressing society's judgments ... Arrow proved that they were wrong. Using a few innocuous-sounding assumptions,[18] he demonstrated that any logically consistent social welfare function is dictatorial – that there is a single individual whose preferences prevail in every situation, even when all other individuals have opposing preferences.

The key point is those "innocuous-sounding assumptions." Because they are very simple, they ignore many factors that enter into real-world social decision making. Again, Ackerman (1997b) summarizes:

[18] The criteria Arrow adopted are that (1) social preferences should be complete (A is either preferred to B or B preferred to A or there is indifference between A and B); (2) social preferences should be transitive (if A is preferred to B and B is preferred to C, then A is preferred to C); (3) if every individual prefers A to B, then society should prefer A to B; (4) there is no "dictator" (i.e., no single voter possesses the power to always determine the group's preference); and (5) social preferences should be independent of irrelevant alternatives; i.e., the social preference of A compared to B should be independent of preferences for other alternatives. For a more technical description and discussion of Arrow's "axioms," see http://plato.stanford.edu/entries/arrows-theorem.

Real decisions are rarely made on such a narrow basis; using only the tools allowed in Arrow's proof, one cannot solve a mundane problem such as the right way to divide a cake among three people. The solutions offered by common sense, either that equal slices are fair, or that the hungriest person should get the most, are excluded, one for using non utility standards of fairness and the other for making interpersonal comparisons of hunger. (Note that majority rule is ethically unattractive here: two people could agree to vote that they should each get half and the third person none.)

Black (1948) proposed a strategy (sometimes termed the median-voter theorem) that obtains unique outcomes in a specific but important class of choice situations. He proved that if, across a set of alternative options, each member of the group making a choice has a preference for one option that is higher than their preference for all others (i.e., their preferences are "single peaked"), then if each option is voted against every other, only one option can achieve a simple majority over all others.[19]

While a number of economists have worked to resolve the problem of choice that Arrow described, perhaps the most attractive solution to date is that proposed by Harsanyi (1955), who observes:

> There is no doubt about the fact that people make, or at least attempt to make, interpersonal comparisons of utility, both in the sense of comparing different persons' total satisfaction and in the sense of comparing increments or decrements in different persons' satisfaction. The problem is only what logical basis, if any, there is for such comparisons.

He argues that rather than aggregating the utilities that describe how individuals would choose when faced with a specific choice situation, one should instead ask, as John Rawles (1972) does, how individuals would want society to make choices if they did not know in advance what specific circumstances they themselves will face and had "an equal *chance* of obtaining any of the social positions." On this basis, Harsanyi is able to define a social welfare function that is equal to "the arithmetic mean of all the individuals in society."

Public policy is not made by simply aggregating the consumption preferences, or even the more broadly defined utilities, of all the individuals who make up a society. Societies have long-established procedures for electing and appointing decision makers, who make choices and implement policies. Bergson (1954) has argued that a key issue is the "counseling" of these public decision makers. Such decision makers will obviously consider *and compare* the interests and preferences of their constituents, but in most cases will also consider a range of ethical, legal, and other issues. At that level the critical role of a policy analyst is to help by exploring alternative framings and applying a range of quantitative and qualitative analytical procedures in order to help provide that "counseling." In a specific decision context, it can then inform what some might choose to view as a social welfare function.

[19] Ties can result when there is an even number of participants in the "single peaked" situation. Ties and deadlock may result when participants have multi-peaked preferences.

READING 2.3

Richard Zeckhauser and Elmer Schaefer, "Chapter 2: Public Policy and Normative Economic Theory," in Raymond Bauer and Kenneth Gergen (eds.), *The Study of Policy Formation*, The Free Press, 1968.

Pages 27–64 provide a compact review of some of the basic ideas of micro- and welfare economics. If you already know some microeconomics you can probably skip this reading.

SUGGESTED RESOURCE TO LEARN MORE ABOUT THE AGGREGATION OF PREFERENCES

For a detailed discussion of different philosophical positions with respect to the aggregation of utilities, see chapter 2 in:

- Matthew D. Adler and Eric A. Posner, *New Foundations of Cost-Benefit Analysis*, Harvard University Press, 236pp., 2006.

See especially pp. 43–52 for a summary and critique of approaches suggested by Kahneman, Griffin, Isbel, and Harsanyi.

2.8 PREFERENCES THAT ARE NOT WELL DEFINED, CHANGE OVER TIME, OR ARE INCONSISTENT

Most of the tools for decision making discussed in the next several chapters assume that people know their preferences – that is, that they have fully articulated utility functions that are sitting in their heads ready to be used or measured. While that may be true in the cases of choices that we make on a regular basis, it is clearly not true for many other choices about things with which we have little or no familiarity. In those cases, people may have to actually construct their preferences (Keeney, 1992). We will explore this issue at greater length in Chapter 5.

The discussion of this chapter also assumes that preferences, and hence utility, are fixed and do not change over time. However, March (1976) observes: "the argument that goal development and choice are independent behaviorally seems clearly false. It seems ... perfectly obvious that a description that assumes that goals come first and action comes later is frequently radically wrong. Human choice behavior is at least as much a process of discovering goals as of acting on them." We will explore this issue at greater length in Chapters 5 and 12.

March (1978) also observes that preferences are frequently not consistent:

From the point of view of ordinary human ideas about choices, as well as many philosophical and behavioral conceptions of choice, the most surprising thing about formal theories of choice is the tendency to treat such terms as values, goals, preferences, tastes, wants and the like as either equivalent or as reducible to a single objective function with properties of completeness and consistency. Suppose that instead of making such an assumption, we viewed the decision maker as confronted simultaneously with several orderings of outcomes. We could give them names, calling one a moral code, another a social role, another a personal taste, or whatever ... [presumably these several orderings could be] independent and irreducible. That is they could not be deduced from each other, and they could not be combined into a single order. Then instead of taking the conventional step of imputing a preference order across these incompatibles by some kind of revealed preference procedure, we [could] treat them as truly incompatible and examine solutions to internal inconsistency that are more in the spirit of our efforts to provide intelligent guidance to collectives in which we accept the incomparability of preferences across individuals.

In the pages that follow, I will make occasional reference to the problem of individuals and organizations choosing goals and values. March has done some of the best thinking on this subject in a paper he titled "The Technology of Foolishness." Using the analogy of play, March (1976) argues:

Playfulness is the deliberate, temporary relaxation of rules in order to explore the possibilities of alternative rules ... My present intent is to propose play as an instrument of intelligence, not a substitute ... Playfulness is a natural outgrowth of our standard view of reason. Play relaxes that insistence to allow us to act "unintelligently" or "irrationally" or "foolishly" to explore alternative ideas of possible purpose and alternative concepts of behavioral consistency. And it does this while maintaining our basic commitment to the necessity of intelligence.

March (1976) suggests a variety of strategies the individual and organizations might adopt during such periods of play: treating goals as hypotheses; treating intuition as real; treating hypocrisy as a transition; treating memory as an enemy; and treating experience as theory.

As you read the paper, bear in mind that March is *not* arguing that these behaviors should be adopted as a general matter. Rather, his suggestion is that during short periods when an individual or organization suspends the normal rules and constraints under which it operates, these strategies may prove helpful as a way to explore and evaluate possible alternative behaviors and goals. Once play stops and the rules are reimposed, some of what has been learned during periods of playfulness might be judged worthy of adoption.

READING 2.4

J.G. March, "Chapter 5: The Technology of Foolishness," in J.G. March and J.P. Olsen (eds.), *Ambiguity and Choice in Organizations*, Universitetsforlaget, pp. 69–81, 1976. This book may be hard to find but a copy of the chapter can be found online at:
www.creatingquality.org/Portals/1/DNNArticleFiles/634631045269246454the%20technology%20of%20foolishness.pdf.

DISCUSSION QUESTIONS FOR READING 2.4

- Why does March say that the argument that goal development and choice are independent is clearly false?
- In what sense does March use the concept of play in this paper?
- When, why, and under what circumstance is March arguing to treat: goals as hypotheses, intuition as real, hypocrisy as transition, memory as an enemy, and experience as theory?
- March concludes his article with five recommendations for how individuals and organizations should consider changing some of their modes of operation. What is your reaction to the advice he offers?

2.9 BACK TO THE BASIC QUESTION: "WHAT IS UTILITY?"

So what is utility? Too often when I have asked students this question after a couple of classes on the subject and several readings, I have gotten answers about possessing things, and about numbers and money. But utility need not be about possession, nor need it be about numbers or be measured in dollars. People derive utility from, that is, they place value on, all sorts of things: watching lovely sunsets, hearing a Mozart symphony, enjoying the view from the top of the *Pic du Midi*, learning that a friend has received a promotion, spending time with a favorite nephew, and viewing a fragment of 18,000-year-old pottery from the Yuchanyan cave. A utility function can include all these and more. Just as it makes sense for me to say:

U_{GM}(eat a Baby Ruth chocolate bar) $\succ$ U_{GM} (eat a Kit Kat bar)

so, too, for me it makes sense to say:

U_{GM}(dinner out with wife, attend symphony) $\succ$ U_{GM}(take-out at McDonalds, night drive from DCA to PIT)

or,

U_{GM}(all Americans have access to health care) $\succ$ U_{GM}(most Americans have access to health care)

In the next chapters, we will explore three analytical strategies, all of which support making choices by maximizing utility, or its expected value. Figure 2.15 provides a very simple taxonomy of these strategies. Chapter 3 discusses benefit–cost (B–C) analysis, which is the most basic. When considering some proposed action or project, this method involves computing all the associated benefits, and then subtracting off all the costs in order to obtain an assessment of "net benefits." B–C analysis has largely been developed and applied by economists. Most applications have done relatively little to describe and

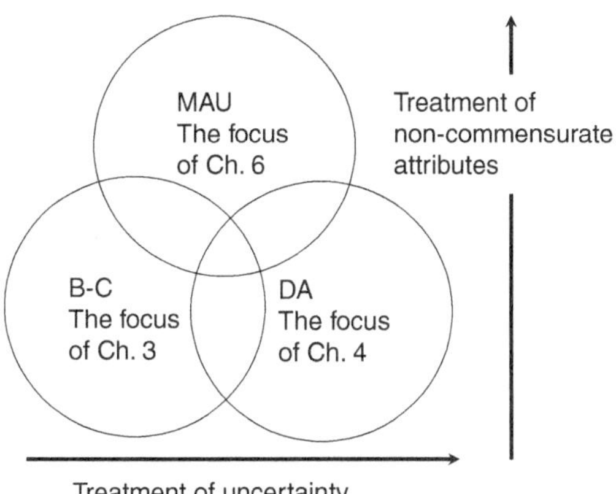

FIGURE 2.15. A simple taxonomy of the three methods of choice that are based on maximizing utility. These methods are the focus of Chapter 3 (benefit–cost analysis), 4 (decision analysis), and 6 (multi-attribute utility theory).

deal with uncertainties, although most of the more recent studies do include sensitivity analyses.

If one adds a systematic treatment of uncertainty to B–C analysis, one ends up with decision analysis. Decision analysis, which is the focus of Chapter 4, also involves a number of other considerations, but evaluating alternatives in the presence of uncertainty is its basic focus.

It is typical in both conventional B–C analysis and in decision analysis to evaluate everything in terms of a single metric of outcome – often dollars, but, especially in the case of decision analysis, also expected utility. As we noted above, utility need not involve just a single factor, that is, it can be "multivariate" in nature. In Chapter 6, we briefly describe a set of methods called "multi-attribute utility theory" that have been developed to deal with situations in which it is important to include a variety of different variables in a decision maker's utility function.

2.10 LIMITS TO THE STRATEGY OF UTILITY MAXIMIZATION

In Parts II and III of this book, we explore the question of whether individuals and groups actually make decisions by maximizing utility. Those discussions largely focus on behavioral issues, including issues that arise from the fact that people and organizations display "bounded rationality," as well as some of the issues of combining different people's preferences that were briefly identified in Section 2.7.

If, for the moment, we ignore cognitive and organizational limitations and assume that utility can be unambiguously defined and is invariant over time, decision strategies that are based on maximizing utility make sense in the context of choices that will be made by a single individual. They may sometimes also make sense if we are considering choices for groups of people who share similar values. However, analysis undertaken with the objective of "maximizing utility" typically does not make sense if the people involved attach very different valuations to the outcomes being considered.

Thus, it is certainly sensible to talk about maximizing utility for a single person who is choosing to buy a car. It may make sense to talk about maximizing utility in designing a parking garage for a town of largely like-minded people, or perhaps even setting an air-quality standard for a country that attaches similar value to the health and welfare of all its citizens.

But, in my view, it makes no sense to talk of choosing a climate policy that maximizes utility for the entire world. That is because there is enormous variation across the values that people from different cultures and regions place on different lifestyles, ecosystems, and climate outcomes and there is no agreed way by which those many different valuations should be combined. A climate policy that is "optimal" for Anglo-American citizens in Milwaukee is not likely to be "optimal" for Inuits living in northern Alaska, or Quechua speakers living in the altiplano of Peru.

That said, in many decision settings that are more socially and culturally homogeneous, there are analytical tools that can be used to aid decision makers in considering the utilities of different individuals and groups that will be affected by their choices (see, for example, chapter 10 of Keeney and Raiffa, 1976). Maximizing utility is the foundation of many of the tools of modern quantitative policy analysis, but before an analyst adopts this framing, they should always think carefully about whether it is an appropriate objective for the problem at hand and should use the formal methods with skepticism and caution.

REFERENCES

Ackerman, F. (1997a). "Utility and Welfare I: The History of Economic Thought," in F. Ackerman, D. Kiron, N.R. Goodwin, J.M. Harris, and K. Gallagher (eds.), *Human Well-Being and Economic Goals*, Island Press, pp. 49–57.

(1997b). "Utility and Welfare II: Modern Economic Alternatives," in F. Ackerman, D. Kiron, N.R. Goodwin, J.M. Harris, and K. Gallagher (eds.), *Human Well-Being and Economic Goals*, Island Press, pp. 81–92.

Adler, D.A. and E.A. Posner (2006). *New Foundations of Cost-Benefit Analysis*, Harvard University Press, 236pp.

Arrow, K.J. (1950). "A Difficulty in the Concept of Social Welfare," *Journal of Political Economy*, *58*, pp. 328–346.

Bentham, J. (1780). *An Introduction to the Principles of Morals and Legislation*. The first edition of this work was printed in 1780 and first published by Clarendon Press in 1789. Republished by Clarendon Press in 1892, 378pp.

Bergson, A. (1954). "On the Concept of Social Welfare," *Quarterly Journal of Economics*, *68*(2), pp. 233–252.

Black, D. (1948). "On the Rationale of Group Decision-Making," *Journal of Political Economy*, *56*(1), pp. 23–34.

Blaug, M. (1985). *Economic Theory in Retrospect*, Cambridge University Press, 737pp.

Cantril, H. (1965). *The Pattern of Human Concerns*, Rutgers University Press, 427pp.

Davis, K.D., S.J. Taylor, A.P. Crawley, M.L. Wood, and D.J. Mikulis (1997). "Functional MRI of Pain- and Attention-Related Activations in the Human Cingulate Cortex," *Journal of Neurophysiology*, *77*(6), pp. 3370–3380.

Easterlin, R.A. (1974). "Does Economic Growth Improve the Human Lot?" in P.A. David and M.W. Reder (eds.), *Nations and Households in Economic Growth: Essays in Honor of Moses Abramovitz*, Academic Press, pp. 89–125. This chapter was reprinted with some revisions as chapter 1 (pp. 13–45) of R.A. Easterlin, *Happiness, Growth and the Life Cycle*, Oxford University Press, 283pp., 2010.

(1995). "Will Raising the Incomes of All Increase the Happiness of All?," *Journal of Economic Behavior and Organization*, *27*, pp. 35–47. This paper was reprinted with some revisions as chapter 2 (pp. 46–55) of R.A. Easterlin, *Happiness, Growth and the Life Cycle*, Oxford University Press, 283pp., 2010.

(2009). "Lost in Transition: Life Satisfaction on the Road to Capitalism?," *Journal of Economic Behavior and Organization*, *71*, pp. 130–145. This chapter was reprinted with some revisions as chapter 4 (pp. 82–110) of R.A. Easterlin, *Happiness, Growth and the Life Cycle*, Oxford University Press, 283pp., 2010.

(2010). *Happiness, Growth and the Life Cycle*, Oxford University Press, 283pp.

Easterlin, R.A., R. Morgan, M. Switek, and F. Wang (2012). "China's Life Satisfaction, 1990–2010," *Proceedings of the National Academy of Science*, *109*, pp. 9775–9780.

Eid, M. and R.J. Larsen (eds.) (2008). *The Science of Subjective Well-Being*, Guilford Press, 546pp.

Frey, B.S. and A. Stutzer (2002). *Happiness and Economics*, Princeton University Press, 220pp.

Gelman, A. and J. Hill (2006). *Data Analysis Using Regression and Multilevel/Hierarchical Models*, Cambridge University Press, 625pp.

Harsanyi, J.C. (1955). "Cardinal Welfare, Individualistic Ethics, and Interpersonal Comparisons of Utility," *Journal of Political Economy*, *63*, pp. 309–321.

Helliwell, J., R. Layard, and J. Sachs (2012). *The World Happiness Report*, The Earth Institute, Columbia University, 167pp. Available at: www.earth.columbia.edu/sitefiles/file/Sachs%20Writing/2012/World%20Happiness%20Report.pdf.

Kahneman, D. (1999). "Objective Happiness," in D. Kahneman, E. Diener, and N. Schwarz (eds.), *Well-Being: The Foundations of Hedonic Psychology*, The Russell Sage Foundation, 593pp.

Kahneman, D., P.W. Wakker, and R. Sarin (1997). "Back to Bentham? Exploration of Experienced Utility," *Quarterly Journal of Economics*, *112*(2), pp. 375–405.

Keeney, R.L. (1992). *Value Focused Thinking: A Path to Creative Decisionmaking*, Harvard University Press, 416pp.

Keeney, R.L. and H. Raiffa (1976). *Decisions with Multiple Objectives: Preferences and Value Tradeoffs*, Wiley, 569pp.

Knight, J. (2012). "Economic Growth and the Human Lot," *Proceedings of the National Academy of Science*, *109*, pp. 9670–9671.

Little, I.M.D. (1952). "Social Choice and Individual Values," *Journal of Political Economy*, *60*(5), pp. 422–432.

March, J.G. (1976). "Chapter 5: The Technology of Foolishness," in J.G. March and J.P. Olsen (eds.), *Ambiguity and Choice in Organizations*, Universitetsforlaget, pp. 69–81.
(1978). "Bounded Rationality, Ambiguity, and the Engineering of Choice," *The Bell Journal of Economics*, *9*(2), pp. 587–608.
Myers, D.G. and E. Diener (1995). "Who Is Happy?," *Psychological Science*, *6*(1), pp. 10–19.
(1996). "The Pursuit of Happiness," *Scientific American*, May, pp. 70–72.
Nettle, D. (2005). *Happiness: The Science behind Your Smile*, Oxford University Press, 216pp.
NRC (2013). *Subjective Well-Being: Measuring Happiness, Suffering, and Other Dimensions of Experience*, National Academy Press, 204pp.
Rawles, J. (1972). *A Theory of Justice*, Clarendon Press, 607pp.
Sagoff, M. (2004). *Price, Principle, and the Environment*, Cambridge University Press, 284pp.
Savage, L.J. (1954). *The Foundations of Statistics*, Wiley, 294pp.
Smith, A. (1776). *An Inquiry into the Nature and Causes of the Wealth of Nations*, republished in 1937 by The Modern Library Random House, 976pp.
Stevens, S.S. (1946). "On the Theory of Scales of Measurement," *Science*, *103*, pp. 677–680.
Stigler, G.J. (1950a). "The Development of Utility Theory I," *Journal of Political Economy*, *58*(4), pp. 307–327.
(1950b). "The Development of Utility Theory II," *Journal of Political Economy*, *58*(5), pp. 373–396.
Strack, F., M. Argyle, and N. Schwarz (eds.) (1991). *Subjective Well-Being: An Interdisciplinary Perspective*, Pergamon, 291pp.
Szpiro, G. (2013). "Value Judgments," *Nature*, *500*, pp. 521–523.
Tukey, J.W. (1977). *Exploratory Data Analysis*, Addison-Wesley, 688pp.
Velleman, P.F. and L. Wilkinson (1993). "Nominal, Ordinal, Interval, and Ratio Typologies Are Misleading," *The American Statistician*, *47*, pp. 65–72.
von Neumann, J. and O. Morgenstern (1944). *Theory of Games and Economic Behavior*, Princeton University Press, 625pp. (3rd ed., 1953, 641pp.).
von Winterfeldt, D. and W. Edwards (1986). *Decision Analysis and Behavioral Research*, Cambridge University Press, 604pp.
White, A.G. (2007). "A Global Projection of Subjective Well-being: A Challenge to Positive Psychology," *Psychtalk*, *56*, pp. 17–20.
Zeckhauser, R. and E. Schaefer (1968). "Public Policy and Normative Economic Theory," in R. Bauer and K. Gergen (eds.), *The Study of Policy Formation*, The Free Press.

3

Benefit–Cost Analysis

Suppose that I am considering whether I should adopt a specific technology or strategy in order to achieve some desired end. Benefit–cost analysis,[1] or B–C, advances a strategy for supporting such decisions. It proposes that I should add up all the benefits (B) and subtract all the costs (C) of the option I am considering. I should only adopt the technology or strategy if net benefits are positive (i.e., B–C > 0).

In many policy applications, B–C analysis is used to assess a single option. However, as shown in Figure 3.1 it can also be used to support decisions between options. What strategy should I use to make my choice? For example, I might pick the technology or strategy that:

- Is the most energy efficient
- Has the highest-quality engineering
- Increases entropy the least
- Wins in a survey of consumer preferences
- Is the one that EDF recommends
- Is the one that OMB recommends
- Is the one that is simplest
- Is the one that is cheapest.

Again, while some of these attributes might figure in my assessment of benefits or costs (i.e., be part of my utility function), B–C argues that in each case I should compute the difference between the sum of all the benefits and the sum of all the costs and then choose the option that maximizes net benefits.

That sounds simple. But if the outcomes lie in the future, how can I be sure I have assessed them fully and correctly (see Chapters 4, 8, and 9)? Equally

[1] Many authors and others refer to "cost–benefit analysis" or CBA. However, I use the term "benefit–cost analysis" or B–C so as to have the dash do double-duty as a minus sign, since the point of such analysis is to compute net benefits, which is benefits *minus* cost.

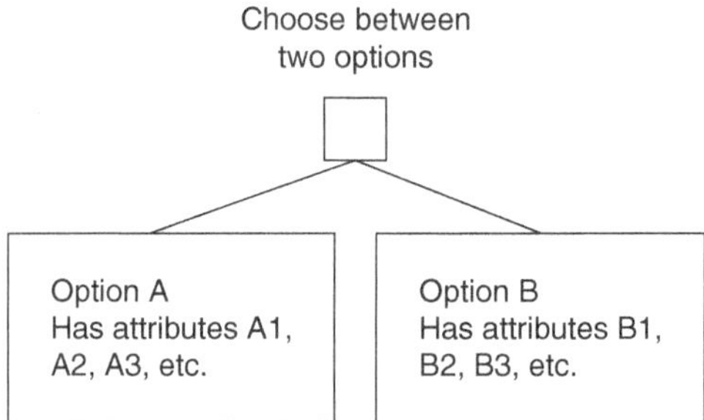

FIGURE 3.1. How should I choose between two options, such as two different technologies, in order to achieve a desired end?

important, how should I measure the benefits and cost? For example, should I measure benefit as P*Q, the price of the product I buy multiplied by the quantity? In Chapter 13, we'll see that this is precisely what Chauncey Starr (1969) did when he wanted to estimate benefits in a classic paper that helped kick off the field of risk analysis. However, economists note that this confuses "total economic value" with "total welfare." We begin this chapter with a very brief review of some of the key ideas and strategies that have been developed to support the performance of B–C analysis. We then explore a number of the issues and limitations that arise in using B–C to address real-world problems.

3.1 B–C BASICS

In a perfectly competitive market, if you buy quantity Q of an infinitely divisible good, you don't just pay the market price P for the last unit of the good that you buy, you pay that price for *all* the goods that you purchase. Suppose, for example, that the good is electricity. We'll ignore intricate rate structures and assume that the price is a flat 15¢/kWh. If you have no electricity at all, you would clearly be willing to pay far more than 15¢/kWh for the first little bit you use so that you can operate a few lights, charge your cellphone, etc. As you use more and more, you will finally reach a point (Q) at which you are no longer willing to pay 15¢ for another kWh. At that point, your marginal utility for an incremental unit of electricity is just equal to its price.

As Figure 3.2 indicates, for every kWh that you bought before you reached that price, you enjoyed a "surplus" in the sense that you received a larger amount of welfare (i.e., you would have been willing to pay more) than your marginal cost. The shaded area in Figure 3.2 is called your "consumer's surplus."

In a market economy with perfect competition, we can estimate a *ceteris paribus* demand curve for the economy as a whole.[2] In that case, the shaded area in Figure 3.2 becomes the "consumer surplus" experienced in that market.

[2] *Ceteris paribus* means "all other things held the same."

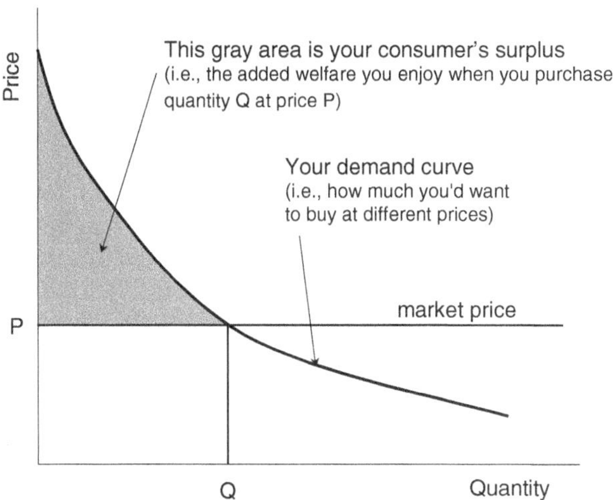

FIGURE 3.2. Illustration of consumer's surplus. Since you pay only P for every unit of quantity Q, but would be willing to pay much more for units before you reach Q, you enjoy a "surplus" in welfare. This illustration is for you as an individual (hence the word "consumer's").

Thus, E.J. Mishan (1973) writes, "for all except marginal change in the amount of good, the market price prevailing in a perfectly competitive setting is an inadequate index of the value [total utility] of a good." Mishan notes that in estimating the *ceteris paribus* demand curve, one is assuming that the population has fixed size and fixed tastes, that prices for all other goods and productive services are fixed, as are "the existing distribution of society's assets among its members," and he reminds us that "a change in any of these things can alter the shape of the demand curve."

Benefit–cost analysis originated in the French civil engineering community as they worked to develop a systematic approach to choosing how to invest in roads, bridges, dams, and other infrastructure. Ekelund and Hébert (1999) explain that the first formal benefit–cost analysis was undertaken in France in 1708.[3] As we noted in Chapter 2, the first person to properly estimate benefit in a B–C analysis by using the concept of consumer surplus was the French engineer Jules Dupuit in 1844. Prior to this time, most analysts had used prices to assess benefits (in much the way that Starr did over 120 years later).

Because the idea was very new, Dupuit went to considerable lengths to explain consumer surplus with examples that involved increasingly higher

[3] In their fascinating book, Ekelund and Hébert (1999) recount in considerable detail how not just benefit–cost analysis but many of the basic ideas of modern microeconomics originated in the French civil engineering community well before British economists developed modern microeconomic theory.

taxes or tolls for the use of a facility such as a bridge. As a concrete example he wrote:

We want to know the utility of a footbridge that is being used free of charge at the rate of 2,080,000 crossings annually. Suppose that a toll of 0 fr.01 would reduce the number of crossings by 330,000, that a tax of 0 fr.02 would reduce it by 294,000, and so on. We then say that for 330,000 crossings the utility is about 0 fr.01 and that for the next 294,000 crossings the utility is about 0 fr.02 and we can then draw up the following table.

330,000	crossings at	0 fr.01	produces a utility of	3300	francs
294,000	"	.02	"	5880	"
260,000	"	.03	"	7800	"
228,000	"	.04	"	9120	"
198,000	"	.05	"	9900	"
170,000	"	.06	"	10,200	"
144,000	"	.07	"	10,080	"
120,000	"	.08	"	9600	"
98,000	"	.09	"	8820	"
78,000	"	.10	"	7800	"
60,000	"	.11	"	6600	"
44,000	"	.12	"	5280	"
30,000	"	.13	"	3900	"
18,000	"	.14	"	2500	"
8000	"	.15	"	1200	"
2,080,000	"			102,000	"

Thus, 102,000 francs would be the absolute utility to society of the bridge. We can find the relative utility by deducting the costs of maintenance and the interest on the capital expended on construction. If the latter sum were to reach or exceed 102,000 francs, the construction would have produced no utility, the difference expressing the loss that would have been made. Such is the calculation to be made in the case where the crossing is free of charge. If there is a toll, we must take only the figures below that of the charge. Thus, for a toll of 0 fr.05, for example, the absolute utility of the bridge is expressed by the sum of the ten last figures or 36,000 francs. (Dupuit, 1844)

The formulation shown in Figure 3.2 is sometimes termed the Marshallian measure of consumer's surplus, after Alfred Marshall (1924). In modern B–C analysis, two other measures of benefit are sometimes used: the "compensating value" (CV) and the "equivalent variation" (EV). As Brent (2006) explains, compensating value proceeds under the assumption that there will be a price reduction due to an increase in output, and asks the amount of compensation that one could take away from consumers and leave them just as well off as they were before the change. In contrast, equivalent variation asks how much compensation one would have to give to consumers in order to forgo the future change. In general, CV yields a smaller value and EV a larger value than the Marshallian measure, although in many cases the values are not dramatically different from the classical Marshallian measure. Readers can find a more detailed discussion of these measures, together with a discussion of various econometric evaluations and applications, in Brent (2006). Readers will find a discussion of the more general issue of willingness to pay versus willingness to accept compensation in Chapter 5.

Much of the practical work in performing B–C analysis entails estimating "shadow prices." Mishan (1973) writes: "There is nothing very special about the notion of a shadow price. In evaluating any project, the economist may effectively 'correct' a number of market prices and, also, may attribute prices to unpriced gains and losses that it is expected to generate." Brent (2006) elaborates:

> Shadow price (social value) determination is at the heart of CBA and public policy. To encourage or discourage an activity one needs to know its social value. If the market price is below its shadow price, then the scale of the activity should be expanded ... Similarly, if the current price is above the shadow price, the activity should be reduced in scale ... The shadow price can be defined as the increase in social welfare resulting from any marginal change in the availability of commodities or factors of production [that is, for good G, the shadow price is the change in social welfare divided by the change in the output of good G].

Often, although not always, shadow prices are estimated as the Lagrange multipliers in a constrained economic optimization. For a detailed discussion, readers are referred to any standard book on B–C analysis such as chapter 4 in Brent (2006).

Often it is necessary to add several consumer surpluses together. For example, if you were doing an analysis of benefits from energy supplied to the home, the consumer surplus for electricity and gas would have to be added together. An economist assuming competitive markets and rational consumers might argue that the order in which the two services are introduced does not matter (Mishan, 1973). In fact, of course, the order may have a significant effect. For example, many consumers would probably not replace their existing electric water heaters if gas subsequently becomes available, this despite the fact that such a replacement would pay for itself very quickly.[4]

In B–C analysis, both the size of the population and its income enter when estimating benefits. For example, Mishan (1973) notes that as population grows, "a bridge or a national park will cater to an increase in the annual number of travelers or visitors over time" and thus produce greater benefit. He argues that this is not because a visitor's "annual visit to the national park provides him with any more utility than it did when he was less rich, but simply because the maximum sum he is willing to pay is higher when his real income,

[4] In a particularly dubious program, some years ago an electric utility in the southern United States made offers to homeowners to replace their existing gas water heaters for free with a new electric water heater (whose operating cost would of course have been much higher).

or welfare is higher." If population grows and per capita income remains fixed, Mishan (1973) notes:

> there will be an increase in the demand for the good produced by an investment project ... [In this case the] bridge or a national park will cater to an increase in the annual number of travelers or visitors over time ... [I]f, at a constant price level, we make our calculations on the basis of money values, any rise in the value of benefits over time ... [due to increased income or population] must be entered into the calculation.

This argument raises a fundamental issue that must be considered when evaluating choices through the use of B–C methods: does the decision maker, or society as a whole, wish to value the policy choice on the basis of how many people will make use of it, and/or how much they are prepared to pay for it? In evaluating a project such as the decision to build a new bridge, the answer is almost certainly yes. However, in making choices about national parks, wilderness areas, or reserves for pristine mid-Pacific coral reefs, the answer is considerably less clear.

There is an obvious problem of valuing a national park, or even more problematic, a wilderness area, solely on the basis of the number of people who visit it and the number of days they spend there. For one thing, overuse may degrade its value. More generally, most people see value in the preservation of such places as an end in itself.

In the resource economics community this issue has given rise to the concept of "existence value," that is, the value that people assign to something that they know is out there, do not personally use, but want to see preserved. Typically this is assessed in terms of "willingness to pay." Of course, even if willingness to pay can be adequately assessed, this formulation can be problematic since willingness to pay is limited by an individual's or a society's income. Should the decision to preserve a mid-Pacific pristine coral reef be based solely on an assessment of the net "willingness to pay" of the U.S. population?

At their root, such questions involve the issue of whether the use or preservation of all things in the natural world should be at the discretion of humankind. Much of Western decision making, including most contemporary economic analysis, has (at least implicitly) adopted the perspective that all the earth is available for human use. However, many are troubled by a too literal interpretation of this view and have argued that not all things involving the use and disposition of the earth (and the heavens) should be subject to human discretion. Rather, adopting a "rights-based" perspective, they argue that some things should lie outside the domain of conventional economic decision making. These questions are discussed at greater length in Chapter 5.

There is no avoiding the reality of income effects or the increasing pressure on services as population increases. However, the fact that both can influence the estimation of B in a B–C analysis can give rise to problematic situations.

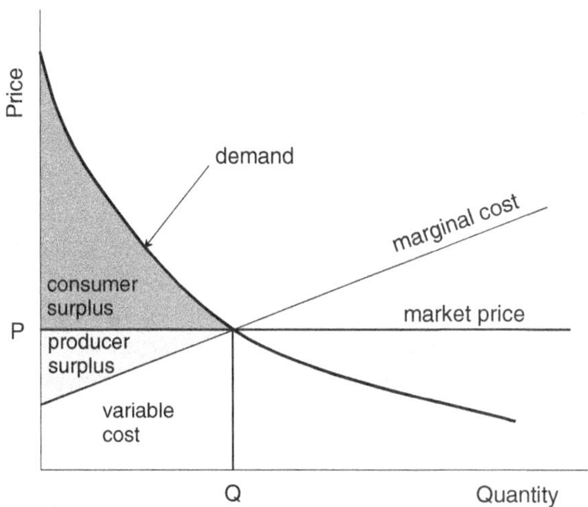

FIGURE 3.3. Producer surplus is the light gray shaded area below the market price and above the marginal cost curve. The sum of the two shaded areas is the benefit.

For example, if an action requires the expenditure of money, then richer people, and richer societies, can afford to spend more.[5] I am able to buy a safer car (a Volvo) than the average resident of India because I can afford the considerably higher cost of all the features that make my more expensive car safer. But, within a society, how should the relation between income effect and something like safety be balanced? For example, within the United States, should airplanes be made safer than inter-city buses simply because the income of those who take the bus is on average lower than that of those who take the plane? The consequences for public policy of the "income effect" are explored at greater length in Chapter 5.

In the preceding discussion, we have focused on the benefits experienced by consumers. However, consumers are not the only ones whose benefits should be considered in a B–C analysis. If they did not receive some benefit from the transaction, the supplier would not be willing to remain in business. To see the benefit or "producer surplus" that the supplier enjoys, we need to consider the marginal cost of supplying the good or service. This is shown in Figure 3.3. The sum of the consumer surplus and producer surplus constitutes the benefit of the good or service. Typically, it is this sum that should be used to estimate B in a B–C analysis.

While estimating consumer surplus and rents and adding them together may seem straightforward, the technical details can become remarkably complicated.

[5] In this context, see Wildavsky (1981), "Richer Is Safer," as well as Keeney (1990), "Mortality Risks Induced by Economic Expenditures."

3.2 PARETO OPTIMALITY

A clearly desirable attribute for any social policy is that while it is beneficial to some, it doesn't make anyone else worse off. A project or allocation that achieves this goal is termed "Pareto-superior" (named for Italian economist Vilfredo Pareto[6]). It is easy to come up with examples of public policies that fail to meet the Pareto standard: for example, taxing people who never leave the city in order to create a national park, or taxing people to develop a vaccine for a disease to which they are already immune. Indeed, it is difficult to think of major policy choices that *do* meet this standard. More typically one must balance the benefits a policy confers on some with the costs imposed on others.

But suppose we *could* identify a policy that we believe is Pareto-superior. A few moments of reflection will suggest several questions that deserve our further attention. For example:

- Do people know a priori what will make them better off?[7]
- Is the policy distributionally unjust? For example, do we want to support all public policies that will make a few billionaires wealthier while not decreasing the wealth of any other member of society? Of course, one could add a requirement for some degree of equity in income distribution (i.e., a low Gini coefficient) to one's utility function, but it is the rare piece of formal analysis that does that.
- Is it really more important to meet individual preferences than to enhance more general community values? B–C analysis as conventionally practiced is utilitarian – equating net social benefit with the economic welfare of the sum of all members of society. While one could specify a utility function in which individuals place value on collective community attributes, again this is almost never done.

Since most projects or policies cannot demonstrate that they are Pareto-superior, the next best thing is to ask whether, if a policy were implemented, the winners could compensate the losers and still come out ahead. If such compensation were paid, in some form that was deemed acceptable to the losers, then the projects or policy would meet the Pareto criterion. Showing that such transfer payments are possible is a standard strategy in B–C analysis and doing this is termed meeting the Kaldor–Hicks (KH) standard (named for the British economist Nicholas Kaldor (1936) and Hungarian/British economist John Hicks (1936), who independently proposed it in slightly different forms).

[6] Ackerman (1997a) provides the interesting (but in this context irrelevant) historical note that "Pareto was an affluent aristocrat who believed that substantial inequality was inevitable and cynically dismissed democratic politics as a fraud – and was made an honorary member of the Italian Senate under Mussolini."

[7] This issue is discussed at greater length in Part III of this book when we turn to a consideration of how individuals make decisions.

In general, the use of such a "potential Pareto criterion" leads to a much better state of affairs, but again some critical reflection yields cases that are troubling. For example, imagine a project that degrades the experience of a handful of American millionaires visiting an exclusive private African game park, while improving dramatically the life of indigenous subsistence farmers who live near the park. Should all those subsistence farmers be asked to compensate the American millionaires?

Another potential problem arises if the changes involved are large enough to modify prices. Moore (2007) observes, "if we were regarding the compensation as being monetary, then a large change would likely change prices, so that monetary compensation which at first seemed adequate might fail to be so after the price changes. Consequently ... the compensation should be in real terms."[8] Finally, as Jones-Lee (1976) notes:

> Under certain circumstances, it is possible for a change from allocation X to allocation Y to represent a potential Pareto improvement and for the change back from the allocation Y to the allocation X also to represent a potential Pareto improvement ... In formal terms the relation of "being potentially Pareto-preferred" is non-symmetric rather than asymmetric and cannot therefore form the basis for a strong (or strict) ordering ... [However], provided that the cost-benefit analyst is aware of the problem and is also careful to point out any instance of its occurrence, then it would not seem to detract too severely from the potential Pareto improvement criterion as a decision-making tool.

In most cases, when one is operating within a single society, and when issues of equity and of people knowing what they value are reasonably straightforward, the Kaldor–Hicks standard seems pretty reasonable – especially if compensation actually takes place. However, in standard B–C analysis, it is often assumed that so long as the transfer *could* take place, and thus have the project or policy meet the Pareto criterion, that alone is sufficient and the transfer does not actually have to be made. In defense of this position John Graham (2008), who directed the Office of Information and Regulatory Affairs (OIRA) in the U.S. Office of Management and Budget (OMB) from 2001 to 2006, writes:

> If society applies the KH test in multiple rulemakings, and if there is considerable mixing of gainers and losers over time, we should expect most citizens in society to become better off than they would have been under the Pareto test ... The more widely the KH test is applied across rulemakings, programs, and agencies, and the more mobile citizens in society are, the more likely it is that different segments of the public will be affected, which means that more mixing of gainers and losers is likely to occur ... As more mixing occurs, a larger percentage of citizens, not just the average citizen, will experience net gains from repeated application of the KH test.

[8] In Moore (2007) this observation is followed by four pages (pp. 416–420) of mathematics that illustrate and work out the details.

DISCUSSION QUESTION

Do you find this statement by John Graham to be persuasive? If so, why; if not, why not?

3.3 B–C VERSUS B/C

When should one report the results of a benefit–cost analysis in terms of net benefit and when is it more appropriate to report them as a ratio of benefits over costs? Mishan (1973) supplies a compact two-page answer. He starts with a simple example. Suppose that one has computed the present value of the benefits and costs for two proposed investment streams (call them options one and two) with the following results:

Option	C	B	B–C	B/C	(B–C)/C
1	100	150	50	1.5	0.5
2	20	50	30	2.5	1.5

Since (B–C)/C = B/C – 1 he then focuses only on assessing when one should use B–C and when one should use (B–C)/C. His bottom line reads: "if we adopt the ... [B–C] method we tacitly assume that the alternative investments are of exactly the size given: no increase is possible. If, however, we adopt the ... [(B–C)/C] method of ranking, we tacitly suppose the opposite; that either stream can be increased in either proportion" (Mishan, 1973). Since in most public policy decision settings one is trying to evaluate one or a few fixed options, in most cases the present value of net benefit (B–C) is what one should be estimating.

3.4 SIMPLE IN THEORY, BUT OFTEN COMPLICATED IN PRACTICE

When performing a B–C calculation, sorting out what should and should not be counted, figuring out what is a transfer payment and hence neither a cost nor a benefit, figuring out where the boundaries for an analysis should be drawn, dealing correctly with issues such as taxes or international trade, avoiding double counting, and valuing externalities and other things that are not traded in markets, along with many similar issues, require careful attention. There are entire books that address these and many other subtleties in the practice of B–C analysis. Readers who plan to actually perform B–C analysis can find useful insight and guidance in the references below. Before attempting to perform a B–C analysis, it is best to have taken a full graduate course or to collaborate with an expert who is familiar with the many nuances involved in producing high-quality analysis.

SUGGESTED RESOURCES TO LEARN TECHNICAL DETAILS ABOUT B–C ANALYSIS

For an older but very compact summary of the basic ideas, see:

- E.J. Mishan, *Economics for Social Decisions: Elements of Cost-Benefit Analysis*, Praeger, 151pp., 1973.

For a very interesting overview followed by a collection of thoughtful excerpts from the literature, see:

- Richard Layard (ed.), *Cost-Benefit Analysis*, Penguin Books, 496pp., 1972.

For a quite comprehensive modern treatment, with an elaboration of many theoretical and practical issues, and a number of worked examples, see:

- Robert J. Brent, *Applied Cost-Benefit Analysis*, 2nd ed., Edward Elgar, 470pp., 2006.

3.5 THE RISE OF B–C ANALYSIS IN GOVERNMENT DECISION MAKING

Hammond (1966) argues that B–C "is peculiarly, and perhaps uniquely, American, stemming as it does from a Constitution in which the antinomies inherent in a federation of sovereign states are compounded by a refusal to allow the Federal Executive Branch discretion over details of expenditure already approved in principle by the Legislative Branch."

While perhaps implied in the Rivers and Harbors Act as early as 1902, most historians date the application of B–C analysis by the U.S. Army Corps of Engineers to the 1920s when the later version of that Act instructed the Corps to begin to apply it to the projects that they were considering. Porter (1995) explains:

> Cost-benefit methods were introduced to promote procedural regularity and to give public evidence of fairness in the selection of water projects. Early in the century, numbers produced by the Corps of Engineers were usually accepted on its authority alone, and there was correspondingly little need for standardization of methods. About 1940, however, economic numbers became objects of bitter controversy, as the Corps was challenged by such powerful interests as utility companies and railroads. The really crucial development in this story was the outbreak of intense bureaucratic conflict between the Corps and other government agencies, especially the Department of Agriculture and the Bureau of Reclamation. The agencies tried to settle their feuds by harmonizing their economic analyses. When negotiation failed as a strategy for achieving uniformity, they were compelled to try to ground their makeshift techniques in economic rationality. On this account, cost-benefit analysis had to be transformed from a collection of local bureaucratic practices into a set of rationalized economic principles. In the American political context of systematic distrust, though, its weakness became strength. Since the 1960s, its champions have claimed for its almost universal validity.

Porter (1995) argues that:

> Cost-benefit analysis was intended from the beginning as a strategy for limiting the play of politics in public investment decisions. In 1936, though, army engineers did not envision that this method would have to be grounded in economic principles, or that it would require volumes of regulations to establish how to do it, or that such regulations might have to be standardized throughout the government and applied to almost every category of public action. The transformation of cost-benefit analysis into a universal standard of rationality, backed up by thousands of pages of rules, cannot be attributed to the megalomania of experts, but rather to bureaucratic conflict in a context of overwhelming public distrust. Though tools like this one can scarcely provide more than a guide to analysis and a language of debate, there has been strong pressure to make them into something more. The ideal of mechanical objectivity has by now been internalized by many practitioners of the method, who would like to see decisions made according to "a routine" that, once set in motion by appropriate value judgments on the part of those politically responsible and accountable, would – like the universe of the deists – run its course without further interference from the top ... This, the ideal of economists, originated as a form of political and bureaucratic culture.

In 1935, the House Flood Control Committee reviewed 1600 projects and recommended a set that had the highest ratio of benefits to costs. However, once the bill moved forward to the full House and Senate, individual members started writing in additional projects, some of which did not have good ratios, and some of which had not even been assessed. The resulting bill became sufficiently embarrassing that it did not pass. In an effort to avoid a repeat of this experience, the 1936 Flood Control Act had specific language that required that benefits exceed costs: "the Federal Government should improve or participate in the improvement of navigable waters or their tributaries including watersheds thereof, for flood-control purposes if the benefits to whomsoever they may accrue are in excess of the estimated costs, and if the lives and social security of people are otherwise adversely affected."

Persky (2001) has observed that:

> Exactly what the Congress meant by "benefits" has always been a bit vague. For modern economists, this uncertainty is only intensified by the separate reference to "lives and social security" ... it seems doubtful that either the Congress or the Corps of that time explicitly commanded any formal application of economic theories of consumer surplus. Thus it was probably only accidental that the choice of the terminology echoed the theoretical traditions of public finance.

The 1936 legislative language launched the Corps on a process of formalizing the strategies they used to compute the benefits and costs of proposed projects. These almost "cookbook-like" procedures began to run into more and more opposition with the growth of the environmental movement in the 1960s. For example, Fox and Herfindahl (1964) noted that no systematic assessment was being performed to determine if projects were being designed to have the optimal size. They also showed that if projects approved in 1962 using a discount rate of 2.6% had instead been assessed using discount rates of 4%, 6%, or 8%, then the fraction of projects for which the "initial gross investment would have a B-C ratio of less than unity ... [would be lower by] 9 percent, 64 percent and 80 percent respectively."

One especially controversial case involved the proposal to build a dam just upstream of the Delaware Water Gap. The proposed Tocks Island Dam would have been the largest dam east of the Mississippi. Benefits the Corps assessed included flood control, water supply, hydroelectric power and recreation services provided through the purchase of 70,000 acres and the construction of many access roads and recreational facilities. Construction of the dam was authorized in the Flood Control Act of 1962. Enormous controversy ensued. In 1975, the Delaware River Commission voted to delay construction. Then, in 1978, Congress voted to apply a "wild and scenic" designation to the relevant section of the Delaware River, thus putting an end to the dam project.

The dam project stimulated a substantial amount of critical analysis in the academic and environmental communities. Under a chapter subheading titled "Analyses are not about what people care about," Robert Socolow (1976) noted that analyses of the sort the Corps had done to support the dam project "are part of the formal debate. We should not be surprised to learn, therefore, that the disciplined analyses brought to bear ... hardly ever do justice to the values in conflict." Socolow noted that in doing its B–C analysis the Corps had used what he terms "golden rules" for generating numbers and choosing analytical strategies in place of performing case-specific analysis:

> Golden rules have been developed that shelter the practitioner of cost-benefit analysis from ... uncertainty about [where to draw the] boundaries [of the analysis]. The analysis becomes stylized, like the folk art of an isolated village. Those costs and benefits that it is permissible to include in the analysis become codified, as do many of the procedures for evaluating their dollar magnitudes. The warping effect on discourse is substantial.

Socolow notes, for example, that an "extraordinary reduction [i.e., narrowing] in the problem's structure" occurs when the Corps evaluation rules are followed on issues such as valuing all recreational activities at $1.35 per visitor per day. "[T]hese oddly formal rules have real consequences – consequences such as extra roads being built through open country to provide the access needed to keep the park populated [and thus justify the large benefit use numbers]." Socolow also comments on "golden numbers," numbers like the flow rate that must be maintained in the Delaware River at Montague, New Jersey, that was chosen years previously through an entirely ad hoc process, but had become enshrined, with no subsequent reexamination, as a hard constraint.

In the United States, the use of B–C analysis in support of virtually all major governmental regulatory decision making is a relatively new phenomenon. Most of the risks and other problems that were being addressed by regulation during the early part of the twentieth century were so obvious, and the costs of addressing them sufficiently modest, that few could argue that the benefits to society did not outweigh the costs.[9] However, as the scope of government regulatory activity continued to expand, more and more people began to argue that government regulation was going too far. Some of these arguments were based on principled considerations of the role of risk in social innovation.[10] Many, however, were motivated by corporate and other interests and did not want to be required to comply with what they saw as an unreasonable regulatory burden.

As concern about regulatory burdens grew, calls began to appear to require that *all* proposed regulation be subjected to a strict B–C evaluation, with the implication that only those that clearly passed such a test be implemented. To this end, in 1981 the Reagan Administration promulgated Executive Order 12291, which stipulated that:

> In promulgating new regulations, reviewing existing regulations, and developing legislative proposals concerning regulation, all agencies, to the extent permitted by law, shall adhere to the following requirements: (a) Administrative decisions shall be based on adequate information concerning the need for and consequences of proposed government action; (b) Regulatory action shall not be undertaken unless the potential benefits to society for the regulation outweigh the potential costs to society; (c) Regulatory objectives shall be chosen to maximize the net benefits to society; (d) Among alternative approaches to any given regulatory objective, the alternative involving the least net cost to society shall be chosen; and (e) Agencies shall set regulatory priorities with the aim of maximizing the aggregate net benefits to society, taking into account the condition of the particular industries affected by regulations, the condition of the national economy, and other regulatory actions contemplated for the future... each agency shall, in connection with every major rule,[11] prepare, and to the extent permitted by law consider, a Regulatory Impact Analysis (EO 12291).

The Office of Information and Regulatory Affairs (OIRA) in the White House Office of Management and Budget began to vet the required B–C analyses, sending some back to Agencies if they did not meet with OIRA's approval.

Not surprisingly, these developments created quite a stir. Subsequent litigation determined that the order did not apply to the actual decisions made in those cases where the authorizing legislation (such as the Clean Air Act)

[9] Note, however, for much of the nineteenth century and the early part of the twentieth century the U.S. Congress refused to implement regulations to limit even the most obvious risks, such as explosions of pressure vessels in steamboats, on the philosophical grounds that these risks were better managed via the courts through tort liability. For details, see the discussion in Section 17.5.

[10] See the discussion of papers by Aaron Wildavsky, Michael Thompson, and William C. Clark in Chapter 10.

[11] A major rule was defined as "any regulation that was likely to result in: 1) An annual effect on the economy of $100 million or more; 2) A major increase in costs or prices for consumers, individual industries, Federal, State, or local government agencies, or geographic regions; or 3) Significant adverse effects on competition, employment, investment, productivity, innovation, or on the ability of United States-based enterprises to compete with foreign-based enterprises in domestic or export markets."

contained no language about balancing benefits with costs. For a time there was concern that OMB might impose what John Graham (2008) has termed a "hard" net benefit test, requiring that the quantitative measure of net benefits must be positive before a regulation could be enacted. In the event, a "soft" test became the norm, in which an argument can be made that the combination of quantitative and qualitative benefits is sufficient to justify a proposed regulation. In the case of regulations such as those promulgated under the Clean Air Act, only a "procedural requirement" was imposed to perform a B–C analysis that would inform OMB, the Congress, and the broader society. However, in these cases there is no formal requirement that the decision maker use the results of the B–C analysis in setting the regulatory standard. Adler and Posner (2006) explain that:

> Prodded by the Office of Management and Budget (OMB), agencies began to perform CBA more routinely than in the past, but these early cost-benefit analyses did not seem to play a decisive role in regulatory decision making, and indeed for most regulations, they continued to be thin rationalizations for decision making on other grounds ... This might explain why President Clinton did not reverse the policy but instead continued the policy of requiring agencies to perform CBA. Clinton's executive order also required agencies to consider equity and other factors absent from Reagan's.

The requirement on Federal regulatory agencies to perform B–C analysis on proposed rules that are then reviewed by OMB's OIRA has continued to this day. Cass Sunstein (2013a), who ran the office from 2009 to 2012, notes that:

> While I was at OIRA, the Obama administration took a number of steps to ensure a disciplined approach. The first step was to promote accountability by recommending that all significant regulations be accompanied by a simple table that offered three things: first, a clear statement of both the quantitative and the qualitative costs and benefits of the proposed or final action; second, a presentation of any uncertainties; and third, similar information for reasonable alternatives to the action. In a related step, OIRA required agencies to include a clear, simple executive summary of any new rules, explaining what they were doing and why and offering a crisp account of the costs and benefits, both quantitative and qualitative. Many federal rules are extremely long and complex, and it is hard for people to know what they are trying to do and why. A clear summary can help a great deal.

Sunstein (2013b) argues that B–C analysis has often served as "a spur to regulation." He notes that:

> If risks do not produce visceral reactions, partly because the underlying activities or outcomes do not produce vivid images, cost-benefit analysis can show that regulatory controls are warranted. The cost-justified elimination of lead in gasoline, brought about by the Reagan administration, is a case in point, and it has had terrific public health benefits. In government [as Director of OIRA under President Obama] I saw a large number of cases in which high benefits and low costs spurred enthusiasm for regulatory initiatives. Rules increasing energy efficiency for appliances made their way through the process in part because their benefits were far higher than their costs...

[Similarly] the Montreal Protocol [limiting the use of CFCs] has been a terrific success story, and cost-benefit analysis helped to make it happen.

Estimating the benefits and cost of a regulation, especially one that has yet to be implemented, poses considerable challenges. One of the most extensive retrospective analyses has been the congressionally mandated evaluation of the costs and benefits of the U.S. Clean Air Act Amendments (EPA, 1997, 2010). The second of these reports that the best estimate of "the net benefit (benefits minus costs) over the entire 1990 to 2010 period of the additional criteria pollutant control programs incorporated in the Post-CAAA case is $510 billion." Considerable sensitivity analysis found B ≥ C across a wide range of assumptions. These reports have been extensively reviewed by the Advisory Council on Clean Air Act Compliance Analysis, made up of independent outside experts convened under the auspices of EPA's Science Advisory Board. In its cover letter to the EPA Administrator communicating its review of the 2010 report, the Council wrote (EPA SAB, 2010):

The Council is impressed with the quality, scope, and presentation of the Second Prospective Report. The report provides a state-of-the-art analysis of the benefits and costs of the 1990 CAAA. It is comprehensive in scope, sophisticated in methodology, and is accessible to both specialist and non-specialist readers. The report includes methodological innovations that enhance our understanding of the benefits and costs of air-quality regulations.

Not all retrospective studies have been as successful or displayed similar high-quality results. Harrington et al. (2000) of Resources for the Future (RFF) performed the first systematic assessment of a number of U.S. Federal regulations. The abstract of their paper reads:

This study compares *ex ante* estimates of the direct costs of individual regulations to *ex post* assessments of the same regulations. For total costs the results support conventional wisdom, namely that the costs of regulations tend to be overestimated. This is true for 14 of the 28 rules in the data set discussed, while for only 3 rules were the *ex ante* estimates too low. For unit costs, however, the story is quite different. At least for EPA and OSHA rules, unit cost estimates are often accurate, and even when they are not, overestimation of abatement costs occurs about as often as underestimation. In contrast, for those rules that use economic incentives, unit costs are consistently overestimated. The difference between the total-cost and the unit-cost results is caused by frequent errors in estimates of the effects of individual rules, which suggests, in turn, that the rule's benefits may also be overestimated. The quantity errors are driven both by difficulties in determining the baseline and by incomplete compliance. In cases of unit-cost overestimation, unanticipated technological innovation appears to be an important factor – especially for economic incentive rules, although procedural and methodological explanations may also apply.

Following this work, OMB (2005) performed a study using a larger sample of regulations in which they also tried to compare the accuracy of costs measured to the accuracy of benefits. OMB invited Harrington to be a reviewer of that report. After performing his review he went on to write an RFF Discussion Paper (Harrington, 2006), in which he reports that "OMB estimates annual benefits in 2004 to be $70 to $277 billion and costs to be $34 to $39 billion, but these estimates omit a great deal; the cost estimate, in particular, is generally acknowledged to be an underestimate." In the same paper Harrington also reviewed two other studies, one by Crain (2005) that was sponsored by the Small Business Administration and a second by OMB. He writes, "I find the Crain report to be deeply problematic and the OMB's *ante/ex post* comparison slightly less so." Clearly one must look very carefully at the details when examining estimates of the costs and benefits of proposed and existing regulations, since performing such assessments poses considerable challenges and they often take place in a highly charged political environment.

3.6 EXAMPLES OF B–C ANALYSIS APPLIED TO PUBLIC DECISION MAKING

The best way to get a sense of the application of B–C analysis is to look at a few applications. However, it is difficult to find examples that do not run to hundreds of pages. Here I urge readers to take a look at a couple of analyses that have been succinctly described in the refereed literature.

Lester Lave once said: "Never believe the executive summary of a B-C analysis." In what follows, I reproduce two executive summaries. However, readers should read the full papers and then consider the several discussion questions I have posed.

READING 3.1

Lester B. Lave, William Wecker, Winthrop Reis et al., "Controlling Emissions from Motor Vehicles: A Benefit-Cost Analysis of Vehicle Emission Control Alternatives," *Environmental Science & Technology*, 24(8), pp. 1128–1135, 1990.

Abstract: U.S. ozone levels exceed the National Ambient Air Quality Standard (NAAQS) of 0.12 ppm in virtually every major urban area and in many nonurban areas in the East (1). Hydrocarbon emissions are a primary contributor to the photochemical reactions that produce ozone (2). These emissions from cars and light duty trucks (LDTs) account for approximately 35% of total man-made hydrocarbon emissions (1).

This article reports the results of a benefit-cost analysis of alternative strategies for controlling emissions from hydrocarbon refueling and evaporative emissions from cars and LDTs. Our analysis accounts for interactions among the different control methods that influence both the costs and benefits of the available strategies. It also examines the role played by variations in temperature conditions and pollution levels across regions and seasons in estimating the costs and benefits.

We have found that the most economically efficient control of refueling and evaporative hydrocarbon emissions from cars and LDTs would result from a mixed strategy that includes fuel volatility controls and controls on service station pumps. The most cost-effective control strategy involves fuel volatility and gasoline pump controls, which can be tailored to each region; the former can be changed with each season. Such flexible controls can be targeted to the specific regions and season where they will do the most good, while avoiding the wasteful cost of controls when and where ozone is not a problem. Vehicle-based controls do not have these advantages.

DISCUSSION QUESTIONS FOR READING 3.1

- What is the decision criterion established by the Clean Air Act?
- What is an EKMA diagram?
- The paper says: "We assume that a reduction in volatile organic compound (VOC) emissions will result in an approximately proportional reduction in VOC concentrations." What is your view of this assumption?
- How are benefits being estimated in this study?[12]
- How do the authors compare current costs with future benefits?
- What, if any, sensitivity analysis do the authors perform?
- When you read this article, did you check who paid for the analysis? If yes, why? If no, why not?

READING 3.2

Alex Hills and M. Granger Morgan, "Telecommunications in Alaskan Villages: A Technical, Economic, and Institutional Analysis," *Science, 211*, pp. 241–248, 1981.

A recently installed satellite system now provides modern long-distance telecommunications services to 100 rural Alaskan villages, most of whose residents are Alaska Natives. In most villages no local telephone or television distribution facilities have yet been installed. Local telephone exchange service appears to be economically marginal unless modest regulatory changes are made. Television delivery presents more difficult problems involving technical and organizational structure. If, after weighing the potential social and cultural effects, village residents elect to acquire television, a delivery system based on low-power transmitters in the villages, local government as the basic organizational and economic unit, and a statewide nonprofit service organization, is the feasible system best suited to village needs.

DISCUSSION QUESTIONS FOR READING 3.2

- In this paper the authors do not perform a B–C analysis for the provision of telephone. What is their justification for doing that? What analytical method do they employ to evaluate alternative strategies for the delivery of a telephone service?

[12] Somehow the authors neglected to reference the source of figure 1, which is Krupnick and Portney (1991).

- How do the authors estimate the benefit of TV service? What limitations might that method entail?
- The authors write: "None of the systems can generate enough revenue from subscriber fees under any pricing scheme (not just marginal cost pricing) to cover operating cost." Yet they claim that some of the systems to supply TV services have a positive value of B–C. How can that be?
- Why do they propose supporting community TV service with a local tax?[13]
- Why do the authors add the extended discussion on "Social Impacts and Local Control"? What do they conclude in this discussion, and why?

The Ford Pinto Case: An especially controversial event in the 1970s, involving the Ford Pinto, raised the issue of B–C analysis in the public consciousness (Birsch and Fielder, 1994). The Pinto was a small low-cost car that Ford developed to compete with VW and small Japanese imports. The gas tank on the Pinto was located between the rear axle and the back bumper. During company testing Ford engineers found that the tank could be easily ruptured if the car was hit from behind, even at relatively low speeds. In addition, such crashes often caused the doors to jam shut, making quick exit difficult. A primary cause of the gas tank ruptures was bolts that stuck out from the differential housing. These bolts punctured and split the tank when it was smashed forward. Ford found that this risk could be minimized by placing a plastic guard over the ends of the bolts (at a cost of just over $2.00/car) and that a wider range of fuel tank risks could be dramatically reduced by covering the outside of the tank, or lining its inside with a bladder, at costs of the order of $8. However, because minimizing production cost was their prime objective, Ford chose not to install these safety features.[14]

Once people started being killed and maimed as a result of fuel fires in Pintos that had been hit from behind, crash investigators outside Ford figured out what was going on and victims and their relatives began to sue Ford. Some of these cases resulted in large monetary damages. In 1977, Mark Dowie published a piece in *Mother Jones* titled "Pinto Madness" that reported that Ford had been aware of this problem but had chosen to do nothing about it in order to keep costs down.[15] Dowie wrote:

> Ford knows the Pinto is a firetrap, yet it has paid out millions to settle damage suits out of court, and it is prepared to spend millions more lobbying against safety standards.

[13] After completing his Ph.D. on this topic, Alex Hills moved back to Alaska and became the governor's telecommunications advisor and had an opportunity to implement many of the results from his analysis. However, the Alaska State Legislature did not adopt his recommendations on how to fund village TV, and simply opted to supply TV services entirely with funds from the Alaskan state budget (a politically easy choice given large revenues from oil operations).

[14] Note that auto manufacturers face hundreds of such cost–safety tradeoffs in every car they design.

[15] A slightly edited version of Dowie's piece along with a number of essays and the Ford B–C memo can be found in Birsch and Fielder (1994).

With a half million cars rolling off the assembly lines each year, Pinto is the biggest selling subcompact in America ... Finally, in 1977 new Pinto models have incorporated a few minor alterations necessary to meet the federal standard that Ford managed to hold off for eight years.

Dowie goes on to assert that "Ford waited eight years because its internal 'cost-benefit analysis,' *which places a dollar value on human life*, said it wasn't profitable to make the changes sooner." This charge had a big impact on the public, and on juries, that were still not particularly aware of the use of B–C methods in the late 1970s. The charge was buttressed by the publicity surrounding an internal Ford memo, subsequently made public when it was attached to a filing Ford made with NHTSA, in opposition to a proposed standard. This memo used a simple B–C analysis to argue that the proposed standard to prevent fires in rollover crashes would not be cost beneficial. Ford estimated the standard would prevent 180 burn deaths and 180 burn injuries and avoid 2100 burned vehicles for a total cost of $49.5 million (using NHTSA's then values of $200,000 per death, $67,000 per injury, and $700 per vehicle).[16] The memo estimated that the cost of implementing preventive designs in 11 million vehicles and 1.5 million light trucks would come to $137 million.

While no B–C analysis by Ford has been reported that explicitly addressed the issue of retrofitting existing Pintos with protection against rear-end crashes, or adding the protective features to new Pintos (before new regulations required them in 1977), many have assumed that similar considerations were responsible for Ford's inaction.

DISCUSSION QUESTIONS ON THE FORD PINTO CASE

Assume that the original Pinto was significantly more susceptible to fire when hit from the rear than other similar vehicles of that era. Suppose, in addition, that Ford had actually performed a B–C analysis similar to the one outlined above in order to decide whether to retrofit existing Pintos. Would they have been justified in doing this? If yes, would they have been justified in using similar values to those used prospectively for an analysis by NHTSA?

READING 3.3

John D. Graham, "Saving Lives through Administrative Law and Economics," *The University of Pennsylvania Law Review*, 157, pp. 395–540, 2008. While it is worth reading this entire paper, here I am suggesting that you read the two sections titled "III D. OIRA as an Advocate of Lifesaving Regulation,

[16] A detailed discussion of the subject of valuing statistical lives lost is provided in Section 5.2.

2001–2006" (pp. 465–480) and "III E. The Benefits and Costs of Federal Rules, 1981–2006" (pp. 481–483).

In the first section (III D), Graham, who headed the U.S. OMB's Office of Information and Regulatory Affairs during the administration of President George W. Bush, presents examples of the role played by B–C analysis in: (1) reducing diesel-engine exhaust; (2) reducing sulfur and nitrogen oxides from coal plants; (3) increasing the fuel efficiency of cars and light trucks. Graham argues that in an administration with a strong "pro-business" orientation, the existence of B–C analyses that showed substantial net benefits was critical in successfully moving some, if not all, proposed regulations forward to implementation. In the second section (III E), Graham summarizes the costs and benefits of the 259 final rules cleared through OIRA. While there are not complete data across this entire interval, he notes that between 1992 and 2006 "the total benefits of major rules ... exceeded the total costs by more than 300%."

DISCUSSION QUESTIONS FOR READING 3.3

- In the case of diesel exhaust, how did OIRA use the existing EPA B–C analysis to persuade senior White House officials that the regulation should be sustained over the objection of several in industry and the conservative Mercatus Center?
- How did that experience lead to regulation of emissions from off-road diesels?
- Graham writes: "In the course of helping to prepare the clear skies proposal, I learned why it can be difficult for benefit cost insights to determine the content of a legislative proposal, especially when complex regional and partisan politics are in play." Describe the issues that arose and how that in turn led to the Clean Air Interstate Rule (CAIR).
- Why did the Bush Administration instruct OIRA to work within existing legal authorities in revising the CAFE standard?
- What is the basis of Graham's argument that sometimes "a benefit-cost approach can lead to more stringent rules than a feasibility analysis"?
- Graham argues that rather than look at the evolution of just the cost of regulation, one should look at the evolution of the net benefits (B–C) of those regulations over time. What is his assertion about that evolution?

While a number of Executive Orders require that B–C analysis be performed for "significant rules," agencies do not always need to show a positive net benefit before adopting a rule. This is particularly true when Congressional legislation mandates that a regulation be adopted, although even in that case agencies go through a full analysis.

A good example is provided by the decision to mandate the phase-in of video rear vision systems in all U.S. passenger cars and light trucks. In February 2008, Congress enacted H.R. 1216, the Cameron Gulbransen Kids Transportation Safety Act of 2007. In support of their final rule to implement the portion of this Act dealing with reducing death and injuries from backing, the National Highway Traffic Safety Administration (NHTSA) produced many hundreds of pages of analysis, took extensive comments, held workshops, and in April 2014 produced a Rear Visibility Final Rule (NHTSA, 2014).

While it is difficult to assess the exact number of fatalities and injuries that result from passenger cars and light trucks backing into people, "NHTSA estimated that backing crashes of all types result in approximately 410 fatalities and 42,000 injuries each year" (NHTSA, 2014). Of the fatalities, they estimated that 31 percent of those killed were under the age of five and that 26 percent of those killed were over the age of seventy.

The NHTSA analysis was complicated by the fact that rear vision systems were already being added to vehicles for other reasons.[17] Hence, they had to make assumptions about the added cost of the mandate above what the market would already do. They conducted a variety of analyses to assess how many deaths might be avoided through the incremental addition of rear vision systems that would result from the mandate. In addition to adopting numbers from Department of Transportation (DoT) guidance on valuing the deaths and injuries,[18] they also estimated the incremental reduction in property loss due to backing that would result. NHTSA conducted various studies to estimate the extent to which rear vision systems would reduce fatalities, since, of course, drivers might sometimes fail to see the person behind them even if they appeared in the visual display. They performed Monte Carlo analysis to address uncertainty and parametric analysis in key variables such as discount rate. Table 3.1 reports their resulting estimates.

[17] Presumably, many customers buy video rear view systems because they make backing easier. However, NHTSA did not make a quantitative assessment of that benefit that all auto-owners will enjoy once the rule is fully in effect.

[18] For a discussion of the issue of valuing statistical lives (VSL) and injuries, see Chapter 5. In their analysis, NHTSA used values for the value of a statistical life (VSL) and injuries from guidance for 2013 published by the Department of Transportation in which DOT adjusted nine studies in the literature on VSL to 2012 dollars and then averaged the results that ranged from $5.17 to $12.93 million per statistical death, obtaining an average VSL of $9.1 million. The DOT guidance excluded values from the literature of $21.65 and $36.17 million on the grounds that these were "implausibly high; industry/occupation risk measure[s]." The DOT guidance observes that based "on wage forecasts from the Congressional Budget Office, we estimate that there will be an expected 1.07 percent annual growth rate in median real wages over the next 30 years (2013–2043). These estimates imply that VSL in future years should be estimated to grow by 1.07 percent per year before discounting to present value." They also advise that injuries should be assessed in terms of a fraction of the VSL using their standard injury severity scale (minor = 0.003VSL; moderate = 0.047VSL; serious = 0.105VSL; severe = 0.266VSL; critical = 0.953VSL). Note the use of three significant figures for these highly normative and uncertain quantities! The DOT guidance can be found at: www.dot.gov/sites/dot.dev/files/docs/VSL%20Guidance%202013.pdf.

TABLE 3.1. *Summary in millions of 2010 dollars of the benefits and costs estimated by NHTSA for the phase-in of rear view video systems in U.S. passenger cars and light trucks from model year 2018 onward as a function of the type of equipment used (180° or 130° camera) and the discount rate (3% or 7%) (NHTSA, 2014).*

	Primary estimate	Low estimate	High estimate	Discount rate
Benefits				
Lifetime monetized	$265	$305	$305	7%
Lifetime monetized	$344	$396	$396	3%
Costs				
Lifetime monetized	$546	$620	$557	7%
Lifetime monetized	$546	$620	$557	3%
Net impact (B-C)				
Lifetime monetized	-$281	-$315	-$252	7%
Lifetime monetized	-$202	-$224	-$161	3%

Note: NHTSA notes that "the Primary Estimate is the lowest installation cost option (which assumes manufacturers will use a 130° camera and will utilize any existing display units already offered in their vehicles). The Low Estimate and High Estimate provide the estimated *minimum and maximum net impacts* possible." Also in this table, costs "do not vary by discount rate because ... only ... the costs that are incurred in order to produce the rear visibility system and install it on the vehicle ... [are included]." See the final rule for details.

NHTSA writes "the agency expects today's final rule to save between 20 and 30 equivalent lives per year ... Using the most up-to-date value of a statistical life from the Department's guidance ... the agency expects the annual benefit of the rule (due to fatality and injury reduction) to be between $206 million and $317 million." As Table 3.1 makes apparent, these benefits are significantly less than the anticipated costs. Depending on assumptions, annual net benefits for this congressionally mandated capability range from –$161 to –$315.

It is interesting to note that, in the final rule, NHTSA references the agency guidance on valuing statistical lives and injuries but does not actually quote the values. Rather, it reports that based on its "estimates for costs and benefits, the net cost per equivalent life saved for rear visibility systems meeting the requirements of today's final rule ranges from $15.9 to $26.3 million. (The range presented is from a 3% to 7% discount rate.)" It also observes that "As backover crash victims are often struck by their immediate family members or caretakers, it is the Department's opinion that an exceptionally high emotional cost, not easily convertible to monetary equivalents, is often inflicted upon the families of backover crash victims."

3.7 LIMITATIONS OF B–C

As B–C analysis has seen greater use as a tool in support of social decision making, it has been subjected to vigorous criticism. Much of this criticism has been ideological – either reflecting a concern that it may result in decisions that the critics oppose, or subject important public decisions to mechanistic processes that ignore non-economic values.

Lester Lave, one of the leading economists of his generation and among the most accomplished practitioners of B–C analysis, also wrote what I think is the best systematic critical assessment of the method.

READING 3.4

Lester B. Lave, "Chapter 6: Benefit-Cost Analysis: Do the Benefits Exceed the Costs?" in Robert W. Hahn (ed.), *Risks, Costs, and Lives Saved: Getting Better Results from Regulation*, Oxford University Press, pp. 104–134, 1996.

This is an important paper worth reading with considerable care. Lave begins his discussion by listing 13 attributes of B–C analysis. The first six are those he argues are needed to make it a useful accounting framework to examine social decisions. The next seven attributes are required if one is to justify using B–C as a tool to optimize social welfare. Lave then explores the limitations of, and justifications for, the Kaldor–Hicks criteria. He provides a brief critique of using a utilitarian framework as the basis for all social decision making. He then explores a number of theoretical problems under headings that read: Is everything for sale?; Situation-specific values; Valuing non-market goods and services; Is efficiency the only important criterion?; and Benefit cost analysis for personal decisions? He discusses a number of more practical operational problems under headings that read: Selecting a valuation concept; Neglecting the primary objective; The correct discount rates; and Valuation in the presence of risks. After discussing a number of other important issues he concludes by arguing that the best use of B–C analysis is *not* as a tool for making social decisions, but rather as a systematic strategy to help inform such decisions. He writes:

With the exception of economists who are utilitarians or unwitting utilitarians, there is general agreement that the option identified as having the largest net benefit does not have a strong claim to being the best social choice. The time has come to purge the utilitarian foundation from benefit-cost analysis. This means identifying the tools as a decision analysis rather than as a means for prescribing optimal decisions. We want to praise the virtues of systematic analysis and straight thinking, not the utilitarian properties of maximizing net benefits in complicated social decisions ...

We need to admit in many cases that a confident benefit-cost analysis is not possible. The basic approach can be used to structure the problem and to give values to parts of the problem, but it simply may not be possible to derive a meaningful estimate of net social benefits. Finally, we need to be more conscious of how we, and the analysis, are used. This is policy analysis, not fundamental research. Partial information can mislead, and analysts can, even inadvertently, become advocates. It is not enough to provide a caveat that such analysis may be underestimating costs and overestimating benefits. We must investigate the extent of the possible bias.

Along with other proponents of benefit-cost analysis, I praise it for forcing analysts to think systematically about social issues, collect data, and do analyses to clarify the implications of decisions. Unfortunately, the median application of the tool not only does not point to the best policy, but tends to mislead. We economists have a great deal of work to do before we can make benefit-cost analysis into the helpful tool that we know it can be.

Finally, in order to understand that Lave is not opposed to all uses of B–C analysis, I suggest:

READING 3.5

Kenneth Arrow, Maureen L. Cropper, George C. Eads, and Robert N. Stavins, "Is There a Role for Benefit-Cost Analysis in Environmental, Health and Safety Regulation?" *Science*, *272*, pp. 221–222, 1996.

DISCUSSION QUESTIONS FOR READINGS 3.4 AND 3.5

- In the piece "Benefit-Cost Analysis: Do the Benefits Exceed the Costs?" Lave lays out a series of criticisms of B–C analysis. Despite all of these concerns, do you believe there are situations in which B–C analysis should be used as part of public policy decision making? If so, please list several examples and explain *how* you think B–C should be used.
- In the beginning of his piece "Benefit-Cost Analysis: Do the Benefits Exceed the Costs?" Lave wrote: "The foundation of benefit-cost analysis is flawed: the tool cannot provide what some economists claim. The practical difficulties are even greater. Even if the techniques might be valid when implemented by a master with unlimited resources for analysis, it is a problematic tool in practice when resources are extremely limited, time is short, and people with little training or experience do the analysis."
- Having written that, how might he defend signing on as a co-author of the Arrow et al. paper in *Science*?

While there is a large literature on the strengths and limitations of B–C analysis, readers who would like a compact overview of the pros and cons might also look at chapter 3 ("What's Wrong with BCA: The Liberal Indictment") and chapter 4 ("In Defense of BCA: Responses to Liberal Critics") in:

- James T. Campen, *Benefit, Cost and Beyond: The Political Economy of Benefit-Cost Analysis*, Ballinger, 240pp, 1986.

3.8 EFFICIENCY VERSUS EQUITY

B–C methods are basically designed to evaluate the efficiency of a proposed line of action. Decision making by democratically elected governments tends to be as or more concerned with issues of equity. As noted in Section 3.2, in principle, issues of equity could be incorporated into B–C analysis. Harberger (1978) has provided an extended, but largely theoretical, discussion of how this might be done using "distributional weights." As he notes, one reason that economists have tended to shy away from the use of such weights is that "it is difficult indeed to tell the difference between a system of distributional weights that decline with income and an alternative system of measurable utility made interpersonally comparable on some basis and characterized by diminishing marginal utility of wealth or income." Boadway (1976) has developed the details of how equity might be integrated with efficiency in B–C analysis if the changes involved are at the margin and if distributional weights have been given. On this latter he observes that "no direction can be given to the policy maker by the economist as to how these [weights] should be arrived at." He suggests that it might be wise to "try out different assumptions about the social welfare function in order to test the sensitivity of any project to equity considerations." Anthoff et al. (2009) provide a concise review of work in this area.

One context in which it has been particularly difficult for analysis to ignore issues of equity has involved attempts to apply B–C and similar methods to assessing global policies to address climate change. In the early stages of work on valuing the impacts of climate change, some economists adopted dramatically different values for a statistical life for impacts in the developed and developing world. "The value put on a death in a developed country, for example, was 15 times higher than in a less industrialized nation" (Masood, 1995). Not surprisingly, this led to a firestorm of protests from commentators across the developing world (Pearce, 1995).[19]

In order to begin to better address this issue, Anthoff et al. (2009) have used "equity weights" in the FUND integrated assessment model, arguing that the "social cost of carbon estimates should be normalized with the marginal utility of consumption of a specific region, if the marginal damage costs are later to be used in a cost-benefit analysis for projects in that region." They ran their analysis for five different socioeconomic development scenarios. From this work they drew four conclusions:

> First, equity-weighted estimates are substantially higher than estimates without equity-weights; equity-weights may even change the sign of the social cost estimates. Second, estimates differ by two orders of magnitude depending on the region to which the equity weights are normalised. Third, equity-weighted estimates are sensitive to the resolution of the impact estimates. Depending on the assumed intraregional income distribution, estimates may be more than twice as high if national rather than regional impacts are

[19] See the additional discussion in Section 5.5.

aggregated. Fourth, variations in the assumed inequality aversion have different impacts in different scenarios, not only because different scenarios have different emissions and hence warming, but also because different scenarios have different income differences, different growth rates, and different vulnerabilities.

In a subsequent paper, Anthoff and Tol (2010) provide a thoughtful critique of the problem of using this approach for national and international decision making. They note:

The aggregation of welfare losses to different countries assumes a supranational perspective. Indeed, the formal derivation of equity weights presumes a global social planner. As an academic exercise, this is fine. However, equity-weighted world wide marginal damage cost estimates for carbon dioxide are also used by the European Commission and the UK Government in their cost-benefit analysis of domestic policies ... This is unusual, because in other domestic policy contexts benefits or costs are not valuated from a supranational planner perspective, let alone by using distributional weights giving more (less) weight to impacts in poor (rich) countries.

In summary they write:

Estimates of the marginal damage costs of carbon dioxide emissions require the aggregation of monetised impacts of climate change over people with different incomes and in different jurisdictions. Implicitly or explicitly, such estimates assume a social welfare function and hence a particular attitude towards equity and justice. We show that previous approaches to equity weighting are inappropriate from a national decision maker's point of view, because domestic impacts are not valued at domestic values. We propose four alternatives (sovereignty, altruism, good neighbour, and compensation) with different views on concern for and liability towards foreigners. The four alternatives imply radically different estimates of the social cost of carbon and hence the optimal intensity of climate policy.

The bottom line is that incorporating equity into B–C methods, especially when those experiencing the costs and benefits are in very different socioeconomic and cultural settings, is at a minimum challenging and should be undertaken with great care and careful reflection. (See Figure 5.6 and associated discussion.)

3.9 GOING OFF THE DEEP END WITH B–C ANALYSIS

In recent years the U.S. regulatory system has become more committed to trying to quantify the net benefits of regulatory policies than virtually any other government in the world. Two recent examples illustrate some of what this focus can lead to.

The first example involves the *Regulatory Impact Analysis for the Final Mercury and Air Toxics Standards* released by the U.S. EPA in December 2011. Since it is 510 pages long, here I will summarize just one key part.

EPA was very slow in implementing controls under the National Emission Standards for Hazardous Air Pollutants (NESHAP) as stipulated in section

112(a) of the Clean Air Act (CAA). Late in 2011 they finalized a rule under this authorization to apply to new and existing coal- and oil-fired electricity generating units. While not strictly part of the process of establishing a standard under the Clean Air Act, the EPA is required by the Office of Management and Budget (OMB) to also prepare a Regulatory Impact Analysis of all new rules. EPA summarizes their analysis as follows:

This rule will reduce emissions of Hazardous Air Pollutants (HAP), including mercury, from the electric power industry. As a co-benefit, the emissions of certain PM2.5 precursors such as SO2 will also decline. EPA estimates that this final rule will yield annual monetized benefits (in 2007$) of between $37 to $90 billion using a 3% discount rate and $33 to $81 billion using a 7% discount rate. The great majority of the estimates are attributable to co-benefits from 4,200 to 11,000 fewer PM2.5-related premature mortalities. The monetized benefits from reductions in mercury emissions, calculated only for children exposed to recreationally caught freshwater fish, are expected to be $0.004 to $0.006 billion in 2016 using a 3% discount rate and $0.0005 to $0.001 billion using a 7% discount rate. The annual social costs, approximated by the compliance costs, are $9.6 billion (2007$) and the annual monetized net benefits are $27 to $80 billion using a 3% discount rate or $24 to $71 billion using a 7% discount rate. As discussed in Chapter 3, costs were annualized using a 6.15% discount rate. The benefits outweigh costs by between 3 to 1 or 9 to 1 depending on the benefit estimate and discount rate used. There are some costs and important benefits that EPA could not monetize, such as other mercury reduction benefits and those for the HAP other than mercury being reduced by this final rule. Upon considering these limitations and uncertainties, it remains clear that the benefits of the MATS are substantial and far outweigh the costs. Employment impacts associated with the final rule are estimated to be small. (EPA, 2011)

In what follows I will only briefly summarize that portion of EPA's analysis that involved estimating and valuing the decrement of the IQ of children exposed to mercury *in utero*. However, it is well worth reading their more than 60 pages of detailed elaboration of how they performed the analysis.

There is uncertainty about the relative contributions to mercury in the environment from natural processes and from human activities such as power plants, the chemical forms this mercury assumes (methylmercury being of particular concern), its fate and transport, and its impacts on people and ecosystems (NRC, 2000). After an extended qualitative discussion of all of these factors, Agency analysts clearly believed that they needed to produce a number. They explain:

EPA chose to focus on quantification of intelligence quotient (IQ) decrements associated with prenatal mercury exposure as the initial endpoint for quantification and valuation of mercury health benefits. Reasons for this initial focus on IQ included the availability of thoroughly-reviewed, high-quality epidemiological studies assessing IQ or related cognitive outcomes suitable for IQ estimation, and the availability of well-established methods and data for economic valuation of avoided IQ deficits, as applied in EPA's previous benefits analyses for childhood lead exposure.

A quantitative assessment was performed of the concentration of mercury in wild-caught fish and how much of that fish is consumed by pregnant women. They then produced an estimate of the "dose-response relationship between maternal mercury body burden and subsequent childhood decrements in IQ using a Bayesian hierarchical model to integrate data from the Faroe Islands, New Zealand, and Seychelles Islands studies." Figure 3.4 summarizes the analytical process EPA used to estimate exposure. Figure 3.5 outlines their strategy for linking census tracts to demographic data and mercury fish tissue samples. The entire analysis is performed nationwide at the census track level, with the population in each divided into four demographic groups: urban/low income, urban/high income, non-urban/low income, and non-urban/high income.

Once they finally obtained an estimate of maternal exposure, their analysis proceeds as follows:

Estimating the IQ decrements in children that result from mothers' ingestion of mercury required two steps. First, based on the estimated average daily maternal ingestion rate, the expected mercury concentration in the hair of exposed pregnant women was estimated as follows:

$$CHgH_n = (0.08)\text{-}1 * (HgI_n/W),$$

where

CHgH = average mercury concentration in maternal hair (ppm) and
W = average body weight for female adults below age 45 (= 64 kg).

... to estimate the expected IQ decrement in offspring resulting from in-utero exposure to mercury through mothers' fish consumption, the following dose-response relationship was applied:

$$dIQ_n = 0.18 * CHgH_n, \quad (4.6)$$

where

dIQ = IQ decrement in exposed mother/child (IQ pts).

... The valuation approach used to assess monetary losses due to IQ decrements ... expresses the loss to an affected individual resulting from IQ decrements in terms of foregone future earnings (net of changes in education costs) for that individual. These losses were estimated using the following equation:

$$Vn = VIQ * dIQi,$$

where

V = present value of net loss per exposed mother/child (2006 dollars) and
VIQ = net loss per change in IQ point.

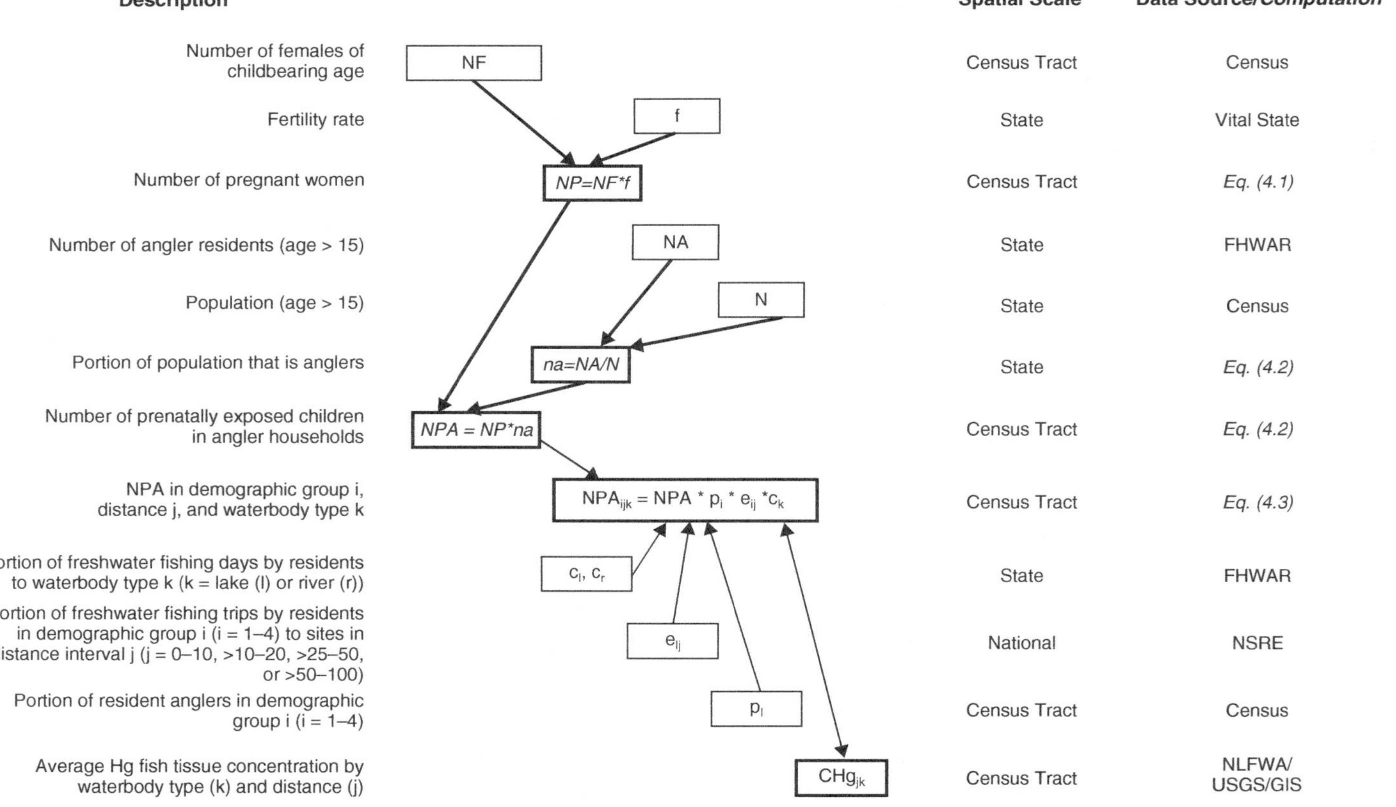

FIGURE 3.4. Factors EPA included in their assessment of exposure to mercury (source: EPA, 2011).

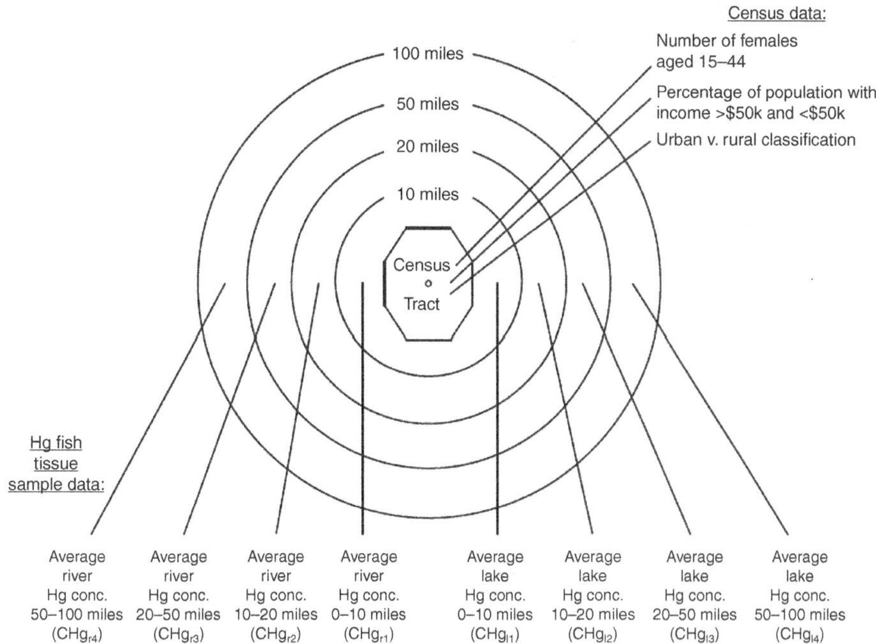

FIGURE 3.5. Summary of how EPA linked census tracts to demographic data and mercury fish tissue samples. The entire analysis is performed nationwide at the census track level, with the population in each divided into four demographic groups (source: EPA, 2011).

The net loss per IQ point decrement is estimated based on the following relationship:

$$VIQ = (z * PVY) - (s * PVS),$$

where

PVY = median present value of lifetime earnings,
PVS = present value of education costs per additional year of schooling,
z = percentage change in PVY per 1-point change in IQ, and
s = years of additional schooling per 1-point increase in IQ.

The estimate for PVY is derived using earnings and labor force participation rate data from the 2006 Current Population Survey (CPS) and assuming (1) an individual born today would begin working at age 16 and retire at age 67; (2) the growth rate of wages is 1% per year, adjusted for survival probabilities and labor force participation by age; and (3) lifetime earnings are discounted back to the year of birth. Using a 3% discount rate, the resulting present value of median lifetime earnings is $555,427 in 2006 dollars.

Estimates of the average effect of a 1-point increase in IQ on lifetime earnings (z) range from a 1.76% increase ... to a 2.379% increase ... The percentage increases in the two studies reflect both the direct impact of IQ on hourly wages and indirect effects on annual earnings as the result of additional schooling and increased labor force participation ...

In addition to this positive net effect on earnings, an increase in IQ is also assumed to have a positive effect on the amount of time spent in school (s) and on associated costs (PVS). The range of estimates for *s* is based on Schwartz (1994) who reports an increase of 0.131 years of schooling per IQ point and Salkever (1995) who reports an increase of 0.1007 years.[20]

The estimate for PVS is derived using an estimate of $16,425 per additional year of schooling in 1992 dollars ..., which is based on U.S. Department of Education data reflecting both direct annual expenditures per student and annual average opportunity cost (i.e., lost income from being in school). We assume these costs are incurred when an individual born today turns 19, based on an average 12.9 years of education among people aged 25 and over in the United States. Discounting at a 3% rate to the year of birth results in an estimate of $13,453 per additional year of schooling in 2006 dollars.

To incorporate (1) uncertainty regarding the size of z and (2) different assumptions regarding the discount rate, the resulting value estimates for the average net loss per IQ point 48 decrement (VIQ) are expressed as a range. Assuming a 3% discount rate, VIQ ranges from $8,013 (using the Schwartz estimate for z and s) to $11,859 (using the Salkever estimates). With a 7% discount rate assumption, the VIQ estimates range from $893 to $1,958.

From here, EPA went on to sum across all census tracts nationwide and add up the results in order to get "the total loss in IQ points due to mercury exposures through consumption of self-caught freshwater fish [which] was estimated to be 25,545 in 2005. For the 2016 base case, the total decrease in IQ points was estimated to be 24,419 (4.4% lower)." Finally, EPA converted this to a present dollar value (assuming five different mercury control scenarios and two different discount rates). They conclude that:

the benefits of the 2016 Toxics Rule scenario (relative to the 2016 base case) are estimated to range between $4.2 million and $6.2 million (assuming a 3% discount rate), because of an estimated 511 point reduction in IQ losses. These benefits are 73% as large as the benefits of the 2016 zero-out scenario (relative to the same 2016 base case). Relative to the *2005* base case, the benefits of the 2016 Toxics Rule scenario range from $13 million to $20 million (3% discount). Despite growth in the exposed population from 2005 to 2016, the changes from the 2005 base case to the 2016 base case account for 69% of these benefits, while the changes from the 2016 base case to the 2016 Toxics Rule account for 31%.

This conclusion is followed by a nine-page discussion of assumptions, limitations, and uncertainties.

One cannot help but be appreciative of the elaborate ends to which the EPA analysts went in this calculation, breaking things down into all their component parts and systematically working through the analysis.

But it is also important to ask ourselves three questions:

1. Do we value bright kids primarily because they can earn more money?

[20] Note the three and four significant figures reported in these and a number of subsequent values.

2. Would our society be justified in deciding to allow childhood exposure to a neurotoxicant if the economic benefits of doing that are sufficiently high?
3. What does it say about us as a society that we have put in place a regulatory system with associated OMB guidance that results in EPA feeling they must go through such elaborate calculations to estimate whether or not we should expose our kids to a neurotoxicant?

SUPPLEMENTAL READING

Resources for the Future has produced a very useful book on regulatory impact analysis that includes three chapters on the Clean Air Mercury Rule as well as chapters on the Clean Air Interstate Rule and the Cooling Water Intakes Structure Rule. See: Winston Harrington, Lisa Heinzerling, and Richard Morgenstern, *Reforming Regulatory Impact Analysis*, Resources for the Future, 246pp., 2009.

The second example, which in my view also "goes off the deep end" in the use of formal quantification of the sort developed for use in B–C analysis, is the work first done in 2010 at the behest of OMB by an interagency working group to estimate "the social cost of carbon." This assessment was motivated in part by the "endangerment" finding that EPA released in December 2009 that greenhouse gases threaten public health and the environment (EPA, 2009). The authors of the "Social Cost of Carbon" report explain that:

> Under Executive Order 12866, agencies are required, to the extent permitted by law, "to assess both the costs and the benefits of the intended regulation and, recognizing that some costs and benefits are difficult to quantify, propose or adopt a regulation only upon a reasoned determination that the benefits of the intended regulation justify its costs." The purpose of the "social cost of carbon" (SCC) estimates presented here is to allow agencies to incorporate the social benefits of reducing carbon dioxide (CO2) emissions into cost-benefit analyses of regulatory actions that have small, or "marginal," impacts on cumulative global emissions ...
>
> The "social cost of carbon" (SCC) is an estimate of the monetized damages associated with an incremental increase in carbon emissions in a given year. It is intended to include (but is not limited to) changes in net agricultural productivity, human health, property damages from increased flood risk, and the value of ecosystem services. We report estimates of the social cost of carbon in dollars per metric ton of carbon dioxide.

On the basis of 50 pages of modeling and other assessment activities, the report recommended:

> four SCC estimates for use in regulatory analyses. For 2010, these estimates are \$5, \$21, \$35, and \$65 (in 2007 dollars). The first three estimates are based on the average SCC across models and socio-economic and emissions scenarios at the 5, 3, and 2.5 percent

TABLE 3.2. *Values of the social cost of carbon dioxide (2015–2020) in 2011 dollars as promulgated by the U.S. Government as of 2013. These values are "dollar-year" and "emission-year" specific. Details can be found at: www.epa.gov/climatechange/Downloads/EPAactivities/scc-fact-sheet.pdf.*

	Average discount rate			
Year	5%	3%	2.5%	3% 95th percentile
2015	$12	$39	$61	$116
2020	$13	$46	$68	$137
2025	$15	$50	$74	$153
2030	$17	$55	$80	$170
2035	$20	$60	$85	$187
2040	$22	$65	$92	$204
2045	$26	$70	$98	$220
2050	$28	$76	$104	$235

discount rates, respectively. The fourth value is included to represent the higher-than-expected impacts from temperature change further out in the tails of the SCC distribution. For this purpose, we use the SCC value for the 95th percentile at a 3 percent discount rate. The central value is the average SCC across models at the 3 percent discount rate. For purposes of capturing the uncertainties involved in regulatory impact analysis, we emphasize the importance and value of considering the full range. These SCC estimates also grow over time. For instance, the central value increases to $24 per ton of CO_2 in 2015 and $26 per ton of CO_2 in 2020.

Since its initial release in 2010, the U.S. Government has continued to update the values it wishes agencies to use for the social cost of carbon. The values reported for 2013 are shown in Table 3.2.

The objective of specifying a social cost of carbon (SCC) is to designate a rate at which we should invest to avoid the costs of climate change. At its heart, the interagency analysis is based on running a number of different integrated assessment models and examining their estimates of cost. As detailed in Section 11.7, these models have a number of limitations. From the point of view of estimating an investment rate to avoid climate change, their biggest limitation is that they basically estimate costs in terms of forgone future consumption – which, when measured in dollar terms, inevitably weights the result toward the change in consumption of high-income populations. While others may disagree, in my view the largest costs of climate change, and the primary reason the United States and other societies should be making investments to minimize or avoid significant change, is to prevent massive and perhaps catastrophic ecological disruption, and to limit the impact on the world's poorest people (i.e., to address issues of global equity). The integrated assessment models used in the interagency exercise do an extremely poor job of dealing with either of these issues.

In 2017, a committee of the U.S. National Academies completed an extensive review of how the social cost of carbon was being estimated. The committee examined "potential approaches, along with their relative merits and challenges, for a comprehensive update to the current methodology" (NRC, 2017). It recommended that a new integrated assessment model be developed. It also recommended much expanded use of expert elicitation. As readers will infer when they read Chapter 9 and Section 11.7, I am unpersuaded that these changes will result in any improvement.

READING 3.6

Interagency Working Group on Social Cost of Carbon, United States Government, "Technical Support Document: Social Cost of Carbon for Regulatory Impact Analysis under Executive Order 12866," U.S. Government, February 2010.

SUPPLEMENTAL READING

Robert S. Pindyck, "Climate Change Policy: What Do the Models Tell Us?," *Journal of Economic Literature, 51*(3), pp. 860–872, 2013.

John Weyant, "Contributions of Integrated Assessment Models," Draft Manuscript, Stanford, 35pp, 2015.

DISCUSSION QUESTIONS FOR READING 3.6

- Do you agree or disagree with Morgan's assessment that the SCC report is an example of B–C type analysis that has "gone off the deep end"? If so, why? If not, why not?
- Some have argued that while the numbers generated by the interagency SCC effort do not adequately reflect the impacts of climate change on ecosystems or on global equity, the effort at least gave OMB a set of numbers supported by a complicated procedure, the details of which do not concern most decision makers. Hence, proponents argue, the effort moves social policy in the right direction, and that fact is more important than the fact that the analysis doesn't really reflect the most important costs to society of climate change. Do you agree?
- Suppose that in place of this interagency undertaking, OMB had instead said: "Because carbon dioxide emissions impact the welfare and ecosystems of the entire planet, it is not sensible to use conventional B–C tools to perform an assessment. In assessing activities and programs that will reduce the emissions of CO_2 and other greenhouse gases, agencies are instructed to perform parametric analysis using a SCC of 20, 40, 80 and 160$/ton of CO_2 and CO_2 equivalent." If you were a staff person at OMB charged with developing a justification for adopting such an approach, what argument would you advance? How would such an instruction have led to more or less defensible regulatory outcomes than the use of the results from the interagency working group?

GENERAL EXERCISE 3.1

Construct a table in which you list all of the strengths and weaknesses of B–C analysis that you can think of.

GENERAL EXERCISE 3.2

Write a short note in which you outline the attributes of private and public decision problems where you believe it would be appropriate to perform a formal B–C analysis and discuss how you believe the results of such an analysis should be used. In doing so, consider at least the following five specific decisions:

1. Deciding whether a company should add a new, more efficient system to manufacture a product they are already making.
2. Deciding whether a highway department should build a new bridge.
3. Deciding whether a new safety system should be required in all new automobiles.
4. Deciding how to set the permissible level of toxic residues allowed in food.
5. Deciding who to marry.

GENERAL EXERCISE 3.3

Write a short note that outlines when, if at all and under what circumstances, you believe that analysts and administrators have a responsibility to argue that assessments they are being asked to perform are not sensible or might better be conducted in some other way?

3.10 B–C VERSUS PRECAUTION

While B–C methods have dominated policy making in the United States, much of the consideration of risk management in Europe has been framed in terms of the precautionary principle.

While ideas of "precaution" have a long history, especially in fields such as public health, Raffensperger and Tickner (1999) provide the following history of the modern development of the principle:

> The principle emerged as an explicit basis of policy during the early 1970s in West Germany as "Vorsorgeprinzip" or the "foresight" principle of German water protection law. At the core of early conceptions of this principle in Germany was the belief that society should seek to avoid environmental damage by careful "forward-looking" planning, blocking the flow of potentially harmful activities. The Vorsorgeprinzip has been invoked to justify the implementation of vigorous policies to tackle river contamination, acid rain, global warming, and North Sea pollution. Implementation of the

foresight principle has given rise to a globally competitive industry in environmental technology and pollution prevention in Germany.

The Precautionary Principle was first introduced internationally in 1984 at the First International Convention on Protection of the North Sea, designed to protect the fragile North Sea ecosystem from further degradation due to the input of persistent toxic substances. At the Second North Sea Conference, ministers noted that "in order to protect the North Sea from possibly damaging effects of the most dangerous substances ... a precautionary approach is addressed which may require action to control inputs of such substances even before a causal link has been established by absolutely clear scientific evidence." Following this conference, the principle was integrated into numerous international conventions and agreements including the Maastricht Treaty, the Barcelona Convention, and the Global Climate Change Convention, among others. The principle guides sustainable development in documents like the 1990 Bergen Ministerial Conference on Sustainable Development and the 1992 United Nations Conference on Environment and Development. It has become a central theme of environmental law and policy in the European Union and many of its member states.

While some have used the idea of precaution to argue to completely ban or avoid any activity for which the associated risks involve uncertainty, the communication from the European Union on this topic is far more nuanced (EU, 2000). It notes that:

The precautionary principle should be considered within a structured approach to the analysis of risk which comprises three elements: risk assessment, risk management, risk communication. The precautionary principle is particularly relevant to the management of risk ... Recourse to the precautionary principle presupposes that potentially dangerous effects deriving from a phenomenon, product or process have been identified, and that scientific evaluation does not allow the risk to be determined with sufficient certainty.

The implementation of an approach based on the precautionary principle should start with a scientific evaluation, as complete as possible, and where possible, identifying at each stage the degree of scientific uncertainty ...

Where action is deemed necessary, measures based on the precautionary principle should be, *inter alia*:

- *proportional* to the chosen level of protection,
- *non-discriminatory* in their application,
- *consistent* with similar measures already taken,
- *based on an examination of the potential benefits and costs* of action or lack of action (including, where appropriate and feasible, an economic cost/benefit analysis),
- *subject to review*, in the light of new scientific data, and
- *capable of assigning responsibility for producing the scientific evidence* necessary for a more comprehensive risk assessment.

DeKay et al. (2002) have demonstrated "how the traditional decision-analytic method can be used to derive decision thresholds for taking precautionary action to avoid a risky activity." They focus particularly on situations in which multiple stakeholders have "differences in their perceptions of the benefit and cost of avoidance" and differences in their perceptions of the accuracy of additional information that may be collected through a test or research program.

In the late 1980s and early 1990s there was considerable concern that exposure to power-frequency (50 and 60 Hz) electric and magnetic fields might give rise to a variety of possible health effects (Nair et al., 1989). My colleagues and I did a considerable amount of risk and other policy analysis. In that context I promoted a strategy that I termed "prudent avoidance." I explained (Morgan, 1992):

> In the public domain, our legal and regulatory institutions have fallen into the unfortunate habit of treating all things as either safe or hazardous. Of course, in our private lives we know the world is not that simple. There are many things (foods, lifestyle choices, possible financial investments) for which our answer to the question "is it risky?" must be "it might be but I don't know." In situations like this, we exercise prudence. Prudence means "exercising sound judgment in practical matters." It means being "cautious, sensible, not rash in conduct."
>
> For example, concerned about the risk of cancer, many of us exercise prudence by eating a bit more fiber, broccoli, and cauliflower than we once did, and a bit less fat and charbroiled meat. We know that the scientific evidence on these dietary changes is mixed and that they offer no assurance of protection from cancer. But, there is some evidence that they might help. The changes don't cost much. You can get used to them, perhaps even grow to like them. So, it seems prudent to make some adjustments.
>
> In public life, we have rather greater difficulty exercising prudence. Our regulatory and legal systems want to classify everything unambiguously as either safe or hazardous.

In that paper I went on to elaborate how both as individuals and as a society we might exercise prudence by taking available steps to avoid exposure when potential risks are uncertain and avoiding exposure costs little or nothing. The approach was adopted in the context of power-frequency fields by a number of U.S. states and several foreign governments.

I can illustrate the concept of prudent avoidance with a personal example. When I measured 60 Hz magnetic fields in my home I discovered that the electric power service drop to our house was attached to the outside wall just on the other side of where my son slept with his head pushed against his bedroom wall. Though I was not persuaded that his nocturnal exposure to a relatively high magnetic field presented any significant risk to his health, as a matter of prudence I moved his bed to a different corner of the room.

I briefly return to the topic of precaution in Section 8.7.

3.11 FINAL THOUGHTS ON B–C

I close this chapter with two observations on B–C analysis that have been offered by thoughtful commentators. First, it is worth repeating Theodore Porter's (1995) historical summary from his book *Trust in Numbers: The Pursuit of Objectivity in Science and Public Life*:

> Cost-benefit analysis was intended from the beginning as a strategy for limiting the play of politics in public investment decisions. In 1936, though, army engineers did not envision that this method would have to be grounded in economic principles, or that it would require volumes of regulations to establish how to do it, or that such regulations might have to be standardized throughout the government and applied to almost every category of public action. The transformation of cost-benefit analysis into a universal standard of rationality, backed up by thousands of pages of rules, cannot be attributed to the megalomania of experts, but rather to bureaucratic conflict in a context of overwhelming public distrust. Though tools like this one can scarcely provide more than a guide to analysis and a language of debate, there has been strong pressure to make them into something more. The ideal of mechanical objectivity has by now been internalized by many practitioners of the method, who would like to see decisions made according to "a routine that, once set in motion by appropriate value judgments on the part of those politically responsible and accountable, would – like the universe of the deists – run its course without further interference from the top."

The second summary comment is drawn from an overview essay written by Frank Ackerman (1997b), who observed:

> The difference between private and social costs must be known to propose policies that internalize externalities. In recent years economists have been hard at work estimating such values. The process recalls an old joke. Graduate school in economics is like a black box, within which a mysterious transformation occurs. In one end go sensible people and out the other come researchers who ask you how much you would pay to avoid having your mother die of cancer.

Later in the same piece, Ackerman concludes: "Cost-benefit analysis is too often promoted from useful servant to foolish master of social decision making, reaching far beyond its limited but effective grasp."

REFERENCES

Ackerman, F. (1997a). "Utility and Welfare II: Modern Economic Alternatives," in F. Ackerman, D. Kiron, N.R. Goodwin, J.M. Harris, and K. Gallagher (eds.), *Human Well-Being and Economic Goals*, Island Press, pp. 81–92.

(1997b). "Applied Welfare Economics: Externalities, Valuation, and Cost-Benefit Analysis," in F. Ackerman, D. Kiron, N.R. Goodwin, J.M. Harris, and K. Gallagher (eds.), *Human Well-Being and Economic Goals*, Island Press, pp. 121–130.

Adler, M.D. and E.A. Posner (2006). *New Foundations of Cost-Benefit Analysis*, Harvard University Press, 236pp.

Anthoff, D., C. Hepburn, and R.S.J. Tol (2009). "Equity Weighting and the Marginal Damaged Cost of Climate Change," *Ecological Economics*, *68*, pp. 836–849.

Anthoff, D. and R.S.J. Tol (2010). "On International Equity and National Decision Making on Climate Change," *Journal of Environmental Economics and Management*, *60*(1), pp. 14–20.

Arrow, K., M.L. Cropper, G.C. Eads, and R.N. Stavins (1996). "Is There a Role for Benefit-Cost Analysis in Environmental, Health and Safety Regulation?," *Science*, *272*, pp. 221–222.

Birsch, D. and J.H. Fielder (eds.) (1994). *The Ford Pinto Case: A Study in Applied Ethics, Business, and Technology*, State University of New York Press, 312pp.

Boadway, R. (1976). "Integrating Equity and Efficiency in Applied Welfare Economics," *Quarterly Journal of Economics*, *90*(4), pp. 541–556.

Brent, R.J. (2006). *Applied Cost-Benefit Analysis*, 2nd ed., Edward Elgar, 470pp.

Campen, J.T. (1986). *Benefit, Cost and Beyond: The Political Economy of Benefit-Cost Analysis*, Ballinger, 240pp.

Crain, W.M. (2005). *The Impact of Regulatory Costs on Small Firms*, No. 264, Office of Advocacy, Small Business Administration, Washington, DC, 87pp.

DeKay, M.L., M.J. Small, P.S. Fischbeck, R.S. Farrow, A. Cullen, J.B. Kadane, L.B. Lave, M.G. Morgan, and K. Takemura (2002). "Risk-Based Decision Analysis in Support of Precautionary Policies," *Journal of Risk Research*, *5*(4), pp. 391–417.

Dupuit, J. (1844). "De la mesure de l'utilité des travaux publics," reprinted in *Revue française d'économie*, *10*, pp. 55–94, 1995. Available at: www.persee.fr/web/revues/home/prescript/article/rfeco_0769-0479_1995_num_10_2_978.

Ekelund, R.B., Jr. and R.F. Hébert (1999). *Secret Origins of Modern Microeconomics: Dupuit and the Engineers*, University of Chicago Press, 468pp.

EO 12291 (1981). "Executive Order 12291–Federal Regulation." Available at: www.archives.gov/federal-register/codification/executive-order/12291.html.

EPA (1997). *The Benefits and Costs of the Clean Air Act, 1970 to 1990*, Report to Congress. Downloadable in sections at: http://yosemite.epa.gov/ee/epa/eerm.nsf/vwRepNumLookup/EE- Fox 0295?OpenDocument.

(2009). *Endangerment and Cause or Contribute Findings for Greenhouse Gases under Section 202(a) of the Clean Air Act; Final Rule*, U.S. Federal Register, *74*(239), pp. 66496–66546.

(2010). *The Benefits and Costs of the Clean Air Act 1990 to 2010*, Report to Congress, EPA-410-R-99-001, 654pp. Available at: www.epa.gov/sites/production/files/2015-07/documents/fullrept.pdf.

(2011). *Regulatory Impact Analysis for the Final Mercury and Air Toxics Standards*, EPA-452/R-11-011, December.

EPA SAB (2010). *Review of the Final Integrated Report for the Second Section 812 Prospective Study of the Benefits and Costs of the Clean Air Act*, 18pp. Available at: http://yosemite.epa.gov/sab/sabproduct.nsf/WebReportsLastFiveCOUNCIL/1E6218DE3BFF682E852577FB005D46F1/$File/EPA-COUNCIL-11-001-unsigned.pdf.

EU (2000). *Communication from the European Commission on the Precautionary Principle*. Available at: www.gdrc.org/u-gov/precaution-4.html.

Fox, I.K. and O.C. Herfindahl (1964). "Attainment of Efficiency in Satisfying Demands for Water Resources," *The American Economic Review*, *54*(3), pp. 198–206.

Graham, J.D. (2008). "Saving Lives through Administrative Law and Economics," *The University of Pennsylvania Law Review*, *157*, pp. 395–540.

Guerry, A.D., S. Polasky, J. Lubchenco et al. (2015). "Natural Capital and Ecosystem Services Informing Decisions: From Promise to Practice," *Proceedings of the National Academy of Science*, *112*(24), pp. 7348–7355.

Hammond, R.J. (1966). "Convention and Limitation in Benefit-Cost Analysis," *Natural Resources Journal*, *6*(2), pp. 195–222.

Harberger, A.C. (1978). "On the Use of Distributional Weights in Social Cost-Benefit Analysis," *Journal of Political Economy*, *86*(2), pp. S87–S120.

Harrington, W. (2006). *Grading Estimates of the Benefits and Costs of Federal Regulation*, RFF Discussion Paper DP 06-39, 44pp.

Harrington, W., L. Heinzerling, and R. Morgenstern (2009). *Reforming Regulatory Impact Analysis*, Resources for the Future, 246pp.

Harrington, W., R.D. Morgenstern, and P. Nelson (2000). "On the Accuracy of Regulatory Cost Estimates," *Journal of Policy Analysis and Management*, *19*(2), pp. 297–322.

Hicks, J. (1936). "Distribution and Economic Progress: A Revised Version," *The Review of Economic Studies*, *4*(1), pp. 1–12.

Hills, A. and M.G. Morgan (1981). "Telecommunications in Alaskan Villages: A Technical, Economic, and Institutional Analysis," *Science*, *211*, pp. 241–248.

Interagency Working Group on Social Cost of Carbon (2010). "Technical Support Document: Social Cost of Carbon for Regulatory Impact Analysis under Executive Order 12866," U.S. Government.

Jones-Lee, M.W. (1976). *The Value of Life: An Economic Analysis*, University of Chicago Press, 162pp.

Kaldor, N. (1936). "Wage Subsidies as a Remedy for Unemployment," *Journal of Political Economy*, pp. 721–742.

Keeney, R.L. (1990). "Mortality Risks Induced by Economic Expenditures," *Risk Analysis*, *10*, pp. 147–159.

Krupnick, A.J. and P.R. Portney (1991). "Controlling Urban Air Pollution: A Benefit-Cost Assessment," *Science*, *252*, pp. 522–528.

Lave, L.B. (1996). "Chapter 6: Benefit-Cost Analysis: Do the Benefits Exceed the Costs?" in R.W. Hahn (ed.), *Risks, Costs, and Lives Saved: Getting Better Results from Regulation*, Oxford University Press, pp. 104–134.

Lave, L.B., W. Wecker, W. Reis et al. (1990). "Controlling Emissions from Motor Vehicles: A Benefit-Cost Analysis of Vehicle Emission Control Alternatives," *Environmental Science & Technology*, *24*(8), pp. 1128–1135.

Layard, R. (ed.) (1972). *Cost-Benefit Analysis*, Penguin Books, 496pp.

Marshall, A. (1924). *Principles of Economics* (8th ed.), Macmillan.

Masood, E. (1995). "Developing Countries Dispute Use of Figures on Climate Change Impact," *Nature*, *376*, p. 374.

Mishan, E.J. (1973). *Economics for Social Decisions: Elements of Cost-Benefit Analysis*, Praeger, 151pp.

Moore, J.C. (2007). *General Equilibrium and Welfare Economics: An Introduction*, Springer, 576pp.

Morgan, M.G. (1992). "Prudent Avoidance," *Public Utility Fortnightly*, *129*(6), pp. 26–29.

Nair, I., M.G. Morgan, and H.K. Florig (1989). *Biological Effects of Power Frequency Electric and Magnetic Fields: Background Paper*, Publ. No. OTA-BP-E-53, Office of Technology Assessment, Congress of the United States.

NHTSA (2014). "Federal Motor Vehicle Safety Standards; Rear Visibility: Final Rule," published in the Federal Register on April 7, 2014. Available at: www.federalregister.gov/articles/2014/04/07/2014-07469/federal-motor-vehicle-safety-standards-rear-visibility.

NRC (2000). *Toxicological Effects of Methylmercury*, Committee on the Toxicological Effects of Methylmercury, Board on Environmental Studies and Toxicology, Commission on Life Sciences, National Academy Press, 344pp.

(2017). *Valuing Climate Damages: Updating Estimation of the Social Cost of Carbon Dioxide*, Committee on Assessing Approaches to Updating the Social Cost of Carbon, U.S. National Academy Press, 394pp.

OMB (2005). *Validating Regulatory Analysis: 2005 Report to Congress on the Costs and Benefits of Federal Regulations and Unfunded Mandates on State, Local, and Tribal Entities*, Office of Management and Budget, U.S. Executive Office of the President, 94pp. Available at: www.whitehouse.gov/omb/inforeg/regpol-reports_congress.html.

Pearce, F. (1995). "Price of Life Sends Temperatures Soaring," *New Scientist*, April 1, p. 5.

Persky, J. (2001). "Cost-Benefit Analysis and the Classical Creed," *Journal of Economic Perspectives*, *15*(4), pp. 199–208.

Pindyck, R.S. (2013). "Climate Change Policy: What Do the Models Tell Us?," *Journal of Economic Literature*, *51*(3), pp. 860–872.

Porter, T.M. (1995). *Trust in Numbers: The Pursuit of Objectivity in Science and Public Life*, Princeton University Press, 310pp.

Raffensperger, C. and J. Tickner (1999). Introduction to *Protecting Public Health and the Environment: Implementing the Precautionary Principle*, Island Press, 385pp.

Socolow, R.H. (1976). "Chapter 1: Failures of Discourse," in H.A. Feiveson, F.W. Sinden, and R.H. Socolow (eds.), *Boundaries of Analysis: An Inquiry into the Tocks Island Dam Controversy*, Ballinger, 417pp.

Starr, C. (1969). "Social Benefits versus Technological Risk," *Science*, *165*, pp. 1232–1238.

Sunstein, C.R. (2013a). "Regulatory Moneyball: What Washington Can Learn from Sports Geeks," *Foreign Affairs*, 92 (May/June), pp. 9–13.

(2013b). *Simpler: The Future of Government*, Simon & Schuster, 260pp.

Weyant, J. (2015). "Contributions of Integrated Assessment Models," Draft Manuscript, Stanford, 35pp.

Wildavsky, A. (1981). "Richer Is Safer," *Financial Analysis Journal*, *37*, pp. 19–22.

4

Decision Analysis

There is of course no reason why conventional B–C analysis can't do a good job of characterizing and analyzing uncertainty. However, until quite recently it has been rare to find much treatment of uncertainty, or even a thorough sensitivity analysis, as part of most B–C analyses.

In Chapter 2, I argued that decision analysis (DA) is basically benefit–cost analysis with a serious treatment of uncertainty.[1] While that is partly true, it leaves out an important distinction. While it can be used to assess choices among alternatives, as practiced, B–C analyses are often focused on assessing the net utility of just a single action, such as a proposed regulation. In contrast, decision analysis supports the maximization of expected utility in the face of uncertainty in situations that involve *choice among multiple options*. Ralph Keeney has offered both an informal and a more formal definition of DA:

> Intuitively, I think of decision analysis as "a formalization of common sense for decision problems that are too complex for informal use of common sense." A more technical definition of decision analysis is "a philosophy, articulated by a set of logical axioms, and a methodology and collection of systematic procedures, based upon those axioms, for responsibly analyzing the complexities inherent in decision problems." (Keeney, 1982)

4.1 DA BASICS

We will discuss the axioms on which DA is based in Section 4.4, but in this section we begin with a quick overview. Suppose that c is the set of choices available to a decision maker and x is the set of the possible outcomes that may result given each choice. Then $p(x|c)$ is the probability of outcome x given

[1] While the term "decision analysis" has now become ubiquitous, many of the same techniques are referred to by other names such as Statistical Decision Theory, Prescriptive Decision Analysis, and Applied Decision Theory in the literature.

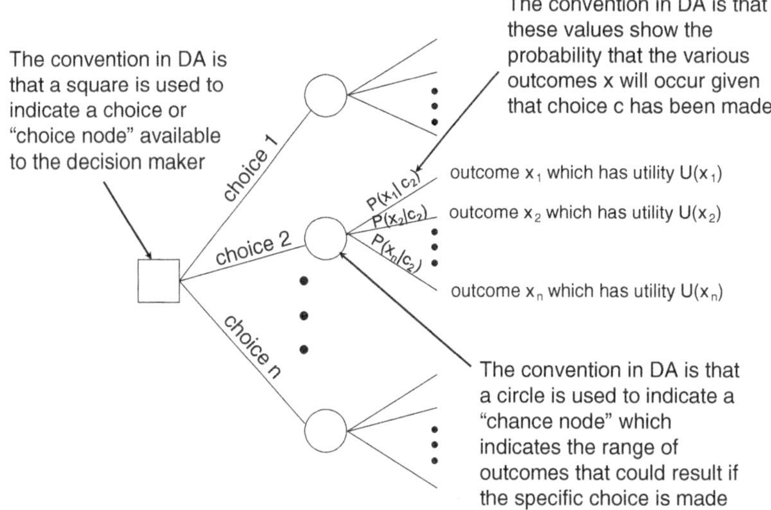

FIGURE 4.1. While it is possible to perform decision analysis using continuous variables, it is far more common to discretize the choices and outcomes and display them as a "decision tree" as shown here.

choice c. If $U(x)$ is the utility that the decision maker attaches to outcome x, then conventional decision analysis finds the choice c that maximizes the decision maker's expected utility:[2]

$$\int_0^\infty p(x \mid c)U(x)dx$$

In conventional applications of DA, the range of possible outcomes x is not treated as a continuous variable but is divided up into several discrete levels and represented using a graphical tree structure.[3] The standard notation is shown in Figure 4.1.

If the $U(x)$ at the end of each branch is the dollar value the decision maker assigns to each outcome x, then the result at the root of each chance node is the expected monetary value across that set of chance outcomes (Figure 4.2A). If, however, the decision maker is risk averse (or possibly even risk seeking), then, rather than using a dollar value for each outcome, the analysis can be

[2] Choosing to maximize expected utility as the decision rule is a normative judgment. One could choose other objectives such as maximizing the minimum welfare, minimizing the maximum possible loss, minimizing regret, etc. The choice of expected utility derives from adopting a set of axioms (see Section 4.4).

[3] For a discussion of the issue of discretizing a continuous distribution for use in a DA, see section 8.4 in Morgan and Henrion (1990) as well as Keefer and Bodily (1983) and Miller and Rice (1983).

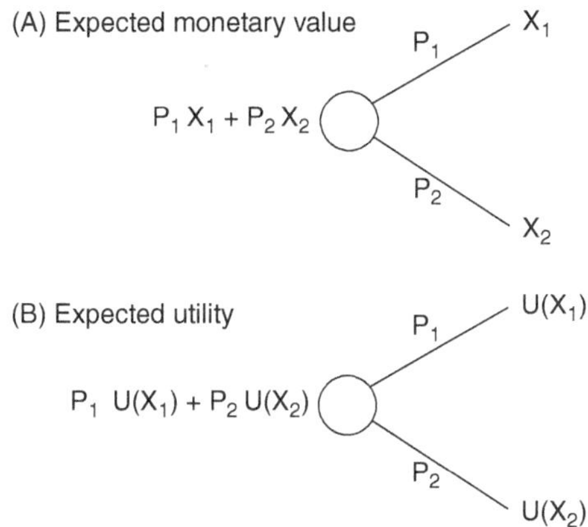

FIGURE 4.2. Evaluation of the expected value of a chance node when outcomes are denoted in monetary terms (A) and when they are denoted in terms of utility values scaled from the decision maker's utility function.

performed using the decision maker's utility for each. In this way, the expected utility of each chance node can be estimated (Figure 4.2B).

In a problem that involves multiple sequential chance outcomes, these dollar values, or utilities, are then propagated back through the tree in order to compute the expected value of each of the branches at the original choice node. The branch at the original choice node that has the highest expected value is then the preferred decision. Once the tree has been solved, the convention is to indicate those choices that are dominated by the best choices by marking them (cutting them off) with a pair of vertical lines (||). If the tree has been solved in terms of utilities, using the decision maker's utility function, the values of the available choices can be converted back into equivalent monetary values by using that function to map back into dollars. As we will see in the example in Section 4.5, the optimal choice when computed strictly in terms of monetary value, and when computed in terms of utility, may not be the same.

For illustrative simplicity, the diagram in Figure 4.1 shows just a single choice among options followed by a single set of probabilistic outcomes. In real decision problems there may be many different choices available, each one of which may then result in a cascade of several possible probabilistic outcomes. In some cases, having made one choice, and obtained an outcome, there may be subsequent opportunities (at a later time) for additional choices. Hence, real decision trees can become very large and complex. Figure 4.3 shows a strategy that is commonly used when reporting such a large tree. To get a sense of how complex real trees can get, suppose that each choice or chance node in the tree shown in Figure 4.3 has only four branches. The final tree would result in $4 \times 4 \times 4 \times 4 \times 4 = 4096$ different end outcomes, making it pretty hard to display the full tree!

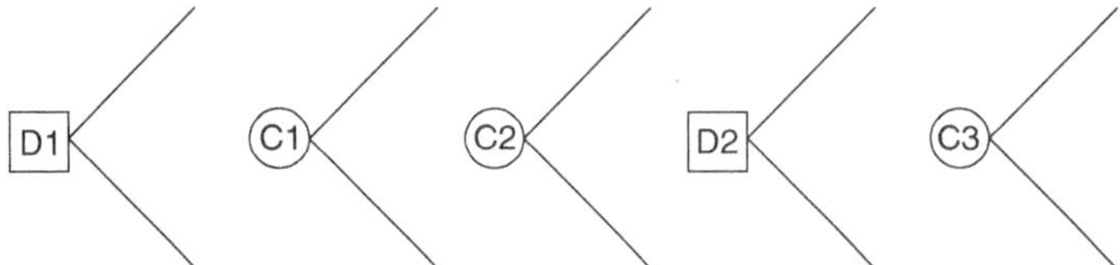

FIGURE 4.3. Because the decision trees for real decision problems can become very large and complicated, it is common in displaying a tree to use a simplified notation of the sort shown here. In this case, chance node C1 is assumed to be placed on the end of all the several branches of the choice options associated with decision node D1. Similarly, chance node C2 is assumed to be placed on the end of all possible outcomes that may result from chance node C1. In some cases, there may also be situations in which, having made a decision and realized the results, a decision maker may have an option to make subsequent decisions (e.g., choice node D2) which in turn will have subsequent uncertain consequences (e.g., chance node C3).

4.2 A SIMPLE WORKED EXAMPLE

If you have never seen a decision analysis, the best way to understand the approach is to start with a very simple worked example. Suppose that you have three investment opportunities. After conferring with a number of analysts you conclude that these opportunities have the following characteristics:

Opportunity A	Opportunity B	Opportunity C
0.1 probability of making 200	0.6 probability of making 200	0.2 probability of making 1000
0.5 probability of making 100	0.4 probability of losing 300	0.3 probability of making 300
0.4 probability of losing 50		0.4 probability of losing 400
		0.1 probability of losing 600

Suppose you have decided to choose the option that will maximize your expected earnings. In this simple case, you hardly need a decision tree, you could just immediately compute the expected value of each. However, for illustration, the tree is shown in Figure 4.4.

The boxes show the expected value of each option. Clearly on the basis of expected earnings, you should choose investment opportunity B.

4.3 STAGES IN A DECISION ANALYSIS

A number of the originators and leading practitioners of decision analysis have created diagrams that lay out the steps that they believe should be followed in structuring and performing an analysis. Two examples are shown in Figure 4.5.

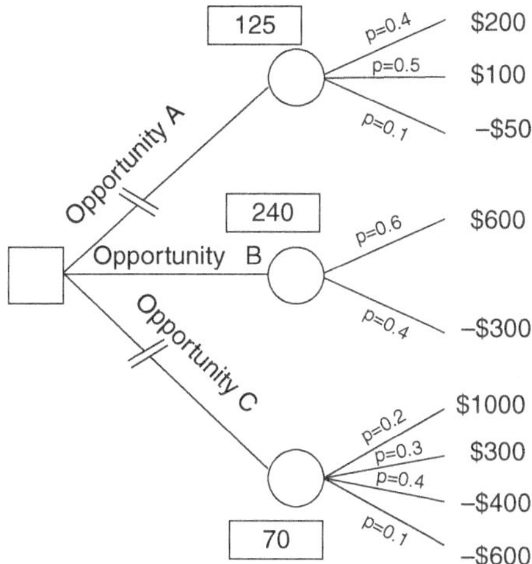

FIGURE 4.4. Illustration of simple decision tree to choose among three investment opportunities.

While the diagrams are different, they display two important similarities. First, they stress the importance of starting with a series of order-of-magnitude assessments to figure out what aspects of the problem are most important. Second, they both adopt a highly iterative framing: basically saying do some analysis, think carefully about the results, refine that analysis, keep doing this until you have adequately understood what matters and are convinced that you have correctly framed the problem.

Both formulations argue that the analyst should begin by identifying the objectives and identifying the alternatives, or choice options, that are available. Then one builds a decision model that relates those alternatives, given the objectives. In order to evaluate alternatives, the decision maker's preferences must be quantified (see Chapters 2 and 9). Then, before moving on to performing a full probabilistic assessment, it is generally a good idea to do some simple deterministic analysis. Doing this both helps the analyst (and decision maker) to better understand the problem, and may also show that some variables are not very important and can be ignored. Once the problem has been set up, one then solves the decision tree (either in terms of expected dollar value or expected utility).

At this point it may be tempting to stop, but that would be a serious mistake. The last critical step after the problem has been structured, and all uncertain variables have been identified, is to conduct a systematic assessment of sensitivities, both in order to refine the analysis and to learn how sensitive the optimal choice is to the specific assumptions that have been made.

This general approach to performing analysis through iteration and refinement should not be unique to formal decision analysis. As outlined in Chapter 1

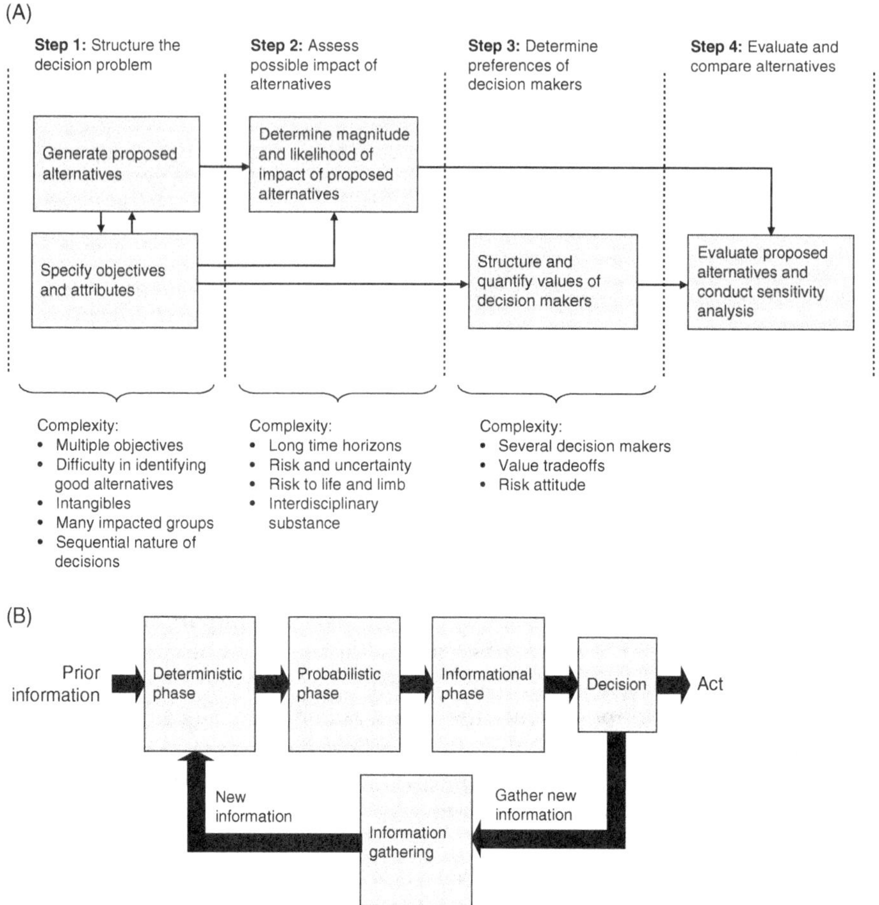

FIGURE 4.5. Two examples of diagrams by different authors illustrating the steps involved in performing a decision analysis. **A.** is redrawn from Keeney (1982). **B.** is redrawn from Howard and Matheson (1984).

and in Morgan and Henrion (1990), it is precisely the approach that should be adopted in any good policy analysis. However, the decision analysis community was among the first to stress this fact.

4.4 THE AXIOMS OF DECISION ANALYSIS

One of the primary advantages of DA over other, more heuristic decision strategies is that it is built up from a set of axioms. Once you have performed a DA following the standard procedures, you can be confident that the results will be consistent with those axioms. Various authors have stated the axioms in more and less technical terms. While slightly less formal and more wordy, Keeney's (1982) statement is among the most easily understandable. It reads as follows:

AXIOM 1A (Generation of Alternatives). *At least two alternatives can be specified.*
For each of the alternatives, there will be a number of possible consequences which might result if the alternatives were followed.

AXIOM 1B (Identification of Consequences). *Possible consequences of each alternative can be identified.*
In identifying consequences, it may be useful to generate a hierarchy of objectives indicating the domains of potential consequences in the problem. Attributes can be specified to provide evaluation scales necessary to indicate the degree to which each objective is achieved.

AXIOM 2 (Quantification of Judgment). *The relative likelihoods (i.e., probabilities) of each possible consequence that could result from each alternative can be specified.*
... there are a number of procedures to assist in specifying relative likelihoods. Such probabilistic estimates are based on available data, information collected, analytical or simulation models, and assessment of experts' judgments [See Chapter 9].

AXIOM 3 (Quantification of Preferences). *The relative desirability (i.e., utility) for all the possible consequences of any alternative can be specified.*
The preferences that should be quantified in a decision problem are those of the decision maker or the decision makers. However, for many problems other individuals share a responsibility for recommending alternatives to the decision makers. In such problems, these individuals may have a responsibility for articulating an appropriate preference structure.[4]

AXIOM 4A (Comparison of Alternatives). *If two alternatives would each result in the same two possible consequences, the alternative yielding the higher chance of the preferred consequence is preferred.*

AXIOM 4B (Transitivity of Preferences). *If one alternative is preferred to a second alternative and if the second alternative is preferred to a third alternative, then the first alternative is preferred to the third alternative.*

AXIOM 4C (Substitution of Consequences). *If an alternative is modified by replacing one of its consequences with a set of consequences and associated probabilities (i.e., a lottery) that is indifferent to the consequence being replaced, then the original and the modified alternatives should be indifferent.*

Axiom 4A is necessary to indicate how various alternatives should be compared.

[4] When a decision maker uses the utility functions of some "expert" as part of their DA, they are saying they are prepared to adopt the expert's values as their own. While sometimes this may be what a decision maker wants to do, it may not always be the case. For example, an ecologist is likely to place a very different value on preserving full ecosystem diversity than many decision makers who may simply want the landscape to look verdant.

Axioms 4B and 4C are often referred to as the constancy axioms. Axiom 4C allows one to reduce complex alternatives involving a variety of possible consequences to simple alternatives referred to in Axiom 4A. It is then easy to compare alternatives. Axiom 4B is necessary to include comparisons of more than two alternatives.

When these axioms are met, Keeney notes, "the main result ... is that the expected utility of an alternative is the indication of its desirability. Alternatives with higher expected utilities should be preferred to those with lower expected utilities."

For other more technical (but logically equivalent) statements of the Axioms of Decision Analysis, see Raiffa and Schlaifer (1961), DeGroot (1969), Brown et al. (1974), Howard and Matheson (1984), von Winterfeldt and Edwards (1986), and Clemen (1996).

READING 4.1

Ralph L. Keeney, "Decision Analysis: An Overview," *Operations Research*, *30*, pp. 803–837, 1982.

The abstract reads:

This article, written for the non-decision analyst, describes what decision analysis is, what it can and cannot do, why one should care to do this, and how one does it. To accomplish these purposes, it is necessary first to describe the decision environment. The article also presents an overview of decision analysis and provides additional sources for its foundations, procedures, history, and applications.

If you have not had any prior exposure to decision analysis, you should read with care. If you have had some prior exposure to decision analysis, you'll probably want to only skim this paper.

4.5 A MORE DETAILED WORKED EXAMPLE[5]

The example in Section 4.2 was very simple. Now let's consider another example, also for a private decision maker,[6] which is sufficiently complex to illustrate a number of other ideas, such as the use of utility, computation of the value of information, and a few other issues.

[5] This example was first developed for an unpublished tutorial on "The role of decision analysis and other quantitative tools in environmental policy analysis" that I prepared for the Chemical Division of the Environmental Directorate of the OECD in 1983.

[6] I specify "private" to imply an individual or a private organization such as a company, in contrast to a decision being made by some governmental (or other public) entity such as a regulator.

Able Chemicals Incorporated is a hypothetical private profit-maximizing firm that operates a large facility that produces a concentrated liquid waste stream of a hypothetical toxic material called TZX. Historically, the company has disposed of this waste stream by diluting it with a large volume of seawater and discharging it through an ocean outfall. However, the company is now under orders by their National Environmental Control Agency to terminate this practice. An acceptable disposable system is being built by Baker Disposal Corporation, and Able holds a contract with Baker to start receiving all of their TZX waste in five years. Until this permanent solution becomes available, Able is considering two interim options: dispersed storage in drums in a series of six small, physically isolated storage buildings, and tank storage in a large, new single-storage tank. In both cases, the storage facilities will be built on an abandoned industrial site that Able already owns. Engineering cost estimates, which are believed to be quite reliable, have been obtained for the two storage options. They are (in some appropriate monetary units, e.g., millions of dollars) 12 for drum storage and 6 for tank storage. For simplicity, assume that issues of time value have been appropriately dealt with in these and all subsequent costs. Also for simplicity we consider all the facilities to be full. The more realistic sequential problem involved with slowly filling the facilities, and then later disposing of the contents once the new treatment facility is available, can be dealt with analytically but is excluded here because that would considerably complicate this example.

On the basis of these costs, tank storage appears to Able to be the preferred solution. However, TZX is a dangerous material. While the costs reported above include insurance costs, and while they believe that insurance can be expected to cover the costs of any small or medium-size accidents, Able Chemical officials are concerned that insurance would not protect them from direct and indirect losses resulting from a major accident. Hence, they have decided to incorporate a consideration of risk in their analysis and have commissioned a quantitative risk assessment and decision analysis. While, in making their final decision, Able management is prepared to consider issues of broader corporate responsibility, they have instructed their analysts to perform this first decision analysis narrowly in terms of the direct economic impacts that an accident would have on Able.

Before an analysis of the relative risk of the various options can be performed, it is necessary to:

- identify the ways in which accidents could occur in each part of the system;
- develop a quantitative estimate of the probability of each of these accidents, paying careful attention to issues such as correlation among variables and common mode failures;
- develop a quantitative estimate of the effects that are likely to be associated with each accident type.

It is clear that handling and transport of the material may be a significant source of risk. However, to simplify our example, let's assume that these risks will be considered in a separate analysis.

In order to produce estimates of accident probabilities and consequences, Able's analysts construct a variety of environmental and risk-assessment models using modeling tools of the sort we will briefly discuss in Chapters 10 and 11. These models rely on available field data, fault trees, and failure mode and effects models that use state-of-the-art air and water pollution transport models. We will assume that Able's analysts have performed a careful and appropriate assessment, and will skip the details.

The assessment concludes that the only way in which a major accident can result from the dispersed storage option is if a fire occurs at one of the storage buildings. Let us assume that simultaneous accidents at more than one building were quantitatively studied but are excluded in our example because they were found to be so unlikely that they do not affect the results of the decision analysis. TZX is not particularly volatile at normal outdoor temperatures. Hence, a small spill on the storage site can be readily confined and cleaned up without causing problems off-site. The concern with fire is that a fire would volatilize some TZX as well as produce toxic combustion by-products. If the exposure levels are high enough, immediate mortality will result. For low-level exposures, no immediate mortality will occur. There is controversy among experts over whether low-level exposure can cause delayed mortality from cancer. Able has had health experts assess the likelihood of two different levels of carcinogenicity (termed high and medium). Finally, the level of exposure that will occur depends upon the weather at the time of the accident.

For the tank storage options, a major accident will occur whenever there is a tank fire or whenever the tank suffers a major rupture without a fire. In the latter cause, the route of exposure is by surface water contamination. This occurs only if seasonal torrential rains occur at the same time as the tank rupture.

Able's lawyers have carefully studied previous liability suits associated with similar large accidents. They estimate Able's probable liability as 2 (same arbitrary monetary units as above) for each immediate death and 1 for each delayed mortality. Able's analysts are not able to produce very precise estimates of the clean-up costs the company would face because these costs depend critically upon the level of clean-up that is required by the National Environmental Control Agency, which Able judges will depend upon the political environment and public opinion that obtains at the time of the accident. Thus, they have estimated clean-up costs for two possible situations: a "high" and an "extraordinary" level of clean-up. They have used a team of political scientists to produce subjective estimates of the probability that these different levels of clean-up will occur.

Finally, Able carries insurance that they are certain will cover the direct capital costs of their losses to storage facilities and which they estimate will cover additional clean-up and liability costs of 20. Of course, if losses are less than 20, only those losses will be covered.

Table 4.1 summarizes all of the data for this (simplified and idealized) problem. These data are used to construct a decision tree as shown in Figure 4.6. The tree is worked through in terms of expected monetary value. The decision with the lowest expected monetary value is the tank storage option, so if Able is prepared to make its decision just on the basis of expected monetary value, then they should still choose the tank storage option. Consider the first top cost entry on the uppermost node of the tree. It reads 10 + (60 + 10 + 25) – Insur. = 85. The first 10 is the capital cost of the five-sixths of the distributed storage that is not destroyed. There is no equivalent term for tank storage since the entire tank is assumed to be lost. Clean-up costs are 60, liability for immediate deaths is 10. Liability for delayed deaths is 25. "Insur." denotes insurance and is ≤ 20 since the insurance never pays more than the loss and never pays more than 20. All values shown are losses; however, minus signs are left off for simplicity.

Risk Aversion: If a decision maker is prepared to accept a sure payment of less than N in place of a chance process that holds a 50:50 chance of yielding a payment of either 0 or 2N, we say they are risk averse. Risk aversion is quite common. While less common, risk-seeking behavior is sometimes also seen.

After studying the results of the decision analysis summarized in Figure 4.6, Able's senior management concluded that they would be crazy to make the decision they face on the basis of expected monetary costs. Able estimates that it could only sustain losses of 400 to 500 before it would go completely bankrupt and disappear as an organization (we will ignore things like loopholes in bankruptcy laws). Thus, a loss of 250 is considerably less than half as terrible an event for Able as a loss of 500, which would put the company out of business. Not surprisingly, Able is risk averse to large losses.

In such circumstances, one cannot use the direct measure of outcome (in this case monetary units) in the decision analysis. It is possible to show, however, that the correct decision will be obtained if instead we substitute the decision maker's utility for money. Using appropriate techniques (see the discussion in Chapters 2 and 5), the analysts have asked Able's executives to think carefully about what various large losses would mean to the company and have produced the utility function shown in Figure 4.7.

Figure 4.8 shows the decision tree once again, this time worked out with utilities. Note that now, with Able's risk aversion to large losses incorporated, the analysis shows that it is in their interest to spend the extra money and choose the system of distributed storage, because of its lower risk of producing a catastrophic accident.

The value of information: One of the largest sources of uncertainty in this analysis involves the level of long-term carcinogenicity (if any) that will result among those exposed to the products in the event of a large TZX fire. This is a question that could be resolved by appropriate scientific research. Given the particular circumstances that Able faces, we can ask how much would it be worth to them to resolve this uncertainty, that is, what is their "expected value

TABLE 4.1. *Hypothetical data developed by Able's analysts on the two storage technologies they are considering.*

Distributed drum storage (six separate sites):

- Capital costs: 12, of which 2 would be lost in accident but covered by insurance.
- Clean-up costs:
  - With favorable weather:
    - High clean-up: 13, extraordinary clean-up: 19
  - With unfavorable weather:
    - High clean-up: 20, extraordinary clean-up: 60
  - Liability for immediate deaths:
    - With favorable weather: none
    - With unfavorable weather: 10
  - Liability for delayed deaths:
    - With favorable weather:
      - High carcinogenicity: 2, medium carcinogenicity: 0.5
    - With unfavorable weather:
      - High carcinogenicity: 25, medium carcinogenicity: 5

Tank storage:

- Capital costs: 6, of which all would be lost in accident and covered by insurance.
- Clean-up costs with fire:
  - With favorable weather:
    - High clean-up: 30, extraordinary clean-up: 90
  - With unfavorable weather:
    - High clean-up: 100, extraordinary clean-up 500
- Liability for immediate deaths with fire:
  - With favorable weather: none
  - With unfavorable weather: 40
- Liability for delayed deaths:
  - With favorable weather:
    - High carcinogenicity: 20, medium carcinogenicity: 5
  - With unfavorable weather:
    - High carcinogenicity: 250, medium carcinogenicity: 50
- Clean-up costs without fire:
  - Without rain:
    - High clean-up: 30, extraordinary clean-up: 10
  - With rain:
    - High clean-up: 200, extraordinary clean-up: 1000
- Liability for immediate deaths without fire:
  - Without rain: none
  - With rain: 4
- Liability for delayed deaths without fire:
  - Without rain:
    - High carcinogenicity: none, medium carcinogenicity: none
  - With rain:
    - High carcinogenicity: 700, medium carcinogenicity: 100

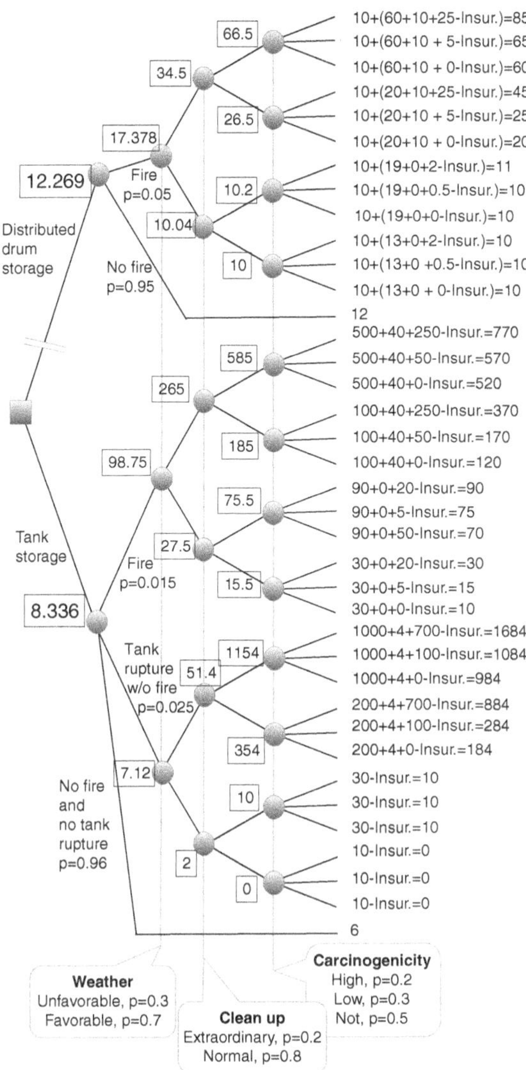

FIGURE 4.6. The decision tree that summarizes the hypothetical toxic waste storage problem faced by Able Chemicals. Data on the tree are discussed in the text and summarized in Table 4.1. Numbers in boxes at the chance nodes of the tree are expected monetary values.

of perfect information" or EVPI for information on carcinogenicity? The EVPI can be defined as:

$$\text{EVPI} = \begin{Bmatrix} \text{Expected value of the} \\ \text{decision made after} \\ \text{the availability of} \\ \text{perfect information} \end{Bmatrix} - \begin{Bmatrix} \text{Expected value of the} \\ \text{decision made prior to} \\ \text{the availability of} \\ \text{perfect information} \end{Bmatrix}$$

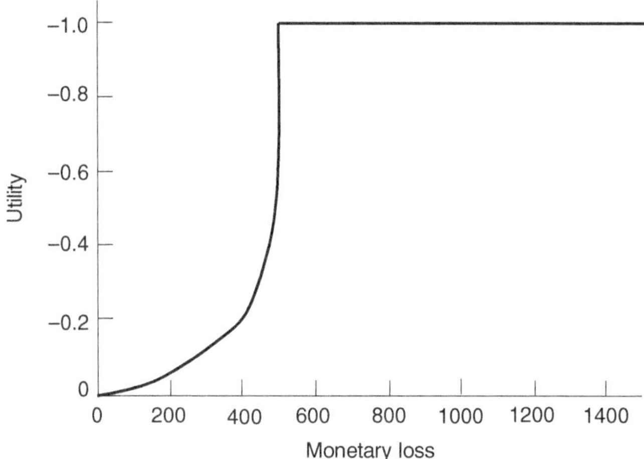

FIGURE 4.7. Able Chemicals' utility function for losses. A loss of 500 will involve the total bankruptcy of the company and hence from Able's point of view is considerably more than twice as undesirable as a loss of 250.

Able currently believes that there is a 0.2 chance of high carcinogenicity, a 0.3 chance of low carcinogenicity, and a 0.5 chance of no carcinogenicity. By evaluating the decision tree as if they knew the answer for each of these three cases, and then combining the answers with weights of 0.2, 0.3, and 0.5, they can estimate what they now expect the value of their decision will be after they have perfect information about the carcinogenicity of TZX. This is illustrated schematically in Figure 4.9.

When this analysis is performed for the model shown in Figure 4.8, one obtains 12.269 −12.214 = 0.055 as the expected value of perfect information. We could go on to talk about the value of partial information but that is more technical than is appropriate here.

Sensitivity analysis: Once one has found their optimal decision in a decision analysis, it is important not to stop without questioning how sensitive the choice is to the important assumptions that have been made. For example, in this problem, one might question using the single value of 20 for insurance recovery. In an actual analysis, one might include this, and several additional variables, among those that are to be treated as uncertain. In order to keep the example simple, we did not do this. However, at this stage it would be nice to know how the decision depends upon the value of insurance (in addition to the replacement value of the storage facility) that we assume. By implementing the decision tree in the Analytica® software environment (see chapter 10 in Morgan and Henrion, 1990), we can easily do this. The result is illustrated in Figure 4.10.

Our assumptions about liability (2 per immediate death, 1 per delayed death) were also quite arbitrary. Figure 4.11 illustrates how this assumption and insurance assumptions together affect the decision.

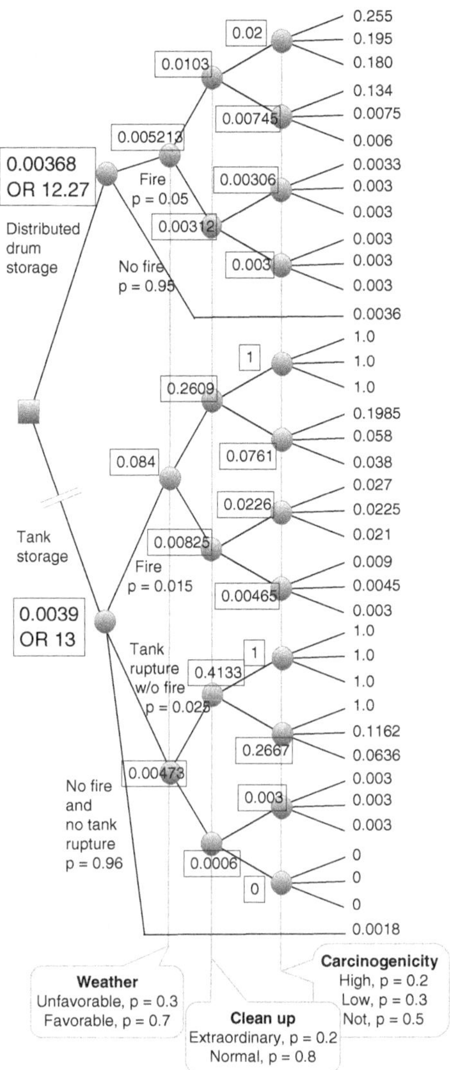

FIGURE 4.8. The same decision tree as shown in Figure 4.6, but this time worked out in terms of utility as defined in Figure 4.7. Because of Able Chemicals' high degree of risk aversion to large losses, in this case the distributed drum storage dominates tank storage. Again, to simplify the drawing, minus signs have been dropped throughout; all utilities and cost figures are losses.

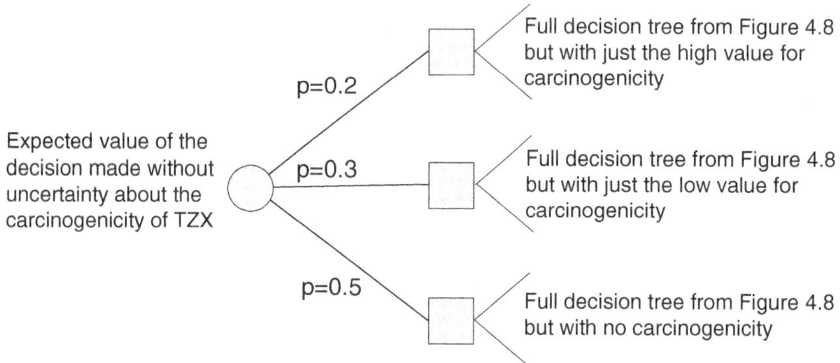

FIGURE 4.9. The expected value of the decision if there were no uncertainty about the carcinogenicity of TZX.

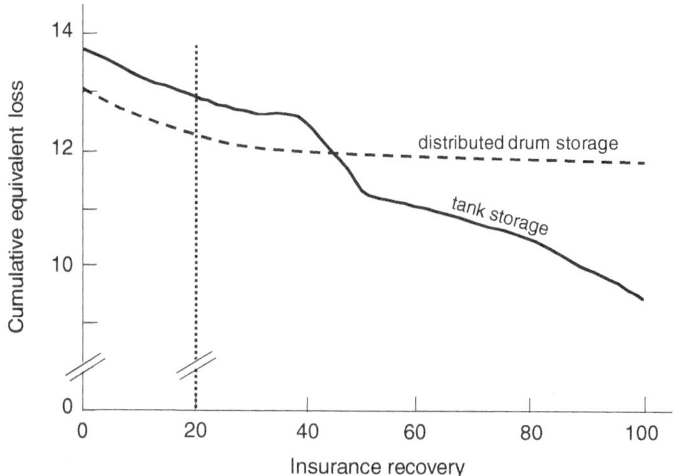

FIGURE 4.10. Illustration of how the optimal decision in Able Chemicals' choice between drum and tank storage depends on the assumed level of insurance recovery.

As a final example, we might examine how the EVPI depends on the level of insurance recovery. This is shown in Figure 4.12.

In a real analysis, we would want to insist on seeing a great deal more sensitivity analysis, but these examples give some idea of the kinds of things one might do.

4.6 OTHER EXAMPLES OF DECISION ANALYSIS

As with examples of B–C, it is difficult to find worked-out examples of DA that do not run to hundreds of pages. However, three are provided in Readings 4.2 to 4.4.

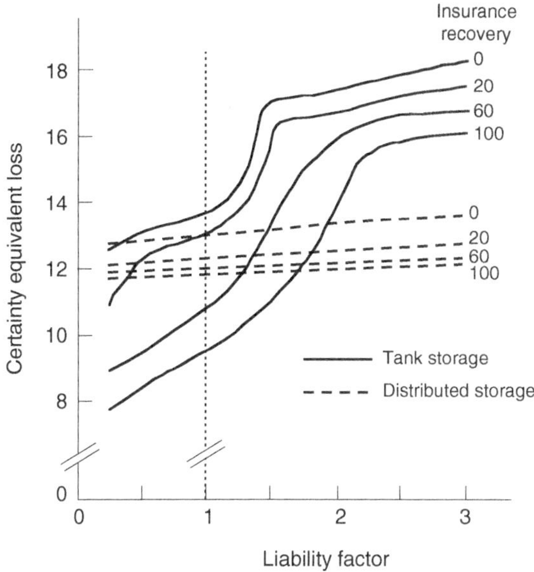

FIGURE 4.11. Illustration of how the optimal decision in Able Chemicals' choice between drum and tank storage depends on the joint values of insurance recovery and the amount of liability incurred.

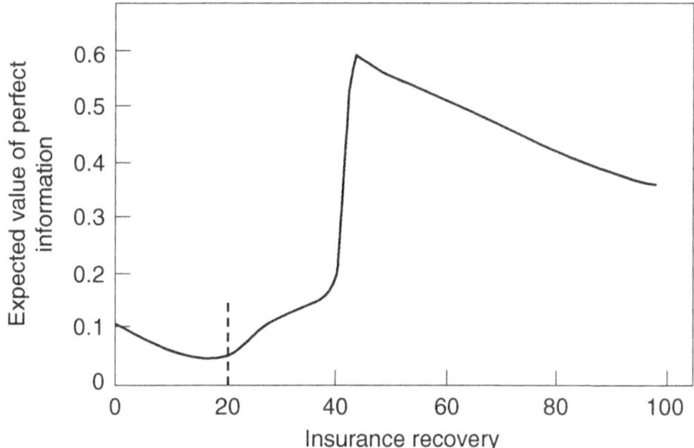

FIGURE 4.12. Illustration of how the EVPI depends on the amount of insurance recovery that is secured after an accident.

READING 4.2

R.A. Howard, J.E. Matheson, and D.W. North, "The Decision to Seed Hurricanes," *Science, 176*, pp. 1191–1202, 1972.

This is a classic early illustration of the use of decision analysis for public-sector decision making. The paper is partly a tutorial, stepping through a number of considerations including the issues of responsibility in the event there is damage, as well as demonstrating an application of Bayes' rule. The paper has no abstract.

READING 4.3

Kelly Klima, M. Granger Morgan, Iris Grossmann, and Kerry Emanuel, "Does It Make Sense to Modify Tropical Cyclones? A Decision Approach," *Environmental Science & Technology*, *45*(10), pp. 4242–4248, 2011.

Abstract: Recent dramatic increases in damages caused by tropical cyclones (TCs) and improved understanding of TC physics have led DHS to fund research on intentional hurricane modification. We present a decision analytic assessment of whether it is potentially cost-effective to attempt to lower the wind speed of TCs approaching South Florida by reducing sea surface temperatures with wind-wave pumps. Using historical data on hurricanes approaching South Florida, we develop prior probabilities of how storms might evolve. The effects of modification are estimated using a modern TC model. The FEMA HAZUS-MH MR3 damage model and census data on the value of property at risk are used to estimate expected economic losses. We compare wind damages after storm modification with damages after implementing hardening strategies protecting buildings. We find that if it were feasible and properly implemented, modification could reduce net losses from an intense storm more than hardening structures. However, hardening provides "fail safe" protection for average storms that might not be achieved if the only option were modification. The effect of natural variability is larger than that of either strategy. Damage from storm surge is modest in the scenario studied but might be abated by modification.

READING 4.4

Steven N. Tani, "Decision Analysis of the Synthetic Fuels Commercialization Program," *AFIPS*, International Workshop on Managing Requirements Knowledge, pp. 23–29, 1978. Available at: www.computer.org/csdl/proceedings/afips/1978/5086/00/50860023.pdf.

This analysis of whether the United States should undertake a synfuel program concluded that doing so was not a good idea. The paper provides a very nice illustration of the use of sensitivity analysis. The work was probably the first example of decision analysis presented at the White House. Despite the conclusion, for various political reasons the United States went ahead and built Great Plains Synfuels Plant (GPSP) in Beulah, North Dakota at a cost of ~$2 billion.

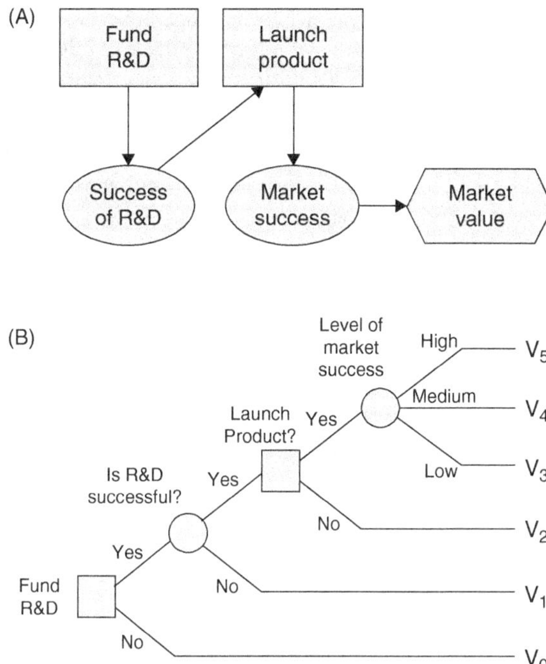

FIGURE 4.13. Illustration of an influence diagram (**A**) and its mapping to a decision tree (**B**).

4.7 INFLUENCE DIAGRAMS AND DECISION TREES

The use of influence diagrams to structure decision problems was pioneered in the Decision Analysis Group at the Stanford Research Institute (SRI) (see, for example, Miller et al., 1976; Smith et al., 1993; Howard and Matheson, 2005). These diagrams offer a very convenient way to represent the relationships among decision and chance variables in a decision problem, as shown in Figure 4.13. Henrion (2012) explains:

> Decision trees and the influence diagrams are complementary views of a decision problem: Decision trees display the set of alternative values for each decision and chance variable as branches coming out of each node. The influence diagram shows the dependencies among the variables more clearly than the decision tree. The decision tree shows more details of possible paths or scenarios as sequences of branches from left to right. But, this detail comes at a steep price: First, you must treat all variables as discrete (a small number of alternatives) even if they are actually continuous. Second, the number of nodes in a decision tree increases exponentially with the number of decision and chance variables.

Howard and Matheson (2005) explain that influence diagrams are

> at once both a formal description of ... [a decision] problem that can be treated by computers and a representation easily understood by people in all walks of life and

degrees of technical proficiency. It thus forms a bridge between qualitative description and quantitative specification ... The reason for the power of this representation is that it can serve at the three levels of specification of relation, function, and number, and in both deterministic and probabilistic cases.

Miller et al. (1976) note that "some influence diagrams do not have corresponding decision trees." In their report, and in subsequent writings such as Howard and Matheson (2005), readers can find details on the graphical formalism for influence diagrams and a discussion of when and how they can be converted to decision trees.

With modest violations of the formalism, influence diagrams are now used in a number of other contexts. For example, influence diagrams are used as the basic user interface for structuring analysis in the Analytica® software environment. Similarly, the "mental model" approach to risk communication (Morgan et al., 2002) uses influence diagrams to represent and compare expert and lay mental models of a risk process (see Chapter 14).

4.8 STRENGTHS AND LIMITATIONS OF DECISION ANALYSIS

The strengths of DA are pretty obvious. It provides a systematic method to frame and analyze complex decision problems in which there are significant amounts of uncertainty. Among practicing decision analysts, Rex Brown (2012) has offered some of the most critical assessments (which another experienced analyst has argued to me informally are overly harsh).

Brown (2012) observes:

Since ideal choice conforms to decision theory norms, one might suppose that [a decision maker] D gets closest to that ideal using an [applied decision theory] ADT model that also obeys those norms. That is not necessarily – indeed, not usually – the case. (However, competent ADT should promote some coherence.) Our initial expectation [several decades ago] that models would revolutionize decision-aiding has certainly not yet come to pass, even in government and business, where most of the earliest applications were attempted.

In support of this claim he lists a number of eminent psychologists and decision analysts who have, in varying degrees, expressed similar views, noting that after a period of considerable optimism that DA would sweep the world, the results have been disappointing.

Brown (2012) argues that this failure of DA to deliver on its early promise derives from two sets of factors. He argues that a first set is not fundamental and might be overcome with better tools and methods. These include:

- Difficulty in capturing all the factors and considerations that enter into the choices made by a decision maker. "An ADT model (such as a decision tree) can only be a partial, imperfectly measured, coherence check on D's

mind-content, since it can only address a few of the countless relevant questions that could draw important material out of D's mind."
- Mis-measured judgments. "Even when D is aware of a consideration, he may not elicit it accurately from his mind-content. In particular, factual judgments are commonly distorted due to emotions (such as vanity, lust, laziness and delusion)."
- Misleading simplification. "Modeling often requires making simplified assumptions, such as 'equivalent substitution'. These can mislead if D does not recognize and adjust for any over-simplification. To effectively use an ADT model, D must have a rare understanding of any mismatch with his perception of reality and how to adjust for it."
- Confusing language that lay users do not understand and do not have the patience to learn about and that decision analysts do not understand is confusing and do not bother to translate into more conventional language.

Brown illustrates each of these with examples, drawn largely from his own work. He argues that at least in principle all of these shortcomings could be overcome with better tools and methods. However, he goes on to argue that there are a number of other limitations that he views as fundamentally inherent to the process itself. He identifies three:

- Misallocated deliberative effort. "The inescapably burdensome challenge of modeling a choice diverts attention from critical decision processes *other than* choice, such as gathering information, identifying new options and acting on the decisions made. Within the choice process, constructing an ADT model can divert effort away from developing sound input."
- Distorting wise normal practice. "D often naturally uses wise decision strategies that are not readily modeled. For example, he takes a series of small incremental steps toward – or away from – a major commitment, interleaving them with gathering information ... In theory, D could prescribe an incremental strategy with a complex 'dynamic programming' ADT model, which evaluates possible strategies, step-by-step." However, Brown notes that "this is prohibitively burdensome" and none of the efforts to implement such a strategy that he or others have tried has proved adequate.
- Ill-fitting estimation models. When an ADT model is approximation, not an identity (as in "population ≡ whites + non-whites"), an error term is needed to make it an identity. If the approximation is poor, allowing for error may be too difficult to be useful. For example, in additive importance-weighted criteria evaluation (noted earlier) criteria may be dangerously incomplete or value-dependent.

Among the strongest critiques of axiomatic decision analysis are those that address the axioms themselves. Accepting these axioms as a basis for rational decision making is a matter of choice. Manski (2013) notes that:

> One may critique the Savage axioms from within axiomatic decision theory or from outside. Internal critiques agree ... that consistency of behavior across hypothetical choice scenarios is a virtue ...
>
> External critiques take issue with the idea that adherence with consistence axioms is virtuous ... a person facing an actual decision problem is not concerned with the consistency of his behavior across hypothetical choice scenarios. He only wants to make a reasonable choice in the setting he actually faces.

Manski goes on to argue that normative decision theory should focus on what he terms "actualist rationality" that promotes "welfare maximization in the choice problem the agent actually faces." He notes that "actualist rationality is *consequentialist* – one values a prescription of decision making for its welfare consequences." In contrast, "the rationality of axiomatic theory is *deontological* – one values consistency of behavior across choice scenarios as a virtue per se."

Manski (2013) writes:

> as I see the matter, there is no unambiguously correct way to choose among undominated actions. Hence I view as misguided that quest by Savage and other axiomatic theorists to prescribe some unique process of rational decision making with partial knowledge. We must face up to the nonexistence of optimal decision criteria and suffice with reasonable ones.

Despite Brown's disappointment that decision analysis has not lived up to his early hopes and the somewhat pessimistic assessments by Manski, in my view (and I would guess theirs as well) decision analysis is a valuable tool that, when used appropriately, can provide valuable insight about a wide range of public- and private-sector problems. As virtually all accomplished practitioners advise, it should not be used as the sole basis for making most decisions, but it can be extremely useful in helping to inform and clarify many complex problems, and deserves much wider thoughtful application.

4.9 A NOTE ON THE HISTORY OF DECISION ANALYSIS

Much of the modern work on the use of DA methods to address problems in policy analysis in the public and private sector is the result of work that originated in the 1960s at Harvard and Stanford.

Two faculty members at the Harvard Business School, Howard Raiffa and Robert Schlaifer, developed the ideas that would become known as decision analysis in their 1961 book *Applied Statistical Decision Theory.* Raiffa also published a simple introductory text that has been widely used in programs in public policy (Raiffa, 1968).

The Decision Analysis Group at the Stanford Research Institute (SRI International) was established in late 1966. It operated in close collaboration with the Department of Engineering Economic Systems at Stanford. A number of DA-related consulting groups grew out of those activities, including groups at SRI and Decision Focus.

Of course, not all experts in decision analysis have come from the Harvard and Stanford "schools." Examples of others include: Morris H. DeGroot (University of Chicago), James S. Dyer (University of Texas at Austin), Peter C. Fischburn (Case Institute of Technology), Max Henrion (Carnegie Mellon), Stephen R. Watson (Cambridge University), Robert Winkler (Chicago), and Detlof von Winterfeldt (University of Michigan) and many others.

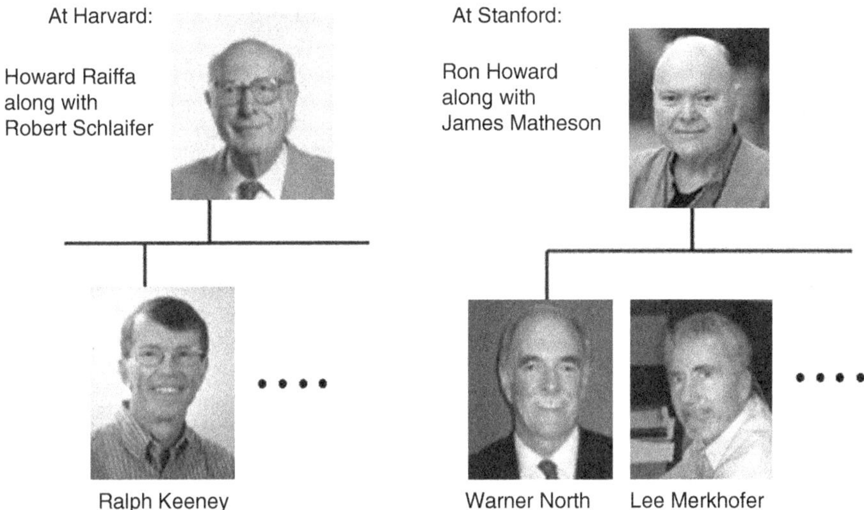

Key players in the two principal "schools" of decision analysis. Photos reproduced with permission from the individuals.

SUGGESTED RESOURCES ON DECISION ANALYSIS

Two of the basic classics of the literature in DA are:

- Howard Raiffa and Robert Schlaifer, *Applied Statistical Decision Theory*, Division of Research, Graduate School of Business Administration, Harvard University, 356pp., 1961.
- Morris H. DeGroot, *Optimal Statistical Decisions*, McGraw-Hill, 489pp., 1969.

Generations of students in public policy learned about DA from a very popular and readable set of instructional notes that Raiffa produced as a book:

- Howard Raiffa, *Decision Analysis: Introductory Lectures on Choices under Uncertainty*, Addison-Wesley, 309pp., 1968.

Other leading textbooks on DA include:

- Detlof von Winterfeldt and Ward Edwards, *Decision Analysis and Behavioral Research*, Cambridge University Press, 604pp., 1986.

- Steven R. Watson and Dennis M. Buede, *Decision Synthesis: The Principles and Practice of Decision Analysis*, Cambridge University Press, 299pp., 1988.
- Robert T. Clemen, *Making Hard Decisions: An Introduction to Decision Analysis*, Duxbury Press, 664pp., 1996.
- J.S. Hammond, R.L. Keeney, and H. Raiffa, *Smart Choices: A Practical Guide to Making Better Decisions*, Harvard Business School Press, 244pp., 1999.
- Rex Brown, *Rational Choice and Judgment: Decision Analysis for the Decider*, Wiley-Interscience, 245pp., 2005.

REFERENCES

Brown, R.V. (2005). *Rational Choice and Judgment: Decision Analysis for the Decider*, Wiley-Interscience, 245pp.

(2012). "Decision Theory as an Aid to Private Choice," *Judgment and Decision Making*, 7(2), pp. 207–223.

Brown, R.V., A.S. Kahr, and C. Peterson (1974). *Decision Analysis: An Overview*, Holt, Rinehart & Winston, 89pp.

Clemen, R.T. (1996). *Making Hard Decisions: An Introduction to Decision Analysis*, Duxbury Press, 664pp.

DeGroot, M.H. (1969). *Optimal Statistical Decisions*, McGraw-Hill, 489pp.

Dyer, J.S. (1990). "Remarks on the Analytic Hierarchy Process," *Management Science*, *36*, pp. 249–258.

Hammond, J.S., R.L. Keeney, and H. Raiffa (1999). *Smart Choices: A Practical Guide to Making Better Decisions*, Harvard Business School Press, 244pp.

Harker, P.T. and L.G. Vargas (1990). "Reply to 'Remarks on the Analytic Hierarchy Process' by J.S. Dyer," *Management Science*, *36*, pp. 269–273.

Henrion, M. (2012). Lumina Corporation website. www.lumina.com/technology/influence-diagrams.

Howard, R.A. and J.E. Matheson (eds.) (1984). *The Principles and Applications of Decision Analysis*, 2 vols., Strategic Decisions Group, 955pp.

(2005). "Influence Diagrams," *Decision Analysis*, 2(3), pp. 127–143.

Howard, R.A., J.E. Matheson, and D.W. North (1972). "The Decision to Seed Hurricanes," *Science*, *176*, pp. 1191–1202.

Keefer, D.L. and S.E. Bodily (1983). "Three Point Approximations for Continuous Random Variables," *Management Science*, *29*, pp. 595–609.

Keeney, R.L. (1982). "Decision Analysis: An Overview," *Operations Research*, *30*, pp. 803–837.

Klima, K., M.G. Morgan, I. Grossmann, and K. Emanuel (2011). "Does It Make Sense to Modify Tropical Cyclones? A Decision Approach," *Environmental Science & Technology*, *45*(10), pp. 4242–4248.

Manski, C.F. (2013). *Public Policy in an Uncertain World: Analysis and Decisions*, Harvard University Press, 199pp.

Miller, A.C., M.W. Merkhofer, R.A. Howard, J.E. Matheson, and T.R. Rice (1976). *Development of Automated Aides for Decision Analysis*, Technical Report, Stanford Research Institute, 214pp.

Miller, A.C. and T.R. Rice (1983). "Discrete Approximations of Continuous Distributions," *Management Science*, *29*, pp. 352–362.

Morgan, M.G., B. Fischhoff, A. Bostrom, and C. Atman (2002). *Risk Communication: A Mental Models Approach*, Cambridge University Press, 351pp.

Morgan, M.G. and M. Henrion with M. Small (1990). *Uncertainty: A Guide to Dealing with Uncertainty in Quantitative Risk and Policy Analysis*, Cambridge University Press, 332pp. (Paperback edition 1992. Latest printing (with revised chapter 10) 1998.)

Raiffa, H. (1968). *Decision Analysis: Introductory Lectures on Choices under Uncertainty*, Addison-Wesley, 309pp.

Raiffa, H. and R. Schlaifer (1961). *Applied Statistical Decision Theory*, Division of Research, Graduate School of Business Administration, Harvard University, 356pp.

Saaty, T.L. (1980). *The Analytic Hierarchy Process*, McGraw-Hill, 287pp.

(1990). "An Exposition on the AHP in Reply to the Paper 'Remarks on the Analytic Hierarchy Process,'" *Management Science*, *36*, pp. 259–268.

Smith, J., E.S. Holtzman, and J.E. Matheson (1993). "Structuring Relationships in Influence Diagrams," *Operations Research*, *41*(2), pp. 280–297.

Tani, S.N. (1978). "Decision Analysis of the Synthetic Fuels Commercialization Program," *AFIPS*, International Workshop on Managing Requirements Knowledge, pp. 23–29.

von Winterfeldt, D. and W. Edwards (1986). *Decision Analysis and Behavioral Research*, Cambridge University Press, 604pp.

Watson, S.R. and D.M. Buede (1988). *Decision Synthesis: The Principles and Practice of Decision Analysis*, Cambridge University Press, 299pp.

5

Valuing Intangibles and Other Non-Market Outcomes

If you are going to use quantitative methods such as B–C or DA for policy analysis, sooner or later it will become necessary to attach a quantitative value to a variety of outcomes that are not valued in a market. For example, if you want to perform a B–C analysis to decide whether a new kind of traffic light or guardrail should be installed on a highway, you will have to attach some value to the change in the risk of death and injury that will result for pedestrians and drivers. If you want to perform a DA of what strategy to adopt to prevent fertilizer runoff and sewage from damaging a lake or a coastal coral reef, you will have to attach some value to the damages that different options cause or prevent.

Of course, you could refuse to do this, arguing that lives or coral are "priceless" or that "sacred" things should not be valued in terms of dollars or measures of utility (that someone might then convert into dollars). However, as soon as you choose to take or not take some action, or choose one option over another, we can estimate the number of lives saved (or lost) and the cost of the action (or inaction), and then combine these two numbers to estimate the implicit rate at which you have chosen to invest to prevent deaths, injuries, or other damages. As discussed later in this chapter, not all issues of valuation entail directly or indirectly assessing a monetary value for outcomes, but since doing that is central to much quantitative policy analysis, we start by exploring methods that are commonly used to make such assessments.

There are basically three strategies that can be adopted to assess the value that people attach to intangible and other non-market outcomes:

1. Observe how people behave, assume that the choices they make are made without constraints and with full knowledge of their own interests and the implications of their actions, and infer a value from those choices.
2. Ask people how much they would be *willing to pay* (WTP) to avoid an undesirable outcome.

3. Ask people how much they *would have to be paid* to accept (WTA) an undesirable outcome.

The standard strategy for addressing options 2 and 3 is called *contingent valuation.*

5.1 INFERRING PEOPLE'S VALUES FROM THE CHOICES THEY MAKE

Sometimes one can estimate how safety or other attributes are valued by observing market transactions. For example, if the exact same automobile is offered with and without a specific safety feature, inferences about the value that consumers place on safety can be drawn from an analysis of purchasing patterns and accident probabilities and outcomes. Of course, doing this assumes that the customers buying those safer cars know and can make use of information about accident probabilities and outcomes.

Activities such as visits to a recreational facility have sometimes been valued using the *cost method.* Since the frequency with which a specific site gets visited typically depends on how far away it is, some approximate estimate of people's willingness to pay to visit a site can be estimated by determining the number of visits people make as a function of distance from the site and the cost per kilometer of travel. This can be done parametric in various attributes of the visitors. Sometimes the method is extended to consider multiple sites that have different attributes.

Often the feature(s) to be valued are bundled with other attributes. For example, people are typically prepared to pay more for a house if it has features such as good access to desirable services (transit, shopping, parks, etc.), is located in a safe neighborhood, has clean air, has good schools, has nice views, is not burdened by aircraft noise, etc. By locating similar homes in a variety of neighborhoods that have different levels of these and other features, one can attempt to estimate the value people attach to each through the use of multivariate regression analysis. This strategy is often referred to as *hedonic pricing.*

Benjamin Franklin (1748) wrote, "time is money." Economists have used that idea as a basis for performing valuation of things such as national parks. Cesario (1976) explains the basic idea:

> At the outset it is important to distinguish between time as a resource and time as a commodity. In the outdoor recreation trip context it is relevant to make the latter interpretation and therefore to be concerned with the value of saving time. If time is saved then it can be employed elsewhere. If time is treated as a resource it has scarcity value and the value of time in this interpretation is the value which one attaches to gaining additional units of it.

Cesario goes on to note that the value of time varies by context and by individual and presents a number of empirical results.

This basic approach has been used in transportation planning (Harrison and Quarmdy, 1969), in valuing consumer products and services such as the Internet in terms of the time spent using them (Goolsbee and Klenow, 2006), valuing attendance at artistic events (Nichols, 2011), and valuing time donated to non-profit organizations by volunteers (Knoepke, 2013).

5.2 THE "VALUE OF A STATISTICAL LIFE" OR VSL

Perhaps the largest literature on inferring people's values from the choices they make involves estimates of the "value of a statistical life" or VSL. This is the value inferred from the marginal rate at which individuals or society are prepared to invest to reduce the probability of death (or injury) when the risk to any single individual is small.

Clearly nobody who is sane, healthy, and not in a dire situation or a villain would be prepared to put a dollar value on whether they, or others, continue to live, nor is that what these estimates are about. So as to avoid confusion, in my own writings I have tried to avoid the use of terms like "value of life" and "VSL" and instead have talked of the rate at which people or society are prepared to invest to reduce the risk of death (or illness or injury).

Economists and others have used several strategies to assess VSL. Section 5.2 outlines how these approaches have evolved. Today the most common approach is to use labor market estimates. The assumption is that among the attributes that people consider when they search for a job is the level of mortality (and morbidity) risk that working in that job entails. The assumption is that as well-informed, rational decision makers, people expect to be paid more to accept an increase in these risks, and that these increments can be inferred by performing regression analysis across large employment data sets of the sort maintained by the U.S. Bureau of Labor Statistics in their Census of Fatal Occupational Injuries (CFOI).

Many of the leading contributions to this literature have been made by economist W. Kip Viscusi and his colleagues. Viscusi (2010) explains that "Examining how workers in the labor market value risks offers the advantage of imputing values from actual risk-taking decisions using large samples with detailed data. Properly designed stated preference studies are a useful supplementary technique for valuing many health risks, such as those for which there is no market evidence." Viscusi explains the basic idea using a figure such as that shown in Figure 5.1. He writes:

> Let $u(w(p))$ be the utility of income when healthy and $v(w(p))$ be the utility of income if killed or injured on the job, where $u',v' > 0$ for any given $w(p)$, and $u'',v'' \leq 0$. Then ... the observed wage-risk tradeoff based on the worker's optimal job choice from the set of available options is given by:
>
> $$w_p = \frac{u - v}{(1-p)u_w + pv_w}.$$

... [The left side of this equation] is the VSL for models in which p pertains to the probability of death. The VSL equals the difference in utility levels between the healthy and the ill health or dead state ... [In Figure 5.1] each worker will choose the wage-risk combination that offers the highest expected utility level given his or her preferences. Worker 1 chooses fatality risk p_1 that offers a wage rate of w_1 (p_1). Worker 2 is willing to face a higher risk of p_2 for a wage w_2 (p_2). The compensating differential that each worker receives for risk is the difference between the wage the worker receives and the value for a risk-free job given by $w(0)$ ...

Conventional hedonic wage models fit a curve that passes through these various points of tangency [x_1, x_2 etc. in Figure 5.1], thus simultaneously reflecting the wage-risk tradeoff for both workers and firms. The median estimate of studies using U.S. data is a VSL of $7 million (2000$s) or $8.7 million (2009$s) based on the meta analysis in Viscusi and Aldy (2003). Thus, the average worker receives an additional $870 to face an annual job fatality risk of 1/10,000.

READING 5.1

W. Kip Viscusi, "Chapter 4: A Survey of Values of Life and Health," in *Fatal Tradeoffs: Public and Private Responsibilities for Risk*, Oxford University Press, pp. 51–74, 1992.

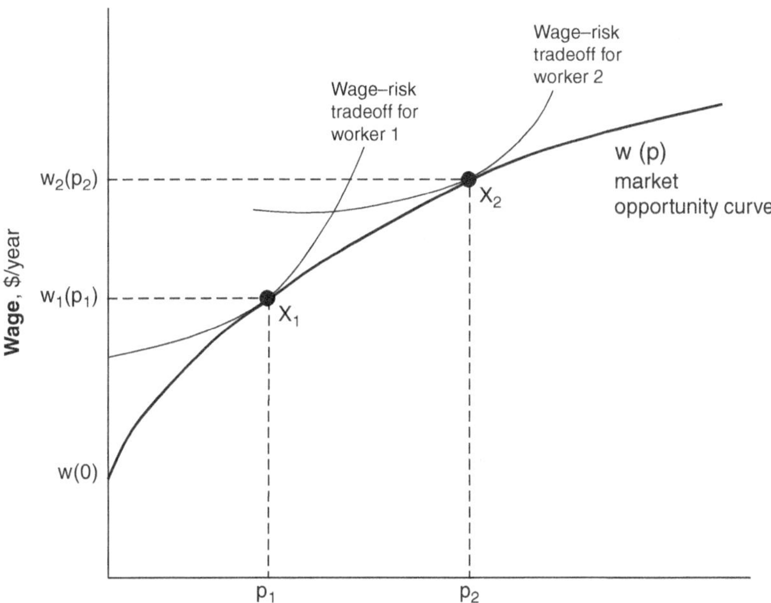

FIGURE 5.1. Standard hedonic labor market model. Redrawn from Viscusi (2010).

READING 5.2

W. Kip Viscusi, "Policy Challenges of the Heterogeneity of the Value of Statistical Life," *Foundations and Trends in Microeconomics*, 6(2), pp. 99–172, 2010.

5.3 A DECISION-ANALYTIC APPROACH TO VALUING ONE'S OWN LIFE

The decision analyst Ron Howard has been a strong proponent of libertarian philosophy. In that context he has argued that other individuals or society have no right to impose a mortality risk on another without their agreement and without compensation (Howard, 1980).[1] Whatever you may think of this position, he has developed a decision analytic framing of how an individual might decide how much compensation they should require before accepting the imposition of a risk or how much they should be willing to pay to eliminate an existing risk (such as a medical condition that carries some low probability of death).[2] He formulated the problem in terms of two decisions involving hypothetical pills:

- a person's decision about how much they would pay to purchase a white pill that if taken would completely eliminate an existing risk he or she faces that carries a mortality risk of p, and
- a person's decision about how much he or she should demand in payment to take a black pill that carries a probability p of causing immediate and painless death.

Of course, even in the absence of the pills and their associated risk, one's future longevity and income are uncertain. These he characterized in terms of a future "life lottery" using standard statistical mortality tables to estimate the probability of continuing to live to enjoy future life or having an endowment to pass along to one's heirs. The two decision trees are shown in the upper part of Figure 5.2. The results obtained by one individual who went through the exercise are shown below.

[1] It is obvious that Howard's view on this issue has evolved since he wrote the paper on "The Decision to Seed Hurricanes" that you read about in Chapter 4. That paper clearly adopts the perspective of a government decision maker.

[2] When Howard presented this formulation at a conference on societal risk assessment at the GM Research Labs, Anita Curran, who was then the Health Commissioner of West Chester County, NY, with extensive experience with regulating restaurants, was incredulous that Howard argued, "I don't like the idea of health commissions making decisions about my life" and called for restaurants to post the risk (in micromorts – units of risks of 10^{-6}) that eating at their establishment would impose, so that individuals could decide whether to patronize them. See Q&A after Howard (1980).

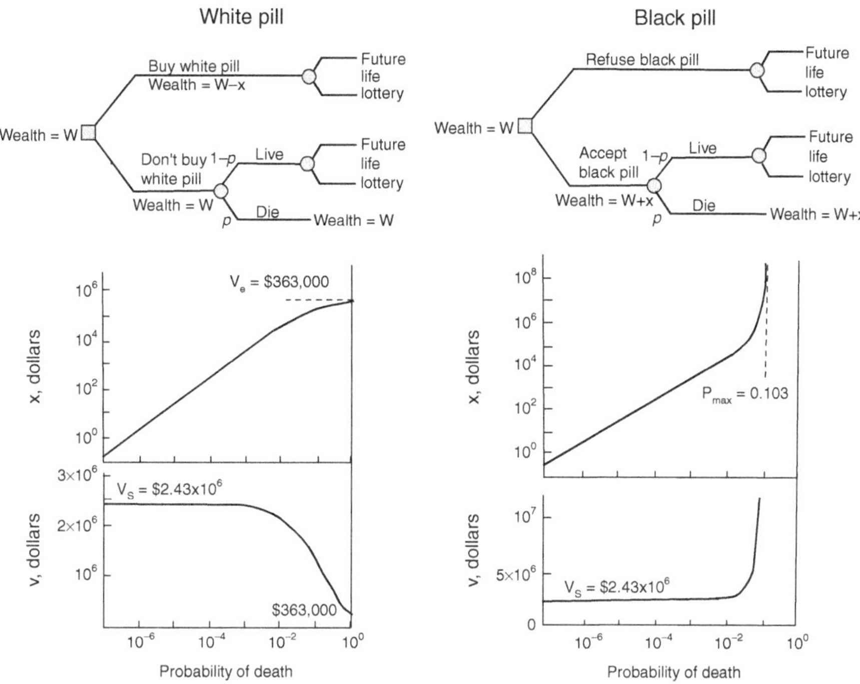

FIGURE 5.2. Illustration of the individual "white pill" and "black pill" personal choice (above), and associated results (below) for a hypothetical respondent in 1980. x = payment to buy the white pill or take the black pill; p = probability of death; v = life value; v_s = value of life at small value of p; v_e = most an individual can pay to obtain the white pill. Figures redrawn from Howard (1980).

The curves in the lower part of Figure 5.2 are instructive. For this individual back in 1980, their low-probability VSL was $2.43 million. Note, however, that in the case of the white pill, as the risk faced becomes larger than about 1/1000, the VSL starts to fall and ultimately drops to $363,000, the maximum amount of resources that this individual believes they can muster to buy the life-saving white pill when faced with an illness or other contingency that will kill them with probability one (i.e., with certainty). This reflects the fact that we all (and, for that matter, society as a whole) face a budget constraint. There is simply a limit, both for us as individuals and for society as a whole, to how much we can afford to pay to reduce risks.

In contrast, the curve for the black pill takes off asymptotically to infinity once the risk reaches about 1/10. This individual might be willing to play Russian roulette with a single round in a ten-chamber pistol for a payment of a billion dollars, but would not agree to play with a six-chamber pistol for any price.

READING 5.3

Ronald A. Howard, "On Making Life and Death Decisions," in Richard S. Schwing and Walter A. Albers (eds.), *Societal Risk Assessment: How Safe Is Safe Enough?*, Plenum, pp. 89–113, 1980.

DISCUSSION QUESTIONS FOR READING 5.3

- While most people find the formulation of the white pill problem to be perfectly acceptable, many find the black pill problem to be very objectionable. Of course, every day of our lives we all run risks of the low magnitudes that Howard is considering. Howard simply uses the hypothetical black pill to reflect that fact. Why, if at all, is a black pill with associated probability of death p any different than accepting payment to drive downtown to run an errand if the risk of dying while doing that also carries a probability p?
- Make yourself a table with probabilities running from 10^{-7} to 10^{0} and see if you can work out the dollar values you would choose, first for the case of the white pill and then for the black.

5.4 EVOLUTION OF APPROACHES TO THE ECONOMIC VALUATION OF LOST LIVES

The first time I encountered the use of the concept of "value of life" in my own work was in a piece of analysis on coal workers' pneumoconiosis (CWP), or black lung disease, done by Lucille Langlois for the Appalachian Regional Commission. In those days it was common to compute a value for a lost life in terms of lost earning power and expenses (Figure 5.3). Langlois (1971) estimated the cost of CWP to individuals as follows:

> the financial loss to a miner *disabled* with CWP would be computed as follows: average annual wage of \$7,000 less 12 percent for taxes, plus 8.5 percent for lost services: \$7,000 – \$840 + \$595 = \$6,755, which is his annual financial loss. In *death* cases, the financial loss to survivors would be: average annual wage of \$7,000, discounted for four years (4 years was chosen as the mean duration of retirement after forced retirement) less the 12 percent for taxes, plus 8.5 percent for lost services, plus 8.5 percent loss of benefits through premature death, and the 26 percent "savings" on consumption of the family head: \$24,822 – \$2,979 + \$2,110 + \$2,110 – \$6,454 = \$19,609.
>
> Welfare and compensation, however, restore some of these economic losses. It is generally estimated that about 10 percent of total loss is replaced in the case of disability, and around 33 percent in death cases ... we arrive at a real annual financial loss of \$6,079 ... for minors totally disabled ... [and] \$13,093 ... to the survivors of each deceased black lung victim ... [which multiplying by the number of cases of disability and deaths] yields an estimated income loss to the underground bituminous mining population of \$23 million a year.

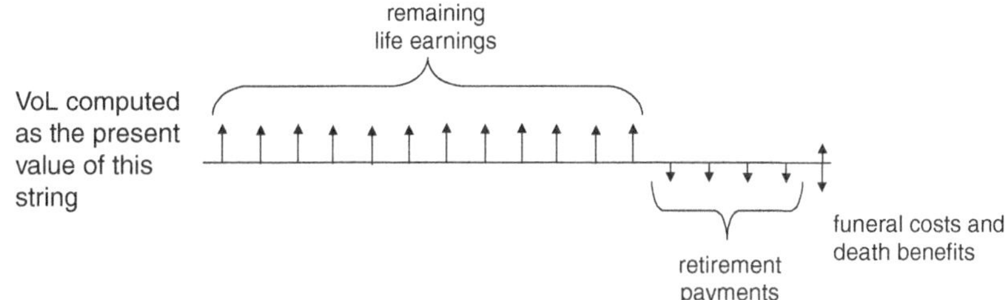

FIGURE 5.3. For almost half-a-century prior to the 1980s, economists and others computed value of life for use in B–C analysis in terms of the present value of future earnings less future expenses. Some (although not Langlois, 1971) even included funeral costs in these calculations. Note that this formulation would result in a negative VoL of many people, such as people (most often women) working full-time at home to raise children and those who are retired. While the formulations have now become much more sophisticated, arguments are still sometimes made that if a smoker dies early, his or her death constitutes a net benefit to society because it no longer has to pay for retirement and other social services (Mansnerus, 1996).

In her calculation, Langlois also computed the value of lost production, the cost of recruiting and training new miners, medical expenses, and similar factors. Adding everything up she concluded that CWP "imposes real annual social and private costs amounting to some $50 million, as opposed to control costs [to limit exposure to coal dust] approaching some $31 million."

Such an approach was pretty much the state of the art in economic assessment in the early 1970s. Writing in 1971, Mishan (1971) summarized as follows:

> Despite repeated expressions of dissatisfaction with the method, the most common way of calculating the economic worth of a person's life and, therefore, loss to the economy consequent upon his decease is that of discounting to the present the person's expected future earnings …
>
> A second method, which might be thought of as more refined than the first, is that of calculating the present discounted value of the losses over time accruing to *others only* as a result of the death of the person at age τ …
>
> A third possible method would repudiate any direct calculation of the losses of potential earnings or spending. Instead it would approach the problem from a "social" point of view. Since society, through its political processes does in fact take decisions on investment expenditures that occasionally increase or reduce the number of deaths, an implicit value of human life can be calculated. This approach receives occasional mention …
>
> [Fourth] the insurance principle is a departure from any of these aforementioned methods. Predicated on the premium a man is willing to pay, and the probability of his being killed as a result of engaging in some specific activity, it is thought possible to calculate the value a man sets on his life.

A concise summary of the evolutions of efforts between 1930 and 1975 to value life and safety improvements can be found in chapter 2 of Jones-Lee (1976). An early analysis by Dublin and Lotka (1930), which Jones-Lee discusses, is very reminiscent of the analysis used 40 years later for the Appalachian Regional Commission, in that it computed "the difference between the discounted present value of [a man's] ... anticipated future earnings and his future anticipated consumption expenditures." The result was an estimate of a value at birth of just under $10,000 (1930$s). Dublin and Lotka included a chapter summarizing work done prior to 1930, which Jones-Lee summarizes as follows:

> Broadly speaking, this literature divides into two groups: that which contains the direct antecedents of Dublin and Lotka's empirical analysis, including the work of Petty, Farr and Lüdtke, the other group comprising more general discussions of the value of a man in the context of "human capital," including the work of Smith, Engle, Nicholson and Marshall. [Citations to these authors can be found in Jones-Lee, 1976.]

Most people have a strong negative reaction to a formulation that values lives in terms of earnings less expenses. Further, such a formulation would place a negative value on people who are not employed and are being compensated in the cash economy.

While it took almost half-a-century, economists and other analysts finally moved on to risk-premium labor market methods and methods based on willingness to pay. The later works reviewed by Jones-Lee display this evolution toward the present more statistical approach to valuing low-probability risks.

Had Langlois (1971) used these later methods to perform estimates for the cost of life loss by coal miners, she would probably have obtained higher values. However, a key assumption in the labor market methods is that there is a free market in which people voluntarily assume greater risk in order to earn greater compensation. As Henry Caudill (1963) has movingly documented, until the latter part of the twentieth century, the assumption that Appalachian coal miners had freedom to move to other jobs, and so assumed the risks of mining voluntarily, was patently absurd.

5.5 USE OF VSL AND SIMILAR MEASURES IN PUBLIC POLICY

Especially in the United States, many government agencies make use of VSL values in making regulatory decisions. In recent years, agencies such as the U.S. Environmental Protection Agency (EPA) and the U.S. Department of Transportation (DOT) have been publishing regular guidance on the VSL values they use in their regulatory decision making. DOT also publishes coefficients by which the VSL should be multiplied to assess the costs of injuries of various levels of seriousness.[3] Readers can easily find the latest recommended values with a few minutes of Internet search.

[3] These coefficients take on values such as 0.003 for "minor," 0.047 for "moderate," 0.105 for "serious," 0.266 for "severe," and 0.593 if "critical," where each level is defined in terms of an Abbreviated Injury Scale (AIS) classification (see: https://en.wikipedia.org/wiki/Abbreviated_Injury_Scale). Note the use of three significant figures!

Readers should consider five questions: (1) should all agencies use the same value? (2) should different values be used for different risks? (3) should different values be used for populations with different levels of income? (4) should different values be used for populations of different age? and (5) should different values be used for populations in which society has made different levels of investment?

Sunstein (2004) has argued at length that the answer is that the value used should vary by risk, income, and age, but that, conditional on that, different agencies should all use the same value. He argues that "In principle, government should not force people to buy protection against statistical risks at a price that seems excessive to them ... At least as a general rule, people should not be required to pay $70 to reduce a risk of 1/100,000 if they are willing to pay no more than $50." As noted in Chapter 3, one consequence of such an argument is that airplanes should be made safer than buses because, on average, the people who fly on airplanes are wealthier, and likely have a higher ability and willingness to pay than those who take the bus. It could also be interpreted to mean (as some economists have argued to EPA) that more should be spent to reduce exposures to low levels of hazardous air or water pollutants in high-income communities than in low-income communities.

If one is addressing an entirely domestic question, such as "should automatic pedestrian avoidance systems be installed on buses," it would then be appropriate to use different levels of VSL in different societies. In an assessment of such technology in Bogotá, Colombia (VSL = $160,000) and New York (VSL = $9 million), Sonia Cecilia Mangones Matos (2015) showed that investing in such technology could be justified in New York but not in Bogotá.

In contrast, as noted in Section 3.8, when economists in Working Group III of the IPCC's second assessment used different VSLs to value impacts from climate change in different countries and then added up the results in order to assess total economic costs, enormous controversy ensued (Pearce, 1995). Given that the developed world (with high VSLs) had produced most of the emissions that cause climate change, using low VSLs to assess damages in the heavily impacted developing world obviously raised serious questions of inter-nation equity![4]

To return to the five questions, if the same population and risk is involved, it is hard to see why there should be variation in the VSL used by different agencies. Of course, if different agencies address different risks to different populations, that might not hold. Sunstein (2004) understands that the answer to question two is complicated by risk perception (see Chapter 13). He might argue that even after one overcomes those perceptual issues (probably an

[4] For some taste of the controversy that arose, see: https://enthusiasmscepticismscience.wordpress.com/2013/01/15/enter-the-economists-the-price-of-life-and-how-the-ipcc-only-just-survived-the-other-chapter-controversy. And: www.bishop-hill.net/blog/2013/2/26/the-price-of-life-the-ipccs-first-and-forgotten-controversy.html.

impossible challenge), cancer deaths should carry a higher VSL than sudden accidental deaths.

There is no avoiding the fact that there is an "income effect" that limits how much an individual can afford to pay, or how much a given society can afford to invest to reduce a risk. The critical issues from a public policy perspective are who bears the cost of the risk abatement, and should that cost be considered at the level of each individual or for the society as a whole. Clearly in the interests of equity, a wealthy society should be prepared to invest more in securing the minimum level of health and safety of its citizens than a poor society can afford to do. But does that mean that the low-cost compact cars poor people can afford should be made as safe as my much more expensive Volvo? My own view is that even the low-cost compact car should meet some minimum level of safety, and that if that means some cross-subsidy from those who purchase expensive cars, that is something that society should do in the interests of equity. However, beyond that, there is no escaping the fact that, in the words of Aaron Wildavsky (1981), "richer is safer."

Sunstein (2004) also argues that because they have fewer years left to live, a lower VSL should apply to older populations. This too raises important issues of equity, complicated by the fact that many older populations may also have more disposable income and thus be able to invest more to avoid a risk. The literature is largely silent on question five. While in some cases people individually cover all the costs of acquiring advanced knowledge and skills, in many cases the development of such "human capital" is subsidized to varying degrees by society.

Assuming it could be adequately assessed, the obvious final issue in considering these questions is whether willingness to pay is even the right metric. As Section 5.3 makes clear, there can be a large difference between willingness to pay to avoid a risk and willingness to accept payment to assume a risk. Should the fact that someone who is very good at math and has chosen to pursue a low-income career teaching inner-city kids as opposed to becoming a "quant" on Wall Street mean that regulators should impose a lower level of protection from a risk that he or she is not voluntarily assuming?

Even if we assume that the same VSL should be used in public decision making across the entire population, there is the issue of how well society is achieving that goal. An economist who has not reflected carefully about his or her own perceptions might argue that in making investments to limit risks, one should invest in such a way as to set the marginal investment per death (and injury) avoided to be equal across all the risks we face. As we will learn in Chapter 13, when people (including many economists when they reflect on it) judge how risky something is and how much should be done to manage it, they consider a variety of other factors such as how equitably a risk is distributed across society, how controllable it is, whether it is assumed voluntarily (skiing) or imposed (chemical plant emissions), etc. On the other hand, it seems

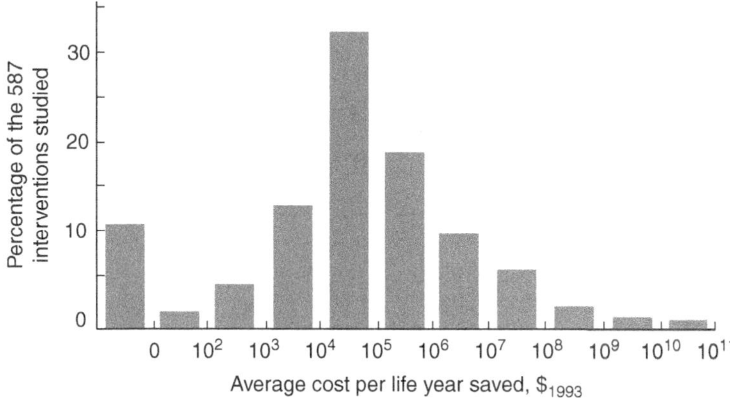

FIGURE 5.4. Distribution of estimates of average cost per life saved (as opposed to marginal cost) in 587 regulatory programs. Note that there is a range of over 10^{11} and that 10% of the interventions are estimated to save both lives and money. Redrawn from Tengs et al. (1995).

unlikely that these other considerations could justify differences in investments to improve safety that vary by more than a few factors of ten.

Suspecting that society's investments in life saving are "haphazard," resulting in very large investments in some things that do little to save lives, while investing little or nothing in other things that could save lots of lives, John Graham and Jim Vaupel (1981) and Tammy Tengs and a number of colleagues (1995, 1996) have undertaken a series of studies to document the distribution of these investments. Tengs et al. (1995) report on a study that examined over 500 assessments that had been made of the cost of safety programs and the number of lives each was thought to save. Figure 5.4 summarizes their results, which span a range of over 100 billion. While this work can be criticized on a number of methodological grounds, the basic conclusion is unassailable: society is seriously under-investing in some life-saving opportunities, while spending way more than it should on some others.

In subsequent work that looked at only that subset of 185 studies for which national cost and effectiveness data were available, Tengs and Graham (1996) asked:

> How many lives could be saved if we were to spend the same amount of money [that is now spent for the 185 risks studied], but invest it in those interventions that, taken together, would save the greatest number of lives possible? Results indicate that if we hold investments constant we could save ... an additional 60,200 lives ... or about twice as many lives saved relative to the status quo. To accomplish these gains we would simply invest in all interventions costing less than ... \$7.57 million [per life saved]. On average we would spend \$183,000 per life saved.

Tengs and Graham (1996) went on to ask how much expenditure might be reduced if the present level of mortality risk were held constant, but the resources reallocated to achieve that level in an optimal way. They estimate a possible savings of $31.1 billion over the status quo.

On the basis of their analysis Tengs and Graham (1996) propose a simple rule of thumb: "invest in all [life-saving] interventions costing less than some threshold (for example, $5 million per life saved) and in none of the interventions costing more."

READING 5.4

T.O. Tengs, M.E. Adams, J.S. Pliskin, D.G. Safran, J.E. Siefel, M.C. Weinstein, and J.D. Graham, "Five-Hundred Life-Saving Interventions and Their Cost-Effectiveness," *Risk Analysis*, *15*(3), pp. 369–390, 1995.

Abstract: We gathered information on the cost-effectiveness of life-saving interventions in the United States from publicly available economic analyses. "Life-saving interventions" were defined as any behavioral and/or technological strategy that reduces the probability of premature death among a specified target population. We defined cost-effectiveness as the net resource costs of an intervention per year of life saved. To improve the comparability of cost-effectiveness ratios arrived at with diverse methods, we established fixed definitional goals and revised published estimates, when necessary and feasible, to meet these goals. The 587 interventions identified ranged from those that save more resources than they cost, to those costing more than 10 billion dollars per year of life saved. Overall, the median intervention costs $42,000 per life-year saved. The median medical intervention costs $19,000/life-year; injury reduction $48,000/life-year; and toxin control $2,800,000/life-year. Cost/life-year ratios and bibliographic references for more than 500 life-saving interventions are provided.

DISCUSSION QUESTIONS FOR READING 5.4

- What methodological problems, if any, do you see in the analysis conducted by Tengs et al. (1995)?
- Tengs and Graham (1996) suggests a simple rule of thumb: "invest in all [life-saving] interventions costing less than some threshold and in none of the interventions costing more." What do you think of such a rule? If such a rule were implemented for government life-saving programs, and the threshold were set somewhere between $5 and $10 million, can you suggest situations in which society might wish to invest more than such a limit? How much more, and why?
- Perhaps some of the actual or proposed regulations that were assessed in this study could also have had other benefits besides reducing deaths and injuries. What is the likelihood that those benefits could change the basic insight from this study?

5.6 CONTINGENT VALUATION (CV)

Assuming that all other Americans pay the same amount, how much would you be willing to pay to preserve a lovely pristine lake in the Adirondack Mountains of upstate New York? How much would you pay to preserve *all* the pristine lakes in the Adirondacks? Is there an amount you would be willing to be compensated (together with all other Americans) to allow a mining or a chemical company to desecrate that pristine lake? These are the sorts of questions, with suitable elaboration and systematic methods, that people are asked to answer in contingent valuation studies.

Economists Norbert Schwarz and Raymond Kopp succinctly define contingent valuation, or CV, as follows:

> CV measures of economic value rely on the same logic that underlies all economic monetary valuation concepts, that is choice. In CV studies choices are posed to people in surveys; analysts then use the responses to these choice questions to construct monetary measures of value. The specific mechanism used to elicit respondents' choices can take a variety of forms including asking survey respondents whether they would purchase, vote or pay for a program or some other well-defined object of choice. It can also be a direct elicitation of the amount each respondent would be willing to pay (WTP) to obtain an object of choice or the amount each respondent would be willing to accept (WTA) in compensation to give it up. (Schwarz and Kopp in the introduction to Kopp et al., 1997)

The use of CV methods began in the 1960s. A big expansion of interest in CV studies and methods was stimulated by efforts by the State of Alaska to value the environmental impacts that resulted when the oil tanker Exxon Valdez ran aground in Prince William Sound, Alaska, in 1989. A study conducted by Carson et al. (1992, 2003) for the State, to assess the lost passive use value resulting from the accident, involved interviews with 1045 randomly selected households across the United States. The study concluded:

> The CV survey revealed that the Exxon Valdez oil spill was spontaneously mentioned by over half the respondents as one of the largest environmental accidents caused by humans anywhere in the world; and over 90 percent of the respondents said they were aware of the spill. The median household willingness to pay for the spill prevention plan was found to be $31. Multiplying this number by an adjusted number of U.S. households results in a damage estimate of $2.8 billion dollars.

Mitchell and Carson (1989) suggest that a well-designed CV study should consist of three parts:

1. A detailed description of the good(s) being valued and their hypothetical circumstance under which it is made available to the respondent.
2. Questions which elicit the respondents' willingness to pay for the good(s) being valued.
3. Questions about respondents' characteristics (for example age, income, etc.), their preferences relevant to the goods being valued, and their use of the good(s).

CV methods are predicated on the assumption that people have well-articulated values for the objects or outcomes that are being valued (see Section 5.6) and that the answers they give relate to their understanding of what they consider to be the relevant attributes of those objects or outcomes.

Using visibility as an example (e.g., in the Grand Canyon or Los Angeles), Fischhoff and Furby (1988) outline how complicated and difficult it can be to correctly identify all the attributes relevant in a hypothetical transaction. In addition to a complete description of the end state, Fischhoff and Furby (1988) note that how that state is reached may also be important to people's valuation. Thus, they argue:

> A scene might be evaluated quite differently if it is seen as reflecting the power of a natural process or the triumph of an unnatural one. For example, evaluations can shift dramatically when the individual realizes that a vivid sunset largely reflects atmospheric pollution (or that a summer haze is due to humidity, rather than smog).

Both economists (Schwarz and Kopp, 1997) and psychologists (Fischhoff and Furby, 1988) agree that in addition to articulating relevant attributes, it is also important to specify the context within which a hypothetical transaction will take place. Fischhoff and Furby (1988) write: "the definition of any good must include any conditioning factors that influence the importance of its attributes. This imparts a certain circularity to the design of [CV] studies, insofar as some knowledge of people's values is needed in order to characterize adequately the stimuli used to reveal those values." As we will see in Section 12.2 when we explore prospect theory, the original reference or target level that is assumed for the change being evaluated can also play an important role (i.e., provide a psychological anchor), because people tend to value things differently depending on how they define the present state and whether the change constitutes a gain or loss with respect to that state. Thus, depending on how a choice is "framed," the same change may be interpreted as either a gain or a loss and result in quite different valuations.

Other factors that Fischhoff and Furby (1988) argue must be addressed in specifying a choice question include the spatial and temporal extent of the change, the timing of the change, and the certainty that the change will actually be made if the transaction is completed. Beyond these, it is important to differentiate between public goods, where everyone enjoys the benefit or harm, and private goods where only those who pay have access and others are excluded.

Given the assumption that people have well-articulated values, much of the attention of the economics community has framed the problem as one of devising adequate instruments to measure those values. Various question and response formats have been used in conjunction with a variety of survey or other elicitation methods. People designing such instruments have paid great attention to devising designs that they believe will minimize bias (e.g., from strategic behavior of respondents who know what they think but give a different answer because they want to influence the policy process in which the CV values will be employed).

When the level of risk is high, then clearly willingness to pay will be limited by the income effect, while willingness to accept will not. However, for very low risks, Graham (2008) argues:

> Under this condition there are no obvious grounds (except for a tiny income effect) for expecting that a person's WTA value for risk imposition will exceed his or her WTP value for avoidance of the same risk. Thus, the minimum price reduction necessary to induce a consumer to purchase a somewhat smaller car with an incremental risk of 1 in 10,000 would be roughly equal to that same customer's maximum WTP for an improved side impact airbag that prevents an incremental annual risk of death of 1 in 10,000 per year.

However, having made this argument, Graham later notes that this equivalency between WTA and WTP is not what one observes in practice.

A serious problem with many CV studies is that results often display little or no sensitivity to quantity: for example, the same willingness to pay for 10 days as for 180 days of improved atmospheric visibility (Tolley and Randall, 1986) or the same willingness to pay to save 2000 migratory waterfowl as to save 200,000 (Schkade and Payne, 1994). Frederick and Fischhoff (1998) have examined this "insensitivity to scope" and concluded that for a variety of reasons such results are not consistent with rational actor economic theory.

Kahneman and Knetsch (1992) raise a range of similar concerns. The abstract reads:

> Contingent valuation surveys in which respondents state their willingness to pay (WTP) for public goods are coming into use in cost-benefit and in litigation over environmental losses. The validity of the method is brought into question by several experimental observations. An embedding effect is demonstrated, in which WTP for a good varies depending on whether it is evaluated on its own or as part of a more inclusive category. The ordering of various public issues by WTP is predicted with significant accuracy by independent ratings of the moral satisfaction associated with contributions to these causes. Contingent valuation responses reflect the willingness to pay for the moral satisfaction of contributing to public goods, not the economic value of these goods.

Additional critical assessments can be found in the collection of papers edited by Hausman (1993).

In an Editor's Comment, the editor of the *Harvard Law Review* (1992) argued that:

> CV is still in a rudimentary state of development ... There are numerous sources of bias and unreliability that are inherent in CV. A fundamental problem is the hypothetical nature of the questions and answers. Unlike the more common marketplace transactions, where consumers must consider income constraints and potential expenditures on other goods, there is no cost to being wrong when answering a CV survey. Therefore there is no incentive to undertake the mental effort to be accurate. CV surveys are also

susceptible to "strategic bias," whereby respondents purposefully misrepresent their WTP in an effort to increase or decrease the amount of money devoted to a resource ...

CV was originally developed to measure use values, such as the opportunity to visit national parks or wilderness areas. The extension of the technique to measurement of nonuse values is especially worrisome [because] ... the hypothetical nature of the survey is intensified when applied to goods with which the respondent may be entirely unfamiliar ...

CV estimates for vastly different sizes and types of resources tend to fall within a similar range ... [For example] an experiment that asked three different groups about their WTP to save 2000, 20,000 or 200,000 birds ... found that ... the average WTP's were virtually identical.

5.7 COMPUTING THE COSTS OF EXTERNALITIES

Once one is able to place a value on deaths or injuries through one of the strategies discussed in Section 5.2, and value other outcomes, such as ecological damage, using contingent valuation, it is then often a reasonably straightforward task to compute the cost of an externality such as air pollution (Matthews, 2001; NRC, 2010; EPA, 2011). In their report *The Hidden Costs of Energy*, a National Academy committee explains the process they used as follows:

Estimating the damages associated with external effects was a multistep process, with most steps entailing assumptions and their associated uncertainties. Our method, based on the "damage function approach," started with estimates of burdens (such as air-pollutant emissions and water-pollutant discharges). Using mathematical models, we then estimated these burdens' resultant ambient concentrations as well as the ensuing exposures. The exposures were then associated with consequent effects, to which we attached monetary values in order to produce damage estimates. One of the ways economists assign monetary values to energy-related adverse effects is to study people's preferences for reducing those effects. The process of placing monetary values on these impacts is analogous to determining the price people are willing to pay for commercial products. We applied these methods to a year close to the present (2005) for which data were available and also to a future year (2030) to gauge the impacts of possible changes in technology. (NRC, 2010)

This approach allowed the committee to reach conclusions such as: "The aggregate damages associated with emissions of SO2, NOx, and PM [but excluding climate change] from these coal-fired facilities in 2005 were approximately $62 billion" and "In 2005, the vehicle sector produced $56 billion in health and other non-climate-change damages, with $36 billion from light-duty vehicles and $20 billion from heavy-duty vehicles" (NRC, 2010).

Under Section 812 of the 1990 Amendments to the Clean Air Act (Public Law 101–549), the U.S. EPA has conducted a number of similar studies. They conclude that their central benefits estimate exceeds costs by a factor of more than 30 to 1, and the high benefits estimate exceeds costs by 90 times, and that even the low benefits estimate exceeds costs by about 3 to 1. Costs were estimated to reach an annual value of $65 billion by the year 2020. Benefits were estimated to reach an annual value of $2 trillion (EPA, 2011).

5.8 ECOSYSTEM SERVICES

As economists and others have worked to apply benefit–cost methods in the evaluation of proposed actions or policies, they have come to understand the importance of including in their analyses some consideration of impacts on, and services provided by, ecosystems. For example, insects provide valuable pollination services for many crops, natural ground cover can reduce the magnitude of flooding, and wetlands often provide water purification functions that would be very costly to replicate if they had to be provided by engineered systems. This realization, coupled with concerns by ecologists and many others who have become alarmed by the growing degradation of ecosystems that has resulted from rapid and often short-sighted economic growth, has given rise to the concept of "ecosystem services."

Brauman et al. (2007) explain:

> Ecosystem services, the benefits that people obtain from ecosystems, are a powerful lens through which to understand human relationships with the environment and to design environmental policy. The explicit inclusion of beneficiaries makes values intrinsic to ecosystem services; whether or not those values are monetized, the ecosystem services framework provides a way to assess trade-offs among alternative scenarios of resource use and land- and seascape change.

Writing some years ago, Mooney and Ehrlich (1997) noted that "while the explicit recognition of ecosystem services is a relatively new phenomenon," for millennia thoughtful people have recognized the key role they play. For example, "Plato understood that the deforestation of Attica led to soil erosion and the drying of springs." Mooney and Ehrlich (1997) went on to observe that "As far as we can determine, the functioning of ecosystems in terms of delivering *services* to humanity was first described in the report of the *Study of Critical Environmental Problems*" (SCEP, 1970).

In a 2000 report to United Nations General Assembly, Secretary-General Kofi Annan observed that:

> The natural environment performs for us, free of charge, basic services without which our species could not survive. The ozone layer screens out ultraviolet rays from the sun that harm people, animals and plants. Ecosystems help purify the air we breathe and the water we drink. They convert wastes into resources and reduce atmospheric carbon levels that would otherwise contribute to global warming. Biodiversity provides a bountiful store of medicines and food products, and it maintains genetic variety that reduces

vulnerability to pests and diseases. But we are degrading, and in some cases destroying, the ability of the environment to continue providing these life-sustaining services for us. (Annan, 2000)

During the five years that followed, a very large international study was conducted that extensively explored and developed these issues. This Millennium Ecosystem Assessment (2005) identified four categories of ecosystem service: (1) provisioning services (e.g., the supply of wood and water); (2) regulating services (e.g., water purification and flood protection); (3) cultural services (e.g., aesthetic and spiritual); and (4) supporting services (e.g., biogeochemical processes and soil formation).

It is clear that ecosystems provide people with many benefits and studying their operation is critically important. However, things get more complicated when one sets out to place economic values on the services that ecosystems provide. While there have been some misguided efforts to value ecosystems *per se* (Costanza et al., 1997; Nature Briefing, 1998), increasingly the community has come to understand that if an economic valuation is to be made it should be on marginal contributions: that is, on comparing the value of leaving a specific ecosystem or portion of an ecosystem in its present state, versus converting it to some other state. Even then, a quantitative monetary valuation may not always be possible or make sense. In this connection, Guerry et al. (2015) argue:

Monetary valuation of ecosystem services is sometimes helpful. Market and nonmarket valuation methods from economics are used to estimate ecosystem service values ... [However,] where monetary valuation is highly contested or lacks robustness, or where monetary value metrics are not relevant to decisions, it is often preferable to report outcomes in biophysical terms or directly in terms of impacts on human health or livelihoods.

Nevertheless, because of the OMB requirement that U.S. government agencies perform benefit–cost analyses on all major rules, the U.S. EPA has placed considerable emphasis on developing and applying methods to quantify environmental services.[5] In that connection, in 2009 the EPA Science Advisory Board conducted a special study on this topic. Table 5.1 summarizes the methods they discuss.

Readers interested in a more general critique of the metaphor of ecosystem services will find a very thoughtful discussion in Norgaard (2010), the abstract of which reads:

What started as a humble metaphor to help us think about our relation to nature has become integral to how we are addressing the future of humanity and the course of

[5] Indeed, in the face of chronically inadequate budgets, this focus on ecosystem services has crowded out much of the most basic work in ecosystem science at EPA.

TABLE 5.1. *Methods to value ecosystem services identified by the EPA Science Advisory Board (2009).*

Method	Form of output/unit	Related concepts(s) of value
Measures of attitudes, preferences, and intentions		
Survey questions eliciting information about attitudes, preferences, and intentions	Attitude scales, preference or importance rankings, behavioral toward depicted environments or conditions	Attitudes and judgments; community-based values
Individual narratives and focus groups	Qualitative summaries and assessments from transcripts	Attitudes and judgments; community-based values
Behavioral observation	Inferences from observations of behavior by individuals interacting with actual or computer-simulated environments	Attitudes and judgments; community-based values
Economic methods		
Market-based methods	Monetary measure of willingness-to pay (WTP) for ecosystem services that contribute to the provision of marketed goods and services	Economic value
Travel cost	Monetary measure of WTP for ecosystem services that affect decisions to visit different locations	Economic value
Hedonic pricing	Monetary measure of marginal WTP or willingness-to-accept (WTA) as revealed by price for houses or wages paid for jobs with different environmental characteristics	Economic value
Averting behavior	Monetary or other measure of WTP as revealed by responses to opportunities to avoid or reduce damages, e.g., through expenditures on protective goods or substitutes	Economic value
Survey questions eliciting stated preferences	Monetary or other measures of WTP or WTA as expressed in survey questions about hypothetical tradeoffs	Economic value
Civic valuation		
Referenda and initiatives	Rankings of alternative options, or monetary or other measure of tradeoffs a community is willing to make, as reflected in community choices	Community-based values; indicator of economic value under some conditions

(*Continued*)

TABLE 5.1. (*cont.*)

Method	Form of output/unit	Related concepts(s) of value
Citizen valuation juries	Rankings of alternative options, or monetary or other measures of required payment or compensation, based on jury-determined assessments of public values	Community-based values; constructed values
Decision science approaches		
Decision science approaches	Attitude weights that reflect tradeoffs individuals are willing to make across attributes, including ecological attributes, for use in assigning scores to alternative policy options	Constructed value
Ecosystem benefit indicators		
Ecosystem benefit indicators	Quantitative spatially differentiated metrics or maps related to supply of or demand for ecosystem services	Indicators of economic value and/or community-based values
Biophysical ranking methods		
Conservation value method	Spatially differentiated index of conservation values across a landscape	Bio-ecological value
Embodied energy analysis	Cost of the total (direct plus indirect) energy required to produce an ecological or economic good or service	Energy-based value
Ecological footprint	Area of an ecosystem (land and/or water) required to support a consumption pattern or population	Bio-ecological value
Cost as a proxy for value		
Replacement cost	Monetary estimate of the cost of replacing an ecosystem service using the next best available alternative	Lower bound on economic value only under limited conditions
Habitat equivalency analysis	Units of habitat (e.g., equivalent acres of habitat) or other compensating changes needed to replace ecosystem services lost through a natural resource injury	Biophysical value; not economic value except under some very limited conditions

biological evolution. The metaphor of nature as a stock that provides a flow of services is insufficient for the difficulties we are in or the task ahead. Indeed, combined with the mistaken presumption that we can analyze a global problem within a partial equilibrium economic framework and reach a new economy project-by-project without major institutional change, the simplicity of the stock-flow framework blinds us to the complexity of the human predicament. The ecosystem services approach can be a part of a larger solution, but its dominance in our characterization of our situation and the solution is blinding us to the ecological, economic, and political complexities of the challenges we actually face.

McCauley (2006) has offered a concise argument against the general use of market valuation of natural systems that is very much in alignment with my own thinking. He writes:

If we mean to make significant and long-lasting gains in conservation, we must strongly assert the primacy of ethics and aesthetics in conservation. We must act quickly to redirect much of the effort now being devoted to the commodification of nature back towards instilling a love for nature in more people ...

To make ecosystem services the foundation of our conservation strategies is to imply – intentionally or otherwise – that nature is only worth conserving when it is, or can be made, profitable. The risk in advocating this position is that we might be taken at our word. Then, if there is a "devaluation" of nature, as in the case of Finca Santa Fe [where coffee was replaced by pineapples so insect pollinators valued at $60,000/year were no longer needed], what are we to tell local stewards who have invested in our ideology, and how can we protect nature from liquidation?

Once one starts to place economic values on natural systems, it is a logical next step to argue that those who value such systems should pay others to preserve them. This has given rise to a large movement focused on payment for ecosystem services (e.g., Pearce, 1995; Kumar and Muradian, 2009; Farley and Costanza, 2010; Naeem et al., 2015). Many of these arguments are focused on the preservation of ecosystems across the developing world. Results from the Millennium Ecosystem Assessment that took place from 2001 to 2005 have often been used to buttress such arguments.[6] One area of payment for ecosystem services that has seen a great deal of attention involves forests, either for ecological preservation or as carbon offsets for development such as fossil-fired power plants. Alix-Garcia and Wolff (2014) have provided an extensive review of experience in this field. They report that "the evaluation literature shows positive results for reforestation and afforestation programs, although the number of studies is quite small. In comparison, the work on avoiding deforestation programs has yielded mixed outcomes."

[6] For a summary of, and links to, the publication of the Millennium Ecosystem Assessment, see: www.millenniumassessment.org/en/index.html.

SUGGESTED RESOURCES TO LEARN TECHNICAL DETAILS ABOUT THE ECONOMIC VALUATION OF NON-MARKET GOODS AND SERVICES

For a comprehensive discussion that lays out a range of methods and makes substantial use of microeconomic theory, see:

- A. Myrick Freeman III, *The Measurement of Environmental and Resource Values: Theory and Methods*, Resources for the Future Press, 516pp., 1993.

For an edited volume with chapters that address theory, methods, and applications, see:

- R.J. Kopp, W.P. Pommerehne, and N. Schwarz, *Determining the Value of Non-Marketed Goods: Economic, Psychological and Policy Relevant Aspects of Contingent Valuation Methods*, Kluwer Academic Publishers, 333pp., 1997.

For a discussion of CV and associated survey methods, see:

- Robert Cameron Mitchell and Richard T. Carson, *Using Surveys to Value Public Goods: The Contingent Valuation Method*, Resources for the Future Press, 463pp., 1989.

For an edited volume with chapters that explore various aspects of CV, see:

- Jerry A. Hausman (ed.), *Contingent Valuation: A Critical Assessment*, North-Holland, 503pp., 1993.

For discussion of the valuation of ecosystem services, see:

- Many papers in the journal *Ecological Economics*, including those in the special issue, "The Dynamics and Value of Ecosystem Service: Integrating Economic and Ecological Perspectives," *Ecological Economics*, *41*(3), 2002.
- Geoffrey Heal, "Valuing Ecosystem Services," *Ecosystems, 3*(1), pp. 24–30, 2000.
- Shuang Liu, Robert Costanza, Stephen Farber, and Austin Troy, "Valuing Ecosystem Services: Theory, Practice, and the Need for Transdisciplinary Synthesis," *Annals of the New York Academy of Sciences*, *1185*(1), pp. 54–78, 2010.
- NRC Report, *Valuing Ecosystem Services: Toward Better Environmental Decision Making*, National Academy Press, 290pp., 2004.
- EPA SAB, *Valuing the Protection of Ecological Systems and Services*, U.S. Environmental Protection Agency, 122pp., 2009.
- Gretchen C. Daily, Stephen Polasky, Joshua Goldstein, Peter M. Kareiva, Harold A. Mooney, Liba Pejchar, Taylor H. Ricketts, James Salzman, and

Robert Shallenberger, "Ecosystem Services in Decision Making: Time to Deliver," *Frontiers in Ecology and the Environment,* 7, pp. 21–28, 2009. The paper includes a description of The Natural Capital Project (www.naturalcapitalproject.org), which is a partnership between Stanford University, The Nature Conservancy, and World Wildlife Fund and others.

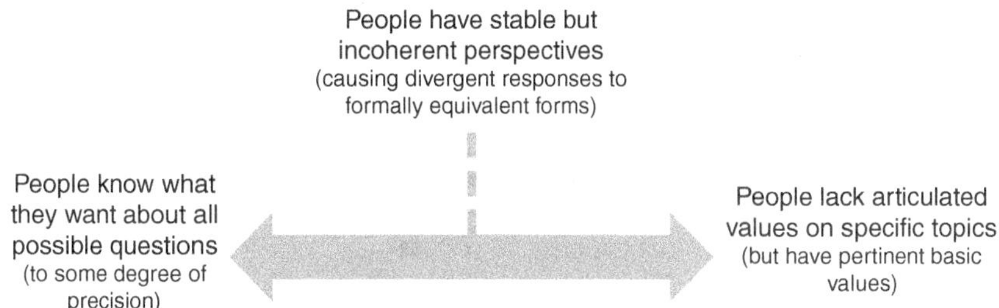

FIGURE 5.5. Fischhoff (1991) lays out this continuum of possibilities that may apply when someone is asked to make a value judgment about some specific issue. He then discusses the errors or problems that might arise if the person eliciting the value judgment assumes that one of these circumstances arises, when in fact a different one actually applies. He goes on to explore the issues that could arise in each case, and how an analyst might address those issues and validate the resulting stated values.

5.9 WHAT IF PEOPLE DON'T HAVE WELL-ARTICULATED UTILITY FUNCTIONS FOR EVERYTHING?

Fischhoff (1991) has outlined a range of the alternative assumptions that economists and various other groups of social scientists make when they seek to elicit judgments from people about how they value something. He lays out a continuum of possibilities that may characterize someone's actual state when making any specific valuation (Figure 5.5) that runs from "well articulated values" to "partially articulated values" to only "basic values" (from which people then have to construct their value judgment about any specific issue). In each case he also outlines the risks of misdiagnosis that might result if asking a respondent to make a value judgment assumes that one of these cases applies, when in fact another obtains.

For example, many of those who design CV studies assume that people have well-articulated values for the issue being assessed. If, however, all that people have is partially articulated or basic values, the answers obtained will likely result in "misplaced precision, reading too much into poorly articulated responses." Table 5.2 lists the conditions that Fischhoff argues favor someone having well-articulated values.

Because many of those who conduct CV studies operate with the assumption that people have well-articulated values, they assume that the problem is

TABLE 5.2. *Conditions that Fischhoff (1991) argues are favorable to someone having well-articulated values.*

Personally familiar (time to think)
Personally consequential (incentive to think)
Publicly discussed (opportunity to hear, share views)
Uncontroversial (stable tastes, no need to justify)
Few consequences (simplicity)
Similar consequences (commensurability)
Experienced consequences (meaningfulness)
Certain consequences (comprehensibility)
Single or compatible roles (absence of conflict)
Diverse appearances (multiple perspectives)
Direct relation to action (concreteness)
Unbundled topic (considered in isolation)
Familiar formulation

one of measurement. Basically they see the question of designing a CV study as: "how can we measure the utility function that is in the respondent's head without biasing them?" For this reason they go to considerable lengths to avoid anything that might influence or shape the respondent's answers.

In contrast, for decision problems with which people have had little or no experience, many psychologists and decision analysts assume that people need help in thinking through and developing their valuations for specific (but typically unfamiliar) outcomes. Indeed, Keeney (1992) has written an entire book outlining how he thinks people should do that (see the discussion in Chapter 6).

READING 5.5

Baruch Fischhoff, "Value Elicitation: Is There Anything in There?," *American Psychologist*, *46*(8), pp. 835–847, 1991.

Abstract: Eliciting people's values is a central pursuit in many areas of social science, including survey research, attitude research, economics, and behavioral decision theory. These disciplines differ considerably in the core assumptions they make about the nature of the values that are available for elicitation. These assumptions lead to very different methodological concerns and interpretations as well as to different risks of reading too much or too little into people's responses. The analysis here characterizes these assumptions and the research paradigms based on them. It also offers an account of how they arise, rooted in the psychological and sociological contexts within which different researchers function.

DISCUSSION QUESTIONS FOR READING 5.5

- Consider the following things:
  - Cappuccino

- Chocolate almond ice cream
- The Toyota Prius
- Red-breasted nuthatches
- The ecology of Lake Umbagogg
- The coral reefs of Glover's Reef off the coast of Belize
- The coral reefs of Tinian and Tatsumi in the Mariana Archipelago
- The ecology of the Olenek River
- The ecology of the Riieser-Larsen Peninsula

For which, if any, would you say you have well-articulated values?

- For those items on the list above for which you judge that you do not have well-articulated values, what sorts of assistance would you want if you decided that you needed to figure out how you value each one?

5.10 VARIATIONS IN BASIC VALUES ACROSS DIFFERENT CULTURES

In the 1950s, anthropologists Kluckholm and Strodbeck (1961) conducted extensive studies of the variations in value orientations across five different communities located in and around the Rimrock region of Arizona (between Phoenix and Flagstaff) in the Southwestern United States. They defined value orientations as "complex but definitely patterned ... principles ... resulting from the interplay of ... the cognitive, the affective, and the directive ... that give order and direction to the ever-flowing stream of human acts and thoughts as they relate to the solution of 'common human' problems." I think it is not too big a stretch to say that their concept of "value orientation" is very similar to what Fischhoff termed "basic values."

While the residents of the five communities they studied were all U.S. citizens, they came from decidedly different cultural backgrounds: two were Native American – Zuni and Rimrock Navaho; one was termed "Spanish-American"; one was Mormon; and one was Texan. These communities had already been extensively studied by anthropologists from Harvard and elsewhere. Through survey methods and statistical analysis Kluckholm and Strodbeck explored how the five cultures differed with respect to their world views about:

- Basic human nature (evil, neutral or a mixture of good and evil, innately good)
- The relationship between humans and nature (subjugation to nature, in harmony with nature, mastery over nature)
- Their orientation with respect to time (past, present, future)[7]

[7] One thing that all people have in common is a finite lifetime so one might be tempted to use time as a common measure to assess impacts that occur across different cultures. There are two problems with such an approach: (1) people have different orientations with respect to how they view time; (2) people in wealthy countries can spend money to "buy time" by hiring others, or using technology, to perform services, and by securing better nutrition and health care to extend life expectancy.

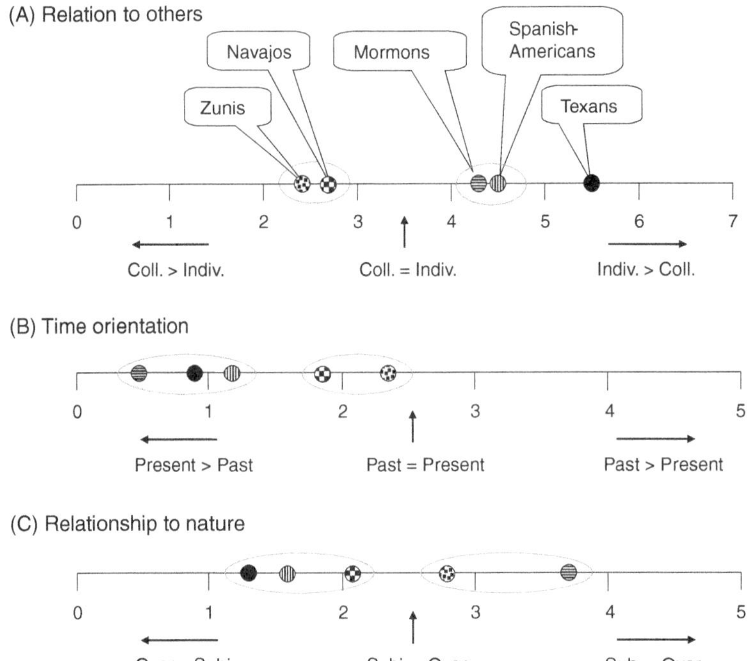

FIGURE 5.6. Three examples of results from the work of Kluckholm and Strodbeck (1961) who studied value orientations among five cultural groups living in the Rimrock area of Arizona in the Southwestern United States. Groupings not in gray ovals are significantly distinct ($p < 0.05$). Drawing modified from Kluckholm and Strodbeck (1961).

- The modality of human activity (being, being-in-becoming, doing)
- Humans' relation to other humans (lineality – i.e., biological relation to others through time, collaterality – i.e., part of a social order, individualism).

Figure 5.6 shows three examples from their extensive findings. As Kluckholm and Strodbeck (1961) explain:

> Among the three dimensions dealing with the relational orientation the [individual – collateral] is the most efficient in discriminating among the five cultures. Three groupings of cultures result. The Texans stand by themselves in showing extreme Individualism; the Mormons and Spanish Americans only slightly favor the Individualistic alternative ...; the Navajo and Zuni form a final grouping which is moderately disposed to a preference for the collateral alternative ... [Figure 5.6A]
>
> The three dimensions generated from the time orientation summaries prove to be highly efficient in designating between culture differences. The [Past–Present] dimension breaks the five communities into two distinct groups. One, composed of the Navaho and Zuni, is more or less indifferent in its preference between the Past and Present. The other (Spanish-American, Texans and Mormons) shows a strong inclination to favor the Present *time* position over the Past one ... [Figure 5.6B].

Finally, Figure 5.6C reproduces one of the findings on humans' relation to nature.

Kluckholm and Strodbeck (1961) provide extensive statistical analysis of their data. Readers who find this study interesting can get a good sense of the study by reading chapters 1, 5, and 10 of their book (Kluckholm and Strodbeck, 1961).[8]

I have briefly described this work here to make the fundamental point that the very nature of people's "basic value" structure or "value orientation" is heavily culturally determined. This may not be a problem so long as an analyst is addressing a problem in which all the key affected parties share the same broad cultural perceptive. It can become more complicated when different cultures are involved, even within a single nation state. Issues of variation in value across cultures can become remarkably complex in the analysis of international and global issues such as the impacts of climate change. However, in too many such analyses, such as most global integrated assessment models that seek optimal solutions, they are completely ignored.

5.11 ARE THERE SOME VALUES THAT SHOULD NOT BE QUANTIFIED?

Economist Nils Soguel (1995) explains that in order to value non-market goods, economic theory "makes the conventional assumption that individuals' preferences are characterized by a substitutability between income and quantities of goods consumed." Methods such as CV are "based on the principle that it is possible to observe how income is allocated among these various goods." By "goods" Soguel is not just talking about soap, cans of soup, vacation trips, and new cars. He includes environmental resources, health, and a wide range of other non-market goods and services.

Should the value of something like a pristine forest or a coral reef in the middle of the Pacific be judged by how much people are willing to spend, either for real or in theory, to protect it? In acquiring soap, cans of soup, vacation trips, and new cars, people and society operate under a budget constraint. Should we assume that all pristine forests and coral reefs are mankind's to exploit, and whether we protect them depends on our willingness to spend or forgo the benefits that might accrue from their exploitation?

In the Book of Genesis in the King James version of the Christian bible, God tells humans to "be fruitful, and multiply, and replenish the earth, and subdue it: and have dominion over the fish of the sea, and over the fowl of the air, and over every living thing that moveth upon the earth." In what some argue is a more accurate rendering of the original Hebrew, the New International Version translates the injunction as: "Be fruitful and increase in number; fill the earth

[8] For a comparison of the Kluckholm and Strodbeck model of cultural orientation with five other different models of cultural dimensions, see Nardon and Steers (2009).

and subdue it. Rule over the fish in the sea and the birds in the sky and over every living creature that moves on the ground."

Over the centuries, many have interpreted this Judeo-Christian mandate to "subdue" and "rule" as basically saying that nature exists for the benefit of humans. That is very much the framing adopted when nature is valued in terms of people's willingness to pay or in terms of "ecosystem services." On the other hand, Bailey (2015) reports that in his 2015 encyclical on climate change Pope Francis argued that Christians have misinterpreted scripture and "must forcefully reject the notion that our being created in God's image and given dominion over the earth justifies absolute domination over other creatures."

In 1964, Rachel Carson argued: "The control of nature is a phrase conceived in arrogance, born of the Neanderthal age of biology and philosophy, when it was supposed that nature exists for the convenience of man." Almost a century before her, John Muir (1875) wrote:

> No dogma taught by the present civilization seems to form so insuperable an obstacle in the way of a right understanding of the relations which culture sustains as to wilderness, as that which declares that the world was made especially for the uses of men. Every animal, plant, and crystal controverts it in the plainest terms. Yet it is taught from century to century as something ever new and precious, and in the resulting darkness the enormous conceit is allowed to go unchallenged.

One difficulty that arose repeatedly in the middle of the twentieth century, when people were concerned about various environmental degradations, was the issue of lack of "standing" – that is, the ability to show sufficient connection to the damage or harm to be allowed to participate as a party in a legal proceeding. Unless they could show that they were directly injured or harmed by an environmental action, courts often ruled that those opposed had no standing. In this connection Christopher Stone (1975), a professor of law at USC, wrote a law review article, later turned into a book, that asked "Should trees have standing?" Stone argued:

> It is not inevitable, nor is it wise, that natural objects should have no rights to seek redress in their own behalf. It is no answer to say that streams and forests cannot speak. Corporations cannot speak either, nor can states, estates, infants, incompetents, municipalities or universities. Lawyers speak for them, as they customarily do for the ordinary citizen who has legal problems.

Stone suggests that we should have a system in which, when a friend of a natural object perceives it to be endangered, they can apply to the court for the creation of a guardianship.

While Stone's vision of legal standing for natural objects has not come to pass, in the years since, the number of circumstances in which concerned parties such as environmental NGOs are deemed to have standing, and thus can intervene in cases involving environmental and ecological damages, has been considerably broadened.

Stone was making a broader argument than that natural objects and systems should be protected for the good of mankind. He writes:

> With what I have been saying so far, my economist friends (unremittent human chauvinists, every one of them!) have no large quarrel in principle ... [But] I propose going beyond gathering up the loose ends of what almost all of us recognize as a legitimate, traditional damage claim. I favor a system in which the guardian would urge before the court injuries not presently cognizable – the death of eagles and inedible crabs, the suffering of sea lions, the loss from the face of the earth of species of commercially valueless birds, the disappearance of a wilderness area. One might, of course, speak of the damages involved as "damages" to us humans in a derivative way.

But, he implies, doing that would still frame the damages in terms of what humans value. Nature has value and should have a right to exist and be protected, quite apart from its use or utility to humans.

Old growth forests or pristine coral reefs are not the only things with which we might be better off if we did not attach an economic or similar quantitative value. Think about issues such as freedom of speech, racial and gender equality, and the right to life, liberty, and the pursuit of happiness. Should these too only be protected to the extent that a society finds the benefits of doing so are greater than the costs?

While an inventive economist might construct utility functions to cover such cases (which might, for example, include values that go off almost to minus infinity in some spots), society does not frame these issues in this way, and in my view, doing so is not helpful. Rather, society addresses such issues by framing them in terms of rights. Rights are based on ethical judgments, not prices determined in markets or through methods such as CV. Legal rights have the important characteristic that the right holders can take action (i.e., sue) through non-market institutions called courts, to maintain or protect their rights.

For example, the 15th Amendment to the U.S. Constitution, adopted in 1870, reads:

> **Section 1.** The right of citizens of the United States to vote shall not be denied or abridged by the United States or by any State on account of race, color, or previous condition of servitude.
> **Section 2.** The Congress shall have power to enforce this article by appropriate legislation.

Because some states were finding ways to deny the right to vote to many African Americans, the Voting Rights Act was passed in 1965 to make sure that this right was properly enforced. The government did not do a B–C analysis to decide if this should be done. A number of subsequent court decisions and administrative actions have affirmed this right.[9]

[9] For details, see: www.justice.gov/crt/about/vot/sec_2/about_sec2.php.

While the U.S. Constitution talks of life, liberty, and the pursuit of happiness as "inalienable rights," the reality is that no rights are absolute in the sense that there is never a situation in which one must not be balanced against another. For example, there are limits to free speech. You can't yell "fire" in a crowded theater. As Stone (1975) notes:

> the lawyer is constantly aware that a right is not, as the layman may think, a concrete entity that one either has or has not. One's life, one's right to vote, one's property, can all be taken away. But those who would infringe on them must go through certain procedures before they can do so. These procedures in turn, are a measure of what we value as a society.

The more fundamental and important the right, the more elaborate the legal procedure and the higher the burden of proof before the right can be abridged.

In recent years, because of requirements by the U.S. Office of Management and Budget (OMB) that major legislation be subject to regulatory review, actions by the U.S. Congress to create or affirm rights have become a bit more complicated. In the United States, we now have ramps at street crossings, public bathrooms with doors wide enough for wheelchairs, and many similar things because of the Americans with Disabilities Act (ADA).[10] Congress begins that Act by stating "physical or mental disabilities in no way diminish a person's *right* to fully participate in all aspects of society" and went on to articulate those rights in some detail. As a consequence of this Act, handicapped persons can sue in court to have their rights enforced.

The Voting Rights Act was passed before OMB regulations were in place requiring a B–C analysis of all major regulations. By the time the ADA was passed, Executive Orders 12866 and 13258 mandated that regulatory reviews in the form of B–C analysis be performed on all regulations with an impact of more than $100 million (see the discussion in Section 3.9). The quotation below is the Department of Justice's explanation from June 30, 2008 of why they did such an analysis.[11] A somewhat similar explanation can be found in the regulatory impact analysis, published on June 23, 2001, that was performed on later amendments to the ADA.[12]

> the Department also received many comments expressing the view that economic analysis is irrelevant with respect to the implementation of a civil rights statute. Under this view, because the ADA is a civil rights statute protecting the rights of individuals with disabilities, regulations designed to implement its protections are necessary regardless of whether quantifiable benefits can be shown to outweigh costs. As these commenters noted, traditional benefit-cost analysis is not designed to measure the inherent value of civil rights protections or to make judgments about fairness or equity.

[10] See: www.ada.gov/pubs/adastatute08.htm.

[11] Available at: www.apta.com/gap/fedreg/documents/nondiscrimination_on_the_basis_of_disability_by_public_accomodations_and_in_commercial_facilities_correction.pdf.

[12] Available at: www.ada.gov/regs2010/RIA_2010regs/DOJ%20ADA%20Final%20RIA.pdf.

The Department is sympathetic to the views expressed by these commenters. However, the Federal laws and regulations that require agencies to express the benefits and costs of regulations in economic terms do not distinguish between regulations that implement civil rights statutes like the ADA and regulations that implement other kinds of laws. The Department also believes that there is much to be gained from the comprehensive identification and description of the benefits of accessibility standards, which are, after all, designed to ensure equal access for everyone. Such benefits include not only the measurable benefits to individuals with disabilities but also the more subtle and far-reaching benefits for society as a whole.

Chapter 2 opened with a classic quotation from Adam Smith's (1776) *Wealth of Nations* in which Smith draws a distinction between "value in use" and "value in exchange." Mark Sagoff has used E.B. White's (1952) children's story, *Charlotte's Web*, to identify three rather than two kinds of value judgments. Sagoff (2004) writes:

I want to call attention to a distinction between three kinds of judgments. First we make judgments as individuals about what is good for or benefits us. For example [the spider] Charlotte could tell which flies were the tastiest, and she trapped those she wanted the most. Wilbur [the pig] wondered, in this context, why Charlotte chose to save his life, since he could do nothing to benefit her or make her better off.

Second we form judgments about what is good in general, right as a matter of principle, or appropriate in view of a particular situation. Charlotte thought it morally better that Wilbur live out his life in peace than show up with an apple in his mouth at Christmas. She valued Wilbur's friendship as a good thing in itself, and she recognized the obligations and responsibilities that friendship creates.

Third we make aesthetic judgments about what is beautiful or is worth appreciating and protecting for its expressive, symbolic, and formal properties. In describing Wilbur as "some pig" and in other ways lauding his aesthetic qualities ... Charlotte convinced Zuckerman [the farmer who owned Wilbur] to spare Wilbur for his intrinsic qualities rather than to slaughter him to provide ham for Christmas dinner.

Sagoff (2004) goes on to argue that:

there is an important difference between saying that something is *good for me* and saying that something is *good in itself*, *good from the point of view of the world*, or *good because of its intrinsic qualities*. I shall take it as a premise that in our political lives we do not pursue merely private conceptions of *the good life* but also public conceptions of *the good society*. We are not concerned only with the way a social decision or outcome affects us. We are concerned with whether the decision or outcome is right, fair, or good in view of values or reasons we believe carry weight with society as a whole.

For an emotional and, in my view, often unrealistic critique of the practice of valuing non-market outcomes, see Ackerman and Heinzerling (2004), who basically argue against any quantification. They write:

It is time to get back to basics – to remember the simple insights that inspired citizens and their representatives, a generation ago, to demand and produce legal protection for health and the environment. To do so, we must give up the idea, reassuring to many, that there is, somewhere, a precise mathematical formula waiting to solve our problems for us. In its place we offer an attitude rather than an algorithm: one that trusts collective, common sense judgments, and is humble in the face of uncertainty, steadfast in confronting urgent problems, and committed to fairness within and beyond this generation.

While it is my belief that we need to address many issues related to health, safety, and the environment using a rights-based formulation, I also believe that in the real world, with finite resources, without mindlessly turning an algorithmic crank we do need to adopt some thoughtful approaches to quantification if we are going to assure equity and rationality in managing the many risks and other important issues we face as individuals and as a society.

SUPPLEMENTAL READING

Mark Sagoff, "Chapter 1: Zuckerman's Dilemma: An Introduction," and "Chapter 2: On the Monument to General Meade or On the Difference between Beliefs and Benefits," in *Price, Principle and the Environment*, Cambridge University Press, pp. 1–56, 2004.

DISCUSSION QUESTIONS FOR SECTION 5.10

- Since valuation is an inherently human activity, what, if anything, does it mean to argue that natural objects and systems should have a value in their own right?
- Do you consider it appropriate that the U.S. Department of Justice has been required to perform a B–C analysis when implementing the Americans with Disabilities Act?
- If no, is there any limit to how much the country and private firms should be required to spend to assure that physical or mental disabilities in no way diminishes a person's *right* to fully participate in all aspects of society?
- If yes, if the OMB directives requiring B–C analysis had been in place when the voting rights and other civil rights laws were passed, should they too have been subjected to a B–C analysis before being implemented?
- How, if at all, do the categories *good for me*, *good in itself*, *good from the point of view of the world*, or *good because of its intrinsic qualities* map into *value in use* and *value in exchange*?
- Sagoff (2004) quotes Goodstein's (1999) textbook as arguing that "Economic analysis is concerned with human welfare or well being. From the economic perspective, the environment should be protected for the material benefit of humanity and not for strictly moral or esthetical reasons." What is your assessment of this argument? To what extent does the concept of "existence value" address the issue?

REFERENCES

Ackerman, F. and L. Heinzerling (2004). *Priceless: On Knowing the Price of Everything and the Value of Nothing*, The New Press, 277pp.

Alix-Garcia, J. and H. Wolff (2014). "Payment for Ecosystem Services from Forests," *Annual Review of Resource Economics*, *6*, pp. 361–380.

Annan, K.A. (2000). *We the People: The Role of the United Nations in the 21st Century*, United Nations Department of Public Information, 80pp. Available at: www.un.org/en/events/pastevents/pdfs/We_The_Peoples.pdf.

Bailey, S.P. (2015). "10 Key Excerpts from Pope Francis's Encyclical on the Environment," *Washington Post*. Available at: www.washingtonpost.com/news/acts-of-faith/wp/2015/06/18/10-key-excerpts-from-pope-franciss-encyclical-on-the-environment.

Brauman, K.A., G.C. Daily, T.K.E. Duarte, and H.A. Mooney (2007). "The Nature and Value of Ecosystem Services: An Overview Highlighting Hydrologic Services," *Annual Review of Environmental Resources*, *32*, pp. 67–98.

Carson, R. (1964). *Silent Spring*, Fawcett Crest, 304pp.

Carson, R.T., R.C. Mitchell, W.M. Hanenmann, R.K. Kopp, S. Presser, and P.A. Ruud (1992). "A Contingent Valuation Study of Lost Passive Use Values Resulting from the Exxon Valdez Oil Spill," A Report to the Attorney General of the State of Alaska, 835pp. Available at http://mpra.ub.uni-muenchen.de/6984.

(2003). "A Contingent Valuation Study of Lost Passive Use Values Resulting from the Exxon Valdez Oil Spill," *Environmental and Resource Economics*, *25*, pp. 257–286.

Caudill, H.M. (1963). *Night Comes to the Cumberlands: A Biography of a Depressed Area*, Little, Brown, 394pp.

Cesario, F.J. (1976). "Value of Time in Recreation Benefit Studies," *Land Economics*, *52*(1), pp. 32–41.

Costanza, R., R. d'Arge, R. de Groot, S. Farber, M. Grasso, B. Hannon, K. Limburg, S. Naeem, R.V. O'Neill, J. Paruelo, R.G. Raskin, P. Sutton, and M. Van den Belt (1997). "The Value of the World's Ecosystem Services and Natural Capital," *Nature*, *387*, pp. 253–260.

Daily, G.C., S. Polasky, J. Goldstein, P.M. Kareiva, H.A. Mooney, L. Pejchar, T.H. Ricketts, J. Salzman, and R. Shallenberger (2009). "Ecosystem Services in Decision Making: Time to Deliver," *Frontiers in Ecology and the Environment*, *7*, pp. 21–28.

Dublin, L.I. and A.J. Lotka (1930). *The Money Value of a Man*, Ronald Press, 264pp.

EPA (2011). *The Benefits and Costs of the Clean Air Act from 1990 to 2020: Summary Report*, U.S. Environmental Protection Agency, 34pp.

EPA SAB (2009). *Valuing the Protection of Ecological Systems and Services*, U.S. Environmental Protection Agency, 122pp.

Farley, J. and R. Costanza (2010). "Payments for Ecosystem Services: From Local to Global," *Ecological Economics*, *69*, pp. 2060–2068.

Fischhoff, B. (1991). "Value Elicitation: Is There Anything in There?," *American Psychologist*, *46*(8), pp. 835–847.

Fischhoff, B. and L. Furby (1988). "Measuring: A Conceptual Framework for Interpreting Transactions with Special Reference to Contingent Valuation of Visibility," *Journal of Risk and Uncertainty*, *1*(2), pp. 147–184.

Franklin, B. (1748). *Advice to a Young Tradesman, Written by an Old One*. The text of Franklin's letter can be found at: www.historycarper.com/1748/01/01/advice-to-a-young-tradesman-written-by-an-old-one.

Frederick, S. and B. Fischhoff (1998). "Scope (in) Sensitivity in Elicited Valuations," *Risk Decision and Policy*, *3*(2), pp. 109–123.

Freeman, A.M., III (1993). *The Measurement of Environmental and Resource Values: Theory and Methods*, Resources for the Future Press, 516pp.

Goodstein, E.S. (1999). *Economics and the Environment*, Prentice Hall, 558pp.

Goolsbee, A. and P.J. Klenow (2006). "Valuing Consumer Products by the Time Spent Using Them: An Application to the Internet," NBER Working Paper No. 11995, 13pp.

Graham, J.D. (2008). "Saving Lives through Administrative Law and Economics," *University of Pennsylvania Law Review*, *157*, pp. 395–540.

Graham, J.D. and J. Vaupel (1981). "Value of a Life: What Difference Does It Make?," *Risk Analysis*, *1*, pp. 692–704.

Guerry, A.D., S. Polasky, J. Lubchenco et al. (2015). "Natural Capital and Ecosystem Services Informing Decisions: From Promise to Practice," *Proceedings of the National Academy of Sciences*, *112*(24), pp. 7348–7355.

Harrison, A.J. and D.A. Quarmdy (1969). "The Value of Time in Transport Planning: A Review," excerpted in R. Layard (ed.), *Cost Benefit Analysis*, Penguin Books, 496pp., 1972.

Harvard Law Review Association (1992). "Ask a Silly Question ... Contingent Valuation of Natural Resource Damage," *Harvard Law Review*, *105*(8), pp. 1981–2000.

Hausman, J.A. (ed.) (1993). *Contingent Valuation: A Critical Assessment*, North-Holland, 503pp.

Heal, G. (2000). "Valuing Ecosystem Services," *Ecosystems*, *3*(1), pp. 24–30.

Helm, D. (2015). *Natural Capital: Valuing the Planet*, Yale University Press, 277pp.

Howard, R. (1980). "On Making Life and Death Decisions," in R.S. Schwing and W.A. Albers Jr. (eds.), *Societal Risk Assessment: How Safe Is Safe Enough?*, Plenum, pp. 89–113.

Jones-Lee, M.W. (1976). *The Value of Life: An Economic Analysis*, University of Chicago Press, 162pp.

Kahneman, D. and J.L. Knetsch (1992). "Valuing Public Goods: The Purchase of Moral Satisfaction," *Journal of Environmental Economics and Management*, *22*(1), pp. 57–70.

Keeney, R.L. (1992). *Value Focused Thinking: A Path to Creative Decisionmaking*, Harvard University Press, 416pp.

Kluckholm, F.R. and F.L. Strodbeck (1961). *Variations in Value Orientations*, Row, Peterson and Company, 450pp.

Knoepke, D. (2013). "Time Is Money: How to Measure the Value of Volunteers," *The Chronicle of Philanthropy*, March 14. Available at: http://philanthropy.com/blogs/measuring-up/time-is-money-how-to-measure-the-value-of-volunteers/55.

Kopp, R.J., W.P. Pommerehne, and N. Schwarz (1997). *Determining the Value of Non-Marketed Goods: Economic, Psychological and Policy Relevant Aspects of Contingent Valuation Methods*, Kluwer Academic Publishers, 333pp.

Kumar P. and R. Muradian (eds.) (2009). *Payment for Ecosystem Services*, Oxford University Press, 308pp.

Langlois, L. (1971). *A Monograph: The Cost and Prevention of Coal Workers' Pneumoconiosis*, Appalachian Regional Commission, 63pp.

Liu, S., R. Costanza, S. Farber, and A. Troy (2010). "Valuing Ecosystem Services: Theory, Practice, and the Need for Transdisciplinary Synthesis," *Annals of the New York Academy of Sciences*, *1185*(1), pp. 54–78.

McCauley, D.J. (2006). "Selling out on Nature," *Nature*, *443*, pp. 27–28.

Mangones Matos, S.C. (2015). "Making the Case for High Technology Buses: Comparison between New York City and Bogota, Colombia," Working Paper, Department of Engineering and Public Policy, Carnegie Mellon, 25pp.

Mansnerus, L. (1996). "Making a Case for Death," *New York Times*, Sunday, May 5.

Matthews, H.S. (2001). "Analysis of the Benefits and Cost of Clean Air," in P.S. Fischbeck and G.S. Farrow (eds.), *Improving Regulation: Cases in Environment Health and Safety*, Resources for the Future, pp. 405–428.

Millennium Ecosystem Assessment (2005). *Our Human Planet: Summary for Decision-Makers*, Island Press, 109pp.

Mishan, E.J. (1971). "The Value of Life," reprinted in R. Layard (ed.), *Cost Benefit Analysis*, Penguin Books, 496pp., 1972.

Mitchell, R.C. and R.T. Carson (1989). *Using Surveys to Value Public Goods: The Contingent Valuation Method*, Resources for the Future Press, 463pp.

Mooney, H.A. and P.R. Ehrlich (1997). "Chapter 2: Ecosystem Services: A Fragmentary History," in G. Daily (ed.), *Nature's Services: Societal Dependence on Natural Ecosystems*, Island Press, 392pp.

Muir, J. (1875). "Wild Wool," *Overland Monthly*, pp. 361–366. Incorporated in 1918 as the first chapter in Muir's book, *Steep Trails*, Houghton Mifflin, 390pp.

Naeem, S., J.C. Ingram, A. Varga et al. (2015). "Get the Science Right When Paying for Nature's Services," *Science*, *347*(6227), pp. 1206–1207.

Nardon, L. and R.M. Steers (2009). "Chapter 1: The Cultural Theory Jungle: Divergence and Convergence in Models of National Culture," in R.S. Bhagat and R.M. Steers (eds.), *Cambridge Handbook of Culture, Organizations, and Work*, Cambridge University Press, 537pp.

Nature Briefing (1998). "Audacious Bid to Value the Planet Whips up a Storm," *Nature*, *395*, p. 430.

Nichols, B. (2011). "Time and Money: Using Federal Data to Measure the Value of Performing Arts Activities," National Endowment for the Arts, NEA Research Note #102, 32pp.

Norgaard, R.B. (2010). "Ecosystem Services: From Eye Opening Metaphor to Complexity Blinder," *Ecological Economics*, pp. 1219–1227.

NRC (2004). *Valuing Ecosystem Services: Toward Better Environmental Decision Making*, National Academy Press, 290pp.

(2010). *Hidden Costs of Energy: Unpriced Consequences of Energy Production and Use*, National Academy Press, 473pp.

Pearce, F. (1995). "Price of Life Sends Temperatures Soaring," *New Scientist*, *146*, p. 5.

Sagoff, M. (2004). *Price, Principle and the Environment*, Cambridge University Press, 284pp.

SCEP (1970). *Man's Impact on the Global Environment: Assessment and Recommendations for Action*, MIT Press, 319pp.

Schkade, D.A. and J.W. Payne (1994). "How People Respond to Contingent Valuation Questions: A Verbal Protocol Analysis of Willingness to Pay for an Environmental Regulation," *Journal of Environmental Economics and Management*, *26*(1), pp. 88–109.

Smith, A. (1776). *An Inquiry into the Nature and Causes of the Wealth of Nations*, republished in 1937 by The Modern Library Random House, 976pp.

Soguel, N.C. (1995). "Introduction," in N.G. Schwab Christie and N.C. Soguel (eds.), *Contingent Valuation, Transport Safety and the Value of Life*, Kluwer Academic Publishers, 193pp.

Stone, C.D. (1975). *Should Trees Have Standing? Toward Legal Rights for Natural Objects*, Discus Books, 118pp.

Sunstein, C. (2004). "Valuing Life: A Plea for Disaggregation," *Duke Law Journal*, *54*(385), pp. 385–444.

Tengs, T.O., M.E. Adams, J.S. Pliskin, D.G. Safran, J.E. Siefel, M.C. Weinstein, and J.D. Graham (1995). "Five-Hundred Life-Saving Interventions and Their Cost-Effectiveness," *Risk Analysis*, *15*(3), pp. 369–390.

Tengs, T.O. and J.D. Graham (1996). "Chapter 8: The Opportunity Costs of Haphazard Investments in Life-Saving," in R.W. Hahn (ed.), *Risks and Costs of Lives Saved*, Oxford University Press, pp. 167–182.

Tolley, G. and A. Randall (1986). *Establishing and Valuing the Effects of Improved Visibility in the Eastern United States*, Report to the U.S. Environmental Protection Agency, University of Chicago Press, 155pp.

Viscusi, W.K. (1992). *Fatal Tradeoffs: Public and Private Responsibilities for Risk*, Oxford University Press, 306pp.

(2010). "Policy Challenges of the Heterogeneity of the Value of Statistical Life," *Foundations and Trends in Microeconomics*, 6(2), pp. 99–172.

Viscusi, W.K. and J.E. Aldy (2003). "The Value of a Statistical Life: A Critical Review of Market Estimates Throughout the World," *Journal of Risk and Uncertainty*, *27*(1), pp. 239–256.

White, E.B. (1952). *Charlotte's Web*, Harper, 184pp.

Wildavsky, A. (1981). "Richer Is Safer," *Financial Analysts Journal*, *37*(2), pp. 19–22.

6

Multi-Attribute Utility Theory and Multi-Criteria Decision Making

With Jared L. Cohon

Multi-Attribute Utility Theory (MAUT) is not so much an alternative to decision analysis (DA) as an extension of it. DA tends to treat all outcomes in terms of some single measure, such as dollars or utility for dollars. As Keeney and Raiffa (1976) explain in the opening paragraph of their classic book *Decisions with Multiple Objectives: Preferences and Value Tradeoffs*, there is a large literature on dealing with the uncertainties in decision problems. Much less attention has been focused on "formalizing the preferences or value side of the problem ... [as opposed to] developing procedures for the assessment of uncertainty." They set up the focus of their book as follows:

> Consider a decision maker who has already decided on the identification and bounding of his problem and has generated the set of alternative actions he wishes to evaluate. Let's assume that he has structured his problem as a decision tree and has assigned probabilities to all the branches of chance nodes ... in complex value problems [of the sort MAUT deals with], consequences at the end of the tree *cannot* be adequately described objectively by a single attribute (e.g., money).

In short, rather than a chance node representing the discretized probabilistic outcome across a distribution of unidimensional outcomes (x), as in Chapter 4, in this formulation each chance node would represent a discretized probabilistic outcome across a q-dimensional space of outcomes ($X_1, X_2, \ldots, X_q$), where each dimension represents an attribute of the outcome that is of concern to the decision maker.[1]

[1] Here we adopt the notation of X_i for attribute *i* which might have n values $x_{i1}, x_{i2}, \ldots x_{in}$, following the notation of Chapter 2.

6.1 MAUT BASICS

Suppose someone needs to choose among alternative transportation technologies. The attributes that might characterize the alternatives could include:

- Convenience of use
- Safety
- Initial capital investment
- Community disruption
- Equity in rider access
- Privacy
- Ongoing operating costs
- Maintenance requirements
- Consequence for energy security
- Pollution
- Greenhouse gas emissions.

You can probably come up with quite a few others.

Many of these attributes are made up of a number of sub-elements. For example, convenience of use might include time to destination, wait times, potential for delays, etc. In addition to a measure of the probability of death or injury, the safety attribute might also include factors such as the number of passengers who could be involved in any accident, the number of strangers in the same compartment, etc. Maintenance could include not only the frequency with which it is required but also a measure of the level of special skills that maintenance personnel would need to have. Pollution could involve factors such as health impacts, economic damages, adverse aesthetic impacts, and ecological impacts.

The existence of multiple attributes makes analysis and decision making more complex. Keeney and Raiffa (1976) explain that:

> In *cost-benefit* analysis, we condense the benefits $B_1,\ldots,B_q$ into a single composite measure, for example, B_0. One usual technique is to introduce a set of conversion factors, w_1, $w_2,\ldots,w_q$ and then define
>
> $$B_0 = w_1 b_1 + \cdots + w_i b_i + \cdots + w_q b_q$$
>
> Of course the units of the measurement of the w_i's are such that the individual summands $w_1 b_1$, $w_2 b_2$, ..., $w_q b_q$ are all in commensurable units. The trick in practice is to find suitable conversion factors [and possibly also non-linear functions to appropriately transform the b_i's].

Why isn't that perfectly sufficient? Certainly, using willingness to pay (WTP), one could try to reduce all the attributes in a problem such as the choice of a transportation system into some single (probably monetary) metric. However, there could be several problems in doing so. Using WTP requires prices, which one would get from market data, or other sources of people's valuations, for example, interviews and surveys. But, some markets have important imperfections, producing prices that do not accurately reflect social value and, thus, significantly affecting benefit estimates. For example, the market prices of transportation alternatives like automobiles do not include all of their externalities such as their contributions to climate change. In other instances, markets may not exist at all. For example, there is no market for equity in rider access. Incorporating attributes like equity into B–C analysis is, therefore, very difficult. And, keep in mind: if something doesn't get a value in B–C analysis – a benefit and/or a cost – that's tantamount to giving it a value of zero.

Many problems also involve benefits and costs that occur at different times. The convention in B–C and DA analysis is to convert these to present values using exponential discounting with some fixed or range of discount rates (see Chapter 7). Rather than adopt some fixed functional form (exponential, hyperbolic, etc.), outcomes that occur at different future moments can be treated as separate attributes in a MAU analysis.

If the attributes can't be made commensurate with WTP or some other conversion factors, we need something else to help decision makers work through the alternatives and the tradeoffs involved. MAUT provides a set of strategies that meet this challenge by explicitly incorporating decision makers' preferences into utility functions defined over the attributes. The utility functions do condense the multiple attributes into one measure, but that measure is the decision maker's utility, and the form of the condensing may be considerably more complicated and nuanced than the w_i's above. The process by which the utility functions are created helps develop insight into the tradeoffs involved and the values that people place on them.

Conceptually the idea of a MAUT is simple. In Figure 2.5 we introduced the idea of a utility space in two dimensions (in that case displaying the utility associated with the quantity consumed of two goods, called A and B). Associated with every point in that space is a utility. We then constructed indifference curves that connected all the points that have the same level of utility. One can do the same thing in an Q-dimensional space involving Q different attributes.

Then for each Q-tuple in that space you could assess a utility $U(x_1, x_2,\ldots,x_q)$. If you have a background in engineering or physics you may find it convenient to think of $U(x_1, x_2,\ldots,x_q)$ as an N-dimensional scalar field. Since it is not easy to draw an Q-dimensional space, Figure 6.1 illustrates the idea using just three dimensions.

That sounds simple enough, until you begin to consider how to assign a U value to every point of interest in an Q-dimensional space. In principle you could go through a large number of Q-tuples, find some way to ask the decision maker to assign a utility value to each point, and then fit a family of multi-dimensional surfaces to the results. Even if all of us carried multi-dimensional utility functions around in our heads, the elicitation task would be formidable! Since we almost certainly do not carry such utility functions around in our heads, the central preoccupation of MAUT is to

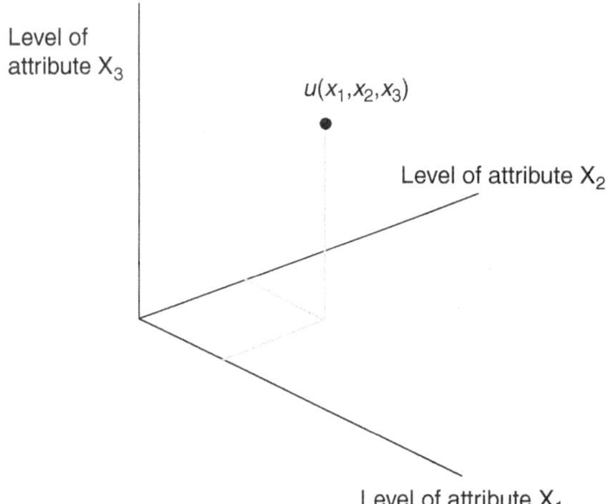

FIGURE 6.1. The objective in developing a multi-attribute utility function is to assign a utility value $u(x_1, x_2,...,x_q)$ to each point in an Q-dimensional space of incommensurate attributes X_i (shown here for a 3-space).

develop feasible strategies to construct such a utility function from a series of more disaggregated judgments. As Keeney (1992) notes, "the components of a multi-objective utility function are single-objective utility functions" combined in some appropriate way.

6.2 CONSTRUCTING MAU FUNCTIONS USING INDEPENDENCE ASSUMPTIONS

The basic contribution of Keeney and Raiffa (1976) was to devise a number of independence assumptions that, if met, allow one to construct a multi-attribute utility function as a weighted sum and/or product of single attribute utility functions, that is as:

$$u(x_1,...,x_q) = \sum_{i=1}^{q} k_i u_i(x_i) + \prod_{i=1}^{q} [\alpha_i + \beta_i u_i(x_i)]$$

where the parameters k_i, α_i, and β_i are derived from an elicitation of the decision maker's preferences using the single attribute utility functions $u_i(x_i)$.

There is quite a range of different cases that the reader can learn about in Keeney and Raiffa (1976), in chapter 7 of Keeney (1980), or in Dyer (2005). Much of this involves posing questions to assess various independence conditions for the relationships among the attributers that, if met, allow simplified utility functions to be used. Here we will outline just a few of the basics to give an idea of the sorts of considerations that are involved.

The first is *preferential independence*. A pair of attributes X_1 and X_2 is said to be preferentially independent if the shape and value of the indifference curves between them does not depend on the value of any other attributes. Since it is not possible to draw a Q-space with Q > 3, this is illustrated in just three dimensions in Figure 6.2. If preferential independence holds, one can elicit a utility function for the tradeoff between X_1 and X_2 and apply it for all values of other attributes (e.g., X_3).

Utility independence occurs when the preference ordering of a lottery involving different levels of an attribute (say X_1) does not depend on the level at which other attributes are fixed. Note that this relationship may not be symmetric. The fact that X_1 is utility independent of X_z does not mean that the reverse is necessarily true.

A set of attributes is said to be *additive independent* if the preference order for lotteries depends only on their marginal probability distributions. Thus, for example, X_1 and X_2 are additive independent if you are indifferent between the following two lotteries:

A 50:50 chance of getting the low value of both attributes X_1 and X_2 or getting the high value of X_1 and X_2

OR

A 50:50 chance of getting the low value of attribute X_1 and the high value of attribute X_2 or getting the high value of X_1 and the low value of X_2.

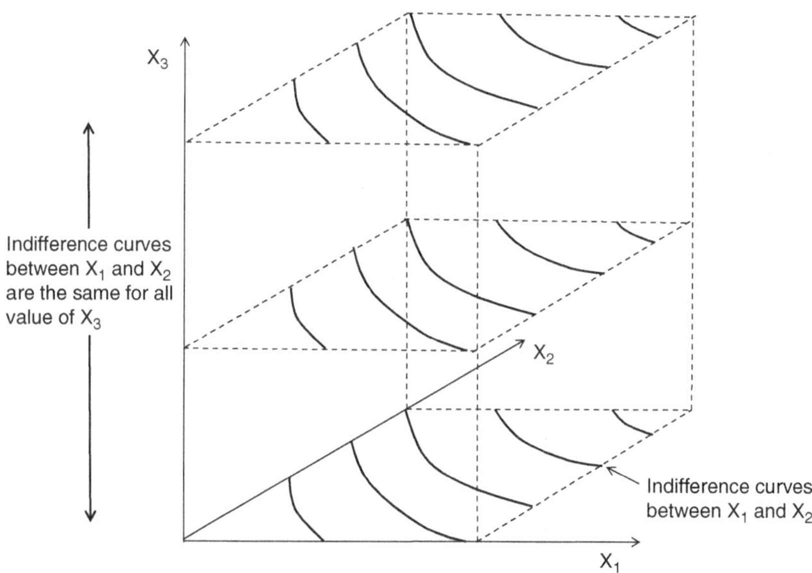

FIGURE 6.2. Illustration (in just three dimensions) of "preferential independence." If the shape of the indifference curves between X_1 and X_2 does not depend on the value of X_3 then X_1 and X_2 are said to preferentially independent.

Both of these lotteries have an equal chance of yielding either a high or low value of X_1 and a high or low value of X_2, thus their marginal probabilities are equal.

Keeney and Raiffa (1976) show that if a set of attributes is additively independent, then the multi-attribute utility function can be represented as the weighted sum of the individual utility functions:

$$u(x_1 \ldots x_q) = \sum_{i=1}^{q} k_i u_i(x_i)$$

This is the simplest form of a MAU function, and is widely used in practice, despite the strong assumptions it requires.

If, on the other hand, the attributes are preferentially independent, a multiplicative mode should be used:

$$u(x_1, \ldots x_q) = \prod_{i=1}^{q} [\alpha_i + \beta_i u_i(x_i)]$$

There are also circumstances under which a combination of the two is appropriate.

6.3 DO PEOPLE HAVE MULTI-ATTRIBUTE UTILITY FUNCTIONS IN THEIR HEADS?

In Section 12.9 we explore literature summarized by Robin Dawes and his colleagues that shows quite persuasively that, without analytical support, most people in most settings simply do not have the ability to perform holistic judgments to make the type of multi-dimensional tradeoffs that are implicit in multi-attribute utility functions. With a few exceptions such as bird watchers or judges in dog shows (Tanaka and Curran, 2001), people are only able to consider attributes one at a time, and the order in which they consider them can significantly change the assessments that they make.[2]

Section 12.9 explains that proper, and even improper or random, weights applied to linear models almost always outperform holistic judgments when

[2] A couple of colleagues who are wine aficionados have argued that a good wine taster can not only determine what vineyard a wine is from but also the year of the vintage. If true, this clearly would involve an impressive multi-attribute holistic judgment. However, several statistical studies suggest that such claims should be viewed with skepticism (Hodgson, 2008; Derbyshire, 2013).

people want to make predictions based on considering the value of a number of different attributes. Taking this observation to its obvious next step, Dawes (1988) writes:

> The inference is simple. Since random and unit weights predict actual outcomes much better than global judgment, intuitive weighting should also. It is then reasonable to conclude that such weights should also outperform global judgment in situations where there is no outcome to predict. That is, the results in the prediction situations can be used as a guide for preference – assuming that methods that can consistently predict better than others when there is an outcome to be predicted will also work better when there is not. Of course, there is no way to check this assumption, because there is no outcome in preference situations. But human intuition would have to have almost magical properties were it to be superior to intuitive weighting when we make choices of what to do, while simultaneously being constantly inferior when we are trying to predict what will happen.

Given the empirical results, and Dawes' argument, how should we think about the development and use of multi-attribute utility functions? Our own view is that there are two answers. First, if in making decisions that they consider to be *very* important, people conclude that they want to make tradeoffs in ways that are non-linear, formal methods for eliciting multi-attribute utility functions provide them with a vehicle by which to do what they cannot do on their own. Second, since there is little evidence that in making decisions people make consistent use of complex non-linear preferences, then using simple linear additive models of utilities, or one of the techniques discussed in the next section, may be perfectly adequate in most circumstances.

READINGS 6.1

Ralph Keeney provides a compact discussion of MAUT together with a detailed transcript of an interview session to elicit a multi-attribute utility function in the context of siting an energy facility in:

- Ralph L. Keeney, "Chapter 7: Evaluating Site Impacts," in *Siting Energy Facilities*, Academic Press, 413pp., 1980.

For an example of an application of MAUT that is "simple and straightforward enough so that the reader can, with diligence and frequent re-examinations of it, conduct relatively straightforward MAUT evaluations," see:

- Ward Edwards and J. Robert Newman, *Multiattribute Evaluation*, Sage Publications, 96pp., 1982. Reprinted as "Chapter 1: Multiattribute Evaluation," in T. Connolly, H.R. Arkes, and K.R. Hammond (eds.), *Judgment and Decision Making: An Interdisciplinary Reader*, Cambridge University Press, pp. 17–34, 2000.

SUGGESTED RESOURCES TO LEARN THE TECHNICAL DETAILS OF CONSTRUCTING MULTI-ATTRIBUTE UTILITY FUNCTIONS

The classic reference is:

- Ralph L. Keeney and Howard Raiffa, *Decisions with Multiple Objectives: Preferences and Value Tradeoffs*, Wiley, 569pp., 1976.

For a somewhat more accessible treatment of the same material, with a detailed transcript of an elicitation interview in the context of a set of alternative energy development scenarios, see:

- Ralph L. Keeney, "Chapter 7: Evaluating Site Impacts," in *Siting Energy Facilities*, Academic Press, pp. 223–327, 1980.

6.4 OTHER MULTIPLE CRITERIA DECISION MAKING (MCDM) METHODS

MAUT provides the theoretical foundation and the most general way for representing preferences. However, the difficulties in applying it, and the expertise required to do so, have led to the development of several alternative techniques for eliciting and approximating decision makers' preferences in multi-attribute settings. Collectively referred to as methods in Multiple Criteria Decision Making (MCDM), each is distinguished from the others by the way in which preferences are captured. In this section we mention a few of the methods and explain one of them for illustration.

MCDM has been a recognized subfield of operations research for 40 years. There is an International Society for MCDM, which holds its international conference every other year and which started the *Journal of Multiple Criteria Decision Analysis*. The hundreds of active researchers in MCDM are basically motivated by the same impetus: "Since I don't have my client's MAU function and I can't get it, what's the best I can do to help the decision maker choose an alternative which is in some sense best for him/her?" Dozens of methods have been created to respond to this challenge, and researchers are still creating more, but certain techniques have emerged as the leaders, notably ELECTRE (Roy, 1968), PROMETHEE (Brans, 1982), and AHP (Saaty, 1980).

MCDM methods all use some simplified representation of preferences such as pairwise comparisons (i.e., is this criterion better or worse than that one, is a common feature). Some such as ELECTRE use thresholds (i.e., the maximum difference in criteria values that a decision maker will accept), to eliminate unattractive alternatives and to shrink the decision space. Some methods seek only to reduce the range of options with the idea that another, more information-intensive MCDM method will be used on the reduced problem to home in on the best solution. However they represent preferences, all of the methods include some processing of the decision maker's responses to move toward a best solution or reduced range of solutions. All of the major techniques have been implemented in commercially available software.

The Analytical Hierarchy Process (AHP) (Saaty, 1977, 1980, 1994) is one of the most widely used MCDM methods. The technique is based entirely on pairwise comparisons made by the decision maker. Following the description in Cohon and Rothley (1997), call a_{ij} the degree to which i is preferred to j, where the i and j can refer to criteria or alternatives and where the degree of preference is expressed on a scale of 1 to 9. If the decision maker is perfectly consistent, then

$$a_{ik} = a_{ij}\, a_{jk} \quad \text{for all } i, j \text{ and } k$$

If the a_{ij}'s represent preferences for the criteria (i.e., a_{ij} is the degree to which X_i is preferred to X_j) and the decision maker is perfectly consistent, then the weights on the criteria would follow this relationship:

$$w_i = \frac{1}{q}\sum_{j=1}^{q} a_{ij} w_j \quad i = 1,\ldots,q$$

where w_i is the weight on attribute X_i and q is the number of criteria.

Decision makers are not, in general, consistent, in which case the set of equations would have no solution. The AHP method gets around this by replacing q with λ_{max}, a variable.

$$w_i = \frac{1}{\lambda_{\max}}\sum_{j=1}^{q_i} a_{ij} w_j \quad i = 1,\ldots,q$$

Saaty (1977) showed that this is an eigenvalue problem and that the vector of weights, $\vec{w}$, is the right eigenvector of the matrix, A, formed by the a_{ij}'s and λ_{max} is its corresponding eigenvalue. Furthermore, Saaty devised an index to measure the degree of consistency:

$$CI = \frac{\lambda_{\max} - q}{q - 1}$$

The value of *CI* from this equation can be compared to *CI* computed for a matrix of the same dimensions as A but comprising randomly generated elements. This provides a basis for judging inconsistency and controlling for it. If *CI* is too large, then the analyst should iterate with the decision maker.

Pairwise comparisons are used to derive weights on all of the criteria and, in the absence of objective data for individual outcomes, criteria scores for individual alternatives. For example, there are no objective measures for evaluating alternative routes for a highway in terms of their aesthetic impacts (one of the criteria). One could use AHP pairwise comparisons to create subjective evaluations, for example, alternative 1 is three times better than alternative 2 in terms of aesthetic impacts. When all of the comparisons are completed, an overall score is determined for each alternative.

The leading software implementation of AHP is Expert Choice, which automates all of the analysis and includes extensive sensitivity analysis features and attractive graphics.[3]

AHP and other MCDM methods have been criticized for their failure to adhere to the axioms of MAUT, which probably shouldn't be surprising since the methods were developed to overcome the complexity and cognitive burdens of extracting MAU functions.

AHP, in particular, has been a focus of intense debate in the literature. Dyer (1990) writes: "The analytic hierarchy process (AHP) is flawed as a procedure for ranking alternatives in that the rankings produced by this procedure are arbitrary." Most of the criticism has focused on AHP's failure to adhere to the principle of transitivity. Indeed, allowing decision makers to be inconsistent is one of AHP's major features. The other major criticism is the technique's vulnerability to irrelevant alternatives. That is, the ranking of the alternatives may change if another alternative is introduced or the order of paired comparisons is changed. Gass (2005), who ultimately comes out on the side of AHP, provides a concise review of these disputes. The key point is that in using AHP or any other MCDM method, one should be aware of the assumptions and possible pitfalls.

READINGS 6.2

James S. Dyer, "Remarks on the Analytic Hierarchy Process," *Management Science*, *36*(3), pp. 249–258, 1990.
Saul I. Gass, "Model World: The Great Debate – MAUT versus AHP," *Interfaces*, *35*(4), pp. 308–312, 2005.

DISCUSSION QUESTIONS FOR READINGS 6.2

- What is your view of the controversy between proponents of MAUT and AHP?
- When might these issues become important in an analysis you perform?

ADDITIONAL RESOURCES ON MCDM

There have been many attempts over the years at comprehensive reviews of MCDM, including MAUT and multiobjective programming (see Section 6.8). The most recent is this volume in Springer's "State of the Art Surveys" series:

[3] Details can be found at expertchoice.com.

- Salvatore Greco, Matthias Ehrgott, and José Rui Figueira (eds.), *Multiple Criteria Decision Analysis: State of the Art Surveys*, *233*, Springer, 1347pp., 2016.

The proceedings of the MCDM Society's biennial meetings provide the most up-to-date, but not necessarily synthesized, view of the field.

In addition, see:

- M. Koksalan, J. Wallenius, and S. Zionts, *Multiple Criteria Decision Making: From Early History to the 21st Century*, World Scientific, 197pp., 2011.
- Terry Connolly, Hal R. Arkes, and Kenneth R. Hammond (eds.), *Judgment and Decision Making: An Interdisciplinary Reader*, Cambridge University Press, 786pp., 2000.

6.5 FIGURING OUT WHAT YOU CARE ABOUT

While Ralph Keeney is one of the most accomplished decision analysts of his generation, he is also one of the most reflective. In a book titled *Value-Focused Thinking: A Path to Creative Decision Making* (Keeney, 1992), he observes:

> Almost all the literature on decision making concerns what to do after the crucial activities of identifying the decision problem, creating alternatives, and specifying objectives ... [However,] it is values that are important to any decision situation. Alternatives are relevant only because they are means to achieve your values. Thus your thinking should focus first on values [what you care about] and later on alternatives that might achieve them.

Keeney argues that before engaging in formal analysis it is important to construct and refine a hierarchy of objectives. Figure 6.3 illustrates such an objective hierarchy for salmon management in the Skeena River in British Columbia, Canada. In this case he was performing an analysis for the Canadian Department of the Environment (DOE) (Keeney, 1977). Several groups would be affected by management choices. Keeney (1992) explains:

> Suppose DOE is considering changing its licensing policy. The new policy may result in a small increase in the number of salmon that return in the Skeena to spawn, or the increase may be large. The change in licensing policy may increase administrative (government) costs. It may lead to better harvests for the lure and net fisherman, but this may leave fewer fish for the sport fishermen and the Indians ... The overall impact on the region may be more employment in canneries ... but less recreational income ... Somehow ... [DOE] must measure each of the possible impacts, balance these in some fair way ... and decide whether to implement the new licensing rules or not.

One way the agency could do this is by developing metrics for each of the end nodes of the objective hierarchy in Figure 6.3, constructing a multi-attribute utility function across those nodes, running the proposed policy through a

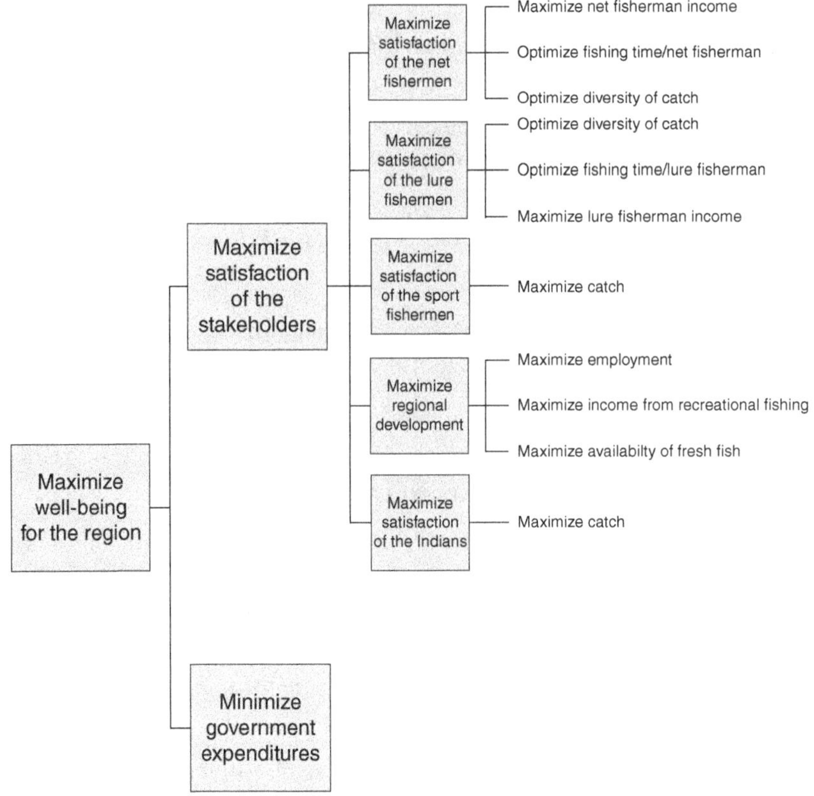

FIGURE 6.3. An example of an objective hierarchy developed by Keeney (1977) for the case of salmon management in the Skeena River in British Columbia, Canada.

set of models to determine the value of each of those metrics, applying the multi-attribute utility function to both the present and proposed situation, and comparing the resulting utilities. Of course when multiple stakeholders are involved, one can also construct separate value trees for each. For an example of a case where this was done for nine different groups concerned about the future of energy policy for Germany, see Keeney et al. (1987).

When a single stakeholder bears both the cost and the benefits of a policy, constructing a MAU model may be analytically complicated and cognitively challenging, but it is at least technically straightforward. When, as in the case of the salmon management example, multiple stakeholders are involved, the decision maker faces the added challenging task of deciding how they want to combine the values and preferences of different parties. One strategy is to simply ask each party and use the results. However, in many cases, a decision maker may instead want to weight the preferences of different stakeholders differently. A private decision maker can obviously do that. It becomes potentially very controversial and politically sensitive if a public decision maker adopts such weightings. For example, suppose that the Administrator of EPA believes Prof. Sue McDonald more than Prof. Sam Smith. Saying that publicly by attaching different weights to how judgments from the two are combined could easily become a big political and legal problem.

DISCUSSION QUESTION

The objective hierarchy illustrated in Figure 6.3 was developed for a decision maker in 1977. If you were going to develop such an objective hierarchy today, would you make modifications, and if so, what would they be?

SUGGESTED RESOURCE TO LEARN ABOUT IDENTIFYING WHAT YOU CARE ABOUT AND CONSTRUCTING A VALUE HIERARCHY

After working with Raiffa on developing MAUT, and applying it to a variety of problems, Keeney wrote a book about how to think systematically about what you (the decision maker) care about. See:

- Ralph L. Keeney, *Value Focused Thinking: A Path to Creative Decisionmaking*, Harvard University Press, 416pp., 1992.

6.6 EXAMPLE APPLICATIONS OF MAUT AND MCDM

Because considerable familiarity with the issues of establishing independence conditions is required to do a good job of applying MAUT methods, the number of good examples of applications of MAUT methods is modest. Keeney (1980) has elaborated applications in a number of contexts related to siting energy facilities.

As an alternative to using contingent valuation (Section 5.6), McDaniels (1996) has illustrated how one can use MAUT methods to evaluate environmental impacts of electric utilities. In this application he worked with the Director of Planning for BP Hydro to construct an "index of environmental impact." His paper provides a very readable account of the process they applied working through steps that involved:

1. Structuring the factors (objectives) important in specifying what is meant by "minimizing environmental impacts."
2. Defining measures of performance, or attributes, for the relevant objectives.
3. Verifying the relevance of assumptions of the basic form of the value model for the index (in this case an additive model was employed).
4. Examining the value tradeoffs between pairs of objectives.
5. Examining the single attribute utility functions.

6. Constructing the utility function.

On the basis of an interview with the Director of Planning, McDaniels identified six attributes that together made up that expert's environmental objectives hierarchy. These were:

- Flora (hectares of mature forest lost)
- Fauna (hectares of prime wildlife habitat lost)
- Wilderness ecosystems (hectares of prime wilderness lost)
- Recreational (hectares of high quality recreation land lost)
- Aesthetics (annual person-years viewing high voltage transmission lines in quality terrain)
- Global environmental impacts (megawatts of fossil fuel [and associated] pollutants).

He then established best and worst outcomes for each, elicited single attribute utility functions for each attribute, and determined that the multi-attribute function should take an additive linear form. He scaled the utility functions elicited over the previously established ranges of worst to best outcome and, by posing questions about tradeoffs, was able to obtain the following weights and ranks for each attribute:

Rank	Attribute	Weight
1	Wilderness	0.372
2	Fauna	0.184
2	Recreation	0.184
4	Flora	0.092
4	Aesthetics	0.092
6	Global Impact	0.076

McDaniels explains:

> the coefficients indicate that, within the ranges defined for the attributes, the effect on wilderness ecosystems is the most important objective, having roughly twice the weight of effects on fauna or recreational use. In turn, effects on fauna or recreation use have roughly twice the weight of effects on flora and aesthetics. Global environmental effects account for only about 7% of the overall impact associated with the environmental objectives, given the range of impacts defined for the attributes.

Other interesting examples of applications of MAUT methods include work on evaluating public preferences in forest land-use choices in Australia (Ananda and Herath, 2005) and on social preferences for health states (Torrance et al., 1982).

MCDM techniques, which were created to overcome the barriers to using MAUT, have been widely used. The Figueira et al. survey (2005) includes chapters devoted to applications in finance, telecommunications, energy, and sustainable development. The *Journal of MCDA* is filled with applications in every issue.[4] In contrast to the elicitation and application of MAU functions, today MCDM methods are being applied thousands of times each year in a wide range of private-sector decision problems.

The use of MCDM in the arena of public policy has been much more limited for reasons discussed in the next section. Given their long national history of applying analysis and citizen engagement in public policy decision making, it is perhaps not surprising that one of the best examples comes from the Netherlands.

In the winter of 1953 a storm in the North Sea broke through protective dikes and resulted in a massive flood that killed 1835 people, displaced roughly 70,000 more, and caused extensive losses to livestock and property. As early as 1937 the Dutch Department of Public Works had identified this vulnerability and developed plans to dam the mouths of many rivers to prevent such events. However, the war delayed efforts and "in the densely populated areas near the river mouths of the Rhine, the Meuse, and the Schelde, it proved very difficult to build new dikes or strengthen the original ones."[5]

In the weeks after the 1953 flood, the Dutch Government created the Delta Commission that designed and began a high-priority program of civil works, the aims of which were to:

1. Drain the areas that flood regularly during high water levels and protect them from the water.
2. Protect the land from getting brackish.[5]

After building barriers in the mouths of several rivers, in 1957 work turned to the Haringvliet estuary, part of the Rhine River delta just south of Rotterdam. By 1971, the 17 60-meter-wide Haringvliet sluices were completed. When they were closed they could close off the estuary from the sea. The Delta Project history[5] explains:

> the Haringvliet dam took the longest time to build. The Haringvliet dam had two functions. Firstly, it had to protect against a potential flood. Secondly, it had to take care of the drainage of water from the Rhine and the Maas into the North Sea. Consequently, the dam had to be an open dam. Seventeen openings regulate the amount of water which flows through the New Waterway to the North Sea. When the water levels near Rotterdam are getting too high, the special drainage sluices can drain off an increased amount of water into the sea.

[4] For example, the 2016 Jan/Feb issue includes papers on the application of MCDM to: the design of mechanical components, the treatment of gastrointestinal disease, vehicle routing, monitoring post-operative heart patients, and benefit–risk assessment of cholesterol-lowering drugs.

[5] These quotations are from the Deltawerken website available at: www.deltawerken.com/Deltaworks/23.html. While the Haringvliet sluices are certainly impressive, if you are ever in the south of the Netherlands make a point of visiting and learning about the even more impressive open dam across the Eastern Schelde. This structure consists of 62 openings, each 40 meters wide. The individual units were fabricated on land and then floated out to be emplaced to make the barrier. The resulting storm surge barrier is one of the largest structures in the world.

In addition to providing flood protection, the dam created significant changes in the local ecology, converting a tidal estuary into a freshwater body with greatly increased sedimentation rates. In 1990, reflecting the shift in attitude towards ecology and water resources, the Dutch government began to explore strategies to restore the ecological health of the Delta. In particular the government wanted to consider new operating rules for the Haringvliet Dam as well as the removal of contaminated settlements by dredging.

Ridgley and Rijsberman (1992) have reported in detail how MCDM methods were used to frame and inform the analysis for this problem.[6]

Deciding how best to manage a dam and whether to dredge in an ecologically sensitive setting is always a challenging problem, requiring sophisticated hydrodynamic and ecological models. But the case of the Rhine River delta is especially complicated because of development and social and economic changes induced by the conversion of the area from a tidal to a freshwater body. With the control provided by the Haringvliet Dam, over the preceding 30 years the Delta had become an important source of freshwater for agricultural, municipal, and industrial uses, and a heavily used recreational resource in an area with its own biological values – but based on freshwater wetland ecology. Reverting back to the conditions of the 1960s before the water structures were built would necessarily have a significant impact on all that had since developed. The determination of the best alternative in this case is clearly a problem with multiple stakeholders and multiple conflicting objectives.

The Dutch government created a four-part hierarchical institutional structure to analyze and address the problem. At the top was the "Consultative Committee," which included high-level officials from all relevant government agencies. This committee was charged with choosing a management plan. One layer down in the hierarchy, representatives of these same agencies joined representatives of stakeholders in a "Coordinating Group." A "Policy Analysis Team," staffed by the Dutch Water Authority, coordinated the analysis. The actual analysis, across the many dimensions of the problem, was carried out by ten "Work Groups." It was at this level where conflicts were identified and resolved. Stakeholders were represented on these Work Groups, giving interested parties a voice in the detailed analysis as well as in the evaluation of the results by the Coordinating Group.

Ridgley and Rijsberman (1992) observe that there was an infinite number of operating schemes for the Haringvliet sluice gates and sediment removal plans (and therefore an infinite number of combinations of the two). However, the planners were able to settle on five different options for sluice gate management ranging from no change from the current management scheme to an option of only closing the sluice gates for storm surge protection. This latter alternative would allow for maximum tidal fluctuation. Five different sediment removal strategies were also identified. Hence, the alternatives consisted of 25

[6] The description provided here draws on the summary prepared by Cohon and Rothley (1997).

possible combinations. Preliminary analysis allowed the 25 alternatives to be reduced to seven that then became the focus of detailed analysis of valuation and decision making.

In the previous section we discussed the importance of the objectives and how time and effort invested early in a project to identify an appropriate set of objectives pay off in a better evaluation end result. This particular case study is one of the finest demonstrations of this point: almost four months of the 14-month-long study were devoted to the creation of an objective hierarchy that consisted of three top-level objectives (ecology, human uses, and the administration). Each of these in turn was elaborated with several sub-objectives with several further stages below them. There was a total of 68 bottom-level objectives; 31 under ecology, 20 under human uses, and 17 under administration. Details on the objective hierarchy can be found in figure 12.18 and table 12.5 in Cohon and Rothley (1997).

Each of the seven alternatives was analyzed and evaluated in terms of the 68 bottom-level objectives. Arriving at a decision required value judgments to be made about the relative importance of each group of objectives. Starting from the bottom of the hierarchy and moving to the top, the analytical hierarchy process (AHP) was used to determine the relative weights of the objectives and arrive at a decision.[7]

The result of the analysis of the Rhine River Delta problem was the selection of an intermediate operating scheme for the sluice gates and the decision to study sediment removal further because of a perceived lack of sufficient information. This was a good result for such a complicated problem, and the use of MCDM was a major factor in coming to a successful resolution.

6.7 LIMITATIONS TO THE USE OF MAUT AND MCDM

Using MAUT to structure and solve problems makes great sense. There are just two problems. First, the process of eliciting all the judgments that are needed in order to work through the independence assumptions and construct a multi-attribute utility function from a set of elicited single attribute utility functions is so complex that few analysts are able to do it properly. Second, many decision makers find the process by which the results emerge to be sufficiently opaque that they basically just have to trust the analyst to have done things right. This is fine if a private decision maker finds a good analyst whom they trust, and wants to use MAUT to assist them in addressing some major problem. In most cases, it simply does not work for public policy making where there are multiple contending parties, and where transparency is often critically important.

[7] Note that having constructed the objective hierarchy, a MA utility function could have then been constructed. Indeed, it would have been interesting to use and compare both methods.

Other MCDM methods are also quite demanding of decision makers, although understanding and articulating pairwise comparisons, for example, is easier on decision makers than the sorts of questioning required by MAUT. The success of any method depends in part on the skill of the analyst, which is especially important for MAUT. The interview skills and understanding of the analyst are probably less important for some of the MCDM methods due to the availability of easy-to-use software.

Public policy presents particular challenges for the use of MCDM techniques. First, there is the question of whose preference information should be represented. As discussed in Chapter 2, public decision makers are, by the very nature of their positions and the policy process, charged with representing their constituents or, more generally, the public interest. This implies that it's the public's preferences (or those of some subset) that matter, but, of course, building the public's MAU function is a wildly impractical idea. This also raises the question, discussed in Chapter 2, of the comparability of different people's utility functions.

In many public policy problems just framing a decision process and even knowing who the decision makers are can be a challenge. In the United States, major policy questions such as determining how the nation should respond to climate change necessarily involves the Office of the President, several executive branch departments, and the Congress. Even very specific public decisions, such as where to put spent nuclear fuel, involve multiple branches of multiple levels of government. These, and similar decisions, also require input from stakeholders and the general public. The prospect of eliciting preferences in any form for such problems is daunting and probably not all that useful.

The nature of the value judgments also poses an enormous challenge for public decision makers. It's one thing to ask a person how much money they would want for certain in exchange for a lottery between two monetary payoffs; it's quite another if the lottery involves something like lives lost. You have to imagine a dialogue in which the analyst asks, "Madame Administrator, how many people would have to die for certain for you to be indifferent between that number of deaths and an even chance of 100 people dying and no one dying?" It may be a reasonable question, but it would be almost impossible for a political decision maker to answer it and not be subjected to withering criticism.

Despite these challenges, the examples presented in the previous section show that in modest ways these methods can play a useful role in public decision making. In both of the examples shown, and especially in the case of the Rhine River Delta, a major contribution was the identification of objectives, i.e., figuring out what decision makers should care about and helping participants learn what is important, both to themselves and to other stakeholders, even if no preferences are ever elicited. This is very much in line with Keeney's observations in the previous section.

6.8 MULTIOBJECTIVE PROGRAMMING

MCDM techniques, including MAUT, are applicable to decision situations in which the alternatives have already been defined. For example, "among a set of five cars that I am considering, which one should I buy?" Or, "which of the three colleges, to which I've been accepted, should I choose to attend?" Similarly, in the case of the Rhine River estuary discussed in Section 6.6, the choice was among 25 combinations of dam operating scenarios and sediment management schemes.

However, there are many situations where the choices cannot be readily defined. Rather, the alternatives are defined by a set of decision variables and constraints, allowing for an infinity of possible paths to take. This requires some analysis to identify specific alternatives that in some sense perform well in terms of the multiple objectives of interest. This is where multiobjective programming (MOP) comes in.

The single-objective mathematical programming problem is:

$$\text{Max}\, X(\bar{y})$$

Subject to:

$$g_{\text{i}}(\bar{y}) \leq b_{\text{i}} \qquad \text{i} = 1,\ldots,\text{m}$$

where $\bar{y}$ is a vector of n decision variables $(y_1, y_2, \ldots\ldots, y_{\text{n}})$, X is the objective function (which we show as being maximized arbitrarily), and there are m constraints.

In a water quality management problem in which we have to determine how much to control combined sewer overflows (CSOs) into a river, the decision variables would be the fraction each CSO is reduced and the water quality parameters of interest. The constraints would include meeting water quality standards (e.g., dissolved oxygen of at least 3 mg/l) and the biochemical and physical relationships that translate pollution inflows into water quality parameter concentrations in the river. The objective function would be to minimize control costs.

The MOP takes the same form, but there are multiple objective functions, say q in all.

$$\text{Max}[\text{X}_1(\bar{y}), \text{X}_2(\bar{y}), \ldots, \text{X}_q(\bar{y})]$$

s.t.

$$g_i(\bar{y}) \leq b_{\text{i}} \qquad i = 1, 2, \ldots, \text{m}$$

In the CSO problem, an additional objective may involve the distribution in costs among the political jurisdictions on the river, reflecting the equity of the control plan.

If all of the objective functions and constraints are linear, this becomes a multiobjective linear program (MOLP) of the following form:

$$\text{Max}\left[\sum_{j=1}^{n} b_{1j}y_j, \sum_{j=1}^{n} b_{2j}y_j, \ldots, \sum_{j=1}^{n} b_{qj}y_j\right]$$

s.t.

$$\sum_{j=1}^{n} a_{ij} y_j \le b_i \quad i = 1, 2, \ldots, \text{m}$$

$$y_j \ge 0 \quad j = 1, 2, \ldots, \text{m}$$

where objective k has the form:

$$\text{X}_k(\bar{y}) = \sum_{j=1}^{n} b_{jk} y_j$$

and we added non-negativity constraints as required by LP solution algorithms.

A solution of an LP is a collection of values of the decision variables, i.e., $\bar{y}'$. $\bar{y}'$ is a feasible solution if all of the constraints are satisfied. In a single objective LP, we find the optimal solution y*, which is a feasible solution that produces the maximum (or minimum) value of the objective function. In an MOLP, we can no longer find an overall optimal solution since the solution that optimizes one of the objectives does not optimize the others, i.e.,

$$\bar{y}^{*k} \ne \bar{y}^{*l}$$

The best we can do is find those solutions of the MOLP which are nondominated (Pareto optimal or noninferior are equivalent terms). A feasible solution is nondominated if there is no other feasible solution that gives more of one objective without giving less of at least one other objective.

Just as with a single-objective LP, a simple two-decisional example (n = 2) allows us to create graphical and intuitive explanations of key concepts. In addition to assuming n = 2, we will also have only two objectives (q = 2). The following sample problem is taken from Cohon (2003).

$$\text{Max } X_1 = 5y_1 - 2y_2$$

$$X_2 = -y_1 + 4y_2$$

s.t.

$$-y_1 + y_2 \le 3$$

$$y_1 \le 6$$

$$y_1 + y_2 \le 8$$

$$y_2 \le 4$$

$$y_1, y_2 \le 0$$

Figure 6.4 displays the feasible region in the decision space for this example problem.

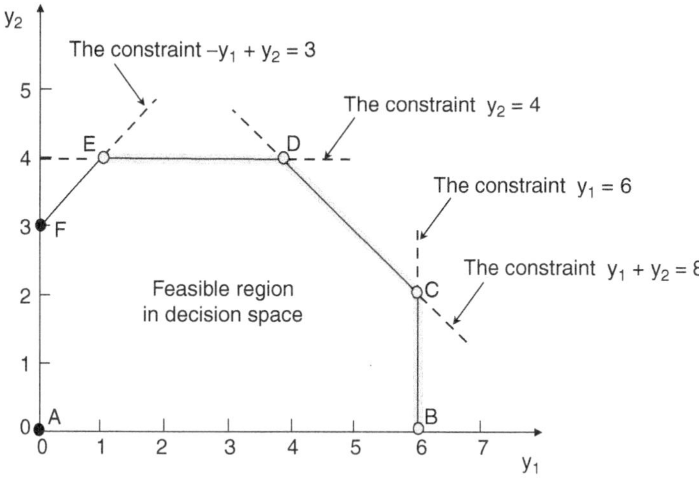

FIGURE 6.4. Graphical illustration of the feasible region in the decision space of the simple multiobjective decision problem. The shaded lines along B–C–D–E delineate the non-dominated set in this space. Figure redrawn from Cohon (2003).

If this were a single-objective problem, we could proceed directly to finding the optimal solution. In the multiobjective case, we determine the set of non-dominated solutions. The first step in doing this is to map the feasible region in decision space into a feasible region in objective space. Table 6.1 shows the values of the decision variables and the objectives at each of the extreme points.

Each of these points is plotted in objective space and then, taking advantage of the linearity of all of the functions, connected with straight lines to create a feasible region in objective space shown in Figure 6.5. The graphical interpretation of nondominance in a maximization problem is that a nondominated solution has no feasible solutions lying in the northeast quadrant with the point in question at the origin. Note that this interpretation only applies in objective space. We can determine by inspection that the nondominated set is the shaded portion of the boundary of the feasible region in objective space: points B, C, D, and E and the lines connecting the adjacent points.

The nondominated set contains powerful information. It shows the range of choices available to solve the problem and, crucially, the tradeoffs among the objectives as one moves through the range of choice. Consider the non-dominated set in objective space in Figure 6.5. Point B is the solution that maximizes objective one, i.e., it would have been the optimal solution of the single objective problem in which we maximized X_1. Point E, at the other end of the nondominated set, maximizes X_2. Notice that the other objective in each case does relatively poorly at these individual optima: $X_2 = -6$ at point B and $X_1 = -3$ at point E. As you move away from either of these end points you are giving up ("trading off") one of the objectives in order to gain some

TABLE 6.1. *Values of the two decision variables and two objectives at the six extreme points A through F in Figure 6.4 (Cohon, 2003).*

	y_1	y_2	$X_1(y_1,y_2) = 5y_1\text{-}2y_2$	$X_2(y_1,y_2) = -y_1+4y_2$
A	0	0	0	0
B	6	0	30	-6
C	6	2	26	2
D	4	4	12	12
E	1	4	-3	15
F	0	3	-6	12

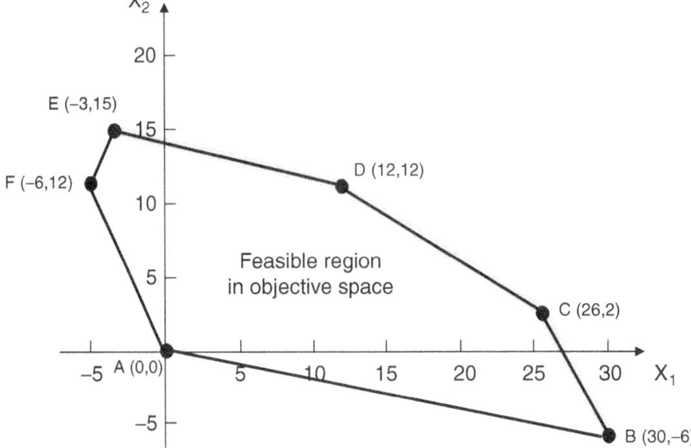

FIGURE 6.5. Graphical illustration of the feasible region in the objective space of the simple multiobjective decision problem. Figure redrawn from Cohon (2003).

amount of the other. The amount that you have to give up of one objective for a gain in the other is the "tradeoff" and is related to the slope of the nondominated set. In moving from point E to point D, for example, we gain five units of X_1 for each unit of X_2 that we give up. This is very valuable information for decision making.

This is as far as we can go with MOP, although it is often far enough. If there are only two or three objectives, a presentation based on illustrations like Figure 6.5 can be enough to support a decision. When there is a large number of objectives the results may overwhelm a decision maker's ability to understand and evaluate tradeoffs. In this case, one could proceed by extracting from the nondominated set a few representative or promising alternatives as input to an MCDM method.

The graphical approach applies only to the simplest demonstration problems. For real problems, we need an algorithm for generating the nondominated set (or, more likely in a real setting, an approximation of it). It's the development of those algorithms that is what the field of MOP has been concerned with.

There are basically two kinds of MOP solution methods: the multiobjective simplex algorithm for MOLP (see Steuer, 1986) and techniques that convert the MOP into a series of single objective problems that we can solve with existing algorithms. The latter class includes the weighting method, the constraint method, and the noninferior set estimation (NISE) method (see Cohon, 2003).

MOP has been applied to a wide range of public decision-making problems, especially in water resources, transportation, and energy facilities (see Cohon, 2003 and Figueira et al., 2005). ReVelle et al. (1991) presented an application to nuclear spent fuel management that provides a good demonstration of the technique. The description of that work that follows is based on Cohon and Rothley (1997).

It has been the policy of the United States for more than three decades that the spent fuel from commercial nuclear power plants should be deposited permanently in an underground repository. However, due to the delays first in agreeing on a site and then in moving ahead with developing it, spent fuel still sits at the reactor sites where it was generated. This state of affairs is a source of concern, leading from time to time to calls for the establishment of temporary above-ground storage facilities. This is the problem analyzed by ReVelle et al. (1991) in response to the then-current interest in so-called "away from reactor" (AFR) waste storage facilities.

Choosing where to site one or more temporary storage facilities is a classic NIMBY ("not in my backyard") problem, further complicated by the problem of choosing the routes over which the waste will be shipped from reactors to storage facilities. Where the storage facility is sited will unavoidably affect shipping routes. Thus, the spent fuel storage problem requires that three questions be answered simultaneously:

- Where should storage facilities be sited?
- If there is more than one facility, to which facility should each reactor send its waste?
- Over which routes should waste be shipped from reactors to storage sites?

ReVelle et al. (1991) formulated this problem as a two-objective zero-one integer linear programming problem:[8]

$$\text{Min}\, Z_1 = \sum_{i=1}^{m}\sum_{j=1}^{n} t_i p_{ij} x_{ij}$$

$$\text{Min}\, Z_2 = \sum_{i=1}^{m}\sum_{j=1}^{n} t_i d_{ij} x_{ij}$$

[8] We have adopted the notation used by ReVelle et al. (1991) in which Z represents objective and x and y are decision variables.

s.t.

$$\sum_{j=1}^{n} x_{ij} = 1 \quad i = 1,\ldots,m$$

$$y_j \geq x_{ij} \quad i = 1,\ldots,m \ and\ j = 1,\ldots,n$$

$$\sum_{j=1}^{m} y_j = f$$

$$x_{ij}y_j = 0,1 \quad i = 1,\ldots,m \ and\ j = 1,\ldots,n$$

where

$$x_{ij} = \begin{cases} 1 & \text{if the spent fuel at reactor } i \text{ is} \\ & \text{assigned to the storage facility at } j \\ 0 & \text{otherwise} \end{cases}$$

$$y_j = \begin{cases} 1 & \text{if a storage facility is established at} \\ & \text{potential site } j \\ 0 & \text{otherwise} \end{cases}$$

t_i = tons of spent fuel at reactor i
p_{ij} = number of people living along the shipping route from reactor i to potential storage site j
d_{ij} = distance in miles of the shipping route from reactor i to potential storage site j
f = number of storage facilities that must be established

The first equation above (Minimize Z_1) is a representation of the risk associated with shipping spent fuel, measured here as the number of people living along shipping routes weighted by the amount of waste shipped along that route. This "person-tons" objective is not an explicit risk measure. It ignores, for example, the probability of radioactive releases and the probability of exposure in the event of releases. Still, it seems to be a relevant characterization of at least public perception of risk (more tons moving past more people). For this problem, that may be more determining than the actuarial risk. The second equation (Minimize Z_2) is an objective related to shipping cost. Here again, a surrogate of "ton-miles" is used, on the grounds that the more weight shipped over longer routes, the higher the cost.

The first of the constraints requires that the waste at every reactor be assigned to one storage facility. The second constraint ensures that assignments can only be made to sites where a storage facility will be established (i.e., $x_{ij} = 1$ only if $y_j = 1$). The third constraint requires that exactly f storage facilities be opened.

Nondominated solutions were obtained for this problem by using the weighting method (see Cohon, 2003). Details on determining the shipping routes to facility locations and the site assignments can be found in ReVelle et al. (1991).

There is an interesting aspect of the solution related to the special nature of this and all other multiobjective integer programming (IP) problems. Because IPs are, by definition, discrete, their nondominated sets consist of unconnected points (i.e., compare Figure 6.6 with the nondominated set for the linear programming problem in Figure 6.5). The nondominated set for the IP is the set of points A, B, C, D, and E and *not* the line segments that connect them.

Figure 6.7 shows the locations of the 119 commercial reactors in the United States as of the end of 1995. Note that the great majority of the reactors are located in the eastern United States. This was the region studied by ReVelle et al. (1991) using a subset of the reactors and data from 1980 and focusing on three potential storage locations at Morris Plains, Illinois, West Valley, New York, and Barnwell, South Carolina. All of these are existing nuclear facilities that are no longer being used. Transportation of spent fuel was assumed to be done by truck on the network of U.S. interstate and other highways.

The IP formulation above, with $f = 2$ (i.e., choose two of the possible storage sites) was used with the weighting method to generate the nondominated set shown in Figure 6.8. As noted above, only the points represent nondominated solutions. Point A is the solution with the lowest value person-tons (i.e., it is the solution that minimizes Z_1). The solution corresponding to this point is shown in the leftmost map in Figure 6.9. Of the three potential storage sites, the two selected are Barnwell, SC and Morris Plains, IL. Figure 6.9 also shows the assignments of the reactors and storage sites to which they ship. We can see that the reactors in Illinois and Michigan ship to Morris Plains in Illinois, and the rest all ship to Barnwell in South Carolina. In order to keep the figure simple we do not show the actual shipping routes.

As we move to solutions down and to the right of A, the cost objective is decreased at the expense of the person-tons objective, which goes up. The unlabeled points between A and B in Figure 6.8 correspond to new nondominated solutions in which the storage sites and assignments are the same as solution A and those shown in the leftmost map in Figure 6.9. These solutions differ from A, and from each other, in the shipping routes that are chosen. As we move from A to B, the routes that avoid population concentrations become longer and are replaced by shorter routes associated with higher populations.

Moving further along the tradeoff curve in Figure 6.8 toward ever lower cost (and higher person-tons) takes us to point B, where there is a shift in

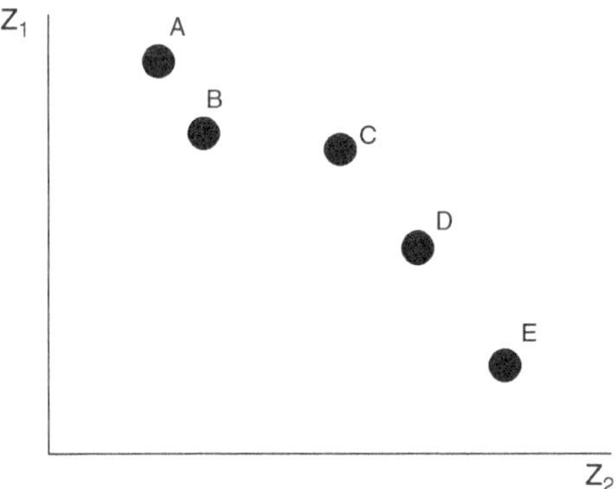

FIGURE 6.6. Nondominated set for a hypothetical two-objective integer program.

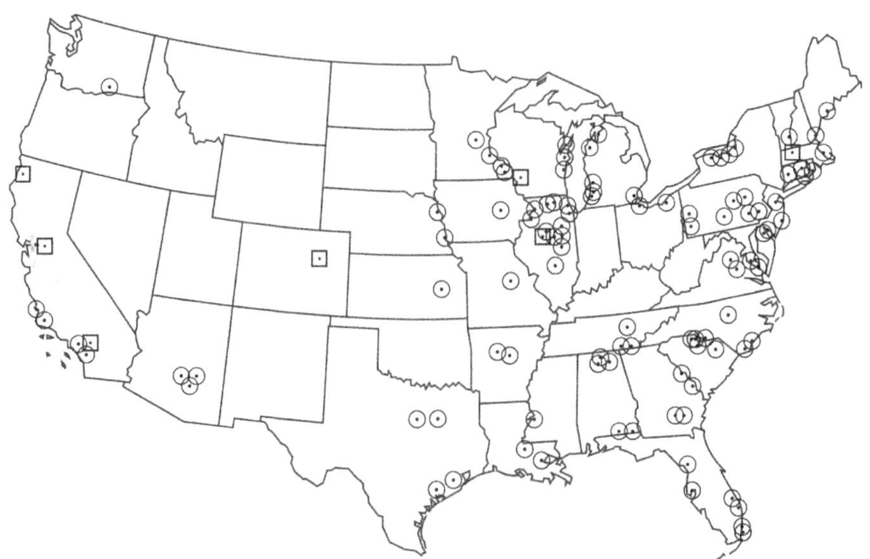

FIGURE 6.7. Location of 119 commercial nuclear reactors in the United States as of the end of 1995 (denoted by ⊙) as well as locations of shut-down reactors that still have fuel on site (denoted by ⊡). Redrawn from ReVelle et al. (1991).

reactor assignments as well as routes. Figure 6.9 shows that at B the reactor in upstate New York reassigns from Barnwell, SC, to Morris Plains, IL. As we move further along the tradeoff curve to point C, not only routes and assignments change, but the set of storage sites also changes to West Valley, NY, and

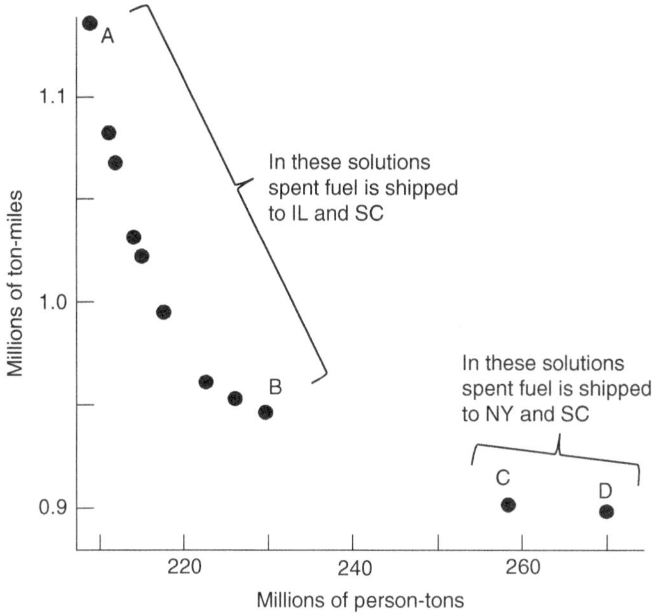

FIGURE 6.8. Approximated nondominated set for the reactor waste transport problem. Modified from ReVelle et al. (1991).

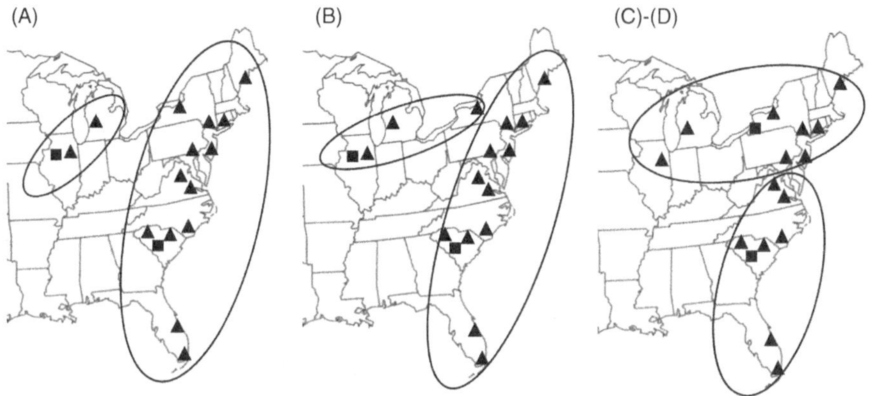

FIGURE 6.9. Reactor assignments and spent fuel storage sites for the solution points A, B, and C in Figure 6.8. Solid triangles are reactors. Solid boxes are storage sites. Note that while the Illinois and South Carolina storage sites are chosen for A and B, the New York site replaces the Illinois site for C-D. Redrawn from ReVelle et al. (1991).

Barnwell, SC. This configuration, with a further change in routing, minimizes the ton-miles objective at Point D.

As analysts, we strive to solve decision problems in a systematic, sensible, repeatable, and defensible manner. This becomes a tall order to fill as the complexity of a decision problem and the number of stakeholders increases. Each party with an interest in the outcome of the decision may advocate a unique set of desirable objectives (see the discussion on negotiation in Section 15.4).

Multiobjective programming and multiple-criteria decision-making techniques can be used to analyze decision problems with more than one objective. The significant feature of MOP and MCDM is that there is no need to convert objectives into a common metric such as dollars. Analysts and decision makers are able to focus their efforts on creating an accurate and complete representation of the decision problem. Using MOP, nondominated alternative solutions are generated independent of the stakeholders' preferences for the importance of the various criteria. The tradeoffs between the objectives for the alternative solutions are explicitly quantified as a result of the analysis. In other words, the decision makers can see exactly what they must give up and what they get with each alternative solution. Using MCDM, the decision makers can invoke their preferences for the various objectives to identify a final preferred solution without the need to convert all the objectives to a common metric such as dollars.

Real-world decision problems are not always readily classified between those appropriate for MOP analysis and those appropriate for MCDM analysis. In fact, it is possible to state almost any decision problem in the format appropriate for either MOP or MCDM methods. The choice of the right analysis method can be based on the analyst's prior experience with the techniques and/or the decision makers' desired results from the analysis. If resources permit, it can often be desirable to compare the results of two or more methods.

REFERENCES

Ananda, J. and G. Herath (2005). "Evaluating Public Risk Preferences in Forest Land-Use Choices Using Multi-Attribute Utility Theory," *Ecological Economics*, 55(3), pp. 408–419.

Brans, J.P. (1982). "L'ingénierie de la Décision: Élaboration d'Instruments d'Aide à la Décision, La Méthode PROMETHEE," in R. Nadeau and M. Landry (eds.), *L'aide à la Décision: Nature, Instruments et Perspectives d'Avenir*, Presses de l'Université Laval, pp. 183–213.

Cohon, J.L. (2003). *Multiobjective Programming and Planning*, Dover Press (originally published by Academic Press in 1978), 333pp.

Cohon, J. and K. Rothley (1997). "Multiobjective Methods," in C. ReVelle and A.E. McGarity (eds.), *Design and Operation of Civil and Environmental Engineering Systems*, Wiley, 752pp.

Connolly, T., H.R. Arkes, and K.R. Hammond (eds.) (2000). *Judgment and Decision Making: An Interdisciplinary Reader*, Cambridge University Press, 786pp.

Dawes, R.M. (1988). *Rational Choice in an Uncertain World*, Harcourt Brace Jovanovich, 346pp.

Derbyshire, R. (2013). "Wine Tasting: It's Junk Science," *Guardian*, June 22. Available at: www.theguardian.com/lifeandstyle/2013/jun/23/wine-tasting-junk-science-analysis.

Dyer, J.S. (1990). "Remarks on the Analytic Hierarchy Process," *Management Science*, *36*(3), pp. 249–258.

(2005). "Chapter 7: MAUT: Multiattribute Utility Theory," in J. Figueira, S. Greco, and M. Ehrgott (eds.), *Multiple Criteria Decision Analysis: State of the Art Surveys*, *78*, Springer, pp. 225–295.

Edwards, W. and J.R. Newman (1982). *Multiattribute Evaluation*, Sage Publications, 96pp. Reprinted as "Chapter 1: Multiattribute Evaluation," in T. Connolly, H.R. Arkes, and K.R. Hammond (eds.), *Judgment and Decision Making: An Interdisciplinary Reader*, Cambridge University Press, pp. 17–34, 2000.

Greco, S., M. Ehrgott, and J.R. Figueira (eds.) (2016). *Multiple Criteria Decision Analysis: State of the Art Surveys*, *233*, Springer, 1347pp.

Gass, S.I. (2005). "Model World: The Great Debate – MAUT versus AHP," *Interfaces*, *35*(4), pp. 308–312.

Hodgson, R.T. (2008). "An Examination of Judge Reliability at a Major U.S. Wine Competition," *Journal of Wine Economics*, *3*(2), pp. 105–113.

Keeney, R.L. (1977). "A Utility Function for Examining Policy Affecting Salmon on the Skeena River," *Journal of the Fisheries Board of Canada*, *34*(1), pp. 49–63.

(1980). "Chapter 7: Evaluating Site Impacts," in *Siting Energy Facilities*, Academic Press, 413pp.

(1992). *Value Focused Thinking: A Path to Creative Decisionmaking*, Harvard University Press, 416pp.

Keeney, R.L. and H. Raiffa (1976). *Decisions with Multiple Objectives: Preferences and Value Tradeoffs*, Wiley, 569pp.

Keeney, R.L., O. Renn, and D. von Winterfeldt (1987). "Structuring Germany's Energy Objectives," *Energy Policy*, *13*, pp. 352–362.

Koksalan, M., J. Wallenius, and S. Zionts (2011). *Multiple Criteria Decision Making: From Early History to the 21st Century*, World Scientific, 197pp.

McDaniels, T.L. (1996). "A Multiattribute Index for Evaluating Environmental Impacts of Electric Utilities," *Journal of Environmental Management*, *46*, pp. 57–66.

ReVelle, C., J.L. Cohon, and D. Shobrys (1991). "Simultaneous Siting and Routing in the Disposal of Hazardous Wastes," *Transportation Science*, *25*(2), pp. 138–145.

Ridgley, M.A. and F.R. Rijsberman (1992). "Multicriteria Evaluation in a Policy Analysis of a Rhine Estuary," *Journal of the American Water Resources Association*, *28*(6), pp. 1095–1110.

Roy, B. (1968). "Classement et Choix en Présence de Points de Vue Multiples (La Méthode ELECTRE)," *La Revue d'Informatique et de Recherche Opérationelle*, *8*, pp. 57–75.

Saaty, T.L. (1977). "A Scaling Method for Priorities in Hierarchical Structures," *Journal of Mathematical Psychology*, *15*, pp. 234–281.

(1980). *The Analytic Hierarchy Process: Planning, Priority Setting, Resource Allocation*, McGraw-Hill, 287pp.

(1994). "How to Make a Decision: The Analytical Hierarchy Process," *Interfaces*, *24*(6), pp. 19–43.

Steuer, R. (1986). *Multiple Criteria Optimization: Theory, Computation, and Application*, Wiley, 546pp.

Tanaka, J.W. and T. Curran (2001). "A Neural Basis for Expert Object Recognition," *Psychological Science*, *12*(1), pp. 43–47.

Torrance, G.W., M.H. Boyle, and S.P. Horwood (1982). "Application of Multi-Attribute Utility Theory to Measure Social Preferences for Health States," *Operations Research*, *30*(6), pp. 1043–1069.

7

Preferences over Time and across Space

In both public and private life, and in much policy analysis, it is often necessary to make judgments about the value of events or outcomes, including benefits and costs, that occur at different moments in time or in different parts of the world. However, the more carefully we look at some of these judgment tasks, the more complicated they become.

There are straightforward methods that are appropriate to use when choosing between financial payments or expenses that involve modest amounts and times. But suppose the judgment involves something that will benefit our grandchildren, or their grandchildren, or the grandchildren of someone we don't even know. Or suppose the cost or the benefit involves someone from a completely different culture who lives in some distant part of the world – either today, or perhaps in the distant future. A few moments of thought will probably persuade most readers that it is not appropriate to use the same strategies to make judgments about those situations as one uses to choose between things like modest financial investments or payments that occur over the course of a few years.

I start the chapter with a consideration of the simple case in which: all costs and benefits are monetary; they are spread out over a fixed time interval that is short compared with the life of the decision maker; they all occur in the decision maker's region of interest; there are no significant uncertainties; and other investment opportunities are not changing. In the chapter's later sections, I discuss a number of situations in which these conditions are not true, with the result that the application of conventional strategies is less appropriate.

7.1 A SIMPLE EXAMPLE OF WHEN TIME DIFFERENCES DO AND DO NOT MATTER

Consider the following simple example. On day zero, you get a call from a non-profit organization in another part of the country that wants to hire you to do a quick consulting job. You really like this NGO and are prepared to do the job for a modest fee. You go online and buy a round-trip airplane ticket for $350. Bright and early on day one, you take a cab to the airport for a cost of $50. When you arrive, you take a free hotel bus to a hotel just across the street from the organization you have come to help. You work there for the next three days. Meals and other expenses are either covered by the organization you are helping or billed to your hotel room. On the morning of the third day, you check out of the hotel, pay your $626 hotel bill, work the balance of the day, and then fly home. You take the $50 cab back to where you live. On the way home, you see on your cellphone that the organization has just electronically transferred your $3000 consulting fee to your checking account. These costs and benefits are displayed along a timeline on the left side of Figure 7.1, in which costs are shown as vectors pointing down and income (i.e., benefits) is shown as vectors pointing up. What is the net economic value to you of this three-day job? You are probably content to compute it as:

Airplane ticket	–350
Airport transport	–50
Hotel bill	–626
Airport transport	–50
Consulting fee	+3000
Net dollar value	+1924

Now consider a second example in which the amounts of money are much larger and the time interval stretches beyond a short period.[1] In this case, it is important to consider the *time value of money*.

Why is a dollar today worth more than a dollar in a few years' time? The simple answer is that I could invest today's dollar, D, in some safe interest-bearing instrument and earn compound interest. If by year t I could have earned an amount of interest I_t, then a payment or cost at that future time t must be equal to $D + I_t$ if it is to have the same present value to me as D has today.

Suppose that a real estate development company is going to build a new office building. The project will be completed in four years, at the end of which time they will sell the building to a client for $300 million dollars. At the beginning of the project in year zero, the company makes a payment of $35 million to the contractor who will be doing the construction work. At the end of year zero, they make payments totaling $5 million for architects, lawyers, and similar costs. At the end of year two, they make a second, larger payment of $62.6 million to the contractor when the building is completed. They don't actually receive the $300-million-dollar payment from the new building

[1] What constitutes "short" depends of course on how much money is involved. Financial companies that handle transactions of many millions of dollars every day arrange to earn interest on money they handle even for a fraction of a day.

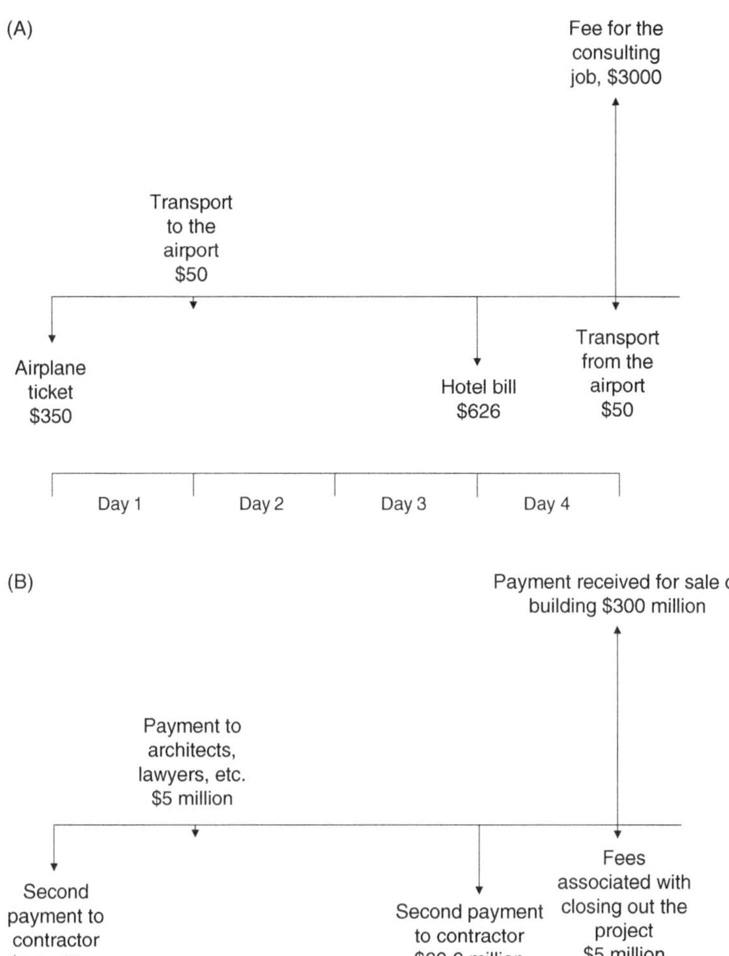

FIGURE 7.1. **A.** Illustration of the costs and benefits along a timeline for the three-day NGO consulting job described in the text. Because the duration of the project is short and the amounts of money involved are modest, you are probably willing to just add up the costs and the payments and say that the dollar value of the job is $1924. **B.** In the case of this real estate development project, which involves much larger amounts of money over a much longer period of time, you would not want to value the project by simply adding up the costs and the payments to compute a value for the project of $192 million. Rather, as described in the text, you would want to discount the future costs and payments using a market interest rate (5% in this example) in order to compute a net present value of $150 million.

owners until the end of year three, at which time they have final legal and other expenses of $5 million. The timeline for this project is shown in Figure 7.1B.

Because both the amounts are so much larger and the time involved so much longer, in this case you would not want to value the project at $192.4 million dollars. Rather, if the guaranteed market rate of interest is 5 percent (compounded annually), you would want to compute the net present dollar value of the project as follows (all values are in millions of dollars):

1st payment to contractor	–35.0	–35.0
Expenses at end of year 1	–5/(1.05) =	–4.8
2nd payment to contractor at the end of year 3	–62.6/(1.05*1.05*1.05) =	–54.1
Expenses at the end of year 4	–50/(1.05*1.05*1.05*1.05) =	–4.1
Sale at end of year 4	+300/(1.05*1.05*1.05*1.05) =	+247.9
	Net present dollar value	+150.0

To generalize, the present or discounted value P of a future amount V after n years is:

$$p = \frac{V_n}{(1+r)^n}$$

where r is the annual rate of compound interest.

Pannell (2006) observes that:

Applied economists typically use a set of simplifying assumptions when applying discounting methods, including the following:

- The discount rate is the actual or implied rate of interest on a financial instrument, commonly a bank account.
- The discount rate is constant over time.
- Tax is not relevant.
- Risk is not relevant, or is included in the discount rate.
- Inflation rates on price of inputs and outputs are identical and constant.
- Productivity growth over time is zero.

Of course, if one is prepared to complicate the analysis, it is not necessary to make any of these assumptions. In an example involving weed management in Australian agriculture, Pannell (2006) has illustrated how a number of these assumptions can be relaxed. When he adds progressively a consideration of taxes, trends in crop yields, and changes in real output prices, the rank ordering among three different future weed management strategies he has analyzed varies dramatically.

Most private commercial decision makers, making decisions in a market economy, would want to use a market discount rate in making their investment decisions. As the discussion later in this chapter makes clear, the situation is considerably more complicated in the case of public-sector decisions. If market rates were applied in such circumstances, society might never choose to build large capital-intensive infrastructure projects such as a subway system, which have large up-front costs and whose benefits accrue over decades or centuries.

While many policy analyses use a single discount rate and use it to compute a project's net present value (NPV), things can get more complicated depending on factors such as the excess social cost of forgone private investment, and how project financing is organized (Feldstein and others in Layard, 1972; Au and Au, 1983).

7.2 EXPONENTIAL DISCOUNTING IN THE EVALUATION OF PROJECTS AND INVESTMENT OPPORTUNITIES

There are a variety of standard formulas used to compute cash flow for the case of compounding done at the end of fixed time periods. These can be found on a variety of websites and in many handbooks of mathematical tables and formulas as well as in basic texts (see, for example, table 2.3 in Park, 2011). Such formulas can be useful if you are doing a lot of engineering economic calculations, but specialized versions can get pretty complicated and confusing.

In doing policy analysis, if one is going to use exponential discounting, an issue that inevitably arises is what rate to employ. Henderson and Bateman (1995) describe the choice as follows:

> The two major numeraires suggested are the opportunity cost of capital ... and the consumption rate of interest. Unfortunately ... the cost of borrowing capital differs among individuals, firms and governments, as do returns on saving. As neither capital nor resources are perfectly mobile, in theory a government must bear in mind that the true opportunity cost of capital varies among economic sectors. If the consumption rate of interest is relevant, whose is it to be? The rate differs among individuals depending on whether they are savers or borrowers ... [indeed a single individual may] simultaneously [be] a borrower and a saver at various real interest rates.

Several authors (Lind, 1982; Lyon, 1990; Henderson and Bateman, 1995) have noted that over time, U.S. government agencies have used rates that range from 2 percent to 12 percent. In 1972, during the Nixon Administration, OMB directed all federal agencies to use a rate of 10 percent. The 1992 revision of OMB Circular A-94 advises:[2]

> The proper discount rate to use depends on whether the benefits and costs are measured in real or nominal terms.
>
> 1. A real discount rate that has been adjusted to eliminate the effect of expected inflation should be used to discount constant-dollar or real benefits and costs.

[2] This circular, titled "Guidelines and Discount Rates for Benefit-Cost Analysis of Federal Programs," is available online at: www.whitehouse.gov/omb/circulars_a094. In addition to discussing discount rates, the circular also provides very detailed instructions on how government agencies should perform benefit–cost analysis.

A real discount rate can be approximated by subtracting expected inflation from a nominal interest rate.
2. A nominal discount rate that reflects expected inflation should be used to discount nominal benefits and costs. Market interest rates are nominal interest rates in this sense.

The circular goes on to argue that a base case analysis should use a 7 percent rate and that sensitivity analysis should then be conducted around that value.

While the convention in most analysis is to use discrete end-of-period compounding, in order to develop an intuitive understanding of time value and discounting, I find it more convenient and informative to adopt a continuous rather than a discretized perspective.[3] If compounding is done on a continuous basis (as opposed to doing it only at the end of discrete time intervals), the NPV of a stream of cash flow is:

$$P = \int_0^\infty \delta(t_i) V(t_i) e^{-rt} dt$$

where $\delta(t_i)$ is a unit delta function at time t_i, $V(t_i)$ is the value of some future cost or benefit that occurs at time t_i, and r is the "discount rate" per unit of time t. Figure 7.2 shows this graphically.

The interest rate that brings the present value of all the positive and negative cash flows along a timeline to zero is termed the "internal rate of return" or IRR. While IRR is sometimes used as a measure in valuing projects, Au and Au (1983) argue that the approach is easily misused and that it is better to use present value or B–C methods in evaluating projects.

Because of its correspondence with the value over time of a safe interest-bearing investment, exponential discounting is most commonly, and appropriately, used in performing economic evaluations of projects that are to be developed over modest periods of time (years to decades) or other similar investment opportunities. However, if a decision maker's preferences across future cash flows (or other benefits and costs) are not analogous to that represented by an interest-bearing investment, there is no inherent reason why the weighting function must be an exponential. For example, if one wants a simple but perhaps more behaviorally realistic mathematical model of time preference, in which the value of the weighting function falls rapidly in the near term, and then less rapidly than exponential in the longer term, one can use "hyperbolic discounting" (see Section 7.8). Going still further, in his work on multi-attribute utility (Chapter 6), Keeney (1980) suggests that time be made an attribute, over which a utility function can be constructed to value outcomes

[3] The discretized version is $P = \sum_{k=1}^{n} \frac{v_k}{(1+i)^k}$.

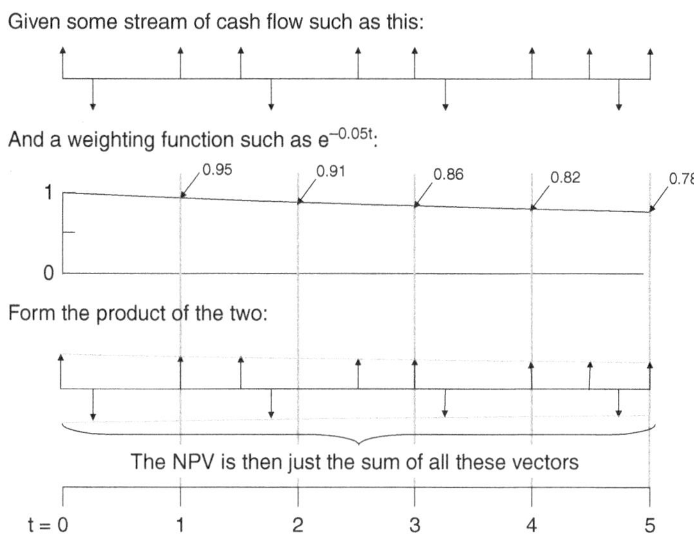

FIGURE 7.2. The present value of a timeline of positive and negative cash flow (above) can be obtained by multiplying it by some appropriate weighting function (in this case $e^{-0.05t}$) and then summing the resulting vectors.

in whatever way a decision maker wishes as a function of when in the future they occur.

SUGGESTED RESOURCES TO LEARN TECHNICAL DETAILS ABOUT ENGINEERING-ECONOMIC ANALYSIS

For a widely used basic text with many basic formulas, worked examples, and advice on using standard computer packages, see:

- Chan S. Park, *Contemporary Engineering Economics*, Prentice Hall, 936pp., 2011. Park has also prepared a companion volume of case studies that provides more detailed worked examples.

For a somewhat more advanced and philosophical treatment, see:

- Tung Au and Thomas Au, *Engineering Economics for Capital Investment Analysis*, Allyn & Bacon, 506pp., 1983.

A valuable resource, originally published jointly with Tung Au and now available for free on the Web, is:

- Chris Hendrickson, *Fundamental Concepts for Owners, Engineers, Architects and Builders*. Available at: http://pmbook.ce.cmu.edu.

7.3 THE ORTHODOXY OF EXPONENTIAL DISCOUNTING

In a classic paper, Samuelson (1937) laid out four assumptions under which it is "possible to arrive theoretically at a precise measure of the marginal utility of *money income* to an individual whose tastes maintain a certain invariance throughout the time under consideration, and during which time the prices of all goods remain constant." Koopmans (1960) and later Bleichrodt et al. (2008) subsequently developed and refined such a preference axiomatization for discounted utility.

It is important to note that when he first advanced his formulation, Samuelson was careful to identify and discuss several serious limitations. He wrote, "it is completely arbitrary to assume that the individual behaves so as to maximize an integral of the form $[J = \int_0^b V(x,t)dt]$." Doing this

> involves the assumption that at every instant of time the individual's satisfaction depends only upon the consumption at that time, and that, furthermore, the individual tries to maximise the sum of instantaneous satisfactions reduced to some comparable base by time discount. As has been suggested ... we might assume that the individual maximizes an integral which contains not only consumption per unit time but also the rate of change of consumption per unit time, and higher derivatives.

He notes further:

> that our equations hold only for an individual who is deciding at the beginning of the period how he will allocate his expenditures over the period. Actually, however, as the individual moves along in time there is a sort of perspective phenomenon in that his view of the future in relation to his instantaneous time position remains invariant, rather than his evaluation of any particular year.

And he concludes that "any connection between utility as discussed here and any welfare concept is disavowed. The idea that the results of such a statistical investigation could have any influence upon ethical judgments of policy is one which deserves the impatience of modern economists." Unfortunately, too many later analysts have overlooked these wise, cautionary words.

7.4 THE USE OF REAL OPTIONS AS AN ALTERNATIVE TO NET PRESENT VALUE

Evaluating a project in terms of its NPV is fine so long as the function it will serve and the environment in which it will operate is not likely to change very much over the project's lifetime.

When that is not the case, a thoughtful decision maker might decide to design the project so that its function will be "robust" in the face of changing future needs and environment.[4] That, of course, can be quite expensive, and if

[4] For a discussion of strategies for robust decision making, see Lempert et al. (2006).

the future is very uncertain, may not end up serving adequately future needs. An alternative is to make smaller investments now that create the "option" of making additional investments in the future that allow new functions as needs and the environment change.

A simple example is a new multi-story building. Suppose that, at the moment, I think I only need five stories. Rather than designing the foundation and the structural elements to support only five stories, I might choose to install a foundation and structural elements that would allow the later addition of several more floors. If I do that, I have bought a "real option" for future expansion. I have no obligation to "exercise" that option, and I may never use it, but the modest investment made now allows me future flexibility that I would otherwise not enjoy.

Greg Hertzler (2006) summarizes:

> the net present value criteria is inadequate for evaluating long-term investments under risk. Adjusting the discount rate can lead to worse, rather than better decisions. Instead, another criteria is needed. Real options theory generalizes the net present value criteria for highly random and nonlinear systems with possibly irreversible outcomes ... Option values can now be calculated for most systems ... are time consistent and can be much larger than a net present value ... Option values are also a way to implement the precautionary principle of environmental management and invest for the long-term future.

Other than to mention this alternative, this book is not the place to elaborate the details of how to implement these ideas. Readers who would like to learn more would be well advised to start with Richard de Neufville and Stefan Scholtes' book, *Flexibility in Engineering Design* (2011), which, as they explain:

> focuses on the challenge of creating best value in large-scale, long-lasting projects. It does this by directly confronting the central problem of design: the difficulty in knowing what to build, at what time. Indeed, to get the best value, we need to have the right facilities in place, when we need them. However, we cannot know what will happen in the future. No matter how hard we try to predict long-term requirements, the forecast is "always wrong." Trends change, surprises occur.

De Neufville and Scholtes discuss strategies for estimating the distribution of future possibilities in complex projects; ways to identify candidate flexibilities that may prove most useful and add value to a project; effective ways to evaluate and select preferred designs; and ways in which to implement effectively flexibility in project design.

Secomandi and Seppi (2014) have applied real options to value what they term "commodity conversion assets." These are devices and systems that deal with the "production, refining, industrial and commercial consumption, and distribution of physical commodities and energy sources such as grains, metals, electricity, coal, crude oil, and natural gas." In order to maximize the market value of commodity conversion assets, they use models of the evolution of commodity prices together with stochastic optimization models of the conversion activities. They observe that "the existence of traded contracts on commodities and energy sources allows commodity conversion assets to be interpreted as real options on the prices of the underlying commodity." They note that real options differ from financial options in a number of ways that may include: decisions at multiple dates; intertemporal linkages across decisions; multiple underlying variables; payoffs determined by operational costs and contractual provisions; engineering-based constraints on operating decisions; and/or quantity decisions rather than binary exercise/no-exercise decisions.

7.5 THE PURE RATE OF TIME PREFERENCE (PRTP) AND THE CONSUMPTION DISCOUNT RATE (CDR)

The modern literature on time value differentiates between two factors: the pure rate of time preference (PRTP) and the consumption discount rate (CDR). Heal (2009) explains:

The PRTP is the δ in the expression

$$\int_0^\infty u(c_t)e^{-\delta t}dt$$

where c_t is aggregate consumption at time t, u is a utility function showing strictly diminishing returns to consumption and we are summing discounted utility over all remaining time. The other discount rate concept, the CDR, is the rate of change of the present value of the marginal utility of consumption, that is, the rate of change of

$$e^{-\delta t}\frac{du(c_t)}{dc_t}$$

Considering the case of the consumption of a single good, the discount factor should then be written as:[5]

$$\rho_t = \delta + \eta(c_t)R(c_t)$$

where ρ_t is the consumption discount rate applied to consumption at time t, $\eta(c_t)$ is the elasticity of the marginal utility of consumption, and $R(c_t)$ is the rate of change of consumption at time t.

Heal (2009) explains that the PRTP (δ):

is the rate at which we discount the welfare of future people *just because they are in the future*: it is, if you like, the rate of intergenerational discrimination ... [T]here are

[5] See Heal (2005) for a review of the evolution of economic thought on this formulation which goes back to Ramsey (1928).

at least two reasons why we may wish to value increments of consumption going to different people differently: one is that they live at different times, which is captured by δ, and the other is that they have different income levels ... A PRTP greater than zero lets us value the utility of future people less than that of present people, *just because they live in the future rather than the present*. They are valued differently even if they have the same incomes. Doing this is making the same kind of judgment as one would make if one valued the utility of people in Asia differently from that of people in Africa, except that we are using different dimensions of the space–time continuum as the basis for differentiation ...

That an increment of consumption is less important to a rich person than to a poor person has long been a staple of utilitarian arguments for income redistribution and progressive taxation ..., and is almost universally accepted. This is reflected in the diminishing marginal utility of consumption, and the rate at which marginal utility falls as consumption rises is captured by $\eta(ct)$ ... [The equation] pulls together time preference and distributional judgments: the rate at which the value of an increment of consumption changes over time, the CDR ρt, equals the PRTP δ plus the rate at which the marginal utility of consumption is falling. This latter is the rate at which consumption is increasing.

7.6 DISCOUNT RATES THAT DECLINE OVER TIME

Some have argued that when valuing something that will occur in the far future it is appropriate to use the lowest discount rate that might plausibly apply (Weitzman, 1998). The basic idea is pretty simple. Consider a range of alternative possible distant futures, each of which has with it an associated discount rate. Because the higher rates discount the futures with which they are associated faster, the lowest rate will ultimately predominate.

Several papers (Newell and Pizer, 2003; Groom et al., 2007; Arrow et al., 2013; Freeman et al., 2015) then go on to argue that empirical results from studies of past investment yields should be applied in performing evaluations of things such as social cost of carbon (see Section 3.9).

While some argue that the value of ecosystems is part of consumption, and so is included in the reduced levels of future consumption that are forecast by integrated assessment models, I have great difficulty being persuaded that the costs of dramatic changes in future ecosystems are adequately reflected in estimates of future consumption.[6] Nor do I believe that variation in the yields on U.S. government bonds over the past decades should drive how I value the possibility that 100 years from now the maple, birch, beech, and white pine ecosystem in the New Hampshire countryside may be replaced by an ecosystem of yellow pine and oak.

[6] For a discussion of integrated assessment models, see Section 11.7.

READINGS 7.1

Geoffrey Heal, "The Economics of Climate Change: A Post-Stern Perspective," *Climatic Change, 96*, pp. 275–297, 2009.

Abstract: What have we learned from the outpouring of literature as a result of the Stern Review of the Economics of Climate Change? A lot. We have explored the model space and the parameter space much more thoroughly. The Stern Review has catalyzed a fundamental rethinking of the economic case for action on climate change. We are in a position to give some conditions that are sufficient to provide a case for strong action on climate change, but we need more work before we have a fully satisfactory account of the relevant economics. In particular, we need to understand better how climate change affects natural capital – the natural environment and the ecosystems comprising it – and how this in turn affects human welfare.

Geoffrey M. Heal and Anthony Millner, "Agreeing to Disagree on Climate Policy," *Proceedings of the National Academy of Science*, *111*(10), pp. 3695–3698, 2014.

Abstract: Disagreements about the value of the utility discount rate – the rate at which our concern for the welfare of future people declines with their distance from us in time – are at the heart of the debate about the appropriate intensity of climate policy. Seemingly small differences in the discount rate yield very different policy prescriptions, and no consensus "correct" value has been identified. We argue that the choice of discount rate is an ethical primitive: there are many different legitimate opinions as to its value, and none should receive a privileged place in economic analysis of climate policy. Rather, we advocate a social choice-based approach in which a diverse set of individual discount rates is aggregated into a "representative" rate. We show that performing this aggregation efficiently leads to a time-dependent discount rate that declines monotonically to the lowest rate in the population. We apply this discounting scheme to calculations of the social cost of carbon recently performed by the U.S. government and show that it provides an attractive compromise between competing ethical positions, and thus provides a possible resolution to the ethical impasse in climate change economics.

DISCUSSION QUESTIONS FOR READINGS 7.1

- How is the pure rate of time preference (PRTP) different from the consumption discount rate (CDR)?
- Why is it important to differentiate between the PRTP and the CDR?
- Under what circumstance might it make sense to assign a negative value to the CDR?
- In the "Agreeing to Disagree" paper Heal and Millner write, "although each member of the group has a constant discount rate δ_i the efficient discount rate for the group as a whole is time-dependent and declines monotonically to the lowest rate in the population." Can you provide an intuitive explanation of this result?

- Adopting the axiomatic views very briefly noted in Section 7.4, Heal's formulation accepts an exponential formulation for time preference. As noted in Section 7.2, Keeney has suggested that time preference could be treated as an attribute in a MAUT model, which means that it could have any shape over time someone might choose. For a topic such as climate change, or the risk posed by large earth-intersecting meteors, can you construct an argument to justify some non-exponential formulation?

MORE DETAILS ON DISCOUNTING IN PUBLIC-SECTOR DECISION MAKING

In the late 1970s and early 1980s, a group of economists embarked on a multi-year project that included an expert conference in March 1977 and the publication of a 468-page book, all focused on the question, "What discount rate should be used to evaluate national energy options and policies?" The underlying assumption of most of this work is that such choices should be made using exponential discounting and the issue is how to choose the "correct" rate. An excellent summary of the issues can be found in:
Robert C. Lind, "Chapter 2: A Primer on the Major Issues Relating to the Discount Rate for Evaluating National Energy Options," pp. 21–94 in Robert C. Lind et al. (eds.), *Discounting for Time and Risk in Energy Policy*, RFF Press, 468pp., 1982.
Lind argues that five factors should enter the decision:

> 1) the social rate of time preference, which is the rate at which society is willing to exchange consumption now for consumption in the future; 2) the consumption rate of interest, which is the rate at which individual consumers are willing to exchange consumption now for consumption in the future; 3) the marginal rate of return on investment in the private sector; 4) the opportunity cost of a public investment, that is, the value of the private investment and consumption forgone as a result of the investment; and 5) risk, which is related to the degree to which variation in the outcome of a public project will affect variation in the payoff from the nation's total assets.

After an extended and most interesting discussion of all these issues, Lind concludes that as of 1982 the social discount rate should be between 2 and 4.6 percent.

Another round of intense discourse about the "correct" rate followed in the late 1990s and the subsequent decades, motivated by concerns about how to deal with time preference in policy decisions related to climate change. Interested readers can find summaries of much of this discourse in:
Paul R. Portney and John Weyant (eds.), *Discounting and Intergenerational Equity*, RFF Press, 186pp., 1999.

The several reports of the IPCC have contained increasingly sophisticated discussions of time preference and a variety of other critical topics. For the discussion by Working Group III in the Fifth Assessment Report, see: "Chapter 3: Social, Economic and Ethical Concepts and Methods," 128pp. in the draft report of Working Group III, Mitigation of Climate Change, IPCC 2014. Available for download at http://mitigation2014.org/report/final-draft.

I find it notable, however, that while the work of Frederick, Loewenstein, and O'Donoghue (Section 7.7) is finally cited in this discussion, which is *much* improved over previous IPCC reports, none of the work of Geoffrey Heal is cited.[7]

7.7 EMPIRICAL STUDIES OF THE TIME PREFERENCES THAT PEOPLE DISPLAY: A LOOK AHEAD TO PART III

Would you and your significant other prefer to enjoy a very fine dinner at a fancy restaurant this weekend and another one in two weeks, or would you prefer to have them both this weekend? Assuming that you can estimate your utility for a fine dinner with your significant other, conventional exponential discounting would have you choosing more now over a pattern of consumption that is spread out over time. However, under many circumstances you would probably choose the first option – that is stretching things out.

There are many such cases in the literature on behavioral social science. These results suggest that in many situations people do not adopt some simple exponential or other function to weight outcomes that will occur at different future moments. Further, if one assumed that they did, Figure 7.3, prepared by Frederick et al. (2002), makes it pretty clear that there is a wide variation in the implicit values used.

We will explore these issues at greater length in Part III. For the moment, simply be warned that assertions, such as the following by Viscusi (1992), should be taken with a very large grain of salt.

> Chief among the results is that the estimated implicit rate of discount that workers use in valuing death risks does not differ in a statistically significant manner from the prevailing rates of return in financial markets during the time periods under study. Thus, there is no evidence to indicate that we should use a different rate of discount when weighting the long-term health benefits of policies that affect life extension as compared with other benefit and cost components that these policies may have. An appropriate *real* rate of return based on market interest rates is a reasonable starting point for this procedure.

Cooper et al. (1994) note that many life-saving programs save lives in the future (and save the lives of people of varying ages). In a telephone survey of 3000

[7] The Carnegie Mellon Center for Climate and Energy Decision Making supported the Frederick et al. work in order to get it into the hands of the authors of the IPCC fourth assessment, but unfortunately that assessment did not cite it.

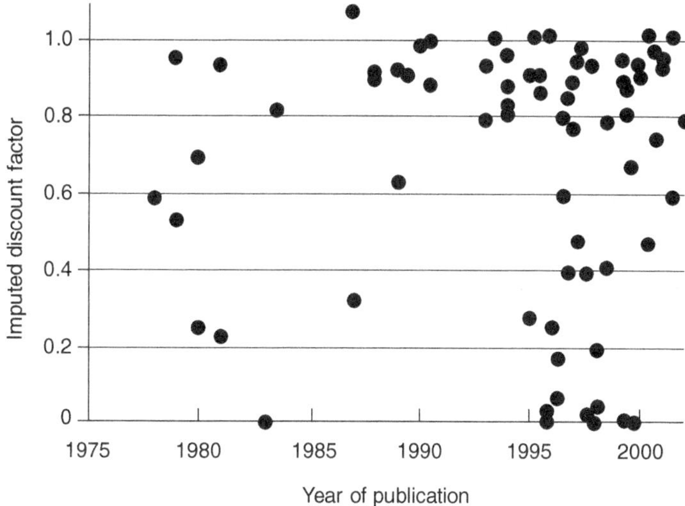

FIGURE 7.3. Published values of discount factors reported in behavioral studies plotted by year of publication. Figure modified from Frederick et al. (2002).

members of the public, they asked respondents to make choices between pairs of hypothetical life-saving programs that saved different numbers of people at different future moments (or different people of different ages[8]). They report that for periods of 5–10 years, respondents' "discount rate for lives saved is almost as high as their discount rate for money." They find a median discount rate of 19.8 percent, which would "require that 2.3 lives be saved five years from now for every life saved today." Over that same period, respondents displayed preferences for money that imply a median discount rate of 20 percent.

When they extend their questions to longer periods, they observe lower discount rates. For example, they report "that 44 lives [must] be saved 100 years from now for every life saved today, implying a discount rate of 3.4% for a 100 year time horizon."[9] If Cooper et al.'s respondents were using exponential discounting, the same discount rates would apply for both 5–10 years and for 50–100 years. The fact that they observe a discount rate that falls as the time interval grows longer is similar to the findings in many other behavioral studies. Such findings have given rise to proposals to use "hyperbolic discounting."

[8] Here our focus is on time preference. On the subject of valuing deaths that occur at different ages, Cooper et al., for example, report that for their median respondent, "saving one 20-year-old is equivalent to saving seven 60-year-olds."

[9] Respondents gave a variety of arguments for preferring to save lives today rather than in the future, of which the three most common were "technological progress provides means to save people in the future" (23% for 5–10 years and 31% for 50–100 years), one should live day-by-day (21% for 5–10 years and 32% for 50–100 years), and "the future is uncertain" (21% for 5–10 years and 15% for 50–100 years).

7.8 HYPERBOLIC DISCOUNTING

Henderson and Bateman (1995) have built on Cooper et al.'s (1994) results and explored their implications. They fit a hyperbolic discount model to the Cooper et al. data, of the form:

$$DF_t = \frac{1}{(1 + r_h t)}$$

where DF_t is the discount factor at time t, t is time in years, and r_h is the (hyperbolic) discount rate. Fitting this model to the data, they obtain a value for r_h of 0.21 with an adjusted R^2 of 99.6. Figure 7.4 compares this result with exponential functions that range from 2 percent to 20 percent. They then provide a thoughtful discussion of the difference between using exponential and hyperbolic discounting for evaluating projects of varying duration. They note that if the Cooper et al. results were interpreted as a true indication of social preference, then for a project of 25 years' duration, an exponential discount rate of 10 percent would be a reasonable choice (i.e., has minimal variation for this hyperbolic function) while an exponential rate of 7 percent would be a better choice for a project with a 100-year duration. They offer this only as an example, noting that there has been insufficient work on eliciting the value of r_h in various contexts.

Henderson and Bateman (1995) conclude that, "at least in the case of lives saved, discounting may be hyperbolic." They go on to note that:

> The necessarily exponential nature of opportunity cost of capital numeraires has perhaps blinded economists to the possibility that the social discount rate may not be exponential. Among behaviorists, however, empirical results have led to standard formulas that are hyperbolic.
>
> In practical cost-benefit analysis the issue is most acute where projects are of an intergenerational nature. However, [there are] enough empirical data to suggest that a definitive shape for the social discount factor curve does not yet exist. If indeed the social discount rate is hyperbolic, the discount rate r_h may be expected to vary over time and across economies for the same reasons that r [the exponential rate] varies ... For intergenerational cost-benefit analysis we suggest adding hyperbolic discount rate results to the normal framework of classical exponential discount rate sensitivity analysis, such that the recognition remains that no single discount rate, hyperbolic or classical, is uniquely correct.

For a discussion of some of the complications and an illustration of how complicated things can become in dealing with time varying discount rates, see Karp (2007).

In a paper titled "Cooperating with the Future," Hauser et al. (2014) have explored the circumstances under which individuals are likely to make consumption choices today at the expense of future generations (i.e., implicitly adopting a high discount rate) and when they are more likely to give serious

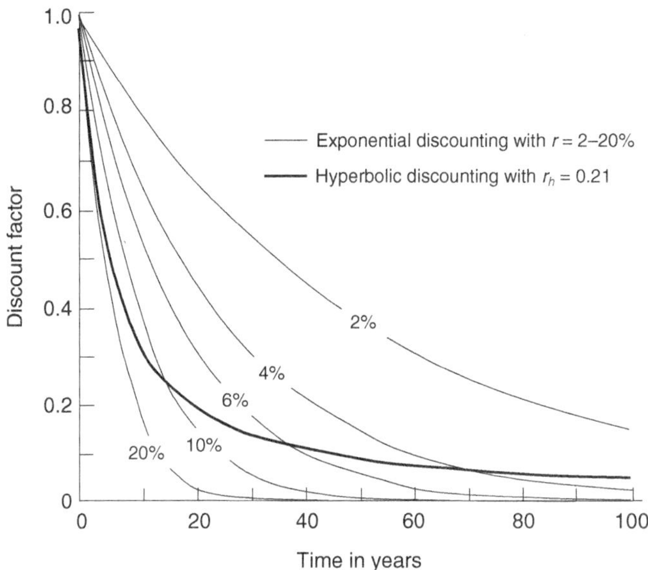

FIGURE 7.4. Comparison of hyperbolic discount inferred from Cooper et al. (1994) with various rates of exponential discounting. Figure modified from Henderson and Bateman (1995).

consideration to future generations in making consumption and similar decisions today. To explore this question they have created an "Intergenerational Goods Game." They report that in that game:

a line-up of successive groups (generations) can each either extract a resource to exhaustion or leave something for the next group. Exhausting the resource maximizes the payoff for the present generation, but leaves all future generations empty-handed ... [We find] that the resource is almost always destroyed if extraction decisions are made individually. This failure to cooperate with the future is driven primarily by a minority of individuals who extract far more than what is sustainable. In contrast, when extractions are democratically decided by vote, the resource is consistently sustained. Voting ... is effective for two reasons. First, it allows a majority of cooperators to restrain defectors. Second, it reassures conditional cooperators ... that their efforts are not futile. Voting, however, only promotes sustainability if it is binding for all involved.

7.9 PREFERENCES THAT CHANGE OVER TIME

March (1978) identifies another problem that arises if an individual's preferences change over time:

If ... we think of the individual as having a distinct, complete and consistent preference relation defined over the outcomes realized in a particular time period, and we imagine that these preferences change over time, then the problem of intertemporal comparisons is more difficult. The problem is technically indistinguishable from the problem of interpersonal comparisons of utilities. When we compare the change in preferences of a single person over time to make tradeoffs across time, we are in the identical position as when we attempt to make comparisons across different individuals at a point in time.

Addressing this same issue, Frederick et al. (2002) write:

A person with time-inconsistent preferences may or may not be aware that her preferences will change over time ... At one extreme, a person could be completely "naïve" and believe that her future preferences will be identical to her current preferences. At the other extreme, a person could be completely "sophisticated" and correctly predict how her preferences will change over time. While casual observation and introspection suggest that people lie somewhere in between these two extremes, behavioral evidence regarding the degree of awareness is quite limited.

We all know the Greek myth of Odysseus asking his crew to tie him to the mast as the ship passed the Sirens so that he would not steer on to the rocks. In that case, Odysseus knew what his future preferences would be and concluded that he should take steps to bind his future actions today, having made the judgment that his present preferences were superior to those that would apply at that moment in the future.

However, in less stark circumstances the situation is far less clear. As individuals and as organizations we learn over time through experience. As March notes, in such circumstances the problem of comparing preferences across time becomes much more challenging, especially if we cannot be certain about how those future preferences will evolve.

7.10 HOW DIFFERENT ARE SPACE AND TIME?

Boroditsky (2000) has shown that there are similarities in the way in which people think about space and time. She has shown that people sometimes use concrete spatial metaphors to understand the more abstract idea of time. Arguing in the other direction, Schelling (1995) has observed that:

Actually, time may serve as a kind of measure of "distance." The people who are going to be living in 2150 I may consider "farther away" than the people who will be living in 2050. They will also be different in racial composition and geographical distribution from the people I most identify with. I observe that in redistributing income via transfer payments, in providing foreign aid, in contributing to charity etc., people are expected to differentiate, and do differentiate, among recipient peoples according to several kinds of distance or proximity. One is geographical: Americans are expected to be more interested in their own cities than in distant cities, their own country than distant countries. Another is political: East Coast Americans are more interested in the people of Los Angeles than in the people of Quebec. Another is cultural: some people are closer in language, religion, and other kinds of heritage. Sheer familiarity seems to matter, and of course kinship does. (Kinship distance has both horizontal and vertical dimensions; just as children are closer than grandchildren, children are closer than nieces and nephews. Time just happens to correlate with vertical distance.)

To be less interested in the welfare of East Africans than former Yugoslavians is less like "discounting" than, perhaps, "depreciating." When we count future welfare less than our own we are depreciating generations that are distant in time, in familiarity, in culture, in kinship, and along other dimensions. (There is no reason to suppose that the depreciation would be exponential. Beyond certain distances there may be no further depreciation for time, culture, geography, race, or kinship.)

In a very similar way, Steininger (2002) notes that:

> We are familiar with the concept of time preference in consumption. Consumption now is preferred over consumption later (our own consumption or analogously consumption by later generations) by a rate which can be measured by the respective partial derivatives ... Similarly, we may prefer consumption at our immediate location to consumption at a distant location (again, either consumption by ourselves or by other people at this distant location). A local consumption increase may be connected to (environmental) costs at a distance ... in optimally evaluating distant costs locally we need to employ a spatial discount factor.

Steininger (2002) has used a contingent valuation approach to assess the case of waste incineration in Austria:

> The issue of waste incineration was thus perfectly available to be used to study the question of spatial preferences of environmental impacts. A questionnaire was sent to 1,100 households in the city of Graz, which were selected on a random basis. Half of them were given the information that the waste incineration in discussion is the one in the city of Graz itself, thus the environmental impact is local ... The other half were given the information that the waste incineration in discussion is to be located at a linear distance of 40 kilometers (within the town of Niklasdorf), however, with the two mountain ranges hindering the exchange of air between this site and the city of Graz ... Both groups were told that the waste incineration plants will be equipped with technology ensuring emission cleaning at the legally required level. However, there is the possibility of installing an additional scrubber for a further cleaning of plant emissions. Both groups were asked ... whether they would vote for such an additional scrubber.

Steininger (2002) concludes:

> Our finding is that indeed there is significant difference between the two subgroups in their willingness to pay. Independent of any natural system emission absorption due to dispersion (as we restrict ourselves to local environmental effects) we find that people do assign less concern to impacts on their neighbours in 40 kilometers distance than to their immediate ones or to themselves. For the fraction of the employed we quantify the private spatial discount rate, with a range for its lower bound between 3.5 and 7.4%. Further, we find that the private spatial discount rate changes with income. A discount rate rising with income implies the poor to be most concerned with the distant.

Hannon (1994) used data developed by Mitchell and Carson (1986) from studies they did of stated public preferences rejecting a hypothetical nuclear power plant and a proposed hypothetical coal-fired power plant to suggest that the percentage of respondents rejecting the plants decreased exponentially with distance from the proposed location. He also used data developed by Colwell et al. (1985) on house prices to assess the effect on housing prices with distance of convenience and noise from a shopping center.

Compared with the enormous literature on time preference, the literature on spatial preference, or, to use Schelling's term, spatial "depreciation," is very sparse. However, in that subset of problems in policy analysis that address a variety of local siting and global issues, it is clearly a topic that deserves very careful consideration.

REFERENCES

Arrow, K., M. Cropper, C. Gollier et al. (2013). "Determining Benefits and Costs for Future Generations," *Science*, *341*, pp. 349–350.

Au, T. and T. Au (1983). *Engineering Economics for Capital Investment Analysis*, Allyn & Bacon, 506pp.

Bleichrodt, H., K.I.M. Rohde, and P.P. Wakker (2008). "Koopmans' Constant Discounting for Intertemporal Choice: A Simplification and a Generalization," *Journal of Mathematical Psychology*, *52*, pp. 341–347.

Boroditsky, L. (2000). "Metaphoric Structuring: Understanding Time through Spatial Metaphors," *Cognition*, *75*, pp. 1–28.

Colwell, P., S. Gujral, and C. Coley (1985). "The Impact of a Shopping Center on the Value of Surrounding Properties," *Real Estate Issues*, *10*(1), pp. 35–39.

Cooper, M.L., A.K. Aydede, and P.R. Portney (1994). "Preferences for Life Saving Programs: How the Public Discounts Time and Age," *Journal of Risk and Uncertainty*, *9*(3), pp. 243–265.

de Neufville, R. and S. Scholtes (2011). *Flexibility in Engineering Design*, MIT Press, 293pp.

Feldstein, M.S. (1972). "The Inadequacy of Weighted Discount Rates," in R. Layard (ed.), *Cost Benefit Analysis*, Penguin Books, pp. 311–331.

Frederick, S., G. Loewenstein, and T. O'Donoghue (2002). "Time Discounting and Time Preference: A Critical Review," *Journal of Economic Literature*, *40*, pp. 351–401.

Freeman, M.C., B. Groom, E. Panopoulou, and T. Pantelidis (2015). "Declining Discount Rates and the Fisher Effect: Inflated Past, Discounted Future," *Journal of Environmental Economics and Management*, *73*, pp. 32–49.

Groom, B., P. Koundouri, E. Panopoulou, and T. Pantelidis (2007). "Discounting the Distant Future: How Much Does Model Selection Affect the Certainty Equivalent Rate?," *Journal of Applied Econometrics*, *22*, pp. 641–656.

Hannon, B. (1994). "Sense of Place: Geographic Discounting by People, Animals and Plants," *Ecological Economics*, *10*, pp. 157–174.

Hauser, O.P., D.G. Rand, A. Peysakhovich, and M.A. Nowak (2014). "Cooperating with the Future," *Nature*, *511*(7508), pp. 220–223.

Heal, G. (2005). "Chapter 12: Intertemporal Welfare Economics and the Environment," in K.-G. Mäler and J.R. Vincent (eds.), *Handbook of Environmental Economics*, Elsevier, pp. 1105–1145.

(2009). "The Economics of Climate Change: A Post-Stern Perspective," *Climatic Change*, *96*, pp. 275–297.

Heal, G.M. and A. Millner (2014). "Agreeing to Disagree on Climate Policy," *Proceedings of the National Academy of Science*, *111*(10), pp. 3695–3698.

Henderson, N. and I. Bateman (1995). "Empirical and Public Choice Evidence for Hyperbolic Social Discount Rates and the Implications of Intergenerational Discounting," *Environmental and Resources Economics*, *5*, pp. 413–423.

Hendrickson, C. (2008). *Fundamental Concepts for Owners, Engineers, Architects and Builders*. Available at: http://pmbook.ce.cmu.edu.

Hertzler, G. (2006). "Chapter 4: Compounding and Discounting under Risk: Net Present Values and Real Option Values," in D.J. Pannell and S.G.M. Schilizzi (eds.), *Economics and the Future: Time and Discounting in Private and Public Decision Making*, Edward Elgar, pp. 37–55.

IPCC (2014). "Chapter 3: Social, Economic and Ethical Concepts and Methods" in the draft report of Working Group III, *Mitigation of Climate Change*, 128pp. Available at: http://mitigation2014.org/report/final-draft.

Karp, L. (2007). "Non-constant Discounting in Continuous Time," *Journal of Economic Theory*, *132*(1), pp. 557–568.

Keeney, R.L. (1980). "Chapter 7: Evaluating Site Impacts," in *Siting Energy Facilities*, Academic Press, 413pp.

Koopmans, T.C. (1960). "Stationary Ordinal Utility and Impatience," *Econometrica*, *28*(2), pp. 287–309.

Layard, R. (ed.) (1972). *Cost Benefit Analysis*, Penguin Books, 496pp.

Lempert, R.J., D.G. Groves, S.W. Popper, and S.C. Bankes (2006). "A General, Analytic Method for Generating Robust Strategies and Narrative Scenarios," *Management Science*, *52*(4), pp. 514–528.

Lind, R.C. (1982). "Introduction," in R.C. Lind, K.J. Arrow, G.R. Corey et al., *Discounting for Time and Risk in Energy Policy*, Johns Hopkins University Press, pp. 1–19.

Lyon, R. (1990). "Federal Discount Rate Policy: The Shadow Price of Capital, and Challenges for Reforms," *Journal of Environmental Economics and Management*, *18*(2), pp. S29–S50.

March, J.G. (1978). "Bounded Rationality, Ambiguity, and the Engineering of Choice," *The Bell Journal of Economics*, *9*(2), pp. 587–608.

Mitchell, R. and R. Carson (1986). "Property Rights, Protest, and the Siting of Hazardous Waste Facilities," Report no. 230, Resources for the Future.

Newell, R.G. and W.A. Pizer (2003). "Regulating Stock Externalities under Uncertainty," *Journal of Environmental Economics and Management*, *45*, pp. 416–432.

Pannell, D.J. (2006). "Chapter 3: Avoiding Simplistic Assumptions in Discounting Cash Flows for Private Decisions," in D.J. Pannell and S.G.M. Schilizzi (eds.), *Economics and the Future: Time and Discounting in Private and Public Decision Making*, Edward Elgar, pp. 25–35.

Park, C.S. (2011). *Contemporary Engineering Economics*, Prentice Hall, 936pp.

Portney, P.R. and Weyant, J. (eds.) (1999). *Discounting and Intergenerational Equity*, RFF Press, 186pp.

Ramsey, F. (1928). "A Mathematical Theory of Saving," *The Economic Journal*, *38*, pp. 543–559.

Samuelson, P. (1937). "A Note on Measurement of Utility," *The Review of Economic Studies*, *4*(2), pp. 155–161.

Schelling, T.C. (1995). "Intergenerational Discounting," *Energy Policy*, *23*, pp. 395–401.

Secomandi, N. and D.J. Seppi (2014). "Real Options and Merchant Operations of Energy and Other Commodities," *Foundations and Trends in Technology, Information and Operations Management*, 6(3–4), pp. 161–331.

Steininger, K. (2002). "Spatial Discounting and the Environment: An Empirical Investigation into Human Preferences," in K. Puttaswamaiah (ed.), *Cost Benefit Analysis: Environmental and Ecological Perspectives*, Transaction Publishers, pp. 253–268.

Viscusi, W.K. (1992). *Fatal Tradeoffs: Public and Private Responsibilities for Risk*, Oxford University Press, 306pp.

Weitzman, M.L. (1998). "Why the Far-Distant Future Should Be Discounted at Its Lowest Possible Rate," *Journal of Environmental Economics and Management*, *36*, pp. 201–208.

PART II

SOME WIDELY USED ANALYSIS TOOLS AND TOPICS

Almost all problems in policy analysis involve uncertainty. However, until the latter part of the twentieth century it was common for policy analysts to largely ignore this fact, use their best estimates of the value of key coefficients, and then perform an analysis that produced a single-value estimate of the "answer." For example, one analyst might say the answer is 8, another might say the answer is 5, and given the absence of any treatment of uncertainty it was often impossible to know if they were saying the same thing or two very different things.

Today there is a well-developed set of tools for dealing with uncertainty in policy analysis. Chapter 8 explores some of these tools and a number of the issues that can arise. One of those issues is the use of expert judgment to obtain quantitative assessments of the value of uncertain quantities using a set of techniques known as "expert elicitation." This topic is explored in Chapter 9.

Most technologies that provide individual and social benefits also carry risks. Hence, it is common for analysts who address issues in science, technology, and public policy to find that they need to perform analysis to assess the nature and magnitude of those risks. This topic of risk analysis is discussed in Chapter 10. Because the equally important topics of risk perception and communication involve human judgment and decision making, a discussion of those topics is postponed until Part III.

The construction and use of many different kinds of models is ubiquitous in the practice of policy analysis. Chapter 11 begins with a brief taxonomy and discussion of such different models and then provides a more extended discussion of issues that can arise when the underlying causal mechanisms and processes being modeled are not well understood and when models are pushed out to, and beyond, their domain of appropriate applicability.

8

Characterizing, Analyzing, and Communicating Uncertainty[1]

Uncertainty is ubiquitous in virtually all fields of human endeavor. As Benjamin Franklin wrote in 1789 in a letter to Jean-Baptiste Leroy, "In this world nothing is certain but death and taxes." And, even in those cases, the timing and nature of the events is often uncertain.

Sometimes uncertainty can be reduced through research. But research can also increase uncertainty when it reveals that we know less about how the world works than we thought we did. While it is important to try to reduce uncertainty when making important decisions, there are many situations in which it is impossible to resolve all-important uncertainties before decisions must be made. In our private lives, we choose where to go to college, what career to pursue, what job to take, whom to marry, whether and when to have children, all in the face of irreducible uncertainty. Similarly, corporations and governments regularly choose what policies to adopt, and where to invest resources, in the face of large and irreducible uncertainty.

In 1990, after a decade of working to develop and demonstrate methods to characterize and deal with uncertainty in risk and other forms of quantitative policy analysis, my colleague Max Henrion and I wrote a book titled *Uncertainty: A Guide to Dealing with Uncertainty in Quantitative Risk and Policy Analysis* (Morgan and Henrion, 1990).[2] Rather than try to condense that book into a single chapter, here I summarize a few key points and then direct the reader to specific chapters in the earlier book for details.

Lest you doubt the importance of considering uncertainty in decision making, consider both a simple private and public example.

[1] Portions of the text in this chapter are derived in edited form from Morgan et al. (2009). My co-authors in that report bear no responsibility for the views expressed in this chapter.

[2] Mitchell Small provided "Chapter 5: Probability Distributions and Statistical Estimation" in Morgan and Henrion (1990).

- Suppose that in your travels you have become stuck in an unpleasant location and there is just one flight a day that will take you home. The hotel concierge tells you that the average time to get to the airport is 25 minutes. If you don't also ask about how often there are traffic jams or other disruptions – that is, ask about the uncertainty in taxi availability and travel time and consider it in your choice of when to leave – there is a good chance you might miss your flight and be stuck for an additional day.
- Suppose that the zoning board for a community situated next to a river is trying to design a set of rules that will protect homeowners from possible floods. If all they do is look at the contour reached by the classically defined 100-year flood, and do not consider other factors such as whether the history of flooding is a "stationary process," many homeowners could face an unpleasant surprise in the future.

8.1 DESCRIBING UNCERTAINTY

By far the most widely used formal language to describe uncertainty is probability.[3] Many of the ideas and much of the vocabulary of probability were first developed in a "frequentist" framework to describe the properties of random processes, such as games of chance, which can be repeated many times. In that case, assuming that the process of interest is stable over time, or "stationary," probability is the value to which the event frequency converges in the long run as the number of trials increases. Thus, in this frequentist or classical framework, probability is a property of a theoretically infinite series of trials, rather than of a single event.

While today some people stick to such a strict classical interpretation of probability, many statisticians, as well as many experimental scientists, adopt a "personalist," "subjectivist," or "Bayesian" view. In many settings, this has the consequence that probability can be used as a statement of a person's degree of belief given all available evidence. In this formulation, probability is not only a function of an event, but also of the state of information i that is available to the person making the assessment. That is, the probability, P, of an event X is represented as $P(X|i)$ where the notation "$|i$" reads "conditional on the information i." Thus, $P(X|i)$ means the probability of X that a person assesses, given all the information available to that person when they made the judgment. In this framework, obviously a person's value of P may change as more or different information becomes available.

In a personalist or Bayesian framework, it is perfectly appropriate to say, based on a subjective interpretation of polling data, results from focus group discussions, and my own reading of the political climate, "I think there is

[3] There are a few alternative "languages" that have been advanced to describe and deal with uncertainty. These are briefly discussed later in this chapter.

an 0.8 probability (or an 80% chance) that Jones will win the next congressional election in this district." However, because it involves the outcome of a single unique future event, such a statement has no meaning in a frequentist framework.

In the face of large amounts of data on a repeating event, and a belief that the process being considered is stationary, the subjectivist probability should reduce to the same value as the classical probability. Thus, for example, if you need to estimate the probability that the mid-morning high-speed Shinkansen train from Kyoto will arrive on time in Tokyo on a Tuesday morning next month, and you have access to a data set of all previous arrival times of that train, you would probably want to simply adopt the (very narrow!) histogram of those times as your probability distribution on arrival time.

Suppose, however, that you want to estimate how long it will take to complete the weekly shopping for a family of four in your community. If you happen to be the person doing the shopping for a family of four on a regular basis in your community, then, as in the case with the Shinkansen, you will have hundreds of observations upon which to rely in estimating a probability distribution. The large amount of data available to you helps you understand that the answer has features that depend on the time of day, day of the week, special occasions, and so on. If you do not shop that often, your ability to estimate how long it will take to do the shopping will be less informed and more likely to be in error. Hence, if you are wise, you will produce quite a wide probability distribution.[4]

Does a subjectivist view mean that one's probability can be completely arbitrary? "No," Morgan and Henrion (1990) answer,

> because if they are legitimate probabilities, they must be consistent with the axioms of probability. For example, if you assign probability p that an event X will occur, you should assign $1-p$ to its complement, [the probability] that X doesn't occur. The probability that one of a set of mutually exclusive events occurs should be the sum of their probabilities. In fact, subjective probabilities should obey the same axioms as objective or frequentist probabilities, otherwise they are not probabilities.

Subjective probabilities are intended to characterize the full spectrum of degrees of belief one might hold about uncertain propositions. However, there exists a long-standing debate as to whether this representation is sufficient. Some judgments may be characterized by a degree of ambiguity or imprecision distinct from estimates of their probability. Writing about financial matters, Knight (1921) contrasted the term *risk* with the term *uncertainty*, using the first to refer to random processes whose statistics were well known and the latter to describe unknown factors, poorly described by quantifiable probabilities. Ellsberg (1961) emphasized the importance of this difference in his famous

[4] Chapter 9 reports that people are systematically overconfident in making most such judgments, that is, they produce probability distributions that are too narrow.

paradox, in which subjects are asked to play a game of chance in which they do not know the probabilities underlying the outcomes of the game.[5] Ellsberg found that many subjects make choices that are inconsistent with any single estimate of probabilities, which nonetheless reflect judgments about which outcomes can be known with the most confidence.

Subjective probabilities seem clearly appropriate for addressing situations in which expert understanding is significant, though incomplete. There is more debate about the most appropriate methods for dealing with situations that involve considerable ignorance or ambiguity. A variety of approaches exist, such as belief functions, certainty factors, second-order probabilities, and fuzzy sets and fuzzy logic, that attempt to quantify the degree of belief in a set of subjective probability judgments.[6] Many of these approaches provide an alternative calculus that relaxes the axioms of probability. In particular, they try to capture the idea that one can gain or lose confidence in one of a mutually exclusive set of events without necessarily gaining or losing confidence in the other events. For instance, a jury in a court of law might hear evidence that makes them doubt the defendant's alibi without necessarily causing them to have more confidence in the prosecution's case.

It is my view that virtually all such cases can be appropriately handled through the use of subjective probability, allowing a wide range of, or a multiple set of, plausible distributions to represent the high levels of uncertainty, and retaining the axioms of probability. As Smithson (1988) explains:

> One of the most frequently invoked motivations for formalisms such as possibility and Shaferian belief theory is that one number is insufficient to represent subjective belief, particularly in the face of what some writers call "ignorance" ... Probabilists reply that we need not invent a new theory to handle uncertainty about probabilities. Instead we may use meta-probabilities [such as second-order probability]. Even such apparently non-probabilistic concepts as possibility can be so represented ... One merely induces a second-order probability distribution over the first-order subjective probabilities.

Much of the literature divides uncertainty into two broad categories, termed opaquely (for those of us who are not Latin scholars) *aleatory* uncertainty and *epistemic* uncertainty. As Paté-Cornell (1996) explains, aleatory uncertainty stems "from variability in known (or observable) populations and, therefore, represents randomness" while epistemic uncertainty "comes from basic lack of

[5] Specifically consider two urns each with 100 balls. In urn 1, the color ratio of red and blue balls is not specified. Urn 2 has 50 red and 50 blue balls. If asked to bet on the color of a ball drawn from one of these urns, most people do not care if the ball is drawn from urn 1 or 2 and give a probability to either color of 0.5. However, when asked to choose an urn when betting on a specified color, most people prefer urn 2. The first outcome implies $p(r_1) = p(r_2) = p(b_1) = p(b_2)$, while the second, it is argued, implies $p(r_1) < p(r_2)$ and $p(b_1) < p(b_2)$. Ellsberg and others discuss this outcome as an illustration of an aversion to ambiguity.

[6] For reviews of these alternative formulations, see Smithson (1988) and Henrion (1999).

knowledge about fundamental phenomena (... also known in the literature as ambiguity)."[7]

While this distinction is common in the more theoretical literature, I believe that it is of limited utility in the context of applied problems involving assessment and decision making in technology and public policy where most key uncertainties involve a combination of the two.

A far more useful categorization for our purposes is the split between "uncertainty about the value of empirical quantities" and "uncertainty about model functional form." The first of these may be either aleatory (the top wind speed that occurred in any Atlantic hurricane in the year 1995) or epistemic (the average global radiative forcing produced by anthropogenic aerosols at the top of the atmosphere during 1995). There is some disagreement within the community of experts about whether it is even appropriate to use the terms epistemic or aleatory when referring to a model.

Empirical quantities represent properties of the real world, which, at least in principle, can be measured. They include:

> quantities in the domains of natural science and engineering, such as the oxidation rate of an atmospheric pollutant, the thermal efficiency of a power plant, the failure rate of a valve, or the carcinogenic potency of a chemical, and quantities in the domain of the social sciences, such as demand elasticities or prices in economics, or amount of judgmental biases in psychology. To be empirical, variables must be measurable, at least in principle, either now or at some time in the future. (Morgan and Henrion, 1990)

Such quantities should be sufficiently well specified that they can pass a clarity test.[8] In such cases it is permissible to express uncertainty about the value of an empirical quantity in the form of a probability distribution. Indeed, I believe that the only types of quantity whose uncertainty may appropriately be represented in probabilistic terms are empirical quantities.[9] "This is because they are the only type of quantity that is both uncertain and can be said to have a *true*, as opposed to an *appropriate* or *good* value."[10]

Uncertainty about the value of an empirical quantity can arise from a variety of sources including: lack of data; inadequate or incomplete measurement; statistical variation arising from measurement instruments and methods; systematic error and the subjective judgments needed to estimate its nature and

[7] The Random House Dictionary defines *aleatory* as "of or pertaining to accidental causes; of luck or chance; unpredictable" and defines *epistemic* as "of or pertaining to knowledge or the conditions for acquiring it."

[8] Often framed as the "Cassandra question" after the Greek prophetess who had the power to precisely foretell the future (see Chapter 9).

[9] This advice is not shared by all authors. For example, Cyert and DeGroot (1987) have treated uncertainty about a decision maker's own value parameters as uncertain. But, see the subsequent discussion of how quantities with the same name may be empirical in some contexts and not in others.

[10] Text in quotation marks in this and the preceding paragraph come directly from Morgan and Henrion (1990).

magnitude; and inherent randomness. Uncertainty about the value of empirical quantities can also arise from sources such as the imprecise use of language in describing the quantity of interest and disagreement among different experts about how to interpret available evidence.

Not all quantities are empirical. Moreover, quantities with the same name may be empirical in some contexts and not in others. For example, quantities that represent a decision maker's own value choice or preference, such as a discount rate (see Chapter 7), a coefficient of risk aversion (see Chapter 2), or the investment rate to prevent mortality (see Chapter 5), represent choices about what they consider to be *appropriate* or *good*. If decision makers are uncertain about what value to adopt, they should perform parametric or "switchover" analysis to explore the implications of alternative choices.[11] However, if an analyst is modeling the behavior of *other* decision makers, and needs to know how they will make such choices, then these same quantities become empirical and can appropriately be represented by a probability distribution.[12]

Some authors refer to some forms of aleatory uncertainty as "variability." There are cases in which the distinction between uncertainty about the value of an empirical quantity and variability in that value (across space, time, or other relevant dimensions) is important. However, in much practical policy analyses, maintaining a distinction between uncertainty and variability is not especially important and maintaining it can give rise to overly complicated and confusing analysis. Some people, who accept only a frequentist view of probability, insist on maintaining the distinction between variability and uncertainty because variability can often be described in terms of histograms or probability distributions based only on a frequentist interpretation.

A model is a simplified approximation of some underlying causal structure. Debates such as whether a dose-response function is really linear, and whether or not it has a threshold below which no health effect occurs, are strictly speaking not about what model is "true."[13] None of these models is a complete, accurate representation of reality. The question is what is a more "useful" representation, given available scientific knowledge and data and the intended use that is to be made of, or decisions to be based on, the analysis. In this sense, uncertainty about model functional form is neither aleatory nor epistemic. The choice of model is partly pragmatic. Good (1962) described such a choice of

[11] In this example, a parametric analysis might ask, "what are the implications of taking the value of life to be 0.5, or 1 or 5, or 10 or 50 million dollars per death averted?" A "switchover" analysis would turn things around and ask "at what value of life does the conclusion I read switch from Policy A to Policy B?" If the policy choice does not depend upon the choice of value across the range of interest, it may not be necessary to further refine the value.

[12] For a more detailed discussion of this and similar distinctions, see the discussion in section 4.3 of Morgan and Henrion (1990).

[13] For a thoughtful discussion of the shape of health damage functions, see Morris (1990).

model as "type II rationality" – how can we choose a model that is a reasonable compromise between the credibility of results and the effort to create and analyze the model (collect data, estimate model parameters, apply expert judgment, compute the results, etc.).

Uncertainty about model functional form can arise from many of the same sources as uncertainty about the value of empirical quantities: inadequate or incomplete measurements and data that prevent the elimination of plausible alternatives; systematic errors that mislead people in their interpretation of underlying mechanisms; inadequate imagination and inventiveness in suggesting or inferring the models that could produce the available data; and disagreement among different experts about how to interpret available evidence.

In most of the discussion that follows, by "model functional form" I will mean a description of how the world works. However, in policy-analytic activities, models may also refer to considerations such as a decision maker's "objectives" and the "decision rules" that he or she applies. These are, of course, normative choices that a decision maker or analyst must make. A fundamental problem, and potential source of uncertainty on the part of those who use results from such analysis, is that the people performing the analysis are often not explicit about the objectives and decision rules they are using. Indeed, sometimes they skip (unknowingly and inconsistently) from one to another in the course of doing an analysis.[14]

The preceding discussion has focused on factors and processes that we know or believe exist, but about which our knowledge is in some way incomplete. There are also things about which we are completely ignorant. While Donald Rumsfeld (2002) was widely lampooned in the popular press, he was absolutely correct when he noted that "there are known unknowns. That is to say, we know there are some things we do not know. But there are also unknown unknowns, the ones we don't know we don't know."

Things we know we do not know can often be addressed and sometimes understood through research. Things about which we do not even recognize we don't know are only revealed by adopting an always-questioning attitude toward evidence. This is often easier said than done. Recognizing the inconsistencies in available evidence can be difficult since, as Thomas Kuhn (1962) has noted, we interpret the world through mental models or "paradigms" that may make it difficult to recognize and pursue important inconstancies.[15] Weick and Sutcliffe (2001) observe that "A recurring source of misperception lies in the temptation to normalize an unexpected event in order to preserve the original expectation. The tendency to normalize is part of a larger tendency to seek confirmation for our expectations and avoid disconfirmations. This pattern ignores vast amounts of data, many of which suggest that trouble is incubating and escalating."

[14] For an example, see National Research Council (1986b).

[15] See the discussion of Kuhn's (1962) notion of "normal science" in Appendix 1 of this book.

Freelance environmental journalist Dianne Dumanoski (1999) captured this issue well when she wrote:

> Scientific ignorance sometimes brings many surprises. Many of the big issues we have reported on involve scientists quibbling about small degrees of uncertainty. For example, at the beginning of the debate on ozone depletion, there were arguments about whether the level of erosion of the ozone layer would be 7% or 13% within 100 years. Yet in 1985, a report came out from the British Antarctic survey, saying there was something upwards to a 50% loss of ozone over Antarctica. This went far beyond any scientist's worst-case scenario. Such a large loss had never been a consideration on anyone's radar screen and it certainly changed the level of the debate once it was discovered. Uncertainty cuts both ways. In some cases, something that was considered a serious problem can turn out to be less of a threat. In other cases, something is considered less serious than it should be and we get surprised.

Perhaps the ever folksy but profound Mark Twain put it best when he noted, "It ain't what you don't know that gets you in trouble. It's what you know for sure that just ain't so."[16]

READING 8.1

M. Granger Morgan and Max Henrion, "Chapter 4: The Nature and Sources of Uncertainty," in *Uncertainty: A Guide to Dealing with Uncertainty in Quantitative Risk and Policy Analysis*, Cambridge University Press, pp. 47–72, 1990.

DISCUSSION QUESTIONS FOR READING 8.1

- What is the difference between a frequentist view and a personalist, or Bayesian, view of probability?
- Why do Morgan and Henrion argue that treating a value parameter as an empirical quantity can sometimes be a mistake? When would it be appropriate to treat a value parameter as an uncertain empirical quantity?
- Morgan and Henrion say that "the orthodox Bayesian view is that linguistic imprecision should simply be eliminated by providing a careful specification of all events and quantities so they can pass the clarity test." What is the basis for this view? Can you describe circumstances in which it might usefully be relaxed?
- What is the difference between uncertainty and variability? In performing analysis, when is it important and not important to maintain the difference?
- What is "switchover analysis" and when is it useful in policy analysis?

[16] www.quotedb.com/quotes/1097.

8.2 THE IMPORTANCE OF QUANTIFYING UNCERTAINTY

A variety of words are used to describe different levels of probability: "probable," "possible," "unlikely," "improbable," "almost impossible," etc. People often ask, why not simply use such words in describing uncertainty about climate change and its impacts?

Such qualitative uncertainty language is inadequate because: (1) the same words can mean very different things to different people; (2) the same words can mean very different things to the same person in different contexts; and (3) important differences in experts' judgments about mechanisms (functional relationships), and about how well key coefficients are known, can be easily masked in qualitative discussions.

Figure 8.1 illustrates the range of meanings that people attached to a set of probability words when asked to do so in a study conducted by Wallsten et al. (1986) in the absence of any specific context. Mosteller and Youtz (1990) performed a review of 20 different studies of the probabilities that respondents attached to 52 different qualitative expressions. They argue that "in spite of the variety of populations, format of question, instructions, and context, the variation of the averages for most of the expressions was modest" and they suggest that it might be possible to establish a general codification that maps words into probabilities. When that paper appeared in *Statistical Science* it was accompanied by eight invited comments (Clark, 1990; Cliff, 1990; Kadane, 1990; Kruskal, 1990; Tanur, 1990; Wallsten and Budescu, 1990; Winkler, 1990; Wolf, 1990).

While several commentators with economics or statistical backgrounds commented favorably on the feasibility of a general codification based on shared natural language meaning, those with psychological backgrounds argued strongly that context and other factors make such an effort infeasible.

For example, Mosteller and Youtz (1990) argued on the basis of their analysis of 20 studies that "likely" appears to mean 0.69 and "unlikely" means 0.16. In a following study in which they asked science writers to map words to probabilities they obtained a median value for "likely" of 0.71 (interquartile range of 0.626 to 0.776) and a median value for "unlikely" of 0.172 (interquartile range of 0.098 to 0.227).

In contrast, Figure 8.2 illustrates the range of numerical probabilities that individual members of the Executive Committee of the EPA Science Advisory Board attached to the words "likely" and "not likely" when those words were being used to describe the probability that a chemical agent is a human carcinogen (Morgan, 1998). Note that, even in this relatively small and expert group, the minimum probability associated with the word "likely" spans four orders of magnitude, the maximum probability associated with the word "not likely" spans more than five orders of magnitude, and there is an actual *overlap* of the probabilities the different experts associated with the two words! Clearly, in this setting the words do not mean roughly the same thing to all

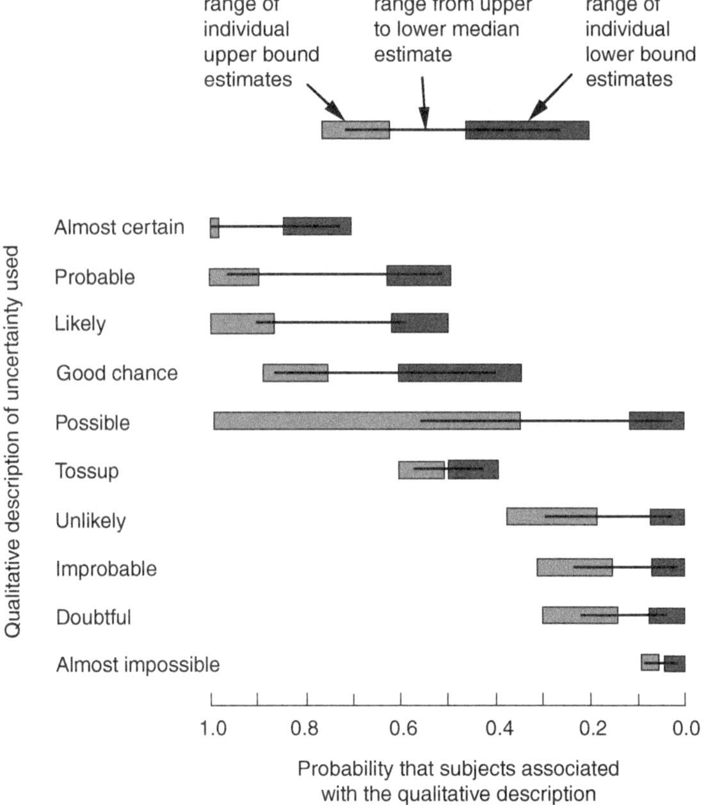

FIGURE 8.1. Range of numerical probabilities that respondents attached to qualitative probability words in the absence of any specific context. Figure redrawn from Wallsten et al. (1986).

experts, and without at least some quantification, such qualitative descriptions of uncertainty convey little, if any, useful information.[17]

While some fields, such as environmental health impact assessment, have been relatively slow to accept the fact that it is important to be explicit about how uncertainty words are mapped into probabilities, and have resisted the use of numerical descriptions of uncertainty (Presidential/Congressional Commission on Risk Assessment and Risk Management, 1997; Morgan, 1998), the climate assessment community has made relatively good, if uneven, progress in recognizing and attempting to deal with this issue. One notable example is the

[17] For an early and thoughtful extended discussion of the use of probability words in the context of national security intelligence assessments, see Kent (1964). For a much more recent discussion of intelligence assessments (in a context where the words are defined), see Mandel and Barnes (2014).

FIGURE 8.2. Results obtained by Morgan (1998) when members of the Executive Committee of the EPA Science Advisory Board were asked to assign numerical probabilities to words that have been proposed for use with the new EPA cancer guidelines (EPA, 1996). Note that, even in this relatively small and expert group, the minimum probability associated with the word "likely" spans four orders of magnitude, the maximum probability associated with the word "not likely" spans more than five orders of magnitude, and there is an overlap of the probabilities the different experts associated with the two words.

guidance document first developed by Moss and Schneider (2000) for authors of the IPCC Third Assessment and the mapping of probability words into specific numerical values employed in the 2001 IPCC reports (IPCC 2001a, b) (Table 8.1). All subsequent IPCC assessments have provided similar guidance and adopted similar practice. The first U.S. National Assessment Synthesis

BOX 8.1 PREDICTING RAINFALL: AN ILLUSTRATION OF FREQUENTIST AND BAYESIAN APPROACHES

Suppose we want to make a prediction about future annual rainfall in San Diego County, California. We have 145 years of past rainfall data that allow the construction of a histogram of past rainfall. Assuming that the same underlying conditions prevail in the future as obtained in the past (i.e., the process is stationary), an analyst adopting a frequentist perspective could use this time series to construct a histogram, as shown below, to make a probabilistic prediction of annual rainfall in some future year.

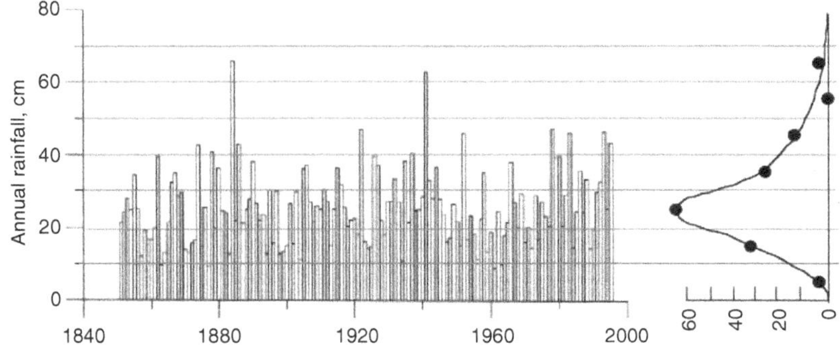

If the analyst wanted to be more sophisticated they could even construct a table of probabilities that is conditional on a variety of specific conditions, such as whether or not it is an El Niño or La Niña year, although it is doubtful how useful that added detail would be for a prediction that is to be made many years in the future.

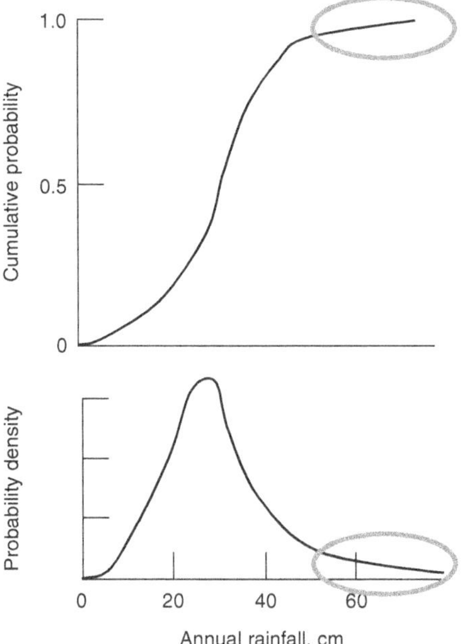

Suppose, however, that our analyst is primarily interested in extreme rainfall events involving 60 cm or more of rain in a year. Because there have been only been two years in the course of the past 145 years in which rainfall has exceeded 60 cm, making such an estimate will have to rely on some expert judgment. If the analyst is prepared to believe that the extreme values will follow some specific probability distribution, that could be used to make the needed estimate. (Rainfall data from Inman et al. (1998).)

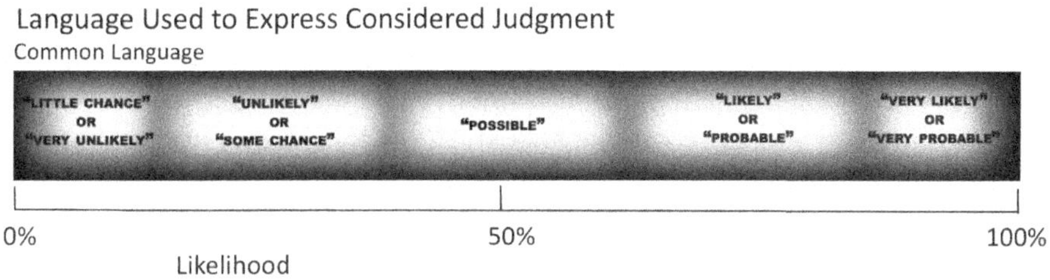

FIGURE 8.3. Mapping of probability words into quantitative subjective probability judgments, used in their two reports, by the members of the National Assessment Synthesis Team of the U.S. National Assessment (2000).

TABLE 8.1. *Mapping of probability words into quantitative subjective probability judgments, used by WG I and II of the IPCC Third Assessment (IPCC, 2001a, b) based on recommendations developed by Moss and Schneider (2000).*

Word	Probability range
Virtually certain	> 0.99
Very likely	0.9–0.99
Likely	0.66–0.9
Medium likelihood	0.33–0.66
Unlikely	0.1–0.33
Very unlikely	0.01–0.1
Exceptionally unlikely	< 0.01

Note: The report of the *IPCC Workshop on Describing Scientific Uncertainties in Climate Change to Support Analysis of Risk and of Options* (2004) observed: "Although WGIII TAR authors (IPCC, 2002c) addressed uncertainties in the WG3-TAR, they did not adopt the Moss and Schneider uncertainty guidelines. The treatment of uncertainty in the WG3-AR4 can be improved over what was done in the TAR."

Team adopted similar strategies (2000). The mapping used in that assessment, which the authors attempted to apply consistently throughout their two reports, is shown in Figure 8.3.

8.3 COGNITIVE CHALLENGES IN ESTIMATING UNCERTAINTY

While our brains are very good at doing many tasks, we do not come hard-wired with statistical processors. Over the past several decades, experimental psychologists have begun to identify and understand a number of the "cognitive heuristics" we use when we make judgments that involve uncertainty.

We will explore these issues at much greater length in Chapters 9 and 12. Here we simply note that both laypeople and experts tend to be systematically overconfident in the face of uncertainty – that is, we produce probability distributions that are much too narrow. Actual values, once they are known, often turn out to lie well outside the tails of the assessed distributions. One reason for this overconfidence, and for other systematic biases that we display when making judgments about uncertainty, is that we make these judgments using a variety of simple "cognitive heuristics" or mental rules of thumb. These simplified judgment procedures serve us well in many day-to-day settings, but, without our realizing it, they can result in significant errors and bias when we make judgments involving uncertainty.

8.4 METHODS AND TOOLS FOR PROPAGATING AND ANALYZING UNCERTAINTY

Once uncertainty in the value of key variables has been defined in terms of probability distributions, a variety of methods are available to propagate it through a model or other analysis to obtain probabilistic results. Doing this analytically becomes difficult in all but a set of special cases. By far the most common method today is to perform stochastic simulation using "Monte Carlo" or some similar procedure. Figure 8.4 illustrates how this is done. Because this topic is covered extensively in Morgan and Henrion (1990), readers are referred to that book for details.

READING 8.2

M. Granger Morgan and Max Henrion, "Chapter 8: The Propagation and Analysis of Uncertainty," in *Uncertainty: A Guide to Dealing with Uncertainty in Quantitative Risk and Policy Analysis*, Cambridge University Press, pp. 172–219, 1990.

DISCUSSION QUESTIONS FOR READING 8.2

- What is the difference between sensitivity analysis and the use of combinatorial scenarios?
- Explain how stochastic simulation based on Monte Carlo analysis works.
- Why are there typically serious limitations in using analytical methods to propagate uncertainty through a model?

- Describe a strategy of converting a continuous probability distribution into a discrete distribution. When and why might an analyst want to do that?
- Why might one want to use stratified sampling or Latin Hyper Cube sampling when performing a stochastic simulation?

While he was at Carnegie Mellon, Max Henrion developed a powerful software tool then called Demos and now called Analytica® that allows one to structure a piece of analysis as an influence diagram, represent the values of key uncertainties as probability distributions, and then propagate those uncertainties through the model to obtain probabilistic answers. Various tools to do sensitivity analysis and ask "what if" questions are provided.

Each node in an Analytica® influence diagram carries fields in which one can specify values or functional relationships, and provide verbal descriptions and documentation including things such as citations to literature. Thus in the process of building the model it becomes self-documenting. Figures 11.6 and 11.7 show the hierarchical nature of an early climate integrated assessment model built in what was then still called Demos (Dowlatabadi and Morgan, 1993). Figure 11.8 shows the top-level nodes of the much more sophisticated model called ICAM-3. As explained in greater detail in Section 11.7, by clicking on the middle button labeled "structure" at the bottom of the top-level diagram the user could turn on or off a variety of alternative model functional forms in order to explore the implication of different model assumptions.

In the ICAM models, in addition to uncertainties about the long-term evolution of the energy system and hence future emissions, uncertainties about the likely response of the climate system, and about the possible impacts of climate change, are so great that a full characterization of coefficient and model uncertainty in a simulation model can lead to probabilistic results that are so broad that they are effectively useless (Casman et al., 1999). Similarly, if one does parametric analysis across different model formulations, one can obtain an enormous range of answers depending on the model form and other inputs that are chosen.

Results like this suggest that there are decided limits to the use of "predictive models" and "optimization" in many assessment and policy settings. This has led several investigators to adopt a very different approach based on the idea of robustness, as opposed to optimality, as the appropriate decision criteria under conditions of irreducible or deep uncertainty. A robust strategy is one that performs well, compared to the alternatives, over the range of alternative futures that are of concern (Lempert et al., 2003, 2006). This has led to the development of an analytical method now known as robust decision making or RDM. Lempert et al. (2013) explain:

RDM rests on a simple concept. Rather than using computer models and data to describe a best-estimate future, RDM runs models on hundreds to thousands of different sets of

Draw random numbers on the interval [0,1] and use them to draw samples from the CDFs of all uncertain input variables (e.g., X_1,X_2, X_3) and compute and record a resulting output Y:

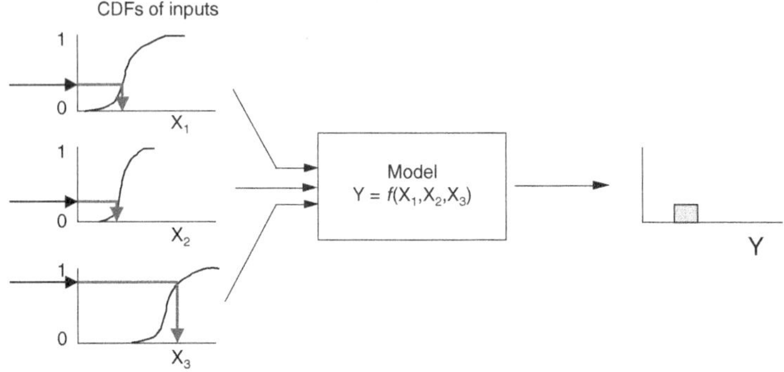

Repeat this process in order to build up a PDF in Y:

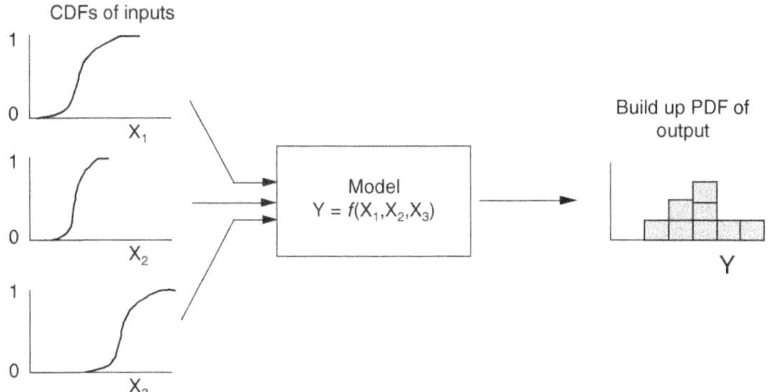

FIGURE 8.4. Illustration of the technique of stochastic simulation.

assumptions to describe how plans perform in a range of possible futures. Analysts then use visualization and statistical analysis of the resulting large database of model runs to help decision-makers distinguish future conditions in which their plans will perform well from those in which they will perform poorly. This information can help decision-makers identify, evaluate, and choose robust decisions – ones that will perform well over a wide range of futures and the better manage surprise.

For details on this approach, including many interesting applications, readers should search for "robust decision making" on the website of the RAND Corporation.

8.5 MAKING DECISIONS IN THE FACE OF UNCERTAINTY

As noted in the introduction to this chapter, both individuals and private and public organizations make decisions in the face of uncertainty all the time.

Sometimes, because decisions must be made, scientific uncertainties are not the determining factor (e.g., Wilbanks and Lee, 1985), and sometimes strategies can be identified that incorporate uncertainties and associated risks into the decision-making calculus (National Research Council, 1986a).

Classical decision analysis (see Chapter 4) provides an axiomatically based normative approach for making decisions when possible outcomes, their probability of occurrence, and the value each holds for the decision maker can be specified (Raiffa and Schlaifer, 1968; Howard and Matheson, 1977; Keeney, 1982). In applying decision analysis, one develops and refines a model that relates the decision makers' choices to important outcomes. One must also determine the decision maker's utility function(s) in order to determine which outcomes are most desirable.[18] One then propagates the uncertainty in various input parameters through the model (appropriately accounting for possible correlation structures among uncertain variables) to generate the expected utility of the various choice options. The best option is typically assumed to be the one with the largest expected utility, although other decision rules are sometimes employed.

As explained in Chapter 4, when the uncertainty is well characterized and the model structure well known, this type of analysis can suggest the statistically optimal strategy to decision makers. In complex and highly uncertain contexts, such as those involved in many climate-related decisions, the conditions needed for the application of conventional decision analysis may not obtain (Morgan et al., 1999; see the discussion in Section 11.7). Where uncertainty is large, efforts can be made to *reduce* the uncertainties – in effect, reducing the width of probability distributions through research to better understand underlying processes. In addition, efforts can be made to *improve understanding* of the uncertainties themselves so that they can be more confidently described and incorporated in decision-making strategies.

Classic decision analysis implicitly assumes that research reduces uncertainty. While eventually it usually does, in complex problems, many years or even many decades may go by during which one's understanding of the problem grows richer, but the amount of uncertainty, as measured by our ability to make specific predictions, remain unchanged, or even grows larger because research reveals processes or complications that had not previously been understood or anticipated. That climate experts understand this is clearly demonstrated in the results from Morgan and Keith (1995) shown in Table 8.2.

Unfortunately, many others do not recognize this fact, or choose to ignore it in policy discussions of topics like climate change. This is not to argue that

[18] Many economists and analysts appear to assume that fully articulated utility functions exist in people's heads for all key outcomes, and that determining them is a matter of measurement. Many psychologists, and some decision analysts, suggest that this is often not the case and that, for many issues, people need help in thinking through and constructing their values (von Winterfeldt and Edwards, 1986; Fischhoff, 1991; Keeney, 1992; Fischhoff, 2005). See the discussion in Chapters 9 and 13.

TABLE 8.2. *In the expert elicitations of climate scientists conducted by Morgan and Keith (1995), experts were asked to design a 15-year-long research program funded at a billion dollars per year that was designed to reduce the uncertainty in our knowledge of climate sensitivity and related issues. Having done this, the experts were asked how much they thought their uncertainty might have changed if they were asked the same question in 15 years. The results below show that, like all good scientists, the experts understand that research does not always reduce uncertainty.*

Expert number	Chance that the experts believe that their uncertainty about the value of climate sensitivity would *grow* by >25% after a 15yr. $\$10^9$/yr. research program
1	10
2	18
3	30 (see note)
4	22
5	30
6	14
7	20
8	25
9	12
10	20
11	40
12	16
13	12
14	18
15	14
16	8

Note: Expert 3 used a different response mode for this question. He gave a 30 percent increase by a factor of ≥ 2.5.

research in understanding climate science, climate impacts, and the likely effectiveness of various climate management policies and technologies is not valuable. Clearly it is, and, in many cases, it can reduce uncertainty. But we should remember that there is value in learning that we knew less than we thought we did, and that in some cases, all the research in the world may not eliminate some key uncertainties.

There are two related strategies that may be especially appealing in the face of high uncertainty. These are:

Resilient Strategies: In this case, the idea is to try to identify the range of future circumstances that one might face, and then seek to identify approaches that will work reasonably well across that range (see discussion above of RDM).

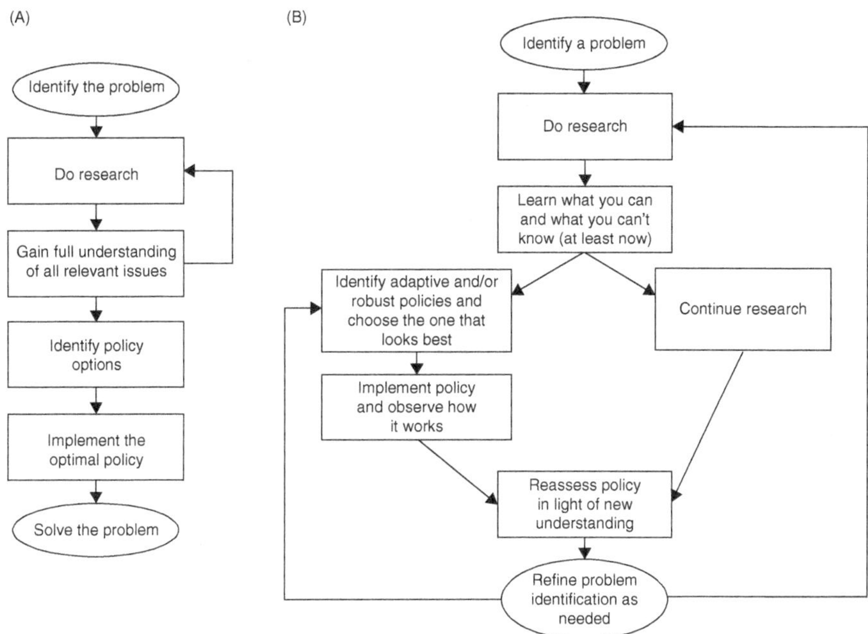

FIGURE 8.5. In the face of high levels of uncertainty, which may not be readily resolved through research, decision makers are best advised to not adopt a decision strategy in which nothing is done until research resolves all key uncertainties (**A**), but rather to adopt an iterative, adaptive, and/or robust strategy (**B**).

Adaptive Strategies: In this case, the idea is to choose strategies that can be modified to achieve better performance as one learns more about the issues at hand and how the future is unfolding.

Both of these approaches stand in rather stark contrast to the idea of developing optimal strategies that has characterized much of the work in the decision analysis and integrated assessment communities, in which it is assumed that a single model accurately reflects the nature of the world, and the task is to choose an optimal strategy in that well-specified world.

The ideas of resilience and adaptation have been strongly informed by the literature in ecology. Particularly nice discussions can be found in Clark (1980) and Lee (1993). A key feature of adaptive strategies is that decision makers learn whatever they can about the problem they face and then make choices based on their best assessment and that of people whose advice they value. They seek strategies that will let them, or those who come after them, modify choices in accordance with insights gained from more experience and research. That is, rather than adopt a decision strategy of the sort shown in Figure 8.5A, in which nothing is done until research resolves all key uncertainties, they adopt an iterative and adaptive strategy that looks more like that shown in

Figure 8.5B. Adaptive strategies work best in situations in which there are not large non-linearities and in which the decision time scales are well matched to the changes being observed in the world.[19]

A familiar example of a robust strategy is portfolio theory as applied in financial investment, which suggests that greater uncertainty (or a lesser capacity to absorb risks) calls for greater portfolio diversification.

Another example arose during the first regional workshop conducted by the U.S. National (Climate) Assessment in Fort Collins, CO. Farmers and ranchers participating in the discussion suggested that, if possible climate change introduces new uncertainties into future climate forecasts, it might be prudent for them to reverse a trend toward highly specialized precision farming and ranching, moving back toward a greater variety of crops and range grasses.

Rather than use models, data, and characterizations of uncertainty to determine a best course of action, which may turn out to be very vulnerable if one or more assumptions turn out not to be true, analyses based on robustness seek to use models, data, and characterizations of uncertainty to determine a course of action that will prove reasonably successful independent of the factors about which we are most uncertain (Lempert et al., 2003).

8.6 SCENARIO ANALYSIS

The development and use of a set of scenarios is a strategy people often use when they are faced with uncertainty. Proponents of these methods often argue that they can be a useful way to "expand your thinking" about a range of possible futures. One long-time proponent of the use of scenarios has been a group at the Shell Oil Company. The developers of Shell's scenarios argue that the story lines they develop "are not forecasts, projections or predictions of what is to come. Nor are they preferred views of the future. Rather, they are plausible alternative futures: they provide reasonable and consistent answers to the 'what if?' questions relevant to business" (Shell International Limited, 2005). In need of some way to address the fact that there is great uncertainty about how future emissions of greenhouse gases will evolve, in 1996 the Intergovernmental Panel on Climate Change (IPCC) adopted a similar strategy, commissioning a group under the leadership of Nebojsa Nakicenovic of the International Institute for Applied Systems Analysis (IIASA) to develop a set of rather detailed "story lines" about how future global society might evolve and what air emissions it would produce. The resulting scenarios were detailed in the IPCC's *Special Report on Emission Scenarios* (SRES) (Nakicenovic and Swart, 2000). In their report the team explains that the SRES scenarios were developed to:

> cover a wide range of the main driving forces of future emissions, from demographic to technological and economic developments ... The set of SRES emissions scenarios is based on an extensive assessment of the literature, six alternative modeling approaches,

[19] See the discussion in chapter 16 of Lindblom (1959), "The Science of Muddling Through," which, to be successful, basically assumes that there are not large non-linearities.

and an "open process" that solicited wide participation and feedback from many groups and individuals. The SRES scenarios include the range of emissions of all relevant species of greenhouse gases (GHGs) and sulfur and their driving forces ... [S]cenarios are used to help review and assess strategy.

As with Shell and others, the SRES team argued that their scenarios were designed to help expand one's thinking. The SRES authors were quite insistent that one should not attach probabilities to any of the scenarios, arguing that all were "equally sound." They wrote: "[The scenarios] ... are neither predictions nor forecasts. Rather, each scenario is one alternative image of how the future might unfold ... Prediction is not possible in such cases" (Nakicenovic and Swart, 2000). From the outset, there was serious debate about the argument that one should not attach probabilities to the SRES scenarios.[20] In a later critique, Morgan and Keith (2008) wrote:

While the authors of scenarios may decline to provide explicit statements about probability, in our view, judgments about the subjective probability of future states of the world lies at the heart of scenario construction. The literature on scenarios often aims to make a sharp distinction between scenarios and forecasts or projections; for example, it is asserted that scenarios are judged by their "feasibility" or "plausibility" rather than their likelihood. We cannot find any sensible interpretation of these terms other than as synonyms for relative subjective probability. Absent a supernatural ability to foresee the future, what could be meant by a statement that one scenario is feasible and another infeasible but that the first is (subjectively) more probable than the second?

Of course, if one is going to use scenarios, it would be good to have them be internally consistent. Schweizer and Kriegler (2012) suggest that one way to do that is with the use of the "cross-impact balance" (CIB) method. They have applied this method to an assessment of the SRES scenarios and report:

Using this method, we find that the four principal storylines employed in the SRES scenarios vary widely in internal consistency. One type of storyline involving highly carbon-intensive development is underrepresented in the SRES scenario set. We conclude that systematic techniques like CIB analysis hold promise for improving scenario development in global change research.

Morgan and Keith argue that because detailed story lines are cognitively compelling they can easily lead to overconfidence, with the result that users may fail to recognize the many other ways in which the future might unfold.[21] Indeed, some proponents of scenarios argue that this is one of their benefits. Gregory (2001) argues:

Practitioners can find several advantages in using scenarios. First, they can use scenarios to enhance a person's or group's expectancies that an event will occur. This can be useful for gaining acceptance of a forecast ... Second, scenarios can be used as a means of

[20] Climatologist Steven Schneider argued at the outset that adding probabilities was essential. Tom Wigley ignored the committee, and performed an analysis assigning equal probability to each scenario. For details, see Morgan and Keith (2008).

[21] See the discussion in Section 12.6.

decreasing existing expectancies ... Third ... scenarios can produce greater commitment in the clients to taking actions described in them.

Not exactly the result one should want if the objective is to "expand your thinking"!

While IPCC continues to build and use scenarios (Moss et al., 2010), Morgan and Keith (2008) argue that a better strategy would be to decompose the quantity of interest into a set of component parts and then:

Using all available models and other formal and informal tools and data at their disposal, a group of analysts (call them the assessment team) should first build as comprehensive a set of arguments for how the quantity of interest (call it *Q)* might end up at high, medium or low levels at the future moments of interest. This should be done by iterating back and forth between independent analysis by each member of the assessment team and collective discussion within the team.

Only after this process has iterated several times, should the team then move on to the task of imposing a parametric consideration of key policy variable(s) (*P*) and constructing a set of probability distributions in the value of *Q* at a future moment of interest, call it $p(Q(t = t_{fut})|\ P)$, a set of distributions at several times, or a continuous time series in $p(Q(t)|P)$.

Additional details on this approach can be found in Morgan and Keith (2008).

While I am not aware of any implementation of the strategy outlined here, Vanessa Schweizer and I have applied a set of simple bounding ideas in order to estimate upper and lower bounds on total U.S. electricity demand in 2050 (Schweizer and Morgan, 2016).

8.7 PRECAUTION

As explained in Section 3.10, the "precautionary principle" is a decision strategy that is often proposed for use in the face of high uncertainty. There are many different notions of what this approach does and does not entail. In some forms it incorporates ideas of resilience or adaptation. In some forms, it can also be shown to be entirely consistent with a decision analytic problem framing (DeKay et al., 2002). However, among some proponents, precaution has often taken the form of advocating complete avoidance of new activities or technologies that hold an uncertain potential to cause adverse impacts, regardless of how remote their probability of occurrence. In this extreme form, the precautionary principle has drawn vigorous criticism from a number of commentators.

For example, Sunstein (2005) argues:

a wide variety of adverse effects may come from inaction, regulation and everything in between. [A better approach] ... would attempt to consider all of these adverse effects, not simply a subset. Such an approach would pursue distributional goals directly by, for example, requiring wealthy countries – the major contributors to the problem of global warming – to pay poor countries to reduce greenhouse gases or to prepare themselves for the relevant risks. When societies face risks of catastrophe, even risks whose likelihood can not be calculated, it is appropriate to act, not to stand by and merely hope.

Writing before "precaution" became widely discussed, Wildavsky (1979) argued that some risk taking is essential to social progress. Thompson (1980) has made very similar arguments in comparing societies and cultures. Precaution is often in the eye of the beholder. Thus, for example, some have argued that while the European Union has been more precautionary with respect to CO_2 emissions in promoting the wide adoption of fuel-efficient diesel automobiles, the United States has been more precautionary with respect to health effects of fine particulate air pollution, stalling the adoption of diesel automobiles until it was possible to substantially reduce their particulate emissions (Wiener and Rogers, 2002).[22]

8.8 COMMUNICATING UNCERTAINTY

Chapter 14 discusses the development of effective communications about risks and other similar issues, focusing in particular on the use of the "mental model method" (Morgan et al., 2002). Here I only note a few of the issues that arise in communicating uncertainty.

It is often argued that one should not try to communicate about uncertainty to non-technical audiences, because laypeople won't understand and decision makers want definitive answers – what Senator Muskie referred to as the ideal of receiving advice from "one-handed scientists."[23] I disagree. Non-technical people deal with uncertainty, and statements of probability, all the time. They don't always reason correctly about probability, but they can generally get the gist (Dawes, 1988).

While they may make errors about the details, for the most part people manage to deal with probabilistic precipitation forecasts from the weather bureau, point spreads at the track, and similar probabilistic information. Similarly, Fischhoff (2012) explains that "behavioral research has found that most people like receiving explicit quantitative expressions of uncertainty (such as credible intervals), can interpret them well enough to extract their main message, and misinterpret verbal expressions of uncertainty (such as 'good' evidence or 'rare' side effects). For most audiences misunderstanding is more likely with verbal expressions." The key issue is to frame things in familiar and understandable terms.

[22] Of course, revelations about how VW programmed their vehicles to bypass emission regulations points up the need to differentiate between policy and actual implementation in the field! See: https://en.wikipedia.org/wiki/Volkswagen_emissions_scandal.

[23] The reference, of course, being to experts who always answered his questions "on the one hand ... but on the other hand ...," the phrase is usually first attributed to Senator Edmund Muskie.

There has been considerable discussion in the literature about whether it is best to present uncertainties to laypeople in terms of odds (e.g., 1 in 1000) or probabilities (e.g., p = 0.001) (Fischhoff et al., 2002). Fischhoff provides the following summary advice:

- Either format will work, if they're used consistently across many presentations.
- If you want people to understand one fact, in isolation, present the result both in terms of odds *and* probabilities.
- In many cases, there's probably more confusion about what is meant by the specific events being discussed than about the numbers attached to them.

Ibrekk and Morgan (1987) reached a similar conclusion in their study of alternative simple graphical displays for communicating uncertainty to non-technical people, arguing for the use of more than one display when communicating a single uncertain result. They also report that "rusty or limited statistical knowledge does not significantly improve the performance of semi-technical or laypersons in interpreting displays that communicate uncertainty" (reported in Morgan and Henrion, 1990).

Patt and Schrag (2003) studied how undergraduate respondents interpreted both probabilities and uncertainty words that specifically relate to climate and weather. They found that these respondents mediated their probability judgments by the severity of the event reported (e.g., hurricane versus snow flurries). They concluded that "in response to a fixed probability scale, people will have a tendency to over-estimate the likelihood of low-magnitude events, and under-estimate the likelihood of high-magnitude events." This is because, "intuitively people use such language to describe both the probability and the magnitude of risks, and they expect communicators to do the same." They suggest that unless analysts make it clear that they are not adjusting their probability estimates up and down depending on the severity of the event described, policy makers' response to assessments are "likely to be biased downward, leading to insufficient efforts to mitigate and adapt to climate change" (Patt and Schrag, 2003).

The presence of high levels of uncertainty offers people who have an agenda an opportunity to "spin the facts." Dowlatabadi reports that when he first started showing probabilistic outputs from Carnegie Mellon's Integrated Climate Assessment Model (ICAM) to staff on Capitol Hill, many of those who thought that climate change was not happening or was not important immediately focused in on the low-impact ends of the model's probabilistic outputs. In contrast, many of those who thought climate change was a very serious problem immediately focused in on the high-impact ends of the model's probabilistic outputs.

This does not mean that one should abandon communicating about uncertainty. Political partisans will spin anything. However, it does mean that communicating uncertainty in key issues requires special care, so that those who really want to understand can do so. As elaborated in Chapter 14, recipients will process any message they receive through their previous knowledge and perception of the issues at hand. Thus, in designing an effective communication, one must first understand what the people who will receive that message already know and think about the topics at hand. One of the clearest findings in the empirical literature on risk communication is that there is no such thing as an expert who can design effective risk communication messages without some empirical evaluation and refinement of those messages with members of the target audience.

While the preceding discussion has dealt with communicating uncertainty in situations in which it is possible to do extensive studies of the relative effectiveness of different communication methods and messages, much of the communication about uncertain events that all of us receive comes from reading or listening to the press.

Philip M. Boffey (quoted in Friedman et al., 1999), editorial-page editor for the *New York Times*, argues that "uncertainty is a smaller problem for science writers than for many other kinds of journalists." He notes that there is enormous uncertainty about what is going on in China or North Korea and that "economics is another area where there is great uncertainty."[24] In contrast, he notes:

> With science writing, the subjects are better defined. One of the reasons why uncertainty is less of a problem for a science journalist is because the scientific material we cover is mostly issued and argued publicly. This is not North Korea or China. While it is true that a journalist cannot view a scientist's lab notes or sit on a peer review committee, the final product is out there in the public. There can be a vigorous public debate about it and reporters and others can see what is happening.

Boffey goes on to note that "one of the problems in journalism is to try to find out what is really happening." While this may be easier than in some other fields, because of peer-reviewed articles and consensus panel mechanisms such as NRC reports, "there is the second level problem of deciding whether these consensus mechanisms are operating properly ... Often the journalist does not have time to investigate ... given the constraints of daily journalism." However, he notes:

> these consensus mechanisms do help the journalist decide where the mainstream opinion is and how and whether to deal with outliers. Should they be part of the debate? In some issues, such as climate change, I do not feel they should be ignored because in this subject, the last major consensus report showed that there were a number of unknowns, so the situation is still fluid.

While it is by no means unique, climate change is perhaps the prototypical example of an issue for which there is a combination of considerable scientific uncertainty, and strong short-term economic and other interests at play.[25]

[24] Note that this was written when China was somewhat less open than it is today.

[25] For an excellent account of this in the context of smoking and health, stratospheric ozone, and climate change, see Oreskes and Conway (2010).

Uncertainty offers the opportunity for various interests to confuse and divert the public discourse in what may already be a very difficult scientific process of seeking improved insight and understanding. Combine this with the limited scientific background of many reporters, the tendency of the press to seek conflict and report "on the one hand, on the other hand" and do so in just a few words and with very short deadlines, it is small wonder that there are problems.

Chemist and Nobel laureate F.S. Roland (quoted in Friedman et al., 1999) notes that: "scientists' reputations depend on their findings being right most of the time. Sometimes, however, there are people who are wrong almost all the time and they are still quoted in the media 20 years later very consistently."

Despite continued discourse within scientific societies and similar professional circles about the importance of scientists interpreting and communicating their findings to the public and to decision makers, freelance environmental writer Dianne Dumanoski (quoted in Friedman et al., 1999) is correct when she observes that "strong peer pressure exists within the scientific community against becoming a visible scientist who communicates with the media and the public." Combined with an environment in which there is high probability that many statements a scientist makes about uncertainties will immediately be seized upon by advocates in an ongoing public debate, it is small wonder that many scientists choose to just keep their heads down, do their research, and limit their communication to publication in scientific journals and presentations at professional scientific meetings.

These problems are well illustrated in an exchange between biological scientist Rita Colwell (then Director of the National Science Foundation), Peggy Girsham of NBC (now with NPR), and Sherry Rowland that is reported by Friedman et al. (1999). Colwell noted that when a scientist talks with a reporter they must be very careful about what they say, especially if they have a theory or findings that run counter to conventional scientific wisdom: "it is very tough to go out there, talk to a reporter, lay your reputation on the line and then be maligned by so called authorities in a very unpleasant way." She noted that this problem is particularly true for women scientists, adding, "I have literally taken slander and public ridicule from a few individuals with clout and that has been very unpleasant." NBC's Girsham noted that, in a way, scientists in such a situation cannot win "because if you are not willing to talk to a reporter, then we [in the press] will look for someone who is willing and may be less cautious about expressing a point of view." Building on this point, Rowland noted that in the early days of the work he and Mario Molina did on stratospheric ozone depletion,

> Molina and I read *Aerosol Age* avidly because we were the "black hats" in every issue. The magazine even went so far as to run an article calling us agents of the Soviet Union's KGB, who were trying to destroy American industry ... what was more disturbing was when scientists on the industry side were quoted by the media, claiming our calculations of how many CFCs were in the stratosphere were off by a factor of 1,000 ... even after we won the Nobel Prize for this research, our politically conservative local newspaper ...

[said that while the] theory had been demonstrated in the laboratory ... scientists with more expertise in atmospheric science had shown that the evidence in the real atmosphere was quite mixed. This ignored the consensus views of the world's atmospheric scientists that the results had been spectacularly confirmed in the real atmosphere.

Clearly, even when a scientist is as careful and balanced as possible, communicating with the public and decision makers about complex and politically contentious scientific issues is not for the fainthearted!

8.9 SOME SIMPLE GUIDANCE ON CHARACTERIZING AND DEALING WITH UNCERTAINTY

In 2009 I served as the lead author for the U.S. Global Change Program in preparing a report (called CCSP 5.2) on the characterization and treatment of uncertainty (Morgan et al., 2009). We concluded that report with the guidance that follows, which applies generally to those performing quantitative policy analysis. I reproduce it below with only minor modifications.

Doing a good job of characterizing and dealing with uncertainty can never be reduced to a simple cookbook. One must always think critically and continually ask questions such as:

- Does what we are doing make sense?
- Are there other important factors which are as, or more, important than the factors we are considering?
- Are there key correlation structures in the problem that are being ignored?
- Are there normative assumptions and judgments about which we are not being explicit?

That said, the following are a few words of guidance to help practitioners on how to do a better job of reporting, characterizing, and analyzing uncertainty. Some of this guidance is based on available literature. However, because doing these things well is often as much an art as it is a science, the recommendations also draw on the very considerable and diverse experience and collective judgment of the writing team.[26]

Reporting Uncertainty

- When qualitative uncertainty words such as "likely" and "unlikely" are used, it is important to clarify the range of subjective probability values that are to be associated with those words. Unless there is some compelling reason

[26] Collectively, the author team that prepared the report (CCSP 5.2) had roughly 200 person-years of experience in addressing these issues both theoretically and in practical analysis in the context of climate and other similar areas.

to do otherwise, we recommend the use of the framework shown below.[27] This approach provides somewhat greater precision and allows some limited indication of secondary uncertainty for those who feel uncomfortable making precise probability judgments.

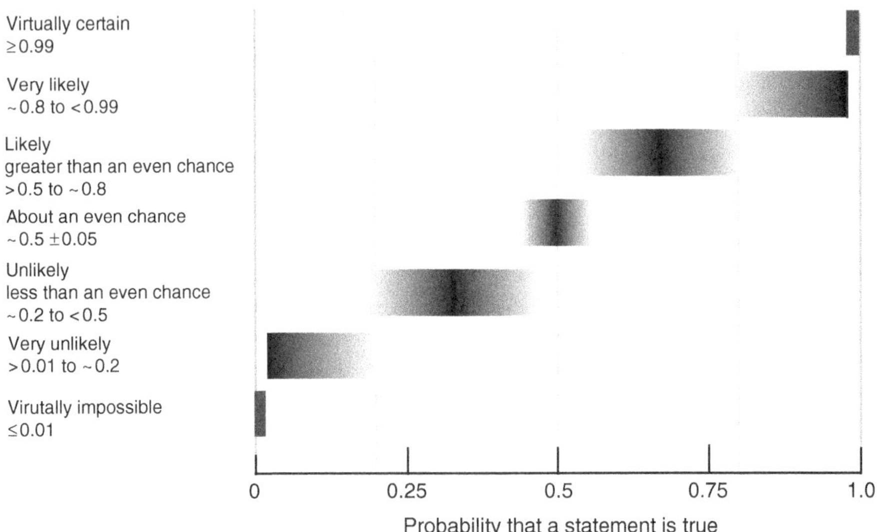

Another strategy is to display the judgment explicitly as shown:

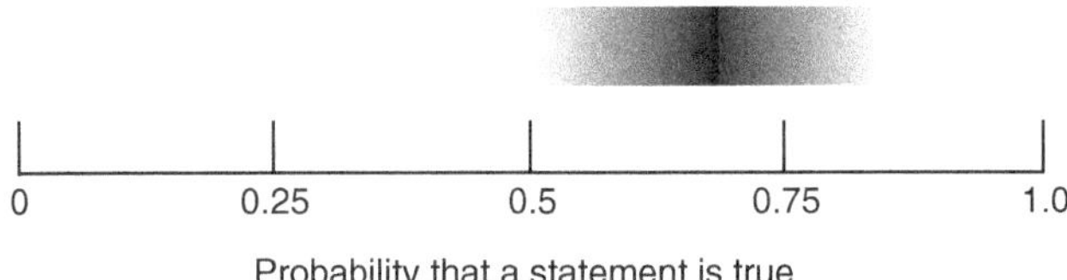

- In any document that reports uncertainties in conventional scientific format (e.g., 3.5±0.7), it is important to be explicit about *what* uncertainty is being included and what is not, and to confirm whether the range is plus or minus

[27] This display divides the interval between 0.99 and 0.01 into five ranges, adding somewhat more resolution across this range than the mapping used by the IPCC–WGI (2001). However, it is far more important to map words into probabilities in a consistent way, *and to be explicit about how that is being done*, than it is to use any specific mapping. Words are inherently imprecise. In the draft version of this diagram, we intentionally included significantly greater overlap between the categories. A number of reviewers were uncomfortable with this overlap, calling for a precise one-to-one mapping between words and probabilities. On the other hand, when a draft of the U.S. National Assessment (2000) produced a diagram with such a precise mapping, reviewers complained about the precise boundaries, with the result that in the final version they were made fuzzy (Figure 2.3). For a more extended discussion of these issues, see section 2 of this report.

one standard deviation. This reporting format is generally not appropriate for large uncertainties or where distributions have a lower or upper bound and hence are not symmetric. In all cases, care should be taken not to report results using more significant figures than are warranted by the associated uncertainty. Often this means overriding default values on standard software such as Microsoft Excel.

- Care should be taken in plotting and labeling the vertical axes when reporting PDFs. The units are probability *density* (i.e., probability per unit interval along the horizontal axis), *not* probability.
- Since many people find it difficult to read and correctly interpret PDFs and CDFs, when space allows it is best practice to plot the CDF above the PDF on the same x-axis (Morgan and Henrion, 1990).
- When many uncertain results must be reported, box plots (first popularized by Tukey, 1977) are often the best way to do this in a compact manner. There are several conventions. Our recommendation is shown below, but what is most important is to be clear about the notation.[28]

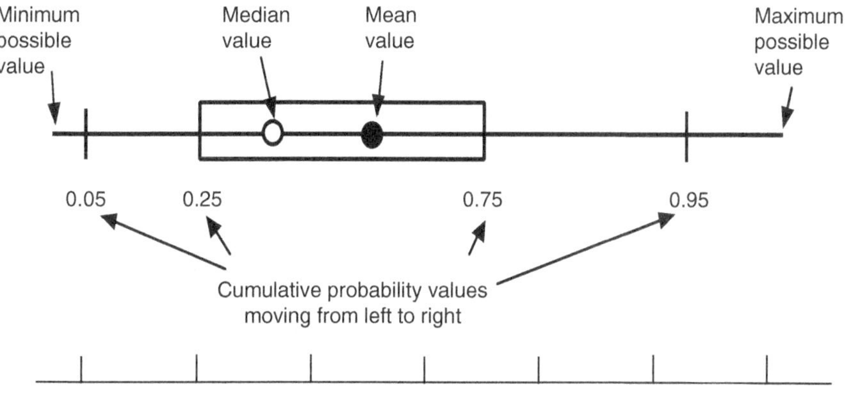

- While there may be a few circumstances in which it is desirable or necessary to address and deal with second-order uncertainty (e.g., how sure an expert is about the shape of an elicited CDF), more often than not the desire to perform such analysis arises from a misunderstanding of the nature of subjective probabilistic statements. When second-order uncertainty is being considered, one should be very careful to determine that the added level of complication will aid in, and will not unnecessarily complicate, subsequent use of the results.

[28] For experimental results on alternative graphical presentations of uncertainty, see Dieckmann et al. (2015).

Characterizing and Analyzing Uncertainty

- Unless there are compelling reasons to do otherwise, conventional probability is the best tool for characterizing and analyzing uncertainty about climate change and its impact.
- The elicitation of expert judgment, often in the form of subjective probability distributions, can be a useful way to combine the formal knowledge in a field as reflected in the literature with the informal knowledge and physical intuition of experts. Elicitation is not a substitute for doing the needed science, but it can be a very useful tool in support of research planning, private decision making, and the formulation of public policy.
- *However*, the design and execution of a good expert elicitation takes time and requires a careful integration of knowledge of the relevant substantive domain with knowledge of behavioral decision science (see Chapter 9).
- When eliciting probability distributions from multiple experts, if they disagree significantly, it is generally better to report the distributions separately. This is especially true if such judgments will subsequently be used as inputs to a model that has a non-linear response (see Chapter 9).
- There is a variety of software tools available to support probabilistic analysis using Monte Carlo and related techniques. As with any powerful analytical tool, their proper use requires careful thought and care.
- In performing uncertainty analysis, it is important to think carefully about possible sources of correlation. One simple procedure for getting a sense of how important this may be is to run the analysis with key variables uncorrelated and then run it again with key variables perfectly correlated. Often, in answering questions about aggregate parameter values, experts assume correlation structures between the various components of the aggregate value being elicited. Sometimes it is important to elicit the component uncertainties separately from the aggregate uncertainty in order to reason out why specific correlation structures are being assumed.
- Methods for describing and dealing with data pedigree (see, for example, Funtowicz and Ravetz, 1990) have not been developed to the point that they can easily be incorporated in probabilistic analysis (see discussion in Chapter 9). However, the quality of the data on which judgments are based is clearly important and should be addressed, especially when uncertain information of varying quality and reliability is combined in a single analysis. At a minimum, investigators should be careful to provide a "traceable account" of where their results and judgments have come from.
- While full probabilistic analysis can be useful, in many contexts, simple parametric analysis, or back-to-front analysis (that works backwards from an end point of interest), may be as or more effective in identifying key unknowns and critical levels of knowledge needed to make better decisions.

- Scenario analysis can sometimes be useful, but also carries risks. Specific detailed scenarios can become cognitively compelling, with the result that people may overlook many other pathways to the same end-points. It is often best to "cut the long causal chains" and focus on the possible range of a few key variables that can most affect outcomes of interest.
- Scenarios, which describe a single point (or line) in a multi-dimensional space, cannot be assigned probabilities. If, as is often the case, it will be useful to assign probabilities to scenarios, they should be defined in terms of intervals in the space of interest, not in terms of point values.
- Variability and uncertainty are not the same thing. Sometimes it is important to draw distinction between the two, but often it is not. A distinction should be made only when it adds clarity for users.
- Analysis that yields predictions is very helpful when our knowledge is sufficient to make meaningful predictions. However, the past history of success in such efforts suggests great caution (see, for example, chapters 3 and 6 in Smil, 2003). When meaningful prediction is not possible, alternative strategies, such as searching for responses or policies that will be robust across a wide range of possible futures, or are easily adaptable, deserve careful consideration.
- For some problems there comes a time when uncertainty is so high that conventional modes of probabilistic analysis (including decision analysis) may no longer make sense. While it is not easy to identify this point, investigators should continually ask themselves whether what they are doing makes sense and whether a much simpler approach, such as a bounding or order-of-magnitude analysis, might be superior (see, for example, Casman et al., 1999).

REFERENCES

Casman, E.A., M.G. Morgan, and H. Dowlatabadi (1999). "Mixed Levels of Uncertainty in Complex Policy Models," *Risk Analysis*, *19*(1), pp. 33–42.

Clark, H.H. (1990). "Comment," *Statistical Science*, *5*, pp. 12–16.

Clark, W.C. (1980). "Witches, Floods and Wonder Drugs," in R.C. Schwing and W.A. Albers, Jr. (eds.), *Societal Risk Assessment*, Plenum, pp. 287–318.

Cliff, N. (1990). "Comment," *Statistical Science*, *5*, pp. 16–18.

Cyert, R.M. and M.H. DeGroot (1987). *Bayesian Analysis and Uncertainty in Economic Theory*, Rowman & Littlefield, 206pp.

Dawes, R.M. (1988). *Rational Choice in an Uncertain World*, Harcourt Brace Jovanovich, 346pp.

DeKay, M.L., M.J. Small, P.S. Fischbeck, R.S. Farrow, A. Cullen, J.B. Kadane, L.B. Lave, M.G. Morgan, and K. Takemura (2002). "Risk-Based Decision Analysis in Support of Precautionary Policies," *Journal of Risk Research*, *5*(4), pp. 391–417.

Dieckmann, N.F., E. Peters and R. Gregory (2015). "At Home on the Range? Lay Interpretations of Numerical Uncertainty Ranges," *Risk Analysis*, *35*(7), pp. 1281–1295.

Dowlatabadi, H. and M.G. Morgan (1993). "A Model Framework for Integrated Studies of the Climate Problem," *Energy Policy*, *21*(3), pp. 209–221.

Ellsberg, D. (1961). "Risk, Ambiguity, and the Savage Axioms," *Quarterly Journal of Economics*, *75*, pp. 643–669.

EPA (1996). *Proposed Guidelines for Cancer Risk Assessment*, Office of Research and Development, U.S. Environmental Protection Agency, Washington, DC, EPA/600P-92/003C.

Fischhoff, B. (1991). "Value Elicitation: Is There Anything in There?," *American Psychologist*, *46*, pp. 835–847.

(2005). "Chapter 18: Cognitive Processes in Stated Preference Methods," in K.-G. Mäleer and J.R. Vincent (eds.), *Handbook of Environmental Economics*, Elsevier, Vol. II, pp. 938–968.

(2012). "Communicating Uncertainty: Fulfilling the Duty to Inform," *Issues in Science and Technology*, *28*(4), pp. 63–70.

Fischhoff, B., A. Bostrom, and M. Jacobs-Quadrel (2002). "Risk Perception and Communication," in R. Detels, J. McEwen, R. Reaglenhole, and H. Tanaka (eds.), *Oxford Textbook of Public Health*, 4th ed., Oxford University Press, Vol. III, pp. 1105–1123.

Franklin, B. (1789). Letter to Jean-Baptiste Leroy.

Friedman, S.M., S. Dunwoody, and C.L. Rogers (1999). *Communicating Uncertainty: Media Coverage of New and Controversial Science*, L. Erlbaum, 277pp.

Funtowicz, S.O. and J.R. Ravetz (1990). *Uncertainty and Quality in Science for Policy*, Kluwer Academic Publishers, 229pp.

Good, I.J. (1962). "How Rational Should a Manager Be?" *Management Science*, *8*(4), pp. 383–393.

Gregory, R. (2001). "Scenarios and Acceptance of Forecasts," in J.S. Armstrong (ed.), *Principles of Forecasting: A Handbook for Researchers and Practitioners*, Kluwer, 849pp.

Henrion, M. (1999) "Uncertainty," in R.A. Wilson and F.C. Keil (eds.), *MIT Encyclopedia of the Cognitive Sciences*, MIT Press, pp. 853–855.

Howard, R.A. and J.E. Matheson (eds.) (1977). *Readings in Decision Analysis*, Decision Analysis Group, SRI International.

Ibrekk, H. and M.G. Morgan (1987). "Graphical Communication of Uncertain Quantities to Nontechnical People," *Risk Analysis*, *7*, pp. 519–529.

Inman, D.L., S.A. Jenkins, and J. Wasyl (1998). "Database for Streamflow and Sediment Flux of California Rivers," SIO Reference 98–9. Scripps Institution of Oceanography, University of California, San Diego.

IPCC (2001a). "Climate Change 2001: The Scientific Basis," in J.T. Houghton et al. (eds.), *Contribution of Working Group I to the Third Assessment Report of the Intergovernmental Panel on Climate Change*, Cambridge University Press, 881pp.

(2001b). "Climate Change 2001: Impacts, Adaptation, and Vulnerability," in J.J. McCarthy et al. (eds.), *Contribution of Working Group II to the Third Assessment Report of the Intergovernmental Panel on Climate Change*, Cambridge University Press, 1032pp.

(2001c). "Climate Change 2001: Mitigation," in B. Metz et al. (eds.), *Contribution of Working Group III to the Third Assessment Report of the Intergovernmental Panel on Climate Change*, Cambridge University Press, 700pp.

(2004). "Workshop Report," in M. Manning et al. (eds.), *Workshop on Describing Scientific Uncertainties in Climate Change to Support Analysis of Risk and of Options*, 146pp. Available at: www.ipcc.ch/pdf/supporting-material/ipcc-workshop-2004-may.pdf.

(2007). "The Physical Science Basis," in S. Solomon et al. (eds.), *Contribution of Working Group I to the Fourth Assessment Report of the Intergovernmental Panel on Climate Change*, Cambridge University Press, 800pp.

Kadane, J.B. (1990). "Comment: Codifying Chance," *Statistical Science*, *5*, pp. 18–20.

Keeney, R.L. (1982). "Decision Analysis: An Overview," *Operations Research*, *30*, pp. 803–837.

(1992). *Value-Focused Thinking: A Path to Creative Decision Making*, Harvard University Press, 416pp.

Kent, S. (1964). "Words of Estimative Probability," *Studies in Intelligence*, *8*(4), pp. 49–65.

Knight, F.H. (1921). *Risk, Uncertainty and Profit*, Houghton Mifflin Company, 381pp.

Kruskal, W. (1990). "Comment," *Statistical Science*, *5*, pp. 20–21.

Kuhn, T.S. (1962). *The Structure of Scientific Revolutions*, University of Chicago Press, 172pp.

Lee, K. (1993). *Compass and Gyroscope: Integrating Science and Politics for the Environment*, Island Press, 243pp.

Lempert, R.J., D.G. Groves, S.W. Popper, and S.C. Bankes (2006). "A General, Analytic Method for Generating Robust Strategies and Narrative Scenarios," *Management Science*, *52*(4), pp. 514–528.

Lempert, R.J., S.W. Popper, and S.C. Bankes (2003). *Shaping the Next One Hundred Years: New Methods for Quantitative, Long-term Policy Analysis*, MR-1626-RPC, RAND, 209pp.

Lempert, R.J., S.W. Popper, D. Groves et al. (2013). "Making Good Decisions Without Predictions," RAND Corporation Research Highlights, 6pp. Only available online at: www.rand.org/pubs/research_briefs/RB9701.html.

Lindblom, C.E. (1959). "The Science of 'Muddling Through,'" *Public Administration Review*, *19*(2), pp. 79–88.

Mandel, D.R. and A. Barnes (2014). "Accuracy of Forecasts in Strategic Intelligence," *Proceedings of the National Academy of Sciences*, *111*(30), pp. 10984–10989.

Morgan, M.G. (1998). "Uncertainty Analysis in Risk Assessment," *Human and Ecological Risk Assessment*, *4*, pp. 25–39.

with H. Dowlatabadi, M. Henrion, D. Keith, R. Lempert, S. McBride, M. Small, and T. Wilbanks (2009). *Best Practice Approaches for Characterizing, Communicating, and Incorporating Scientific Uncertainty in Climate Decision Making*, U.S. Climate Change Science Program Synthesis and Assessment Product (CCSP 5.2), 89pp.

Morgan, M.G., B. Fischhoff, A. Bostrom, and C.J. Atman (2002). *Risk Communication: A Mental Models Approach*, Cambridge University Press, 351pp.

Morgan, M.G. and M. Henrion (1990). *Uncertainty: A Guide to Dealing with Uncertainty in Quantitative Risk and Policy Analysis*, Cambridge University Press, 332pp.

Morgan, M.G., M. Kandlikar, J. Risbey, and H. Dowlatabadi (1999). "Why Conventional Tools for Policy Analysis Are Often Inadequate for Problems of Global Change," *Climatic Change*, *41*, pp. 271–281.

Morgan, M.G. and D. Keith (1995). "Subjective Judgments by Climate Experts," *Environmental Science & Technology*, *29*(10), pp. 468–476.

(2008). "Improving the Way We Think about Projecting Future Energy Use and Emissions of Carbon Dioxide," *Climatic Change*, *90*(3), pp. 189–215.

Morris, S.C. (1990). *Cancer Risk Assessment: A Quantitative Approach*, M. Dekker, 408pp.

Moss, R. and S.H. Schneider (2000). "Uncertainties in the IPCC TAR: Recommendations to Lead Authors for More Consistent Assessment and Reporting," in R. Pachauri et al. (eds.), *Guidance Papers on the Cross Cutting Issues of the Third Assessment Report of the IPCC*, World Meteorological Organisation, pp. 33–51.

Moss, R.H., J.A. Edmonds, K.A. Hibbard et al. (2010). "The Next Generation of Scenarios for Climate Change Research and Assessment," *Nature*, *463*, pp. 747–756.

Mosteller, F. and C. Youtz (1990). "Quantifying Probabilistic Expressions," *Statistical Science*, *5*, pp. 2–12.

Nakicenovic, N. and R. Swart (eds.) (2000). *Special Report on Emissions Scenarios*, Cambridge University Press, 612pp.

National Assessment Synthesis Team (2000). "Climate Change Impacts on the United States: The Potential Consequences of Climate Variability and Change," U.S. Global Change Research Program. Available at: www.globalchange.gov/browse/reports/climate-change-impacts-united-states-potential-consequences-climate-variability-and.

National Research Council (1986a). *Understanding Risk: Informing Decisions in a Democratic Society*, National Academy Press, 250pp.

(1986b). *Scientific Basis for Risk Assessment and Management of Uranium Mill Tailings*, Committee on Uranium Mill Tailings Report, National Academy Press, 264pp.

Oreskes, N. and E.M. Conway (2010). *Merchants of Doubt: How a Handful of Scientists Obscured the Truth on Issues from Tobacco Smoke to Global Warming*, Bloomsbury Press, 355pp.

Paté-Cornell, M.E. (1996). "Uncertainties in Risk Analysis: Six Levels of Treatment," *Reliability Engineering and System Safety*, *54*, pp. 95–111.

Patt, A.G. and D.P. Schrag (2003.) "Using Specific Language to Describe Risk and Probability," *Climatic Change*, *61*, pp. 17–30.

Presidential/Congressional Commission on Risk Assessment and Risk Management (1997). Vol. I: *Framework for Environmental Health Risk Management*; Vol. II: *Risk Assessment and Risk Management in Regulatory Decision-Making*. Available at: http://cfpub.epa.gov/ncea/cfm/recordisplay.cfm?deid=55006.

Raiffa, H. and R. Schlaifer (1968). *Applied Statistical Decision Theory*, MIT Press, 356pp.

Rumsfeld, D. (2002). News briefing as quoted by M. Shermer, *Scientific American*, *293*, September 2005, p. 38.

Schweizer, V.J. and E. Kriegler (2012). "Improving Environmental Change Research with Systematic Techniques for Qualitative Scenarios," *Environmental Research Letters*, 7(4), p. 044011.

Schweizer, V.J. and M.G. Morgan (2016), "Bounding U.S. Electricity Demand in 2050," *Technology Forecasting & Social Change*, *105*, pp. 215–223.

Shell International Limited (2005). *Shell Global Scenarios 2025*. Available at: www-static.shell.com/content/dam/shell/static/aboutshell/downloads/our-strategy/shell-global-scenarios/exsum-23052005.pdf.

Smil, V. (2003). *Energy at the Crossroads*, MIT Press, 448pp.

Smithson, M. (1988). *Ignorance and Uncertainty: Emerging Paradigms*, Springer-Verlag, 393pp.

Sunstein, C.R. (2005). *Laws of Fear: Beyond the Precautionary Principle*, Cambridge University Press, 234pp.

Tanur, J.M. (1990). "Comment: On the Possible Dangers of Isolation," *Statistical Science*, *5*, pp. 21–22.

Thompson, M. (1980). "Aesthetics of Risk: Culture or Context," in R.C. Schwing and W.A. Albers (eds.), *Societal Risk Analysis*, Plenum, pp. 273–285.

Tukey, J.W. (1977). *Exploratory Data Analysis*, Addison-Wesley, 688pp.

von Winterfeldt, D. and W. Edwards (1986). *Decision Analysis and Behavioral Research*, Cambridge University Press, 624pp.

Wallsten, T.S. and D.V. Budescu (1990). "Comment," *Statistical Science*, *5*, pp. 23–26.

Wallsten, T.S., D.V. Budescu, A. Rapoport, R. Zwick, and B. Forsyth (1986). "Measuring the Vague Meanings of Probability Terms," *Journal of Experimental Psychology: General*, *155*(4), pp. 348–365.

Weick, K. and K. Sutcliffe (2001). *Managing the Unexpected: Assuring High Performance in an Age of Uncertainty*, Wiley, 200pp.

Wiener, J.B. and M.D. Rogers (2002). "Comparing Precaution in the United States and Europe," *Journal of Risk Research*, *5*(4), pp. 317–349.

Wilbanks, T. and R. Lee (1985) "Policy Analysis in Theory and Practice," in T.R. Lakshmanan and B. Johansson (eds.), *Large-Scale Energy Projects: Assessment of Regional Consequences*, North-Holland, pp. 273–303.

Wildavsky, A. (1979). "No Risk Is the Highest Risk of All," *American Scientist*, *67*, pp. 32–37.

Winkler, R.L. (1990). "Comment: Representing and Communicating Uncertainty," *Statistical Science*, *5*, pp. 26–30.

Wolf, C., Jr. (1990). "Comment," *Statistical Science*, *5*, pp. 31–32.

9

Expert Elicitation[1]

Society often calls upon experts for advice that requires judgments that go beyond well-established knowledge. In providing such judgments, it is common practice to use simulation models, engineering-economic assessment, and similar tools. While such analytical strategies can provide valuable insight, they can never hope to include all relevant factors. In such situations, the community of applied decision analysis has long employed quantitative expert judgments in the form of subjective probability distributions that have been "elicited" from relevant experts. Most such applications have been undertaken in support of decisions being made by private parties (Spetzler and Staël von Holstein, 1975; Garthwaite et al., 2005; O'Hagan et al., 2006; Hora, 2007). Sometimes the resulting distributions are used directly, sometimes they are fitted to formal functions and used in various Bayesian decision models (DeGroot, 1970; Garthwaite et al., 2005).

The use of expert elicitation in public-sector decision making has been less common. Several studies have explored issues such as the health impacts of fine particle air pollution (Morgan et al., 1978, 1984; Cooke, 1991; Cooke et al., 2007; Roman et al., 2008; Knol et al., 2009; Hoek et al., 2010) and of lead pollution (Wallsten and Whitfield, 1989), the likely nature and extent of climate change (NDU, 1978; Morgan and Keith, 1995; Morgan et al., 2006; Zickfeld et al., 2010), the various impacts that may result from climate change (Morgan et al., 2001; Zickfeld et al., 2007), herbicide-tolerant oilseed crops (Krayer von Krauss et al., 2004), and the likely cost and performance of various energy technologies (Curtright et al., 2008; Chan et al., 2011; Anadon et al., 2012, 2013; Abdulla et al., 2013). EPA has begun to make use of elicitation methods to address uncertain issues in environmental science (EPA, 2011), and folks in both DOE and FDA have expressed interest in possibly using the method.

[1] Most of the text in this chapter first appeared as Morgan (2014). Thanks to the *Proceedings of the National Academy of Sciences* for permission to reuse it in this book.

Done well, expert elicitation can make a valuable contribution to informed decision making. Done poorly, it can lead to useless or even misleading results that lead decision makers astray, alienate experts, and wrongly discredit the entire approach. In what follows, I draw upon relevant literature and 35 years of personal experience in designing and conducting substantively detailed expert elicitations, in order to suggest when it does and does not make sense to perform elicitations, how they should be designed and conducted, and how I believe the results should, and should not, be used. In contrast to much of the literature in Bayesian decision making and applied decision analysis, my focus is on developing detailed descriptions of the state of understanding in some field of science or technology.

9.1 ARE THERE ANY EXPERTS?

In order to conduct an expert elicitation, there must be experts whose knowledge can support informed judgment and prediction about the issues of interest. There are many topics about which people have extensive knowledge that provides little or no basis for making informed predictive judgments. The further one moves away from questions whose answers involve matters of fact that are largely dependent upon empirical natural or social science and well-validated models, into realms in which individual and social behavior determine the outcomes of interest, the more one should ask whether expertise, with predictive capability, exists. For example, given a specified time series of future radiative forcing and other relevant physical variables, in my view, it is reasonable to ask climate scientists to make probabilistic judgments about average global temperature 150 years in the future. I am far less persuaded that it makes sense to ask "experts" questions that entail an assessment of how the stock market, or the price of natural gas, will evolve over the next 25 years, or what the value of global GDP will be 150 years in the future.

9.2 THE INTERPRETATION OF PROBABILITY

A subjectivist or Bayesian interpretation of probability (DeGroot, 1970; Good, 1971; de Finetti, 1974; Jaynes, 2003) is employed when one makes subjective probabilistic assessments of the present or future value of uncertain quantities, the state of the world, or the nature of the processes that govern the world. In such situations, probability is viewed as a statement of an individual's belief, informed by all formal and informal evidence that he or she has available. As noted in Chapter 8, while they are subjective, such judgments cannot be arbitrary. They must conform to the laws of probability. Further, when large quantities of evidence are available on identical repeated events, one's subjective probability should converge to the classical frequentist interpretation of probability.

Partly as a result of their different training and professional cultures, different groups of experts display different views about the appropriateness of making subjective probabilistic judgments, and have different levels of willingness to make such judgments. While every natural scientist and engineer I have ever interviewed seemed to think naturally in terms of subjective probabilities, others, such as some experts in the health sciences, have been far less comfortable with such formulations. For example, some years ago, my colleagues and I conducted an expert elicitation among a group of different types of health experts in an effort to gain insight about health damages that could result from chronic exposure to sub-micron sulfate air pollution. One of our experts, an inhalation toxicologist, tried repeatedly to answer our questions to provide a subjective probability distribution on the slope of a health damage function, but simply could not bring himself to provide such answers. After framing our questions in several different ways, and always reaching an impasse, we suspended the elicitation. Some days later the expert came back to us saying he'd been thinking about it, that the questions we'd been asking made sense, and that he wanted to try again. However, when we did that, he once again found that he could not bring himself to make the necessary quantitative judgments. While this may be an extreme case, I believe that it also reflects a broader difference among fields.

Fifteen years ago, the Presidential/Congressional Commission on Risk Assessment and Risk Management (1997), almost all of whose members were medical professionals, argued that natural scientists should provide probabilistic assessments of exposures, and economists should provide probabilistic assessments of damages, but that health experts should provide only a deterministic treatment of the health damage functions associated with environmental exposures. This reticence to engage in making quantitative subjective judgments has led some to draw an overly sharp distinction between "variability" and "uncertainty" – with the claim that only the former should be described in terms of distributions (i.e., with histograms). While, as I suggested in Chapter 8, there are certainly situations in which it is important to distinguish variability from uncertainty, there are also many decision contexts in which distinguishing between the two simply adds unnecessary complication.

9.3 QUALITATIVE UNCERTAINTY WORDS ARE NOT SUFFICIENT

As explained in Chapter 8, there is clear evidence that without some quantification, the use of qualitative words such as "likely" and "unlikely" to describe uncertainty can mask important, often critical, differences between the views of different experts (see Figures 8.1 and 8.2). The problem arises because the same words can mean very different things to different people, as well as different things to the same person in different contexts. Figure 8.1 summarizes the range of quantitative values that respondents attached to various probability words, independent of any specific context, in a study conducted by

Wallsten et al. (1986). Wardekker et al. (2008) report similar findings in more recent studies undertaken in the Netherlands to improve the communication of uncertainty in results from environmental assessments. Figure 8.2 summarizes the range of quantitative values that members of the EPA Science Advisory Board attached to probability words used to describe the likelihood that a chemical agent is a human carcinogen. Such results make a compelling case for at least some quantification when assessing the value of uncertain coefficients or the likelihood of uncertain events. The climate assessment community has taken this lesson to heart, providing mappings of probability words into quantitative values in most assessment reports (Moss and Schneider, 2000; National Assessment Synthesis Team, 2001; Morgan et al., 2009).

9.4 COGNITIVE HEURISTICS AND BIAS

We humans are not equipped with a competent mental statistical processor. Rather, in making judgments in the face of uncertainty, we unconsciously employ a variety of cognitive heuristics. As a consequence, when asked to make probabilistic judgments, either in a formal elicitation or in any less formal setting, people's judgments are often biased. Two of the cognitive heuristics that are most relevant to expert elicitation are called "availability" and "anchoring and adjustment." These heuristics, which have been extensively studied by Kahneman and Tversky (Tversky and Kahneman, 1974; Kahneman et al., 1982), are discussed in detail in Chapter 12. Here I give a brief overview.

Through the operation of availability, people assess the frequency of a class, or the probability of an event, by the ease with which instances or occurrences can be brought to mind. In performing elicitation, the objective should be to obtain an expert's carefully considered judgment based on a systematic consideration of all relevant evidence. For this reason, one should take care to adopt strategies designed to help the expert being interviewed to avoid overlooking relevant evidence.

When presented with an estimation task, if people start with a first value (i.e., an anchor) and then adjust up and down from that value, they typically do not adjust sufficiently. Kahneman and Tversky call this second heuristic anchoring and adjustment. In order to minimize the influence of this heuristic when eliciting probability distributions, it is standard procedure *not* to begin with questions that ask about "best" or most probable values but rather to first ask about extremes: "What is the highest (lowest) value you can imagine for coefficient X?" or "Please give me a value for coefficient X for which you think there is only one chance in 100 that the actual value of X could be larger (smaller)." Having obtained an estimate of an upper (lower) bound, it is then standard practice to ask the expert to imagine that the uncertainty about the coefficient's value has been resolved and the actual value has turned out to be 10 or 15 percent larger (smaller) than the bound they offered. We then ask the expert: "Can you offer an explanation of how that might be possible?" Sometimes experts can offer a perfectly plausible physical explanation, at which point we ask them to revise their bound. After obtaining estimates of upper and lower bounds on the value of a coefficient of interest, we then go on to elicit intermediate values across the probability distribution ("What is the probability that the value of X is greater (less) than Y?") If results seem to be unduly scattered, changing the question format may help: "Give me a value of X such that the odds that the true value is greater (less) than 1 in Z (or probability P)."

To support such interviews, the decision analysis community has developed adjustable "probability wheels" on which the size of a colored pie-slice portion of a wheel can be adjusted so that respondents can compare their assessments of probability to the size of the slice and adjust it up and down until the size of the slice corresponds to their judged probability (see Figure B9.3 on p. 267). While such aids may be helpful for decision analysts who are dealing with clients with limited numeracy, when we have shown such an aid to an expert in science or technology they have typically toyed with it in a bemused way and then set it aside to give direct quantitative responses.

Only after filling in a number of intervening points in a cumulative distribution function does one finally ask for a median or best estimate, sketch the resulting distribution, and show it to the expert for their assessment and possible revision.

9.5 UBIQUITOUS OVERCONFIDENCE

One reason for adopting this rather elaborate procedure is that there is strong evidence that most such judgments are overconfident (see Chapter 12). A standard measure of overconfidence is the "surprise index," the fraction of true values that lie outside an assessor's 98 percent confidence interval when answering questions for which the true answer is known (e.g., the length of the Panama canal). Figure 9.1 reports a summary of results from 21 different studies involving over 10,000 such assessment questions. Note that none yields the target value for the surprise index of 2 percent and over half yielded values of 30 percent or more! Lest the reader infer that such overconfidence is only observed in judgments made by lay respondents, Figure 9.2 shows the evolution over time of the recommended values for the speed of light. Similar results exist for other physical quantities.

Calibration is a widely used measure of the performance of someone making subjective probabilistic judgments. Lichtenstein et al. (1982) explain that an assessor (judge) is well calibrated "if, over the long run, for all propositions assigned a given probability, the proportion that is true equals the probability that is assigned. Judges' calibration can be empirically evaluated by observing their probability assessments, verifying the associated propositions, and then observing the proportion that is true in each response category." With a

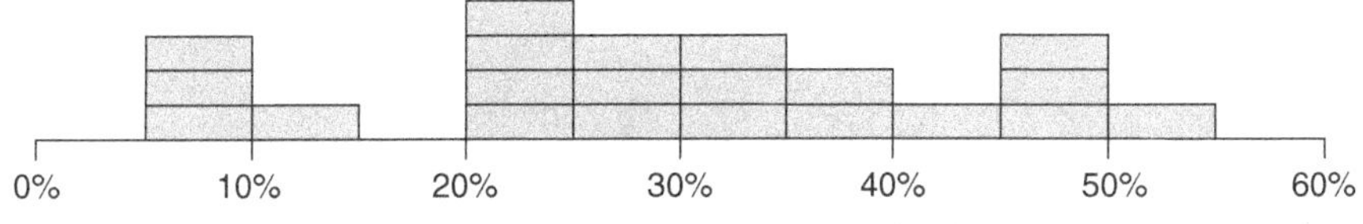

FIGURE 9.1. Summary of the value of the "surprise index" (ideal value = 2%) observed in 21 different studies involving over 10,000 assessment questions. These results indicate clearly the ubiquitous tendency to overconfidence (i.e., assessed probabilities that are too narrow). A more detailed summary is provided in Morgan and Henrion (1990).

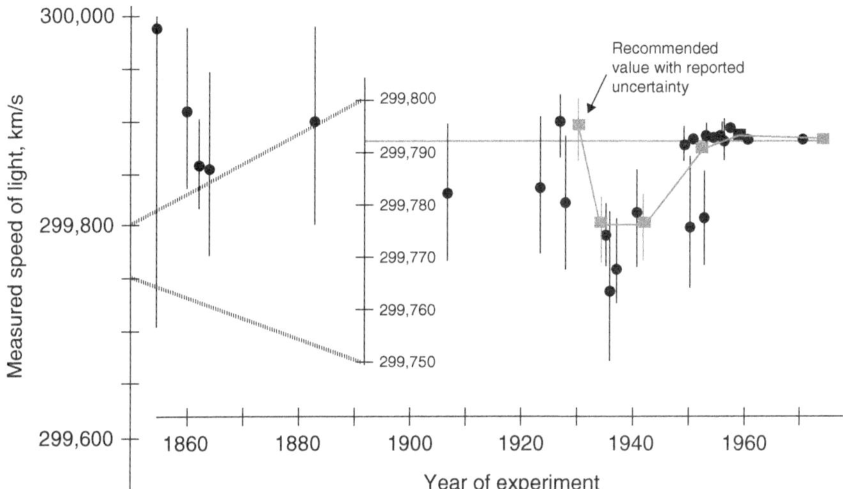

FIGURE 9.2. Published estimates of the speed of light. The light gray boxes that start in 1930 are the recommended values from the particle physics group that presumably include an effort to consider uncertainty arising from systematic error. Note that for over two decades the reported confidence intervals on these recommended values did not include the present best-measured value. Henrion and Fischhoff (1986), from which this figure is combined and redrawn, report that the same overconfidence is observed in the recommended values of a number of other physical constants.

few exceptions, such as weather forecasters who make daily precipitation forecasts aided by computer models and receive regular feedback on how well they are performing (Murphy and Winkler, 1977; Charba and Klein, 1980), most people making subjective judgments are not very well calibrated. Figure 9.3 shows examples of very poorly calibrated results from clinical diagnosis of pneumonia (Christensen-Szalanski and Bushyhead, 1981) and of very well calibrated probabilistic precipitation judgments by U.S. weather forecasters (Charba and Klein, 1980).

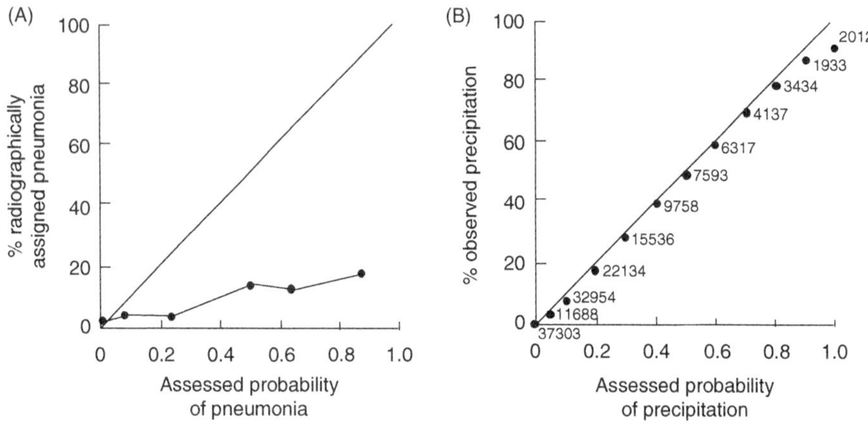

FIGURE 9.3. Illustration of two extremes in expert calibration. **A.** Assessment of probability of pneumonia (based on observed symptoms) in 1531 first-time patients by nine physicians as compared with radiographically assigned cases of pneumonia as reported by Christensen-Szalanski and Bushyhead (1981). **B.** Once-daily U.S. Weather Service precipitation forecasts for 87 stations are compared with actual occurrence of precipitation (April 1977 to March 1979) as reported by Charba and Klein (1980). The small numbers adjacent to each point report the number of forecasts.

Lichtenstein et al. (1982) found that probability judgments tend to be too high when questions are hard, and too low when questions are easy, where "hard" and "easy" questions were classified in terms of the percentage of correct answers made by a reference group. One possible explanation is that assessors partition their responses according to some fixed "cut-off value." The hard/easy effect would result if that value remains constant as the difficulty of the question changes. Lichtenstein et al. (1982) suggest that the hard/easy effect may result because of "an inability to change the cutoffs involved in the transformation from feelings of certainty to probabilistic responses."

While good calibration is rare, it is not unique to weather forecasters. Using a remarkable data set, Mandel and Barnes (2014) have assessed the performance of 1514 strategic intelligence forecasts abstracted from intelligence reports produced by the Canadian Government's strategic intelligence analysis unit. They find that:

both discrimination and calibration of forecasts was very good. Discrimination was better for senior (versus junior) analysts and for easier (versus harder) forecasts. Miscalibration was mainly due to underconfidence such that analysts assigned more uncertainty than needed given their high level of discrimination. Underconfidence was more pronounced for harder (versus easier) forecasts and for forecasts deemed more (versus less) important for policy decision making. Despite the observed underconfidence, there was a paucity of forecasts in the least informative 0.4–0.6 probability range. Recalibrating the forecasts substantially reduced underconfidence. The findings offer cause for tempered optimism about the accuracy of strategic intelligence forecasts and indicate that intelligence producers aim to promote informativeness while avoiding overstatement.

If an assessor is asked a large enough set of questions to make it possible to plot a calibration curve, one might be tempted to simply adjust his or her assessed probabilities (e.g., when the expert says $p = 0.7$, adjust it to 0.8). While recalibration can sometimes make sense, Kadane and Fischhoff (2013) have shown that for assessed probabilities that conform to the basic laws of probability (i.e., are coherent) such a procedure is not justified.

9.6 DEVELOPING A PROTOCOL

A primary output of many expert elicitations is a set of subjective probability distributions on the value of quantities of interest, such as an oxidation rate or the slope of a health damage function. A simply hypothetical example of an elicitation procedure to obtain a set of probability distributions is shown in Box 9.1 at the end of this chapter.

However, often the objective is broader than simply eliciting a number of distributions. Rather, it is to obtain an expert's characterization of the state of knowledge about a general topic or problem area, in which the elicitation of specific probability distributions may be only one of a number of tasks. Either way, the development of a good elicitation protocol requires considerable time and care, and multiple iterations on format and question wording. Working with colleagues who are familiar with the domain and its literature, one can usually build a much longer list of questions than it is reasonable to have an expert answer in a session of a few hours or the better part of a day. If the objectives of the elicitation have not already been sharply defined, this is the time to do that. A sharp focus can help the pruning process and sometimes the pruning can help to sharpen the focus.

Questions that are posed in an expert elicitation should pass what is commonly termed a clairvoyant test. The question, "What will be the price of gasoline next year?" fails such a test. Without specifying the octane, and when and where that gasoline is to be purchased, a clairvoyant cannot provide a precise answer to this question.

The best experts have comprehensive mental models of all of the various factors that may influence the value of an uncertain quantity, as well as which of those factors most contribute to its uncertainty. However, not all of that knowledge may be comparably accessible. Since the objective of an elicitation should be to obtain each expert's "best considered judgment," it is important to help them keep all of those factors in mind as they answer specific questions in an elicitation. To assist in that process, we have often used a variety of graphical aids such as summary tables and influence diagrams that illustrate the relation between key factors that influence the value of interest.

For a simple example, see pp. 4 and 5 of the protocol used in Curtright et al. (2008), available at: http://pubs.acs.org/doi/suppl/10.1021/es8014088/suppl_file/es8014088_si_001.pdf.

My colleagues and I have also made frequent use of card-sorting tasks, in which, working iteratively with the group of experts before we visit them, we develop a set of cards, each of which lists a factor that may influence the value of interest (blank cards are included so that an expert can add, modify, or combine factors). After discussing and possibly refining or modifying the factors, the expert is then asked to sort the cards, first in terms of the strength of influence, and then a second time in terms of how much each factor contributes to uncertainty in the value of the quantity of interest. Such an exercise helps experts to differentiate between strength of influences versus source of uncertainty, and to focus on the most important of the latter in formulating their probabilistic responses. For an example, see pp. 5–7 of the protocol used in Zickfeld et al. (2010), available at: www.pnas.org/content/suppl/2010/06/28/0908906107.DCSupplemental/Appendix.pdf.

Similarly, when we have done an elicitation on a future technology, such as carbon capture and geological sequestration for coal-fired power plants, we have taken the question apart into component pieces, rather than simply asking for holistic judgments about the entire system (Rao et al., 2006).

In choosing the questions that will be posed, it is important to draw a clear distinction between questions of fact and questions whose answers largely entail normative judgments. It may be appropriate in some circumstances to ask experts what they believe a specific group's preferences are, or will be. However, one should take care to distinguish such questions from those in which, using methods similar to those employed in expert elicitation, experts' *own* value judgments are elicited. An example of the former would be questions of fact, such as the implicit "value of a statistical life" that a specific socioeconomic group can be expected to display in making a well-specified risky decision. An example of the latter would be normative questions about what value of a statistical life society *should* adopt in making regulatory decisions. While it may be interesting to learn what value of a statistical life an economist thinks society should adopt, or what level of protection an ecologist thinks society should afford a particular species or habitat, such questions are not about issues of fact, and thus are more appropriately handled as part of an "opinion survey."

In most of the elicitations I have conducted, I have involved an excellent post-doc or junior colleague, who has not yet established a reputation or a professional stake in the field, but has performed a recent systematic review of the relevant literature. Upon hearing a particular response from an expert, they may observe: "That response would appear to be at odds with work reported by Group X." Sometimes the expert will respond, "Oh yes, I had forgotten about that," and adjust their answer. More often they say something more along the lines of: "Yes, I know, but I really discount the work of Group X because I have grave doubts about how they calibrate their instrument." When I have described this proactive procedure to some colleagues who work in survey research they have expressed concern that such an intervention may inappropriately influence an expert's response. While I am not aware of literature on this point, in most of the elicitations that I have conducted in areas of natural science, such as air chemistry or climate change, it is my experience that the experts are intimately familiar with and have assessed each other's work, and it is most unlikely that anything I or my colleagues say during an elicitation session will change their judgment once they have considered all relevant evidence. When that is not the case, care should be taken ahead of time to provide literature packets, reviews, and summaries so that all experts come to the questions with a comparable familiarity with available knowledge.

In contrast to political or similar polling, the objective of most expert elicitation is not to obtain a statistically representative sample of the views of a population. Rather, it is to gain an understanding of the range of responsible expert judgments and interpretations across the field of interest. Thus, in selecting the group of experts, care must be taken to include people who represent all the major perspectives and interpretations that exist within the community. This can typically be achieved by a careful reading of the literature and discussion with experts, who can identify the views of their various peers. In the elicitations we have conducted, we have often constructed tables of the experts sorted by background and technical perspective. Because we have always worked with a collaborator who was an expert in the field and with the relevant literatures, we have not felt it necessary to use more formal procedures for sorting and selecting participants.

When results from an expert elicitation are to be used as input to regulatory or other public policy decision making (by EPA, FDA, etc.), perceived legitimacy or fairness becomes especially important (Clark et al., 2011). In such cases, a more systematic approach should be used in the selection of experts. Knol et al. (2010) outline a number of more formal procedures that they and others have used in order to select experts. In their expert elicitation of the health impacts from PM2.5 conducted for EPA, Roman et al. (2008) used a two-part selection process that employed publication counts and peer-nomination of experts. The EPA White Paper (2011) on expert elicitation provides a discussion of these issues.

There is no "right answer" to the question "how many experts are needed for a good elicitation?" The answer depends on the nature of the field. If virtually all experts adopt similar basic models of the underlying science, then as few as five or six might suffice. In most cases, since experts will have a diversity of opinions about the underlying science, a larger group will be necessary to obtain adequate coverage of the range of opinions.

When we have published the results from expert elicitations, in most cases, we have identified the experts involved, but have not linked individual experts to specific results (although in a few cases experts familiar with the views of their colleagues have been able to privately identify who said what). In many cases, providing such limited anonymity is important so that experts can provide their considered judgment unconstrained by corporate, political, or other considerations. The EPA White Paper (2011) on expert elicitation observes that given "current norms within the scientific community, experts may be unwilling to participate and share their judgments honestly if they fear a need to defend any judgments that divert from the mainstream or conflict with positions taken by their institutions." While I agree, I find troubling the extension of this argument made by Aspinall (2010), who suggests that an advantage of combining results elicited from several experts "is that it encourages experts wary of getting involved in policy advice: the structured, neutral procedure, and the collective nature of the result reassures experts and relieves them of the burden of sole responsibility." Experts should be providing their careful considered judgments, and too much anonymity may result in their taking those judgments less seriously.

Writing in the specific context of elicitations done in support of environmental impact assessment, Knol et al. (2010) describe a seven-step approach to developing and conducting expert elicitations. Despite the title (which sounds like the authors might be offering a "cook-book"), their treatment is thoughtful and nuanced. It explores many of the issues discussed in the preceding paragraphs, reaching broadly similar conclusions.

While I have argued that the development of an elicitation protocol should be an iterative process, requiring considerable effort, pretesting, and refining, not everyone agrees. For example, Aspinall (2010) argues that "the speed with which ... elicitations can be conducted is one of their advantages," and cites a study of the virulence of biological agents conducted in just two days "with a few days of preparatory work." I've no doubt that in this case, in a study of a very focused topic with an intensive couple of days of preparation, it was possible to develop a quality study. However, one needs to be careful not to encourage the development of "quick and dirty" expert elicitations.

9.7 COMPUTER TOOLS TO SUPPORT OR PERFORM ELICITATION

A variety of computer tools have been developed and used in support of expert elicitation (Devillee and Knol, 2011). Some of these are quite specific to the process of elicitation (O'Hagan et al., 2010; Morris et al., 2014); others, such as tools for constructing influence diagrams and Bayesian belief nets, are much more general in nature. For example, in our own work, we have had experts who chose to perform runs of their own computer models to gain insights before answering specific questions we have posed. Using specialized software tools to summarize literature or construct influence diagrams or similar aids can also be very helpful.

While I have found no published literature that evaluates them, several investigators have developed software to perform the actual elicitation, posing questions to establish ranges and seek probabilistic judgments that allow the construction of probability distributions. In at least one case, the software also supports a card-sorting exercise prior to performing the elicitation. Such tools might be useful, if used in conjunction with a face-to-face elicitation. It is an open question whether experts working on their own will devote the same degree of serious consideration in responding to an automated elicitation system that they clearly do when responding to a well-developed protocol during a face-to-face interview with attentive and technically knowledgeable interviewers sitting with them in their office.

9.8 UNCERTAINTY ABOUT MODEL FUNCTIONAL FORM

A few investigators have conducted studies in which the assumptions about the functional form of a set of underlying causal processes are explicitly identified and experts are asked to make judgments about the likelihood that each is a correct description of underlying physical reality. Evans et al. (1994a, b) developed and demonstrated such methods in the context of health experts' judgments about low-dose cancer risk from exposure to formaldehyde in environmental and occupational settings. The method employed the construction of probability trees that allowed experts to make judgments about the relative likelihood that alternative models of possible pharmacokinetic and pharmacodynamic processes correctly describe the biological processes that are involved. Budnitz et al. (1995, 1997, 1998) have employed a set of deliberative processes designed to support a group of experts in developing a "composite probability distribution [that] represents the overall scientific community." The process they developed is very labor intensive and uses experts as "evaluators" of alternative causal models and their implications rather than as "proponents" of one or another model. It would be highly desirable to apply procedures such as those developed and demonstrated by Evans et al. (1994a, b) and Budnitz et al. (1995, 1998) in assessment processes such as those used by the Intergovernmental Panel on Climate Change (IPCC). However, resource constraints, and the limited familiarity that most experts have with decision science, probably make such an effort infeasible.

As elaborated in Chapter 11, in contrast to integrated assessment models of climate change that adopt fixed model structures and fixed functional relationships among variables, Dowlatabadi and I (Dowlatabadi and Morgan, 1993; Morgan and Dowlatabadi, 1996) populated our Integrated Climate Assessment Model (ICAM) with switches that allow the user to explore the implications of a wide range of plausible alternative functional forms. In addition to alternative assumptions about climate science and impacts, ICAM also allows users to explore models that employ a variety of different approaches to time preference, and allows a variety of different behavioral responses (e.g., nations may or may not defect from a global carbon tax regime as tax rates become high). In exploring a wide range of alternative model functional forms, it became clear that we could get an *enormous* variety of answers depending on the range of plausible assumptions we made about the structure of the model and which regional decision maker we considered. Rarely was any emission abatement policy optimal for all regions. Rarely were any results stochastically dominant. We concluded that it is indefensible to use integrated assessment models that have a fixed functional form in an effort to find a single "globally optimal" climate policy.

Finally, Refsgaard et al. (2005) have suggested a variety of different strategies that can be used to explore the implications of what they term "uncertainty due to model structure error."

9.9 CONFIDENCE, SECOND-ORDER UNCERTAINTY, AND PEDIGREE

The nature and quality of the evidence that experts draw upon to make probabilistic judgments is often highly variable. In developing guidance on the treatment of uncertainty for IPCC, Moss and Schneider (2000) distinguished between the amount of evidence available to support a judgment and the degree of consensus within the scientific community. When both are high, they term the state of knowledge as "well established." When evidence is modest but agreement is high, they term the state "established but incomplete"; when the reverse is true they say "there are competing explanations." When both evidence and agreement are low, they describe the situation as "speculative."

The IPCC has continued to use a two-dimensional formulation. However, for the fifth assessment (Mastrandrea et al., 2010), the interpretation evolved to:

- Confidence in the validity of a finding, based on the type, amount, quality, and consistency of evidence (e.g., mechanistic understanding, theory, data, models, expert judgment) and the degree of agreement ...
- Quantified measures of uncertainty in a finding expressed probabilistically (based on statistical analysis of observations or model results, or expert judgment).

Rather than quantify "confidence" the guidance document explains that the level of confidence in a probabilistic assessment should be "expressed using [one of] five qualifiers: 'very low,' 'low,' 'medium,' 'high,' and 'very high.' " The guidance explains that "levels of confidence are intended to synthesize author teams' judgments about the validity of findings as determined through their evaluation of evidence and agreement, and to communicate their relative level of confidence qualitatively." In addition, a mapping is provided between probability words and probability values. Hence, in the IPCC's fifth assessment report (2013) one reads statements such as: "In the Northern Hemisphere, 1983–2012 was likely the warmest 30-year period of the last 1400 years (medium confidence)." In that statement, the IPCC maps the word "likely" to a probability range of 66–100 percent. Statements such as this are basically an alternative to reporting a second-order uncertainty, that is, to reporting an assessment of the probability that one's single value assessed probability is correct. For a graphical display, see the second figure in Section 8.9.

Funtowicz and Ravetz (1990) further refined these ideas, by introducing a five-element vector to describe uncertain quantities. The elements in their NUSAP characterization of an uncertain quantity are: *numeral* (typically a best estimate); *unit* (the units in which the value is measured); *spread* and *assessment* (which are simple and more complete descriptions of uncertainty about the value of the quantity); and *pedigree*, which is intended to "convey an evaluative account of the production process of the quantitative information" – typically in the form of a matrix of qualitative values.

Assigning a pedigree to each uncertain quantity is an appealing idea, but implementing it in practice becomes rather complicated. Van der Sluijs and coworkers (2005a, b) have made several attempts to implement the NUSAP idea in environmental assessments. Assessing and propagating a pedigree matrix of qualitative values through a quantitative model obviously requires one to focus on those variables that have greatest influence on the output of interest. The results become rather complex and, in my view, their utility to decision makers remains an open question.

9.10 DIVERSITY IN EXPERT OPINION

It is common in assessment processes, such as those conducted by the IPCC, to convene panels of experts and ask them to produce consensus judgments of the value of key uncertain quantities. In most cases, this is done informally. While the cognitive biases described above certainly operate in such circumstances, there is typically no way to assess their impact or control their influence in such informal settings. In several of the elicitations of individual experts that my colleagues and I have conducted on issues related to climate change, we have obtained significantly wider ranges of values than those reported by the analogous IPCC consensus process.

Figure 9.4 compares results of the values of radiative forcing by aerosols as assessed by the IPCC fourth assessment (IPCC, 2007) with distributions elicited at about the same time from 24 aerosol experts (Morgan et al., 2006). Note that several experts place significant probability outside of the bounds that result if one simply adds the upper bound of the direct and cloud albedo estimates from the IPCC fourth assessment.

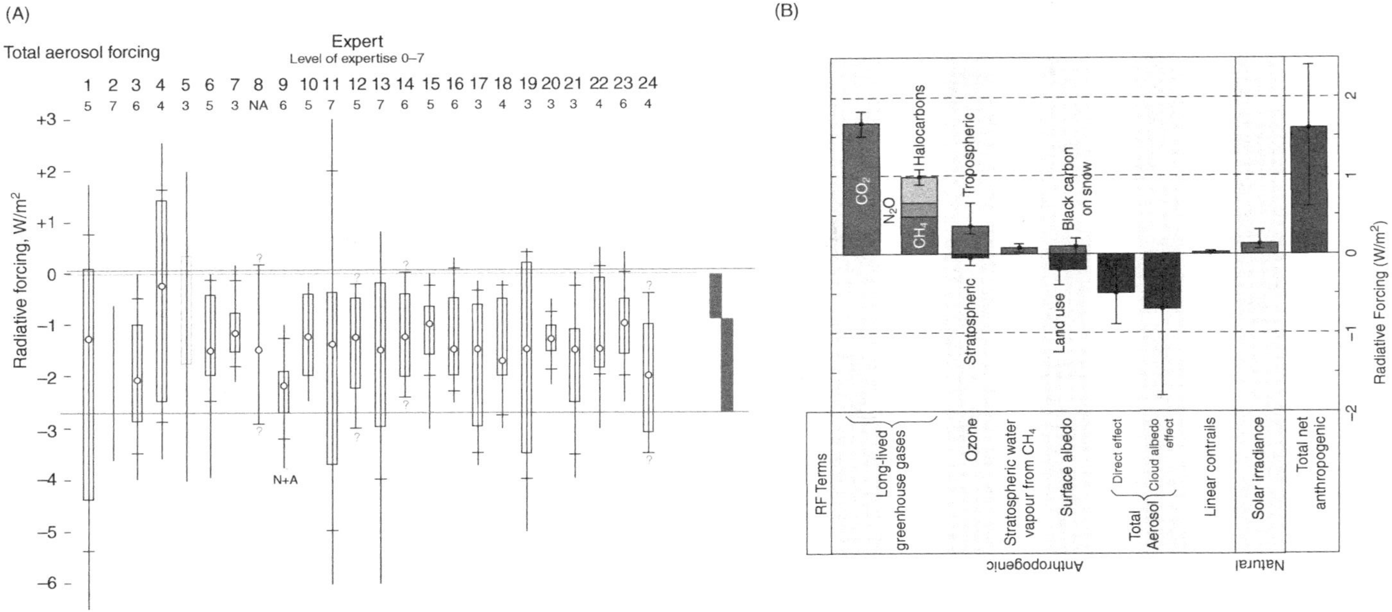

FIGURE 9.4. Comparison of individually assessed value of total radiative forcing produced by aerosols (15) (**A**) with the summary assessment produced by the fourth IPCC assessment (IPCC, 2007) (**B**). Note that many of the individual assessments reported in **A.** involve a wider range of uncertainty than IPCC consensus summary. The summary that was provided in the third assessment (IPCC, 2001) included only a portion of the indirect effects and the range was narrower.

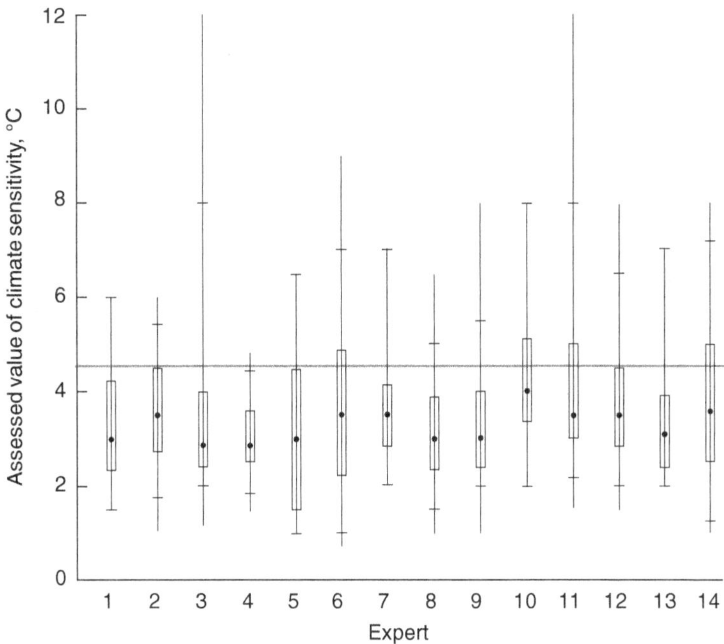

FIGURE 9.5. Individual expert assessments of the value of climate sensitivity as reported in Zickfeld et al. (2010) compared with the IPCC assessment by Schneider et al. (2007) that there is between an 0.05 and 0.17 probability that climate sensitivity is >4.5°C (i.e., above the horizontal line). The assessed expert distributions place probability of between 0.07 and 0.37 above 4.5°C.

Figure 9.5 compares results from an elicitation of the values of climate sensitivity (Zickfeld et al., 2010) with the IPCC fourth assessment (IPCC, 2007) that estimated that the "equilibrium climate sensitivity is likely to lie in the range 2 – 4.5°C, with a most likely value of about 3°C." IPCC defined likely as a 0.66–0.90 probability, which in chapter 19 of Working Group II (68) (Schneider et al., 2007) was interpreted as a 0.05–0.17 probability that climate sensitivity is >4.5°C. Ten of the 14 elicited distributions reported in Figure 9.5 placed more than 0.17 of their probability above 4.5°C.

Without arguing that these results from individual elicitations are more appropriate or informative than IPCC consensus judgments, the difference does suggest that IPCC and similar groups might be well advised to adopt a strategy that uses both approaches. For example, after the experts involved in an assessment team have individually reviewed all the available evidence, an elicitation of probability distributions for key parameters of interest might be performed with each individual team member. The results could then be used as inputs to the group deliberations in which the team develops their collective assessment.

Oppenheimer et al. (2007), Aspinall (2010), and the EPA White Paper (2011) all argue that an advantage of expert elicitation is that results can clearly display different schools of thought within an expert community. The EPA (2011) writes:

> differences in response may result from different paradigms by which the experts view the world and the data. This often is true when the experts come from different disciplinary backgrounds. Experts tend to trust data obtained through methods with which they have direct experience. For example, when one is trying to estimate the relationship between exposure to a substance and increased morbidity or mortality, epidemiologists may tend to find epidemiological data compelling while being more suspect of toxicological studies on animals. Toxicologists may have the opposite preference. In this situation, the variability among the findings represents a spectrum of beliefs and weights that experts from different fields place on the various types of evidence. In such cases, reconciling the differences may be imprudent.

In the context of climate change, Oppenheimer et al. (2007) argue that "with the general credibility of the science of climate change established, it is now equally important that policy-makers understand the more extreme possibilities that consensus may exclude or downplay."

Figure 9.6 provides a striking example of two quite different schools of thought that existed in 2005 within the community of oceanographers on the topic of possible collapse of the Atlantic Meridional Overturning Circulation (AMOC) in the face of global warming. After reviewing literature on paleoclimate change and model simulations, in its 2007 assessment, IPCC Working Group II (Schneider et al., 2007) wrote: "The third line of evidence, not assessed by Working Group I, relies on expert elicitations (sometimes combined with the analysis of simple climate models). These [A]MOC projections show a large spread, with some suggesting a substantial likelihood of triggering a [A]MOC threshold response within this century." However, Figure 9.6 was not reproduced in the report.

9.11 COMBINING EXPERT JUDGMENTS

There is a large literature on strategies to combine experts' probabilistic judgments, excellent overviews of which can be found in the writings of Clemen and Winkler (1999, 2007). Clearly, there are circumstances in which combining the judgments of different experts is a sensible thing to do. However, if the experts make very different judgments about the relevant underlying science, or if the uncertain value that is being assessed will be used as an input to a non-linear model, then it is best *not* to combine the separate judgments, but rather to run separate analyses in order to explore how much the difference in expert opinions affects the outcome of interest. For example, in early work on the health impacts of fine particle air pollution, we found that differences among air pollution experts made relatively little difference in assessments of health impact as compared with the wide range of different functional models and views expressed by health experts (Morgan et al., 1978).

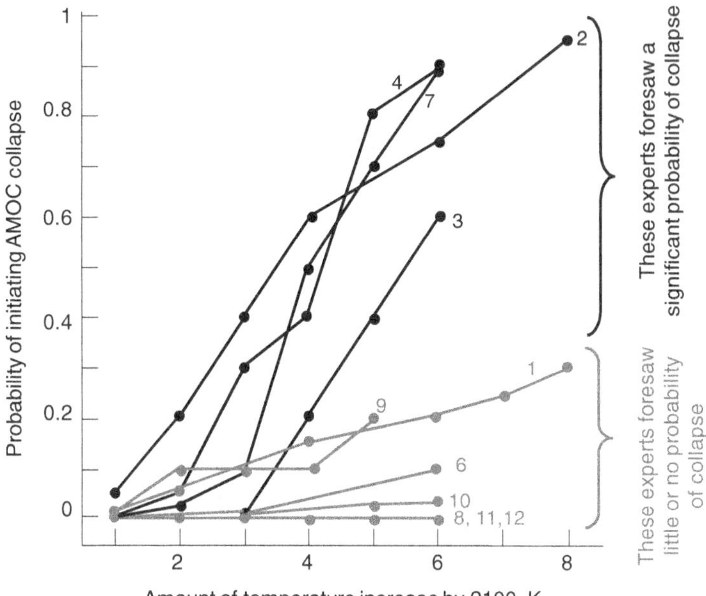

FIGURE 9.6. Expert elicitation can be effective in displaying the range of opinions that exist within a scientific community. This plot displays clearly the two quite different schools of thought that existed roughly a decade ago within the community of oceanographers about the probability "that a collapse of the AMOC will occur or will be irreversibly triggered as a function of the global mean temperature increase realized in the year 2100." Each curve shows the subjective judgments of one of 12 experts. Collapse was defined as a reduction in AMOC strength by more than 90% relative to present-day. Figure from Zickfeld et al. (2007).

Cooke and colleagues (1991, 2008) have worked extensively on developing and applying methods to assess the quality of expert judgments and support the combining of those judgments. In an approach he and his co-workers term the "classical method," experts are asked to make judgments about a number of "seed" questions – questions about the value of quantities in the same general domain as the topic of interest, but for which true values can be found. By performing a product of a calibration score and an information score (a measure of assessed confidence interval), and dropping those experts whose calibration score is lower than a cut-off value, the performance of experts is evaluated, and only those who achieve a high enough score are used to produce a combined distribution. It remains an open question just how diagnostic this procedure is for assessing the quality of expert judgments on complex scientific questions for which answers cannot be known for at least many years in the future. Withholding various numbers of seed questions and treating them as the target quantities of interest has allowed some evaluation of the screening method.

On the basis of an examination of 14 studies that used the classical method, Clemen (2008) concluded that "the overall out-of-sample performance of Cooke's method appears to be no better than EQ [the use of equal weights on all experts]; the two methods have similar median combination scores, but EQ has less variability and better accuracy." Similarly, Lin and Cheng (2009) concluded that while sometimes the performance weight method was superior it did not always outperform EQ. However, more recently, in a much larger study using data from 33 different expert elicitations, Colson and Cooke (2017) have demonstrated quite persuasively that in most cases the use of performance-based weights is superior to the use of equal weights.

While Cooke's method has been used in a number of applications (Cooke, 1991; Aspinall, 2010), it is potentially problematic in situations, such as the assessment of health damage functions or various quantities in climate science, in which different experts make very different assumptions about the nature of the underlying causal mechanisms. As noted above, depending upon how the results will be used, combining the judgments of experts (by any procedure) may not be appropriate. It would also be problematic if one were to exclude some experts who represent plausible, but poorly represented, alternative views about the science. The history of science is replete with examples in which the minority opinion about uncertain science ultimately proved to be correct.

A special case in the literature on combining expert judgments involves the combination of judgments about binary events (either the event happens or it does not). In laboratory studies Karvetski et al. (2013) showed that by eliciting extra judgments to determine how coherent a judgment is, adjusting the resulting set of judgments to make them more coherent, and then weighting those adjusted judgments on the basis of original coherence, a significant improvement in performance could be achieved.

In the early 1950s, a group of investigators at RAND developed a strategy to obtain group judgment that they termed the Delphi Method. This method was first used in classified studies conducted for the U.S. Air Force on bombing requirements (Dalkey and Helmer, 1972). When that work was declassified a decade later (Dalkey and Helmer, 1972), the method became popular as a strategy for developing group consensus about the value of unknown parameters or various normative or policy issues. Criticisms of the method soon began to appear. With support from the U.S. Air Force, Harold Sackman (1975), another RAND analyst, performed an assessment of the technique, the conclusions of which were highly critical: "Delphi consensus is specious consensus." He recommended that the use of "conventional Delphi be dropped … until its principles, methods and fundamental applications can be experimentally established as scientifically tenable." Fifteen years later, after an extensive review conducted for the Dutch government of a much larger body of literature, Woudenberg (1991) reached a very similar conclusion, writing: "A Delphi is extremely efficient in obtaining consensus, but this consensus is not based on genuine agreement; rather, it is the result of ... strong group pressure to conformity."

Delphi continues to be widely used. A number of more recent authors clearly do not agree with these negative conclusions. For example, Rowe and Wright (1999) identified and reviewed 27 evaluative studies.[2] They report that "evidence for Delphi effectiveness is equivocal, but results generally support its advantage over first round/staticized group aggregates." Drawing on insights from literature in social psychology, Bolger and Wright (2011) explore a variety of factors that are likely to result in participants changing their judgments over the course of a multi-round Delphi study. They argue that "Delphi usually does better than freely interacting groups, or simply taking the average of initial opinion." Most of the studies they cite do not entail the use of the very detailed feedback of reasons for judgments, such as those employed in the initial RAND studies, that was "integral to early implementations of Delphi." They report that the "few studies into the effects of providing reasons as feedback have provided mixed results."

9.12 CONCLUDING THOUGHTS AND ADVICE

Some may find it tempting to view expert elicitation as a low-cost, low-effort alternative to doing serious research and analysis. It is neither. Rather, expert elicitation should build upon the best available research and analysis and be undertaken only when, given those, the state of knowledge will remain insufficient to support timely informed assessment and decision making.

If expert elicitation is to obtain careful considered judgments from the experts involved, elicitation protocols must be developed through careful iterative refinement. Draft protocols should be pilot tested with quasi-experts (such as advanced graduate students or post-doctoral fellows) in order to assure that question formulations are workable and can be understood. Such iterative refinement is essential because there are always many more things one would like to ask than time and experts' patience will allow. This process of iterative refinement can often take several months or longer. In most cases, true experts are a rare resource that must be conserved and treated with care. A few shoddy studies can sour an entire expert community to participation.

Most of the elicitations my colleagues and I have performed have been conducted using face-to-face interviews in experts' offices where the expert can readily access relevant data and analytic and model results. In many cases, we have prepared concise literature summaries or other materials, and have employed card-sorting and other tasks to encourage experts to systematically identify all relevant factors that may influence a value of interest or contribute to its uncertainty. While well-informed experts obviously know and have thought about all of these things, it is important to make sure that they do not

[2] See also Bolger and Rowe (2014).

overlook any of them when they are asked to make quantitative judgments. Indeed, when an answer seems to be at odds with such evidence it is important to push for explanations and justifications. If it becomes clear that respondents have not thought about some of the relevant evidence, then care should be taken to identify the bounds of their expertise and appropriately limit the use of, and generalizations drawn from, their judgments.

Because experts are human, there is simply no way to eliminate cognitive bias and overconfidence. The best one can hope to do is to work hard to minimize its influence. It is important to acknowledge this, brief experts on the issue, and design elicitation procedures that work to achieve this objective. Of course, the same cognitive biases arise in the deliberations of less formal consensus panels – but, in those cases, they are virtually never acknowledged or addressed. The performance of consensus expert panels might be improved if panel members first performed individual elicitations before they begin their group deliberations.

It is tempting to want to combine the judgments of multiple experts in order to obtain *the* answer. Sometimes this makes sense. However, if different experts base their judgments on very different models of the way in which the world works, or if they produce quite different judgments that will be used as the input to a non-linear model, then combining judgments does not make sense. It is always important to remember that science is not a matter of "majority vote." Sometimes it is the minority outlier who ultimately turns out to have been correct. Ignoring that fact can lead to results that do not serve the needs of decision makers.

READING 9.1

Read one of the following papers:

- M. Granger Morgan and David Keith, "Subjective Judgments by Climate Experts," *Environmental Science & Technology*, *29*(10), pp. 468–476, 1995.
- M. Granger Morgan, Louis F. Pitelka, and Elena Shevliakova, "Elicitation of Expert Judgments of Climate Impacts on Forest Ecosystems," *Climatic Change*, *49*(3), pp. 279–307, 2001.
- Kirsten Zickfeld, Anders Levermann, M. Granger Morgan, Till Kuhlbrodt, Stefan Rahmstorf, and David W. Keith, "Expert Judgments on the Response on the Atlantic Meridional Overturning Circulation to Climate Change," *Climatic Change*, *82*, pp. 235–265, 2007.
- Aimee E. Curtright, M. Granger Morgan, and David W. Keith, "Expert Assessments of Future Photovoltaic Technologies," *Environmental Science & Technology*, *42*(24), pp. 9031–9038, 2008.
- Henry A. Roman, Katherine D. Walker, Tyra L. Walsh, Lisa Conner, Harvey M. Richmond, Bryan J. Hubbell, and Patrick L. Kinney, "Expert

Judgment Assessment of the Mortality Impact of Changes in Ambient Fine Particulate Matter in the U.S.," *Environmental Science & Technology*, *42*, pp. 2268–2274, 2008.

- Kirsten Zickfeld, M. Granger Morgan, David Frame, and David W. Keith, "Expert Judgments about Transient Climate Response to Alternative Future Trajectories of Radiative Forcing," *Proceedings of the National Academy of Sciences*, *107*, pp. 12451–12456, 2010.

Then, choose some uncertain quantity about which a friend has "expert" knowledge. Carefully design a question that you will pose to your friend in order to elicit a CDF of that quantity. Write out the question. Read it to your friend and perform any necessary revisions in the wording. Then perform the elicitation using methods of the type discussed in this chapter and in the reading. Write up the results describing how you proceeded, what result you obtained, and any concerns you have with what transpired.

BOX 9.1 A SIMPLE ILLUSTRATION OF THE PROCESS OF ELICITING A SUBJECTIVE PROBABILITY DISTRIBUTION

As the main text explains, a well-developed protocol for expert elicitation may entail a variety of activities, only some of which involve asking an expert to assess the likely value of an uncertain coefficient as a subjective probability distribution.

An example of the protocol used in Zickfeld et al. (2010) can be found at: www.pnas.org/content/suppl/2010/06/28/0908906107.DCSupplemental/Appendix.pdf.

The protocol used in Abdulla et al. (2013) can be found in Appendix S2 at: www.pnas.org/content/suppl/2013/05/22/1300195110.DCSupplemental/sapp.pdf.

This box provides a very simple illustration of how the actual process of eliciting a probability distribution might proceed.

Suppose that I have a colleague who has driven to the airport midday from our offices many times. It is midday now and the colleague is sitting next to me in my office. I want to elicit a probability distribution that provides their judgment of how long he believes it will take him to drive to the airport if they leave for the parking lot to get his car right now.

First, we should probably break the question up into at least three parts:

1. Time to get to his car
2. Time to drive to the airport
3. Time to get from his car to the gate

For simplicity in this illustration I'll focus on just part 2.

Before I ask my colleague any questions, we need to agree on some general assumptions. I am interested in their judgment assuming normal traffic at this hour, no major accidents, no presidential motorcades, no ice storms, no terrorist attacks, etc. We also assume that their car starts, has adequate gas, and has no mechanical problems.

Having agreed on these general assumptions, the interview dialogue might run something like this:

Me: Once you are in your car what is the maximum amount of time you could expect it to take to drive to the airport right now?
Colleague: 50 minutes.
Me: Has it ever taken you any longer than that?
Colleague: Yeah, once it took 60 minutes and I missed my flight.
Me: With normal traffic could it take longer than that?
Colleague: I suppose maybe 65 minutes.
Me: Do you want to up your maximum time from 50 to 65?
Colleague: Yeah, I guess I should.
Me: OK, now what's the minimum time for the drive to the airport?
Colleague: So, now I know that you're going to push me on this, so let's see, it is 30 miles and the speed limit is 55, but everyone drives 60. So 30 miles at 60 mph, that's 30 minutes. Sometimes I push it a bit more so I'll say between 25 and 30 minutes.

This dialogue results in my marking the range illustrated in Figure B9.1. The objective in these initial exchanges is to get all the evidence brought to mind for my colleague so as to minimize the impact of the heuristic of "availability" (see main text). In doing this, it is common to use strategies such as counter examples, so as to establish as wide a range as possible and minimize overconfidence. In more technical examples, a common strategy is to say something like "You said the minimum [maximum] value is X. Suppose that when the actual value becomes known it turns out to be 0.95 [1.05] X. Can you think of any way in which that might occur?" If the expert can offer an explanation, then he or she might decide to increase the bounds.

Continuing with the airport drive-time example, having established the range, I would then start to ask questions such as:

Me: What's the probability that your drive to the airport will take less than 60 minutes?
Colleague: 0.98.
Me: What's the probability that the drive will take more than 40 minutes?
Colleague: 0.65.
Me: What's the probability ... etc.

Through a series of such questions we would build up a distribution of the sort shown in Figure B9.2. If my colleague's estimates appear to be scattered, I might also phrase questions in the form "Give me a time such that you think there is at least a 30 percent chance you can drive to the airport in less time than that."

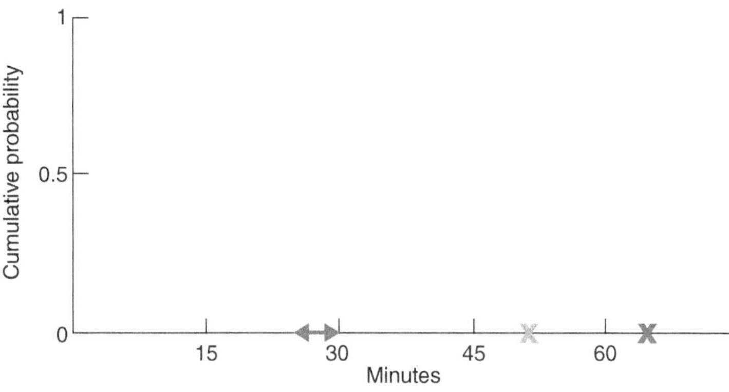

FIGURE B9.1. Upper and lower bounds on the time it will take my colleague to drive to the airport.

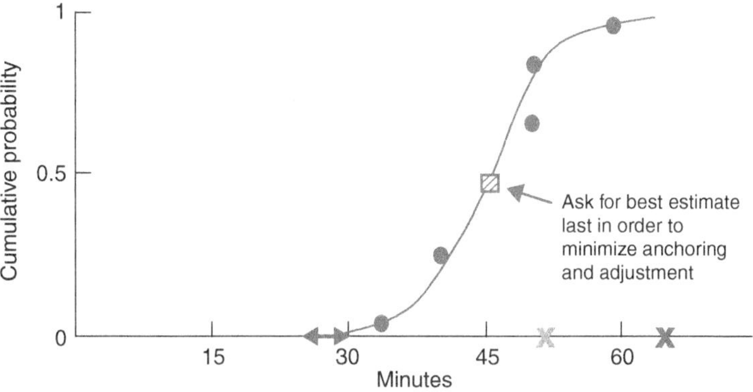

FIGURE B9.2. Elicited distribution of the time it will take for my colleague to drive to the airport.

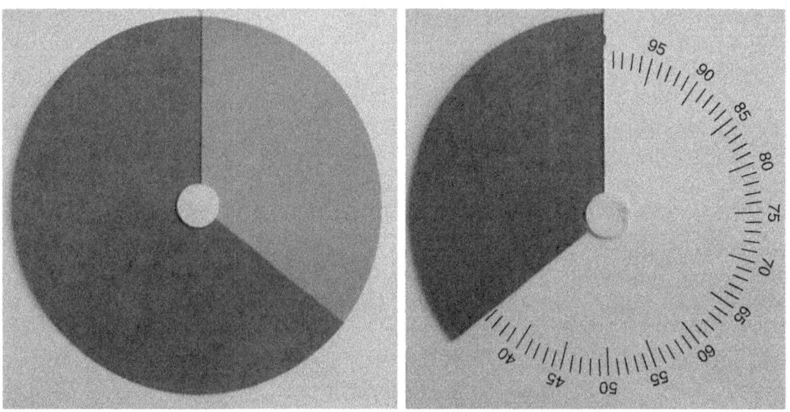

FIGURE B9.3. Example of the sort of probability wheel that is sometimes used by the decision analysis community when eliciting experts who are not particularly numerate. Respondents are asked to adjust the size of the dark pie section (left) to match their probability. The value can then be read off the scale on the back (right). The specific wheel shown was made by Decision Focus, Inc.

Finally, while I will ask my colleague for a best or median estimate, I will not pose that question until I have completed all my other questions so as to minimize the influence of the heuristic of "anchoring and adjustment" (see main text).

In virtually all the elicitations I have run, the experts have been very numerate and have chosen to answer questions directly in terms of probabilities. When respondents are not very numerate, folks in the decision analysis community sometimes ask the expert to respond by adjusting the colored section of a probability wheel of the sort shown in Figure B9.3.

REFERENCES

Abdulla, A., I. Azevedo, and M.G. Morgan (2013). "Expert Assessments of the Cost of Light Water Small Modular Reactors," *Proceedings of the National Academy of Sciences*, *110*(24), pp. 9686–9691.

Anadon, L.D., V. Bosetti, M. Bunn, and A. Lee (2012). "Expert Judgments about RD&D and the Future of Nuclear Energy," *Environmental Science & Technology*, *41*(21), pp. 11497–11504.

Anadon, L.D., G.F. Nemet, and E. Verdolini (2013). "The Future Costs of Nuclear Power using Multiple Expert Elicitations: Effects of RD&D and Elicitation Design," *Environmental Research Letters*, *8*(3), p. 034020.

Aspinall, W. (2010). "A Route to More Tractable Expert Advice," *Nature*, *463*, pp. 294–295.

Bolger, F. and G. Rowe (2014). "Delphi: Somewhere between Scylla and Charybdis?," *Proceedings of the National Academy of Science*, *111*(41), p. E4284.

Bolger, F. and G. Wright (2011). "Improving the Delphi Process: Lessons from Social Psychological Research," *Technological Forecasting and Social Change*, *78*(9), pp. 1500–1513.

Budnitz, R.J. et al. (1995). "Recommendations for Probabilistic Seismic Hazard Analysis: Guidance on Uncertainty and the Use of Experts," UCRL-ID 122160, Lawrence Livermore National Laboratory.

et al. (1997). "Recommendations for Probabilistic Seismic Hazard Analysis: Guidance on Uncertainty and Use of Experts," NUREG/CR-6372, Vol. II, U.S. Nuclear Regulatory Commission.

Budnitz, R.J., G. Apostolakis, D.M. Boore, L.S. Cluff, K.J. Coppersmith, C.A. Cornell, and P.A. Morris (1998). "Use of Technical Expert Panels: Applications to Probabilistic Seismic Hazard Analysis," *Risk Analysis*, *18*(4), pp. 463–469.

Chan, G., L.D. Anadon, M. Chan, and A. Lee (2011). "Expert Elicitation of Cost, Performance, and RD&D Budgets for Coal Power with CCS," *Energy Procedia*, *4*, pp. 2685–2692.

Charba, J.P. and W.H. Klein (1980). "Skill in Precipitation Forecasting in the National Weather Service," *Bulletin of the American Meteorological Society*, *61*, pp. 1546–1555.

Christensen-Szalanski, J.J.J. and J.B. Bushyhead (1981). "Physicians' Use of Probabilistic Information in a Real Clinical Setting," *Journal of Experimental Psychology: Human Perception and Performance*, 7(4), pp. 928–935.

Clark, W.C., T.P. Tomich, M. van Noordwijk, D. Guston, D. Catacutan, N.M. Dickson, and E. McNie (2011). "Boundary Work for Sustainable Development: Natural Resource Management at the Consultative Group on International Agricultural Research (CGIAR)," *Proceedings of the National Academy of Sciences*, *113*(17), 8pp.

Clemen, R.T. (2008). "Comment on Cooke's Classical Method," *Reliability Engineering and System Safety*, *93*, pp. 760–765.

Clemen, R.T. and R.L. Winkler (1999). "Combining Probability Distributions from Experts in Risk Analysis," *Risk Analysis*, *19*, pp. 187–203.

(2007). "Chapter 9: Aggregating Probability Distributions," in W. Edwards, R.F. Miles Jr., and D. von Winterfeldt (eds.), *Advances in Decision Analysis: From Foundations to Applications*, Cambridge University Press, pp. 154–176.

Colson, A.R. and R.M. Cooke (2017). "Cross Validation for the Classical Model of Structured Expert Judgment," *Reliability Engineering and System Safety*, *163*, pp. 109–120.

Cooke, R.M. (1991). *Experts in Uncertainty: Opinion and Subjective Probability in Science*, Oxford University Press, 336pp.

Cooke, R.M. and L.L.H.J. Goossens (2008). "TU Delft Expert Judgment Data Base," *Reliability Engineering and System Safety*, *93*, pp. 657–674.

Cooke, R.M., A.M. Wilson, J.T. Tuomisto, O. Morales, M. Tainio, and J.S. Evans (2007). "A Probabilistic Characterization of the Relationship between Fine Particulate Matter and Mortality: Elicitation of European Experts," *Environmental Science & Technology*, *41*, pp. 6598–6605.

Curtright, A.E., M.G. Morgan, and D.W. Keith (2008). "Expert Assessment of Future Photovoltaic Technology," *Environmental Science & Technology*, *42*(24), pp. 9031–9038.

Dalkey, N. and O. Helmer (1972). "An Experimental Application of the Delphi Method to the Use of Experts," RAND Corporation report RM- 727/1- (Abridged).

de Finetti, B. (1974). *Theory of Probability: A Critical Introductory Treatment*, Wiley, 2 vols.

DeGroot, M.H. (1970). *Optimal Statistical Decisions*, McGraw-Hill, 489pp.

Devilee, J.L.A. and A.B. Knol (2011). "Software to Support Expert Elicitation: An Exploratory Study of Existing Software Packages," RIVM Letter Report 630003001/2011 (Dutch National Institute of Public Health and Environment), 98pp. Available at: www.rivm.nl/en/Documents_and_publications/Scientific/Reports/2012/mei/Software_to_support_expert_elicitation_An_exploratory_study_of_existing_software_packages.

Dowlatabadi, H. and M.G. Morgan (1993). "A Model Framework for Integrated Studies of the Climate Problem," *Energy Policy*, *21*(3), pp. 209–221.

EPA (2011). "Expert Elicitation Task Force White Paper." Available at: www.epa.gov/stpc/pdfs/ee-white-paper-final.pdf.

Evans, J.S., J.D. Graham, D.M. Gray, and R.L. Sielken, Jr. (1994a). "A Distributional Approach to Characterizing Low-Dose Cancer Risk," *Risk Analysis*, *14*(1), pp. 25–34.

Evans, J.S., G.M. Gray, R.L. Sielken, A.E. Smith, C. Valdezflores, and J.D. Graham (1994b). "Using of Probabilistic Expert Judgment in Uncertainty Analysis of Carcinogenic Potency," *Regulatory Toxicology and Pharmacology*, *20* (1 pt.1), pp. 15–36.

Funtowicz, S.O. and J.R. Ravetz (1990). *Uncertainty and Quality in Science for Policy*, Kluwer, 229pp.

Garthwaite, P.H., J.B. Kadane, and A. O'Hagan (2005). "Statistical Methods for Eliciting Probability Distributions," *Journal of the American Statistical Association*, *100*, pp. 680–700.

Good, I.J. (1971). "46656 Varieties of Bayesians," *The American Statistician*, *25*(5), pp. 62–63.

Henrion, M. and B. Fischhoff (1986). "Assessing Uncertainty in Physical Constants," *American Journal of Physics*, *54*(9), pp. 791–798.

Hoek, G., H. Boogaard, A. Knol et al. (2010). "Concentration Response Functions for Ultrafine Particles and All-Cause Mortality and Hospital Admissions: Results of a European Expert Panel Elicitation," *Environmental Science & Technology*, *44*, pp. 476–482.

Hora, S.C. (2007). "Chapter 9: Eliciting Probability from Experts," in E.W. Ward, R.F. Miles Jr., and D. von Winterfeldt (eds.), *Advances in Decision Analysis: From Foundations to Applications*, Cambridge University Press, pp. 129–153.

IPCC (2001). "Climate Change 2001: The Scientific Basis," in J.T. Houghton et al. (eds.), *Contribution of Working Group I to the Third Assessment Report of the Intergovernmental Panel on Climate Change*, Cambridge University Press, 881pp.

(2007). "Climate Change 2007: The Physical Science Basis," in S. Solomon et al. (eds.), *Contribution of Working Group I to the Fourth Assessment Report of the Intergovernmental Panel on Climate Change*, Cambridge University Press, 800pp.

(2013). "Summary for Policymakers in Climate Change 2013: The Physical Science Basis," in T.F. Stocker et al. (eds.), *Contribution of Working Group I to the Fifth Assessment Report of the Intergovernmental Panel on Climate Change*, Cambridge University Press.

Jaynes, E.T. (2003). *Probability Theory: The Logic of Science*, Cambridge University Press, 727pp.

Kadane, J. and B. Fischhoff (2013). "A Cautionary Note of Global Recalibration," *Judgment and Decision Making*, *8*(1), pp. 25–28.

Kahneman, D., P. Slovic, and A. Tversky (eds.) (1982). *Judgment under Uncertainty: Heuristics and Biases*, Cambridge University Press, 555pp.

Karvetski, C.W., K.C. Olson, D.R. Mandel, and C.R. Twardy (2013). "Probabilistic Coherence Weighting for Optimizing Expert Forecasts," *Decision Analysis*, *10*, pp. 305–326.

Knol, A.B., J.J. de Hartog, H. Boogaard et al. (2009). "Expert Elicitation on Ultrafine Particles: Likelihood of Health Effects and Causal Pathways," *Particle and Fibre Toxicology*, *6*, p. 19.

Knol, A.B., P. Slottje, J.P. van der Sluijs, and E. Lebret (2010). "The Use of Expert Elicitation in Environmental Health Impact Assessment: A Seven Step Procedure," *Environmental Health*, *9*, p. 19.

Krayer von Krauss, M.P., E.A. Casman, and M.J. Small (2004). "Elicitation of Expert Judgments of Uncertainty in the Risk Assessment of Herbicide-Tolerant Oilseed Crops," *Risk Analysis*, *24*(6), pp. 1515–1527.

Lichtenstein, S., B. Fischhoff, and L. Phillips (1982). "Chapter 22: Calibration of Probabilities: The State of the Art to 1980," in D. Kahneman, P. Slovic, and A. Tversky (eds.), *Judgment under Uncertainty: Heuristics and Biases*, Cambridge University Press, pp. 306–334.

Lin, S.W. and C.H. Cheng (2009). "The Reliability of Aggregated Probability Judgments Obtained through Cooke's Classical Method," *Journal of Modeling in Management*, *4*, pp. 149–161.

Mandel, D. and A. Barnes (2014). "Accuracy of Forecasts in Strategic Intelligence," *Proceedings of the National Academy of Sciences*, *111*(30), pp. 10984–10989.

Mastrandrea, M.D. et al. (2010). "Guidance Note for Lead Authors of the IPCC Fifth Assessment Report on Consistent Treatment of Uncertainties, Intergovernmental Panel on Climate Change (IPCC)." Available at: www.ipcc.ch/pdf/supporting-material/uncertainty-guidance-note.pdf.

Morgan, M.G. (2014). "The Use (and Abuse) of Expert Elicitation in Support of Decision Making for Public Policy," *PNAS*, *111*(20), pp. 7176–7184.

Morgan, M.G., P. Adams, and D.W. Keith (2006). "Elicitation of Expert Judgments of Aerosol Forcing," *Climatic Change*, *75*, pp. 195–214.

Morgan, M.G. and H. Dowlatabadi (1996). "Learning from Integrated Assessment of Climate Change," *Climatic Change*, *34*, pp. 337–368.

Morgan, M.G. with H. Dowlatabadi, M. Henrion, D. Keith, R. Lempert, S. McBride, M. Small, and T. Wilbanks (2009). *CCSP 5.2 Best Practice Approaches for Characterizing, Communicating, and Incorporating Scientific Uncertainty in Decisionmaking*, Report by the Climate Change Science Program and the Subcommittee on Global Change Research, National Oceanic and Atmospheric Administration, 96pp.

Morgan, M.G. and M. Henrion with a chapter by M. Small (1990). *Uncertainty: A Guide to Dealing with Uncertainty in Quantitative Risk and Policy Analysis*, Cambridge University Press, 332pp.

Morgan, M.G. and D. Keith (1995). "Subjective Judgments by Climate Experts," *Environmental Science & Technology*, *29*(10), pp. 468A–476A.

Morgan, M.G., S.C. Morris, M. Henrion, D.A.L. Amaral, and W.R. Rish (1984). "Technical Uncertainty in Quantitative Policy Analysis: A Sulfur Air Pollution Example," *Risk Analysis*, *4*, pp. 201–216.

Morgan, M.G., S.C. Morris, W.R. Rish, and A.K. Meier (1978). "Sulfur Control in Coal-Fired Power Plants: A Probabilistic Approach to Policy Analysis," *Journal of the Air Pollution Control Association*, *28*, pp. 993–997.

Morgan, M.G., L.F. Pitelka, and E. Shevliakova (2001). "Elicitation of Expert Judgments of Climate Change Impacts on Forest Ecosystems," *Climatic Change*, *49*(3), pp. 279–307.

Morris, D.E., J.E. Oakley, and J.A. Crowe (2014). "A Web-Based Tool for Eliciting Probability Distributions from Experts," *Environmental Modelling and Software*, *52*, pp. 1–4.

Moss, R. and S.H. Schneider (2000). "Uncertainties in the IPCC TAR: Recommendations to Lead Authors for More Consistent Assessment and Reporting," in R. Pachauri et al. (eds.), *Guidance Papers on the Cross Cutting Issues of the Third Assessment Report of the IPCC*, pp. 33–51. Available at: www.ipcc.ch/pdf/supportingmaterial/guidance-papers-3.

Murphy, A.H. and R.L. Winkler (1977). "Can Weather Forecasters Formulate Reliable Probability Forecasts of Precipitation and Temperature?," *National Weather Digest*, *2*, pp. 2–9(a).

National Assessment Synthesis Team (2001). *Climate Change Impacts on the United States: The Potential Consequences of Climate Variability and Change*, Cambridge University Press, 612pp.

NDU (1978). "February," in *Climate Change to the Year 2000: A Survey of Expert Opinion*, Report published by the National Defense University in cooperation with the U.S. Department of Agriculture, the Defense Advanced Research Projects Agency, the National Oceanic and Atmospheric Administration, and Institute for the Future. [For a critique, see Stewart, T.R. and M.H. Glantz (1985). "Expert Judgment and Climate Forecasting: A Methodological Critique of Climate Change to the Year 2000," *Climatic Change*, *7*, pp. 159–183.]

O'Hagan, A., C.E. Buck, A. Daneshkhah, J.R. Eiser, P.H. Garthwaite, D.J. Jenkinson, J.E. Oakley, and T. Rakow (2006). *Uncertain Judgments: Eliciting Experts' Probabilities*, John Wiley & Sons, 321pp.

O'Hagan, A. and J.E. Oakley (2010). "SHELF: The Sheffield Elicitation Framework, Version 2.0, School of Mathematics and Statistics," University of Sheffield. Available at: www.tonyohagan.co.uk/shelf.

Oppenheimer, M., B.C. O'Neill, M. Webster, and S. Agerwala (2007). "The Limit of Consensus," *Science*, *317*, pp. 1505–1506.

Presidential/Congressional Commission on Risk Assessment and Risk Management (1997). Vol. I: *Framework for Environmental Health Risk Management*; Vol. II: *Risk Assessment and Risk Management in Regulatory Decision Making*. Available at: http://cfpub.epa.gov/ncea/cfm/recordisplay.cfm?deid=55006.

Rao, A.B., E.S. Rubin, D.W. Keith, and M.G. Morgan (2006). "Evaluation of Potential Cost Reductions from Improved Amine-Based CO_2 Capture Systems," *Energy Policy*, *34*, pp. 3765–3772.

Refsgaard, J.C., J.P. Van der Sluijs, J. Brown, and P. Van der Keur (2005). "A Framework for Dealing with Uncertainty Due to Model Structure Error," *Water Resources*, *29*, pp. 1586–1597.

Roman, H.A., K.D. Walker, T.L. Walsh, L. Conner, H.M. Richmond, B.J. Hubbell, and P.L. Kinney (2008). "Expert Judgment Assessment of the Mortality Impact of Changes in Ambient Fine Particulate Matter in the U.S.," *Environmental Science & Technology*, *42*, pp. 2268–2274.

Rowe, G. and G. Wright (1999). "The Delphi Technique as a Forecasting Tool: Issues and Analysis," *International Journal of Forecasting*, *15*(4), pp. 353–375.

Sackman, H. (1975). *Delphi Critique: Expert Opinion, Forecasting, and Group Process*, Lexington Books, 142pp.

Schneider, S. et al. (2007). "Climate Change 2007: Impacts, Adaptation, and Vulnerabilities," in M.L. Parry et al. (eds.), *Contribution of Working Group II to the Fourth Assessment Report of the Intergovernmental Panel on Climate Change*, Cambridge University Press, pp. 779–810.

Spetzler, C.S. and C.-A.S. Staël von Holstein (1975). "Probability Encoding in Decision Analysis," *Management Science*, *22*(3), pp. 340–358.

Tversky, A. and D. Kahneman (1974). "Judgments under Uncertainty: Heuristics and Biases," *Science*, *185*(4157), pp. 1124–1131.

Van der Sluijs, J.P., M. Craye, S. Funtowicz, P. Kloprogge, J. Ravetz, and J. Risbey (2005a). "Combining Quantitative and Qualitative Measures of Uncertainty in Model-Based Environmental Assessment: The NUSAP System," *Risk Analysis*, *25*(2), pp. 481–492.

Van der Sluijs, J.P., J.S. Risbey, and J. Ravetz (2005b). "Uncertainty Assessment of VOC Emissions from Paint in the Netherlands using the NUSAP System," *Environmental Monitoring and Assessment*, *105*, pp. 229–259.

Wallsten, T.S., D.V. Budescu, A. Rapoport, R. Zwick, and B. Forsyth (1986). "Measuring the Vague Meanings of Probability Terms," *Journal of Experimental Psychology: General*, *155*(4), pp. 348–365.

Wallsten, T.S. and R.G. Whitfield (1989). "A Risk Assessment for Selected Lead-Induced Health Effects: An Example of a General Methodology," *Risk Analysis*, *9*(2), pp. 197–207.

Wardekker, J.A., J.P. van der Sluijs, P.H.M. Janssen, P. Kloprogge, and A.C. Petersen (2008). "Uncertainty Communication in Environmental Assessments: Views from the Dutch Science–Policy Interface," *Environmental Science and Policy*, *11*, pp. 627–641.

Woudenberg, F. (1991). "An Evaluation of Delphi," *Technology Forecasting and Social Change*, *40*(2), pp. 131–150.

Zickfeld, K., A. Levermann, M.G. Morgan, T. Kuhlbrodt, S. Rahmstorf, and D.W. Keith (2007). "Expert Judgments on the Response on the Atlantic Meridional Overturning Circulation to Climate Change," *Climatic Change*, *82*, pp. 235–265.

Zickfeld, K., M.G. Morgan, D. Frame, and D.W. Keith (2010). "Expert Judgments about Transient Climate Response to Alternative Future Trajectories of Radiative Forcing," *Proceedings of the National Academy of Sciences*, *107*, pp. 12451–12456.

10

Risk Analysis[1]

Statistical evidence shows that the residents of most developed nations live longer, healthier, and wealthier lives today than they did at any time in the past. Yet concerns about risk to health, safety, and the environment are ubiquitous. Perhaps we are more concerned about risks today precisely because we have more to lose and because we have more disposable income to spend on risk reduction. Such economic factors are undoubtedly important, but they probably do not tell the whole story. Why, for example, do risks from newer technologies such as microwave ovens, which when used properly present virtually no probability of death or injury, often get more attention than older, well-established risks like motorcycles, which in the United States routinely result in roughly 4500 deaths and 80–90,000 injuries each year?[2] Why do people who have slept under an electric blanket every night for decades suddenly become terrified about possible adverse health effects when a new high-voltage power line is built several hundred meters from their home?

Our ancestors, more resigned to death, disease, and injury as a common feature of their lives, understood that nothing in life is risk-free. However, modern society has done so well in reducing risks that now many people seem to forget that no activity or technology can be absolutely safe. Since no technology or activity is without risk, the real problem is deciding how to balance the benefits they bring against their cost and the risks they may impose to health, safety, and the environment. The answer to the simple question "How safe is safe enough?" is complicated and is contextually dependent. In this chapter, the

[1] Portions of the text in this chapter are derived from two articles originally published in *IEEE Spectrum*: M. Granger Morgan, "Probing the Question of Technology-Induced Risk," *IEEE Spectrum, 18*(11), pp. 58–64, 1981 November; and M. Granger Morgan, "Choosing and Managing Technology-Induced Risk," *IEEE Spectrum, 18*(12), pp. 53–60, 1981 December. Thanks to IEEE for permission to edit and reuse portions of these papers.

[2] For details, see Insurance Information Institute at www.iii.org/issue-update/motorcycle-crashes.

primary focus is on assessing and managing risks. We postpone most discussion of issues of risk perception until after we have laid some foundations in Chapter 12 on how people think and make decisions about things that are uncertain. Most of the examples in this chapter are drawn from a U.S. context, but similar issues and concerns arise all around the world.[3]

10.1 A FRAMEWORK FOR THINKING ABOUT RISK

Figure 10.1 is a simple four-stage framework for thinking about risk. Starting on the left, there are human activities and the natural environment, either or both of which may initiate a set of processes that expose objects and processes in the natural and human environment to the possibility of change. For example, a power plant may emit sulfur dioxide gas (SO_2). Atmospheric processes transport and disperse the SO_2, convert some of it into sulfate aerosol, and lose some of the gas and particles through processes of wet and dry deposition. As indicated by the box labeled "exposure processes," people, plants, and other things get exposed. The second box, labeled "effects processes," represents the effects on objects and processes in the natural and human environment that arise as a result of the exposure. For example, people may experience health effects, alfalfa grown in sulfate-poor soil may grow larger,[4] and sunsets may get redder. In most cases people only notice some of the changes that occur. What they notice is characterized by the third box, labeled "human perception processes."[5] Finally, having observed a change, people value it, as indicated by the final box labeled "human valuation processes" – the output of which is shown as assessed "costs and benefits." Note that in describing the changes, I wrote alfalfa "may grow *larger*" and "sunsets may get *redder*" as opposed to writing "may grow *better*" and "sunsets may get *prettier*." *Larger* and *redder* are statements about the state of the world. *Better* and *prettier* are normative statements that a human observer might make after applying valuation processes.

While no model or assessment can be absolutely free of value judgments, I have separated the model into two parts because most qualified analysts should be able to model the processes in the left two boxes, making relatively few value judgments. In most cases, almost any competent risk analyst could be expected to obtain very similar results. In contrast, the processes in the right two boxes are inherently value-based. People with different mental models and

[3] For a U.S.–EU comparison, see Wiener et al. (2011).

[4] Alfalfa plants absorb the SO_2 through their stomata, but as long as the concentration of SO_2 in the air is low, toxic levels do not build up in the plants. Instead, the SO_2 is metabolized by the plant into sulfates and other sulfur compounds, some of which are needed for healthy plant growth and might not be otherwise present if the alfalfa happens to be growing in sulfate-poor soil.

[5] There is, of course, the additional issue of whether the changes that people observe are actually attributed to the hazard. This has been an especially important issue in the context of climate change, but for simplicity we do not address that issue here.

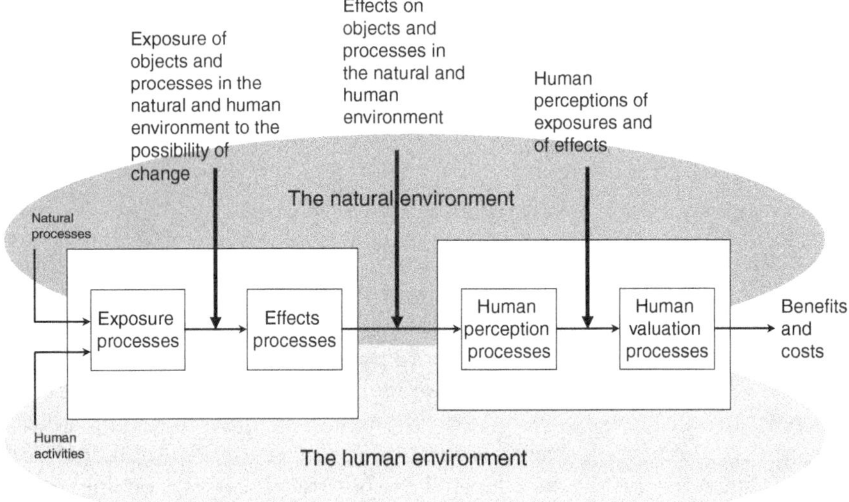

FIGURE 10.1. A simple four-stage diagram for thinking about risk.

different preferences and values could be expected to notice different changes and reach quite different conclusions about how they value those changes.

10.2 RISK IS INHERENTLY UNCERTAIN

Most dictionaries define risk as "the exposure to a chance of injury or loss." There are two key words in that definition: *chance* and *loss*. We typically do not consider chance events that have good outcomes, such as winning a few hundred dollars in a lottery,[6] to be risks.

The chance, or probabilistic, element of risk may arise because:

1. The values of all the important variables involved are not or cannot be known, and/or precise projections cannot be made;
2. The physics, chemistry, and biology of the processes involved are not fully understood and no one knows how to build adequate predictive models; or,
3. The processes involved are inherently probabilistic, or at least so complex that it is infeasible to construct and solve predictive models.

In addition, the extent to which a process is viewed as certain or uncertain often depends upon individual perspectives. An individual driver is likely to view

[6] In most cases, the consequences of winning a few hundred dollars in a lottery are likely to be only positive. However, winning a very large lottery could have negative (as well as positive) impacts on the winner's life.

TABLE 10.1. *Risks inherently involve some element of chance or uncertainty. That uncertainty can be introduced through exposure or effects processes, or both.*

	Probabilistic exposure	Deterministic exposure
Probabilistic effect	*Getting stung by a bee* People engaged in normal day-to-day activities do not usually get stung by bees, but there is always a small exposure probability. Once stung, most people simply have a painful bite, but there is always the possibility of a life-threatening allergic reaction.	*Routine dental X-ray* Exposure to dental X-rays as part of a regular check up is deterministic in that the patient chooses to have the procedure. The possible health effects (cancer) from exposure to low levels of ionizing radiation are inherently probabilistic.
Deterministic effect	*Being on top of a large gas main explosion* The chance that any given individual will be right next to a large gas main when it explodes is very low, but if they are unfortunate enough to be there at the instant, they will certainly be killed.	Situations in which both exposure and effect are deterministic are typically not defined as a risk.

automobile accidents as highly unpredictable events. But an insurance company can usually predict with remarkable precision the number of accidents that will occur among its many thousands of policyholders during the coming year (and use that prediction to accurately forecast likely damage claims).

The probabilistic element in risk can be introduced through exposure processes, or through effects processes, or both – yielding three possible combinations: a probabilistic exposure followed by a probabilistic effect, a deterministic exposure followed by a probabilistic effect, or a probabilistic exposure followed by a deterministic effect, as shown in Table 10.1. A situation in which both exposure and effect is deterministic is typically *not* considered an example of a risk, since there is no chance involved.

This three-way classification seems simple enough until it is applied. Then, depending upon the example, it becomes clear why so many of the heated arguments about risk revolve around questions of where to draw the system boundaries and how to classify things. For example, some surgeons might argue that the risk of failure of a surgical implant constitutes an example of certain deterministic exposure (inserting the device) with probabilistic effect (stemming from such unpredictable complications as infection, rejection, and device failure).

On the other hand, a malpractice lawyer might categorize this as a case of probabilistic exposure (the same injury treated by different doctors will receive different treatments) with deterministic effects (the surgeon used poor technique so the infection occurred, or he damaged the device while inserting it, with the result that it ultimately failed).

BOX 10.1 ILLUSTRATION OF EXPOSURE AND EFFECTS PROCESSES

A couple of decades ago, in writing for a more general audience than the readers of this book, I illustrated the first two steps of this model with an example of a visit I made with my family to the Denver Mint. In the course of the tour I noticed that the ceilings in some of the workrooms had been sprayed with a layer of soundproofing material to deaden the noise from the machinery. The application was obviously old and some of that material had begun to flake; strands of fibers could be seen dangling here and there, gently wafting in the breeze from open windows and ventilating fans. In some places visitors could have reached up from the tour balcony and touched the ceiling.

Did this old, flaking ceiling represent a health risk? I do not know, and if it did I am sure that it has long ago been remediated. However, the framework of Figure 10.1 illustrates how we might perform a risk assessment.

Through age, vibration, air motion, and perhaps human contact, pieces of ceiling fiber were falling off. The physics and chemistry of the situation determined how many of these fibers fell off and whether they fell off only as large chunks or also as very small particles in a size range that could be readily inhaled. Other factors that probably influenced the amount and size of dust particles in the air included the way in which the janitors and maintenance people cleaned the machinery and floors, as well as the air-circulation patterns that were set up by the fans and open windows. Together all of these factors make up the processes that could expose visitors and workers to the possibility of inhaling very fine particles. By conducting a series of observations and setting up some monitors, a clear sense of the concentration in the air could be readily obtained.

The human upper respiratory system is remarkably good at filtering out dust and other larger particles. But particles in the size range from a fraction of a micron to a few microns can enter deep into the lungs. Hence if the exposure process produced micron-sized ceiling particles in the air, then some of these particles were probably ending up in the lungs of workers and a few in the lungs of visitors.

What is the possible effect of inhaling such particles and having a few lodged deep in the lungs? In the short run, unless they acted as an allergen and triggered an asthma attack, there probably would be no effects at all.

Dust is present in the air all the time and, in this case, the amount of ceiling dust was fairly low. In the long run, the situation is less clear, depending strongly on the chemical and physical properties of the particles, which could be readily determined through some simple laboratory procedures.

If the material was not hazardous, sooner or later any particles that entered people's lungs would be cleared through natural processes. However, there is also a possibility that the ceiling materials included mineral fibers, perhaps asbestos. If this were so, then there would be a very small chance that 10 or 20 years after any given particle became lodged in a cell in the lining of the lung, a cancer would develop. If the lung happened to belong to a smoker, the chance of cancer from exposure to asbestos might be as much as 15 times greater than the chance for a nonsmoker.

The information about the uncertainty associated with risk processes usually fits into one or more of the following five categories:

1. Good direct statistical evidence on the process of interest is available. This is clearly the most desirable situation, but is rare for most categories of risk problems.
2. The process can be disaggregated with analytical tools (such as fault trees, event trees, and various stochastic models) into sub-processes, for which good statistical evidence is available. Aggregate probabilities can then be constructed.
3. No good data are available for the process under consideration, but good data are available for a similar process and these data may be adapted or extended for use either directly or as part of a disaggregated model.
4. The direct and indirect evidence that is available is poor or incomplete and it is necessary to rely to a very substantial extent on the physical intuition and the subjective judgment of technical experts.
5. There is little or no available evidence, and even the experts have little basis on which to produce a subjective judgment (i.e., there is a high level of "ignorance").

Unfortunately, a very substantial fraction of the risk problems with which society must deal falls into categories 3, 4, or 5.

10.3 RISK IS A MULTI-ATTRIBUTE CONCEPT

With a definition like "the exposure to a chance of injury or loss," it is tempting to define risk as:

$$\text{Risk} = (\text{probability of an event})(\text{cost of that event})$$

If the damages take the form of excess deaths, this definition could then be rewritten as:

Risk = (probability of death from X)(number of deaths caused by X)($/death)

Indeed, many people have adopted such simple definitions. However, because risk involves people's perception and valuation processes, such a definition is typically *not* adequate. Consider the following seven hypothetical examples of risk, all of which produce the same expected number of deaths, D, when considered on an annual basis. Despite this fact, most readers will perceive and value these risks very differently.

Case 1: People have begun to buy small, two-passenger electric automobiles to do their local shopping. These slow vehicles are occasionally involved in fatal accidents, often with larger conventional vehicles. While they are much cheaper, these small cars are not as safe as larger cars. The incremental expected number of deaths for the current fleet of small cars is D deaths per year.

Case 2: Commuter airlines that fly twin-engine aircraft to small airports are becoming increasingly important around the world. Viewed in terms of fatalities per passenger-mile, they are generally quite safe. The commuter airline system in one country now operates with an annual expected rate of accidental deaths of D deaths per year. Over the past few years, crashes had a fatality rate of between 0 and 20 deaths per crash.

Case 3: The residential community of Willowbend is three miles downstream from a large earthen dam that is part of a regional irrigation and flood-control project. Should the dam fail abruptly, it has been estimated that approximately half of the N people living in Willowbend would die. The best available estimate on the annual probability of failure for such dams is P. The product $P \times N/2$ yields an annual expected statistical mortality rate of D deaths per year.

Case 4: Coal plays an important part in the energy picture of the world. Underground coal mining is dangerous, but it usually does not require a very large fraction of a country's workforce. In one country, accidental coal mine deaths are now averaging D deaths per year.

Case 5: Twenty years ago, workers in a major chemical industry were routinely exposed to a compound whose trade name was TZX. Nobody thought very much about the situation. It has since been learned that TZX causes a fatal degenerative disease of the central nervous system. Last year D deaths were attributed worldwide to occupational exposure to TZX in the early 1960s.

Case 6: On a per-passenger-mile basis, the charter bus lines of most developed countries have an excellent record. In one country, the mortality rate is averaging about D deaths per year. Indeed, there were precisely D deaths last year, and they all occurred in just one accident in which a charter tour bus, carrying the award-winning high-school concert band from a small, traditional rural town, went out of control and over an embankment.

Case 7: Sulfur air pollution is produced when coal is burned to generate electric power. It is difficult to estimate the health impact of coal-fired power plants because neither the exposure processes nor the effects processes are fully understood. For a given coal-fired power plant, it is estimated that the most likely value of the impact on excess mortality from chronic exposure (that is, death occurring at least one year earlier than it would without the presence of the pollutant) is D deaths per year. But it is also estimated that there is a 20 percent probability of no increase in mortality and a 10 percent chance that the increase is as great as 4D deaths per year.

Despite the fact that all of these cases involve the same expected annual mortality rate, most people do not react to each case in the same way. Why?

Here we simply note a few of the things that differ among these hypothetical cases. After discussing some of the modern literature on human mental processes in Chapter 12, we will return to examine empirical results on risk perception in Chapter 13.

The number of people killed in each event is clearly one factor that varies. In the electric auto case, D people are killed in between D/2 and D individual separate accidents. In cases 2 and 6, most or all of the D deaths occur in a single event. In the case of the dam failure, many more than D deaths occur, but the event has a low probability of occurring in any given year so the annual value of the expected mortality is D. In the case of the power plants, most deaths occur decades in the future.

The spatial distribution of the deaths also varies. Aircraft and dam accidents happen in one or a few localized places. Air pollution, by contrast, affects people over a very wide area.

The charter bus accident differs from most of the other accidents because all of the victims are socially related and their deaths will have a profound impact on the remaining residents of a small, traditional rural town. The coal mine example differs because a few workers bear a high individual risk in order to produce a benefit that is shared by many – raising issues of equity. Death is immediate in the case of most risks involving accidents but occurs years after initial exposure in cases such as the TZX and sulfur air-pollution examples. Finally, the values of P and D may be known quite precisely for cases 1, 2, 4, and 6, but they may be extremely uncertain for cases 3, 5, and 7.

The different attributes and circumstances involved in these cases clearly matter to most people when they think about risks, and what risks they are prepared to accept for themselves, for their families and friends, and for society as a whole. The multi-attribute nature of risk is explored in greater detail in Chapter 13.

10.4 MODELS OF EXPOSURE AND EFFECTS PROCESS

Exposure and effects processes can be continuous, as in chronic exposure to air or water pollution, or they can involve discrete events, as in an airplane crash or a plant explosion. Depending on the needs of the assessment, a variety of models are available to estimate exposures, ranging from simple box models, to Gaussian plume models, to much more complex Lagrangian and Eularian models with imbedded chemistry. A general overview is provided in Morgan and McMichael (1981). On the air side, readers can find details in Seinfeld and Pandis (2006) and Zannetti (2003–2010); on the water side, in Wellen et al. (2015), Karcher et al. (2012), and Thomann and Mueller (1987).[7]

Fault trees, event trees, and failure mode and effects analysis are standard tools with which to address discrete events. In the area of risk analysis, these tools first came to prominence as a result of their use in the initial Rasmussen nuclear safety study (WASH-1400, 1975; Rasmussen, 1981). The basic strategy in this work, which has been followed in various forms by many probabilistic risk analyses in the years since, was to lay out a set of event trees that identify all the pathways by which an undesired outcome (such as a pipe break in the reactor's cooling system) might occur. An example is shown in Figure 10.2. The probability of each branch in that event tree (e.g., whether or not electric power remains available) is estimated using fault trees, an example of which is shown in Figure 10.3. The probabilities for each of the input variables are estimated from industry and other experience with similar systems. Today, large data sets of past events have been developed and the production of probabilistic risk assessment for systems such as nuclear and process chemical plants has become a major business.

After laying out all the imaginable routes to a major reactor accident, and estimating the exposure that could result from each, the Rasmussen study then summed the probabilities of each to estimate the probability of events of varying magnitude. The result is shown in Figure 10.4.

While event trees are often the best we can do in developing an estimate of a failure probability, they have the disadvantage that they are only as good as analysts' ability to imagine and analyze every sequence that could lead to the failure of interest. In this connection, the results from a study by Fischhoff et al. (1978) sound a note of caution. In that study, college students and experienced auto mechanics were asked to look at various versions of an event tree of the sort shown in Figure 10.5.

Different groups of respondents received trees that had between four and eight branches and different degrees of detail. In cases when some of the branches were left out, the excluded branches were implicitly lumped into the "all other problems" branch. Respondents were asked to assess probabilities across the branches for why a car might not start. The amount of probability that respondents assigned to "all other problems" did not change anywhere near as much as it should have as more or fewer branches were lumped into the category "all other problems." This suggests that "out of sight is out of mind."

[7] For additional discussion, see Chapter 11.

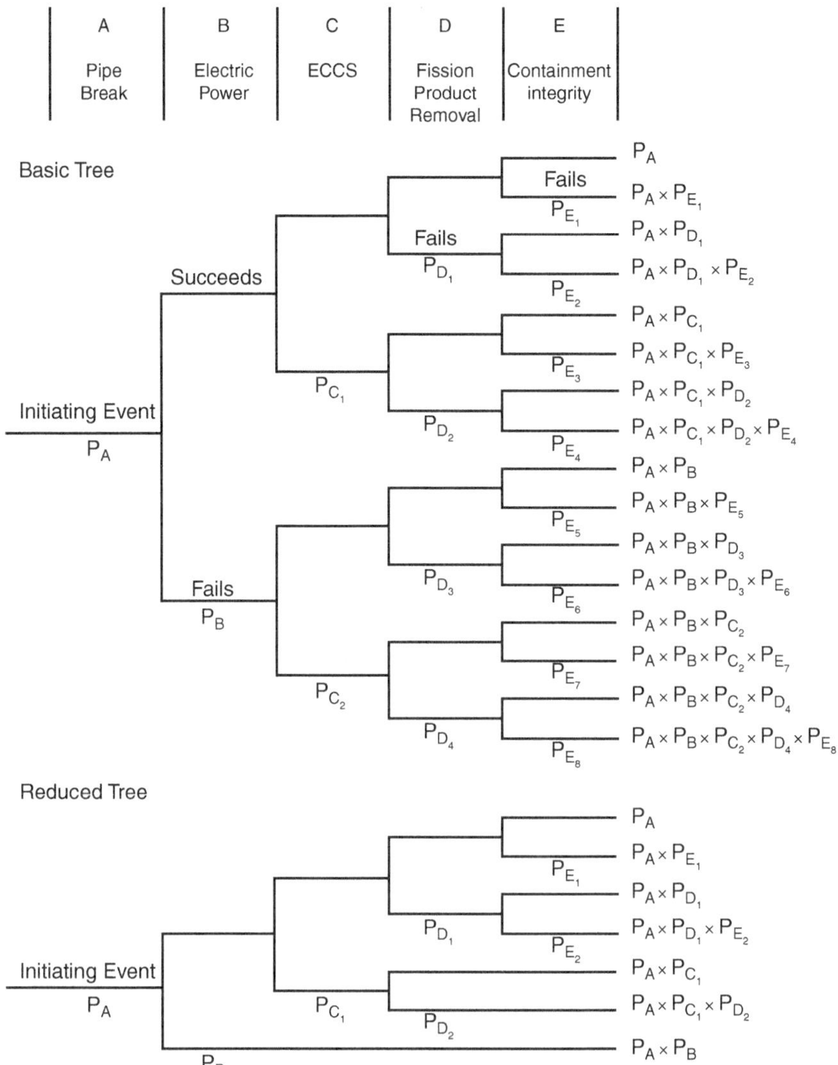

FIGURE 10.2. Example of an event tree leading to a large loss of cooling accident. Reproduced from WASH-1400 (1975).

Without some help it is cognitively difficult to anticipate all the routes that might lead to an event of concern.

In order to construct comprehensive event and fault trees, analysts should seek multiple independent assessments, engage in repeated brainstorming, and seek review by others. Even then, they may not be assured of "getting it all." Troubling as this may be, there is probably no viable alternative.

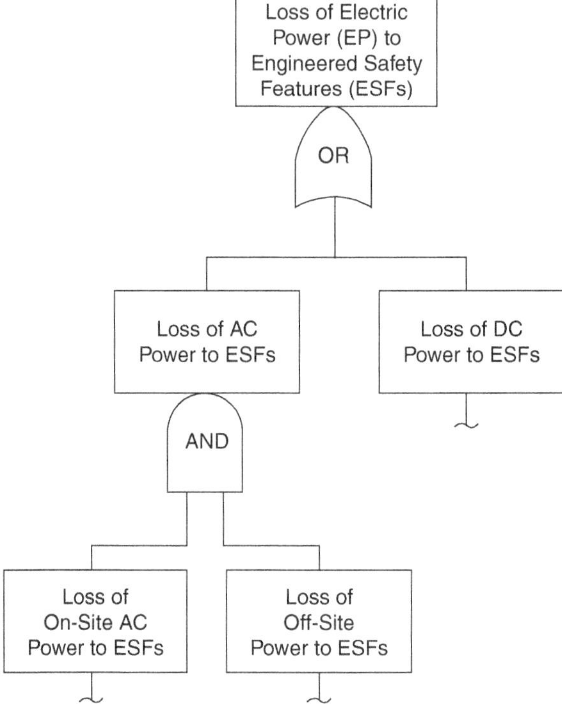

FIGURE 10.3. Example of a fault tree to estimate the probability that electric power is not available to a component in an event tree. Reproduced from WASH-1400 (1975).

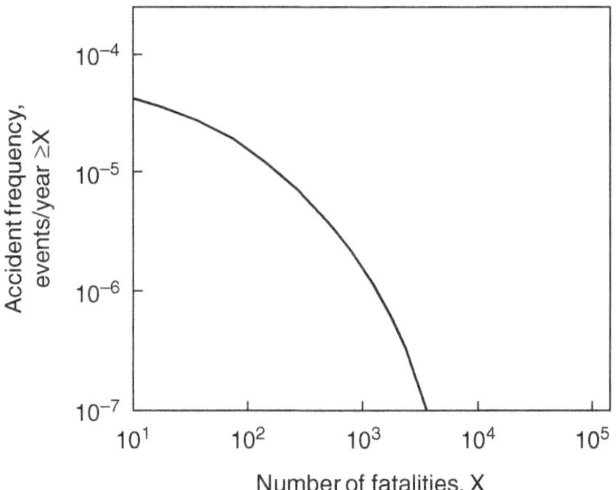

FIGURE 10.4. Example from WASH-1400 (1975) of final estimates of the probability of numbers of deaths that could be caused by 100 nuclear power plants in the United States.

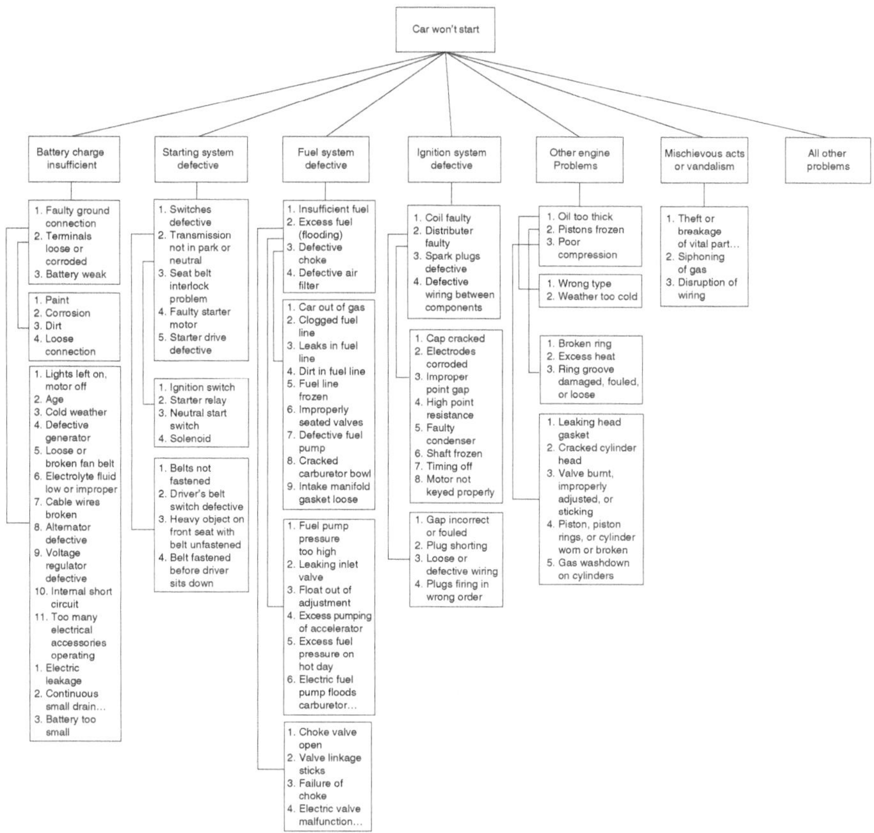

FIGURE 10.5. Event tree used by Fischhoff et al. (1978) in an experiment conducted with college students and auto mechanics. The amount of probability that respondents assigned to the right hand branch "all other problems" was insufficiently sensitive to how much of the tree had been included or deleted and implicitly included in that branch. Note that this tree is for cars with carburetors and that for a while U.S. cars were required to have seatbelt ignition interlocks. This requirement was later abandoned because of customer opposition, safety, and other concerns. Redrawn from Slovic et al. (1980).

The simplest models of effects processes involve a linear relationship between exposure (e.g., as measured by the time integral of the concentration of a pollutant) and the resulting change. Such linear models can be constructed with and without a minimum threshold. Hypothetical examples of such linear "effects functions," with and without thresholds, are shown in Figure 10.6. When the change involves a health impact, it is common to refer to effects functions as "dose-response functions." An example of dose-response functions for cigarette smoking, based on epidemiological evidence, is shown in Figure 10.7.

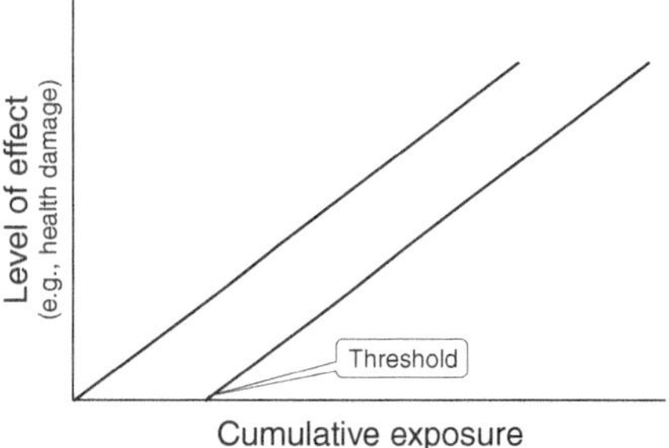

FIGURE 10.6. Examples of linear effects functions. Note that the right-hand example has a threshold below which exposure causes to change.

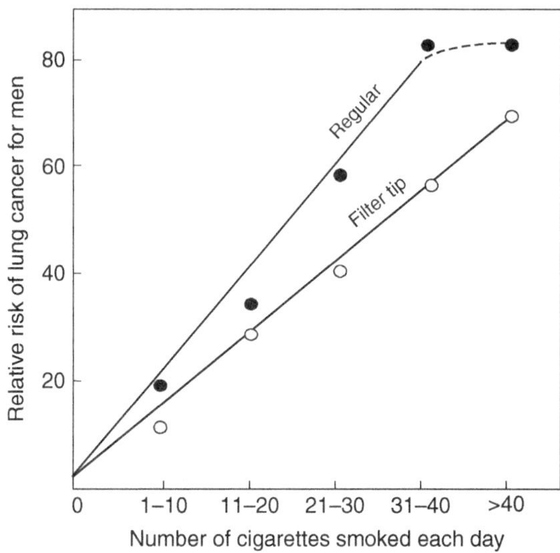

FIGURE 10.7. An example of a dose-response function based on epidemiological evidence for lung cancer and cigarette smoking among males who have been smoking for ten years or longer. Data from Wynder and Hoffmann (1979).

In more recent years, Pope et al. (2011) have used prospective cohort data collected from a sample of 1.2 million adults by the American Cancer Society as part of the Cancer Prevention Study in order to produce estimates of dose-response functions for the mortality impacts of exposure to fine particles smaller than 2.5 microns ($PM_{2.5}$) for both lung cancer and cardiovascular diseases. They conclude that: "At low exposure levels, cardiovascular deaths are projected to account for most of the burden of disease, whereas at high levels of $PM_{2.5}$, lung cancer becomes proportionately more important." Their results are reproduced in Figure 10.8.

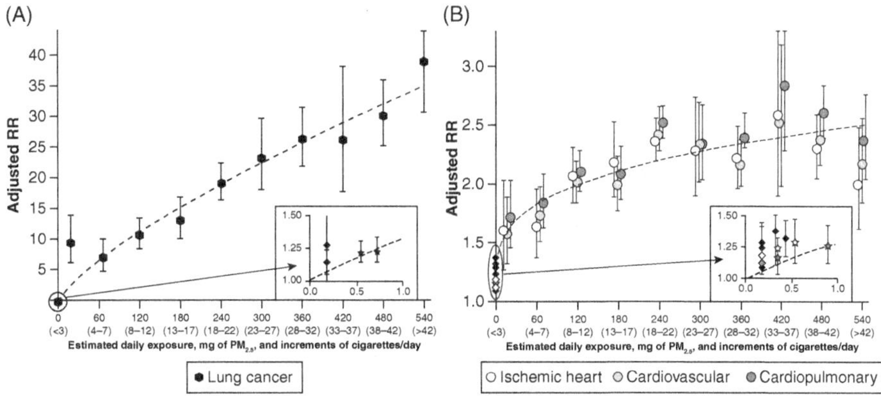

FIGURE 10.8. Adjusted relative risk (RR) with 95% confidence intervals (CIs) of lung cancer mortality (**A**) and IHD, cardiovascular, and cardiopulmonary mortality (**B**) plotted against estimated daily exposure of $PM_{2.5}$ (milligrams) and increments of cigarette smoking relative to never-smokers (cigarettes/day) as reported by Pope et al. (2011). Diamonds represent comparative mortality risk estimates (with 95% CIs) for $PM_{2.5}$ from air pollution from the comparative studies ... Stars represent comparable pooled RR estimates (with 95% CIs) associated with SHS exposure from comparative studies ... The dotted lines represent the non-linear power function fit through the origin and the estimates (including active smoking, SHS, ambient $PM_{2.5}$). Estimated doses from different increments of active smoking are dramatically larger than estimated doses from ambient air pollution or SHS; therefore, associations at lower exposure levels (due to ambient air pollution and SHS) are shown as insets with a magnified scale.

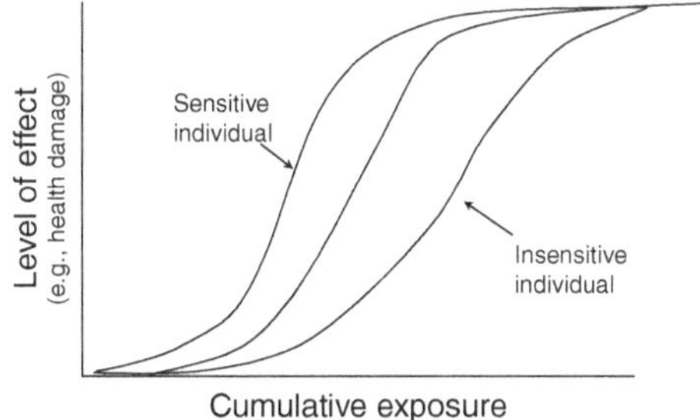

FIGURE 10.9. Examples of non-linear effects functions. Different individuals in a population may display different degrees of sensitivity.

Of course, the response to the time integral of exposure may not be linear. It may be that it takes some minimum amount of exposure to cause any change, after which impact may rise rapidly. However, at a certain level impacts may saturate. Hypothetical examples of such effects functions, which may be different for different individuals, are shown in the left side of Figure 10.9. Some effects functions actually have both positive and negative

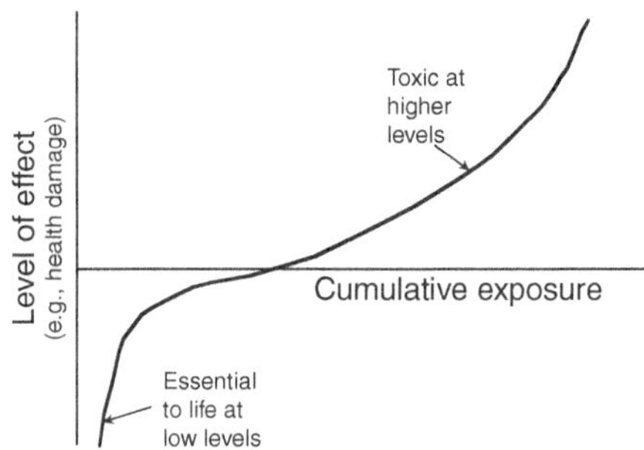

FIGURE 10.10. Example of a dose-response function in which very low levels of a material, such as a metal, is essential to life, but high levels are toxic.

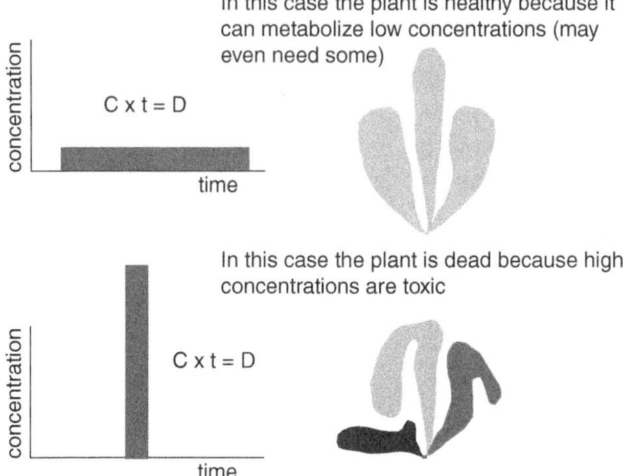

FIGURE 10.11. Example of a dynamic effects function in which the resulting change depends upon the time series of the exposure, and not just its time integral.

values. For example, there are various trace metals that our bodies need in low amounts. If we are deficient in things like fluoride or copper we experience adverse health consequences. On the other hand, if concentrations become too large, the result can be serious toxicity. This is illustrated in the right side of Figure 10.10.

All of these examples assume that there is a one-to-one mapping between the integral of exposure and the resulting change. Of course, if the system being exposed is something living, such as a plant, animal, or person, that assumption may not be valid. Living things can metabolize pollutants and otherwise respond dynamically. A hypothetical example of the results a dynamic effects function might produce for a plant that can metabolize a pollutant at low level is shown in Figure 10.11.

For a thoughtful discussion of possible alternative functional forms for cancer-related dose-response functions, see Morris (1990).

READINGS 10.1

A very useful collection of papers on risk assessment can be found in Glickman and Gough (1990). The following four papers, reprinted in that collection, provide a good cross-section of different approaches to risk analysis:

- Bruce Ames,[8] Renae Magaw, and Lois S. Gold, "Ranking Possible Carcinogenic Hazards," *Science, 236*, pp. 271–280, 1987.
- Mary C. White, Peter F. Infante, and Kenneth C. Chu, "A Quantitative Estimate of Leukemia Mortality Associated with Occupational Exposure to Benzene," *Risk Analysis, 2*(3), pp. 195–204, 1982.
- Norman C. Rasmussen,[9] "The Application of Probabilistic Risk Assessment Techniques to Energy Technologies," *Annual Reviews of Energy*, 6, pp. 123–138, 1981.
- Ralph L. Keeney, Ram B. Kulkarni, and Keshavan Nair, "Assessing the Risk of an LNG Terminal," *Technology Review, 81*(1), pp. 64–72, 1978. In reading the Keeney paper, focus on understanding the method.

In addition:

- Edmund A.C. Crouch and Richard Wilson, "Chapter 7: Everyday Life: A Catalogue of Risks," in *Risk/Benefit Analysis*, Ballinger, pp. 165–193, 1982.

DISCUSSION QUESTION FOR READINGS 10.1

- I included the Crouch and Wilson paper because it is a good compact summary. However, the paper was published in 1982, so some of the data are now rather out of date. Pick two examples where you think the value today might be quite different, find the current value, and discuss why the change has occurred.

10.5 CAUSES OF DEATH

Sooner or later everybody dies from something. The age-specific mortality curve is a convenient way to show the probability of death as a function of

[8] The "Ames test," named after Bruce Ames, exposes bacteria to chemical agents and looks for mutations. Many agents that yield a positive Ames test also turn out to be human carcinogens. See: http://en.wikipedia.org/wiki/Ames_test.

[9] Norman Rasmussen was a Professor of Nuclear Engineering who led the first probabilistic assessment of the risks of LWRs and BWRs that led to a report widely known as WASH-1400. See: http://en.wikipedia.org/wiki/WASH_1400.

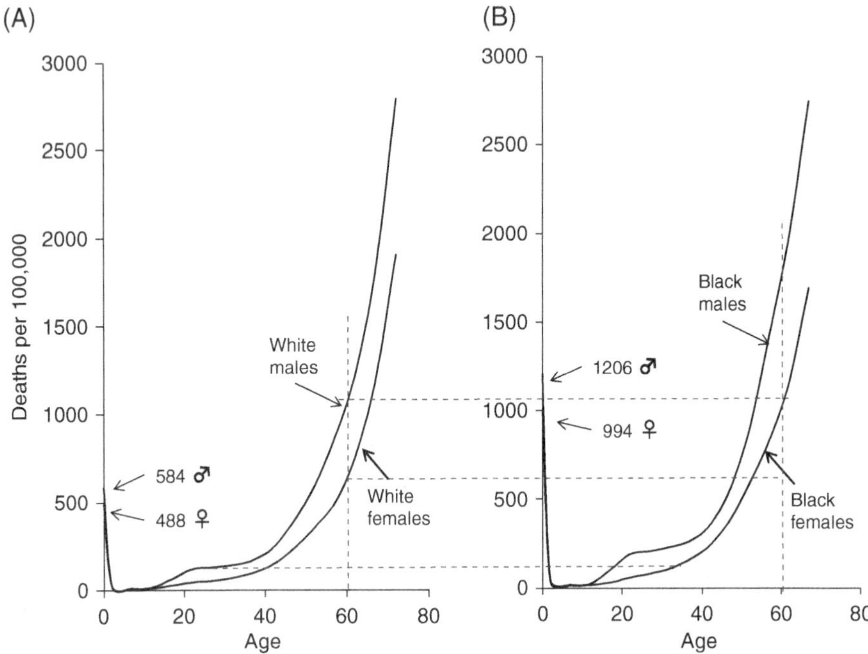

FIGURE 10.12. U.S. age-specific mortality curves in deaths/100,000 in 2010 by sex (**A**) for whites and (**B**) comparison with blacks. Data from U.S. CDC.

age (usually reported in deaths per 100,000 in an age cohort). Figure 10.12 shows age- and race-specific mortality curves for the U.S. population in 2010. Figure 10.13 shows how life expectancy has evolved over the course of the twentieth century, and Figure 10.14 shows how causes of death evolved in the United States over the second half of the twentieth century. Table 10.2 reports the magnitude of some common causes of death in the United States. For data at the global level, see the Global Burden of Disease studies at www.healthdata.org/gbd.

In recent years, while U.S. mortality rates have continued to fall for most age and socioeconomic cohorts, Case and Deaton (2015) report an alarming reversal among middle-aged white non-Hispanic men and women, especially those with only a high school education or less. They report that the increase is "largely accounted for by increasing death rates from drug and alcohol poisonings, suicide, and chronic liver diseases and cirrhosis." Case and Deaton note that similar trends are observed in self-reported measures of well-being. They speculate that this reversal is the result of a serious decline in the economic and social prospects for men and women and their families in this cohort. A similar trend is not observed in the same cohort in Europe, where there is a stronger societal "safety net."

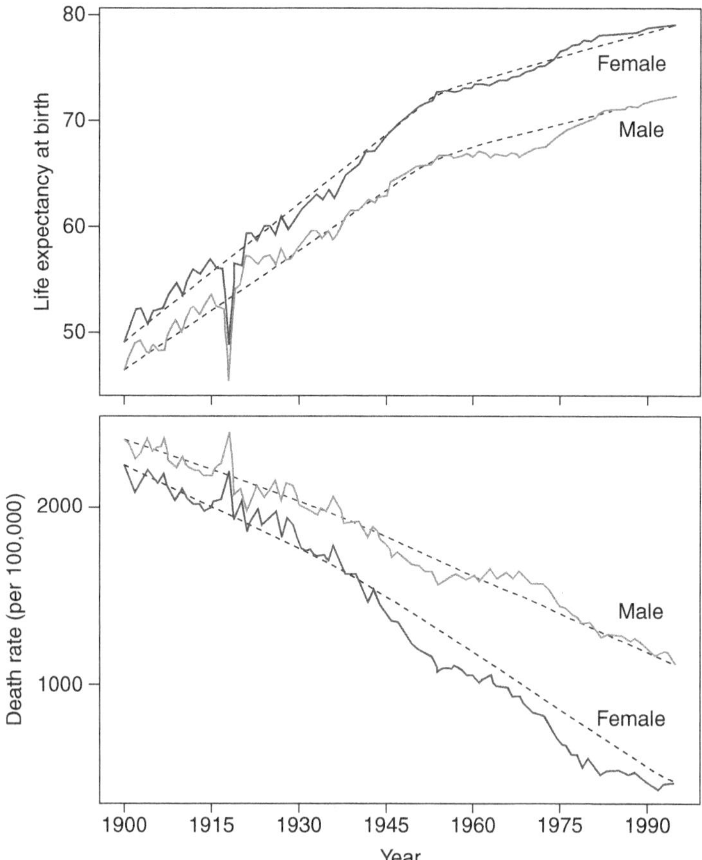

FIGURE 10.13. Evolution of U.S. life expectancy. Note the large drop in 1918 that resulted from the global influenza epidemic. From Wilmoth (1998). Reprinted with permission from AAAS.

10.6 MANAGING RISK

Since risk cannot be eliminated, the problem people face, individually and collectively, is to decide how much risk they will live with and how much time, energy, and other resources they want to devote to managing that risk. To address these issues, analytical tools can be built that will allow the processes in Figure 10.1 to be understood and described for specific tasks. In choosing a risk-management strategy, it is important to remember that many of the activities that one might adopt to reduce risk also carry risks, resulting in a need to consider risk–risk tradeoffs. Graham and Wiener (1995) have proposed a framework for thinking about such tradeoffs, presented nine case studies to illustrate how the need for tradeoffs can arise, and suggested some strategies to minimize the likelihood that such tradeoffs will arise.

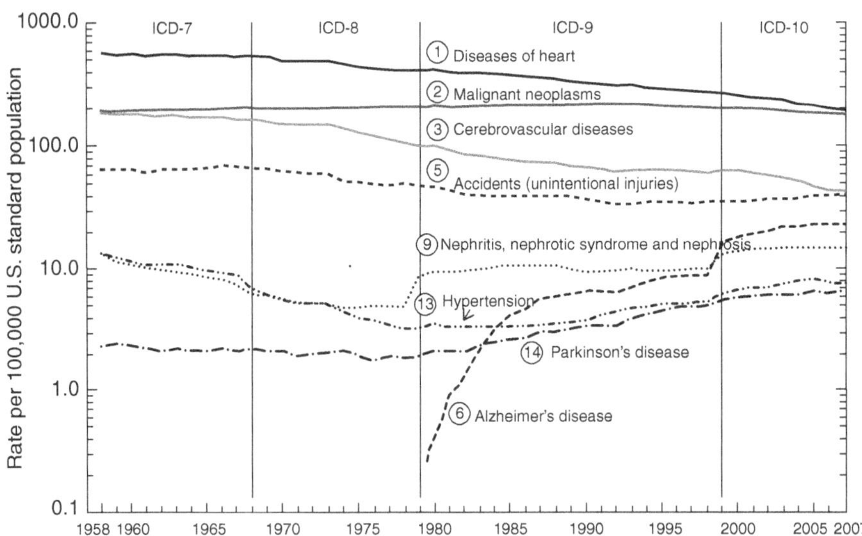

FIGURE 10.14. Evolution of U.S. age-adjusted death rate by selected leading causes of death, 1958–2010 (source: CDC/NCHS, National Vital Statistics System, Mortality). Notes: ICD is the International Classification of Diseases. Circled numbers indicate ranking of conditions as leading causes of death in 2010. Rates for 2001–2009 are revised using updated intercensal estimates and may differ from rates previously published.

In selecting a strategy for managing risk, it is also important to consider the alternative social and technical implications of risk-management philosophies and to select philosophies that are compatible with the goals of society. Then a set of incentives and institutions must be created or evolve that will implant them.

There are basically five strategies that can be adopted to manage a risk:

1. The natural or human environment can be modified so the causal factors no longer occur.
2. Exposure processes can be modified.
3. Effects processes can be modified.
4. The way in which people perceive and value effects can be modified.
5. After the fact, the risk can be mitigated or compensated.

These five options are illustrated in Figure 10.15.

As Table 10.3 makes clear, different options make sense for different hazards. For example, modifying the environment might make sense for lawns in the desert southwest, but obviously doing away with the use of electricity does not make sense for hazards related to electric power. Modifying exposure processes makes sense for many hazards. Modifying effects processes makes far more sense for hazards such as auto accidents than it does for handguns. Mitigating, or compensating after the fact, is often not a very appealing

TABLE 10.2. *Data on mortality from a number of well-known risks. Remember that, since sooner or later we all die from something, everyone's lifetime odds of dying are 1 in 1.*

Cause of death	Approximate number of Americans who die each year from this cause	Approximate odds that the average American will die from this cause
Diseases (all kinds)	2,400,000	1 in 1.1
Heart disease	611,000	1 in 4.2
Cancer (all kinds)	585,000	1 in 4.4
Accidents (all kinds)	131,000	1 in 20
Diabetes	76,000	1 in 34
Suicide	41,000	1 in 63
Auto accidents	35,000	1 in 74
Homicide	16,000	1 in 160
Viral hepatitis	8157	1 in 320
Asthma	3600	1 in 720
Drowning	3400	1 in 760
Fire	3000	1 in 870
Pregnancy and related (only♀)	1100	1 in 1175
Accidental electrocution	1000	1 in 2600
Firearm accident	500	1 in 5200
Appendicitis	370	1 in 7000
Car-train accidents	270	1 in 9600
Tornado	110	1 In 24,000
Floods	70	1 in 37,000
Lightning	32	1 in 81,000
Fireworks	8	1 in 325,000
Botulism	1	1 in 2,600,000

Note: The values shown are for 2013, or in some cases for a ten-year average ending around 2013. There are several reasons why this table uses the words "approximately" and "average American." The numbers of deaths change a bit each year, and some are uncertain for other reasons. Not all people face the same risk. For example, a careful middle-aged driver in a full-sized car on a week-day morning faces a much lower risk of being killed in an auto accident than a carefree teenager driving a subcompact car on a Saturday night. The numbers in this table are primarily based on statistics published by the U.S. Government. They have not been corrected with the age-specific values from life tables.

strategy, although clearly carrying insurance and having good emergency and medical response systems in place are very important as a way to limit total damages. In the case of nuclear power, the government indemnification provided by the Price-Anderson Act has been essential to allowing that industry to develop.

Working to modify people's perceptions and valuations raises ethically complicated issues (see Chapter 14 on risk communication). Working to help people develop a realistic understanding of the science of known or potential hazards is clearly appropriate and socially desirable so as to avoid wasteful

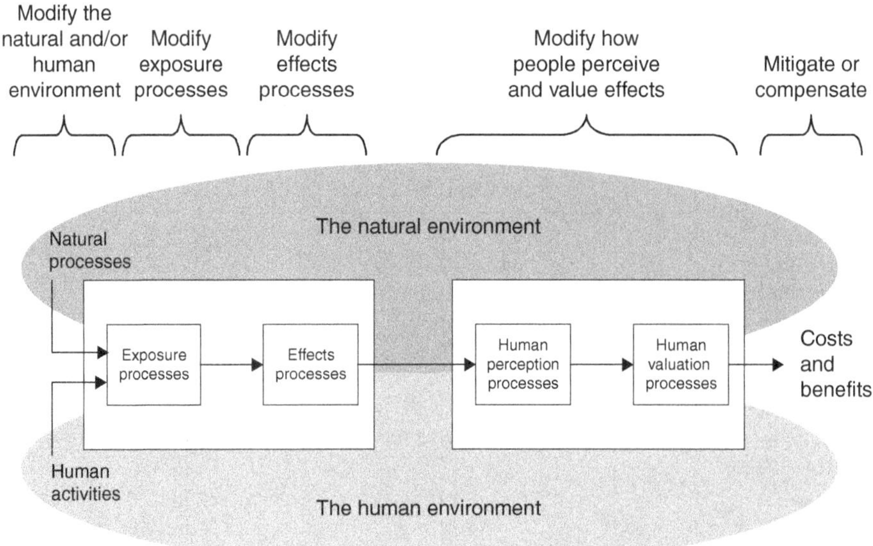

FIGURE 10.15. Illustration of five strategies for managing risk.

investments in risk management that achieve little or no improvement in safety. On the other hand, advertising and lobbying activities by interested parties with the objective of getting individuals and society to minimize or ignore real hazards (Oreskes and Conway, 2010; Mayer, 2016) raises serious ethical issues (Morgan and Lave, 1990). Of course, in a free democratic society there is probably no way to prevent at least some activity by powerful economic interests and scientific "hired guns."

Once a set of strategies has been chosen to manage the risk posed by a hazard that arises from something that also confers social or individual benefit, the obvious next question is "How much should the risk be abated?" If abating the risk costs nothing, the obvious answer is reduce it to zero: get rid of the risk. But risk abatement almost always does cost money and time. When it is impossible to eliminate the risk completely with easy low-cost strategies, the question becomes, "How much risk abatement should we buy?"

If the risk arises from some human activity or technological system, one should first ask whether, given the expected levels of risk, the activity or technology is necessary. In the case of medical diagnostic X-rays, the answer is yes. In the case of shoe-fitting fluoroscopes, of the sort described in the boxed section on aluminum house wire, the answer is clearly no.

Various criteria can be used to decide how much risk abatement to buy. Two of the most common are "acceptable risk" and "optimal risk." "Acceptable" implies a threshold level below which risk will be tolerated. "Optimal" implies

TABLE 10.3. *Examples of risk-management strategies that might be adopted for different hazards. Note that one management strategy does not fit all. Different strategies make more sense for different risks.*

Example hazard	Modify the natural and/or human environment	Modify exposure processes	Modify effects processes	Modify how people perceive and value effects	Mitigate or compensate
Occupant injury in auto accidents	Live close to work and walk Build rapid transit systems	Change speed limit Crack down on drunk drivers Train people to drive defensively	Wear seat belts Add more air bags Re-engineer vehicle	Advertise how cars are now so much safer Reinforce the perception that driver is "above average"	Carry auto insurance Operate good emergency medical systems Sue the other driver
Possible health effects from exposure to power-frequency magnetic fields from distribution lines	Stop using electricity	Place distribution lines away from people Move to another home	Unclear since it is unclear what (if any) mechanism causes health effect	Help people to understand the science Place distribution lines underground	Maintain good health systems Sue the power company
Getting shot by a hand gun	Eliminate poverty, inequality, anger, prejudice, and mental illness	Ban hand guns Mandatory background checks Impose harsh penalties on crimes with guns Avoid high-crime areas	Wear bulletproof clothing Duck	Advertise and lobby against politicians who are against gun control	Carry health insurance Operate good emergency medical systems Sue person who shot you

(*Continued*)

TABLE 10.3. (*cont.,*)

Example hazard	Modify the natural and/or human environment	Modify exposure processes	Modify effects processes	Modify how people perceive and value effects	Mitigate or compensate
Aluminum house wire	Stop using electricity	Replace Al wire with Cu Clean and add ointment to connections Inspect	Install smoke detectors Flashlights and smoke- hoods at bedside Hold fire drills	Advertise and lobby politicians and contractors that Al wire is not a hazard	Carry home insurance Good, fast fire department
Cataracts from the RF radiation from microwave ovens	Use conventional gas or electric ovens	Design ovens with good shielding Design ovens with reliable door interlocks Educate users	Provide users with Faraday shielding goggles or helmets	Help people to understand the science Advertise that microwave ovens are safe	Carry health insurance Provide cornea transplants Sue manufacturer and/or supplier
Nuclear power	Stop using electricity	Generate electricity from non-nuclear sources Good plant back-up systems to avoid releases Don't locate plants near people	Stock potassium iodine pills that can be used to minimize dose to the thyroid	Help people to develop a realistic understanding of the risks Advertise and lobby that our nuclear plants are safer than others	Maintain rapid emergency response and evacuation plans Provide federal insurance guarantee Sue manufacturer and/or power company
Power lawn mowers	Don't plant lawns	Don't cut the grass Use hand mower Require safety interlocks	Wear steel-tip shoes	Advertise that new mowers are safe	Carry health insurance Operate good emergency medical systems Sue the manufacturer

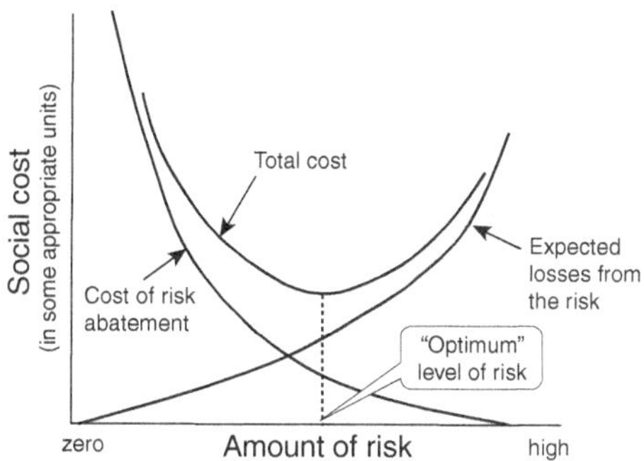

FIGURE 10.16. If it were possible to quantify risks and their associated costs, then most economists would argue that the choice of how much risk abatement to choose boils down to finding the level that minimizes total social cost. However, attempts to do such analysis by replacing "risk" with "expected mortality" often evoke significant displeasure because this ignores the multi-attribute nature of risk.

a tradeoff that minimizes the sum of all damages from a risk with the costs of abating that risk. This idea is illustrated in Figure 10.16. While attractive in concept, given the complexity of quantifying risk, implementing it is often impossible in practice.

AN EXAMPLE: ALUMINUM HOUSE WIRE

For about a decade beginning in the late 1960s, aluminum wiring was used instead of traditional copper in new and renovated houses. Aluminum was substituted because it was less costly. However, over time, aluminum can develop a surface oxide layer that has high resistivity, so connections may become warm whenever the circuit is used. As the circuit is cycled on and off through daily household use, the resulting heating and cooling of the connection does two things: it contributes to the loosening of mechanical contacts, and it aids the further growth of the high-resistance oxide layer. Sooner or later the high-resistance connection may become so hot that insulation melts off the wires, plastic connection caps char and fall away, and, if there is other combustible material nearby, a fire may start, and in some cases the building may burn down.

We can use the risks posed by aluminum wiring to consider the five risk-management strategies in Figure 10.15. Not using electricity would obviously do away with the risk, but that is not a practical option. However, some risks are easily dealt with in this way. For example, in the 1940s many shoe stores installed fluoroscope machines that let customers check how well shoes fit. As a kid in the 1950s, my oldest sister and I had great fun watching our toe bones as we wiggled them in our new shoes. But by then people had begun to realize that these machines produced dangerous and unnecessary exposure to X-rays. Soon after, the machines were junked.

The second approach, modifying or avoiding exposure processes, does make sense in the aluminum wire example. It includes such strategies as not using aluminum wire in the first place; replacing existing aluminum with copper; cleaning and treating the aluminum with a special ointment that inhibits oxide formation and inspecting the contacts periodically; and not using large loads on circuits suspected of containing aluminum wire. It would also include the strategy of disconnecting circuits suspected of containing a problem until they are fixed.

The third approach, modifying or avoiding effects processes, is also workable. It includes installing smoke detectors, placing rope ladders for emergency escape next to windows in upper floors, placing flashlights and smoke hoods at everybody's bedside for use in the event of a house fire, and occasionally holding family fire drills.

As with many other risks, when the problem of aluminum wiring was first discovered, some industry lawyers and lobbyists mounted arguments that the risk was being overblown. Today nobody would exercise the fourth option of trying to persuade homeowners that aluminum wiring is actually not a risk. However, we see this option exercised frequently in the case of other real or imagined risks. Despite overwhelming evidence that smoking cigarettes causes lung cancer and other adverse health impacts, the tobacco industry continues to work to minimize the risks in the mind of the public. A strategy of "out of sight is out of mind" can be one way to change public perceptions. It is unclear whether exposure to power-frequency magnetic fields can cause health risks – but utilities have found that putting distribution lines underground reduces the level of public concern, this despite the fact that because the lines are now closer, in some cases field strengths on some sidewalks may be greater than when the lines were placed overhead.

The final strategy is mitigating or compensating for effects once they have occurred. In the case of aluminum house wiring, this might include having a fast and capable local fire department and carrying adequate fire insurance. In general, such after-the-fact strategies are less satisfactory than those that avoid or reduce the hazard.

Some have argued that if society wants to be rational about risk abatement, it should operate so that a dollar spent in one place will buy the same amount of risk reduction as a dollar spent in any other place (Figure 10.16). But as noted in Section 10.3, and discussed further in Chapter 13, risk is a multi-attribute concept. Hence, it is not surprising that most people do not to want to measure risk simply in terms of expected mortality and morbidity. For example, on the basis of investments made on the basis of cost-per-death-averted, most people want to spend somewhat more to prevent deaths in airliners, which in a crash typically kill many people at a time, than they want to spend to prevent isolated deaths in automobiles. Yet even if we accept some variations of this sort, it is probably not socially desirable to have differences of many orders of magnitude in spending on different kinds of risk abatement.

As discussed in Section 5.5, computing the marginal investment per life saved for risk-abatement programs is extremely difficult. As a second-best strategy, John Graham and colleagues (Graham and Vaupel, 1981; Tengs et al., 1995) have compiled a large number of published estimates of the average cost of a number of life-saving programs together with estimates of the amount of life saving these investments have achieved or could achieve. The results shown in Figure 5.4 span a range of more than a factor of 10^{11} in the average cost per life saved. While clearly some range in investment rates should be expected, it seems clear that this enormous range is not socially optimal. Presumably this very large range results in part from the rather stochastic way in which we, and society, consider and address different risks. Rather than looking systematically across all the hazards all the time, both as individuals and as a society we typically consider one risk and then another as a variety of salient events focus our attention. Ramsberg and Sjöberg (1997) have estimated a range in cost per life saved of roughly 10^7 in Sweden. In light of the multi-attribute nature of risk, some variation in the average (or marginal) rate of investment to prevent mortality should be expected. However, it is difficult to believe that, if risks were considered systematically, society would want the range to be so wide. While the Tengs et al. (1995; Tengs and Graham, 1996) results include some proposed strategies that were never implemented, and are subject to other criticisms, they, together with work by Morrall (1986, 2003), Ramsberg and Sjöberg (1997), and others, suggest that we should be paying significantly more attention to looking comparatively across the investments we make in managing risks.[10]

A number of institutional structures have evolved to implement risk-management procedures. Of these, the four most important are:

1. Tort and other common law – particularly those laws related to negligence, liability, nuisance, and trespass.
2. Insurance – offered either by private companies, through joint private/government arrangements, or directly by government programs.
3. Voluntary standard-setting organizations such as the Underwriters Laboratory, the American Society of Testing and Materials, the National Fire Protection Association, the American National Standards Institute, and engineering societies such as the IEEE and ASME.[11]
4. Mandatory government standards or regulations.

[10] For an example of the ongoing controversy over such studies, see the critique by Heinzerling (1998) and response by Morrall (2003).

[11] Sometimes a voluntary standard developed by such an organization is subsequently picked up and converted into a mandatory standard by a government regulatory organization.

The decision to regulate raises important questions. Does the government have the right to impose a small involuntary cost on many of its citizens in order to make a few or even most people safer? Today probably most U.S. residents would answer yes to this question if the net benefits of regulation very clearly exceed the net costs. But there are other philosophical perspectives besides this utilitarian one. Libertarian and other philosophies place far greater emphasis on individual rights. Thus, it is important to understand that the decision to rely on government regulation, as opposed to tort law or insurance, is an ethical decision about which not all reasonable people will agree.

One-hundred and fifty years ago only the tort law and insurance mechanisms were in general use. The first technological risk to be regulated by the U.S. Government was that of steamboat boiler explosions. As explained in Section 17.5, it took over fifty years, several hundred accidents, and more than 3000 deaths before Congress finally decided that tort law alone could not adequately control fly-by-night operators, overcame its reluctance to meddle in private enterprise, and passed an effective regulatory law (Burke, 1966). Regulation of technologically based risks did not become a major activity until after the innovations of the New Deal in the 1930s.

Most of the government regulatory agencies that today dominate our approach to risk management have been created since 1945. Figure 10.17 is a plot prepared by EPRI that catalogs regulations that apply to the electric power industry that have been developed in the period from 1870 to the late 1990s. Note in Figure 10.17 the particularly rapid rise of regulation in the decades since 1970. The electricity industry is by no means unique. Similar plots could be created for almost any other major U.S. industrial sector.

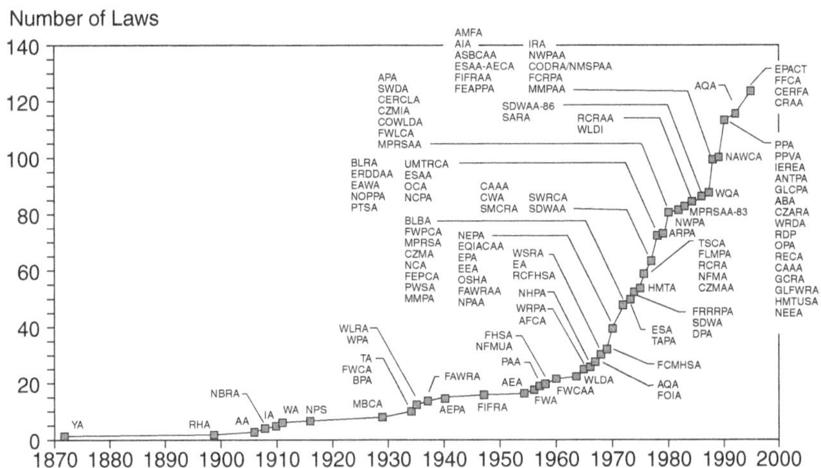

FIGURE 10.17. A cataloguing of regulations that have been applied to the U.S. electricity industry over the period from 1870 through the late 1990s. Similar plots could be developed for almost any other major U.S. industrial sector (source: EPRI).

Design standards specify in detail the way a device or system may be built and operated. Good examples of this are the pressure vessel code of the American Society of Mechanical Engineers and the data-encryption standard of the National Bureau of Standards. In contrast, performance standards specify the way a device must perform in a given situation, leaving designers free to meet that objective as they think best. In general, performance standards are better, because they allow room for innovation, although in many cases, demonstrating that the specified performance can be met poses a challenge (Notarianni, 2000; Notarianni and Fischbeck, 2001).

Standards often take the form of a threshold, as with the exposure thresholds specified in many regulations of the Occupational Safety and Health Administration or the ambient air-pollution concentration thresholds specified by the U.S. Environmental Protection Agency under the Clean Air Act.

An approach that most economists find theoretically attractive is the externality tax. This requires that someone who operates a system that imposes some social cost pay a tax that is roughly equal to the non-market costs, such as damage from pollution, that are imposed as a result of the activity. Such a tax has the effect of "internalizing" the social cost, so that it becomes cost-effective for the operator to buy just the amount of risk-abatement technology that is socially optimal. An early context in which this approach saw a major application involved the control of pollution in the Rhine River valley in Germany, where the 1976 Effluent Tax Act imposed a tax on industries proportional to the amount of pollution they discharged into the river (Möller-Gulland et al., 2011). A closely related strategy that involves capping the amount of emissions that are allowed and then allowing trading among emitting parties, called "cap and trade," is now in use in the United States for sulfur air pollution and in Europe for carbon dioxide. Efforts are being made around the world to extend the application of such strategies more generally to the control of carbon dioxide.[12]

Several groups have worked on assessing and improving our current approaches to risk assessment and risk. The result has been a number of new and proposed institutional arrangements. The Carter Administration made major attempts at regulatory reform. A principal vehicle was Executive Order 12044 that, among other things, stipulated that regulatory agencies had to

[12] Note that cap and trade systems should only be applied to situations in which the pollutant is well mixed since otherwise the given quantity of pollution being traded may be producing quite different amounts of harm. For this reason, efforts in the United States to implement a cap and trade regime for mercury pollution are potentially problematic. The same issue also applies to emission taxes. In principle the units traded or taxed could be weighted as a function of the emission location, time, etc., but that adds a degree of complexity that in most cases would make implementation impractical. For a range of views on the relative attractiveness of regulations based on cap and trade and on emission tax, see: http://e360.yale.edu/feature/putting_a_price_on_carbon_an_emissions_cap_or_a_tax/2148.

perform an analysis for any regulations that would have significant economic impact. The Reagan Administration replaced this order with another (Executive Order 12291) that requires all executive agencies to prepare a regulatory impact analysis to assist them in selecting regulatory approaches in which the "potential benefits to society from the regulation outweigh the potential costs to society." Every subsequent presidency has issued similar orders (see discussion in Chapter 3). Such analyses are required only for "major rules" that are likely to have an economic impact of $100 million a year or more or significant adverse effects on competition, employment, investment productivity, innovation or on the ability of U.S.-based enterprises to compete with foreign-based enterprises in domestic or export markets; or will result in a major increase in costs or prices in the economy.

SUGGESTED RESOURCES TO LEARN MORE ABOUT REGULATION

- Paul S. Fischbeck and R. Scott Farrow (eds.), *Improving Regulation: Cases in Environment, Health and Safety*, Resources for the Future, 461pp., 2001.
- Lester B. Lave, *The Strategy of Social Regulation: Decision Frameworks for Policy*, Brookings, 166pp., 1981.
- Jonathan B. Wiener, M.D. Rogers, J.K. Hammitt, and P.H. Sand (eds.), *The Reality of Precaution: Comparing Risk Regulation in the United States and Europe*, RFF Press, 582pp., 2011.

In thinking about improving existing risk-management systems, five issues deserve special attention:

1. Many existing risk-management systems still do not do a good enough job of characterizing and dealing with uncertainty.
2. Most risk-management systems are focused too narrowly on specific classes of risks. They frequently miss the big picture. For example, flood-control measures, such as dams, reduce the risks from routine floods but often increase the risk of occasional large floods. Many efforts at ecosystem management, such as insect pest control, reflect similar difficulties. With separate air, water, and solid-waste divisions, the Environmental Protection Agency still has trouble dealing with the coupled air, water, and solid-waste effluents of large-process industries.
3. Most risk-management systems seem committed to providing immediate global solutions. We have not learned how to encourage different approaches to the same problem so we can go slowly and select the one found to work best or so a broad approach can be adapted to local circumstances.
4. In the continuing attempt to assign blame, which the adversarial world view promotes, most risk-management systems have not become very

good at adapting, at being flexible, and at being willing to admit and learn from mistakes.[13]

5. Most risk-management systems generally do not do a very good job of promoting consensus, collaboration, and cooperation among the major actors in the area in which they are operating.[14]

10.7 THE RISK OF WORRYING (TOO MUCH) ABOUT RISK

Risk is a fascinating subject – so fascinating that it is easy to get completely wrapped up in it and forget that there are risks and other costs involved in worrying about risk. Real or imagined risks are everywhere, and ever-increasing levels of resources are devoted to their management resources that in some cases might otherwise go toward advancing science and technology, improving productivity, or enriching culture.

A number of authors have written about striking a social balance between risk seeking and risk avoiding. It is hard to move individuals back and forth between a risk-seeking and a risk-avoiding view of life, but that is probably not a bad thing. The danger comes from gradually moving everyone in a society to just one end of this continuum. If people become completely preoccupied with risk reduction on a piecemeal risk-by-risk basis, they are likely to build a society that is stagnant and has very little freedom.

Yet no reasonable person would argue that society should forget about risk. Instead it must perform a continual balancing act, retaining a diversity of risk takers and risk avoiders, because both contribute certain strengths. Together, we must design institutions and strategies for risk management that take a wide perspective and that are flexible and adaptable. In short, people must learn that living with, managing, and adapting to risk is what life is all about.

READINGS 10.2

- Aaron Wildavsky, "No Risk Is the Highest Risk of All," *American Scientist*, 67, Jan–Feb, pp. 32–37, 1979. Reprinted in T.S. Glickman and M. Gough, *Readings in Risk*, Resources for the Future, pp. 120–128, 1990.
- William C. Clark, "Witches, Floods and Wonder Drugs," in R.C. Schwing and W.A. Albers Jr. (eds.), *Societal Risk Assessment: How Safe Is Safe Enough?*, Plenum, pp. 287–318, 1980.

[13] One obvious exception is the U.S. Transportation Research Board (TRB). When an accident happens, the TRB mounts an investigation that is independent of arguments about who is to blame. The results of TRB investigations have been critical to improving transportation safety, especially in air travel, in both the United States and around the world.

[14] The past few decades have witnessed the emergence of negotiated rule making in which a regulatory agency and a group of regulated parties sit down to work out an arrangement that is acceptable to all. See, for example, EPA SAB (2001).

- Michael Thompson, "Aesthetics of Risk: Culture or Context," in R.C. Schwing and W.A. Albers Jr. (eds.), *Societal Risk Assessment: How Safe Is Safe Enough?*, Plenum, pp. 273–285, 1980.
- Ralph L. Keeney, "Understanding Life-Threatening Risks," *Risk Analysis*, *15*, pp. 627–637, 1995.

DISCUSSION QUESTIONS FOR READINGS 10.2

- What does Wildavsky mean when he says "by trying to make ourselves super-safe ... we may end up super-sorry"?
- A central idea raised by both Wildavsky and Clark is the importance of "stopping rules." What is a stopping rule and how should it be developed and applied?
- What is the essence of the argument related to floods advanced by Clark?
- What is the point of Thompson's long discourse on Buddhists and Hindus?
- Why does Thompson frame some of his argument in terms of the "aesthetics of risk taking"? For many years a significant proportion of construction workers in high steel in the United States were Native Americans from the Mohawk and other Iroquois Tribes. Similarly, high trapeze artists have been dominated by a few families such as the Wallendas. Can you construct a possible analogy to Thompson's argument?
- What is your view of Keeney's argument that "total risk to an individual can not be reduced; only the causes and timing can be transferred"?
- What does Keeney mean when he argues that "conservatism is not always conservative"?

BOX 10.2 COMPACT SUMMARY DEVELOPED BY THE U.S. ENVIRONMENTAL PROTECTION AGENCY OF RISK ASSESSMENT AND MANAGEMENT AT THE AGENCY

- 1970s: EPA was involved with risk assessment practices since the Agency's early days, although risk assessment per se was not a formally recognized process then. EPA completed its first risk-assessment document in December 1975: *Quantitative Risk Assessment for Community Exposure to Vinyl Chloride* (Kuzmack and McGaughy, 1975). The next significant document appeared in 1976: *Interim Procedures and Guidelines for Health Risk and Economic Impact Assessments of Suspected Carcinogens* (Train, 1976). The preamble of this document, signed by the Administrator, signaled the Agency's intent that "rigorous assessments of health risk and economic impact will be undertaken as part of the regulatory process." A general framework described a process to be followed in analyzing cancer risks of pesticides, and the document recommended that the health data be analyzed independently of the economic impact analysis.

- 1980s: EPA announced the availability of water quality criteria documents for 64 contaminants. This was the first application of quantitative procedures developed by EPA to a large number of carcinogens, and the first EPA document describing quantitative procedures used in risk assessment.

  Then in 1983, the National Academy of Science (NAS) published *Risk Assessment in the Federal Government: Managing the Process* (NRC, 1983, commonly referred to as the "Red Book"). EPA has integrated the principles of risk assessment from this groundbreaking report into its practices to this day. The following year, EPA published *Risk Assessment and Management Framework for Decision Making* (US EPA, 1984), which emphasizes making the risk-assessment process transparent, describing the assessment's strengths and weaknesses more fully, and providing plausible alternatives within the assessment. Also in the 1980s, EPA released the *Integrated Risk Information System (IRIS)*, a database of human health effects that may result from exposure to various substances found in the environment.
- 1990s: Shortly after the publication of the Red Book, EPA began issuing a series of guidelines for conducting risk assessments (e.g., in 1986 for cancer, mutagenicity, chemical mixtures, developmental toxicology, and in 1992 for estimating exposures). Although EPA efforts focused initially on human health risk assessment, the basic model was adapted to ecological risk assessment in the 1990s to deal with risks to plants, animals, and whole ecosystems.

  Over time, the NAS expanded on its risk-assessment principles in a series of subsequent reports, including *Pesticides in the Diets of Infants and Children* (NRC, 1993), *Science and Judgment in Risk Assessment* (NRC, 1994), also known as the "Blue Book," and *Understanding Risk: Informing Decisions in a Democratic Society* (NRC, 1996). For example, the NAS places equal emphasis on fully characterizing the scope, uncertainties, limitations, and strengths of the assessment and on the social dimensions of interacting with decision makers and other users of the assessment in an iterative, analytic-deliberative process. The purpose of this process is to ensure that the assessments meet the intended objectives and are understandable. EPA risk-assessment practices have evolved over time along with this progression of thought and in many cases helped drive the evolution of thinking on risk assessment.

REFERENCES

Ames, B.N., R. Magaw, and L.S. Gold (1987). "Ranking Possible Carcinogenic Hazards," *Science*, *236*, pp. 271–280.

Burke, J.G. (1966). "Bursting Boilers and the Federal Power," *Technology and Culture*, *7*, pp. 1–23.

Case, A. and A. Deaton (2015). "Rising Morbidity and Mortality in Midlife among White Non-Hispanic Americans in the 21st Century," *Proceedings of the National Academy of Science*, *112*(49), pp. 15078–15083.

Clark, W.C. (1980). "Witches, Floods and Wonder Drugs," in R.C. Schwing and W.A. Albers Jr. (eds.), *Societal Risk Assessment: How Safe Is Safe Enough?*, Plenum, pp. 287–318.

Crouch, E.A.C. and R. Wilson (1982). *Risk/Benefit Analysis*, Ballinger, 218pp.

EPA SAB (2001). *Improved Science-Based Environmental Stakeholder Processes: A Commentary by the EPA Science Advisory Board*, EPA-SAB-EC-COM-01-006, 25pp. Available at: http://yosemite.epa.gov/sab/sabproduct.nsf/cee3f-362f1a1344e8525718e004ea078/$file/eecm01006_report_appna-e.pdf.

Fischbeck, P.S. and R.S. Farrow (eds.) (2001). *Improving Regulation: Cases in Environment, Health and Safety*, Resources for the Future, 461pp.

Fischhoff, B., P. Slovic, and S. Lichtenstein (1978). "Fault Trees: Sensitivity of Estimated Failure Probabilities to Problem Representation," *Journal of Experimental Psychology: Human Perception and Performance*, *4*, pp. 342–355.

Glickman, T.S. and M. Gough (1990). *Readings in Risk*, Resources for the Future, distributed by Johns Hopkins University Press, 262pp.

Graham, J.D. and J. Vaupel (1981). "Value of Life: What Difference Does It Make?," *Risk Analysis*, *1*, pp. 692–704.

Graham, J.D. and J.B. Wiener (1995). *Risk versus Risk: Trade-offs in Protecting Health and the Environment*, Harvard University Press, 337pp.

Heinzerling, L. (1998). "Regulatory Costs of Mythic Proportions," *The Yale Law Journal*, *107*(7), pp. 1981–2070.

Karcher, S.C., J.M. VanBriesen, and C.T. Nietch (2012). *Assessing the Challenges Associated with Developing an Integrated Modeling Approach for Predicting and Managing Water Quality and Quantity from the Watershed through the Drinking Water Treatment System*, U.S. EPA Office of Research and Development, EPA/600/R-12/030, 55pp.

Keeney, R.L. (1995). "Understanding Life-Threatening Risks," *Risk Analysis*, *15*, pp. 627–637.

Keeney, R.L., R.B. Kulkarni, and K. Nair (1978). "Assessing the Risk of an LNG Terminal," *Technology Review*, *81*(1), pp. 64–72.

Kuzmack, A.M. and R.E. McGaughy (1975). *Quantitative Risk Assessment for Community Exposure to Vinyl Chloride*, U.S. Environmental Protection Agency, 122pp.

Lave, L.B. (1981). *The Strategy of Social Regulation: Decision Frameworks for Policy*, Brookings, 166pp.

Mayer, J. (2016). *Dark Money: The Hidden History of the Billionaires behind the Rise of the Radical Right*, Doubleday, 449pp.

Möller-Gulland, J., K. McGlade, and M. Lago (2011). "Effluent Tax in Germany," EPI Water Report WP3 EX-POST, Evaluating Economic Policy Instrument for Sustainable Water Management in Europe, 39pp. Available at: www.feem-project.net/epiwater/docs/d32-d6-1/CS14_Germany.pdf.

Morgan, M.G. (1981a) "Probing the Question of Technology-Induced Risk," *IEEE Spectrum*, *18*(11), pp. 58–64.

(1981b) "Choosing and Managing Technology-Induced Risk," *IEEE Spectrum*, *18*(12), pp. 53–60.

Morgan, M.G. and L.B. Lave (1990). "Ethical Considerations in Risk Communication Practice and Research," guest editorial in *Risk Analysis*, *10*(3), pp. 355–358.

Morgan, M.G. and F.C. McMichael (1981). "A Characterization and Critical Discussion of Models and Their Use in Environmental Policy," *Policy Sciences*, *14*, pp. 345–370.

Morrall, J.F., III (1986). "A Review of the Record," *Regulation*, pp. 25–34.

III (2003). "Saving Lives: A Review of the Record," AEI-Brookings Joint Center Working Paper 03-6, 28pp.

Morris, S.C. (1990). *Cancer Risk Assessment: A Quantitative Approach*, M. Dekker, 408pp.

Notarianni, K.A. (2000). "The Role of Uncertainty in Improving Fire Protection Regulation," Ph.D. thesis, Department of Engineering and Public Policy, Carnegie Mellon University, 256pp.

Notarianni, K.A. and P.S. Fischbeck (2001). "Performance with Uncertainty: A Process for Implementing Performance-Based Fire Regulations," in P.S. Fischbeck and G.S. Farrow (eds.), *Improving Regulation: Cases in Environment Health and Safety*, Resources for the Future, pp. 233–256.

NRC (1983). *Risk Assessment in the Federal Government: Managing the Process*, National Academies Press, 191 pp.

(1993). *Pesticides in the Diets of Infants and Children*, National Academies Press, 386pp.

(1994). *Science and Judgment in Risk Assessment*, National Academies Press, 651pp.

(1996). *Understanding Risk: Informing Decisions in a Democratic Society*, National Academies Press, 249pp.

Oreskes, N. and E.M. Conway (2010). *Merchants of Doubt*, Bloomsbury Press, 355pp.

Pope, C.A., III, R.T. Burnett, M.C. Turner, A. Cohen, D. Krewski, M. Jerrett, S.M. Gapstur, and M.J. Thun (2011). "Lung Cancer and Cardiovascular Disease Mortality Associated with Ambient Air Pollution and Cigarette Smoke: Shape of the Exposure–Response Relationships," *Environmental Health Perspectives*, *119*(11), pp. 1616–1621.

Ramsberg, J.A.L. and L. Sjöberg (1997). "The Cost-Effectiveness of Lifesaving Interventions in Sweden," *Risk Analysis*, *17*(4), pp. 467–478.

Rasmussen, N.C. (1981). "The Application of Probabilistic Risk Assessment Techniques to Energy Technologies," *Annual Reviews of Energy*, *6*, pp. 123–138.

Seinfeld, J.H. and S. Pandis (2006). *Atmospheric Chemistry and Physics: From Air Pollution to Climate Change*, Wiley, 1203pp.

Slovic, P., B. Fischhoff, and S. Lichtenstein (1980). "Facts and Fears: Understanding Perceived Risk," in R.S. Schwing and W.A. Albers Jr. (eds.), *Societal Risk Assessment: How Safe Is Safe Enough?*, Plenum, pp. 181–214.

Tengs, T.O., M.E. Adams, J.S. Pliskin, D.G. Safran, J.E. Siegel, M.C. Weinstein, and J.D. Graham (1995). "Five-Hundred Live Saving Interventions and Their Cost-Effectiveness," *Risk Analysis*, *15*, pp. 369–390.

Tengs, T.O. and J.D. Graham (1996). "Chapter 8: The Opportunity Costs of Social Investments in Life-Saving," in R.W. Hahn (ed.), *Risks and Costs of Lives Saved*, Oxford University Press, pp. 167–182.

Thomann, R.V. and J.A. Mueller (1987). *Principles of Surface Water Quality Modeling and Control*, Harper & Row, 644pp.

Thompson, M. (1980). "Aesthetics of Risk: Culture or Context," in R.C. Schwing and W.A. Albers Jr. (eds.), *Societal Risk Assessment: How Safe Is Safe Enough?*, Plenum, pp. 273–285.

Train, R. (1976). "Interim Procedures and Guidelines for Health Risk and Economic Impact Assessments of Suspected Carcinogens," EPA Office of the Administrator, 15pp.

US EPA (1984). "Risk Assessment and Management: Framework for Decision Making," US EPA 600-9-85, 37pp.

WASH-1400 (1975). *Reactor Safety Study: An Assessment of Accident Risks in U.S. Commercial Nuclear Power Plants*, NUREG-75/014 (WASH-1400), 207pp.

Wellen, C., A.-R. Kamran-Disfani, and G.B. Arhonditsis (2015). "Evaluation of the Current State of Distributed Watershed Nutrient Water Quality Modeling," *Environmental Science & Technology*, *49*(6), pp. 3278–3290.

White, M.C., P.F. Infante, and K.C. Chu (1982). "A Quantitative Estimate of Leukemia Mortality Associated with Occupational Exposure to Benzene," *Risk Analysis*, *2*(3), pp. 195–204.

Wiener, J.B., M.D. Rogers, J.K. Hammitt, and P.H. Sand (eds.) (2011). *The Reality of Precaution: Comparing Risk Regulation in the United States and Europe*, RFF Press/Earthscan/Routledge, 582pp.

Wildavsky, A. (1979). "No Risk Is the Highest Risk of All," *American Scientist*, *67*, Jan.–Feb., pp. 32–37.

Wilmoth, J.R. (1998). "The Future of Human Longevity: A Demographer's Perspective," *Science*, *280*, pp. 395–397.

Wynder, E.L. and D. Hoffmann (1979). "Tobacco and Health: A Societal Challenge," *The New England Journal of Medicine*, *300*, pp. 894–903.

Zannetti, P. (ed.) (2003–2010). *Air Quality Modeling: Theories, Methodologies, Computational Techniques, and Available Databases and Software*, Vol. I, Fundamentals; Vol. II, Advanced Topics; Vol. III, Special Issues; Vol. IV, Advances and Updates, EnviroComp and Air & Waste Management Association.

11

The Use of Models in Policy Analysis

The word "model" can mean many things. Greenberger et al. (1976) offer the taxonomy shown in Figure 11.1. Our focus in this chapter is on that subset that he terms mathematical and computer models. Humans have been building mathematical models of the natural world for thousands of years. The use of such models in modern natural science has its roots in the fifteenth century with the work of people like Newton and Kepler.

In Greenberger's classification, "schematic models" are things like blueprints of a building, "physical models" are things such as an airfoil that is tested in a wind tunnel, and "role playing" models are things like war games or economic market games (both of which may of course be supported by symbolic models). Today, mathematical models, and their computer implementations, are an integral part of virtually all work in the natural sciences.

While some computer models simply consist of the automation of mathematical models, many are more complex. Some mathematical models (e.g., certain sets of differential equations) cannot be solved (or easily solved) in closed form, so computational methods are used to obtain approximate solutions. When the value of key model coefficients is not known, models are often run as "stochastic simulations," that is, by evaluating them many times with different sets of possible coefficient values drawn from input probability distributions that are used to build up a probability distribution in the value of the output.

Many simulation models are run simply to understand how a complicated system is likely to behave. Others are run as optimizations, in order to determine a set of coefficient values that produce the "best" performance when assessed against some objective function.

In 1991 John Sterman observed that:

> Computer modeling of social and economic systems is only about three decades old. Yet in that time, computer models have been used to analyze everything from inventory management in corporations to the performance of national economies, from the

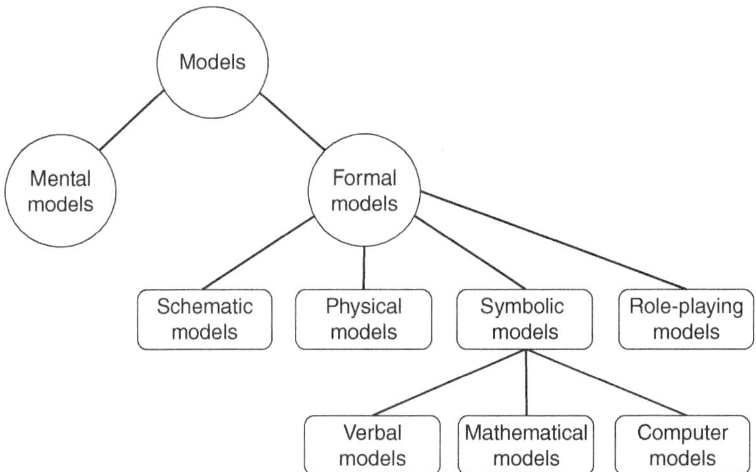

FIGURE 11.1. A taxonomy of "classes of models" as suggested by Greenberger et al. (1976).

optimal distribution of fire stations in New York City to the interplay of global population, resources, food, and pollution.

Many of the best policy models are small and simple and present relatively modest computational demands for modern digital computers. These attributes flow directly from the requirement that to be useful and defensible, policy models must be understandable, easily described to others, and modest enough to be vigorously exercised to explore the implications of uncertainty and of alternative assumptions and policies.

Of course, many models are not small and simple. In the case of models of well-understood processes in natural science or engineering (e.g., a computational fluid dynamic assessment of an aircraft or wind-turbine blade), such complexity is entirely appropriate. However, as one moves to the realm of models for policy analysis that involves large amounts of economic and behavioral content, size and complexity can become more problematic. Too many such models are large or complex because their authors gave too little thought to why and how they were being built and how they should be used. Writing about large policy models over forty years ago, House and McLeod (1977) argued that such models were often "oversold and underdelivered."[1] Unfortunately, too often today the situation is the same.

Building models can be intellectually challenging and great fun. Many of us who have built models have argued that the insights and lessons learned

[1] In addition to an extended discussion of issues in the development and use of large policy models, House and McLeod (1977) provide detailed descriptions of many early modeling efforts such as SEAS (Strategic Environmental Assessment System) and GEM (General Environmental Model).

during the process of constructing the model have often been more valuable than the outputs from running the models. At the same time, if a model is going be used in making important policy, design, or other decisions, validating the results becomes very important. In some cases it is possible to directly compare model results with outcomes from experiments or similar activities (e.g., a computational fluid dynamics model can be validated by comparing its output with data from wind tunnel tests). In the case of time series models, it may be possible to do back casting, that is, to start the model at some past moment with data from that moment and run it forward to see how well it predicts the present. However, in many cases model validation poses very considerable challenges, a few of which are discussed in the sections that follow.

11.1 TYPES OF MODELS COMMONLY USED IN TECHNICALLY FOCUSED POLICY ANALYSIS

The next six sections of this chapter discuss briefly a number of different types of models and model applications that are commonly used by analysts working in the area of technology and public policy. As in other sections of this book, my objective is not to provide a detailed "how to" discussion but rather to help readers to develop a broad critical overview.

In Section 11.2, I briefly discuss what I have termed simple engineering, economic, and policy models. These include most of the wide variety of models that are built and used by practitioners of science, technology, and policy research and analysis.

Most readers of this book are probably familiar with conservation laws such as the conservation of mass and energy. These laws provide a very useful basis for performing many types of analysis (Figure 11.2). For example, if one captures air pollution at the source, the mass that is no longer released to the atmosphere must either end up as a liquid or solid waste (or a product). Conservation laws may be second nature to students of science and engineering, but it took the U.S. Environmental Protection Agency many years before they began to understand the importance of adopting a "multimedia approach" to environmental controls. Robert Dunlap, Fran McMichael, and a number of other investigators in Carnegie Mellon's Department of Engineering and Public Policy played a key role in helping them to reach this understanding. Models for Environmental Impact Assessment are discussed in Section 11.3.

Building on the strategy of "tracking the mass," these ideas have been extended more recently to perform "life cycle analysis" (LCA) on a wide variety of goods and services. Sometimes referred to as "cradle to grave" analysis, LCA attempts to identify and catalog all of the energy and material inputs and outputs during the creation, use, and disposal of a good or the provision of a service. LCA is discussed in Section 11.4.

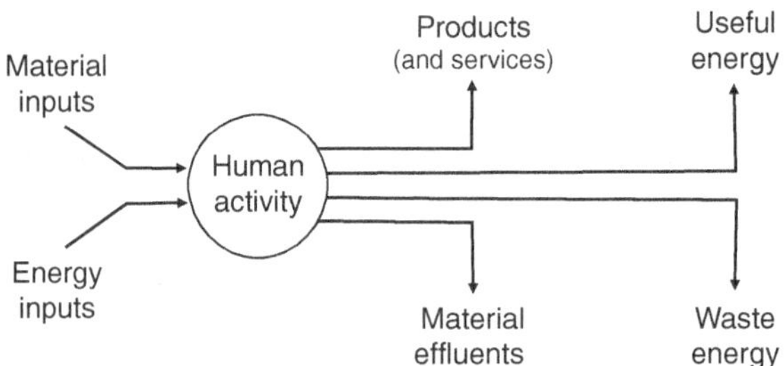

FIGURE 11.2. Because mass and energy are conserved, a very useful way to model many human activities is to track their flow through the system.

Of course, human activities are embedded in the economy. A variety of models are used to assess and predict the performance of the economy (discussed in Section 11.5). Often these are coupled with models of the energy system (discussed in Section 11.6). Extending such integration further leads to a family of "integrated assessment" (IA) models (discussed in Section 11.7).

The analysis of problems in technology and public policy frequently requires inputs from much larger models of physical, biological, ecological, or social systems. Because such models are often very computationally intensive, and do not lend themselves to the sort of iterative "what if" application that characterizes good policy analysis, a variety of methods are available to extract key insights, for example by generating "response surfaces," that allow their results to be incorporated into simpler, more flexible policy models (discussed in Section 11.9).

Finally, while to date they have received relatively little application in policy analysis, there is growing interest in the use of agent-based models. In such models, each individual or organization in a system of interest is given a set of behavioral rules and the agents then interact in the computer environment, often producing important and unanticipated emergent consequences. There is growing use of such models in fields such as epidemiology, where simple rules that describe the behavior of, and interaction among, individuals can result in complex and often counterintuitive results. Since most such agent-based models involve a considerable behavioral component, I have postponed a discussion of such models to Section 15.7.

11.2 SIMPLE ENGINEERING, ECONOMIC, AND POLICY MODELS

The advice to "make things as simple as possible, but not simpler" has been attributed to Albert Einstein as well as a number of others.[2] Independent of

[2] See: http://quoteinvestigator.com/2011/05/13/einstein-simple/#more-2363.

who first offered the advice, it should be taken to heart by anyone building models for use in analyzing problems in technology and public policy.

While performing classical engineering-economic evaluation of specific engineering projects or activities is one element of engineering, economic, and policy models, here I have in mind a much wider set of simple models developed to assess and provide insight about a variety of technologies and the policies that might be used to govern them.

Virtually all students of civil engineering take at least one course in engineering economic analysis. However, relatively few students in other fields of engineering or science take such a course as an undergraduate. Readers who are not familiar with the classic tools for valuing capital investments can find a comprehensive treatment in Au and Au (1992). For a somewhat broader discussion of many of the same ideas, see the Web-based book by Chris Hendrickson and Tung Au titled *Project Management and Construction* that is available online at http://pmbook.ce.cmu.edu.

While net present value and similar calculations are part of many engineering, economic, and policy models, such models are also built to implement simple order of magnitude calculations (Harte, 1988), B–C and decision analysis, and to apply other analytic strategies of the sort we have discussed in Chapters 3 to 7.[3] Such models are typically built using either a conventional programming language, or in environments such as Excel, Matlab® (see: www.mathworks.com), and Mathematica® (see: www.wolfram.com/mathematica).

Because the adequate treatment of uncertainty and performing sensitivity analysis is such an important component of good quantitative policy analysis (see Chapter 8), a number of tools have been developed to support these procedures. From my perspective the best of these is Analytica®, developed by my colleague Max Henrion (for details, including worked examples, see: www.lumina.com). Models built in Analytica® start with influence diagrams into which formal mathematical relationships can be added. Coefficients can be represented as single values, as arrays of values, or as full probability distributions. A variety of tools make it very easy to perform sensitivity analysis and assess the relative contribution of the uncertainty in different coefficients to the uncertainty in resulting outputs. Details, including tutorials, many worked examples (some of which can be run live online), and other information are available at www.lumina.com.

Many who make extensive use of spreadsheets find the system @risk® attractive because it allows one to convert spreadsheet models into stochastic simulations (see: www.palisade.com/risk). For a discussion of why he believes the Analytica® environment is superior to those based on spreadsheets, see Henrion (2004).

[3] For a slightly different perspective on such tools than that adopted in the earlier chapters of this book, see Benjamin and Cornell (1970).

11.3 MODELS FOR ENVIRONMENTAL IMPACT ASSESSMENT[4]

Many different kinds of models are used in environmental impact assessment. Most engineers and scientists working on problems in this field limit their activities to a handful of model types. While most understand that there is a wider array of model types in use, they tend to think about environmental impact assessment models largely in terms of the types of models they themselves employ. Thus, a terrestrial ecologist, a hydrologist, and an aerosol physicist are likely to answer the question "What is an environmental impact assessment model?" in rather different ways. An introduction to physical and chemical environmental models can be found in Schnoor (1996) and Seinfeld and Pandis (2006). For an introduction to ecological models, see Ågren and Andersson (2012), Ford (2009), and Smith and Smith (2007).

Environmental impact assessment models, and their various sub-components, can be classified along a continuum that runs from discrete impact assessment models to holistic impact assessment models. Discrete models operate under the assumption that the processes being modeled can be treated incrementally in the context of a stable background system. In contrast, holistic models provide a general dynamic description of the environmental system. With such models, a particular perturbation can be imposed over time on one or several parts of the system, and the model can be used to estimate how these perturbations will modify the overall operation of the environmental system.

In addition to classifying environmental assessment models on the discrete/holistic continuum, models can also be usefully classified by media (e.g., air, water, soil) and by structural type (e.g., point source, line source, regional source, and long-range transport). These models can be implemented in a variety of ways:

1. As simple box type transport models.
2. As models based on Gaussian plume dispersion.
3. As more complex Lagrangian models that can be thought of as modeling the trajectories of individual particles or fluid elements through time.
4. As more complex Eulerian models that can be thought of as modeling the properties of the fluid at a set of fixed points across space.

In addition, regional problems are sometimes approached by ignoring the details of transport and transformation processes and attempting to directly relate emissions to ambient concentrations either in a linear way, as in the "linear rollback models" used as quick and dirty tools in addressing some regional air-quality problems, or in more sophisticated ways that involve the statistical fitting of emission data to ambient concentration data, as a function of varying meteorological and other environmental factors, for a given location. There are, however, risks involved in adopting such an approach if there is significant

[4] Portions of the text in this section are derived from Morgan and McMichael (1981).

chemistry involved, since in the case of both smog and sub-micron fine particles, reducing the concentration of one atmospheric pollutant may not reduce, and in some cases may even increase, the concentration of the pollutant of primary concern (Seinfeld and Pandis, 2006).[5]

11.4 LIFE CYCLE METHODS

Life cycle analysis is a method for addressing such deceptively simple questions as: which type of supermarket bag is more environmentally benign – paper or plastic? As Hendrickson et al. (2006) note: "This simple question at the grocery store checkout counter might seem to sort those who care about the quality of the environment and the sustainability of our economy from ignorant or apathetic shoppers. We know that the correct answer is 'paper,' because it is a 'natural' product rather than some chemical." Using this and other simple examples, Hendrickson et al. (2006) observe that many people are surprised by the results obtained from life cycle assessments that point out that:

> paper bags, paper cups, (or even ceramic cups), [and] cloth diapers were not obviously superior in terms of using less energy and materials, producing less waste, or even disposal at the end of life. Paper requires cutting trees and transporting them to a paper mill, both of which use a good deal of energy. Papermaking results in air emissions (the sulfite process) and water discharges of chlorine and biological waste ... After use, [unless it is recycled] the [paper] bag goes to a landfill where it gradually decays, releasing methane ... Perhaps most surprisingly, washing a ceramic cup by hand uses a good deal of hot water and soap, resulting in discharges of wastewater that has to be treated and the expenditure of a substantial amount of fuel to heat the water, although washing the cup in a fully loaded dish washer uses less soap and hot water per cup. In short, it is not obvious which product is more environmentally benign and more sustainable.

The International Standard ISO 14040 (ISO, 1997) defines life cycle analysis (LCA) as:

> a technique for assessing the environmental aspects and potential impacts associated with a product, by
>
> - compiling an inventory of relevant inputs and outputs of a product system;
> - evaluating the potential environmental impacts associated with those inputs and outputs;
> - interpreting the results of the inventory analysis and impact assessment phases in relation to the objectives of the study.
>
> LCA studies the environmental aspects and potential impacts throughout a product's life (i.e., cradle-to-grave) from raw material acquisition through production, use and disposal. The general categories of environmental impacts needing consideration include resource use, human health, and ecological consequences.

[5] See the Milford et al. (1989) example in Section 11.9.

A key issue in LCA is choosing where to draw the boundaries around the system or activity that is being analyzed. For example, if one of the inputs is steel, do you only include the steel that is purchased to go into the product, or do you also include the steel that was used to build the steel mill and construct the railroad that was used to transport the iron ore, coal, coke, and finished steel, etc.? If you include the latter, how should you appropriately apportion a small fraction of that steel to the product of interest? Similarly, if the product requires electricity or fuel, how far back up the fuel and equipment supply chain should the analysis go in assessing the impacts of that energy input?

In performing LCA, analysts have adopted two quite different approaches: bottom-up engineering assessment and top-down economy-wide assessment. Bottom-up strategies draw a boundary around the inputs, products, and waste streams that are judged to impose the largest impacts. Because it looks in detail at each of the components of the product or service, as long as the boundary has been chosen with care the results can be quite accurate.

Top-down analysis, originally developed by H. Scott Matthews and colleagues, uses an input-output table for the entire economy, in which energy use and associated pollution have been linked to each cell. The tool is now available on the Web at www.eiolca.net. This tool has been used extensively by analysts. As the EIO-LCA website explains:

> Results from using the EIO-LCA on-line tool provide guidance on the relative impacts of different types of products, materials, services, or industries with respect to resource use and emissions throughout the supply chain. Thus, the effect of producing an automobile would include not only the impacts at the final assembly facility, but also the impact from mining metal ores, making electronic parts, forming windows, etc. that are needed for parts to build the car.

Of course, because the EIO-LCA system works with a 428 × 428 input-output table of the U.S. economy, it yields results on a coarser scale than more detailed bottom-up analysis. However, those performing bottom-up analysis are well advised to also make use of the tool, so as to be sure they have not missed a major source of impact when drawing the boundary for their analysis. In at least some cases a comparison of results from a top-down EIO-LCA analysis have yielded impacts that are several times larger than those found in an engineering bottom-up analysis – this because in drawing the boundary, the latter neglected to include some element(s) that had large impacts.

Readers who would like to learn more about LCA and its applications should start with Matthews and Hendrickson (2015).

11.5 MODELS OF THE ECONOMY

A wide variety of economic models have been developed for many different purposes. Unlike the case of environmental and LCA models, I am not aware of any good general reference on different types of economic models. Holcombe (1989) has written a thoughtful but rather philosophical book, but it does not provide a straightforward comparison of different modeling approaches. More recently, Rodrik (2015) has written a general discussion of economics that focuses throughout on the importance of a wide range of models in economics – from very simple to full general equilibrium. But, as with Holcombe, his treatment, while highly readable, is high level and philosophical.

The simplest strategy to forecast the future value of an economic variable is to fit a linear or non-linear curve to the time series of the past performance of that variable and project it into the future. If the forecast duration is not very long, and the variable's past performance has been "well behaved," such a simple strategy is often perfectly adequate and may perform as well as, or better than, more sophisticated methods.

The economic input-output tables discussed above provide a static linear description of an economy. For example, each row in such a table might describe the production from a particular economic sector, call it S. Then each column entry for that row would indicate the economic contribution required from all other sectors to produce a unit of S. Horowitz and Planting (2009) explain that the U.S. Bureau of Economic Analysis maintains two tables, a "use table" that shows the uses of commodities by intermediate and final users and a "make table" that shows the production of commodities by industries in which the rows present the industries and the columns display the commodities that the industries produce.

> For example, for the bakery products industry, the use table shows the amount (in dollars) of flour, eggs, yeast, and other inputs that are necessary to produce baked goods and the secondary products of the industry, such as flour mixes and frozen food. (Horowitz and Planting, 2009)

Input-output tables can be used to support a variety of economic analysis when the activities being considered are sufficiently modest in scale that they will not have a major impact on the values in the table, and they will take place over a time span that is short enough that the values in the table are unlikely to experience significant change. Most nations maintain input-output tables of their economies that are updated periodically. Tables for the U.S. economy can be found through the U.S. Department of Commerce Bureau of Economic Analysis at www.bea.gov/industry/io_annual.htm. For a detailed discussion of the interpretation and use of input-output tables, see the BEA document *Concepts and Methods of the U.S. Input-Output Accounts* (Horowitz and Planting, 2009).

While input-output tables deal with an entire economy, in many cases a more local approach may be sufficient. Using an appropriate elasticity for the commodity or service of interest, one can examine the impact of a change in the price of that good or service, assuming that all other things remain unchanged. This approach is termed "partial equilibrium analysis." If, in addition, one allows the price of substitutes and complements to change, but holds all other prices fixed, one engages in what is often termed "comparative statics." Holcombe (1989) offers the following simple illustration:

> Comparative statics really does not look at changes over time, but rather estimates two different possible situations that hypothetically could exist at the same time. There is a certain price and quantity exchanged in the domestic coffee market, for example. If a tariff were placed on imported tea, this would raise the price of tea which would cause people to substitute into coffee. The increased demand for coffee would cause an increase in the price and an increase in the quantity exchanged. This illustration of comparative statics does not say that placing a tariff on tea will raise the price of coffee. It says that, if there were a tariff on tea, the price of coffee would be higher than it actually is at the moment. In other words, all other things held equal the important barrier on tea will increase the price of coffee.

In this example, the analyst needed price elasticities for both tea and coffee. Such values are typically obtained by applying econometric methods to past time series.

As a result of the development of large and fast computers it has become possible to run dynamic models of entire economies. These models are termed "computational general equilibrium" (CGE) models. These models use a large database analogous to the information contained in an economic input-output table, together with estimates of elasticities. When a modification is made to some part of the economy (e.g., a tax or regulation is added or a new technology is introduced that results in a change of the price of a product or service), a CGE model is able to propagate the impact of those changes as they ripple out through the economy. An important technical issue in the development and use of CGE models involves strategies to assure that the model will converge to an equilibrium.

In theory, if all the necessary data were available, a CGE model should be superior to other types of economic models. In practice, depending on the application, this is not always the case. In this connection, West (1995) has provided a comparison of applying an input-output (IO) model, an IO model combined with a set of econometric analyses (IOE) that captures household income, and a full CGE model to the problem of assessing the economic impact of tourism in Queensland, Australia. While readers should not generalize from the results, West (1995) reports estimates of the short-term tourism impact obtained with the IO model to be 38 percent higher than those for the CGE model, with the IOE model producing intermediate values.

In the context of CGE models, McKitrick (1998) cautions "that choice of functional forms affects not only industry-specific results, but aggregate results as well, even for small policy shocks."

CGE models may be either static (i.e., operated to find an equilibrium for a single moment in time) or dynamic (i.e., operated to find an equilibrium over some future time path). As the duration of the forecast becomes longer, a wide range of issues such as changing regulations, changing resource availability, and changing technology all complicate matters and add uncertainty. A collection of papers discussing a number of technical details involved in the development and use of CGE models can be found in the edited volume by Scarf and Shoven (1984).

Readers planning to make use of results from economic models would be well advised to consider two observations offered by Holcombe (1989):

> based on only a few initial facts, economists are often willing to make sweeping predictions about the future consequences of those initial conditions. Tell an economist that a drought in Colombia has damaged this year's coffee crop and economists will be ready to predict that the price of coffee will rise, and since tea is now relatively cheaper compared to coffee, people will drink less coffee and more tea ... unless, of course, income effects are taken into account.

And:

> prediction in economics is not prediction about what people will do, but rather is prediction about how people's behavior will change if certain conditions change. There is an important difference. The predictions are made based on the assumption that people will act in the future according to the same "laws" that they did in the past. The laws in fact do not compel people to behave that way, and often they do not. But if people are in general successful in acting to satisfy their wants with the means at hand, then it is reasonable to think that under similar future circumstances they will behave similarly.

11.6 MODELS OF ENERGY SUPPLY AND USE

A variety of models have been developed to analyze and make projections about the future performance of the energy system. Perhaps the most widely used is the National Energy Modeling System (NEMS), which was developed and is maintained by the U.S. Department of Energy's Energy Information Administration (EIA). EIA (2009) explains that NEMS:

> is a computer-based, energy-economy modeling system of [the] U.S. ... NEMS projects the production, imports, conversion, consumption, and prices of energy, subject to assumptions on macroeconomic and financial factors, world energy markets, resource availability and costs, behavioral and technological choice criteria, cost and performance characteristics of energy technologies, and demographics.

As shown in Figure 11.3, NEMS consists of a set of modules for the commercial, industrial, transportation, and residential sectors, a set for each energy supply sector (e.g., coal, oil and gas, renewables, etc.), a module covering international energy activities, a macro-economic activity module, and an integrating module. The model is spatially disaggregated across nine major U.S. census regions.

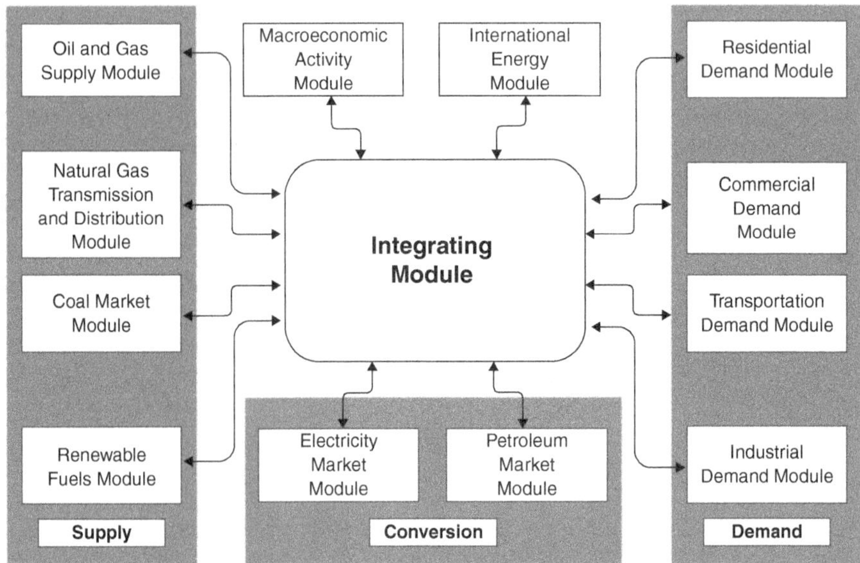

FIGURE 11.3. Basic structure of the NEMS model (source: www.eia.gov/oiaf/aeo/overview/figure_2.html).

EIA (2009) explains:

A key feature of NEMS is the representation of technology and technology improvement over time. Five of the sectors – residential, commercial, transportation, electricity generation, and refining – include extensive treatment of individual technologies and their characteristics, such as the initial capital cost, operating cost, date of availability, efficiency, and other characteristics specific to the particular technology. For example, technological progress in lighting technologies results in a gradual reduction in cost and is modeled as a function of time in these end-use sectors. In addition, the electricity sector accounts for technological optimism in the capital costs of first-of-a-kind generating technologies and for a decline in cost as experience with the technologies is gained both domestically and internationally. In each of these sectors, equipment choices are made for individual technologies as new equipment is needed to meet growing demand for energy services or to replace retired equipment.

In the other sectors – industrial, oil and gas supply, and coal supply – the treatment of technologies is more limited due to a lack of data on individual technologies. In the industrial sector, only the combined heat and power and motor technologies are explicitly considered and characterized. Cost reductions resulting from technological progress in combined heat and power technologies are represented as a function of time as experience with the technologies grows. Technological progress is not explicitly modeled for the industrial motor technologies. Other technologies in the energy-intensive industries are represented by technology bundles, with technology possibility curves representing efficiency improvement over time. In the oil and gas supply sector, technological progress is represented by econometrically estimated improvements in finding rates, success rates, and costs. Productivity improvements over time represent technological progress in coal production.

It is difficult to find details on the workings of the individual modules in NEMS; indeed, the Macroeconomic Activity Module is a proprietary CGE model developed and supported by IHS Global Insight, Inc. However, Gabriel et al. (2001) provide a very useful discussion of how the various sub-models are integrated.

Convergence can be a serious issue in a large model like NEMS. Gabriel et al. (2001) note:

While the convergence problems have been managed, NEMS modelers and other researchers wish to improve the speed of convergence of the current approach when starting solutions are not necessarily "close" to a previous solution. For example, because of new uses of NEMS when simulating new policies (e.g., the Kyoto Protocol on greenhouse gases), convergence problems can arise. One such strategy for achieving these goals is to model the NEMS equilibrium as a nonlinear complementarity problem (NCP) or a related variational inequality (VI). These more general formats have several benefits. First, and perhaps most importantly, from a modeling perspective, the NCP/VI format allows one to collectively handle all the NEMS modules together. NEMS is a collection of mathematical programs (currently linear programs) and nonlinear econometric demand and linking equations, with each module passing estimates of some of the equilibrium fuel prices and quantities to other modules ... Second, the NCP/VI approach is helpful for more accurate checking of the termination conditions for the equilibrium computations ... convergence within a particular module is declared when no appreciable changes occur between successive iterates ... These estimates of equilibria are then passed on to other modules ... note that if NEMS were reformulated as an NCP or VI, with appropriate algorithms, there would be less dependence on ad hoc procedures, given the more general NCP/VI format. Third, for several of the NEMS modules relating to specific sectors of the energy market, estimates of equilibrium fuel prices and quantities are determined from the dual variables of the associated linear programs. In fact, the equilibrium prices are functions of the dual values via certain "linking equations" that deviate from perfect competition and cause prices to differ from marginal costs.

NEMS is by no means the only model for analyzing and forecasting the energy system. John Weyant (2012) explains that:

The oil embargo of 1973 brought economic and political chaos to the oil-importing world. A particularly devastating attribute of the embargo was its unexpectedness. It was difficult for the world's economies to adjust to a sudden reduction in oil availability. In addition, it established a new world order in petroleum which had implications that were enigmatic to almost everyone. The stable conditions that had characterized the world energy system for almost a quarter-century provided neither experience nor incentive for anyone to try to understand its workings very well. During that earlier era, conditions each year were presumed to differ little and in predictable ways from those existing during the previous years.

The unfamiliar circumstances created by the 1973 embargo coupled with rising concern about environmental issues, especially in the United States and Western Europe, provided the motivation for the birth of a new discipline known as energy-environmental policy modeling ... [With such models] analysts attempt to capture the essence of important relationships characterizing the energy system with simple mathematical equations ...

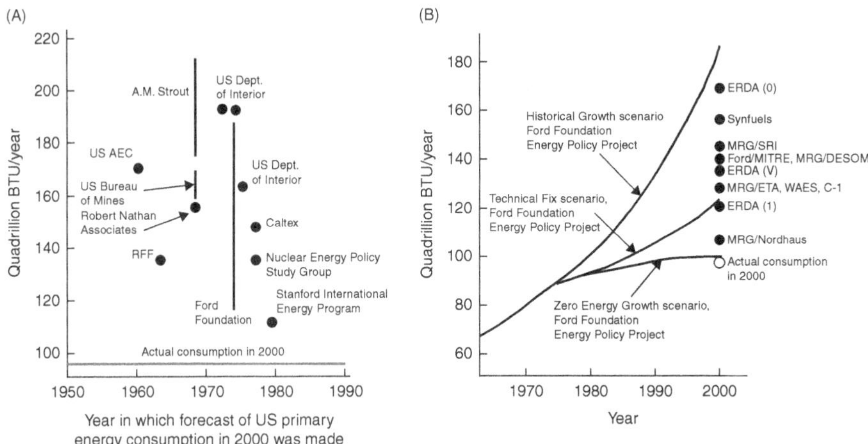

FIGURE 11.4. Comparisons of performance of forecasts of U.S. primary consumption for the year 2000: (**A**) made in the 1960s to 1980s (Smil, 2003). Note that even those that provided uncertainty bands did not include the actual value (line at the bottom of the figure); (**B**) made by the Ford Foundation Energy Project (1974) and others. Note that actual consumption lay just below the Ford project's lowest scenario (Greenberger, 1983).

The models have increased in number and matured over the last thirty years, but at the same time the energy and environmental policy issues of most interest have become more global and required a much more inter-disciplinary approach. The impact of this continual increase in complexity has been somewhat offset by improvements on computers and solution algorithms, but significant challenges remain in formulating interesting questions, analyzing them sufficiently and especially in communicating ever more complicated results to the appropriate decision makers.

As these models proliferated, and began to offer quite different insights and "answers," the need arose to compare them, understand sources of disagreement, and refine the strategies and assumptions they made. Since 1976 this function has been performed under Weyant's leadership, by the Energy Modeling Forum.[6]

There have been far too few retrospective analyses of the ability of experts and their models to produce good projections of key variables such as future energy consumption. Greenberger (1983), Huntington (1994), and Smil (2000, 2003) were among the first to observe that nobody is very good at making accurate forecasts (Figure 11.4). Other retrospective assessments have been performed by Craig et al. (2002), Flyvbjerg et al. (2003), Koomey et al. (2003), Linderoth (2002), O'Neil and Desai (2005), and Winebrake and Sakva (2006). As this book went to press, at Carnegie Mellon Lynn Kaak was doing interesting work on applying empirical prediction intervals to attach uncertainty to EIA energy-related forecasts.

[6] For details, see: https://emf.stanford.edu.

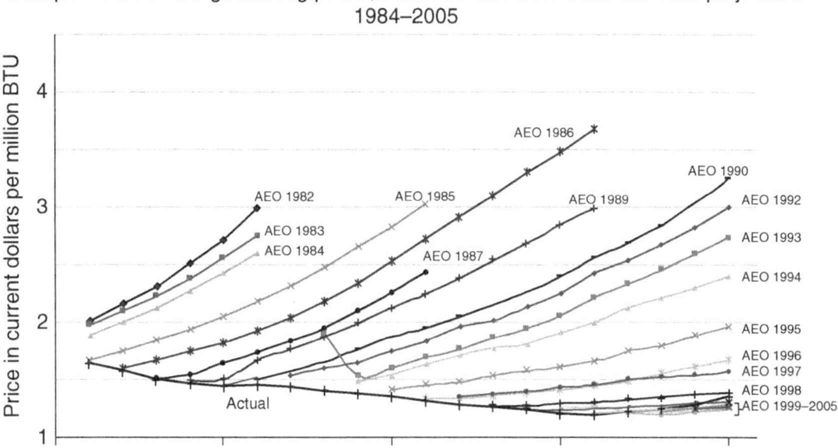

FIGURE 11.5. Example of EIA forecasts of the future cost of coal to electric generating plants compared with actual. Compiled by Adam Newcomer.

Demographic projection is another field in which some limited but valuable work has been done on retrospectively evaluating past forecasts and developing improved methods for describing uncertainties in future forecasts (Keyfitz, 1981; Lutz and Goldstein, 2004; Raftery et al., 2012).

Of course, none of these forecasts was made by EIA using the NEMS model. While there may have been slight improvements as a result in recent years, and EIA has now begun to provide some modest discussion of uncertainty, the results in Figure 11.5 suggest that making reliable forecasts continues to be a serious challenge.

11.7 INTEGRATED ASSESSMENT MODELS

The rise of concern about the environmental consequences of long-range transport of sulfur and nitrogen air pollution and associated acid rain prompted the development of a family of integrated assessment models (IAMs) that combine models of physical and socioeconomic process with models of physical, ecological, and environmental impacts, in order to help decision makers frame the issues and think about the policy response.

Three quite different types of models were developed. In Europe, where there was no significant controversy over whether acid rain was a problem, the RAINS model was created and used to allocate commitments for emission reductions among different EU member states (Alcamo et al., 1990). In the United States the situation was quite different. Reluctant to take any regulatory action, the Reagan Administration argued that the topic required further study and launched the National Acid Precipitation Assessment Program (NAPAP).

In addition to mounting a variety of scientific field studies, federal support was provided for the development of two integrated assessment models. The first was undertaken as a collaborative effort among several of the national labs of the U.S. Department of Energy. Each lab developed highly detailed, science-based sub-models with the idea that later they would be combined in order to produce an integrated tool for decision support. In the end, they were never adequately integrated to provide such a capability.

In contrast, in the Department of Engineering and Public Policy at Carnegie Mellon, Ed Rubin led an effort that was focused specifically on supporting decisions in the face of significant uncertainty. The result of this project was a single integrated model developed in DEMOS called ADAM (Acid Deposition Assessment Model).[7] All of the key parameter uncertainties were represented as full probability distributions (Rubin et al., 1990, 1992). Analysis performed with the ADAM model concluded that, despite the various uncertainties, a U.S. acid rain control program had clear environmental benefits. Rubin et al. (1990) estimated that in the Adirondack Park in upstate New York, "an additional 50 lakes ... would be expected to recover [and be able to support trout] as a result of [a proposed] 10 Mtpy emissions reduction. For boundary waters [a region in northern Minnesota], an increase of six lakes supporting trout would be expected."

The ADAM model made it clear that, despite the various uncertainties, acid rain posed significant environmental risk, and that regulatory action could be justified. Shortly after this conclusion became apparent, federal funding for the project ended.

The NAPAP work continued for some additional years. Rubin (1991) has written an evaluation of the program, the abstract for which reads:

> Concluding ten years of study, the U.S. National Acid Precipitation Assessment Program (NAPAP) recently issued its integrated assessment report designed to provide guidance to policy makers on the sources and effects of acid deposition, and the costs and benefits of alternative control measures. This paper focuses on an evaluation of the benefit-cost implications of acid rain controls as revealed by two of the five major questions addressed in the NAPAP assessment framework. While the NAPAP effort made significant scientific contributions to the study of acid deposition, key gaps are found in the assessment of benefits and costs most relevant to policy decisions. Lessons learned from NAPAP may be helpful in avoiding similar problems in assessing emerging environmental issues such as global climate change.

On the basis of the experience Rubin and his colleagues had in building and using the ADAM model, a number of us argued that integrated assessment held the potential to significantly assist policy makers in the context of the problem of climate change (Rubin et al., 1991; Lave et al., 1992; Dowlatabadi and Morgan, 1993). Table 11.1 lists some of the reasons we made this argument.

[7] DEMOS was the early version of the system now distributed commercially by Lumina Decision Systems as Analytica®.

TABLE 11.1. *Reasons for performing integrated assessment (from Morgan and Dowlatabadi, 1996).*

To develop better understanding of:
- The structure of the problem
- The dynamics of the problem
- The factors and variables that drive the problem

To guide future analysis and research by:
- Identifying important missing parts of the problem
- Identifying limits to existing analytical tools
- Establishing research priorities

To get policy insight and answers that:
- Identify *the* policy
- Identify the strengths, weaknesses, and pitfalls of proposed policies and actions
- Identify things that it does not make sense to do

In addition to a large multi-year effort on performing climate integrated assessment at Carnegie Mellon (described below), a number of other groups in the United States and Europe also built such models. In an article they wrote for *Annual Review of Energy and the Environment*, Parson and Fisher-Vanden (1997) classify integrated assessment models into three broad categories: (1) those that emphasize emission dynamics and optimization; (2) those that emphasize uncertainty; and (3) those that emphasize fine spatial detail in the characterization of atmospheric change, impacts, and feedbacks. Weyant (2015) notes that, to date, roughly 20 integrated assessment models have been developed and offers a two-part classification: (1) "detailed process (DP) IAMs" that "focus on climate change mitigation options and climate change impacts in some detail without necessarily aggregating all the impacts into a single measure of projected climate damages" and (2) "more highly aggregated global-scale analysis that focuses on calculating optimal global carbon emissions trajectories and carbon prices that maximize global welfare" that he terms (BC) IAMs. One of the best-known examples of the former is the family of models developed by the Joint Global Change Research Institute run by Pacific Northwest Laboratories and the University of Maryland (see www.globalchange.umd.edu). Probably the best-known example of the latter are the DICE and RICE models developed by Nordhaus and Boyer (2000).

At Carnegie Mellon we began doing climate-related integrated assessment by constructing various influence diagrams in order to begin to understand the interactions that were likely to be most important. Then Lave and Dowlatabadi (1993) performed a simple parametric analysis in which they assumed several different levels of impact from climate change on U.S. GDP in the year 2040 and several different levels of cost to abate CO_2 emissions. They concluded that "At least for the next decade, the prior judgments that decision makers bring to the

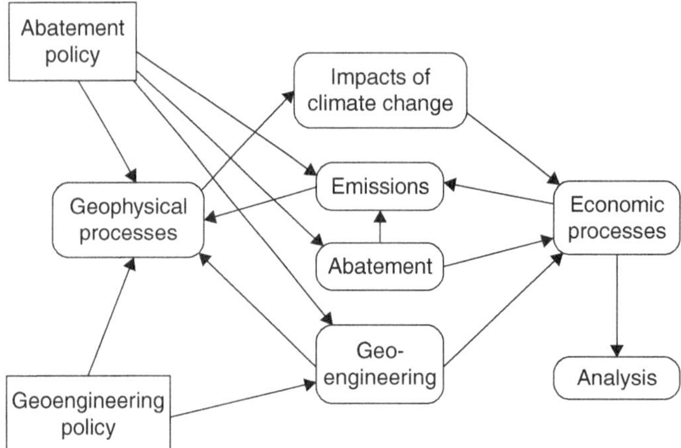

FIGURE 11.6. Top-level influence diagram that shows the structure of ICAM-1.

problem, the decision rules they employ (e.g., expected value versus minimizing maximum loss), could be far more important in controlling ... policy conclusions ... than the results of scientific discoveries over that period." From there we went on to build the ICAM-1 model in Analytica®. This model divided the world into two regions (developed "north" and less developed "south"), used 25-year time steps, and ran until 2100. The basic structure of ICAM-1 is shown in Figure 11.6. The hierarchical nature of the model is illustrated in Figure 11.7.

In a paper reporting on our work with ICAM-1, we wrote:

> The idea of an assessment framework is that the structure and assumptions of the sub-elements, and indeed even the relationship between those sub-elements, is not fixed. Rather it is the central focus of on-going analysis. Various alternative sub-models may be substituted, and their implications explored. These may be as simple as a few variables or they may involve reduced form or response surface descriptions of very complex models.
>
> ... Because uncertainty is so important, it should be easy to represent uncertain quantities as probability distributions, propagate probabilistic values through the models and perform various kinds of deterministic and stochastic sensitivity and uncertainty analysis ...
>
> ... [We found] that the choice of decision rule plays a key role in the selection of mitigation policies, that given a decision rule, uncertainty in key variables can make it difficult or impossible to differentiate between the outcome of alternative policies and that the model parameters that contribute the most uncertainty to outcomes depend on the choice of policy, the discount rate and the geographical region being considered. (Dowlatabadi and Morgan, 1993)

Under Hadi Dowlatabadi's leadership we went on to build ICAM-2, which divided the world into seven regions and treated 2000 variables as uncertain. We developed PDFs from the literature and from a set of expert elicitation of climate scientists (Morgan and Keith, 1995).

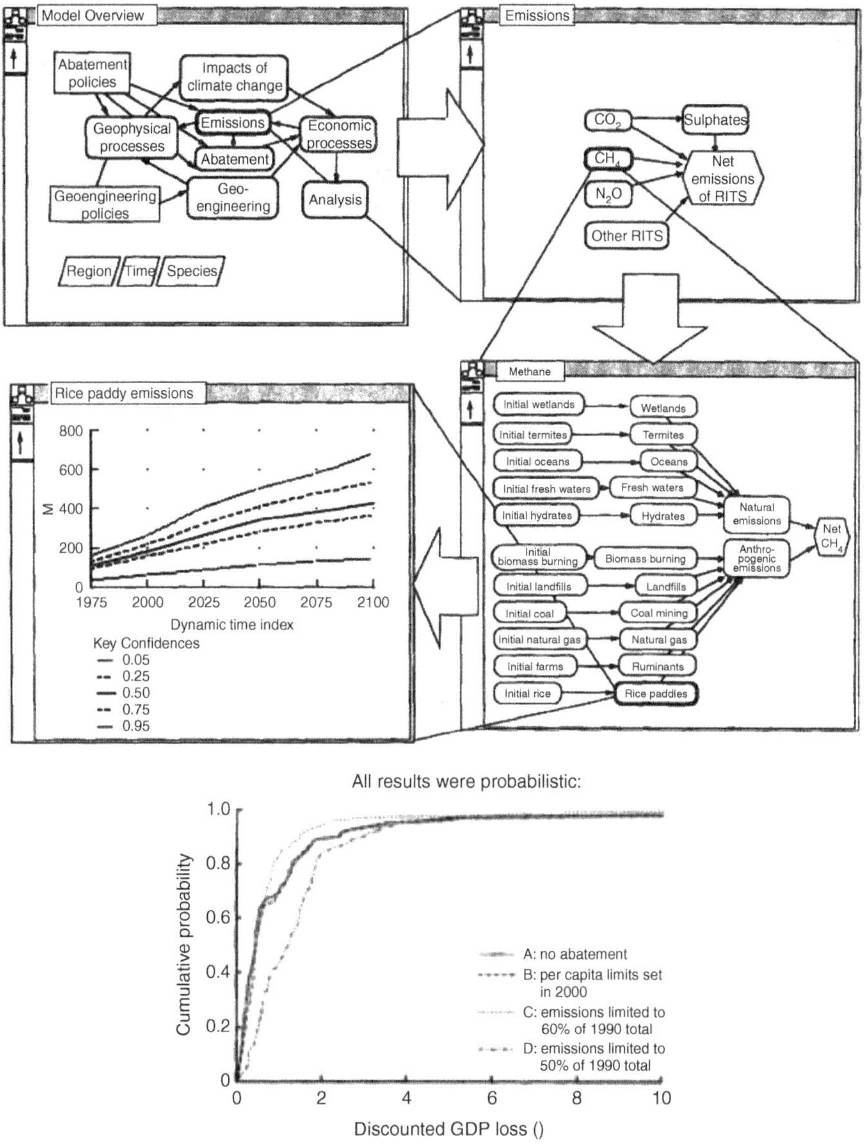

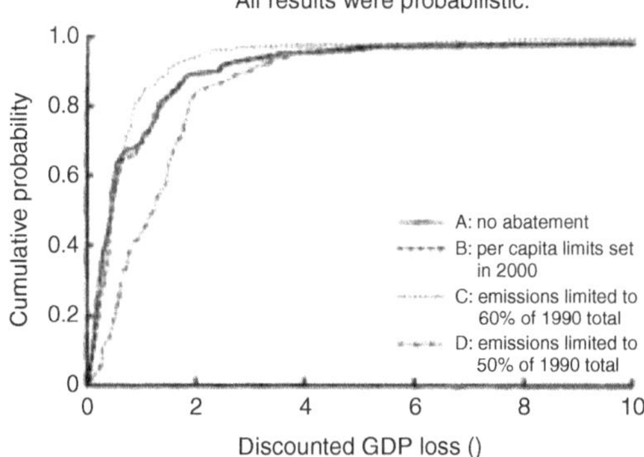

FIGURE 11.7. Illustration of the hierarchical structure of ICAM-1. By clicking on a node such as the one labeled emissions, the user moves down a level in the model hierarchy to see the various sources of modeled emissions of greenhouse gases. Then by clicking on "CH4" (methane), one moves down another level in the model to see all the various global sources of methane. Clicking on "rice paddy emissions" and asking for a plot of a probabilistic time series results in the plot at the lower left (Dowlatabadi and Morgan, 1993).

We populated ICAM-2 with switches that allowed the user to examine the implications of adopting alternative plausible model structures. These included the option of making alternative assumptions about things such as the response of the energy system; the rate of discovery of new resources or diffusion of new technologies; ecological responses; demographic models; and the treatment of air pollution including aerosols. Later, in ICAM-3 we added switches that allowed the user to choose alternative assumptions about things like: the treatment of time preference; the global warming potential (GWP) of different gases and aerosols; capital lifetime; whether or not "tax revolts" occur, etc.

A view of the top-level influence diagram for ICAM-2 and 3 is shown in Figure 11.8.

We populated ICAM-3 with separate autonomous adaptive agents in each region of the world. These agents were given simple decision rules (which could be changed with different settings of switches). The agent in each region observed the evolving model world and reacted according to those rules – for example, leaving a global control regime if carbon taxes got too high in a simulation in which the switch to allow tax revolts was turned on.

We also explored the consequences of applying a number of different decision rules such as minimize ecological impacts, minimize economic impacts, as well as various combinations.

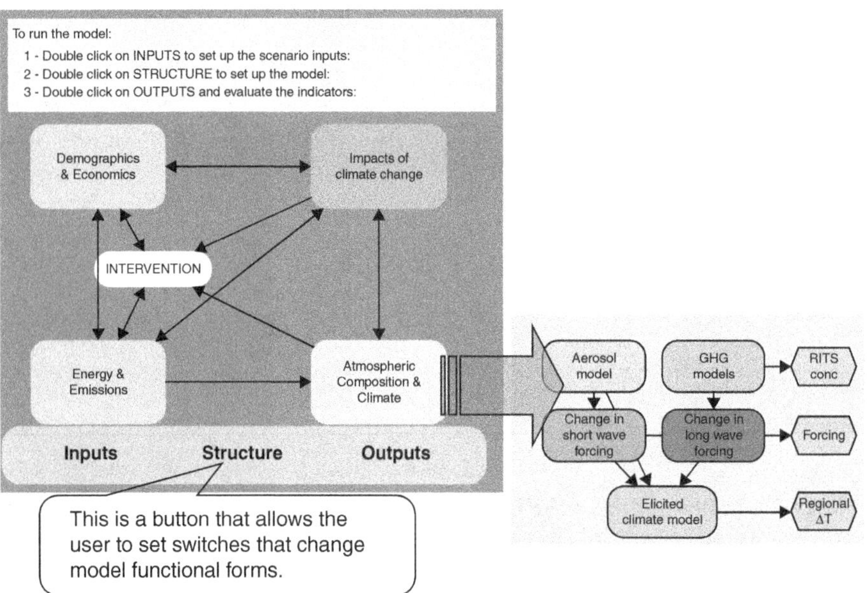

FIGURE 11.8. Illustration of the top-level influence diagram for ICAM-2 and 3, together with a display one level down for the set of models of atmospheric composition and climate. In addition to treating roughly 2000 variables as uncertain, this model is populated with multiple switches that can be used to turn on and off a variety of alternative model functional forms.

In a 1996 paper that discussed what we'd learned in four progressively more detailed rounds of integrated assessment, we argued:

> Integrated assessment is neither an end in itself, nor a one shot proposition. The most useful results from doing integrated assessment will typically not be "answers" to specific policy questions. Rather they will be insights about the nature and structure of the climate problem, about what matters, and about what we still need to learn. (Morgan and Dowlatabadi, 1996)

In drawing on the insights over 35 years of work by the Energy Modeling Forum, Weyant (2012) reached a similar conclusion:

> the avalanche of detailed quantitative results produced by the models has often tended to blind model users to the insights they can provide ... [Harvard's Bill Hogan captures this view when he says] "it is not the individual results of a model that are so important; it is the improved user appreciation of the policy problem that is the greatest contribution of modeling." ... [T]he purpose of energy-environmental policy modeling is to develop insights ... not precise numerical forecasts.

In ICAM-2 and 3 we found that:

- We could get an *enormous* variety of answers depending on the range of plausible assumptions we made about the structure of the model and which regional decision maker we considered;
- Rarely was any policy optimal for all regions;
- Rarely were any results stochastically dominant.

In Casman et al. (1999) we noted that:

> uncertainty about the appropriate functional form of different sub-models is sufficiently large, and the difficulty of constructing all plausible alternatives sufficiently great, that it is often best to report results parametrically across a set of combinations of different model structural assumptions, in much the same way that one reports the results of parametric sensitivity studies of coefficient uncertainty. For example, in an application of ICAM-2 designed to explore the probability that a specific carbon tax policy ... would yield net positive benefits, we found that the probability ranged from 0.15 to 0.95 for the world as a whole, depending upon the structural assumptions made.

Quantitative details supporting these findings are provided in Casman et al. (1999).

Pindyck (2013) is similarly pessimistic about the value of using integrated assessment models to search for optimal policies or to perform meaningful B–C analysis in support of estimates of the social cost of carbon (see Section 3.9). He writes: "IAMs are of little or no value in evaluating alternative climate change policies and estimating SCC. On the contrary, an IAM-based analysis suggests a level of knowledge and precision that is non-existent, and allows the modeler to obtain almost any desired result." Unfortunately, in dismissing the utility of integrated assessment, Pindyck ignores the first two classes of motivation (achieving better understanding and guiding future analysis and research) listed in Table 11.1. The process of building and using integrated assessment models has helped the climate community to better identify and understand many key complexities. Unfortunately, too many of those who have built or used such models have gone on to treat their outputs as making reliable predictions about the real world.[8]

While in our work with ICAM we were focused on exploring the implications of uncertainty in coefficient values and model functional form, most of the rest of the integrated assessment community was focused on using a single model, often with fixed coefficients, and a single global utility maximizing decision maker, in order to develop recommendations for globally optimal climate policy. In Morgan and Dowlatabadi (1996) we concluded that our studies with ICAM led us to believe:

> that the first impressions gained from a "global commoner" model may confuse more than they clarify. At the international level, at least a dozen different nations will make choices which could have significant climate implications. Many of those choices will not be made by single national decision-making authorities, but rather through the individual choices of millions of organizations and individual citizens, and they will be driven by local interests and conditions. This distributed decision making is one of the most fundamental characteristics of the climate problem.

Again, in the context of modeling in support of U.S. domestic energy policy, Weyant (2012) has made a rather similar observation: "Analysts may have a strong preference for policies that are optimal from the point of view of some narrowly or ill-defined (say maximizing welfare assuming markets are perfectly competitive when they are definitely not) criteria, but decision makers rarely develop such preferences." Of course, integrated assessment models are not the only modeling efforts that have attempted to anticipate social and economic evolution on a large scale over timescales of many decades. For example, Forrester (1971) and Meadows et al. (1972) used system dynamics to produce such forecasts.[9] A similar effort, which combined results from a large number of different models and data sets, is provided by the Global 2000 Report to the President (GTS, 1980).

In a paper titled "Limits and Possibilities of Large-Scale Long-Range Models," Ayres (1984) outlines four major problems in creating such models:

- weakness in the received economic and other theories;
- limitations of statistical methods;

[8] Rose et al. (2014) have performed a particularly interesting analysis of the three different IAMs (DICE, FUND, and PAGE) used by the United States in estimating the social cost of carbon. They take each separate part of each model (estimate of future emissions; emissions to climate change; climate change to impacts and damages), drive them with identical inputs, and find that each yields very different outputs.

[9] Boyd (1972) demonstrates that the pessimistic conclusions of the Forrester model can be reversed with the addition of a variable to deal with technological change and "multipliers to express the effect of technology on other state variables." He concludes, "the world dynamic simulation is far from useful as a policy tool, and, even within his own framework, Forrester was unjustified in making such strong policy recommendations."

- the ubiquity of non-linearity;
- preoccupation with determinism.[10]

Ayres (1984) provides a discussion of each of these problems. With respect to the issue of determinism he notes that in physics, despite fundamental indeterminacy at the micro-scale, it is possible to construct probability distributions that allow for a considerable degree of determinacy at a macro-scale (e.g., using Newtonian mechanics to predict the orbits of planets). Thus, he writes:

> In the case of societal modeling, it is natural to suggest that perhaps a similar rule might hold: that the effects of indeterminacy (or free will) can be ignored on the macro-scale ... [But] if we believe that leaders do occasionally lead, that history would not be the same if Napoléon or Hitler had never been born, that policy is not a sham, that policymakers do exist – both as individuals and as institutions – then macro-indeterminacy cannot be ignored in models.

Ayres concludes that as a result of indeterminacy and the mathematical characteristics of large non-linear systems (including chaotic behavior), producing meaningful long-run forecasts may not be possible. He argues that with long-range social and economic models, "The best forecasts in the world can do no better than indicate a range of possibilities. No model can do better."

11.8 LIMITS OF STANDARD ANALYTICAL TOOLS

The deeper we got into doing integrated assessment of the climate problem, the more concerned we became that too many of the standard analytic tools that we and others routinely use in doing policy analysis are not appropriate for addressing a number of issues related to climate change (Morgan et al., 1999).

Most of the analysis that uses conventional tools of policy analysis makes some or all of the following assumptions:

1. There is a single (public-sector) decision maker who faces a single problem (in the context of a single polity);
2. Values are known (or knowable) and static;
3. The decision maker should select a policy by maximizing expected utility;
4. The impacts involved are of manageable size and can be valued at the margin;
5. Time preference is accurately described by conventional exponential discounting of future costs and benefits;
6. The system under study can reasonably be treated as linear;
7. Uncertainty is modest and manageable.

[10] Ayres terms the fourth the "Selden Paradox," in reference to Hari Selden, a character from Isaac Asimov's *Foundation* science fiction novels who was developing a comprehensive mathematical model, based on the laws of large numbers, that could predict critical stages in the macro-level evolution of society.

We saw an illustration of the sorts of problems that can arise when standard tools are applied without reflecting on their applicability in Sections 3.8 and 5.5, in which economists in Working Group III of the IPCC's second assessment used different "life values" for different countries around the world and then added them up to assess a total global cost.

Before someone picks up any of the conventional tools of policy analysis (e.g., B–C analysis, decision analysis, MAUT, contingent valuation of non-market goods and events, etc.) and applies them to a climate or other problem that lies well out along any axis in Figure 11.9B, they should think very carefully about the appropriateness of the assumptions on which those analytical tools are based. In some cases it may be necessary to consider adopting, or developing, different, more appropriate, analytical approaches and methods.

11.9 USING LARGE RESEARCH AND SCIENTIFIC MODELS IN POLICY APPLICATIONS[11]

It is inevitable that policy analysts will occasionally want to make use of large and complex models developed for engineering design, or as part of scientific research. Such models are frequently unwieldy, incomplete, may be expensive to run, and usually are not suitable for use in the kind of iterative probing approach to analysis summarized in Figure 1.4.

Using techniques discussed in chapter 8 of their book *Uncertainty*, Morgan and Henrion (1990) argue that it is often possible to do more uncertainty analysis on such models than is typically done. But while these techniques can be extremely useful, they will not turn a large complex scientific research model into a flexible, easily exercised policy model.

One appropriate way to use large scientific models in the policy process is to abstract and simplify from their structure and outputs. In some cases this can be done directly by producing a response surface over the relevant model domain (i.e., across ranges of important variables) that can be used in policy studies. An example of the use of this strategy can be found in work done by Milford et al. (1989), in which she repeatedly simulated a large atmospheric pollution model of the Los Angeles basin in order to produce a number of response surfaces that display its complex non-linear performance across different parts of the Los Angeles air basin, shown in Figure 11.10. Another example is work by Fischbeck et al. (2015), who made multiple runs of the IECM simulation tool for coal-fired power plants (IECM, 2015) in order to produce a response surface that has allowed them to characterize the performance of all coal-fired electric power plants in the United States in order to provide states and other decision makers with decision support in meeting the requirements of section 111 of the U.S. Clean Air Act.

[11] Portions of the text in this section and Section 11.10 are based on chapter 11 of Morgan and Henrion (1990).

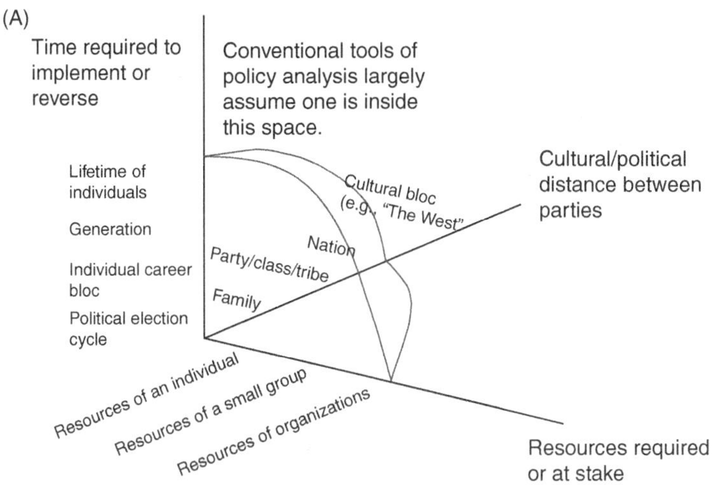

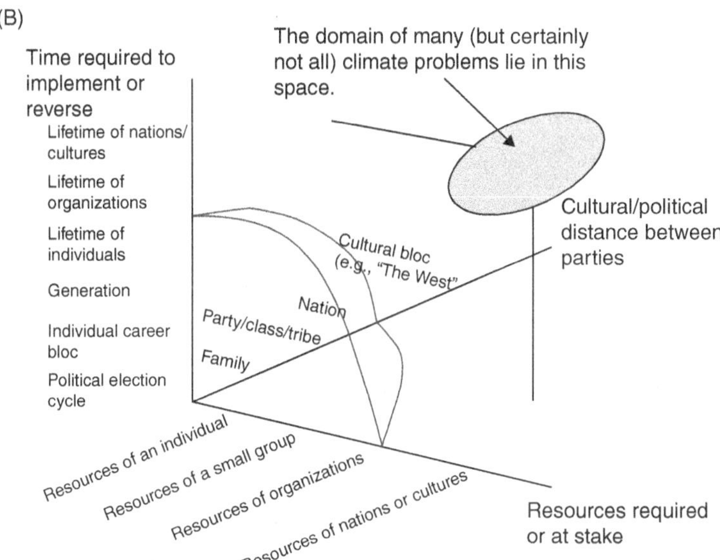

FIGURE 11.9. While it is appropriate to apply the conventional tools of policy analysis to most problems that lie in the inner part of the space shown in **A.**, for problems such as some aspects of climate change, that involve issues that lie well outside that space, analysts should not make use of those tools without first carefully examining the appropriateness of the assumptions on which they are based, **B.**

Another strategy that may be possible once a big research model has been built and empirically validated is to extract one or more simplified analytical models that provides satisfactory results over those model domains of interest to the policy process. These simplified models can then be exercised repeatedly

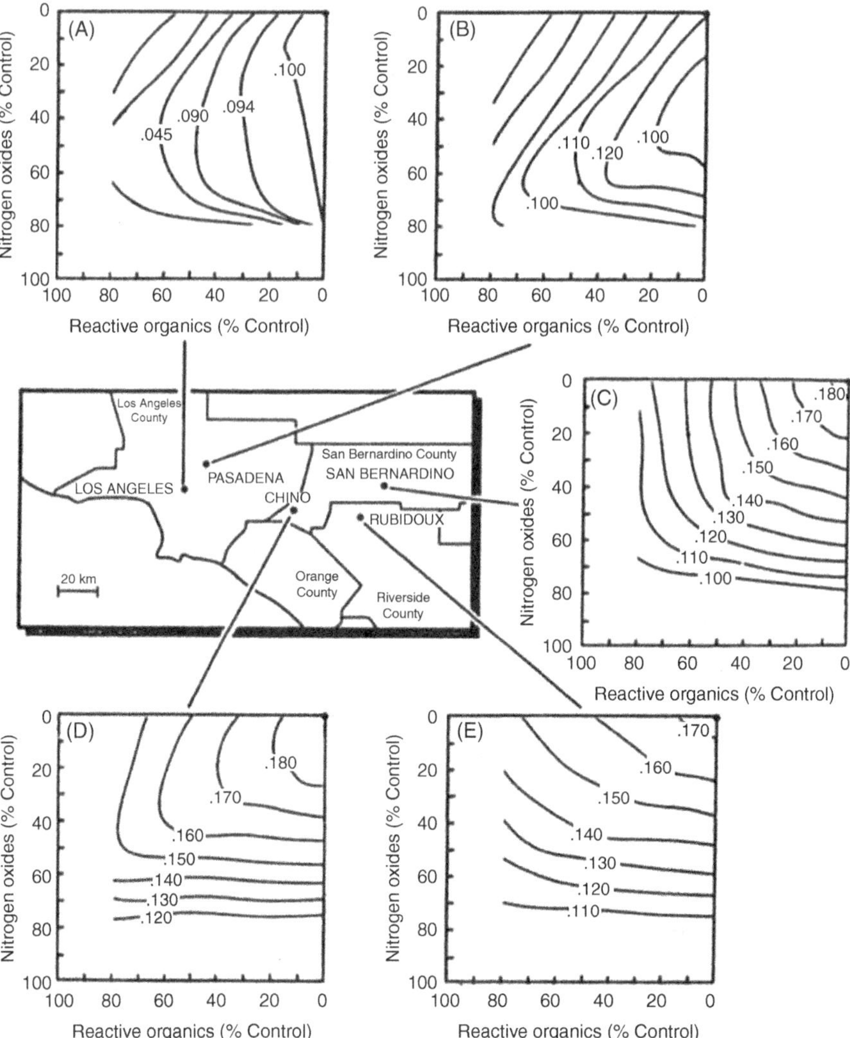

FIGURE 11.10. Isopleths displaying the response of peak ozone concentrations at locations across the Los Angeles basin to spatially uniform reductions in NOx (vertical axes) and reactive organics (horizontal axes). Note that in these EKMA-like diagrams a decrease in one pollutant may not lead to a decrease, and may even lead to an increase in ozone level. These results were obtained by Jana Milford as part of her Ph.D. research at Carnegie Mellon. Details can be found in Milford et al. (1989).

to explore various policy alternatives. Simplistic models of complex systems that have been built without empirical validation can be useless or even dangerous. In contrast, a simple model that abstracts the relevant empirically validated insights from a complex scientific model for use in a specific policy problem can be a powerful and valuable tool.

In circumstances where neither a response surface nor a simplified extracted model are feasible, experts may be able to use insights from selected runs of their large models together with a number of smaller models to construct bounding, scaling, or other arguments. Using these together with professional judgment, they may be able to offer useful advice and guidance for policy purposes. Except when standard well-validated engineering design models are being used, the one thing it is almost never appropriate to do is to run a big deterministic research model just once and then adopt its output as policy gospel.

The key point to remember is that without thorough and systematic modeling and analysis of the uncertainty of the problem, you cannot be sure that the results of a model, especially a very large and complex one, provide meaningful results.

11.10 SOME THOUGHTS ON "LARGE" AND "COMPLEX" MODELS

Large models are models requiring large amounts of human, computational, or other resources in their construction and operation. If they are organized so that their structure and their outputs are easy to understand, and so their solution is straightforward, large models may not be complex.

The definition of complexity has been a topic of interest in a number of fields. Warren Weaver (1948) has defined two kinds of complexity. By "disorganized complexity" he meant "a problem in which the number of variables is very large, and one in which each of the many variables has a behavior which is individually erratic, or perhaps totally unknown." He argued that probabilistic techniques have made excellent progress in characterizing the bulk properties of such systems, and cited examples ranging from thermodynamics to the operation of telephone switching centers. In contrast, he argued that "organized complexity" involves problems in which probabilistic approaches cannot cope but in which it is necessary to deal explicitly with a large number of variables. Although Weaver did not say so, it seems apparent that whether a complex system is organized or disorganized in his terminology depends largely on the level at which one is trying to explain its behavior.

Jay Forrester (1969) defines a complex system as a "high-order, multiple loop, nonlinear feedback structure." He places great emphasis on feedback and non-linearity, arguing that these features are likely to lead to "counter intuitive behavior in complex systems."

Herb Simon (1981) provides an especially useful discussion. He informally defines a complex system as:

> One made up of a large number of parts that interact in a non-simple way. In such systems the whole is more than the sum of the parts, not in an ultimate, metaphysical sense but in the important pragmatic sense that, given the properties of the parts and the laws of interaction, it is not a trivial matter to infer the properties of the whole.

He argues:

> How complex or simple the structure is depends critically upon the way in which we describe it. Most of the complex structures found in the world are enormously redundant, and we can use this redundancy to simplify their description. But to use it, to achieve this simplification, we must find the right representation.

Simon argues that most, perhaps all, of the world's human and natural systems are hierarchical in structure, that is, they are either "decomposable" into subsystems whose interactions are negligible, or are "nearly decomposable," that is, they are decomposable into subsystems "in which the interactions among the subsystems are weak but not negligible." Indeed, if this were not true of some complex systems, such systems would be very difficult to detect or understand, since it is probably only by understanding the interaction of subsystems that we are cognitively capable of building up an understanding of the whole.

Simon argues that it is unlikely that complex physical, biological, or social systems would evolve that are not hierarchical, since the various sub-elements of these systems need to have been individually stable long enough for the larger system to be built up or to evolve. This has the interesting implication that in trying to understand any particular behavior of a complex hierarchical system, there are some natural limits or boundaries to the detail with which all aspects of the subsystems involved must be understood. To use a physical example, much can be understood about atoms and molecules without paying detailed attention to subatomic particles. Similarly, much can be understood about geology, oceanography, or atmospheric science without paying detailed attention to atoms and molecules. Everything in this world interacts with everything else, but for most behaviors a modest subset of those interactions is far more important than all the others. That is, the system is decomposable, or at worst nearly decomposable, into a hierarchical structure. Such a decomposition may be required along several different dimensions, for example, across space or over time.

Electric power systems provide a good example of a system often analyzed through decomposition according to timescale. Electric fault processes can involve timescales of fractions of seconds; voltage and frequency transients can involve periods of seconds to minutes; questions of economic dispatch and load management typically involve timescales of minutes to hours; and expansion planning involves timescales of years to decades. Rather than constructing a single model that spans the entire problem space from milliseconds to decades, different models are used to study each of the different issues.

If we apply Simon's perspective to policy problems, the implication is that the process of modeling for policy analysis should be the process of identifying, isolating, and understanding just those aspects of the system and their interactions that matter for the particular problem of interest.

11.11 MODEL COMPLEXITY SHOULD MATCH THE ANALYST'S LEVEL OF UNDERSTANDING[12]

Analysts often find themselves pressed to run a model into portions of its phase space that are not well understood, and for which the underlying assumptions and understanding upon which the model was built are no longer applicable.[13] This issue often arises for complex models in which different sub-models may become unreliable at different rates. A common example involves running a time-stepped integrated assessment model far into the future. The economic portions of such a model may only be appropriate for a decade or less, while the geophysical portions may be good for many decades or more.

Several strategies can be used to deal with such situations. For example, for a model that produces output as a time series, a plot can be added that displays the assessed probability of model failure over time. Similarly, possible alternative "surprises" can be assigned probabilities, modeled separately, and combined. Examples of both of these strategies are provided in Casman et al. (1999).

When I asked a colleague who is a Bayesian theorist how one should deal with the problem of pushing a model into less well-understood portions of its phase space, the advice I got was to specify the (perhaps infinite) set of all priors and models that fit the constraints imposed by whatever limited knowledge is available. Probability weights (which might all be equal) should then be applied across this set, and the problem should be solved for all cases. While this may make theoretical sense, it also means that the less you know about the system being modeled, the more complex your modeling strategy becomes. Such an approach would not pass the laugh test in real-world policy circles!

As an alternative, in Casman et al. (1999) we proposed a strategy in which, over time, one shifts between models, moving from more detailed to progressively simpler order-of-magnitude models, and perhaps ultimately to simple bounding analysis. That is, we propose to deal with the more distant future (or, to be more general, with the less well-understood regions of the model phase space) by building very simple models, which are based on order-of-magnitude estimates when possible, and using bounding considerations such as material and energy balance and carrying capacity, when best estimates are no longer meaningful. Such a strategy is illustrated graphically in Figure 11.11. This example starts with a detailed model that is likely to only be reliable for a few years. Gradually weight is shifted over from this model to a much simpler model based on order-of-magnitude considerations. Finally, in the long term, it is only possible to bound the result, without giving a best estimate. The weighting functions that are used to combine models, and make the switch from one

[12] Portions of the text in this section have been reworked from Casman et al. (1999).

[13] The Random House unabridged dictionary defines a phase space as "a hypothetical space constructed so as to have as many coordinates as are necessary to define the state of a given ... system."

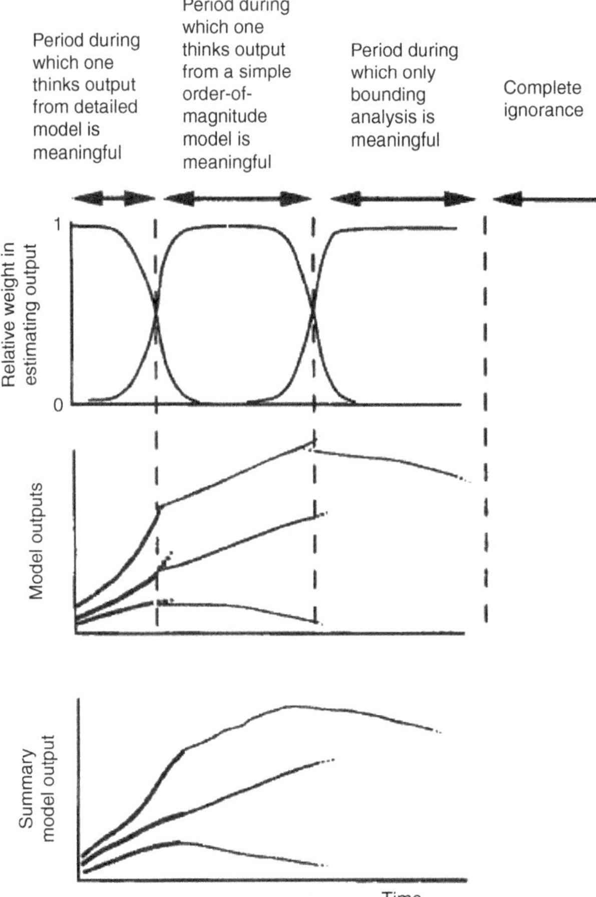

FIGURE 11.11. Schematic illustration of the strategy of switching to progressively simpler models as one moves into less well-understood regions of the problem phase space, in this case, over time. One starts with a detailed model that is likely to only be reliable for a few years. Gradually one moves over to a much simpler model based on order-of-magnitude considerations. Finally, in the long term, one can only bound the result, without giving best estimates. The weighting functions for combining the models are based on subjective judgment. While the illustration shows three models over time, there is no reason why the number cannot be more or fewer than three. Figure from Casman et al. (1999).

model to another over time, must, of course, be based on subjective judgment. While the illustration shows three models over time, there is no reason why the number cannot be more or less than three. In Casman et al. (1999), we provide a simple illustration, gradually switching from the rather detailed demographic model in ICAM-3 to a bounding analysis based upon the work of demographer J.E. Cohen (1995).

To many who have thought about it, the use of order-of-magnitude and bounding analysis in situations where uncertainty is very high may seem like an obvious strategy. However, persuading others that this is sometimes the best that we can do can be very challenging. My colleagues and I have learned this firsthand when we have gone through multiple rounds of reviews before we could publish bounding analyses of the environmental factors that contribute to lung cancer (Casman et al., 2004; Ha-Duong et al., 2004; Casman and Morgan, 2005) or the range of possible U.S. electricity consumption that could result in the year 2050 (Schweizer and Morgan, 2016). Nevertheless, I firmly believe that bounding analysis is a technique that has been seriously neglected and deserves much wider application (Morgan, 2001).

REFERENCES

Ågren, G. and F. Andersson (2012). *Terrestrial Ecosystem Ecology: Principles and Applications*, Cambridge University Press, 330pp.

Alcamo, J., R. Shaw, and L. Hordijk (eds.) (1990). *The RAINS Model of Acidification: Science and Strategies in Europe*, Kluwer, 402pp.

Au, T. and T.P. Au (1992). *Engineering Economics for Capital Investment Analysis*, Prentice Hall, 540pp.

Ayres, R.U. (1984). "Limits and Possibilities of Large-Scale Long-Range Societal Models," *Technological Forecasting and Social Change*, *25*(4), pp. 297–308.

Benjamin, J.R. and C.A. Cornell (1970). *Probability, Statistics, and Decision for Civil Engineers*, McGraw-Hill, 684pp.

Boyd, R. (1972). "World Dynamics: A Note," *Science*, *177*, pp. 516–519.

Casman, E.A., M. Ha-Duong, and M.G. Morgan (2004). "Response to Sander Greenland's Critique of Bounding Analysis," *Risk Analysis*, *24*(5), pp. 1093–1096.

Casman, E.A. and M.G. Morgan (2005). "Use of Expert Judgment to Bound Lung Cancer Risks," *Environmental Science & Technology*, *39*, pp. 5911–5920.

Casman, E.A., M.G. Morgan, and H. Dowlatabadi (1999). "Mixed Levels of Uncertainty in Complex Policy Models," *Risk Analysis*, *19*(1), pp. 33–42.

Cohen, J.E. (1995). "Population Growth and Earth's Human Carrying Capacity," *Science*, *269*, pp. 341–346.

Craig, P.P., A. Gadgil, and J.G. Koomey (2002). "What Can History Teach US? Examination of Long-Term Energy Forecasts for the United States," *Annual Review of Energy and the Environment*, *27*, pp. 83–118.

Dowlatabadi, H. and M.G. Morgan (1993). "A Model Framework for Integrated Studies of the Climate Problem," *Energy Policy*, *21*(3), pp. 209–221.

EIA (2009). *The National Energy Modeling System: An Overview 2009*, DOE/EIA-0581, 77pp. Available at: www.eia.gov/forecasts/aeo/nems/overview/pdf/0581(2009).pdf.

Fischbeck, P., H. Zhai, and J. Anderson et al. (2015). "A Techno-Economic Decision Support Tool for Guiding States' Responses to the EPA Clean Power Plan." Available at: www.cmu.edu/energy/cleanpowerplantool.

Flyvbjerg, B., M.K. Skamris Holm, and S.L. Buhl (2003). "How Common and How Large Are Cost Overruns in Transport Infrastructure Projects?," *Transport Review*, *23*(1), pp. 71–88.

Ford, A. (2009). *Modeling the Environment*, Island Press, 380pp.

Ford Foundation Energy Project (1974). *A Time to Choose: America's Energy Future*, Ballenger, 511pp.

Forrester, J.W. (1969). *Urban Dynamics*, MIT Press, 285pp.

(1971). *World Dynamics*, Wright-Allen Press, 142pp.

Gabriel, S.A., A.S. Kydes, and P. Whitman (2001). "The National Energy Modeling System: A Large-Scale Energy-Economic Equilibrium Model," *Operations Research*, *49*(1), pp. 14–25.

Greenberger, M. (1983). *Caught Unawares: The Energy Decade in Retrospect*, Ballinger, 415pp.

Greenberger, M., M.A. Crenson, and B.L. Crissy (1976). *Models in the Policy Process: Public Decision Making in the Computer Era*, Russell Sage Foundation/ Basic Books, 355pp.

GTS (1980). *The Global 2000 Report to the President: Entering the Twenty-First Century*, ed. by G.O. Barney, 3 vols., Council on Environmental Quality and the Department of State.

Ha-Duong, M.E., A. Casman, and M.G. Morgan (2004). "Bounding Poorly Characterized Risks: A Lung Cancer Example," *Risk Analysis*, *24*(5), pp. 1071–1084.

Harte, J. (1988). *Consider a Spherical Cow: A Course in Environmental Problem Solving*, University Science Books, 283pp.

Hendrickson, C. and T. Au (2008). *Project Management and Construction: Fundamental Concepts for Owners, Engineers, Architects and Builders*. Online book available at: http://pmbook.ce.cmu.edu.

Hendrickson, C.T., L.B. Lave, and H.S. Matthews (2006). *Environmental Life Cycle Assessment of Goods and Services: An Input-Output Approach*, Resources for the Future, 262pp.

Henrion, M. (2004). "What's Wrong with Spreadsheets: And How To Fix Them With Analytica," 16pp. Available at: www.lumina.com/uploads/technology/Whats%20 wrong%20with%20spreadsheets.pdf.

Holcombe, R.G. (1989). *Economic Models and Methodology*, Greenwood Press, 201pp.

Horowitz, K.J. and M.A. Planting (2009). *Concepts and Methods of the Input-Output Accounts*, Bureau of Economic Analysis, U.S. Department of Commerce, 266pp. Available at: www.bea.gov/papers/pdf/IOmanual_092906.pdf.

House, P.W. and J. McLeod (1977). *Large Scale Models for Policy Evaluation*, Wiley-Interscience, 326pp.

Huntington, H.G. (1994). "Oil Price Forecasting in the 1980s: What Went Wrong?," *The Energy Journal*, *15*, pp. 1–22.

IECM (2015). *The Integrated Environmental Control Model*. Available at: www.cmu. edu/epp/iecm.

ISO (1997). "ISO Standard 14040: Environmental Management – Life Cycle Assessment: Principles and Framework," International Standard Organization, 12pp.

(2006). "ISO 14040: Environmental Management – Life Cycle Assessment: Principles and Framework," International Standards Organization. Available online at www. iso.org/iso/catalogue_detail?csnumber=37456.

Keyfitz, N. (1981). "The Limits of Population Forecasting," *Population and Development Review*, 7(4), pp. 579–593.

Koomey, J., P. Craig, A. Gadgil, and D. Lorenzetti (2003). "Improving Long-Range Energy Modeling: A Plea for Historical Retrospectives," *The Energy Journal*, *24*, pp. 75–92.

Lave, L.B. and H. Dowlatabadi (1993). "Climate Change: The Effects of Personal Beliefs and Scientific Uncertainty," *Engineering Science &Technology*, *27*(10), pp. 1962–1972.

Lave, L.B., H. Dowlatabadi, G.J. McRae, M.G. Morgan, and E.S. Rubin (1992). "Uncertainties of Climate Change," *Nature*, *355*, p. 197.

Linderoth, H. (2002). "Forecast Errors in IEA-Countries' Energy Consumption," *Energy Policy*, *30*, pp. 53–61.

Lutz, W. and J.R. Goldstein (2004). "Introduction: How to Deal With Uncertainty in Population Forecasting?" *International Statistical Review*, *72*(1), pp. 1–4.

McKitrick, R.R. (1998). "The Econometric Critique of Computable General Equilibrium Modeling: The Role of Functional Forms," *Economic Modelling*, *15*(4), pp. 543–573.

Matthews, H.S. and C.T. Hendrickson (2015). *Life Cycle Assessment: Quantitative Approaches for Decisions That Matter*, 241pp. Only available at: https://cmu.app.box.com/s/5mnzyq1y3gcyjrveubf4/1/2746878222.

Meadows, D.H., D.L. Meadows, J. Randers, and W.W. Behrens (1972). *The Limits to Growth: A Report for the Club of Rome's Project on the Predicament of Mankind*, Universe Books, 205pp.

Milford, J.B., A.G. Russell, and G.J. McRae (1989). "A New Approach to Photochemical Pollution Control: Implications of Spatial Patterns in Pollutant Responses to Reductions in Nitrogen Oxides and Reactive Organic Gas Emissions," *Environmental Science & Technology*, *23*(10), pp. 1290–1301.

Morgan, M.G. (2001). "The Neglected Art of Bounding Analysis," Viewpoint, *Environmental Science & Technology*, *35*, pp. 162A–164A.

Morgan, M.G. and H. Dowlatabadi (1996). "Learning from Integrated Assessment of Climate Change," *Climatic Change*, *34*, pp. 337–368.

Morgan, M.G. and M. Henrion (1990). *Uncertainty: A Guide to Dealing with Uncertainty in Quantitative Risk and Policy Analysis*, Cambridge University Press, 332pp.

Morgan, M.G., M. Kandlikar, J. Risbey, and H. Dowlatabadi (1999). "Why Conventional Tools for Policy Analysis Are Often Inadequate for Problems of Global Change," *Climatic Change*, *41*, pp. 271–281.

Morgan, M.G. and D. Keith (1995). "Subjective Judgments by Climate Experts," *Environmental Science & Technology*, *29*(10), pp. 468A–476A.

Morgan, M.G. and F.C. McMichael (1981). "A Characterization and Critical Discussion of Models and Their Use in Environmental Policy," *Policy Sciences*, *14*, pp. 345–370.

Nordhaus, W.D. and J. Boyer (2000). *Warming the World: Economic Models of Global Warming*, MIT Press, 232pp.

O'Neil, B.C. and M. Desai (2005). "Accuracy of Past Projections of U.S. Energy Consumption," *Energy Policy*, *33*, pp. 979–993.

Parson, E.A. and K. Fisher-Vanden (1997). "Integrated Assessment Models of Global Climate Change," *Annual Reviews of Energy and the Environment*, *22*, pp. 589–628.

Pindyck, R.S. (2013). "Climate Change Policy: What Do the Models Tell Us?," *Journal of Economic Literature*, *51*(3), pp. 860–872.

Raftery, A.E., N. Li, H. Ševčíková, P. Gerland, and G.K. Heilig (2012). "Bayesian Probabilistic Population Projections for All Countries," *Proceedings of the National Academy of Sciences*, *109*(35), pp. 13915–13921.

Rodrik, D. (2015). *Economics Rules: The Rights and Wrongs of the Dismal Science*, W.W. Norton & Company, 253pp.

Rose, S., D. Turner, G. Blanford, J. Bistline, F. de la Chesnaye, and T. Wilson (2014). *Understanding the Social Cost of Carbon: A Technical Assessment – Executive Summary*, EPRI, 18pp.

Rubin, E.S. (1991). "Benefit-Cost Implications of Acid Rain Controls: An Evaluation of the NAPAP Integrated Assessment," *Journal of the Air & Waste Management Association*, *41*(7), pp. 914–921.

Rubin, E.S., C.N. Bloyd, M.J. Small, R.J. Marnicio, and M. Henrion (1990). "Atmospheric Deposition Assessment Model: Applications to Regional Aquatic Acidification in Eastern North America," in J. Kamari (ed.), *Impact Models to Assess Regional Acidification*, Kluwer Academic Publishers, pp. 253–284.

Rubin, E.S., L.B. Lave, and M.G. Morgan (1991). "Keeping Climate Research Relevant," *Issues in Science and Technology*, *8*(2), pp. 47–55.

Rubin, E.S., M.J. Small, C.N. Bloyd, and M. Henrion (1992). "Integrated Assessment of Acid Deposition Effects on Lake Acidification," *Journal of Environmental Engineering*, *118*(1), pp. 120–134.

Scarf, H.E. and J.B. Shoven (eds.) (1984). *Applied General Equilibrium Analysis*, Cambridge University Press, 538pp.

Schnoor, J.L. (1996). *Environmental Modeling: Fate and Transport of Pollutants in Water, Air, and Soil*, John Wiley & Sons, 682pp.

Schweizer, V. and M.G. Morgan (2016). "Bounding U.S. Electricity Demand in 2050," *Technological Forecasting & Social Change*, pp. 215–223.

Seinfeld, J.H. and S.N. Pandis (2006). *Atmospheric Chemistry and Physics: From Air Pollution to Climate Change*, Wiley, 1203pp.

Simon, H.A. (1981). *Science of the Artificial*, 2nd ed., MIT press, 247pp.

Smil, V. (2000). "Perils of Long-Range Energy Forecasting: Reflections on Looking Far Ahead," *Technology Forecasting and Social Change*, *65*, pp. 251–264.

(2003). *Energy at the Crossroads: Global Perspectives and Uncertainties*, MIT Press, 427pp.

Smith, J. and P. Smith (2007). *Introduction to Environmental Modeling*, Oxford University Press, 180pp.

Sterman, J.D. (1991). "A Skeptic's Guide to Computer Models," *Managing a Nation: The Microcomputer Software Catalog*, 2, pp. 209–229.

Weaver, W. (1948). "Science and Complexity," *American Scientist*, *36*, pp. 536–544.

West, G.R. (1995). "Comparison of Input–Output, Input–Output + Econometric and Computable General Equilibrium Impact Models at the Regional Level," *Economic Systems Research*, *7*(2), pp. 209–227.

Weyant, J.P. (2012). "Lessons Learned from Past Energy-Environmental Inter-Model Comparison Projects: With Opportunities and Challenges Remaining," Energy Modeling Forum and Department of Management Science and Engineering, Stanford University, 175pp.

Weyant, J. (2015). "Contributions of Integrated Assessment Models," draft book chapter, Stanford University, 35pp.

Winebrake, J.J. and D. Sakva (2006). "An Evaluation of Errors in U.S. Energy Forecasts: 1982–2003," *Energy Policy*, *34*, pp. 3475–3483.

PART III

HOW INDIVIDUALS AND ORGANIZATIONS ACTUALLY MAKE DECISIONS

It is all well and good to argue that people should behave as rational, utility-maximizing decision makers. However, there is compelling experimental evidence that shows that in many situations people do not behave in this way, and perhaps don't even want to, even if they could. Chapter 12 provides a very compact introduction to this empirical literature, mostly developed by psychologists and other behavioral social scientists over the course of the last few decades, and discusses a number of the implications of what has been learned. The bottom line is that people are "boundedly rational" – that is, even when we want to, our mental processing capabilities limit how close we can get to the ideal of performing as a rational actor engaged in maximizing utility.

For policy analysts dealing with issues that involve science and technology, an important and closely related topic is how people (not just the general public – *all* of us) perceive and think about risk. The degree to which something constitutes a "risk" turns out to be a multi-attribute issue – certainly depending on the expected number of deaths and injuries, but also depending in important ways on a range of other attributes. These issues are explored in Chapter 13. Then in Chapter 14 we move on to the topic of how to develop effective communications about risks. The examples in this chapter are largely drawn from technical topics, but the approach that is outlined is more widely applicable.

Many policy choices, including many of those that are most important, are not the result of decisions made by single individuals. Rather they are the emergent consequence of the interactions within organizations populated by participants operating with "bounded rationality." In order to be effective, policy analysts need to have a basic understanding of these processes of organizational behavior. While the literature in this field is enormous, Chapter 15 provides an overview and discussion of a small number of key ideas.

12

Human Mental Processes for Perception, Memory, and Decision Making

With the exception of a few parts of Chapters 9 and 10, everything we have discussed until now has assumed that people act and make decisions as utility-maximizing rational actors. That assumption provides a useful basis for doing analysis to help people make decisions, but it falls short when we are trying to anticipate how people perceive and remember things that are important to the formulation of public policy, or how they are likely to make decisions in the presence of uncertainty. These issues are in the domain of a special branch of empirical social science, largely developed by experts in psychology, that is now often called "decision science" or the science of "judgment and decision making." I say *empirical* social science because this important understanding has grown out of a solid base of carefully designed experimental studies, studies whose results, like those in other fields of science, have been repeatedly replicated and verified.

Fischhoff (2010) explains:

> Over the past 40 years, the study of judgment and decision making has spread widely, first to social psychology ... then to application areas like accounting, health, and finance, finally penetrating mainstream economics under the banner of behavioral economics. That success owes something to the power of the approach, which liberated researchers previously bound by rational-actor models for describing behavior. It also owes something to the fascination of results that address a central aspect of the human condition, individuals' competence to manage their own affairs.

There is obviously no way to cover all the insights from this body of research in a single chapter, or, for that matter, in just a course or two. Here I do four things: outline a few of the key experimental results, suggest a few original papers that I urge you to read to get a sense of what empirical studies in this field look like, suggest that you read some excellent summary accounts of key ideas written by Robin Dawes (1988), and recommend a few other books to which interested readers can turn for more detail.

12.1 TWO KINDS OF THINKING

Cautioning that it is only a metaphor to help understand a much more complex set of cognitive processes, the psychologist Daniel Kahneman (2011) has argued that it is useful to think of human thought as consisting of two "systems." System 1 is fast, automatic, effortless, intuitive, and strongly influenced by affect (i.e., feeling or emotion). In contrast, System 2 is much slower, requires significant mental effort, and is more systematic. Asked "what is 2 times 2," System 1 automatically and effortlessly generates "4." Asked "what is 19 times 36," most of us have to resort to System 2 to figure it out. Indeed, while we would use the algorithm we have learned to perform such a calculation, many of us would also have to resort to paper and pencil, finding it too difficult to retain the intermediate products in our short-term memory.

The same sort of automatic processing occurs in many domains. When you first learned to drive you had to think carefully about every move you made. Now, except in unusual situations, you drive effortlessly without really thinking about it.

Slovic et al. (2004) argue that both systems are often needed for good decision making: "Even such prototypical analytic exercises as proving a mathematical theorem or selecting a move in chess benefit from experiential guidance, the mathematician senses whether the proof 'looks good' and the chess master gauges whether a contemplated move 'feels right', based upon stored knowledge of a large number of winning patterns" (DeGroot, 1965 as paraphrased by Slovic et al., 2004). Psychologists working in the general area of risk and decision making under uncertainty are somewhat divided about the role played by emotions and feelings (i.e., affect) in making risk and related judgments. Some (e.g., Sjöberg, 2006) argue that such influences are minor, others (e.g., Loewenstein, 1996; Loewenstein et al., 2001) assign them a dominant role. Agreeing with Slovic et al.'s conclusion that both are often important, Wardman (2006) suggests that the most effective responses "may in fact occur when they are driven by both affective and deliberative-analytical considerations, and that it is the absence of one or the other that may cause problems."

The cartoonist Garry Trudeau has illustrated the difference between System 1 and 2 in a cartoon he titled "Street Calculus" (Figure 12.1). While we probably should, most of us do not perform the sort of systematic analysis Trudeau implies. Rather, when we encounter someone on the street, System 1 produces a snap judgment, perhaps unconsciously informed by instantaneous observation of some of the factors Trudeau lists, but certainly not in the same systematic way.

Street Calculus

FIGURE 12.1. Illustration of the difference between System 1 and System 2 in a cartoon by Garry Trudeau.

12.2 FRAMING EFFECTS AND PROSPECT THEORY

How something is brought to our attention, that is, how it is "framed," can make a big difference in how we evaluate it. People's judgments about two problems that are logically identical can be readily reversed by presenting them with different framings.

Robyn Dawes (1988) offers a simple example involving money:

Imagine that I have given you $200. I now offer you more, in the form of one of two options:

Option 1: I will give you an additional $100.
Option 2: I will toss a fair coin. If it lands heads I will give you an additional $200; if it lands tails, I will give you no additional money.

Most people select option 1...

Now consider a variation of this. I begin by giving you $400, but there is a slight penalty involved. You must choose one of the penalty options:

Penalty Option 1: You must give me back $100.
Penalty Option 2: I will toss a fair coin. If it lands heads you must give me back $200; if it lands tails, you may keep all the money I gave you.

Presented with this hypothetical choice most people select penalty option 2.

Take a few moments to think carefully about the first and second examples. They are logically identical. As Dawes notes in both cases, "You are presented with a choice between a certainty of $300 ... or a 50:50 chance of obtaining $200 or $400." Yet depending upon how the choice is presented, how it is "framed," people make different choices.

The effect is not limited to choices involving money. Amos Tversky and Daniel Kahneman (1981) presented 152 subjects with the following choice:

Imagine that the U.S. is preparing for the outbreak of an unusual Asian disease, which is expected to kill 600 people. Two alternative programs to combat the disease have been proposed. Assume that the exact scientific estimate of the consequences of the programs are as follows:

- If Program A is adopted, 200 people will be saved. [chosen by 72% of respondents]
- If Program B is adopted, there is 1/3 probability that 600 people will be saved, and 2/3 probability that no people will be saved. [chosen by 28% of respondents]

Which of the two programs would you favor?

They report that "The majority choice in this problem is risk averse: the prospect of certainly saving 200 lives is more attractive than a risky prospect of equal expected value, that is, a one-in-three chance of saving 600 lives."

A second group of 155 subjects was presented with the following choice:

Imagine that the U.S. is preparing for the outbreak of an unusual Asian disease, which is expected to kill 600 people. Two alternative programs to combat the disease have been proposed. Assume that the exact scientific estimate of the consequences of the programs are as follows:

- If Program C is adopted, 400 people will die. [chosen by 22% of respondents]
- If Program D is adopted, there is 1/3 probability that nobody will die, and 2/3 probability that 600 people will die. [chosen by 78% of respondents]

Which of the two programs would you favor?

In this case the majority of respondents were risk seeking, choosing program D over program C.

Again, if you think about it for a moment, you will see that the choice between the options in the two problem statements is logically identical. The only difference is that in the first case, outcomes were framed in terms of saving lives (i.e., a gain) and in the second case, in terms of losing lives (i.e., a loss).[1]

Dawes (1988) notes that, with great consistency in studies about making choices about risk, "people opted for avoiding risk when questions were framed in terms of saving lives. However, when they were asked to state how serious it would be for various numbers of people in society to lose their lives, they consistently indicated that such seriousness *accelerated* with number of lives lost."

From these and a variety of similar studies, Tversky and Kahneman (1981) explain that they have observed such reversals in "groups of respondents, including university faculty and physicians" in a wide variety of situations in which respondents display "contradictory attitudes toward risks involving gains and losses." They conclude that in assessing the value of a gain or loss, people tend not to make judgments in terms of the overall state of the world, or their total well-being, but rather with respect to their present status. Their utility judgments are generally not symmetric about that assessed status. Even a modest loss of a given size is seen as producing a greater loss in utility than a gain of the same amount. Tversky and Kahneman have termed this phenomenon "prospect theory." An example of the sort of utility curve that results is shown in Figure 12.2.

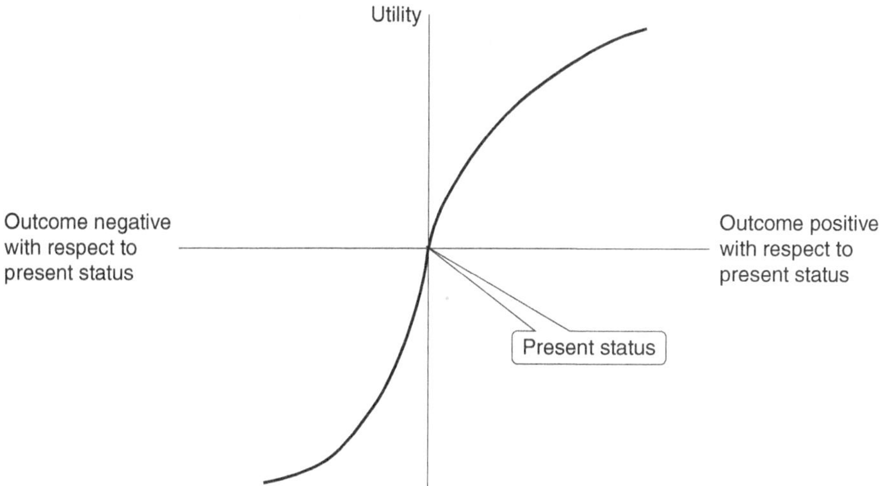

FIGURE 12.2. A typical utility curve implied by prospect theory in which people are risk averse with respect to gains and risk seeking with respect to loss.

[1] Unwilling to abandon the notion that humans are (at least boundedly) rational, under a heading of "widespread irrationality or occasional cognitive illusions," economist Charles Manski (2013) has questioned the broad conclusions about human judgment that Kahneman and Tversky draw (pp. 109–111), while at the same time acknowledging that their specific experimental findings are very robust.

As in the example cited above, by framing a problem in such a way that it shifts a person's assessment of the present status, preference reversals in choice often result.

READINGS 12.1

Chapter 3 in Robyn M. Dawes, *Rational Choice in an Uncertain World*, Harcourt Brace Jovanovich, 346pp., 1988, *OR*, if you cannot find a copy of the older Dawes book, chapters 13 and 10 in Reid Hastie and Robyn M. Dawes, *Rational Choice in an Uncertain World*, Sage, 372pp., 2001. I prefer the earlier Dawes book because it is more concise.[2]

Amos Tversky and Daniel Kahneman, "The Framing of Decisions and the Psychology of Choice," *Science*, *211*, pp. 453–458, 1981.

Abstract: The psychological principles that govern the perception of decision problems and the evaluation of probabilities and outcomes produce predictable shifts of preference when the same problem is framed in different ways. Reversals of preference are demonstrated in choices regarding monetary outcomes, both hypothetical and real, and in questions pertaining to the loss of human lives. The effects of frames on preferences are compared to the effects of perspectives on perceptual appearance. The dependence of preferences on the formulation of decision problems is a significant concern for the theory of rational choice.

DISCUSSION QUESTIONS FOR READINGS 12.1

- What is a "framing effect"?
- Dawes quotes Kahneman and Tversky as writing "Our perceptual apparatus is attuned to the evaluation of changes or differences rather than to the evaluation of absolute magnitudes." What is the relevance of this argument to the idea of "prospect theory"?
- Under what circumstances could it be important to consider framing effects and prospect theory in designing a public policy?

Keysar et al. (2012) have run a series of experiments in which they asked subjects to perform a variety of tasks in judgment and decision making, both in their native language and in a second language that they have studied for some years. Using many of the classic questions from the work of Kahneman and Tversky, Keysar et al. (2012) report that when people respond to these questions using the foreign language, biases resulting from framing effects and loss aversion are dramatically reduced. They conclude that this is because "a foreign language provides greater cognitive and emotional distance than a native tongue does." In

[2] I also prefer it because when I read it I can almost hear Robyn Dawes, who for many years was a good friend and colleague on the faculty at Carnegie Mellon.

short, if one can induce greater use of what Kahneman has termed System 2, it appears to be possible to reduce some of the cognitive biases that otherwise arise automatically, as a result of the operation of System 1.

12.3 UBIQUITOUS OVERCONFIDENCE[3]

In Section 9.5, I argued that all of us tend to be systematically overconfident in our probabilistic judgments. But there is no need for you to take my word for it. Without looking up the answers, please take a piece of paper and write down three numbers for each of the canals shown in Figure 12.3. In each case, estimate:

A length for which you believe there is only a 5% chance that the canal could be shorter.	—	Your best estimate of how long the canal is.	—	A length for which you believe there is only a 5% chance that the canal could be longer.

1. Cape Cod Canal

Allows ships to avoid going around Cape Cod, MA

2. Houston Ship Channel

Allows ships to travel from the sea to Houston, TX

3. Panama Canal

Allows ships to pass from the Caribbean to the Pacific

4. The Soo Canal

Allows ships to travel from Lake Michigan to Lake Superior

5. The Suez Canal

Allows ships to pass from the Mediterranean to the Red Sea

6. The Welland Canal

Allows ships to bypass Niagara Falls

FIGURE 12.3. For each of the six ship canals shown, write three lengths on a piece of paper: a length for which you think there is only a 5% chance the canal could be shorter, your best estimate, and a length for which you think there is only a 5% chance the canal could be longer. It is best to estimate the two extremes before you make your best estimate. Images from Wikimedia.

[3] Portions of the text in this section are derived in edited form from Morgan et al. (2009).

Given the discussion in Chapter 9, you should first estimate the two extremes before you produce your best estimate. Once you have written down all 18 numbers, you can check your answers against the table at the end of this chapter.

People tend to be systematically overconfident in the face of uncertainty. One consequence of this is that when they are asked to make probabilistic judgments of the sort you just made about the length of various canals, they typically produce probability distributions that are much too narrow. As previously noted in Chapter 9, actual values, once they are known, often turn out to lie well outside the tails of their assessed distribution.

This is well illustrated with the data in the summary table reproduced on the left side of Figure 12.4. This table reports results from laboratory studies in

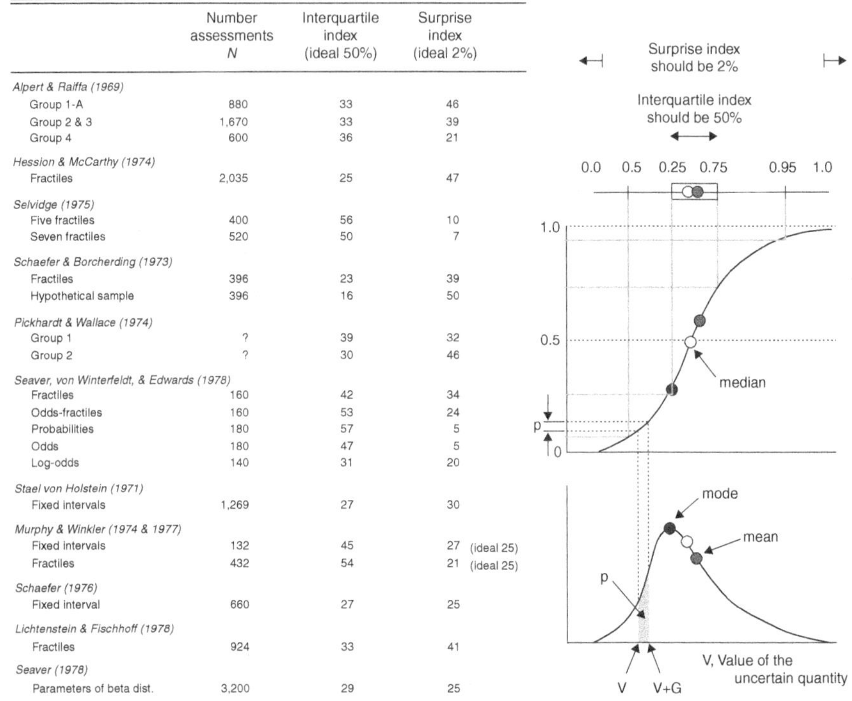

	Number assessments *N*	Interquartile index (ideal 50%)	Surprise index (ideal 2%)
Alpert & Raiffa (1969)			
Group 1-A	880	33	46
Group 2 & 3	1,670	33	39
Group 4	600	36	21
Hession & McCarthy (1974)			
Fractiles	2,035	25	47
Selvidge (1975)			
Five fractiles	400	56	10
Seven fractiles	520	50	7
Schaefer & Borcherding (1973)			
Fractiles	396	23	39
Hypothetical sample	396	16	50
Pickhardt & Wallace (1974)			
Group 1	?	39	32
Group 2	?	30	46
Seaver, von Winterfeldt, & Edwards (1978)			
Fractiles	160	42	34
Odds-fractiles	160	53	24
Probabilities	180	57	5
Odds	180	47	5
Log-odds	140	31	20
Stael von Holstein (1971)			
Fixed intervals	1,269	27	30
Murphy & Winkler (1974 & 1977)			
Fixed intervals	132	45	27 (ideal 25)
Fractiles	432	54	21 (ideal 25)
Schaefer (1976)			
Fixed interval	660	27	25
Lichtenstein & Fischhoff (1978)			
Fractiles	924	33	41
Seaver (1978)			
Parameters of beta dist.	3,200	29	25

FIGURE 12.4. Summary of data from different studies in which, using a variety of methods, people were asked to produce probability distributions on the value of well-known quantities (such as the distance between two locations), so that their distributions can be subsequently checked against true values. The results clearly demonstrate that people are systematically overconfident (i.e., produce subjective probability distributions that are too narrow) when they make such judgments. The table is reproduced from Morgan and Henrion (1990) who, in compiling it, drew in part on Lichtenstein et al. (1982). Definitions of interquartile index and surprise index are shown in the diagram on the right.

which, using a variety of elicitation methods, subjects were asked to produce probability distributions to indicate their estimates of the value of a number of well-known quantities. If the respondents were "well calibrated," then the true value of the judged quantities should fall within the 0.25 to 0.75 interval of their probability distribution about half the time. The frequency with which the true value actually falls within that interval is called the interquartile index. Similarly, the frequency with which the true value lies below the 0.01 or above the 0.99 probability values in their distribution is termed the "surprise index." Thus, for a well-calibrated respondent, the surprise index should be 2 percent.

In the results of the experimental studies reported in Figure 12.4, interquartile indices ranged between 20 and 40 percent rather than the 50 percent they should have been, and surprise indices ranged from a low of 5 percent (2.5 times larger than it should have been) to 50 percent (25 times larger than it should have been). Figure 9.1 presents a histogram of surprise indices for these studies.

Overconfidence is not unique to non-technical judgments. Henrion and Fischhoff (1986) have examined the evolution of published estimates of a number of basic physical constants, as compared to the best modern values. Figure 9.2 shows results for the speed of light. While one might expect error bars associated with published experimental results not to include all possible sources of uncertainty, the "recommended values" do attempt to include all uncertainties, including possible systematic errors. Note that for a period of approximately 25 years during the early part of the last century, the one standard deviation error bar being reported for the recommended values did not include the current best estimate. Similar results obtain for recommended values of other basic physical quantities such as Planck's constant, the charge and mass of the electron, and Avogadro's number. For details, see Henrion and Fischhoff (1986) from which Figure 9.2 was redrawn.

12.4 COGNITIVE HEURISTICS AND BIASES[4]

Virtually all important private and public decisions must be made in the face of deep uncertainty that, while it may be reduced through careful analysis, typically cannot be eliminated. Given that fact, it is important to consider how well we humans are equipped to make judgments about, and in the face of, uncertainty. In Chapter 8 I noted that while our brains are very good at doing many tasks, we do not come hard-wired with statistical processors. Instead, typically without being aware of it, we use a variety of "cognitive heuristics" or mental short cuts.

Thinking about uncertainty is not the only context in which our brains employ heuristics. For example, while most of us are unaware of it, in judging how far it is to a distant mountain, we are influenced by how sharp we perceive

[4] Portions of the text in this section are derived in edited form from Morgan et al. (2009).

its image to be. When air quality is poor, we are likely to judge the mountain to be further away than it actually is. When the air is exceptionally clean, we are likely to judge the mountain to be closer than it actually is.

Three cognitive heuristics are especially relevant in the context of decision making under uncertainty: availability, anchoring and adjustment, and representativeness (Tversky and Kahneman, 1974). For a comprehensive review of much of the literature, see Kahneman et al. (1982).

When people judge the frequency of an uncertain event, they often do so by the ease with which they can recall such events from the past, or imagine such events occurring. This *availability heuristic* serves us well in many situations. For example, suppose that I want to judge the likelihood of encountering a traffic police car on the way to the airport in mid-afternoon on a normal workday. Since I have driven that route many times at that time of day, the ease with which I can recall such encounters from the past is probably proportional to the likelihood that I will encounter a police car today. However, if I wanted to make the same judgment for a drive to the airport at 3:30 am (a time at which I have never made that drive), using availability may not yield a reliable judgment.

A classic illustration of the availability heuristic in action is provided in Figure 12.5A, which shows results from a set of experimental studies conducted by Lichtenstein et al. (1978) in which well-educated Americans were told that 50,000 people die each year in the United States from motor vehicle accidents,[5] and were then asked to estimate the number of deaths that occurred each year from a number of other causes. While there is scale compression – the likelihood of high-probability events is underestimated by about an order of magnitude, and the likelihood of low-probability events is overestimated by a couple orders of magnitude – the fine structure of the results turns out to be very replicable and clearly shows the operation of availability. Many people die of stroke or from diabetes, but the only time most people hear about such deaths is when a famous person or close relative dies. Thus, as a consequence of availability, the probability of dying from stroke or diabetes is underestimated. Botulism poisoning is very rare, but whenever anyone dies from botulism poisoning, anywhere in the world, the event is likely to be covered in the news and we all hear about it. We also hear news reports of many deaths from tornadoes. Thus, through the operation of availability, the probability of death from botulism poisoning and tornadoes is overestimated. In short, judgments can be dramatically affected by what gets our attention. Things that come readily to mind are likely to have a large effect on our probabilistic judgments. Things that do not come readily to mind may be ignored; or, in the words of the fourteenth-century proverb, all too often "out of sight is out of mind."

[5] Today, while Americans drive more, thanks to safer cars and roads and reduced tolerance for drunk driving, the number has fallen to about 40,000 deaths per year.

We can illustrate the heuristic of *anchoring and adjustment* with results from a similar experiment in which Lichtenstein et al. (1978) made no mention of deaths from motor vehicle accidents but instead told a different group of respondents that about 1000 people die each year in the United States from electrocution. Figure 12.5B shows the resulting trend lines for the two experiments.

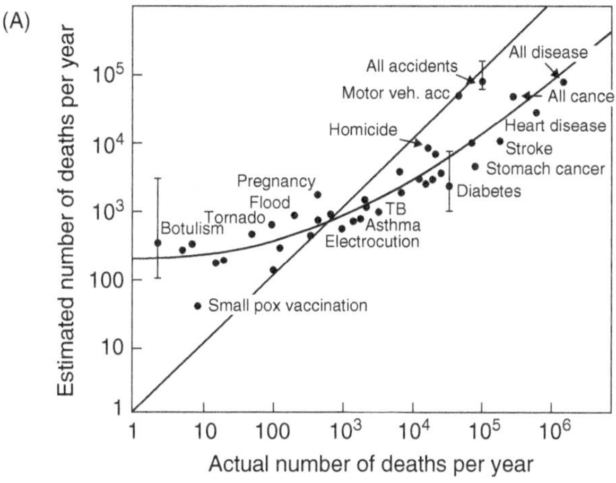

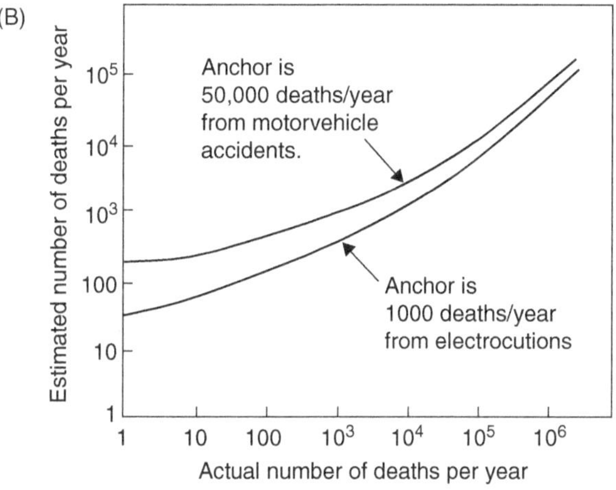

FIGURE 12.5. Illustration of (**A**) the heuristic of availability and of (**B**) anchoring and adjustment. In **A**, note that diabetes and stroke lie below the trend line and that botulism and tornadoes lie above the trend line. This is a result of the availability heuristic – we do not learn of most diabetes and stroke deaths and we do learn of most botulism deaths and many tornado deaths via news reports. **B** replicates the same study with an anchor of 1000 deaths/year. Due to the influence of this lower anchor through the heuristic of anchoring and adjustment, the mean trend line has moved down. Figures are redrawn from Lichtenstein et al. (1978).

Because in this case respondents started with the much lower "anchor" (1000 rather than 50,000), all of their estimates are systematically lower.

One of the most striking experimental demonstrations of anchoring and adjustment was reported by Tversky and Kahneman (1974):

> In a demonstration of the anchoring effect, subjects were asked to estimate various quantities stated in percentages (for example, the percentage of African countries in the United Nations). For each quantity, a number between 0 and 100 was determined by spinning a wheel of fortune in the subject's presence. The subjects were instructed to indicate first whether that number was higher or lower than the value of the quantity, and then to estimate the value of the quantity by moving upward or downward from the given quantity. Different groups were given different numbers for each quantity, and these arbitrary numbers had a marked effect on the estimates. For example, the median estimates of the percentage of African countries in the United Nations were 25 and 45 for groups that received 10 and 65, respectively, as starting points.[6] Payoffs for accuracy did not reduce the anchoring effect.

Very similar results are reported for similarly posed questions about other quantities such as "what is the percentage of people in the U.S. today who are age 55 or older."

The third heuristic, called *representativeness*, says that people expect to see, in single instantiations, properties that they know that a process displays in the large. Thus, for example, people judge the sequence of coin tosses HHHTTT to be less likely than the sequence HTHHTH because the former looks less random than the latter, and they know that the process of tossing a fair coin is a random process. In fact, all specific sequences of six outcomes of the toss of a fair coin are equally likely to occur.

Kahneman and Tversky (1973) conducted extensive studies of representative thinking. In one set of studies they selected three different groups of subjects, all of whom were graduate students majoring in psychology in three major U.S. universities. Subjects in the first, called the "base-rate group" (n = 69), were asked to judge the percentage of college students enrolled in each of nine fields of specialization. Subjects in the second, called the "similarity group" (n = 65), were given a personality sketch of a student named Tom W. and asked to rank the nine fields in terms of "how similar is Tom W. to the typical graduate student" in each of the nine fields. The personality sketch of Tom W. read as follows:

> Tom W. is of high intelligence, although lacking in true creativity. He has a need for order and clarity, and for neat and tidy systems in which every detail finds its appropriate place. His writing is rather dull and mechanical, occasionally enlivened by somewhat corny puns and by flashes of imagination of the sci-fi type. He has a strong drive for competence. He seems to have little feel and little sympathy for other people

[6] Hastie and Dawes (2001) report that at the time the experiment was conducted, the actual proportion of African nations in the United Nations was 35 percent.

and does not enjoy interacting with others. Self-centered, he nonetheless has a deep moral sense.

The third "prediction group" (n = 114) received the same personality sketch of Tom W. along with the following additional information:

> The preceding personality sketch of Tom W. was written during Tom's senior year in high school by a psychologist, on the basis of projective tests. Tom W. is currently a graduate student. Please rank the following nine fields of graduate specialization in order of the likelihood that Tom W. is now a graduate student in each of these fields.

Kahneman and Tversky report that the product-moment correlations between the judged likelihood and similarity was 0.97 while the correlation between judged likelihood and base rate was −0.65. They conclude that "judgments of likelihood essentially coincide with judgments of similarity and are quite unlike the estimates of base rates. This result provides a direct confirmation of the hypothesis that people predict by representativeness or similarity."

In the same paper, Kahneman and Tversky (1973) go on to describe an elegant study in which they make the base rates very apparent to experimental subjects. These studies involved judgments about five personality sketches said to have been drawn from a group of 70 engineers and 30 lawyers (or in a parallel study, 30 engineers and 70 lawyers). Again, despite the explicitly listed base rate, judgments were influenced much more strongly by similarity. However, when faced with the question:

> Suppose now that you are given no information whatsoever about an individual chosen at random from the sample. The probability that this man is one of the 30 engineers in the sample of 100 is ________%.

subjects did report correctly using the ratio from the base rate.

These same subjects were presented with the following personality sketch, which obviously contains no career-relevant information about the man:

> Dick is a 30-year-old man. He is married with no children. A man of high ability and high motivation, he promises to be quite successful in his field. He is well liked by his colleagues.

Subjects in this case recognized that the sketch contained no relevant information. However, rather than respond with the base rate (70:30 or 30:70), they responded 50:50. Kahneman and Tversky conclude: "Evidently, people respond differently when given no specific evidence and when given worthless evidence. When no specific evidence is given, the prior probabilities are properly utilized; when worthless specific evidence is given, prior probabilities are ignored."

The details of the experimental design and analysis in this paper are very elegant. Readers would be well advised to read the original paper.

READINGS 12.2

Daniel Kahneman and Amos Tversky, "On the Psychology of Prediction," *Psychological Review*, *80*, pp. 237–251, 1973.

Abstract: Intuitive predictions follow a judgmental heuristic – representativeness. By this heuristic, people predict the outcome that appears most representative of the evidence. Consequently, intuitive predictions are insensitive to the reliability of the evidence or to the prior probability of the outcome, in violation of the logic of statistical prediction. The hypothesis that people predict by representativeness is supported in a series of studies with both naive and sophisticated subjects. It is shown that the ranking of outcomes by likelihood coincides with their ranking by representativeness and that people erroneously predict rare events and extreme values if these happen to be representative. The experience of unjustified confidence in predictions and the prevalence of fallacious intuitions concerning statistical regression are traced to the representativeness heuristic.

Chapters 5 and 6 in Robyn M. Dawes, *Rational Choice in an Uncertain World,* Harcourt Brace Jovanovich, 346pp., 1988, *OR*, if you cannot find a copy of the older Dawes book, chapters 4, 5, and 6 in Reid Hastie and Robyn M. Dawes, *Rational Choice in an Uncertain World,* Sage, 372pp., 2001. As noted above, I prefer the earlier Dawes book because it is more concise.

DISCUSSION QUESTIONS FOR READINGS 12.2

- Give a precise definition of the heuristic of availability and a specific example of its operation and consequence.
- Give a precise definition of the heuristic of representativeness and a specific example of its operation and consequence.
- Give a precise definition of the heuristic of anchoring and adjustment and a specific example of its operation and consequence.
- Describe a situation in which you might want to adopt a strategy of anchoring and adjustment.

12.5 HINDSIGHT BIAS

It is tempting to think of memory as being like a recording system that preserves images and text for later recall. However, there is considerable evidence that memory contains strong synthetic elements and can be highly selective in what is or is not retained. What one remembers depends in critical ways on how experiences are encoded, and can also be dramatically shaped, or reshaped, by subsequent experiences. Perhaps the most compelling are examples from "recovered memory therapy," in which subjects develop false memories (confabulations) of things, such as childhood sexual assaults, that never actually occurred.

However, even when no such processes are at play, the accuracy with which we recall how well we anticipated that future events would unfold is biased in such a way as to leave us thinking that our predictive capabilities were much better than they actually were (and are). This phenomenon, first formally studied by Baruch Fischhoff, is termed *hindsight bias*. Kahneman (2011) describes the initial work as follows:

> Together with Ruth Beyth ... Fischhoff conducted a survey before President Richard Nixon visited China and Russia in 1972. There respondents assigned probabilities to fifteen possible outcomes of Nixon's diplomatic initiatives. Would Mao Zedong agree to meet with Nixon? Might the United States grant diplomatic recognition to China?...
>
> After Nixon's return ... Fischhoff and Beyth asked the same people to recall the probability that they had originally assigned to the fifteen possible outcomes ... If an event had actually occurred, people exaggerated the probability they had assigned to it earlier. If the possible event had not come to pass, the participants erroneously recalled that they had always considered it unlikely.

Fischhoff (1975) conducted a number of additional studies demonstrating the same result. In discussing these he observes:

> Reporting an outcome's occurrence consistently increases its perceived likelihood and alters the judged relevance of data describing the situation preceding the event ...
>
> Subjects are either unaware of outcome knowledge having an effect on their perception or, if aware, they are unable to ignore or rescind that effect ...
>
> It might be asked whether the failure to empathize with ourselves in a more ignorant state is not paralleled by a failure to empathize with outcome-ignorant others. How well people manage to reconstruct the perception that others had before the occurrence of some event is a critical question for historians ...
>
> ... undiagnosed creeping determinism not only biases people's impressions of what they would have known without outcome knowledge, but also their impressions of what they themselves or others actually *did* know in foresight.

Summarizing the results from the range of studies, he concludes:

> In the short run, failure to ignore outcome knowledge holds substantial benefits. It is quite flattering to believe, or lead others to believe, that we would have known all along what we could only have known with outcome knowledge ...
>
> When we attempt to understand past events, we implicitly test the hypothesis or rules we use to interpret and anticipate the world around us. If, in hindsight we systematically underestimate the surprises which the past held and holds for us, we are subjecting those hypotheses to inordinately weak tests and, presumably, finding little reason to change them. Thus, the very outcome knowledge which gives us the feeling that we understand what the past was all about may prevent us from learning anything from it.

Fifteen years later, Hawkins and Hastie (1990) reviewed a range of subsequent studies, identified and explored a number of different mechanisms that might contribute to hindsight bias, and concluded that a "creeping determinism" mechanism "is the most common mechanism underlying observed hindsight bias." Drawing a conclusion very similar to that reached by Fischhoff, they write:

> For the theoretical psychologist, the most important implications of research on hindsight bias derive from the relation between hindsight and adaptive learning from experience. The three mechanisms that we believe are the primary sources of the bias – selective

memory, evidence evaluation, and evidence integration model – constitute the chief mechanisms for adaptive learning and proficient judgment in natural environments. In a sense, hindsight biases represent the dark side of successful learning and judgment.

As an informative exercise, the reader might start a practice of writing down their views on a range of issues, filing them away, and then, without looking at those previous notes, writing about the same issues some years later. A subsequent comparison of the two sets of notes can be *very* enlightening!

12.6 SCENARIOS AND SCENARIO THINKING[7]

When people and organizations want to think about the future, they often construct scenarios. For example, as noted in Chapter 8, the Intergovernmental Panel on Climate Change, the joint effort of the World Meteorological Organization (WMO) and United Nations Environment Program (UNEP) that produces massive reviews of the state of knowledge about climate change (IPCC, 1995, 2001, 2007), has made extensive use of scenarios (Nakićenović et al., 2000; Moss et al., 2010; van Vuuren et al., 2011) as a vehicle to assess possible future emissions of carbon dioxide and other greenhouse gases. Many others, including a number of major oil companies such as Shell Oil, have made extensive use of scenarios.[8]

Many of these scenarios involve complex "story lines" that lay out, often in elaborate detail, how a specific future may unfold. In most cases, the developers of scenarios insist that no probability should be attached to the scenarios they develop; rather, these should be used to help expand people's thinking.

Whether and how well scenarios, especially detailed ones, can do this is entirely unclear. The more detail that one adds to a story line, the lower the probability that that specific future will come to pass. However, when people judge the probability of a story, their assessment often goes up as more detail is added.

The problem is clearly illustrated in a study conducted by Slovic et al. (1976) in which subjects were given the personality sketch of a student named Tom W., identical to the one quoted above. In a first treatment, subjects were asked to assess the probability that "Tom W. will select journalism as his college major." In a second treatment, subjects were asked what is the probability that "Tom W. will select journalism as his college major but become unhappy with his choice?" Finally, in a third treatment, subjects were asked what is the probability that "Tom W. will select journalism as his college major but become unhappy with his choice and switch to engineering?"

Since each of the latter cases is a *subset* of the earlier cases, the assessed probabilities should *decline* as more and more details are added. In fact, the

[7] Portions of the text in this section are reworked from Morgan and Keith (2008).

[8] For details, see www.shell.com/global/future-energy/scenarios.html as well as http://en.wikipedia.org/wiki/Scenario_planning.

reverse was found. The assessed probabilities *grew* from 0.21 for the simplest case to 0.39 and then to 0.40 for the most detailed "story line."

Lest one conclude that this dismaying result is the consequence of some unique detail of the study design, Tversky and Kahneman (1983) ran a whole series of studies in which they tried various manipulations designed to induce respondents to give responses that did not reflect such a "conjunction fallacy." They began with some "indirect and subtle" questions in which subjects were asked to judge the probability of simple and compound events. They "expected that even naive respondents would notice the repetition of some attributes, alone and in conjunction with others, and that they would apply the conjunction rule and rank the conjunction below its constituents. This expectation was violated, not only by statistically naive undergraduates, but even by highly sophisticated respondents." They then ran a series of studies that made the conjunction more and more obvious. In the simplest formulation, they provided a personality sketch of a woman named Linda and then asked respondents to indicate which of the following two statements was more likely to be true:

"Linda is a bank teller."
"Linda is a bank teller and is active in the feminist movement."

Eighty-five percent of respondents chose the latter statement as more probable! Subsequent manipulations designed to explain and focus respondents' attention on the conjunction fallacy never managed to reduce the fraction of wrong answers below 56 percent.

Tversky and Kahneman (1983) have demonstrated similar problems among several expert groups, such as physicians engaged in making medical judgments about the relationship between symptoms and disease. Redelmeier et al. (1995) extended that work with physicians, to demonstrate similar findings in much greater detail. Fox and Birke (2002) have conducted detailed studies in which they asked lawyers to make judgments about trial outcomes, and again obtained similar results. Tversky and Kahneman (1983) have demonstrated similar findings in studies involving scenarios about the future. For example, subjects found the conjunction of an earthquake and a flood in California in which 1000 people drown some time in 1983 roughly 40 percent more probable than the simpler case of a flood somewhere in North America in which 1000 people drown some time in 1983.

Particularly telling for those who propose the use of scenarios in forecasting, Tversky and Kahneman (1983) conducted studies with 115 participants at the July 1982 Second International Congress on Forecasting in which they repeatedly found violations of the conjunction rule in probabilistic judgments involving comparisons between simple and compound forecasts. For example, the probability of "a 30% drop in the consumption of oil in the USA in 1983" was judged to be 0.22 while the probability of "a dramatic increase in oil prices and a 30% drop in the consumption of oil in the USA in 1983" was judged to be 0.36.

While I quoted Gregory (2001) in Chapter 8, his argument is worth repeating here:

> Practitioners can find several advantages in using scenarios. First, they can use scenarios to enhance a person's or group's expectancies that an event will occur. This can be useful for gaining acceptance of a forecast ... Second, scenarios can be used as a means of decreasing existing expectancies ... Third ... scenarios can produce greater commitment in the clients to taking actions described in them.

Gregory supports these claims by citing much of the same literature that we have described above. Surreptitiously shaping someone's views through such manipulation may be standard practice in political or advertising settings. In my view, it is *not* appropriate in policy analysis, where the objective should be to give analysts, planners, and decision makers balanced and unbiased assessments on which to base their decisions. I read Gregory's enthusiastic endorsement of the advantages of using one or a few detailed scenarios as a compelling argument against their use in policy analysis.

The largely separate literature on war gaming also suggests problems that may arise from the use of detailed scenarios (Bracken, 1977; Brewer and Shubik, 1979; Goldberg et al., 1990). There has long been a concern that participants in such games can over-generalize from the specific story line developed and played in the game. Bracken (1977) performed a most interesting analysis of ways in which the use of scenarios in strategic war gaming has led to unintended and sometimes undesirable consequences. He analyzed a series of military war games and identified examples of what he terms "diverting, learning, and suppression." By diverting, he means a process by which war gaming, and the often-detailed scenarios on which such games are based, may divert attention from key elements that deserve attention. Learning refers not just to the learning that specific participants take from the experience but also to a collective view that may emerge, often quite indirectly and unconsciously, among decision makers. While Bracken identifies some instances in which this has been a very positive development, he also identifies a number of cases in which the consequences were extremely negative, noting in a subsequent paper that "gaming and simulation can also reinforce biases and narrow the span of an organization's attention" (Bracken, 1990). Finally, on suppression, Bracken (1977) notes:

> There is a well-known tendency for individuals to suppress both unpleasant memories and future possibilities ... The extension from individual suppression to group and, in some instances, even organizational suppression is a surprisingly easy step ... It is convenient to consider two forms of suppression ... outcomes that for some reason are undesirable may be suppressed and this can be termed suppression by commission. Alternatively, suppression may occur by omission. The omission of problem scenarios or strategies ... can be a convenient method for avoiding unpleasant eventualism.

There is clearly a risk of suppression occurring when scenarios for use in energy, climate, or similar analyses are constructed in a public setting in which future outcomes such as negative economic development in some regions, pandemics, or regional nuclear war are excluded because they are politically unacceptable.

READING 12.3

Chapter 7 in Robyn M. Dawes, *Rational Choice in an Uncertain World,* Harcourt Brace Jovanovich, 346pp., 1988, *OR*, if you cannot find a copy of the older Dawes book, chapter 7 in Reid Hastie and Robyn M. Dawes, *Rational Choice in an Uncertain World,* Sage, 372pp., 2001. As noted above, I prefer the earlier Dawes book because it is more concise.

DISCUSSION QUESTIONS FOR READING 12.3

- What cognitive heuristic makes a long multi-condition scenario seem more likely than one consisting of just one or two conditions?
- How could one use a Venn diagram to illustrate the erroneous assessments of probability that can result from scenario thinking?
- What is the nature of Dawes' argument with respect to "scenarios about ourselves"?

12.7 (NOT) HONORING SUNK COSTS

The expression "What's done is done" dates back to the early thirteenth century. Wikipedia tells us that the expression derives from an earlier French expression. Other languages have similar sayings such as "Et Hanaaseh Ein Lehashiv" in Hebrew and "A lo hecho, pecho" in Spanish.[9]

In one way or another, such aphorisms remind us that in deciding how to proceed now and in the future, you should *not* consider investments that have already been made or costs already incurred but only the resources you have and the options you face at the moment of decision.[10] Dawes (1988) provides a simple but compelling example:

> You and your companion have driven half-way to a resort. Responding to a reduced-rate advertisement, you have made a nonrefundable $100 deposit to spend the weekend there. Both you and your companion feel slightly bad physically and out of sorts psychologically. *Your assessment of the situation is that you and your companion would have a much more pleasurable weekend at home.* Your companion says it is "too bad" you have reserved the room because you both would much rather spend the time at home, but you can't afford to waste $100. You agree. Further, you both agree that given the way you both feel, it is extraordinarily unlikely you will have a better time at the

[9] http://en.wikipedia.org/wiki/What's_done_is_done.

[10] Of course, some of those past investments may have created the resources and the options that you have today. Those, and the opportunities they offer, should be considered. What should not be considered is the magnitude of the investments made to create them.

resort than you would at home. Do you drive on or turn back? If you drive on, you are behaving as if you prefer paying $100 to be where you don't want to be than to be where you want to be.

... The moment you paid the $100 your net assets decreased by $100. That decrease occurred several days before your drive half-way to the resort. Is the fact that your net assets have decreased by $100 sufficient reason for deciding to spend the weekend at a place you don't want to be?

... If the $100 could be refunded, you would certainly return home ... What does that imply? Once the deposit was made, you had a certain net asset level. Now, if you could only get a refund and thereby *increase* your net assets by $100, you would be willing to do what you prefer to do – otherwise [you will] not. That's rational? ... The $100 *you have already paid* is technically termed a *sunk cost*. Rationally, sunk costs *should not affect decisions about the future*.

Because choices made today can only influence the future, and one has no control today over what has already happened, in making choices today rational decision makers should consider their present preferences and the assets and opportunities they have available at the time of their decision. Summarizing, Dawes (1988) notes that in making such decisions "the past is relevant only insofar as it provides information about possible and probable futures."

Many people do honor sunk costs. For example, they open separate "mental accounts" for different issues rather than thinking in terms of total net assets (see Section 12.2). Thus, it is common in policy circles to be accused of being a "flip-flopper" if one does not stick with a past position, even though it no longer makes sense. Of course, the possibility that this may occur is a *future* event. If it is not likely to be easy to explain the change, it may make sense to include this fact in one's assessment of the choice options available today.

READING 12.4

Chapter 2 in Robyn M. Dawes, *Rational Choice in an Uncertain World,* Harcourt Brace Jovanovich, 346pp., 1988, *OR*, if you cannot find a copy of the older Dawes book, chapter 2, sections 2.5 and 2.6, in Reid Hastie and Robyn M. Dawes, *Rational Choice in an Uncertain World*, Sage, 372pp., 2001. As noted above, I prefer the earlier Dawes book because it is more concise.

DISCUSSION QUESTIONS FOR READING 12.4

- Why does Dawes argue that it is not rational to honor sunk costs?
- Past investments can create opportunities for future choice. Is Dawes arguing that these opportunities should be ignored?

12.8 ORDER EFFECTS IN SEARCH

Faced with a choice among a number of options, each with different values across a set of attributes, a rational utility-maximizing decision maker reviews them all and chooses the one that is best. In doing that, the decision maker's choice should not be affected by the order in which different options, or their attributes, are considered. By now the reader should have concluded that, in the real world, such decision makers do not exist,[11] and so should be able to guess that the order in which different options, or their attributes, are considered, and what they are compared to (i.e., how the choice is "framed"), will indeed have a significant impact on a decision maker's choices.

In the context of organizational decision making (see Chapter 15), March and Simon (1958) have described an alternative search strategy based on "bounded rationality" that they call "satisficing." They note that such a strategy produces satisfactory (as opposed to optimal) results if "(1) there exists a set of criteria that describes minimally satisfactory alternatives, and (2) the alternative in question meets or exceeds these criteria." We will return to a more extended discussion of satisficing in Chapter 15. Here, we limit the discussion to a brief review of a couple of empirical studies of difficulties that arise when people try to make choices among multiple options, each of which may involve several attributes.

An experimental illustration of how the order in which options are presented influences choice was reported by Nisbett and Wilson (1977). They describe two studies that showed clearly a position effect in choice among similar consumer goods. They write:

> In both studies, conducted in commercial establishments under the guise of a consumer survey, passersby were invited to evaluate articles of clothing – four different nightgowns in one study (378 subjects) and four identical pairs of nylon stockings in the other (52 subjects). Subjects were asked to say which article of clothing was the best quality and, when they announced a choice, were asked why they had chosen the article they had. There was a pronounced left-to-right position effect, such that the right-most object in the array was heavily overchosen. For the stockings, the effect was quite large, with the right-most stockings being preferred over the left-most by a factor of almost four to one.

However, when subjects were asked to explain the basis of their choice, "no subject ever mentioned spontaneously the position of the article in the array. And, when asked directly about a possible effect of the position of the article, virtually all subjects denied it, usually with a worried glance at the interviewer suggesting that they felt either that they had misunderstood the question or were dealing with a madman" (Nisbett and Wilson, 1977).

Huber and Puto (1983) have demonstrated that adding an additional option to a choice set (a decoy) that is inferior to one of the options can move the choice from one of the superior options to another, depending on the attributes of the decoy. They summarize:

[11] Unless, of course, they employ analytical support.

> What happens to the share of choices each item receives when the choice set boundaries are extended by adding a new item that is extremely good on one dimension but poor on the others? First, there is a substitution effect whereby the new item takes choice share mainly from similar items in the set. Second, there is an attraction effect resulting in a general shift of preference toward the added item. Experimental studies show that choice patterns conflict with current theoretical and common-sense ideas about the effect of added alternatives on choice.

Such decoy effects are widely employed in marketing, and are also employed in situations involving social or political choice. These effects have much in common with the more general issue of framing effects discussed above. Dawes (1988, pp. 61–62) quotes at length an example in which Senator Warren Magnuson reversed a Senate vote that looked sure to reject an amendment, not by listing all the attributes, but by recasting the choice in terms of presidential versus congressional prerogative.

Recognizing that in many real-world circumstances it is impossible to do exhaustive systematic comparison of alternatives, both because of time constraints and because of cognitive limitations, Dawes (1988) outlines a number of strategies that one can use to get close to a good outcome when dealing with a large search space. One, termed "elimination by aspect," was first proposed by Tversky (1972). Under this procedure, one ranks the aspects or attributes from most to least desirable. Then, options that do poorly on the most important attribute are discarded, after which options that don't do well on the next most important attribute are discarded, and so on. Dawes (1988) summarizes:

> If the aspects are considered in the same order as their desirability, this form of bounded rationality results in reasonably good choice – although it involves no compensatory (weighting) mechanisms. If the aspects are chosen probabilistically in proportion to their importance (one of Tversky's "models"), the procedure is somewhat less satisficing. If they are chosen ad hoc on the basis of the ease with which they "come to mind" it is a decidedly flawed procedure.

READING 12.5

Chapter 4 in Robyn M. Dawes, *Rational Choice in an Uncertain World,* Harcourt Brace Jovanovich, 346pp., 1988, *OR*, if you cannot find a copy of the older Dawes book, chapter 11 in Reid Hastie and Robyn M. Dawes, *Rational Choice in an Uncertain World*, Sage, 372pp., 2001. As noted above, I prefer the earlier Dawes book because it is more concise.

DISCUSSION QUESTIONS FOR READING 12.5

- What are some of the consequences that Dawes argues can arise as a result of "order effects"?
- What simple strategies does Dawes recommend in an effort to minimize the impact of order effects?

12.9 THE POWER OF SIMPLE LINEAR MODELS

We like to think that in making complex choices among options that involve several different attributes we are able to keep all those attributes present in our mind and make effective holistic judgments. However, there is compelling evidence that under most circumstances, and for most choices, we are unable to do this, unless we employ formal analytical methods of the sort discussed in Chapter 6.

Arguing for the use of a statistical analytical approach, Dawes et al. (1989) write:

> In the clinical method the decision-maker combines or processes information in his or her head. In the actuarial or statistical method the human judge is eliminated and conclusions rest solely on empirically established relations between data and the condition or event of interest. A life insurance agent uses the clinical method if data on risk factors are combined through personal judgment. The agent uses the actuarial method if data are entered into a formula, or tables and charts that contain empirical information relating these background data to life expectancy.

Dawes (1979, 1989, 2002) has reviewed the evidence repeatedly and argues that rather than try to make holistic judgments about things like which students to admit to a graduate program, whether to release a prisoner on parole, or what treatment to prescribe to a psychiatric patient, better outcomes can almost always be achieved if one identifies a set of relevant indicator measures, weights them, and adds up the results. In summary, Dawes (1979) explains:

> Proper linear models are those in which predictor variables are given weights in such a way that the resulting linear composite optimally predicts some criterion of interest. Examples of proper linear models are standard regression analysis, discriminant function analysis, and ridge regression analysis. Research indicates that when a numerical criterion variable (e.g., graduate grade point average) is to be predicted from numerical predictor variables, proper linear models out-perform clinical intuition. Improper linear models are those in which the weights of the predictor variables are obtained by some non-optimal method; for example, they may be obtained on the basis of intuition, derived from simulating a clinical judge's predictions, or set to be equal.

Such improper linear models are superior to clinical intuition when predicting a numerical criterion from numerical predictors. In fact, unit (i.e., equal) weighting is quite robust for making such predictions (Dawes, 1979).

Indeed, even weights that are randomly assigned (but with the correct sign) can do better than most clinical (i.e., holistic) judgments. While people are good at observing their environment (i.e., assessing some of the relevant measures) they are poor at combining those measures into a summary judgment.

Most people find these claims counterintuitive. However, in the following reading, Dawes (1988) has provided a good qualitative explanation of why these results hold.

READING 12.6

Chapter 10 in Robyn M. Dawes, *Rational Choice in an Uncertain World*, Harcourt Brace Jovanovich, 346pp., 1988, *OR*, if you cannot find a copy of the older Dawes book, chapter 3, sections 3.3–3.6, in Reid Hastie and Robyn M. Dawes, *Rational Choice in an Uncertain World*, Sage, 372pp., 2001. As noted above, I prefer the earlier Dawes book because it is more concise.

DISCUSSION QUESTIONS FOR READING 12.6

- What is Dawes' basic argument about the power of simple linear models?
- Dawes reports that many professionals have been extremely slow to accept the implications of the findings in this literature. Why might that be?
- What implications, if any, do you believe these findings might have for those performing analysis based on MAUT (see Chapter 6)?

12.10 INDIVIDUAL AND SOCIAL DILEMMAS

The prisoner's dilemma is a classic two-person game that is the simplest example of a wide set of individual and social dilemmas that have been used in the study of human decision making. Here is the description of the basic game from Wikipedia:

> Two members of a criminal gang are arrested and imprisoned. Each prisoner is in solitary confinement with no means of speaking to or exchanging messages with the other. The prosecutors do not have enough evidence to convict the pair on the principal charge. They hope to get both sentenced to a year in prison on a lesser charge. Simultaneously, the prosecutors offer each prisoner a Faustian bargain. Each prisoner is given the opportunity either to: betray the other by testifying that the other committed the crime, or to cooperate with the other by remaining silent. Here is the offer:
>
> - If A and B each betray the other, each of them serves 2 years in prison
> - If A betrays B but B remains silent, A will be set free and B will serve 3 years in prison (and vice versa)
> - If A and B both remain silent, both of them will only serve 1 year in prison (on the lesser charge).

The simple "payout matrix" for this game is shown in Figure 12.6. Clearly, the "dominating strategy" is for both players to opt for strategy two.

Variations of this simple two-dimensional game have been widely used to study a variety of behavioral issues including social comparison (McClintock and McNeel, 1966), the evolution of cooperation (Axelrod, 2006), and a variety of other behaviors (Dawes, 1980).

	Prisoner B stays silent (i.e., cooperates)	Prisoner B betrays (i.e., defects)
Prisoner A stays silent (i.e., cooperates)	Each serves one year	A gets 3 years B goes free
Prisoner A betrays (i.e., defects)	A goes free B gets 3 years	Each serves 3 years

FIGURE 12.6. Payout matrix for the simple two-player prisoner's dilemma.

More generally Dawes (1980) explains:

> Interest in social dilemmas – particularly those resulting from overpopulation, resource depletion, and pollution – has grown dramatically in the past 10 years ... Such dilemmas are defined by two simple properties: (a) each individual receives a higher payoff for a socially defecting choice (e.g., having additional children, using all the energy available, polluting his or her neighbors) than for a socially cooperative choice, no matter what the other individuals in society do, but (b) all individuals are better off if all cooperate than if all defect. While many thinkers have simply pointed out that our most pressing societal problems result from such dilemmas, most have addressed themselves to the question of how to get people to cooperate. Answers have ranged from imposition of a dictatorship (Leviathan) to "mutual coercion mutually agreed upon," to appeals to conscience.

Dawes (1980) has demonstrated that behavior is very different in repeat play games, where if a player defects they can expect retaliation in subsequent plays.

We will return to related topics in Chapter 15 when we explore the work of Thomas Schelling (1978/2006) on micro motives and macro behavior and work by Raiffa (1982, 2002) on negotiation.

12.11 WRAPPING UP

This chapter has only scratched the surface in describing important scientific understanding about human mental processes for perception, memory, and decision making. As Dawes (1988) has summarized: "Mental processes that systematically lead us to make irrational decisions include honoring sunk costs, being swayed by framing and grouping effects, systematically misjudging probabilities on the basis of representativeness or availability, and thinking in scenario terms." None of these issues arises because people are lazy or pernicious. Instead, they are the result of the way in which human cognitive processes function. It is essential that practitioners in policy analysis develop an understanding of these processes so that they can factor them into the recommendations that they make, and the communications that they develop.

SUGGESTED RESOURCES TO LEARN MORE ABOUT HUMAN MENTAL PROCESSES

An easy way to learn more about many of the ideas discussed in this chapter is to read from two excellent edited collections of papers:

- Daniel Kahneman, Paul Slovic, and Amos Tversky, *Judgment under Uncertainty: Heuristics and Biases*, Cambridge University Press, 555pp., 1982.
- Daniel Kahneman and Amos Tversky, *Choices, Value and Frames*, Cambridge University Press, 840pp., 2000.

A more popular treatment of much of the same material can be found in:

- Daniel Kahneman, *Thinking Fast and Slow*, Farrar, Straus and Giroux, 499pp., 2011.

ANSWERS TO THE CANAL QUESTIONS

If you are like most people (and you have not cheated), in a number of cases the actual length will lie outside of the 90 percent confidence intervals that you estimated, that is, your estimates were overconfident.

Canal	Length in miles	Length in kilometers
1. Cape Cod	17.5	28.2
2. Houston Ship Channel	50.6	81.4
3. Panama Canal	50.7	81.6
4. Soo Canal	1.3	2.1
5. Suez Canal	101	163
6. Welland Canal	27	43

Of course, in this case since Figure 12.3 follows a section heading that reads "ubiquitous overconfidence," perhaps you took the hint and spread your distribution out more than you might have without that hint.

REFERENCES

Axelrod, R.M. (2006). *The Evolution of Cooperation*, Basic Books, 241pp.

Bracken, P. (1977). "Unintended Consequences of Strategic Gaming," *Simulation and Gaming*, *8*, pp. 283–318.

(1990). "Gaming in Hierarchical Defense Organizations," in A.C. Goldberg, D. van Opstal, and J.H. Barkley (eds.), *Avoiding the Brink: Theory and Practice in Crisis Management*, Brassey's, 138pp.

Brewer, G.D. and M. Shubik (1979). *The War Game: A Critique of Military Problem Solving*, Harvard University Press, 385pp.

Dawes, R.M. (1979). "The Robust Beauty of Improper Linear Models in Decision Making," *American psychologist*, *34*(7), pp. 571–582.

(1980). "Social Dilemmas," *Annual Review of Psychology*, *31*, pp. 169–193.

(1988). *Rational Choice in an Uncertain World*, Harcourt Brace Jovanovich, 346pp.

(2002). "The Ethics of Using or Not Using Statistical Prediction Rules in Psychological Practice and Related Consulting Activities," *Philosophy of Science*, *69*(S3), S178–S184.
Dawes, R.M., D. Faust, and P.E. Meehl (1989). "Clinical Versus Actuarial Judgment," *Science*, *243*, pp. 1668–1674.
DeGroot, M. (1965). *Thought and Choice in Chess*, Basic Books, 463pp.
Fischhoff, B. (1975). "Hindsight ≠ Foresight: The Effect of Outcome Knowledge on Judgment under Uncertainty," *Journal of Experimental Psychology*, *1*, pp. 288–299.
(2010). "Judgment and Decision Making," *WIREs Cognitive Science*, *1*(5), pp. 724–735.
Fox, C.R. and R. Birke (2002). "Forecasting Trial Outcomes: Lawyers Assign Higher Probability to Possibilities That Are Described in Greater Detail," *Law and Human Behavior*, *26*, pp. 159–173.
Goldberg, A.C., D. van Opstal, and J.H. Barkley (eds.) (1990). *Avoiding the Brink: Theory and Practice in Crisis Management*, Brassey's, 138pp.
Gregory, W.L. (2001). "Scenarios and Acceptance of Forecasts," in J.S. Armstrong (ed.), *Principles of Forecasting: A Handbook for Researchers and Practitioners*, Kluwer, 849pp.
Hastie, R. and R.M. Dawes (2001). *Rational Choice in an Uncertain World*, Sage, 372pp.
Hawkins, S.A. and R. Hastie (1990). "Hindsight: Biased Judgments of Past Events after the Outcome Is Known," *Psychological Bulletin*, *107*, pp. 311–327.
Henrion, M. and B. Fischhoff (1986). "Assessing Uncertainty in Physical Constants," *American Journal of Physics*, *54*(9), pp. 791–798.
Huber, J. and C. Puto (1983). "Market Boundaries and Product Choice: Illustrating Attraction and Substitution Effects," *Journal of Consumer Research*, *10*, pp. 31–44.
IPCC (Intergovernmental Panel on Climate Change) (1995). *Climate Change 1995*. Available at: www.ipcc.ch.
(2001). *Climate Change 2001*. Available at: www.ipcc.ch.
(2007). *Climate Change 2007*. Available at: www.ipcc.ch.
Kahneman, D. (2011). *Thinking Fast and Slow*, Farrar, Straus and Giroux, 499pp.
Kahneman, D., P. Slovic, and A. Tversky (1982). *Judgment under Uncertainty: Heuristics and Biases*, Cambridge University Press, 555pp.
Kahneman, D. and A. Tversky (1973). "On the Psychology of Prediction," *Psychological Review*, *80*, pp. 237–251.
(2000). *Choices, Value and Frames*, Cambridge University Press, 840pp.
Keysar, B., S.K. Hayakawa, and S.G. An (2012). "The Foreign Language Effect: Thinking in a Foreign Tongue Reduces Decision Biases," *Psychological Science*, *23*, pp. 661–668.
Lichtenstein, S., B. Fischhoff, and L.D. Phillips (1982). "Calibration of Probabilities: The State of the Art to 1980," in D. Kahneman, P. Slovic, and A. Tversky (eds.), *Judgment under Uncertainty: Heuristics and Biases*, Cambridge University Press, pp. 306–334.
Lichtenstein, S., P. Slovic, B. Fischhoff, M. Layman, and B. Combs (1978). "Judged Frequency of Lethal Events," *Journal of Experimental Psychology: Human Learning and Memory*, *4*(6), pp. 551–578.
Loewenstein, G.F. (1996). "Out of Control: Visceral Influences on Behavior," *Organizational Behavior and Human Decision Processes*, *65*(3), 272–292.
Loewenstein, G.F., E.U. Weber, C.K. Hsee, and E.S. Welch (2001). "Risk as Feelings," *Psychological Bulletin*, *127*(2), pp. 267–286.
McClintock, C.G. and S.P. McNeel (1966). "Reward Level and Game Playing Behavior," *Journal of Conflict Resolution*, *10*(1), pp. 98–102.

Manski, C.F. (2013). *Public Policy in an Uncertain World: Analysis and Decisions*, Harvard University Press, 199pp.

March, J.G. and H.S. Simon (1958). *Organizations*, Wiley, 262pp.

Morgan, M.G. with H. Dowlatabadi, M. Henrion, D. Keith, R. Lempert, S. McBride, M. Small, and T. Wilbanks (2009). *Best Practice Approaches for Characterizing, Communicating, and Incorporating Scientific Uncertainty in Climate Decision Making*, Synthesis and Assessment Product 5.2, report by the U.S. Climate Change Science Program and the Subcommittee on Global Change Research, 89pp.

Morgan, M.G. and M. Henrion (1990). *Uncertainty: A Guide to Dealing with Uncertainty in Quantitative Risk and Policy Analysis*, Cambridge University Press, 332pp.

Morgan, M.G. and D.W. Keith (2008). "Improving the Way We Think about Projecting Future Energy Use and Emissions of Carbon Dioxide," *Climatic Change*, *90*, pp. 198–215.

Moss, R., J.A. Edmonds, K.A. Hibbard et al. (2010). "The Next Generation of Scenarios for Climate Change Research and Assessment," *Nature*, *463*, pp. 747–756.

Nakićenović, N. and R. Swart (2000). *Special Report on Emissions Scenarios: A Special Report of Working Group III of the Intergovernmental Panel on Climate Change*, Cambridge University Press, 599pp. Available at: www.ipcc.ch/ipccreports/sres/emission/index.php?idp=0.

Nisbett, R.E. and T.D. Wilson (1977). "Telling More Than We Can Know: Verbal Reports on Mental Processes," *Psychological Review*, *84*, pp. 231–259.

Raiffa, H. (1982). *The Art and Science of Negotiation*, Harvard University Press, 373pp.

with J. Richardson and D. Metcalfe (2002). *Negotiation Analysis*, Harvard University Press, 548pp.

Redelmeier, D.A., D.J. Koehler, V. Liberman, and A. Tversky (1995). "Probability Judgment in Medicine: Discounting Unspecified Possibilities," *Medical Decision Making*, *15*, pp. 227–230.

Schelling, T.C. (1978, 2006). *Micromotives and Macro Behavior*, W.W. Norton and Co., 252pp. in 1978, 270pp. in 2006.

Sjöberg, L. (2006). "Will the Real Meaning of Affect Please Stand up?" *Journal of Risk Research*, *9*(2), pp. 101–108.

Slovic, P., M.L. Finucane, E. Peters, and D.G. MacGregor (2004). "Risk as Analysis and Risk as Feelings: Some Thoughts about Affect, Reason, Risk and Rationality," *Risk Analysis*, *24*(2), pp. 311–322.

Slovic, P., B. Fischhoff, and S. Lichtenstein (1976). "Cognitive Processes and Societal Risk Taking," in J.S. Carroll and J.W. Payne (eds.), *Cognition and Social Behavior*, Halsted Press Division of Wiley, pp. 7–36.

Tversky, A. (1972). "Elimination by Aspects: A Theory of Choice," *Psychological Review*, *79*, pp. 281–299.

Tversky, A. and D. Kahneman (1974). "Judgment under Uncertainty: Heuristics and Biases," *Science*, *185*(4157), pp. 1124–1131.

(1981). "The Framing of Decisions and the Psychology of Choice," *Science*, *211*, pp. 453–458.

(1983). "Extensional versus Intuitive Reasoning: The Conjunction Fallacy in Probability Judgment," *Psychological Review*, *90*, pp. 293–315.

van Vuuren, D.P., J. Edmonds, M. Kainuma et al. (2011). "The Representative Concentration Pathways: An Overview," *Climatic Change*, *109*, pp. 5–31.

Wardman, J.K. (2006). "Toward a Critical Discourse on Affect and Risk Perception," *Journal of Risk Research*, *9*(2), pp. 109–124.

13

Risk Perception and Risk Ranking

While many of the technologies used in modern society provide great benefits, they also create hazards. Understanding the nature and magnitude of the resulting risks in quantitative terms is important. But if risk management and regulation are to be effective, it is important that decision makers also understand how people perceive the risks created by such hazards.

In the 1960s, most experts characterized the risk created by some hazardous activity or technology in terms of the expected number of deaths or injuries. In its classic study of the risks of nuclear power, the Rasmussen Report (WASH-1400, 1975) elaborated this representation, arguing that risk events that lead to large numbers of deaths occurred much less frequently than those that caused only a small number of deaths. To the results shown in Figure 10.4, the authors added similar curves for a variety of hazards as shown in Figure 13.1. Having made this comparison, the implicit argument was that since society accepts these other, much larger risks, it should obviously accept nuclear power. For many years, a more individually focused comparison that nuclear proponents often made was with the risk of contracting cancer from eating peanut butter (which contains trace amounts of aflatoxin).[1] It was common to argue that the risk of living five miles from nuclear plants for 50 years is the same as traveling ten miles by bicycle or eating 40 tablespoons of peanut butter and then to argue, if you don't worry about going ten miles on a bicycle or eating peanut butter, then you also shouldn't worry about the risks from nuclear power plants.

Despite the fact that this analysis suggested that the risk of nuclear power was several orders of magnitude lower than almost any other risk faced by

[1] A Web search of nuclear power and peanut butter will yield dozens of examples. See, for example, *DOE Handbook General Employee Radiological Training*, DOE-HDBK-1131-98, December 2007, 27pp. Available at: http://energy.gov/sites/prod/files/2013/07/f2/hdbk1131-98reaffirm.pdf. Probably as a result of research in risk perception, more recent DOE documents have dropped the peanut butter comparison.

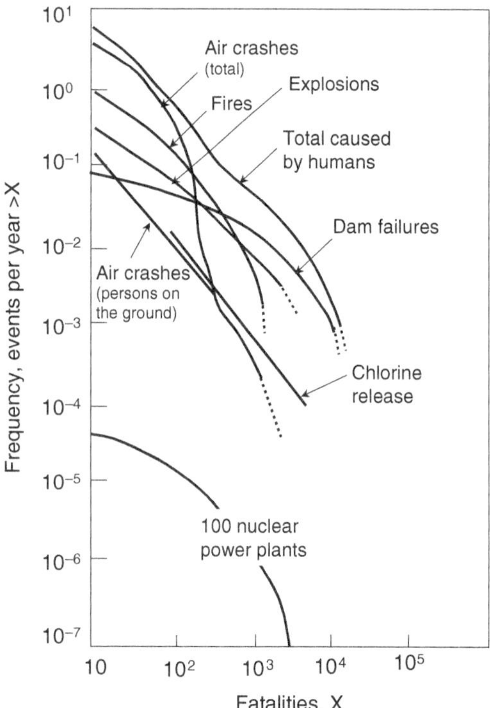

FIGURE 13.1. Estimates of the frequency of accidents as a function of the number of deaths they produce. This figure was prepared for the Rasmussen Reactor Safety Study (WASH-1400, 1975), which used it to suggest that nuclear power should be socially acceptable because its "risks" lay well below virtually all other potential major causes of deaths caused by humans. Redrawn from WASH-1400.

modern society, nuclear engineers were dismayed that such arguments did not appear to assuage public fears.

13.1 STARR ON ACCEPTABLE RISK

Puzzled by the lack of public acceptance, nuclear engineer Chauncey Starr published a set of back-of-the-envelope analyses in *Science* in which he argued that the general public had a very different willingness to accept risks depending on whether they were voluntary or involuntary (Starr, 1969).[2] Assuming that the benefit associated with a risky activity could be approximated by the amount that society or individuals spent to engage in the activity, Starr summarized this argument in Figure 13.2. In the same paper, Starr went on to advance a number of other hypotheses about the social acceptability of risks.

[2] At the time, Starr was Dean of Engineering and Applied Science at the University of California Los Angeles. Shortly thereafter he became the founding president of the Electric Power Research Institute (EPRI).

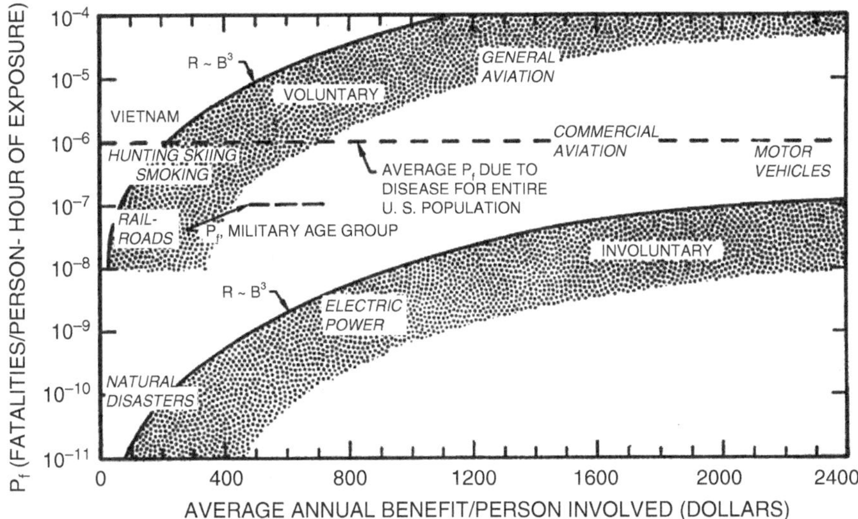

FIGURE 13.2. This plot reports the results of a set of back-of-the-envelope calculations that Starr (1969) used in order to argue that, for a given level of risk, people are willing to voluntarily assume risks that are about three orders of magnitude higher than the risks they will accept on an involuntary basis. Subsequent empirical studies by psychologists demonstrated that, while several different attributes of a risk factored in determining its acceptability, the voluntary/involuntary distinction is probably not the most important of those. From Starr (1969). Reprinted with permission from AAAS.

READING 13.1

Chauncey Starr, "Social Benefits versus Technological Risk," *Science*, *165*, pp. 1232–1238, 1969.

Abstract: In this article I offer an approach for establishing a quantitative measure of benefit relative to cost for an important element in our spectrum of social values – specifically, for accidental deaths arising from technological developments in public use. The analysis is based on two assumptions. The first is that historical national accident records are adequate for revealing consistent patterns of fatalities in the public use of technology. (That this may not always be so is evidenced by the paucity of data relating to the effects of environmental pollution.) The second assumption is that such historically revealed social preferences and costs are sufficiently enduring to permit their use for predictive purposes. In the absence of economic or sociological theory, which might give better results, this empirical approach provides some interesting insights into accepted social values relative to personal risk. Because this methodology is based on historical data, it does not serve to distinguish what is "best" for society from what is "traditionally acceptable."

DISCUSSION QUESTIONS FOR READING 13.1

- Starr uses the product P*Q as an estimate of social benefit. What are the limitations of that assumption?

- What other attributes of a risk might be correlated with whether it is voluntary or involuntary?

HOMEWORK

Check the robustness of the conclusions drawn in the Starr paper by:

1. Choosing one or two risks not included in Figure 13.2, finding the necessary data, and doing a set of calculations to add this point to Figure 13.2. As you do this, recall the issues addressed in Chapter 7. In addition, do the best job you can of estimating the *uncertainty* associated with your point(s). Make a copy of Figure 13.2 and add your new point(s) and the associated uncertainty bars. In writing up your work, explain what you did and cite the references you used. Do the results support or contradict the argument advanced by Starr?
2. Performing any other "validating calculation" that you can think of to check the robustness of one of the other arguments about risks that Starr advances in his paper.

Write up these two calculations along with a brief summary evaluation. Explain your calculations and reference the sources you used in your write-up.

You may find some of the numbers you need in the *Statistical Abstract of the US* and in various almanacs or in *Accident Facts*. For a more international perspective, see the statistical reports of the World Health Organization. If you choose some form of cancer, see CDC's Interactive Cancer Atlas. Although many of the numbers are now somewhat out of date, you might get useful ideas from Richard Wilson (1979); chapter 7 in Wilson and Crouch (1982).

13.2 PUBLIC ASSESSMENT OF CAUSES OF DEATH

At about the same time that Starr was getting interested in risk perception, three psychologists at Decision Research in Eugene, Oregon were beginning to also think about these issues. Paul Slovic, Baruch Fischhoff, and Sarah Lichtenstein were not comfortable with the simple voluntary/involuntary arguments Starr had advanced. They embarked on a series of empirical studies using subjects such as students at the University of Oregon and members of the Oregon League of Women Voters. Their studies sought to learn how well laypeople are able to judge the number of deaths that are associated with a wide range of risks and what factors people find important in assessing the level of risk. In the first of a series of studies, they asked questions of the following form for a wide variety of pairs of hazards: "Considering the U.S. population as a whole, which is the more likely risk of death: emphysema or stroke? How many times more likely?"

Lichtenstein et al. (1978) found that when comparing pairs of risks, subjects were typically able to identify the one that yielded more annual deaths so long as the difference between the death rates was greater than about a factor of two. However, respondents did not do very well on assessing the ratios. For example, for a series of questions for which the true ratio was 1000 to 1, the average values of the answers to the individual questions ranged from less than 2 to 1 to roughly 5000 to 1.

Lichtenstein et al. found considerable scale compression in the estimates. The number of deaths assessed for very common causes of death was typically underestimated, while the number of deaths assessed for rare causes of death was systematically overestimated (see Figure 12.5A). They explained:

> We believe that when people estimate these likelihoods, they do so on the basis of a) how easy it is to *imagine* someone dying from such a cause, b) how many instances of such an event they can remember happening to someone they know, c) publicity about such events in the news media, or d) special features of the event that make it stand out in one's mind.

They also found that much of the fine structure in Figure 12.5A is not random, but can be reliably reproduced from study to study. Indeed, one of these replications was done by an early cohort of students in the graduate core course in Engineering and Public Policy at Carnegie Mellon University that led to this book (Engineering and Public Policy, 1983).

As noted in Chapter 12, in addition to being a classic illustration of the heuristic of availability, a second part of this study has also become one of the classic illustrations of the heuristic of anchoring and adjustment. In the initial study, people were told that there were 50,000 deaths a year from motor vehicle accidents.[3] In a repetition of the study, respondents were told there were 1000 deaths a year from electrocutions. As noted in Chapter 12, due to this lower anchor, the entire curve shifted down.

13.3 FACTORS THAT SHAPE RISK JUDGMENTS

While the work of Lichtenstein et al. (1978) demonstrated that people have a reasonable ability to assess the *relative* number of deaths associated with a variety of hazards, Slovic et al. (1980) also demonstrated that if people are asked to rank those same hazards in terms of how "risky" they are, one gets a rather different ordering. This difference arises because, as noted in Chapter 10, people view risk as a multi-attribute concept. While the number of deaths or injuries that are caused by a hazard do matter, a variety of other attributes (beyond just voluntary versus involuntary) also matter. Fischhoff et al. (1978) showed this by asking respondents to evaluate each of 30 hazards against a variety of attributes. An example of the sorts of assessment that respondents were asked to make for each hazard is shown in Figure 13.3.

In a subsequent study (Slovic et al., 1980), the investigators asked lay respondents to assess each of 90 hazards in terms of 18 risk characteristics

[3] Thanks in large part to safer motor vehicles, safer roads, and vigorous programs to limit drunk driving, today, despite the fact more miles are being driven, that number is considerably lower in the United States. See: http://en.wikipedia.org/wiki/List_of_motor_vehicle_deaths_in_U.S._by_year.

Voluntariness of risk

Do people face this risk voluntarily? If some of the risks are voluntarily undertaken and some are not, mark an appropriate spot towards the center of the scale.

risk assumed voluntarily	1	2	3	4	5	6	7	risk assumed involuntarily

Immediacy of effect

To what extent is the risk of death immediate—or is death likely to occur at some later time?

effect immediate	1	2	3	4	5	6	7	effect delayed

Knowledge about risk

To what extent are the risks known precisely by the persons who are exposed to those risks?

risk level known precisely	1	2	3	4	5	6	7	risk level not known

To what extent are the risks known to science?

risk level known precisely	1	2	3	4	5	6	7	risk level not known

Control over risk

If you are exposed to the risk, to what extent can you, by personal skill or diligence, avoid death?

personal risk can't be controlled	1	2	3	4	5	6	7	personal risk can be controlled

Newness

Is this risk new and novel or old and familiar?

new	1	2	3	4	5	6	7	old

Chronic-catastrophic

Is this a risk that kills people one at a time (chronic risk) or a risk that kills large numbers of people at once (catastrophic risk)?

chronic	1	2	3	4	5	6	7	catastrophic

Common-dread

Is this a risk that people have learned to live with and can think about reasonably calmly, or is it one that people have great dread for—on the level of a gut reaction?

common	1	2	3	4	5	6	7	dread

Severity of consequences

When the risk from the activity is realized in the form of a mishap or illness, how likely is it that the consequence will be fatal?

certain not to be fatal	1	2	3	4	5	6	7	certain to be fatal

FIGURE 13.3. Example of the types of assessments that lay respondents were asked to make for each of a variety of hazards in studies by Slovic et al. (1980). Similar assessments were performed in a variety of subsequent replications (see, for example, Jenni, 1997).

(instead of the 9 shown in Figure 13.3). By performing a factor analysis on the results, they found that characteristics could be clustered into three factors (i.e., groups of characteristics among which there is high correlation). The resulting "factor space" is shown in Figure 13.4.

When one examines these and similar results in detail, several conclusions emerge. First, the results are quite robust. A number of replications by Slovic, Fischhoff, and others (e.g., Jenni, 1997) have all yielded results that locate risks in approximately the same locations in this space (Figure 13.5). Second, the

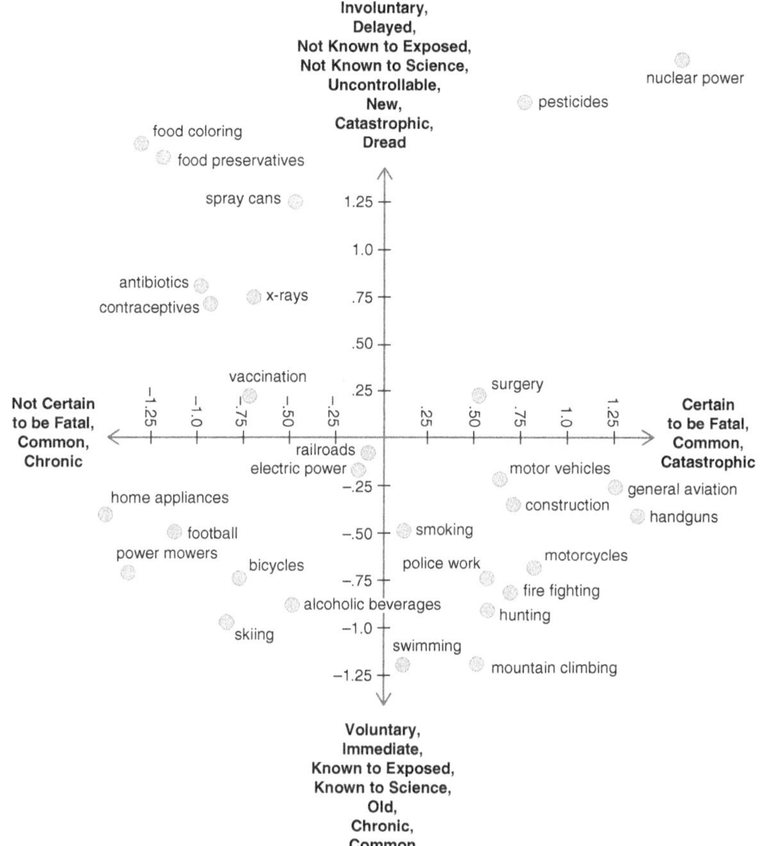

FIGURE 13.4. Risk factor space. When risks are evaluated against a set of different characteristics, Fischhoff et al. (1978) found they could be sorted into three groups or factors. Two are shown in this diagram. A third factor, the number of people exposed to each hazard, is not shown (it would be a third axis perpendicular to the page). This is a simplified diagram for 30 risks. For a diagram that maps 90 risks into this space, see Slovic et al. (1980). These results are very robust and similar sortings have been found in studies conducted with a variety of groups (e.g., Jenni, 1997). Figure from Fischhoff and Kadvany (2011). For a more detailed display that shows the location of 90 different risks in this space, see Slovic et al. (1980).

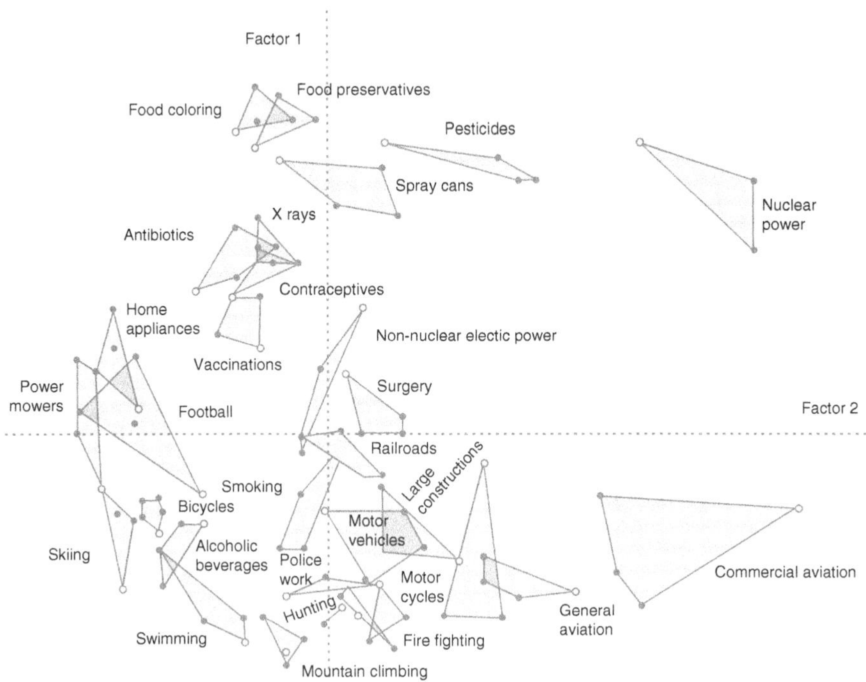

FIGURE 13.5. The Fischhoff et al. (1978) factor space study has been repeated multiple times by a variety of investigators. This figure shows the results of replications conducted with four different groups. Open circles are responses from risk experts. Figure courtesy of Paul Slovic.

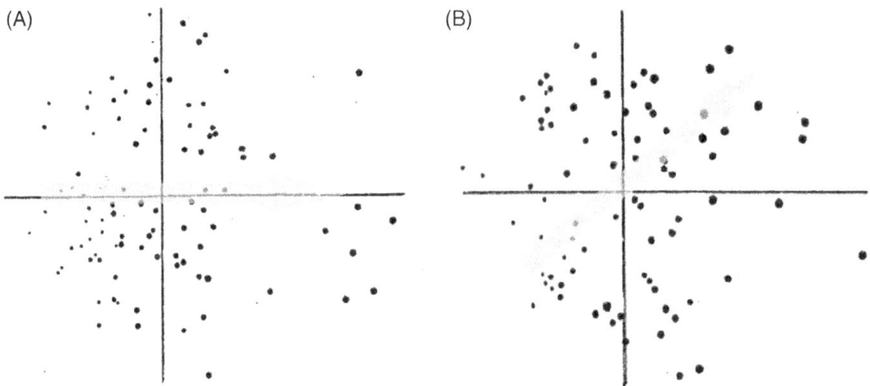

FIGURE 13.6. Where a risk falls in the factor space provides a rough indication of: A. how much people are likely to want to see it regulated, and B. how much "signal potential" they will attach to an event. Figure adapted from Slovic (1987).

place where a specific risk is located in this space says a great deal about how people are likely to perceive it. As shown in the left side of Figure 13.6, the further to the right a risk is located in this space, the higher the likelihood that people will want to see it regulated (Slovic, 1987).

The right side of Figure 13.6 displays "signal potential," by which is meant the extent to which an event signals some more fundamental problem (Slovic, 1987). For example, if in February in Minnesota a car skids off a corner on a slick, ice-covered road, people will be troubled, but say, "too bad, but sometimes accidents like this happen." On the other hand, if a new model car loses its brakes and goes off a corner on a clean dry road, people may wonder if there is a basic design or manufacturing problem that could affect all cars of that make. The latter is an example of an event with high signal potential. The further up into the right-hand quadrant in the factor space a risk lies, the greater the likelihood that people will view any event involving that risk as having signal potential – that is, as suggesting that there may be some underlying general problem that needs attention.

In the 1980s, when my colleagues and I started studying the issue of possible health risks from exposure to power-frequency electric and magnetic fields, we replicated the risk factor space study including that potential hazard, and found that it lay well up in the upper right corner (Morgan et al., 1985). Whenever a new hazard comes to public attention, performing such an analysis is one strategy that can be used to gain insight about how it may play out in subsequent public discourse.

Not all people face the same risks. In a study at Carnegie Mellon, we asked three generations of subjects (high school students, parents, grandparents) to construct their own lists of concerns and then to answer questions about the five risks that most concerned them (Fischer et al., 1991). The abstract of this paper reads:

> An unusual questionnaire was used to explore what risks concern laypeople. It asked respondents to list, in their own words, as many risks of personal concern as they could. They then selected the five risks of greatest concern and answered a set of specific questions about each. A coding scheme was developed for categorizing these responses and was shown to have good reliability. The questionnaire was administered to a heterogeneous convenience sample of subjects. They reported a very broad range of risks of concern, which differed in plausible ways as a function of their gender and age. Females and student-age subjects were generally more concerned about the environment, whereas males and older subjects were more likely to mention health and safety risks. Both the extent of the risk-reduction actions that they reported and their expressed willingness to pay for future risk reductions were greater for risks that presented a direct personal threat (e.g., health risks) than for risks that posed a diffuse threat to the environment or to people in general (e.g., pollution). Respondents perceived themselves as bearing primary responsibility for managing threats to their own health, but generally saw government as bearing a heavier responsibility for managing environmental risks (especially for pollutants) and war. The questionnaire instrument and coding structure developed for this work are well suited to a variety of future research applications. They provide a way to identify the risks that concern lay groups, as well as to track the evolution of those concerns over time.

READINGS 13.2

Sarah Lichtenstein, Paul Slovic, Baruch Fischhoff, Mark Layman, and Barbara Combs, "Judged Frequency of Lethal Events," *Journal of Experimental Psychology: Human Learning and Memory*, *4*(6), pp. 551–578, 1978.

Abstract: A series of experiments studied how people judged the frequency of death from various causes. The judgments exhibited a highly consistent but systematically biased subjective scale of frequency. Two kinds of bias were identified: (a) a tendency to overestimate small frequencies and underestimate large ones, and (b) a tendency to exaggerate the frequency of some specific causes and to underestimate the frequency of others, and any given level of objective frequency. These biases were traced to a number of possible sources including disproportionate exposure, memorability, or imaginability of various events. Subjects were unable to correct for these sources of bias when specifically instructed to avoid them. Comparisons with previous laboratory studies are discussed, along with methods for improving frequency judgments and the implications of the present findings for the management of social hazards.

Paul Slovic, Baruch Fischhoff, and Sarah Lichtenstein, "Facts and Fears: Understanding Perceived Risk," in R.S. Schwing and W.A. Albers Jr. (eds.), *Societal Risk Assessment: How Safe Is Safe Enough?*, Plenum, pp. 181–214, 1980.

Abstract: Subjective judgments, whether by experts or lay people, are a major component of any risk assessment. If such judgments are faulty, efforts at public and environmental protection are likely to be misdirected. The present paper begins with an analysis of biases exhibited by lay people and experts when they make judgments about risk. Next the similarities and difference between lay and expert evaluations are examined in the context of a specific set of activities and technologies. Finally, some special issues are discussed, including the difficulty of reconciling divergent opinions about risk, the possible irrelevance of voluntariness as a determinant of acceptable risk, the importance of catastrophic potential in determining perceptions and triggering social conflict, and the need to facilitate public participation in the management of hazards.

DISCUSSION QUESTIONS FOR READINGS 13.2

- Why is it important for risk managers and regulators to understand people's subjective judgments about risk?
- What is the implication of the fact that when asked to rank order the numbers of deaths or injuries caused by a hazard, people get the order about right, but when asked to rank those same hazards in terms of how risky they are, people produce a rather different order?
- Contrast the empirical findings of Slovic, Fischhoff, and Lichtenstein with the early arguments advanced by Starr.

13.4 COMPARING AND RANKING RISKS[4]

In light of the complexity of risk perception, it should be clear to readers that making risk comparisons that are balanced and do not lead people astray requires considerable care. Problems are likely to arise if one simply compares on the basis of a single measure such as number of deaths. Problems also arise when comparisons are not made in a neutral way, but are instead used as a vehicle to try to persuade people that they should accept a particular risk.

Recognizing these problems, but believing that risk comparisons could nevertheless be very useful, Covello et al. (1988) produced a guidance document for chemical plant managers that offered advice on how to avoid pitfalls when performing risk comparisons. Not only did the authors offer a list of 14 strategies that they judged to be increasingly less acceptable, but they also created sample text to illustrate each one.

Because they had conveniently provided these textual examples, we conducted an experiment in which we devised seven rating scales that were designed to tap different elements of Covello et al.'s definition of "acceptable" (Roth et al., 1990). We then asked four diverse groups of subjects to use these scales to judge the acceptability of the 14 sample statements that Covello et al. had composed. We "found no correlation between the judgments of acceptability produced by our subjects and those predicted by Covello et al."

I do not interpret this finding as saying Covello et al. did a bad job. Rather, it provides clear evidence of an insight that will be a central theme of Chapter 14 on risk communication: nobody is very good at figuring out in the abstract what strategies work best in risk communication. In developing a communication of any sort, including comparisons, there is simply no substitute for adopting an empirical approach.

Regulatory agencies and other organizations that are responsible for managing large numbers of risks often look for strategies they can use to set priorities. While some economists have argued that risks across society should all be managed so that the marginal reduction in deaths and injuries per dollar invested is equal across all risks, the discussion in Section 13.3 indicates clearly that most people want other factors to be considered.

Beginning in the late 1980s the U.S. Environmental Protection Agency (EPA) began to be concerned about how systematically they were pursuing their regulatory and research agendas. A landmark report, *Unfinished Business* (EPA, 1987), summarized the judgments of 75 staff members ranking the risks addressed by EPA's existing programs, as well as risks that it might one day regulate. A similar process, undertaken by EPA's Science Advisory Board, resulted in *Reducing Risk: Setting Priorities and Strategies for Environmental Protection* (EPA, 1990). Based on the framework that these reports created, EPA established a program to encourage state and local risk-ranking exercises.

[4] Some of the historical discussion in this section is based upon Fischhoff and Morgan (2009).

After supporting several dozen such exercises, EPA published *A Guidebook to Comparing Risks and Setting Environmental Priorities* (EPA, 1993), with thoughtful advice on conducting respectful, scientifically informed deliberations. Seeing its foundational work as done, EPA funded two regional centers to support additional ranking.

Central to EPA's approach was letting participants drive the process, in terms of which risks are ranked and how "risk" should be defined. Technical experts were to be entrusted with creating risk estimates relevant to participants' concerns. One price paid for this flexibility and responsiveness is reduced transparency. Individuals who were not in a ranking group must trust the work of those who were, because the rationale for their ranking is not made explicit. A second price is limited comparability. Without a standard definition of "risk," one cannot tell whether different groups have reached consistent conclusions, nor can one pool rank results across domains so as to assess overall priorities.

Building on this EPA work, at Carnegie Mellon a number of us developed and demonstrated a set of ranking methods in which risk experts define and categorize the risks to be ranked, identify a set of relevant risk attributes, and characterize the risks in a set of standardized risk summary sheets, which are then used by lay or other groups in structured ranking exercises (DeKay et al., 2001; Florig et al., 2001; Morgan et al., 2001). This approach is shown diagrammatically in Figure 13.7. Because of the prior work on risk attributes (Slovic et al., 1980), choosing attributes to rank risks to health, safety, and the environment was relatively straightforward. In order to conduct empirical assessments of the method, we developed an environment in which respondents were asked to rank risks to children in a hypothetical Centerville Middle School (Florig et al., 2001). Risk summary sheets were developed to describe 22 different risks students faced in that school. Each risk was described in multi-attribute terms as shown in the left side of Figure 13.8. Because the previous risk-attribute literature was limited to health and safety, in order to extend the work to environmental risks we had to extend those previous studies and identify a set of relevant environmental attributes (Willis et al., 2004, 2005; Willis and DeKay, 2007). In order to test these methods empirically, we created a second test bed (the hypothetical DePaul county, in which Centerville school was located). An example of a risk-attributed sheet for this second test bed is shown in the right side of Figure 13.8.

We conducted both individual and group rankings in both test beds. Participants reported high levels of satisfaction with their group's decision-making processes and the resulting rankings, and these reports were corroborated by regression analyses. Risk rankings were similar across individuals and groups, even though individuals and groups did not always agree on the relative importance of risk attributes. Agreement among participants increased over the course of the exercise, perhaps because the materials and deliberations

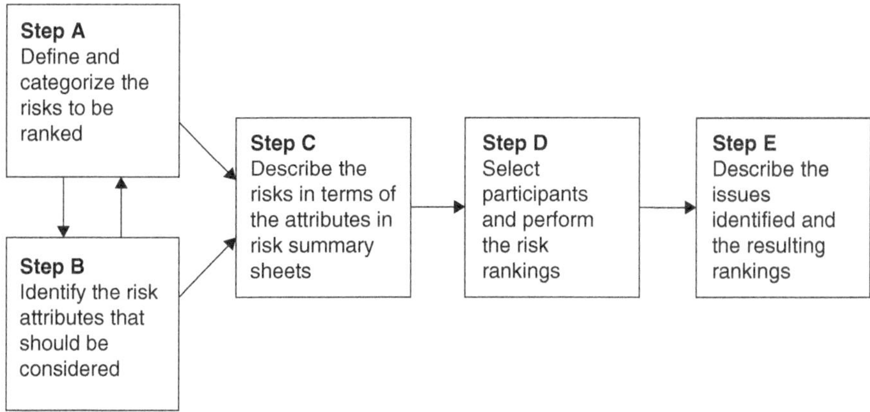

FIGURE 13.7. Steps in the Carnegie Mellon strategy for systematic risk ranking.

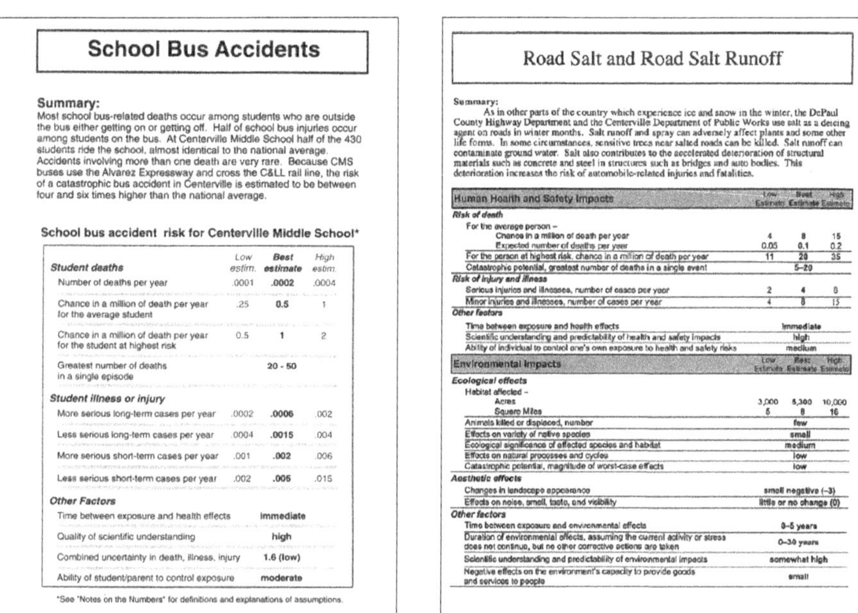

School Bus Accidents

Summary:
Most school bus-related deaths occur among students who are outside the bus either getting on or getting off. Half of school bus injuries occur among students on the bus. At Centerville Middle School half of the 430 students ride the school, almost identical to the national average. Accidents involving more than one death are very rare. Because CMS buses use the Alvarez Expressway and cross the C&LL rail line, the risk of a catastrophic bus accident in Centerville is estimated to be between four and six times higher than the national average.

School bus accident risk for Centerville Middle School*

Student deaths	*Low estim.*	***Best estimate***	*High estim.*
Number of deaths per year	.0001	**.0002**	.0004
Chance in a million of death per year for the average student	.25	**0.5**	1
Chance in a million of death per year for the student at highest risk	0.5	**1**	2
Greatest number of deaths in a single episode		**20 - 50**	
Student illness or injury			
More serious long-term cases per year	.0002	**.0006**	.002
Less serious long-term cases per year	.0004	**.0015**	.004
More serious short-term cases per year	.001	**.002**	.006
Less serious short-term cases per year	.002	**.005**	.015
Other Factors			
Time between exposure and health effects		**immediate**	
Quality of scientific understanding		**high**	
Combined uncertainty in death, illness, injury		**1.6 (low)**	
Ability of student/parent to control exposure		**moderate**	

*See "Notes on the Numbers" for definitions and explanations of assumptions.

Road Salt and Road Salt Runoff

Summary:
As in other parts of the country which experience ice and snow in the winter, the DePaul County Highway Department and the Centerville Department of Public Works use salt as a deicing agent on roads in winter months. Salt runoff and spray can adversely affect plants and some other life forms. In some circumstances, sensitive trees near salted roads can be killed. Salt runoff can contaminate ground water. Salt also contributes to the accelerated deterioration of structural materials such as concrete and steel in structures such as bridges and auto bodies. This deterioration increases the risk of automobile-related injuries and fatalities.

Human Health and Safety Impacts	Low Estimate	Best Estimate	High Estimate
Risk of death			
For the average person –			
Chance in a million of death per year	4	8	15
Expected number of deaths per year	0.05	0.1	0.2
For the person at highest risk, chance in a million of death per year	11	20	35
Catastrophic potential, greatest number of deaths in a single event		5–20	
Risk of injury and illness			
Serious injuries and illnesses, number of cases per year	2	4	8
Minor injuries and illnesses, number of cases per year	4	8	15
Other factors			
Time between exposure and health effects		immediate	
Scientific understanding and predictability of health and safety impacts		high	
Ability of individual to control one's own exposure to health and safety risks		medium	

Environmental Impacts	Low Estimate	Best Estimate	High Estimate
Ecological effects			
Habitat affected –			
Acres	3,000	5,300	10,000
Square Miles	5	8	16
Animals killed or displaced, number		few	
Effects on variety of native species		small	
Ecological significance of affected species and habitat		medium	
Effects on natural processes and cycles		low	
Catastrophic potential, magnitude of worst-case effects		low	
Aesthetic effects			
Changes in landscape appearance		small negative (–3)	
Effects on noise, smell, taste, and visibility		little or no change (0)	
Other factors			
Time between exposure and environmental effects		0–5 years	
Duration of environmental effects, assuming the current activity or stress does not continue, but no other corrective actions are taken		0–30 years	
Scientific understanding and predictability of environmental impacts		somewhat high	
Negative effects on the environment's capacity to provide goods and services to people		small	

FIGURE 13.8. Layout of the front page of the risk summary sheet used in experiments to rank 22 risks to health and safety in the hypothetical "Centerville Middle School" (left) and in experiments to rank ten environmental risks in the hypothetical "DePaul County."

helped participants to correct their misconceptions and clarify their values. In the studies using the DePaul County test bed, overall, health and safety attributes were judged more important than environmental attributes. However, the overlap between the rankings of the two sets of attributes suggests that some

BOX 13.1 PAPERS REPORTING ON RESULTS FROM THE CARNEGIE MELLON PROJECT TO DEVELOP AND EVALUATE A SYSTEMATIC APPROACH TO RISK RANKING

- M. Granger Morgan, H. Keith Florig, Michael DeKay, Paul Fischbeck, Kara Morgan, Karen Jenni, and Baruch Fischhoff, "Categorizing Risks for Risk Ranking," *Risk Analysis*, *20*(1), pp. 49–58, 2000.
- H. Keith Florig, M. Granger Morgan, Kara M. Morgan, Karen E. Jenni, Baruch Fischhoff, Paul S. Fischbeck, and Michael L. DeKay, "A Deliberative Method for Ranking Risks (I): Overview and Test Bed Development," *Risk Analysis*, *21*(5), pp. 913–921, 2001.
- Kara M. Morgan, Michael L. DeKay, Paul S. Fischbeck, M. Granger Morgan, and Baruch Fischhoff, "A Deliberative Method for Ranking Risks (II): Evaluation of Validity and Agreement among Risk Managers," *Risk Analysis*, *21*(5), pp. 923–937, 2001.
- Henry H. Willis, Michael L. DeKay, M. Granger Morgan, H. Keith Florig, and Paul S. Fischbeck, "Ecological Risk Ranking: Development and Evaluation of a Method for Improving Public Participation in Environmental Decision Making," *Risk Analysis*, *24*, pp. 363–378, April 2004.
- Henry H. Willis, Michael L. DeKay, Baruch Fischhoff, and M. Granger Morgan, "Aggregate, Disaggregate, and Hybrid Analyses of Ecological Risk Perceptions," *Risk Analysis*, *25*(2), pp. 405–428, 2005.
- Henry H. Willis and Michael L. DeKay, "The Roles of Group Membership, Beliefs, and Norms in Ecological Risk Perception," *Risk Analysis*, *27*, pp. 1365–1380, 2007.

information about environmental impacts is important to participants' judgments in comparative risk-assessment tasks.

As part of our risk-ranking work, we conducted extensive studies of consistency and agreement across ranking methods and from group to group. See the papers listed in Box 13.1 for additional details.

13.5 RECENT SUMMARIES OF WORK ON RISK PERCEPTION

Since the work by Slovic, Fischhoff, and Lichtenstein in the late 1970s and early 1980s, the literature on risk perception has exploded. The ideas summarized above are what most technical people addressing issues of risk most need to know. Those readers interested in a more complete exploration of this literature could start with:

- Paul Slovic, *The Perception of Risk*, Earthscan, 473pp., 2000.
- Baruch Fischhoff and John Kadvany, *Risk: A Very Short Introduction*, Oxford University Press, 162pp., 2011.

REFERENCES

Covello, V.T., P.M. Sandman, and P. Slovic (1988). *Risk Communication, Risk Statistics, and Risk Comparisons: A Manual for Plant Managers*, Chemical Manufacturers Association, 57pp.

DeKay, M.L., H.K. Florig, P.S. Fischbeck, M.G. Morgan, K.M. Morgan, B. Fischhoff, and K.E. Jenni (2001). "The Use of Public Risk Ranking in Regulatory Development," in P.S. Fischbeck and G.S. Farrow (eds.), *Improving Regulation: Cases in Environment Health and Safety*, Resources for the Future, pp. 208–232.

Engineering and Public Policy (1983). "On Judging the Frequency of Lethal Events: A Replication," *Risk Analysis*, *3*, pp. 11–16.

EPA (1987). *Unfinished Business: A Comparative Assessment of Environmental Problems*, Office of Policy, Planning and Evaluation, 119pp.

(1990). *Reducing Risk: Setting Priorities and Strategies for Environmental Protection*, Report SAB-EC-90-021 of the EPA Science Advisory Board, 25pp.

(1993). *A Guidebook to Comparing Risks and Setting Environmental Priorities*, EPA 230 8-93-003, Office of Policy, Planning and Evaluation, 226pp.

Fischer, G.W., M.G. Morgan, B. Fischhoff, I. Nair, and L.B. Lave (1991). "What Risks Are People Concerned about?," *Risk Analysis*, *11*(2), pp. 303–314.

Fischhoff, B. and M.G. Morgan (2009). "The Science and Practice of Risk Ranking," *Horizons*, *10*(3), pp. 40–47.

Fischhoff, B. and J. Kadvany (2011). *Risk: A Very Short Introduction*, Oxford University Press, 162pp.

Fischhoff, B., P. Slovic, S. Lichtenstein, S. Read, and B. Combs (1978). "How Safe Is Safe Enough? A Psychometric Study of Attitudes towards Technological Risks and Benefits," *Policy Sciences*, *9*(2), pp. 127–152.

Florig, H.K., M.G. Morgan, K.M. Morgan, K.E. Jenni, B. Fischhoff, P.S. Fischbeck, and M.L. DeKay (2001). "A Deliberative Method for Ranking Risks (I): Overview and Test Bed Development," *Risk Analysis*, *21*(5), pp. 913–921.

Glickman, T.S. and M. Gough (1990). *Readings in Risk*, RFF Press – Routledge, 280pp.

Jenni, K.E. (1997). "Attributes for Risk Evaluation," Ph.D. thesis, Department of Engineering and Public Policy, Carnegie Mellon University, 241pp.

Lichtenstein, S., P. Slovic, B. Fischhoff, M. Layman, and B. Combs (1978). "Judged Frequency of Lethal Events," *Journal of Experimental Psychology: Human Learning and Memory*, *4*(6), pp. 551–578.

Morgan, K.M., M.L. DeKay, P.S. Fischbeck, M.G. Morgan, and B. Fischhoff (2001). "A Deliberative Method for Ranking Risks (II): Evaluation of Validity and Agreement among Risk Managers," *Risk Analysis*, *21*(5), pp. 923–937.

Morgan, M.G., H.K. Florig, M. DeKay, P. Fischbeck, K. Morgan, K. Jenni, and B. Fischhoff (2000). "Categorizing Risks for Risk Ranking," *Risk Analysis*, *20*(1), pp. 49–58.

Morgan, M.G., P. Slovic, I. Nair, D. Geisler, D. MacGregor, B. Fischhoff, D. Lincoln, and H.K. Florig (1985). "Power Line Frequency Electric and Magnetic Fields: A Pilot Study of Risk Perception," *Risk Analysis*, *5*, pp. 139–150.

Roth, E., M.G. Morgan, B. Fischhoff, L.B. Lave, and A. Bostrom (1990). "What Do We Know about Making Risk Comparisons?," *Risk Analysis*, *10*(3), pp. 375–392.

Slovic, P. (1987). "Perception of Risk," *Science*, *236*(4779), pp. 280–285.

(2000). *The Perception of Risk*, Earthscan, 473pp.

Slovic, P., B. Fischhoff, and S. Lichtenstein (1980). "Facts and Fears: Understanding Perceived Risk," in R.S. Schwing and W.A. Albers Jr. (eds.), *Societal Risk Assessment: How Safe Is Safe Enough?*, Plenum, pp. 181–214.

Starr, C. (1969). "Social Benefits versus Technological Risk," *Science*, *165*, pp. 1232–1238.

WASH-1400 (1975). *Reactor Safety Study: An Assessment of Accident Risks in U.S. Commercial Nuclear Power Plants*, NUREG-75/014, WASH-1400, 207pp.

Willis, H.H. and M.L. DeKay (2007). "The Roles of Group Membership, Beliefs, and Norms in Ecological Risk Perception," *Risk Analysis*, *27*, pp. 1365–1380.

Willis, H.H., M.L. DeKay, M.G. Morgan, H.K. Florig, and P.S. Fischbeck (2004). "Ecological Risk Ranking: Development and Evaluation of a Method for Improving Public Participation in Environmental Decision Making," *Risk Analysis*, *24*, pp. 363–378.

Willis, H.H., M.L. DeKay, B. Fischhoff, and M.G. Morgan (2005). "Aggregate, Disaggregate, and Hybrid Analyses of Ecological Risk Perceptions," *Risk Analysis*, *25*(2), pp. 405–428.

Wilson, R. (1979). "Analyzing the Daily Risks of Life," *Technology Review*, *81*, pp. 41–46. Reprinted in T.S. Glickman and M. Gough, *Readings in Risk*, RFF Press – Routledge, pp. 55–59, 1990.

Wilson, R. and E.A.C. Crouch (1982). *Risk/Benefit Analysis*, Ballinger, 219pp.

14

Risk Communication[1]

In the words of Aaron Wildavsky (1981), "richer is safer." As a society becomes more affluent, many of the risks that it faces diminish. Those that remain are often less immediate and more subtle. However, because people who live in such societies need to devote less time to meeting basic needs, and have more resources available for use in reducing the risks they face, interest in understanding and managing risks tends to grow as societies become better off. Public demand grows for information about risks, and pressure grows on governments, corporations, and others to provide information – that is, to engage in "risk communication."

The authors of such communication typically argue that their objective is to supply people with the information they need to make informed decisions about risks to health, safety, and the environment. Although everyone agrees that "risk communication" involves telling someone something about risk, often that is the extent of the agreement. To many of the manufacturers or managers of technologies that create risks, "risk communication" means persuading the public that the risk from their technology is small and should be ignored. In such contexts, Sheila Jasanoff (1989) has suggested that "risk communication is often a code [word] for brainwashing by experts or industry."

As the field of risk analysis matured in the 1980s, discussion about the importance of risk communication began to grow. People from state and federal agencies, from private companies, and from non-profit advocacy organizations began giving speeches about how important it is to have good risk

[1] Portions of the text in this chapter are derived in edited form from Morgan et al. (1992). My four co-authors in that paper bear no responsibility for the views expressed in this chapter. I thank *Environmental Science & Technology* and the American Chemical Society for permission to reuse previously published text. The chapter also draws on ideas presented in greater detail in Morgan et al. (2002) to which readers should refer if they wish to implement the "mental model" method for risk communication.

communication. But, while lots of people were talking about it, and a variety of people had ideas about how it should be done, nobody had conducted the necessary empirical studies to determine how good risk communications could be developed.

Finally, in 1987, the National Science Foundation issued a call for proposals for a group to undertake systematic empirical studies of this topic. My colleagues Baruch Fischhoff, Lester Lave, and I were fortunate to write the winning proposal. This support, along with support from the Electric Power Research Institute, launched us on a multi-year program of studies designed to understand various aspects of risk communication and, with the assistance of Ph.D. students Ann Bostrom and Cynthia Atman, to create an empirically based approach to developing risk communication messages – what is now known as the "mental model" approach to risk communication (Atman et al., 1994; Bostrom et al., 1994b; Morgan et al., 2002).[2]

The single most important insight about risk communication to result from this work is that *there is no such thing as an expert who can tell you the best content or format for a risk communication message*, or how a specific audience will interpret it. To learn those things, you must iteratively test and refine the message, working with people of the sort who make up the target audience. This chapter outlines a set of procedures for doing that.

The basic ethical judgment that underlies the approach we developed is that risk communication should strive to supply people with the understanding and information they need to make their own informed, independent judgments about risks to health, safety, and the environment and about whether and how society should address them (Morgan and Lave, 1990). In the language from Chapter 12, our focus is on providing the information that people need to make decisions using the slower deliberative processes that Kahneman has termed Mental System 2. This approach is particularly relevant in situations in which people have adequate time to reflect and make informed judgments – which, except in emergency situations, is the case for most of the significant risks that most of us face.

Of course, as the literature on "risks as feeling" suggests, risk communication strategies could also be designed that are focused on System 1 (Slovic et al., 2004). This is what many interested parties, such as some corporations or environmental NGOs, try to do as they work to persuade people that something is, or is not, a serious risk. Probably the most respectable strategies that focus on Mental System 1 are those framed in terms of nudges.[3]

[2] While this project produced a great deal of interesting applied social science, supported some or all of five Ph.D.s, and assisted in the production of over 30 refereed publications, at its heart it was an engineering enterprise designed to produce an empirically based method that could be widely used to produce effective risk communication messages. In addition to Atman, Bostrom, Fischhoff, and Lave, other collaborators in this effort included Greg Fischer, Gordon Hester, Michael Maharik, John Merz, and Emilie Roth.

[3] For a thoughtful elaboration of these ideas, see Thaler and Sunstein (2008).

This involves ordering options and framing information in ways that induce desired behaviors. While often based more on seat-of-the-pants judgment than systematic empirical work, this is basically the strategy adopted by much modern advertising. Clearly, whether risk-related nudges work to an individual's advantage and interests depends upon who designs them.

As the discussion below will make clear, developing the empirical evidence that is needed to create good risk communications takes time. There are some situations in which a risk is so imminent that there is no time to engage in such empirical study. However, it is rare that such risks cannot be anticipated long before they become reality. Responsible public health and similar authorities should conduct the necessary anticipatory work for such risks so that when the need arises, they have empirically validated messages available that can be tailored to the specific circumstances of the risk at hand. Nudges, or even direct orders ("evacuate *now*!"), may also be appropriate and necessary in such circumstances.

14.1 WHAT INFORMATION DO PEOPLE NEED TO KNOW ABOUT A RISK?

If laypeople were trained decision analysts, it would be straightforward to determine what information they need. A decision analysis would be constructed for each decision that they face, their current knowledge would be assessed, and the additional information they need to help them distinguish among the available options would be determined. For example, homeowners deciding whether to test for radon would need to know the likelihood that their house has a high radon level (i.e., the nature of the underlying geology), the health risk of various radon levels (i.e., the shape of the health damage function, conditional on personal factors such as smoking), the cost and accuracy of testing procedures, and the cost and efficacy of possible remediation measures. Sometimes people do not need to know much in order to make an informed decision. For example, the probability of having a radon problem might be so small that individuals would gain nothing by testing.

The minimum information content for a risk communication should be the information people will require for the decisions they face. Remarkably, many of the risk communications that we have examined do not contain: key information such as numbers that allow an assessment of the magnitude of the risks; or, any indication of the confidence that can be placed in risk estimates. In their stead are recommendations such as "practice safe sex" or "if your measured radon level is above the standard, hire an approved contractor." The implicit assumption of these communications is that people will know how to convert general advice into specific action or will let others do the decision analysis for them, trusting an "expert" to apply the best scientific evidence to identify the course of action that is in their best interest. That trust could be strained or misplaced whenever the expert has a vested interest in which actions are taken, has values that are different from the client's, or disagrees with other experts.

Even when trust is complete and appropriate, numbers alone may not suffice. Especially when they involve very small quantities (e.g., 0.00001) or are expressed in unfamiliar units (e.g., 10^{-5}), the numbers simply may not "speak" to people. To get an intuitive feeling for the nature and magnitude of a risk, people may need some understanding of the physical processes that create and regulate it. Moreover, independent knowledge of the substance of an issue provides one basis for evaluating experts' pronouncements and engaging in an informed way in public discourse.

Substantive information may be even more important in pre- and post-decision activities. Long before they make any decisions, people may be monitoring public discussion of a hazard, trying to establish some competence in the issues, and formulating options for future action. After an option has been chosen, implementing it (or making midcourse corrections) can require further knowledge of how things work.

Analogous issues arise when control over hazards is exercised through political processes. Laypeople must decide whether to support or oppose a technology, as well as how to express those beliefs. A substantive understanding of risk processes may be important for evaluating the competence of those responsible for managing a hazard.

While it is important that a risk communication contain the information that people need to make the decisions they face, care must also be taken not to fill it up with so much detail that it is difficult or impossible for people to extract the key facts. This is particularly a problem for academically inclined experts, who find all the details about a risk fascinating and can't resist the temptation to share them all, whether or not they are needed for the decision that people face.

In order to think systematically about what people may need to know about a risk, we have adopted the strategy of constructing an expert influence diagram.[4] Figure 14.1 shows such a diagram for managing the risk of radon in a house built above a crawl space. This diagram was developed iteratively with a group of experts who reviewed successive drafts.

The development of such an expert influence diagram, against which lay knowledge can be compared, constitutes the first step in the five-step approach to risk communication summarized in Table 14.1.

[4] As explained in Section 4.7, if such diagrams are constructed according to strict rules, they can be mapped into decision trees. However, influence diagrams are much more intuitive than decision trees for displaying the functional relationships among variables. Since influence diagrams used in the development of risk communication are typically not converted to actual decision trees, those rules can be somewhat relaxed.

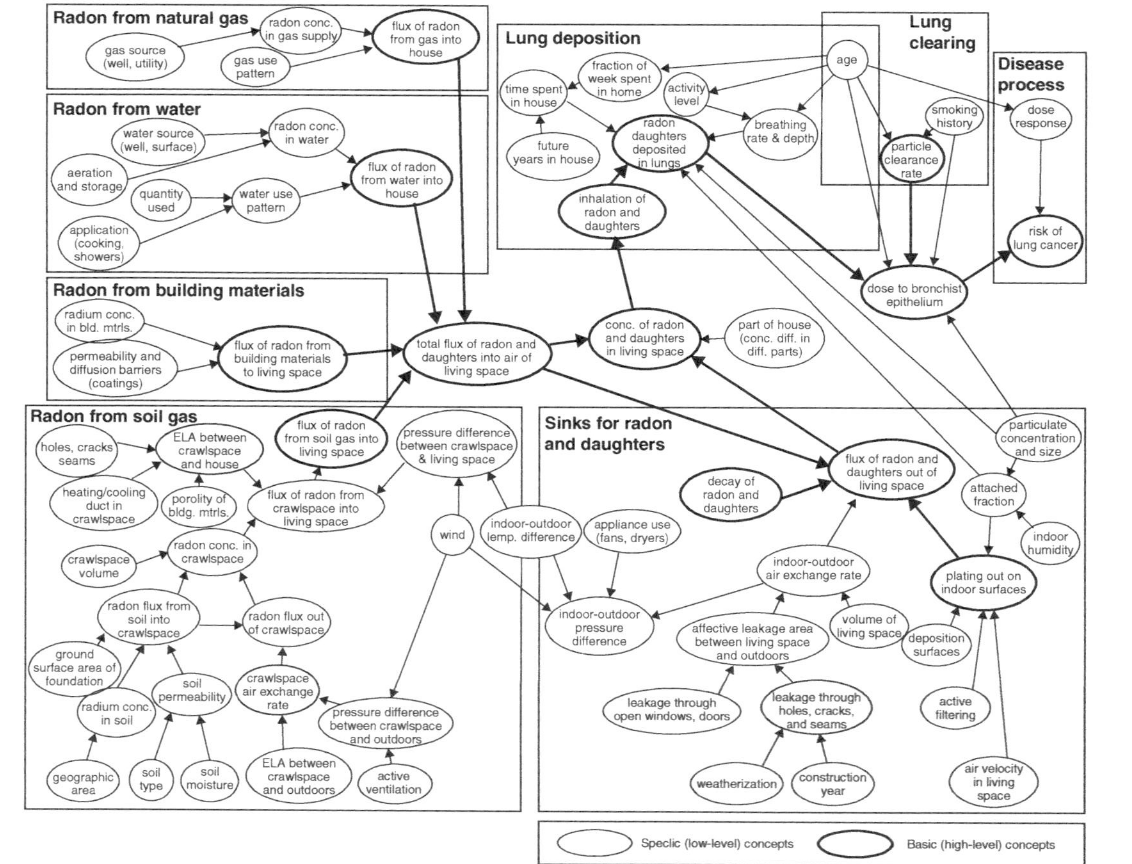

FIGURE 14.1. Expert influence diagram of factors to consider in a decision about the risk of radon in a house built over a crawl space.

TABLE 14.1. *The five steps in the "mental model approach" to risk communication developed in EPP at Carnegie Mellon.*

Step 1: Create an expert model: Review current scientific knowledge about the processes that determine the nature and magnitude of the risk. Summarize it explicitly, from the perspective of what can be done about the risk, subjecting the result to external review and assessing it in terms of information relevance. Represent this knowledge in the form of an influence diagram and subject it to review by technical experts with differing perspectives in order to ensure balance and authoritativeness. Revise as needed.

Step 2: Conduct mental models interviews: Conduct open-ended interviews eliciting people's beliefs about the hazard, expressed in their own terms. Later stages of the interview protocol should be shaped by the expert influence diagram, so that it covers potentially relevant topics. It should allow for the expression of both correct and incorrect beliefs and ensure that the respondents' intent is clear to the interviewer. Develop an appropriate coding scheme and code and summarize the results. Responses should be analyzed in terms of how well these mental models correspond to the expert model captured in the influence diagram.

Step 3: Conduct a closed-form survey: Create a confirmatory questionnaire whose items capture the beliefs expressed in the open-ended interviews and the expert model. Administer it to larger groups, sampled appropriately from the intended audience, in order to estimate the population prevalence of these beliefs.

Step 4: Prepare a draft communication: Use the results from the structured interviews as compared with the expert diagram to identify those elements of knowledge that it is most important to communicate, those gaps in knowledge that it is most important to fill, and those incorrect beliefs that it is most important to correct. Draft a communication in appropriate lay language using higher-level organizers, supporting figures, and similar aids.

Step 5: Evaluate communication: Test and refine the communication with individuals selected from the target population, using one-on-one read-aloud interviews, focus groups, closed-form questionnaires, and/or problem-solving tasks. Refine the communication as needed and repeat this process until the communication is effective and is understood as intended.

14.2 MENTAL MODELS INTERVIEWS

The traditional approach to developing a risk communication involves a simple two-step process:

- Find one or more health or safety specialists who know a lot about the risk and ask them what they think people should be told.
- Give the resulting material to a "communications expert" to package it for a lay audience.

Three things are missing in this traditional approach. It doesn't involve any systematic assessment of: (1) what people already know; (2) what people need to know in order to make the decisions that they face; and, (3) how people actually interpret and understand the communication.

People process new information in the context of their existing knowledge and beliefs. If they know *nothing* about a topic, then a new message may be incomprehensible. If they have erroneous beliefs, then they may misconstrue the message. For example, even science students who get good grades will graft new knowledge onto fundamentally incorrect naive "mental models" of concepts, such as "inertia," for a long time, before finally replacing them with technically correct models (Nussbaum and Novick, 1982; Posner et al., 1982; Clement, 1983; Driver, 1983; Schauble et al., 1991).

Mental models play significant roles in how people acquire new skills, operate equipment, follow instructions, and think about how the world works (Craik, 1943; Gentner and Stephens, 1983; Johnson-Laird, 1983; Norman, 1983; Murphy and Wright, 1984; Rouse and Morris, 1986; Carroll and Olson, 1987). As a result, communicators need to know the nature and extent of a recipient's knowledge and beliefs if they are to design messages that will not be dismissed, misinterpreted, or allowed to coexist with misconceptions.

It is fine to say that before we can develop an appropriate risk communication we need to know the recipient's mental model of the risk – but how can we do that? We could design and administer a survey instrument, but the problem with that is that any such instrument will of necessity contain information. People are smart. Once they get the survey they will start making inferences based on the information contained in, or implied by, the survey's questions. As a result, we will not be able to tell if the answers we are getting reflect the respondent's prior knowledge about the risk or the inferences that they are making based on the information contained in the survey questions.

For this reason, instead of asking directed questions, we begin step 2 of the process with an open-ended approach. For example: "tell me about radon in homes" or "tell me about climate change." In answering such questions, most people can only offer a few sentences. However, those few sentences often contain five or ten different concepts. If the interviewer has been trained to keep track of all the things that are mentioned, they can then go on to ask follow-up questions on each one.

For example, the interviewer might say "you mentioned that radon comes into a house through the cellar, tell me more about that." By systematically recording on a work sheet all the concepts that the respondent introduces, and then following up on each, a well-trained interviewer can often sustain a conversation for 10–20 minutes, while introducing no new ideas of their own.[5]

[5] Conducting such an interview requires practice and self-restraint. When we first began to consider using this approach in 1988, we sent several of our engineering Ph.D. students out to interview their friends and neighbors about radon in homes. When we transcribed the tape recordings, the results were hilarious. A few moments into most of the interviews, the lay respondents had figured out that here was someone who knows about radon and they had begun busily extracting information from the Ph.D. student interviewer. In order to do a good job of interviewing, one must practice, record the interviews, and then review them carefully to make sure that no new information is being introduced inadvertently.

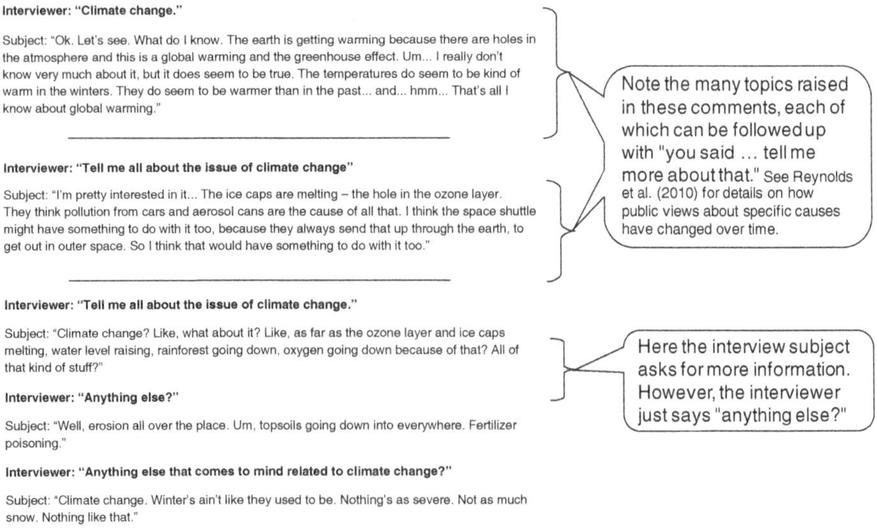

FIGURE 14.2. Three examples of the opening question in mental model interviews conducted with lay respondents by Ann Bostrom on the topic of climate change.

Three examples of opening interviews conducted by Ann Bostrom on the subject of climate change are shown in Figure 14.2.

Once the interview has exhausted what can be easily learned without introducing any information, it moves on to a second phase that explores the various sections of the expert influence diagram. As an example, Table 14.2 reproduces a portion of the protocol used in one of our interviews about radon. To ensure that respondents have ample opportunities to address all aspects of the expert influence diagram, as the interview proceeds, we provide increasingly directed prompts, in this case exploring exposure, effects, and risk-management processes.[6]

Interviews should be recorded and transcribed. Then their content should be coded using a set of categories derived from the expert diagram, but also including erroneous, peripheral, and background beliefs that are not part of the expert diagram that emerged in the interviews. The coding scheme must represent the elicited knowledge and beliefs in a way that is sensitive, neither omitting nor distorting beliefs; practical, in terms of the resources needed for analysis; reducible to summary statistics; reliable across investigators; comparable across studies; and informative regarding the design of communications. Details on these issues can be found in Morgan et al. (2002) and in Bostrom et al. (1992).

Using relatively heterogeneous opportunity samples, we have found that the number of different concepts that arise in the course of conducting a

[6] Another strategy we have used to identify possible misconceptions that may not become apparent during the interview is to ask respondents to engage in a photo-sorting task in which respondents are asked to describe what each of several dozen photographs shows and to explain why each either is or is not relevant to the risk at hand. Details can be found in chapter 4 of Morgan et al. (2002).

TABLE 14.2. *Excerpt from an interview protocol for radon.*

"What I'd like to ask you to do is just talk to me about radon: that is, tell me what you know about radon and any risks it poses."

Basic prompts:

Anything else?

Can you tell me more?

Anything else – don't worry about whether it's right, just tell me what comes to mind.

Can you explain why?

Exposure processes

Source of radon

Can you tell me (more) about where radon comes from?

Can you tell me (more) about how radon gets into homes?

You told me that – (e.g., radon leaks in through the basement) – can you tell me more about that?

Can you tell me (more) about the things that determine how much radon there is in a home?

Can you tell me (more) about how radon moves around in a home once it gets in?

Is the level of radon usually the same in all parts of a house? Can you tell me more about that?

Concentration and movement in home

Can you tell me (more) about the things that determine how much radon there is in a home?

Can you tell me (more) about how much variation there is in the amount of radon in different homes?

The protocol continues similarly to explore the other parts of the expert influence diagram.

series of mental model interviews approach an asymptotic limit after 15 to 20 interviews. Figure 14.3 illustrates this result for two different risks: "radon in homes" and "space launch of nuclear energy sources."

Most of the mental model interviews that we have conducted have revealed a good understanding on the part of the general public of key aspects of the risks they face. At the same time, in almost all cases, we have also found misconceptions that, if not corrected, would be likely to lead people to reach incorrect conclusions and make inappropriate risk-management choices.

For example, we found that some of our respondents believed that radon is a permanent contaminant. While wrong, this is a sensible inference based on stories they have heard about contamination by some persistent pesticides and contamination by long-lived radionuclides. However, such a misconception might lead some to not test, because, for example, if they found a problem, that would mean they could not sell their house with a clear conscience because they could not afford extensive remodeling. In our interviews, we encountered one respondent who, believing this erroneous "permanent contamination" model, had been

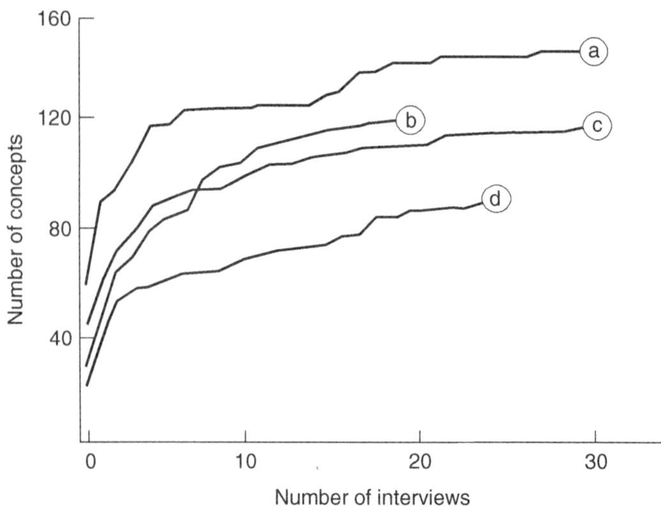

FIGURE 14.3. Illustration of the fact that the number of new concepts encountered in mental model interviews reaches an asymptote after a few dozen interviews. Curves **a** through **c** are for three groups considering risks posed by space launch of vehicles with on-board nuclear power sources (**a** = technical experts; **b** = general public; **c** = environmentalists). Curve **d** is for lay respondents on radon. Figure redrawn from Maharik (1991).

persuaded by a contractor to unnecessarily replace all the rugs, paint, and wallpaper in her home. We also encountered respondents who thought that radon results from decaying garbage. They had heard the word "decay" in discussions of radon, did not know about radioactive decay, and so inferred that since their home was not near any old garbage dumps, they did not have a problem.

Similarly, in research on perceptions of climate change, we and Kempton (1991) have found confusion between the concepts of stratospheric ozone depletion and the greenhouse effect. In fact, in interviews we conducted in the early 1990s some of our U.S. interviewees suggested that giving up hairspray (which once contained, but no longer contains, the powerful greenhouse gas chlorofluorocarbon, or CFC, as a propellant) was one of the best things they could do to help to slow global warming. Potentially more serious was many respondents' failure to mention any link between the greenhouse effect and energy consumption (Bostrom et al., 1994a; Read et al., 1994).[7]

In studies of the lay understanding of possible risks from power-frequency electric fields, we have found that many laypeople do not understand that the strength of the electric fields associated with a power line decreases rapidly with distances (i.e., as $\sim 1/r^2$). The result is that they believe that any line they can see will expose them. Hence, they place little or no value on widening power-line

[7] A follow-up study 15 years later that used the same survey instrument showed some improvement, but not as much as one would have hoped in light of all the intervening press coverage and public discourse on the topic of climate change (Reynolds et al., 2010).

rights-of-way as a strategy to reduce exposure (Morgan et al., 1990). Once we had begun to suspect this was the case, we confirmed it with survey instruments that had formats such as that shown in Figure 14.4. Example results are shown in Figure 14.5.

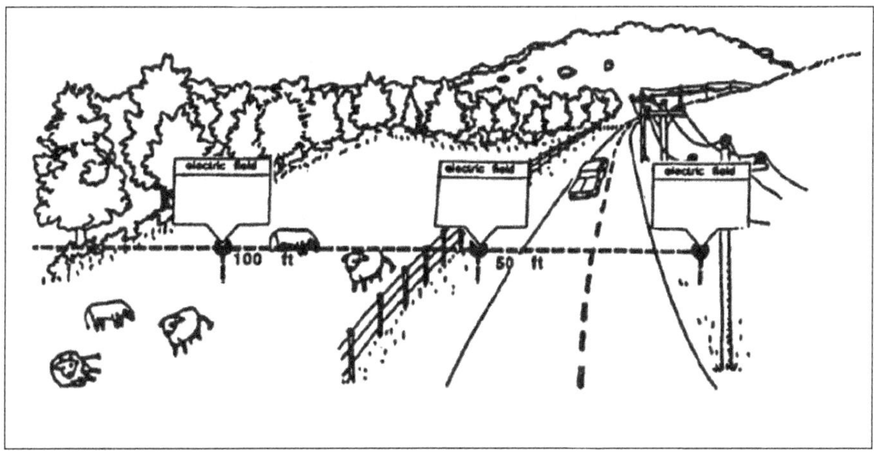

FIGURE 14.4. Example of a survey question designed to assess how people believe field strength depends on distance from a power line. Respondents were asked to assume that the field at the box closest to the line is 100 and were asked to write 100 in that box. Then they were asked to write the numbers they thought appropriate to describe the strength of the field at the two boxes further from the line. From Morgan et al. (1990).

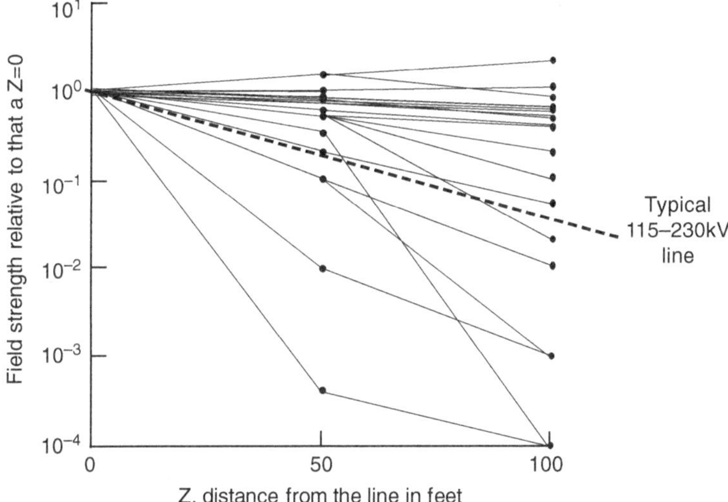

FIGURE 14.5. Normalized results from a sample of 32 lay respondents who estimated how electric field strength varied as a function of distance from a power line. Note that most either do not believe that field strength decreases significantly with distance or believe that it decreases much more slowly than $1/r^2$. From Morgan et al. (1990).

Interested readers can find more examples of important misconceptions in Morgan et al. (2002).

14.3 STRUCTURED INTERVIEWS FOLLOWED BY CLOSED-FORM SURVEYS

Open-ended interviews are essential for allowing the structure of people's mental models to emerge and, in particular, for identifying the set of misconceptions that could lead to erroneous risk-management decisions if uncorrected. However, the labor intensity of the interview procedure makes it impossible to use the results to reliably estimate the frequency with which each such belief is held in the population for which the communication is being developed. Indeed, it would be hazardous to do so, since one might be led to invest considerable effort in correcting a misconception held by only one very inventive respondent – and, because risk communication is at best an inexact tool, perhaps spread that misconception more widely.[8]

Having identified a plausible set of concepts and misperceptions, the next step is to determine how prevalent they are. To do that, the concepts and misperceptions that have been identified in the mental model interviews are used to create a closed-form questionnaire for estimating the prevalence of different beliefs.

These questionnaires are typically in true/false form. Developing questions in lay language that have unambiguous correct answers requires considerable care. In order to be assured that respondents will read questions in the way that they are intended, we subject them to "read-aloud" protocols in which lay respondents read the question out loud and then say whatever comes into their mind as they consider how to answer.

The questions posed should address all significant expert and non-expert concepts, translating abstract technical material into concrete language appropriate for lay respondents. To satisfy that requirement, there is no substitute for iteratively testing successive drafts with subjects similar to the eventual respondents. For example, the test that we developed for radon included 58 statements. Respondents could answer "true," "maybe true," "don't know," "maybe false," or "false." Details can be found in chapter 5 of Morgan et al. (2002).

[8] As an extreme example, one respondent to a mental model interview we conducted near a proposed new power line in upstate New York told us that "radiation" leaks out of nuclear power plants, travels out along the power lines, and then leaks off on to people. In subsequent studies, we were able to clearly demonstrate that this was the very inventive view of a single person and not a belief shared by others. However, had we not done those follow-up studies and had addressed and tried to correct this model in our communication, we would probably have spread the misconception to a number of others.

14.4 DEVELOPMENT AND EVALUATION OF COMMUNICATION MATERIALS

The results of the closed-form survey provide an idea of which concepts are missing that are important to the risk decisions people face, as well as which potentially serious misconceptions are widely shared. As explained below, we have used several different strategies in developing the message, focusing on communicating those facts that the expert diagram suggests that people most need to know, and correcting those few misconceptions that could most lead people astray as they decide how to act.

It is not realistic to expect people to absorb more than a few key concepts, so in preparing the draft message one must be careful to pare things down to the essentials. To assist in reading, we provide a variety of aids, such as a simple summary and a table of contents, clear section headings (often in the form of questions that are followed by answers), a glossary, simple figures and diagrams, and various boxes that spell out details.

Having produced a first draft, we move to the crucial final step of Table 14.1: testing the materials with people who will use them. This is done through one-on-one read-aloud protocols in which laypeople read the material out loud, saying everything that comes to mind as they read. It is also done with focus groups that work through the materials section by section.

While we work very hard to produce a first draft that is appropriate, we have always found things that needed to be revised when we have done the evaluation. Sometimes these are simply rewording a sentence or two. However, sometimes the necessary changes have included performing a basic restructuring or adding an entire new summary. Tone can be as important as content. In an early draft of a communication on the risks of launching spacecraft with a nuclear power source on board (essential for deep space missions far from the sun where solar power is not adequate), we had made some simple neutral comparison to the Challenger accident. In the focus groups, we discovered that people read this as suggesting that the authors were a bunch of cold, heartless technocrats, and this reaction shaped the way they interpreted much of the material. As soon as we modified the reference so that it referred to the "tragic explosion that caused the Challenger accident," the problem was resolved. Problems may not just be verbal. In a draft brochure on power-frequency electric and magnetic fields, the montage of images on the draft cover included a lab rat in an exposure system – this because much of the biological evidence had been gathered with such systems. In read-aloud studies, several people responded "yuck ... I don't want to read something with a rat on the cover." We substituted a female technician in a lab coat looking through a microscope, and the problem was resolved.

These examples clearly demonstrate the importance of adopting an empirical approach. Sitting in our office there is no way we would come up with many of the misconceptions or interpretations we have observed, nor be able to judge how common each is.

14.5 ARE THE RESULTS ANY BETTER?

The process this chapter has outlined (which is explained in far greater detail in Morgan et al., 2002) clearly requires a lot of effort. What do we know about how well it works?

The most detailed evaluation we have done involved studies with radon. In those studies, we had found that important pieces of the basic model of indoor radon exposure and effects processes were often missing from our respondents' mental models (e.g., radon decays quickly, radon causes lung cancer). Adding these high-level concepts might in itself delete or replace erroneous beliefs. Other erroneous beliefs (e.g., radon causes breast cancer), peripheral beliefs (e.g., radon comes from industrial wastes), and indiscriminate beliefs (e.g., radon makes you sick) seem to be derived from mental models of various hazardous processes rather than a core mental model for radon. As a result, they need to be addressed individually. Based on these results, we designed two brochures. A hierarchical structure for each brochure was derived from a decision-analytic perspective. One (CMU-DN) traced the Directed Network of the influence diagram. The other (CMU-DT) adopted a Decision-Tree framework, stressing the choices that people had to make. Both used higher-level organizers that have been found to improve the comprehension and retention of textual material (Krug et al., 1989). These organizers included a table of contents, clear section headings, and a summary. Both brochures contained identical illustrations, a glossary, and a boxed section discussing the assumptions underlying EPA's recommended exposure levels and the attendant risks.

These two brochures were tested against the 1986 version of EPA's widely distributed *Citizen's Guide to Radon* (EPA, 1986). CMU-DN included all basic exposure concepts in the expert influence diagram and CMU-DT included 89 percent; EPA included 78 percent. Each brochure covered 80 percent of the basic effects concepts. EPA covered a much higher percentage of specific effects concepts (50 percent versus 13 percent). The only higher-level organizers that EPA used were section headings.

In tests we ran, the three brochures were compared on a battery of measures, including our open-ended interview, our true/false test, a multiple-choice test commissioned by EPA (Desvousges et al., 1989), a short problem-solving task, and verbal protocols of individuals reading the text. In addition to exploiting the respective strengths of these different procedures, this battery of tests allowed our brochures and EPA's to be evaluated with questionnaires developed by both groups. In general, subjects reading the two CMU brochures performed similarly, and significantly better, than those reading the EPA brochure (Atman, 1990; Bostrom, 1990). The greatest superiority of performance was observed with questions requiring inferences on topics not mentioned explicitly in the brochures; these dealt predominantly with detection and mitigation. People who used the CMU brochures also gave more detailed recommendations when asked to produce advice for a neighbor with a radon problem.

Respondents were equally able to recall or recognize material mentioned explicitly in their brochure. Each group performed significantly better than a control group in all respects. Although subjects of EPA's test did more poorly on the tests derived from the mental models perspective, there was no overall difference in performance on the EPA-commissioned test.

Performance on two individual questions deserves note. More subjects who read the EPA brochure knew that health effects from radon were delayed. However, when asked what homeowners could do to reduce high radon levels in their home, 43 percent of EPA subjects answered "Don't know" and 9 percent answered, "There is no way to fix the problem." This contrasts with the 100 percent of CMU-DN and 96 percent of CMU-DT subjects who answered, "Hire a contractor to fix the problem."

Risk communications are complex entities and it is difficult to determine which features cause which impacts. We believe that the advantage of the CMU brochures lay in several common features not shared by the original EPA brochure: their decision-analytic structure emphasized action-related information, which facilitates inferences; our preparatory descriptive research focused the content of our brochures on gaps and flaws in recipients' mental models; and our use of principles from the research literature in reading comprehension directed the design. One possible additional advantage was that each CMU brochure was written by a single individual, aided by advice from others. On the other hand, the EPA's brochure was written by a committee consisting of members from diverse backgrounds. Perhaps that compromised its coherence.[9]

After completing our studies, we briefed the authors of the EPA brochure on our findings and to their credit they made significant improvements in the next edition.

Although their approaches differed, the projects producing the EPA and CMU brochures both showed a commitment to empirical validation. By contrast, much of the advice about risk communication available in the literature, or offered by consultants, lacks such commitment.[10]

Perhaps the most carefully prepared and widely circulated guidance is a manual for plant managers produced by three leading risk experts for the Chemical Manufacturers Association (Covello et al., 1988). It focuses on the pitfalls of comparing risks, enumerates and rank orders (from best to poorest) 14 different strategies for making risk comparisons, and then concludes with 14 paragraph-length illustrations of risk comparisons described with labels

[9] Note that all these results were obtained with relatively small, albeit quite heterogeneous, populations in western Pennsylvania. However, it is likely that the prevalence of particular beliefs vary more across population groups than with the repertoire of thought processes involved in making inferences or absorbing new material.

[10] For an evaluation of a risk communication brochure we developed on power-frequency electric and magnetic fields, see MacGregor et al. (1994).

ranging from "very acceptable" to "very unacceptable." However, as noted in Section 13.4, in the evaluation we conducted, we found no correlation between the acceptability judgments predicted by the manual and those produced by our subjects.

One possible reason for the failure of these predictions is that the manual's authors knew too much (from their own previous research) to produce truly unacceptable comparisons. More important than identifying the specific reasons for this failure is the general cautionary message: because we all have experience in dealing with risks, it is tempting to assume that our intuitions are shared by others. Often they are not. Effective risk communication requires careful empirical research. A poor risk communication can cause more public health (and economic) damage than the risks it attempts to describe. One should no more release an untested communication than an untested product (Fischhoff, 1985).

Critics argue that all risk communication is manipulative, designed to sell unsuspecting recipients on the communicator's political agenda. My colleagues and I believe that, with careful design and evaluation, it is possible to develop balanced materials that provide lay audiences with the information they need to make informed decisions about the risks they face. However, design must start with an examination of what choices people face, what beliefs they hold, and what expert knowledge exists.

Research on risk communication is still a work in progress. Much "conventional wisdom" withers when subjected to empirical examination. As a result, when developing communications for lay audiences, we see no substitute for the kind of empirical exploration and validation that is outlined in Table 14.1.

This process must be iterative, insofar as even the most careful risk communicators are unlikely to get things right the first few times around. Communicators are not to be trusted in their speculations regarding others' perceptions. The legacy of undisciplined claims is miscommunication, whose price is paid in increased conflict and forgone technological opportunities.

READERS INTERESTED IN LEARNING MORE ABOUT, AND APPLYING, THE MENTAL MODEL APPROACH TO DEVELOPING RISK COMMUNICATION SHOULD SEE

- M. Granger Morgan, Baruch Fischhoff, Ann Bostrom, and Cynthia Atman, *Risk Communication: A Mental Models Approach*, 351pp., Cambridge University Press, New York, 2002.

Chapter 2 of that book provides a concise overview. Subsequent chapters discuss and offer examples of each of the steps outlined in Table 14.1. Samples of a number of the risk communication materials that we have developed can be found in that book's appendix A.

14.6 COMMUNICATION TO WHAT END?

The methods described in this chapter were primarily developed to assist individuals making decisions about managing the risks they face personally. However, both the examples on power-frequency fields and climate illustrate that the same approaches can be employed to help members of society to develop the understanding they need to engage as informed participants in public discourse about how society should address such risks. While he bears no responsibility for my interpretation, Figure 14.6 displays a framework that Bill Clark suggested to me for framing these issues. The horizontal axis reflects the degree to which there is consensus about the science among the relevant domain experts. As elaborated in Morgan et al. (1992), when there is not consensus we have tried very hard to explain the nature of the disagreements. For example, in a risk communication on power-frequency electric and magnetic fields that we developed for the U.S. EPA, we wrote the following:

> Scientists do not agree.
>
> Some careful responsible scientists examine all the scientific evidence and remain unconvinced that there are any significant health risks from 60 Hz fields. Others, equally careful and responsible, look at the same evidence and conclude that there may be risks. The disagreements result because the available scientific evidence is complex. Current knowledge is fragmentary and insufficient to explain everything that is observed. Responsible scientists can have legitimate disagreements about how the available evidence should be interpreted. Until more scientific studies are done these disagreements will remain and simple yes or no answers to questions about possible health risks will not be possible.
>
> As with many controversial technical problems, there are a number of experts and other people on both sides of the issue who are very sure they are right. Because these people hold more extreme views, which can produce more colorful news stories, the press often gives them more attention.
>
> This unbalanced press coverage can either convey the impression that the experts are completely confused, or that they have "sold out" to some special interest. For most experts working on 60 Hz fields, neither of these impressions is correct.

Later in that same brochure we go on to outline a strategy of "prudent avoidance" that individuals and society might adopt in the face of this uncertainty. We also include a personal response to the question, "Dr. Morgan, what have you done?"[11]

Of course, in public decision making, helping people to develop an understanding of the nature and extent of scientific understanding of a risk only addresses a piece of the problem. Some discussion of the broader issues of reaching public consensus and policy formation can be found in Chapters 15 and 16. There are also relevant literatures in the sociology of science that explore the production of knowledge (see, for example, Guston, 2001; Jasanoff, 2004; Nowotny et al., 2006).

[11] The entire risk communication brochure on 60 Hz fields, as well as several other brochures developed using the mental model approach, is reproduced in an appendix of Morgan et al. (1992).

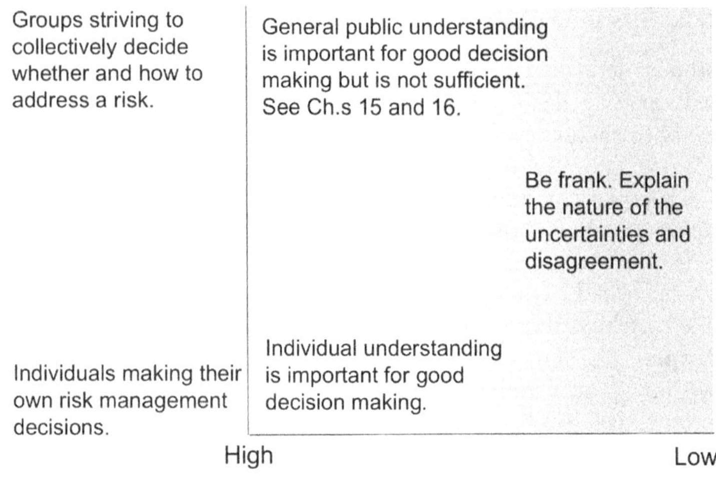

FIGURE 14.6. A simple framework for considering the different contexts in which a risk communication may be developed and used.

For risks ranging from cigarette smoking to ozone depletion and climate change, the process of reaching collective judgments about how society should address a risk is often considerably complicated by interested parties who work hard to confuse, and inject doubt into, the public discourse (Oreskes and Conway, 2010).

REFERENCES

Atman, C.J. (1990). "Network Structures as a Foundation for Risk Communication: An Investigation of Structure and Format Differences," Ph.D. thesis, Department of Engineering and Public Policy, Carnegie Mellon University, 131pp.

Atman, C.J., A. Bostrom, B. Fischhoff, and M.G. Morgan (1994). "Designing Risk Communications: Completing and Correcting Mental Models of Hazardous Processes, Part I," *Risk Analysis*, *14*(5), pp. 779–788. Also reprinted as chapter 18 in in S. Gerrard, R.K. Turner, and I. Bateman (eds.), *Environmental Risk Planning and Management*, Edward Elgar Publishers, pp. 251–260, 2001.

Bostrom, A. (1990). "A Mental Models Approach to Exploring Perceptions of Hazardous Processes," Ph.D. thesis, School of Urban and Public Affairs, Carnegie Mellon University, 279pp.

Bostrom, A., C.J. Atman, B. Fischhoff, and M.G. Morgan (1994b). "Evaluating Risk Communications: Completing and Correcting Mental Models of Hazardous Processes, Part II," *Risk Analysis*, *14*(5), pp. 789–798. Also reprinted as chapter 18 in S. Gerrard, R.K. Turner, and I. Bateman (eds.), *Environmental Risk Planning and Management*, Edward Elgar Publishers, pp. 261–270, 2001.

Bostrom, A., B. Fischhoff, and M.G. Morgan (1992). "Characterizing Mental Models of Hazardous Processes: A Methodology and an Application to Radon," *Journal of Social Issues*, *48*(4), pp. 85–100.

Bostrom, A., M.G. Morgan, B. Fischhoff, and D. Read (1994a). "What Do People Know about Global Climate Change? Part I: Mental Models," *Risk Analysis*, *14*(6), pp. 959–970.

Carroll, J.M. and J.R. Olson (eds.) (1987). *Mental Models in Human–Computer Interaction*, National Academy Press, 39pp.

Clement, J. (1983). "A Conceptual Model Discussed by Galileo and Used Intuitively by Physics Students," in D. Gentner and A.L. Stevens (eds.), *Mental Models*, Erlbaum, pp. 325–339.

Covello, V.T., P.M. Sandman, and P. Slovic (1988). *Risk Communication, Risk Statistics, and Risk Comparisons: A Manual for Plant Managers*, Chemical Manufacturers Association, 57pp.

Craik, K. (1943). *The Nature of Explanation*, Cambridge University Press, 123pp.

Desvousges, W.H., V.K. Smith, and H.H. Rink, III (1992). "Communicating Radon Risks Effectively: The Maryland Experience," *Journal of Public Policy & Marketing*, pp. 68–78.

Driver, R. (1983). *The Pupil as Scientist*, Taylor & Francis, 119pp.

EPA and U.S. DHHS (1986). *A Citizen's Guide to Radon*, OPA-86-004, Office of Air and Radiation, 16pp.

Fischhoff, B. (1985). "Managing Risk Perceptions," *Issues in Science and Technology*, *2*(1), pp. 83–96.

Gentner, D. and A.L. Stephens (eds.) (1983). *Mental Models*, Erlbaum, 348pp.

Guston, D.H. (2001). "Boundary Organizations in Environmental Policy and Science: An Introduction," *Science, Technology, & Human Values*, *26*(4), pp. 399–408.

Jasanoff, S. (1989). Talk presented at the Symposium on Managing the Problem of Industrial Hazards: The International Policy Issues, National Academy of Sciences, Washington, DC, February 27.

(ed.) (2004). *States of Knowledge: The Co-production of Science and Social Order*, Routledge, 317pp.

Johnson-Laird, P. (1983). *Mental Models: Towards a Cognitive Science of Language, Inference, and Consciousness*, Harvard University Press, 513pp.

Kempton, W. (1991). "Lay Perspectives on Global Climate Change," *Global Environmental Change*, *1*(3), pp. 183–208.

Krug, D., B. George, S.A. Hannon, and J.A. Glover (1989). "The Effect of Outlines and Headings on Readers' Recall of Text," *Contemporary Educational Psychology*, *14*(2), pp. 111–123.

MacGregor, D.G., P. Slovic, and M.G. Morgan (1994). "Perception of Risks from Electromagnetic Fields: A Psychometric Evaluation of a Risk-Communication Approach," *Risk Analysis*, *14*(5), pp. 815–828.

Maharik, M. (1991). "Public Perception of the Risks of an Unfamiliar Technology: The Case of Using Nuclear Energy Sources for Space Missions," Ph.D. thesis, Department of Engineering and Public Policy, Carnegie Mellon University, 230pp.

Morgan, M.G., B. Fischhoff, A. Bostrom, and C.J. Atman (2002). *Risk Communication: A Mental Models Approach*, Cambridge University Press, 351pp.

Morgan, M.G., B. Fischhoff, A. Bostrom, L. Lave, and C.J. Atman (1992). "Communicating Risk to the Public," *Environmental Science & Technology*, *26*(11), pp. 2048–2056.

Morgan, M.G., H.K. Florig, I. Nair, C. Cortes, K. Marsh, and K. Pavlosky (1990b). "Lay Understanding of Power-Frequency Fields," *Bioelectromagnetics*, *11*, pp. 313–335.

Morgan, M.G. and L. Lave (1990a). "Ethical Considerations in Risk Communication Practice and Research," Guest Editorial, *Risk Analysis*, *10*(3), pp. 355–358.

Murphy, G.L. and J.C. Wright (1984). "Changes in Conceptual Structure with Expertise: Differences between Real-World Experts and Novices," *Journal of Experimental Psychology: Learning, Memory, and Cognition*, *10*, pp. 144–155.

Norman, D. (1983). "Some Observations on Mental Models," in D. Gentner and A.L. Steven (eds.), *Mental Models*, Erlbaum, pp. 7–14.

Nowotny, H., P. Scott, and M. Gibbons (2006). "Re-thinking Science: Mode 2 in Societal Context," in E.G. Carayannis and D.F.J. Campbell (eds.), *Knowledge Creation, Diffusion, and Use in Innovation Networks and Knowledge Clusters: A Comparative Systems Approach across the United States, Europe and Asia*, Praeger, pp. 39–51.

Nussbaum, J. and S. Novick (1982). "Alternative Frameworks, Conceptual Conflict and Accommodation: Toward a Principled Teaching Strategy," *Instructional Science*, *11*, pp. 183–200.

Oreskes, N. and E.M. Conway (2010). *Merchants of Doubt*, Bloomsbury, 355pp.

Posner, G.J., K.A. Strike, P.W. Hewson et al. (1982). "Accommodation of a Scientific Conception: Towards a Theory of Conceptual Change," *Science Education*, *66*, pp. 211–227.

Read, D., A. Bostrom, M.G. Morgan, B. Fischhoff, and T. Smuts (1994). "What Do People Know about Global Climate Change? Part II: Survey Studies of Educated Laypeople," *Risk Analysis*, *14*(6), pp. 971–982.

Reynolds, T., A. Bostrom, D. Read, and M.G. Morgan (2010). "Now What Do People Know about Climate Change?," *Risk Analysis*, *30*(10), pp. 1520–1538.

Roth, E., M.G. Morgan, B. Fischhoff, L.B. Lave, and A. Bostrom (1990). "What Do We Know about Making Risk Comparisons?," *Risk Analysis*, *10*(3), pp. 375–392.

Rouse, W.B. and N.M. Morris (1986). "On Looking into the Black Box: Prospects and Limits in the Search for Mental Models," *Psychological Bulletin*, *100*, pp. 349–363.

Schauble, L., R. Glaser, K. Raghavan et al. (1991). "Causal Models and Experimental Strategies in Scientific Reasoning," *Journal of the Learning Sciences*, *1*, pp. 201–238.

Slovic, P., M.L. Finucane, E. Peters, and D.G. MacGregor (2004). "Risk as Analysis and Risk as Feelings: Some Thoughts about Affect, Reason, Risk and Rationality," *Risk Analysis*, *24*, pp. 311–322.

Thaler, R.H. and C.R. Sunstein (2008). *Nudge: Improving Decisions about Health, Wealth, and Happiness*, Yale University Press, 293pp.

Wildavsky, A. (1981). "Richer Is Safer," *Financial Analysts Journal*, *37*(2), pp. 19–22.

15

Organizational Behavior and Decision Making

Many, perhaps even most, important decisions are not made by individuals. Rather they are made by, or emerge from, organizations. For this reason, it is important to consider how organizations operate and produce choice outcomes. The literature on organizational behavior, and on how decisions happen in organizations, is large and continues to grow. Much of it is focused on advising managers on how to improve their more qualitative inter-personal management skills and achieve the outcomes they desire (see, for example, Altman and Hodgetts, 1979; Robbins, 2003; Locke, 2009; Easterby-Smith and Lyles, 2011). Here, we are less concerned with those issues than with gaining some understanding of the basic processes by which organizations behave and arrive at choices.

It is common in day-to-day discourse to discuss organizations, such as companies or governments, as if they are single, rational, utility-maximizing entities. We say things like:

"General Motors brought out this new car because it wants to appeal to young working women under the age of 35."

"The U.S. provided economic aid to Pakistan because it saw that as a way to limit the spread of radical terrorist groups."

"The NGO Environmental Defense chose to team with the Royal Society and the Science Academies of the Third World in a project on the governance of solar radiation management because it believed that the benefits of doing so would outweigh the risks."

While sometimes such a "single rational actor framing" is a sensible way to explain an organization's decisions, often a decision is the emergent consequence of much more complex internal behavioral and bureaucratic processes.

Using decisions made by the United States and the Soviet Union during the Cuban Missile Crisis in the fall of 1962, Graham Allison (1971) has provided an example of the different factors that can influence organizational decision making, and the strengths and limitations of different analytical frameworks, or "windows," that one can use to interpret and attempt to explain such a complex set of decisions. This work is briefly discussed in Section 15.1.

Most introductory textbooks in microeconomics lay out a model of decision making by firms that assumes that firms act as unitary utility-maximizing rational actors. As March (2008) explains:

> In classical theories of the firm ... an organization is transformed into an individual by assuming that markets (particularly markets for labor, capital and products) convert conflicting demands [among individuals] into prices. In this perspective, entrepreneurs are imagined to impose their goals on an organization in exchange for mutually satisfactory wages paid to workers, returns on investment paid to capital, and product characteristics paid to customers.

This model was already well developed when, in the 1950s, Carnegie Mellon created its Graduate School of Industrial Administration (GSIA – now called the Tepper School of Business). In building this new school, the university assembled an interdisciplinary faculty that, rather than only taking their research questions from the microeconomic literature, went out and studied how real firms operated (Simon, 1945–1997; March and Simon, 1958, 1993; Cyert and March, 1963). What they found led to a group of insights about decision making in organizations that is now commonly termed the "Carnegie School of Behavioral Social Science."[1] A number of the key insights that grew out of this work are described in Section 15.2.

Section 15.3 on "garbage can" models explores the way in which different parties with different agendas sometimes "pile on" when a decision or choice opportunity opens up.

Negotiation is a key element of reaching decisions both within and between organizations. Section 15.4 briefly summarizes results from the formal study of negotiation processes led by Howard Raiffa and others in the Program on Negotiation.

Organizations do not always perform as well as they should. Classical microeconomic theory provides very little insight about the mechanisms that customers or members can employ to induce improved performance or make a change to another organization. This is the topic of a lovely little book-length essay called *Exit, Voice and Loyalty: Responses to the Decline of Firms, Organizations and States* that Albert Hirschman (1970) wrote while he was a visitor at Stanford on leave from his faculty appointment at Harvard in the turbulent 1960s. The discussion in Section 15.5 is brief because it is far better for readers to read the original.

Some organizations manage complex socio-technical systems. Section 15.6 explores circumstances and organizational structures that can increase or decrease the chances that serious accidents may happen.

[1] "Carnegie" rather than "Carnegie Mellon" since this work was done in the Carnegie Institute of Technology before its merger in 1967 with the Mellon Institute of Science that gave rise to what is now Carnegie Mellon University.

Using computers that had less computational power than most of us now carry around in our pockets, Simon and others at GSIA worked on building agent-based models of the operation of firms. In the late 1970s, Thomas Schelling used similar ideas, using simple strategies such as placing coins on a large checkerboard rather than computers, to explore questions such as why communities seemed to become segregated even when most of the residents would have preferred that not to happen. The advent of modern computers, with their ability to do large numbers of computations and store large quantities of data, have given rise to a whole new set of computational strategies to study social processes and organizations. These models populate the system of interest with large numbers of autonomous but interacting agents, each with their own decision rules. When these systems are turned loose in the computer, many social processes become apparent as "emergent properties" that more conventional approaches in the social sciences have found difficult to explain. Section 15.7 provides a very brief look at this field, now often called "computational social science."

Studies of how individual workers operate within commercial organizations date back more than a century. While this literature is rather less central to the themes of this book, Section 15.8 summarizes a few of the key developments that may be relevant to students of technology and public policy.

15.1 DIFFERENT VIEWS THROUGH DIFFERENT WINDOWS

Graham Allison (1971) has used a case study of the Cuban Missile Crisis to illustrate the very different perspectives and insights that one gains in applying different analytical frameworks in interpreting a complex process of decisions such as those made by the former Soviet Union, Cuba, and the United States leading up to and during the Cuban Missile Crisis in October 1962.[2] Because

[2] A personal note: I was in my senior year of college in the fall of 1962. I can still distinctly remember sitting with others in our residence hall watching President Kennedy's address to the nation on television. Most of us thought the country was on the brink of nuclear war. In this connection Graham Allison (2012) has written, "Fifty years ago, the Cuban missile crisis brought the world to the brink of nuclear disaster. During the standoff, U.S. President John F. Kennedy thought the chance of escalation to war was 'between 1 in 3 and even,' and what we have learned in later decades has done nothing to lengthen those odds. We now know, for example, that in addition to nuclear-armed ballistic missiles, the Soviet Union had deployed 100 tactical nuclear weapons to Cuba, and the local Soviet commander there could have launched these weapons without additional codes or commands from Moscow. The U.S. air strike and invasion that were scheduled for the third week of the confrontation would likely have triggered a nuclear response against American ships and troops, and perhaps even Miami. The resulting war might have led to the deaths of 100 million Americans and over 100 million Russians." More recently still, it has been learned that Russian submarine B-59, which the U.S. Navy forced to surface in international waters, was armed with nuclear torpedoes. The submarine Captain, Valentin Grigorievitch Savitsky, had been out of contact with the surface, did not know if war had broken out, and wanted to launch. While other officers supported this decision, he was prevented from doing so by Captain Vasili Alexandrovich Arkhipov, thus averting what could have easily been the start of a nuclear war. See: http://en.wikipedia.org/wiki/Vasili_Arkhipov.

recent years have seen the release of far more details about the specifics of the crisis than were available in 1971, especially from sources in the former Soviet Union, Allison subsequently collaborated with Philip Zelikow to produce a revised edition in 1999.

While details on the crisis have continued to emerge,[3] *here we are interested in understanding the three analytical perspectives* that Allison elaborates, rather than the evolving historical details.

The first of these analytical perspectives (Model I) is a rational actor model in which the national players are treated as single unitary decision makers. This is the standard framing adopted by most news reporting and commentary and much of the literature in international relations. In this framework, Allison lists several hypotheses for why the Soviet Union might have chosen to locate nuclear missiles in Cuba: as a bargaining chip for use in ongoing arms control negotiations; as a "diverting trap" in connection with possible Soviet designs on Berlin; as a guarantee against a U.S. invasion of Cuba; to change the Cold War balance of power.

The second perspective (Model II) adopts an organizational process model. Under this model, factors such as the "standard operating procedures" of the different sub-national organizations are emphasized. For example, the KGB was responsible for bringing the missiles into Cuba. Since the KGB's standard operating procedure was to do everything with deep secrecy, they took great care to disguise the fact that they were importing the missiles. However, when the Strategic Rocket Forces installed the missiles, they too used their standard operating procedures – the same procedures they employed when installing strategic missile launch sites in the Soviet Union. Hence, while the United States did not detect the missiles being sent in, as soon as a U2 flew a high-altitude photo-reconnaissance flight over Cuba, U.S. photo interpreters immediately spotted the telltale images of Russian missile launch sites. As a unitary actor, the Soviet Union would not have wanted this outcome – it occurred because organizations charged with executing their assigned missions did so by applying the standard operating procedures they had developed and used for years. On the U.S. side, similar issues are illustrated by the repeated claims that an air strike on Cuba would entail as many as 500 sorties (because that was the predefined plan on the shelf) and the discussion of how the Navy would impose and operate a blockade. In this latter context, Allison describes attempts by Secretary of Defense Robert McNamara to assure that the U.S. Navy would apply the blockade in a nuanced way that was sensitive to political and diplomatic needs. The Chief of Naval Operations resisted, waving the Manual of Naval Regulations in McNamara's face, shouting "It's all in there," to which McNamara is reported to have replied, "I don't give a damn what John Paul Jones would have done, I want to know what you are going to do now." The

[3] For the recent historical accounts and documentation, see Coleman (2012); Munton and Welch (2012). For a most interesting compilation of primary documents, see Bredhoff (2012).

key point is that large organizations cannot improvise quickly – they develop and practice detailed standard procedures to deal with specific contingencies, and when they execute them they have great difficulty tuning them to deal with circumstances that do not correspond to the basic assumptions on which the plans were built.

The third perspective (Model III) applies a bureaucratic politics paradigm. In this case the specific nature of actions emerge from the interplay among actors in a complex bureaucracy in which each of the players is jockeying to advance their own local agendas and preserve and augment their own power. As Allison puts it, in this perspective "where you stand depends upon where you sit." He illustrates this model through references to the infighting for power within the Soviet Presidium and Central Committee and the process by which the Executive Committee, which Kennedy had assembled to help advise him on how to deal with the crisis, led ultimately to his choosing to impose a blockade, rather than mount an air strike or invasion.

It is clear from Allison's account that, in this specific case, elements of all three models came into play. In less dramatic situations, Models II and III play an even greater role in most government problem solving and decision making. While there are limits to how much attention the top levels of the U.S. Government can devote to any specific issue, for a pressing issue of national security such as the missile crisis, the Executive Office of the President is able to briefly seize the reins of governance and, within the limits discussed by Allison, take charge and make things happen. That has not always been true in other national governments. For example, van Wolferen's (1990) account of the internal workings of the Japanese Government in the 1980s describes an environment in which Model III is pre-eminent. He argues that it is tempting to view the Japanese Government as an "authoritarian bureaucratic state," but notes that:

> to try to pinpoint just who among the bureaucrats is in charge is to get lost again at once. Pressed to endorse decisions their respective ministries object to, the administrative vice-ministers will not give in to each other ... controversial issues always result in impasses, because there is simply no way to break a deadlock caused by a reluctant ministry.
>
> Intense rivalry among officials has long prevented their achieving a general dominance over Japanese policy-making. By the same token, territorial jealousies among ministries and agencies ... obstruct the formulation of needed unified national policies.

Van Wolferen (1990) goes on to observe that "from out of this huge system [it is impossible to identify] ... anything that can really be called a state." While the existence of a state is implied, "the working of the System inevitably negates effects that would be normal anywhere else in the industrialized world." He cautions that:

> One must be careful ... not to see the system as monolithic ... Indeed any component of the System that might aspire [to be in charge] ... would promptly find the other

components lining up against it. The preservation of its own power is the primary priority of every system component ...

For domestic purposes, this System without a core works reasonably well, even though areas of social malfunction tend to go on malfunctioning for lack of decisive action. Japan trundles along while officials, politicians and businessmen tinker endlessly with minor policy adjustments.

However, describing the Japan of the 1980s as a "paralyzed superpower," van Wolferen argues that Japan had no way to take definitive international action. "The political give-and-take among the System's components interferes with the nation's need to deal with the rest of the world." He concludes that:

From an international perspective, the Japanese System in its present shape is an anachronism. It might have fitted a poor and isolated Japan, but it is unsuitable for Japan as an international partner. Its finely meshed all-Japanese components are glaringly deficient in providing the country with an effective means to establish a *modus vivendi* with a potentially very hostile world.

Not surprisingly, van Wolferen's account created considerable controversy.[4] Whether it provides a fully accurate description of how the Japanese system functioned in the 1980s, or functions today, is less important for our purposes than the fact that it is an account of organizational decision making (or lack thereof) that is almost entirely dominated by Allison's Model III.

READING 15.1

Graham T. Allison, *Essence of Decision: Evaluating the Cuban Missile Crisis*, Scott, Foresman and Company, 338pp., 1971, *OR*, a later and longer edition that contains an updated discussion of the historical record: Graham T. Allison and Philip Zelikow, *Essence of Decision: Explaining the Cuban Missile Crisis*, 2nd ed., Longman, 416pp., 1999.

The point of this reading assignment is to understand the three alternative models that Allison develops to explain the crisis. So, *focus on the models*. Substantive details of the crisis are of secondary importance for our purposes. In addition, pay close attention to the section of chapter 3 titled "Organization Theory and Economics," which provides a concise summary of many of the key ideas discussed in the next section of this chapter. Because our focus is on Allison's three models, *feel free to skim those parts of the book that are not developing or explaining the models.*

EXERCISE AND DISCUSSION QUESTIONS FOR READING 15.1

- After you have gained an understanding of Allison's three models, choose some institutional decision with which you are familiar and prepare

[4] For a discussion, see: http://en.wikipedia.org/wiki/The_Enigma_of_Japanese_Power.

about half a page that describes the decision from each of the three perspectives that Allison adopts.

- In what sorts of circumstances are Allison's Model II and Model III likely to have the greatest descriptive power?
- It is common for people to discuss the actions and decisions of organizations and governments solely in terms of Allison's Model I. How might that lead to problems or to the misdiagnosis of situations?

While the Allison analysis of the Cuban Missile Crisis is a convenient way to introduce the ideas explored in this chapter, another interesting and quite different analysis of the same events is provided by Gibson (2012a, b). In 2001, most of the tape recordings of the ExCom deliberations were made available to the public.[5] Gibson has subjected these deliberations to modern methods of conversation analysis. He argues (Gibson, 2012a) that while the decision process used by the Kennedy Administration's ExCom is sometimes "held up as a model of rational decision making," in fact, McNamara's recollection that the ExCom "was not going through an unemotional, orderly and comprehensive decision process" is much closer to the reality revealed in the tapes (Gibson, 2012b).

Gibson (2012a) finds that "Kennedy was susceptible to persuasion ... shaped by conversational viscidities and exigencies." These include such issues as "the rules of turn-taking and expectations that one say something relevant to whatever was said last," processes that "are not easily put to the service of comparing the consequences of competing courses of action." After providing an analysis of the deliberations, noting for example the role played by interruption as a conversational vehicle for the active "suppression" of certain topics such as the risks of allowing the Soviets to bring the missiles to operational readiness, Gibson (2012a) concludes:

> The same process could have had a different ending. Had a consensus in favor of the blockade been forged even a day sooner, for instance, it might have gone into effect in time for the Navy to intercept the *Aleksandrovsk*. Given that this ship was under orders to sink itself rather than be boarded ... that would have sent history careening down a different path entirely.
>
> The lesson for scientists, advisors and policy makers is that the details and mechanics of conversation matter. Talk is useful for decision making, but its conventions do not ensure that sustained attention is given to all the things that could go wrong. Given enough time, all branches of the decision tree might receive their due, but during a crisis time is in short supply, and the hardest decisions might require that some branches are neglected and even willfully abandoned.

Gibson (2012b) observes that "sociologists are deeply uncomfortable with the idea that events of historical importance are dependent on the vagaries of talk

[5] Available at: http://millercenter.org/scripps/archive/presidentialrecordings/kennedy/1962/10_1962.

and gesture, or indeed of any small scale occurrence." However, it appears that "the course of history may sometimes hinge on small, localized events including, but not limited to, face-to-face interactions." In more technical terms, the process might be thought of as quasi-chaotic. Without some strong constraining influence, small changes may send subsequent developments down entirely different paths.

15.2 THE CARNEGIE SCHOOL OF ORGANIZATIONAL DECISION MAKING

From the late 1940s through the early 1960s, a small group of faculty in the newly created Graduate School of Industrial Administration (GSIA) in the Carnegie Institute of Technology (now Carnegie Mellon University) transformed how the world thought about business and other organizations.[6] The intellectual leaders of this effort included Herbert Simon,[7] James March, and Richard Cyert.[8]

Simon (1945–1997) began to argue that rational actor models of individuals failed to capture a number of key behavioral elements that shaped the operation of organizations.[9] Because individuals have "bounded rationality," he noted that "it is impossible for the behavior of a single, isolated individual to reach any high degree of rationality. The number of alternatives he must explore is so great, the information he would need to evaluate them so vast that even an approximation to objective rationality is hard to conceive."

Choices, which are the key to the operation of any organization, take place with a constrained set of assumptions or "givens." An organization can shape the environment in which those choices are made, permitting "stable expectations to be formed by each member of the group ... Such stable expectations are an essential precondition to a rational consideration of the consequences of action in social groups." Further, Simon argues, "organizations and institutions provide the general stimulus and attention-directors that channelize the behaviors of the members of the group, and provide those members with

[6] A somewhat different set of new thinking about organizations developed in Europe a couple of decades later. For an historical account of the two quite different developments, see March (2007).

[7] Simon's Ph.D. was in political science, but that hardly defines the intellectual spaces in which he worked. When he won the Nobel Prize in Economics in 1978 for the work outlined here, he was no longer based in Carnegie Mellon's business school, but rather was collaborating with computer scientist Allen Newell, occupying a joint appointment between psychology and computer science. While certainly not the only factor, Simon's career was an important contributor to shaping the culture of interdisciplinary education and research that is such a notable characteristic of Carnegie Mellon University that made possible the creation of the Department of Engineering and Public Policy.

[8] For a compact review of much of this literature, see pp. 64–78 in Allison (1971).

[9] There have been many later editions of *Administrative Behavior*. While Simon added some additional chapters to the later editions, he kept the original 11 chapters unchanged.

the intermediate objectives that stimulate action." Simon summarized the mechanisms that an organization employs to influence the decisions of its members as:

- Division of work among its members, thus directing and limiting individuals' attention;
- Establishing standard practices so that specific tasks are done in specific ways;
- Transmitting decisions through the ranks through established systems of authority and influence;
- Providing both formal and informal "channels of communication running in all directions"; and
- Training and indoctrinating its members so that they acquire "knowledge, skill and identifications or loyalties" that enable them to make decisions by themselves in a way that is consistent with the way the organization would like them to decide.

Having laid out this framing, Simon explored a variety of issues including the maintenance of equilibrium in organizations, the roles of authority and communication, and strategies used to achieve "efficiency."

Building on these ideas, and using formal models similar in structure to influence diagrams, March and Simon (1958) set out to "eliminate ... the artificialities of the classical description of the employees as an instrument" (what they called the "machine model") and to "replace this abstraction with a new one that recognizes that members of organizations have wants, motives, and drives and are limited in their knowledge and in their capacities to learn and solve problems." They begin by building models of the various factors that influence the nature of an individual's motivations within an organization and their decision to participate. They argue that these factors go well beyond those acknowledged in earlier machine models of individuals in organizations.

Building on these models, they then develop models first of intergroup conflict and then of organizational reaction to conflict. They argue that organizations "react to conflict by four major processes: 1) problem solving, 2) persuasion, 3) bargaining, and 4) politics." They explain that the latter is similar to bargaining except that "the arena of bargaining is not taken as fixed by the participants." They suggest that the more organizational conflict results from individual difference in judgment and opinion, "the greater the use of analytic procedures" that assist individuals to reconcile their different views and come to a shared decision by searching for additional information on the available alternatives and the associated consequences. Conversely, they argue, "the more organizational conflict represents intergroup differences, the greater the use of bargaining."

Problem solving and persuasion, they argue, "represent attempts to secure private as well as public agreement to decisions" and that these processes are analytic in nature.

March and Simon (1958) note that the processes of problem solving and persuasion are very different in their impacts on the organization than the process of bargaining:

> Bargaining almost necessarily places strains on the status and power systems of the organization. If those who are formally more powerful prevail, this results in a more forceful perception of status and power difference in the organization (generally dysfunctional in our culture). If they do not prevail, their position is weakened. Furthermore, bargaining acknowledges and legitimizes heterogeneity of goals in the organization. Such a legitimation removes a possible technique of control available to the organizational hierarchy.
>
> Because of these consequences of bargaining, we predict that the organizational hierarchy will perceive (and react to) all conflict as though it were in fact individual rather than intergroup conflict ... [that is] almost all disputes in the organization will be defined as problems in analysis ... and the initial reaction to conflict will be problem-solving and persuasion ... [S]uch reactions will persist even when they appear to be inappropriate ... [with] greater explicit emphasis on common goals where they do not exist than where they do, and that bargaining (when it occurs) will frequently be concealed within an analytic framework.

To this mix of models, March and Simon (1958) add "cognitive limits on rationality" of the sort discussed in Chapter 12. They provide a critique of the conventional utility-maximizing rational actor model of individuals in an organization and then introduce three modifications. In many cases, they argue, a stimulus triggers a set of routinized and problem-solving responses. Search may be initiated, but once a solution is found it will typically be adopted with little further thought or search when similar circumstances arise in the future.

They observe that "most human decision-making, whether individual or organizational, is concerned with the discovery and selection of satisfactory alternatives; only in exceptional cases is it concerned with discovery and selection of optimal alternatives." This is the idea of "satisficing," previously discussed in Chapter 12.

Finally, they introduce the idea of "performance programs," detailed predefined routines that individuals and organizations execute when faced with a specific stimulus. They explain: "For example, the sounding of an alarm gong in a fire station initiates such a program. So does the appearance of a relief applicant at a social worker's desk. So does the appearance of an automobile chassis in front of the work station of a worker on the assembly line." Such "performance programs" are essentially the standard operating procedures we encountered above in Allison. March and Simon examine a number of performance programs in some detail. They observe that:

> The amount and kinds of discretion ... available to the organizational participant are a function of his performance program and in particular the extent to which the program specifies activities (means) and the extent to which it specifies product or outcome (ends) ... The further the program goes in the latter direction, the more discretion it allows for the person implementing the program to supply the means–end connection.

March and Simon (1958) observe that "the whole pattern of programmed activity in an organization is a complicated mosaic of program executions, each initiated by appropriate program-evoking steps."

They identify a number of cognitive processes that reinforce a tendency toward selective attention to subgoals. Because at any one time people can only attend to a limited number of things, organizations break up their activities into sub-tasks, and develop programs for each. The result is that "members of an organizational unit [tend] to evaluate action only in terms of subgoals, even when these are in conflict with the goals of the large organization."

Communication is an obviously important part of the effective functioning of any organization. March and Simon (1958) develop and explore a taxonomy of a number of different classes of formal and informal communication within organizations and analyze their importance and the coordinating functions they perform. Organizations tend to develop their own sets of concepts and vocabularies. Communications framed in terms of those concepts tend to be better understood than those that are not.

Information is typically summarized using classification schemes. A process March and Simon (1958) term "uncertainty absorption" occurs when this happens since, given the transformations and condensation that have occurred, "the recipient of a communication is severely limited in his ability to judge its correctness." On the other hand, transferring and expecting individuals to process all the raw data has typically not been feasible. "Both the amount and the locus of uncertainty absorption affect the influence structure of the organization." As a consequence, "uncertainty absorption is frequently used, consciously and unconsciously, as a technique for acquiring and exercising power."

Many of the decision rules employed in a firm are not explicit. However, writing thirty years later in the context of an increasingly automated world, March and Sproull (1990) observe that:

> When the decision relevance of information is made explicit, the information can be corrupted by strategic actors. For example, revealing the decision rule relating information on costs and benefits to investment decisions is an invitation to biased estimates. Establishing acceptable risk makes the assessment of risk a political process. These complications are well known to managers, but decision-support technologies often require managers to make their decision rules explicit. Thus they often increase decision makers' vulnerability to strategic manipulation.

In a final chapter on planning and innovation in organizations, March and Simon (1958) argue that so long as formal and informal objectives or goals are being met at some acceptable level, people and organizational units continue to execute their established programs. However, when they are not being met, sooner or later this will be noticed and problem solving will ensue. Problem solving is basically a process of search and sorting. It may be as simple as searching individual or collective memory for things that have worked in the past. It may also entail the synthesis of new approaches and the development of new programs. Because considerable effort is required to synthesize a new program (i.e., they entail considerable sunk cost), there is often reluctance to make major changes and a preference, whenever feasible, to make minor modifications to existing programs. Again, March and Sproull (1990) observe:

> Increasing competence within an existing technology (or knowledge structure such as a scientific paradigm) makes it difficult to shift to new and potentially better technologies. In effect, learning drives out the experimentation on which it depends ... an organization or an individual may become so expert at an old technology that shifting to newer (and in principle better) technology will lead to decreased performance, in the short run.

March and Sproull term this phenomenon a "competence trap."

Many of the theoretical ideas developed by March and Simon were subsequently further assessed through detailed field studies conducted in a number of firms, extended, and reported in another landmark book by Cyert and March (1963). In the preface to the second edition of *A Behavioral Theory of the Firm*, Cyert and March (1986) wrote:

> We had an agenda [when we first published this book] in 1963. We thought that research on economics and research on organizations should have something to say to each other. We thought that the theory of the firm should be connected to empirical observations of firms ... We thought that the analytical forms used in theories of firms and other organizations were inadequate for the tasks, that they required different kinds of models and different kinds of modeling techniques.

The authors note that the approach they took was "somewhat deviant from dominant ideas" when the book first appeared, but that now "a number of the ideas discussed in the book have become part of received doctrine."

The classical treatment, they explain, "treats two main areas – the conditions for maximum net revenue and the analysis of shifts in equilibrium positions."[10] This approach assumes that the sole objective of the firm is to maximize its profits and that in doing so, they have access to perfect knowledge about their circumstances and about the market in which they operate. Cyert and March point out that in observing how real firms operate, they find that neither of these assumptions is correct. From there they go on, using observations gathered in studies of the actual operation of firms, to define a firm or similar organizations as a "coalition of individuals, some organized into subcoalitions" and ask how such coalitions hold together and develop shared goals. Somewhat in contrast to March and Simon, they argue that this occurs through bargaining and "side payments." These they define in very broad terms, not just money, but also power, responsibility, and the other things that members of the coalition want. It is, they argue, "primarily through bargaining within the active group that ... *organizational objectives* arise. Side payment, far from being the incidental distribution of a fixed, transferable booty, represents the central process of goal

[10] In an appendix to chapter 2, they lay out the relevant mathematical formalism.

specification. That is, a significant number of these payments are in the form of policy commitments."

Having developed an organizational goal, the next question the firm faces is stabilizing that goal, since the process of negotiating and bargaining is a continual process. Cyert and March identify three mechanisms that help to contribute to goal stabilization: the establishment of the budget; the allocation of functions (so that each part has a limited set of responsibilities); and institutional memory. Goals shift largely as a result of experience, which, over time, focuses finite attention on to specific issues.

Cyert and March (1963) elaborate the ideas of choice procedures and "standard operating procedures" in some detail. They identify three major features for the choice procedures used in firms:

1. *Avoid uncertainty:* Rather than looking for ways of dealing with uncertainty through certainty equivalents, the firm looks for procedures that minimize the need for predicting uncertain future events. One method uses short-run feedback as a trigger to action, another accepts (and enforces) standardized decision rules.
2. *Maintain the rule:* Once it has determined a feasible set of decision procedures, the organization abandons them only under duress. The problems associated with continuously redesigning a system as complex as a modern firm are large enough to make organizations caution about change.
3. *Use simple rules:* The firms rely on individual "judgment" to provide flexibility around simple rules. One of the most common forms of a decision rule consists in a basic, simple procedure and the specification of a set of "considerations" describing under which the procedure may be modified.

Standard operating procedures are most commonly developed in firms to deal with task performance rules (how to make a part), the creation and maintenance of records and reports, the handling of information, and the development and dissemination of plans (ranging from "short term budgets of operating expenses to long-run plans for capital expenditures"). Cyert and March explain and elaborate on each in some detail. They argue that the development and use of standard operating procedures have effects on and shape: individual goals within the organization; individual perception of the state of the environment; the range of alternatives an organization and its members consider; and the managerial decision rules that are used.

Another important source of standard operating procedures are those that professionals bring to the organization. Experts trained in fields such as accounting, engineering, or public health bring with them a repertoire of standard strategies for framing and addressing problems that are the norm in these fields.

Before turning to a set of detailed cases and applications, Cyert and March (1963) summarize their theoretical framework in terms of four assumptions:

1. Multiple changing acceptable-level goals. The criterion of choice is that the alternative selected meets all the demands (goals) of the coalition.
2. An approximate sequential consideration of alternatives. The first satisfactory alternative evoked is accepted. Where an existing policy satisfies the goal, there is little search for alternatives. Where failure occurs, search is intensified.
3. The organization seeks to avoid uncertainty by following regular procedures and a policy of reacting to feedback rather than forecasting the environment.
4. The organization uses standard operating procedures and rules of thumb to make and implement choices. In the short run these procedures dominate the decision made.

Search is a key idea in much of the literature of the Carnegie School. March (1988) summarizes:

> [The] simple theory of search has been used to illuminate two broad kinds of phenomena in organizational decision-making. The first is the way in which an organization directs energies among its various activities and goals. Organizations vary their search efforts in response to patterns of success and failure ... when faced with risky alternatives, managers do not simply assess as part of a package of exogenously determined attributes, but actively seek to redefine alternatives, looking for options that retain the opportunities, but eliminate dangers ... Such behavior fits into a theory that sees choice as driven by attention allocation, less naturally into a theory that sees choice as driven by explicit optimization.
>
> The second set of phenomena illuminated by such a theory of search involves organizational slack, i.e., resources and effort directed toward activities that cannot be justified easily in terms of their immediate contribution to organizational objectives. Slack increases during periods of success and declines during periods of failure ... By providing an inventory of unexplored efficiencies, slack serves to smooth performance in the face of a variable environment ... [It can also] be interpreted as forms of search. Slack search proceeds without the explicit organizational targets that distinguish problem oriented search ... Thus, it is less likely to solve immediate problems, more likely to be directed to subunit or individual objectives, and more likely to discover distinctly new alternatives.

15.3 GARBAGE CAN MODELS OF ORGANIZATIONAL DECISION MAKING

Classic decision science of the sort discussed in Chapter 4 tends to frame decision processes in linear terms, starting with a stated problem, then articulating decision alternatives, performing an assessment of outcomes, and then making a choice based on an assessment of the expected value of those outcomes. In contrast, March and colleagues (Cohen et al., 1976) argue decision making in an organization is often more like a "garbage can into which various problems and solutions are dumped by participants." As these get stirred around, and perhaps dumped into other cans, different bits get stuck together and result in different outcomes. Of course, the problem with such a model, and with the reality that it represents, is that in many cases it is difficult a priori to anticipate where things will end up. Once a choice opportunity has arisen, different individuals and groups within an organization may use it as a vehicle to address issues that are of concern to them and to promote solutions that they favor.

If you do not like the analogy of different bits of garbage sticking together and resulting in different re-combinations of problems and outcomes, March and Romelaer (1976) have offered an alternative analogy based on a bizarre game of soccer:

> Consider a round, sloped, multi-goal field on which individuals play soccer. Many different people (but not everyone) can join the game (or leave it) at different times. Some people can throw balls into the game or remove them. While they are in the game, individuals try to kick whatever ball comes near them in the directions of the goals they like, and away from goals they wish to avoid. The slope of the field produces a bias in how the balls fall and what goals are reached. But the course of a specific decision and the actual outcomes are not easily anticipated. After the fact, they may look rather obvious; and usually normatively reassuring.

The key point is that once a choice opportunity arises it may lead to a wide array of unanticipated outcomes, some in domains at some considerable distance from the issues that were the initial problem focus. We will see more discussion of the "recombinant" nature of this process when we discuss J.W. Kingdon's model of the policy process in Chapter 16 (Kingdon, 1984).

While it may not be possible to anticipate what will "come out of the woodwork" once a choice opportunity has arisen, the realization that such things are possible, or even likely, often results in people preferring to live with an existing suboptimal system rather than run the risk of undertaking a major rework with the possibility that things may not work out as planned. For example, whatever your perspective, it is clear that the U.S. Clean Air Act is not a perfect regulatory framework. However, many people who value its "rights-based" framing are reluctant to allow a major overhaul to be launched for fear that the entire framing might be recast in terms of maximizing benefit–cost.

READING 15.2

Johan P. Olsen, "Reorganization as a Garbage Can," in James G. March and Johan P. Olsen (eds.), *Ambiguity and Choice in Organizations*, 2nd ed., Universitetsforlaget, pp. 314–337, 1976.

DISCUSSION QUESTIONS FOR READING 15.2

- What does Olsen mean when he writes "reorganization is a garbage can"?
- What were the objectives of the senior faculty in the Department of Physics at the University of Oslo? What were the objectives of the more junior faculty members?
- What were the follow-on consequences across the university of the efforts to reorganize the Department of Physics?
- What broader implications do you draw from the garbage can model for any activity that involves embarking on a new policy initiative?

15.4 THE IMPORTANCE OF NEGOTIATION

Both within and between organizations, negotiation is key to resolving differences and arriving at agreed outcomes. In Chapter 12 we briefly mentioned game theory in the context of single and repeat play prisoners' dilemma games. Raiffa (2002) has provided a very helpful plain-language comparison between game theory and negotiation analysis (Table 15.1).

Raiffa (2002) notes that:

> When thinking about joint decisions, our first inclination is to concentrate on the final decision ... The final decision is of central importance, but joint decision opportunities crop up throughout a negotiation, not just at the crunch ... [These include] what issues to discuss ... the rules of conduct ... [whether to invite] a mediator to take part ... post agreement settlements, and [agreeing to ignore] a subset of issues.

While communication between the parties can be important, sometimes it is easier to reach an agreement if the negotiators focus on the outcome without being too open about their respective objectives and motivations (Raiffa, 1982).

Raiffa has devised a variety of very informative graphic displays to illustrate the processes involved in negotiations. Figure 15.1 illustrates a simple version of one in which two parties are negotiating over making a sale. The seller has a minimum price s they will accept, and the seller has a maximum price b they will pay. So long as $b > s$ there is a possibility of closing the deal.

Raiffa (1982, 2002) and his colleagues in the Program on Negotiation explored a wide range of issues that readers likely to be engaged in negotiation will find very useful.[11]

15.5 EXIT, VOICE, AND LOYALTY

What options do individuals have when an organization with which they are involved is not performing as well as it should? This is the question economist Albert O. Hirschman (1970) explores in a book-length essay titled *Exit,*

[11] For details on the Program on Negotiation, see: http://en.wikipedia.org/wiki/Program_on_Negotiation.

TABLE 15.1. *Comparison of game theory with negotiation theory (Raiffa, 2002).*

Game theory	Negotiation theory
• You have to act (doing nothing is an act) • Your payoff depends on what you do and what the other designated players do • You do not know what they *will* do – but you know what they *could* do • They do not know what you will do	• You and the other individuals can make mutually agreed-upon joint decisions • Your payoffs depend on the consequences of the joint decisions or on each party's go-it-alone alternatives • You can reciprocally and directly communicate with each other – about what you want, what you have, what you will do if you don't agree, or anything else. The communications might be honest, or might not • You can be creative in the decisions you make

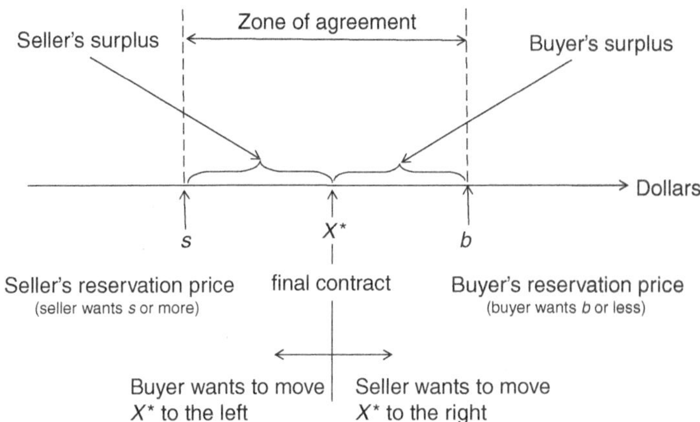

FIGURE 15.1. Illustration of a simple negotiation between a seller and buyer who are seeking a mutually acceptable selling price x^*. Since in this case $b > s$, an agreement is possible. Figure redrawn and modified from Raiffa (1982).

Voice and Loyalty: Responses to Decline in Firms, Organizations and States.[12] Hirschman begins his treatment focusing on individual firms but then broadens

[12] Hirschman (1915–2012) had a remarkable career. He was born in Berlin during the Weimar Republic. He studied economics in Berlin, Paris, and London, ultimately earning a Ph.D. in economics from the University of Trieste. He fought against Franco in Spain and then against the Nazis in France, after which he helped many to escape to the United States via Portugal. He held positions at Berkeley, with the OSS and the Federal Reserve, served for the World Bank and as an independent consultant in Colombia, was a visitor at Yale, held faculty positions at Columbia and Harvard, and ended up at the Institute for Advanced Studies at Princeton, all the while writing prodigiously. Much of his work focused on offering new insights on issues of development in the developing world. For a most interesting biography, which includes the backstory on how *Exit, Voice and Loyalty* came to be written, see Adelman (2013).

it to include a wide variety of other organizations such as "voluntary associations, trade unions, and political parties."

When the quality of a firm's products or services falls, Hirschman argues that customers may react by simply buying from a different firm (a strategy he terms "exit") or by complaining to the firm's management in the hopes that this will result in an improvement in quality (a strategy he terms "voice"). In two brief chapters Hirschman articulates these ideas, and notes that they involve an extension of classical microeconomic theory in which all firms and customers enjoy full knowledge and react without inertia. Voice enters when customers believe they can do something to improve the quality of product or service provided by firm (or organization) A and for various reasons are reluctant to switch immediately to B. Hirschman (1970) notes that a decision to stick with the deteriorating A is based on:

1. An evaluation of the chances of getting the firm or organization producing "back on track," through one's own action or that of others; and
2. A judgment that it is worthwhile, for a variety of reasons, to trade the certainty of B, which is available here and now, against those chances.

Loyalty, a concept not included in conventional microeconomic theory, can serve to delay exit, that is, "it can neutralize within certain limits the tendency of the most quality-conscious customers or members to be the first to exit." Whether and how loyalty influences voice is more complex. Figure 15.2 illustrates some of the arguments that Hirschman develops. He notes that "high fees for entering an organization and stiff penalties for exit are among the main devices generating or reinforcing loyalty in such a way as to repress either exit or voice or both." He notes that entry in some organizations (family, nationality) may occur without cost (e.g., as a matter of birth). He also explores the fact that in some contexts (such as public schools) one cannot fully exit (you can send your kids to a private school, but you still live in the community that experiences the consequences of bad public schools).

Hirschman (1970) uses his formulation to explore why political parties may move to extreme positions. In political parties that have activist members located at the extremes:

> a shift toward the center which antagonizes the captive but activist members is likely to be resisted more strenuously than a radical shift, even though the latter might lead to exit of the non-captive members and voters. One could conjecture that radicalization of political movement predicted by this model would assert itself the more strongly the longer the interval between elections; for electoral considerations can be expected to exert some restraining influence on the power of the captive party members. But this whole matter is further complicated by the phenomena of organizational loyalty.

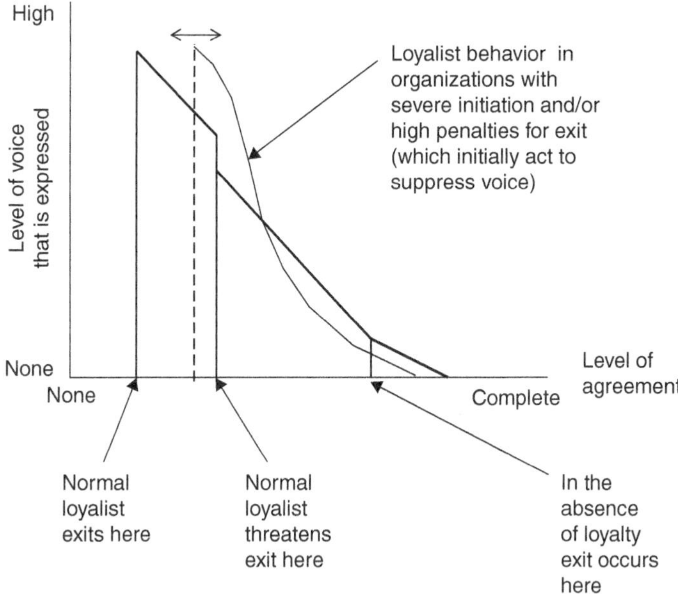

FIGURE 15.2. Hirschman's illustration of how loyalist behavior influences the decision to exit from an organization. Figure redrawn and modified from Hirschman (1970).

READING 15.3

Albert O. Hirschman, *Exit, Voice and Loyalty: Responses to Decline in Firms, Organizations and States*, Harvard University Press, 1970. Read pp. 1–5, 21–43, and 62–119.

DISCUSSION QUESTIONS FOR READING 15.3

- What does Hirschman argue he was concerned about in undertaking this work?
- Give examples from your own experience of the concepts of exit and voice.
- What is the idea of "voice as a residual of exit"?
- How does loyalty relate to exit and voice? Give examples from your own experience of the concept of loyalty.
- Discuss exit and voice in American ideology and practice. What might be the consequences if more people holding important public office in the United States were prepared to exercise exit with voice? Give examples.

15.6 NORMAL ACCIDENTS VERSUS HIGH-RELIABILITY ORGANIZATIONS

While there have always been accidents caused by human systems and actions as well as natural causes, the past century has witnessed the emergence of growing numbers of complex coupled socio-technical systems that involve potentially hazardous materials or activities. An obvious question is whether these systems, and the organizations that manage them, can operate in such a way as to avoid catastrophic outcomes. Two quite different schools of thought have emerged with respect to this question.

Charles Perrow (1984) argues that such systems will inevitably fail and result in accidents – events he describes as "normal accidents." In assessments of systems ranging from nuclear power plants to petrochemical plants, aircraft and air operations, marine shipping, dams, space launch, and others, he argues that because of tight coupling, non-linearity, organizational lapses, and a number of other factors, sooner or later accidents in such systems are inevitable. He argues that such systems can be divided into three categories:

> The first would be systems that are hopeless and should be abandoned because the inevitable risks outweigh any reasonable benefits (nuclear weapons and nuclear power); the second, systems that we are either unlikely to be able to do without but which could be made less risky with considerable effort (some marine transport), or where the expected benefits are so substantial that some risks should be run, but not as many as we are now running (DNA research and production). Finally, the third group includes those systems which, while hardly self-correcting in all respects, are self correcting to some degree and could be further improved with quite modest efforts (chemical plants, airliners and air traffic control ...).[13]

Of course, there are some systems that, while they involve highly hazardous environments, have been run safely without disasters for many years. Beginning in the 1980s, Todd La Porte and his colleagues in a group at the University of California, Berkeley conducted extensive observational studies in order to understand the strategies such "high-reliability" organizations adopt in order to maintain their excellent safety records (La Porte and Consolini, 1991; La Porte, 1996; Rochlin, 1996; Bourrier, 2011).

Bourrier (2011) explains that:

> The group first identified three organizations that to their knowledge continuously met and often surpassed the criteria set by society for reliable performance: (i) The Air Traffic Control System (Federal Aviation Administration); (ii) Electric Operations and Power Generation Departments (Pacific Gas and Electric Company) and (iii) The peacetime flight operations of the US Navy's Carrier Group 3 and its two nuclear aircraft carriers USS Enterprise (CVN 65) and USS Carl Vinson (CVN 70). Later, the nuclear production at PGE's Diablo Canyon plant (Pacific Gas and Electric Company) was included.

[13] Examples provided in parentheses are part of the quotation from Perrow (1984).

La Porte (1996) summarizes attributes of high-reliability organizations as follows:

1. Extraordinary *technical competence* ultimately shapes authority relations and decision processes among operating personnel who are often consummately skilled at what they do ... Sustaining very high levels of competence, effectiveness and operator commitment is secured, in part, by a combination of high organizational status and visibility for the activities that enhance reliability ...
2. HROs achieve *rigorously high operational performance* of the technical systems accompanied by stringent quality assurance (QA) measures in maintenance ... Extensive performance data bases that track and calibrate technical operations proved an *unambiguous* description of the systems status. This becomes ... [the information] upon which awareness and interpretations of system readiness from a variety of perspectives are widely available and often nourish competition between groups formally responsible for safety ...
3. ... Effective performance calls for considerable flexibility and "organizational slack" to insure safety and protect performance resilience. *Structural flexibility and redundancy* [is achieved through] ... overlapping activities that can provide backup ... first line supervisors [who are] trained for multiple jobs ... [and] jobs and work groups designed in ways that limit the interdependence of incompatible functions.
4. ... collegial patterns of authority based on skill and functional authority ... decision dynamics are characterized by flexible, dispersed operational decision-making, and sustained efforts to improve, including rewards for the discovery of incipient error.
5. Decision making within shifting authority patterns, especially operating decisions, tend to be decentralized ...
6. Once determined, decisions are executed often very quickly, with little chance for review, recovery or alteration. HROs therefore put an unusual premium on increasing the likelihood that decisions will be based on the best information available ... [and made by operating personnel with a high degree of technical understanding of the system].

While this description is somewhat abstract, Pool (1997) has provided an excellent specific illustration of these concepts in the context of the peacetime operation of U.S. Naval aircraft carriers.

Leveson et al. (2009) have provided a comparison of the normal accidents and high-reliability organization literature and then, based on work they did following the Challenger and other space-related mishaps, suggest a "top-down systems approach to organizational safety." While a useful contribution, their analysis strikes me as overly optimistic about system analysts' ability to anticipate and model all relevant interactions,[14] and rather underplays the importance of learning in actual field operations.

[14] See the discussion of fault trees for a car that will not start (Section 10.4) as well as the more general discussion of cognitive limitations in Chapter 12.

READING 15.4

Robert Pool, "Chapter 8: Managing the Faustian Bargain," in *Beyond Engineering: How Society Shapes Technology*, Oxford University Press, pp. 249–277, 1997.

DISCUSSION QUESTIONS FOR READING 15.4

- Pool quotes Alvin Weinberg as describing the adoption of nuclear power as involving a "Faustian Bargain." What is a Faustian Bargain and why did Weinberg make this statement?
- Why did the accident happen at the Union Carbide plant at Bhopal, India?
- What does the Challenger accident have in common with the Bhopal chemical plant accident?
- What are the primary attributes of a "high-reliability organization"?
- Describe why La Porte argues that a U.S. Navy aircraft carrier is an example of a high-reliability organization.

15.7 AGENT-BASED MODELS OF SOCIAL PROCESSES AND ORGANIZATIONS

Society and organizations are made up of individuals. Each of these "agents" has a particular set of preferences and applies their own decision rules when faced with choices. Thus, the overall behavior of a society or organization results from the sum of all those individual behaviors, choices, and the interactions that occur among them.

Long before computers became powerful enough to model each separate agent in a social system together with all their interactions, the economist Thomas Schelling understood the importance of these processes. One of his first forays into this area was in the context of working to understand segregation in residential communities. Schelling (1978, 2006)[15] writes:

> Some vivid dynamics can be generated by any reader with a half-hour to spare, a role of pennies and roll of dimes, a tabletop, a large sheet of paper ...
>
> [Divide the sheet of paper] into one-inch squares ... and find some device for selecting squares at random ... place dimes and pennies on some of the squares and suppose them to represent the members of two homogeneous groups – men and women, blacks

[15] As with several of the classic books discussed in this chapter, there are two editions of Schelling's *Micromotives and Macrobehavior*. As far as I can tell, the only difference between the 1978 and the 2006 editions is that the 2006 version includes a new Preface and a final chapter that reproduces Schelling's lecture on the occasion of his receiving the 2005 Nobel Prize in Economics.

and whites, French-speaking and English-speaking, officers and enlisted men [etc.] ... We can spread them at random or put them in a contrived pattern. We can use equal numbers of dimes and pennies or let one be a minority. And, we can stipulate various rules for individual decision.

Schelling goes on to demonstrate what happens when very simple decision rules are applied that are apparently socially benign (e.g., equal number of the two types and each wants only a third or more of their neighbors to be like themselves). Assuming there are some unoccupied spaces on the board, individuals (dimes and pennies) move at random to achieve the desired mix of neighbors. Rather quickly one ends up with two segregated neighborhoods – not what any individual party (agent) wanted, but the emergent property of each exercising their simple decision rules.[16]

Schelling (1978, 2006) explores a large number of examples (in areas as diverse as seating patterns in auditoriums, sending Christmas cards, patterns of traffic flows, support for public radio, the growth and decline of attendance at seminars, and sales of used cars), most of which demonstrate that it is wrong to assume "that the self-serving behavior of individuals should usually lead to collectively satisfactory results." He further demonstrates that there is "nothing particularly attractive about an equilibrium." Indeed, in many cases the equilibria that result from individuals' choices (micromotives) give rise to social outcomes (macrobehaviors) that are undesirable. He discusses a number of strategies that can be employed to limit or offset those outcomes.

READING 15.5

Thomas C. Schelling, *Micromotives and Macrobehavior*, W.W. Norton and Co., either 1978 or 2006. Read pp. 11–43; 83–133; 147–155; and 213–243. I have selected sections that are particularly relevant for our purposes. However, some readers will probably find Schelling's treatment so fascinating that you will end up reading more. If you can find the time, it will be well worth your while.

DISCUSSION QUESTIONS FOR READING 15.5

- Outline Schelling's example of seating patterns in an auditorium.
- Outline Schelling's example of the distribution of men and women in dining halls of co-ed college dorms.

[16] For additional discussion of the mathematics of segregation, see Hayes (2013) as well as http://ccl.northwestern.edu/netlogo/models/Segregation.

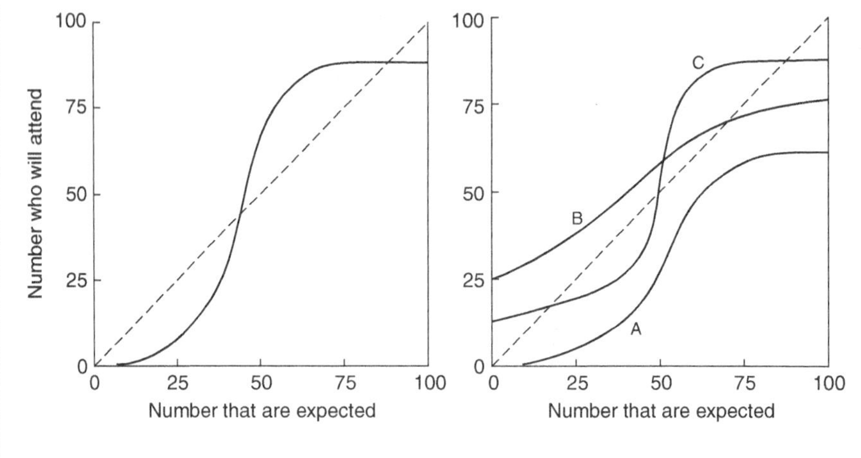

- Explain the two figures above, that have been redrawn from Schelling (1978, 2006).
- Explain "the market for lemons."

The growth of computer power has witnessed the emergence of a new field of "computational social science." It is now possible to construct models with millions of separate agents, each of which is endowed with a reasonably complex set of behavioral rules, and each of which interacts in prescribed ways with other agents in the model. This micro-bottom-up approach stands in strong contrast to more conventional macro-top-down approaches that have characterized much economics, sociology, and other social science in the past. The latter has developed general aggregated models such as demand and supply curves, often using empirical tools such as regression analysis. Agent-based models seek to produce and explore such observed "emergent" behaviors through bottom-up simulations.

Such models have been able to qualitatively replicate many macro-behaviors (Epstein and Axtell, 1996). While it can be difficult to develop the data needed to calibrate an agent's rules, rapid progress is being made. There are some striking examples of success, such as the agent-based simulation of the depopulation and ultimate abandonment by the Native American Anasazi people in Long House Valley, Arizona, calibrated with extensive archeological evidence (Axtell et al., 2002; Diamond, 2012). A second remarkable example, discussed in Section 16.5, involves the evolution of the complex traditional system of "water temples" and associated religious rituals that evolved in Bali to manage the allocation of water between farms and to control pests. Not surprisingly, in both these cases the results reported are sensitive to how the models are calibrated as well as several other factors (Janssen, 2007, 2009).

Agent-based models are seeing considerable application to studies of stock market and other economic bubbles, crashes, and similar phenomena in economic systems. For a brief overview of some of this work, see Battiston et al. (2016).

READING 15.6

Joshua M. Epstein, "Prelude and Chapter 1: Agent-Based Computational Models and Generative Social Science," in Joshua M. Epstein (ed.), *Generative Social Science: Studies in Agent-Based Computational Modeling*, Princeton University Press, 356pp., 2006.

DISCUSSION QUESTION FOR READING 15.6

- What are the potential advantages and disadvantages of agent-based approaches when compared with more traditional models and methods of analysis of social systems?

The literature in this area is growing rapidly. Details on the application to Long House Valley, Arizona can be found in:

- R.A. Axtell et al., "Population Growth and Collapse in a Multiagent Model of the Kayenta Anasazi in Long House Valley," *PNAS*, *99*, suppl. 3, pp. 7275–7279, May 14, 2002.
- Jared M. Diamond, "Life With the Artificial Anasazi," *Nature*, *419*, pp. 567–569, October 2012.
- Jonathan Rauch, "Seeing Around Corners," *The Atlantic Monthly*, April 2002.
- Marco A. Janssen, "Understanding Artificial Anasazi," *Journal of Artificial Societies and Social Simulation*, *12*(4), p. 13, 2009. Available at: http://jasss.soc.surrey.ac.uk/12/4/13.html.

For a discussion of the abandonment of settlements by the Anasazi that is focused on Mesa Verde, see:

- Richard Monastersky, "And Then There Were None," *Nature*, 527, pp. 26–29, 2015.

15.8 STUDIES OF THE BEHAVIOR OF INDIVIDUALS WITHIN COMMERCIAL ORGANIZATIONS

While less central to the focus of this book, the final section of this chapter provides a brief summary of three of the most influential early studies of the behavior of individuals within commercial organizations.

Taylor and Scientific Management: Frederick Taylor (1911) began his classic book *The Principles of Scientific Management* by citing President Theodore Roosevelt's call to use natural resources more efficiently. He observed:

We can see and feel the waste of material things. Awkward, inefficient or ill-directed movements of men,[17] however, leave nothing visible or tangible behind them. Their appreciation calls for an act of memory, and effort of imagination. And for this reason, even though our daily loss from this source is greater than from our waste of material things, the one has stirred us deeply, while the other has moved us but little. (Taylor, 1911)

Taylor (1911) argued that in field studies he had observed that most workers are working well below their potential and that time and motion studies that break the work up into sub-tasks could dramatically improve output. Acknowledging that this might result in some worker pushback, he argued that those who participate should be compensated with "special incentives" such as better pay, promotion, or shorter hours. He argued that such a program should have four features: (1) "develop a science for each element of a man's work, which replaces the old rule of thumb"; (2) "scientifically select and then train, teach and develop the workmen"; (3) "heartily cooperate with the men so as to insure all of the work [is] being done in accordance with the principles of the science that has been developed"; and (4) take steps to "assure an almost equal division of the work and responsibilities between the management and the workmen."

Taylor outlined how he had applied these steps in a variety of applications from loading pig iron onto rail cars, to laying brick, to inspecting ball bearings for bicycle wheels, or managing the operations of metal cutting in a machine shop. Despite his stress on management–worker collaboration, to the modern reader Taylor's attitude toward workers often comes across as condescending and elitist. Nevertheless, in the early part of the twentieth century, his work had a major impact on several decades of thinking in industrial management.[18]

The Hawthorne Studies: In 1927, officials in a Western Electric plant that manufactured devices for the Bell Telephone Company began a series of what they thought would be rather straightforward studies to explore how lighting levels affected worker productivity (Mayo, 1933; Roethlisberger et al., 1941). Initial results from these studies conducted with five women suggested that many factors other than simple light levels were more important in determining worker productivity. As the study progressed, Western Electric officials recruited the involvement of the National Research Council and investigators from Harvard and MIT who helped to design and conduct later studies involving tasks such as relay assembly, mica splitting,[19] and a stage in the assembly of switches for central office equipment called connector and selector

[17] Given the norms of the era in which Taylor worked, it is not surprising that all workers in his examples are men.

[18] Taylor's work is an example of the "machine model" of employees referenced by March and Simon (1958) in Section 15.2.

[19] The mineral mica came to workers in blocks several inches on a side. Workers were required to split off and then test sheets of mica a few mils thick for use as insulating material.

bank wiring. By the time the studies were concluded in 1932, roughly 20,000 Western Electric employees had been involved in the studies.

While the details of these many studies are fascinating, here I summarize just two key sets of findings. The first, now widely known as the Hawthorne Effect,[20] found that productivity increases appeared to result more from the simple fact that management was paying special attention to workers, and seeking their views, than from many of the specific interventions that were being made. Studies suggested that issues such as fatigue and monotony were much more psychological than physical and that benefits from doing things like scheduling regular breaks was less related to physical recovery than to the fact that such changes indicated to employees that the employer was showing care for the workers and encouraging their social interactions and morale.

In summarizing insights from several studies, Roethlisberger et al. (1941) observe that "Sometimes attempts to make the employees more efficient [by rearranging work patterns] unwittingly deprived them of the very things which gave meaning to work, their cultural traditions of craftsmanship, their personal interrelation." Similarly, Mayo (1933) notes that providing workers with an understanding of their "work situation" is of critical importance in the maintenance of workplace morale. He argues that, because individuals are not mindless machines, as the design of production operations becomes more complex, "the more necessary it is that there shall be a method of communicating understanding 'down the line.' "

In the bank wiring experiments, the investigators found that the 14 men in these experiments divided into two cliques. After considering and rejecting explanations of clique formation based on factors such as job type and spatial distribution, the investigators concluded that clique membership basically was determined by how much work conformed to four norms (Roethlisberger et al., 1941):

1. You should not turn out too much work. If you do, you are a "rate buster."
2. You should not turn out too little work. If you do, you are a "chisler."
3. You should not tell a supervisor anything that will react to the detriment of an associate. If you do, you are a "squealer."
4. You should not attempt to maintain social distance or act officious. If you are an inspector, for example, you should not act like one.

After extended discussion of a variety of possible explanations of the source of these norms, the investigators conclude that they were not the result of a rational economic, income-maximizing assessment of the workers' situation but rather "resulted primarily from the position of the group in the total company structure and its consequent relations with other groups within the company." That is, issues of social relations dominated rational economic models.

[20] This term was coined by H.A. Landsberger (1958).

More generally, across the set of studies, Roethlisberger et al. (1941) report that "None of the results ... gave the slightest substantiation to the theory that the worker is primarily motivated by economic interest. The evidence indicated that the efficacy of wage incentives is so dependent on its relation to other factors that it is impossible to separate it out as a thing in itself having an independent effect." The investigators further report that "most of the dissatisfaction with wages implied that the employee is just as much concerned with wage differentials, that is the relation of his wages to the wages of other workmen, as with the absolute amount of his wages." While based on smaller numbers of subjects than one would like, this finding is remarkably similar to results reported in Section 2.3 indicating that above a minimum income threshold, relative income within a social group is a more important contributor to happiness than absolute income.

The decades following the Hawthorne Studies saw significant critical commentary by sociologists, political scientists, and others who were focused on issues of industrial relations, labor collective bargaining, and similar topics. Landsberger (1958) has reviewed these criticisms and concludes that they are more reflective of theoretical and ideological disagreements with the broader conclusions that Mayo (1933) and others drew from the studies, than with any of the findings reported in the studies themselves.

Herzberg studies of job satisfaction: In the 1950s, Frederick Herzberg and his colleagues conducted an extensive set of qualitative studies in which they interviewed workers, asking for specific details about development in the course of their work lives that contributed to, or detracted from, their job satisfaction. Interviews were transcribed and then subjected to extensive content analysis.

Herzberg et al. (1959) found that three factors had the greatest impact on contributing to positive job satisfaction: the nature of the work itself, the extent of responsibility given to workers, and the opportunity that workers had to achieve advancement. Factors that most contributed to negative job satisfaction were: "company policy and administration; supervision (both technical and interpersonal relationships); and working conditions." Salary entered both as a contributor to and detractor from job satisfaction. They note, however, that "as an affector[21] of job attitudes salary has more potency as a job dissatisfier than as a job satisfier ... when salary occurred as a ... [dissatisfier] it revolved around the unfairness of the wage system ... and this almost always referred to the increases in salaries rather than the absolute values." On the satisfaction side, salary was mentioned as a form of positive recognition for good work well done.

While the Herzberg et al. (1959) studies were based on extensive analysis of interviews, since then formal survey methods have been developed that allow

[21] This is not a typo. The word is "affector" as in "affect" (to cause satisfaction or dissatisfaction), not "effecter" as in "to cause."

similar questions about job satisfaction to be explored through the collection of larger data sets that can be subjected to statistical analysis (Hackman and Oldham, 1975).

SUGGESTED RESOURCES TO LEARN MORE ABOUT ORGANIZATIONS AND ORGANIZATIONAL DECISION MAKING

- James G. March, *Decisions and Organizations*, Basil Blackwell, 458pp., 1988.
- James G. March, *A Primer on Decision Making: How Decisions Happen*, The Free Press, 289pp., 1994.
- Zur Shapira (ed.), *Organizational Decision Making*, Cambridge Series on Judgment and Decision Making, Cambridge University Press, 397pp., 1997.

For a discussion of organizational studies as they are influenced by cultural differences, see:

- Rabi S. Bhagat and Richard M. Steers (eds.), *Cambridge Handbook of Culture, Organizations, and Work*, Cambridge University Press, 537pp., 2009.

15.9 WRAPPING UP

I began this chapter by arguing that many decisions are the emergent consequence of a complex interplay within organizations. This is true in corporations, in NGOs, in universities, and also in governments. Sometimes the choices and actions of individuals can make a big difference, but more often it is the interactions among many different individuals and groups, within and outside an organization, that shape important outcomes.

The next chapter explores some of the processes that play out in the development of public policy, and the role that analysis can play in those processes. A consideration of organizational behavior is relevant both in managing the processes that shape how policy is developed, and in evaluating the likely effectiveness of alternative policy designs and strategies. Both of these activities are at least as much an art as a science. I am not able to offer simple clear advice on how the literature reviewed in this chapter should be incorporated into thinking about the processes of developing and implementing policy. However, I am confident that the development and implementation of policy is much less likely to be successful if it is undertaken without some knowledge and consideration of how individuals develop preferences and actually make decisions (Chapter 12), and of the complexity of interplay among those preferences and decisions in organizations as described in this chapter.

REFERENCES

Adelman, J. (2013). *Worldly Philosopher: The Odyssey of Albert O. Hirschman*, Princeton University Press, 740pp.

Allison, G.T. (1971). *Essence of Decision: Explaining the Cuban Missile Crisis*, Scott, Foresman and Co., 338pp.; and a later expanded edition with Philip Zelikow (1999), Longman, 416pp.

(2012). "The Cuban Missile Crisis at 50: Lessons for U.S. Foreign Policy Today," *Foreign Affairs*, Jul./Aug. edition, pp. 11–16.

Altman, S. and R.M. Hodgetts (1979). *Readings in Organizational Behavior*, W.B. Saunders and Co., 367pp.

Axtell, R.A., J.M. Epstein, J.S. Dean, G.J. Gumerman, A.C. Swedlund, J. Harburger, S. Chakravarty, R. Hammond, J. Parker, and M. Parker (2002). "Population Growth and Collapse in a Multiagent Model of the Kayenta Anasazi in Long House Valley," *PNAS*, *99*, suppl. 3, pp. 7275–7279.

Battiston, S., J.D. Farmer, A. Flache et al. (2016). "Complexity Theory and Financial Regulation," *Science*, *351*, pp. 818–819.

Bhagat, R.S. and R.M. Steers (eds.) (2009). *Cambridge Handbook of Culture, Organizations, and Work*, Cambridge University Press, 537pp.

Bourrier, M. (2011). "The Legacy of the High Reliability Organization Project," *Journal of Contingencies and Crisis Management*, *19*, pp. 9–13.

Bredhoff, S. (2012). *To the Brink: JFK and the Cuban Missile Crisis*, The Foundation for the National Archives, 90pp.

Cohen, M.D., J.G. March, and J.A. Olsen (1976). "Chapter 2: People, Problems, Solutions and the Ambiguity of Relevance," in J.G. March and J.P. Olsen (eds.), *Ambiguity and Choice in Organizations*, Universitetsforlaget, pp. 24–37.

Coleman, D.G. (2012). *The Fourteenth Day: JFK and the Aftermath of the Cuban Missile Crisis*, W.W. Norton & Co., 259pp.

Cyert, R.M. and J.G. March, with contributions by G.P.E. Clarkson and others (1963). *A Behavioral Theory of the Firm*, Prentice-Hall, 332pp.; 2nd ed. (1986), Blackwell, 252pp.

Diamond, J.M. (2012). "Life with the Artificial Anasazi," *Nature*, *419*, pp. 567–569.

Easterby-Smith, M. and M.A. Lyles (2011). *Handbook of Organizational Learning and Knowledge Management*, 2nd ed., Wiley, 711pp.

Epstein, J.M. (ed.) (2006). *Generative Social Science: Studies in Agent-Based Computational Modeling*, Princeton University Press, 356pp.

Epstein, J.M. and R.L. Axtell (1996). *Growing Artificial Societies: Social Science from the Bottom up*, Brookings Institution Press, 208pp.

Gibson, D.E. (2012a). "Decisions at the Brink," *Nature*, *487*, pp. 27–29.

(2012b). *Talk at the Brink: Deliberation and Decision during the Cuban Missile Crisis*, Princeton University Press, 218pp.

Hackman, J.R. and G.R. Oldham (1975). "Development of the Job Diagnostic Survey," *Journal of Applied Psychology*, *60*, pp. 159–170.

Hayes, B. (2013). "The Math of Segregation," *American Scientist*, *101*, pp. 338–341.

Herzberg, F., B. Mausner, and B.B. Snyderman (1959). *The Motivation to Work*, Vol. I, Transaction Publishers, 157pp.

Hirschman, A.O. (1970). *Exit, Voice and Loyalty: Responses to Decline in Firms, Organizations and States*, Harvard University Press, 176pp.

Janssen, M.A. (2007). "Coordination in Irrigation Systems: An Analysis of the Lansing–Kremer Model of Bali," *Agricultural Systems*, *93*(1), pp. 170–190.

(2009). "Understanding Artificial Anasazi," *Journal of Artificial Societies and Social Simulation*, *12*(4), p. 13.

Kingdon, J.W. (1984). *Agendas, Alternatives, and Public Policies*, Little, Brown and Company, 240pp.

Landsberger, H.A. (1958). *Hawthorne Revisited: Management and the Worker, Its Critics, and Developments in Human Relations in Industry*, Cornell University, 119pp.

La Porte, T.R. (1996). "High Reliability Organizations: Unlikely, Demanding and at Risk," *Journal of Contingencies and Crisis Management*, *4*(2), pp. 60–71.

La Porte, T.R. and P.M. Consolini (1991). "Working in Practice But Not in Theory: Theoretical Challenges of High-Reliability Organizations," *Journal of Public Administration Research and Theory: J-PART*, *1*(1), pp. 19–48.

Leveson, N., N. Dulac, K. Marais, and J. Carol (2009). "Moving beyond Normal Accidents and High Reliability Organizations: A Systems Approach to Safety in Complex Systems," *Organization Studies*, *30*(2–3), pp. 227–249.

Locke, E.A. (2009). *Handbook of Principles of Organizational Behavior*, 2nd ed., Wiley, 651pp.

March, J.G. (1988). *Decisions and Organizations*, Basil Blackwell, 458pp.

(1994). *A Primer on Decision Making: How Decisions Happen*, The Free Press, 289pp.

(2007). "The Study of Organizations and Organizing since 1945," *Organization Studies*, *28*(1), pp. 9–19. Available at: http://oss.sagepub.com/content/28/1/9.

(2008). *Explorations in Organizations*, Stanford University Press, 464pp.

March, J.G. and P. Romelaer (1976). "Chapter 12: Position and Presence in the Drift of Decisions," in J.G. March and J.P. Olsen (eds.), *Ambiguity and Choice in Organizations*, Universitetsforlaget, pp. 251–276.

March, J.G. and H.A. Simon, with H. Guetzkow (1958). *Organizations*, Wiley, 262pp.

March, J.G. and H.A. Simon (1993). *Organizations*, 2nd ed., Blackwell, 287pp.

March, J.G. and L.S. Sproull (1990). "Chapter 5: Technology, Management and Competitive Advantage," in P.S. Goodman and L.S. Sproull (eds.), *Technology and Organizations*, Jossey-Bass, pp. 144–173.

Mayo, E. (1933). *The Human Problems of an Industrial Civilization*, Macmillan, 194pp.

Monastersky, R. (2015). "And Then There Were None," *Nature*, *527*, pp. 26–29.

Munton, D. and D.A. Welch (2012). *The Cuban Missile Crisis: A Concise History*, Oxford University Press, 123pp.

Olsen, J.P. (1976). "Reorganization as a Garbage Can," in J.G. March and J.P. Olsen (eds.), *Ambiguity and Choice in Organizations*, 2nd ed., Universitetsforlaget, pp. 314–337.

Perrow, C. (1984). *Normal Accidents: Living with High-Risk Technologies*, Basic Books, 386pp.

Pool, R. (1997). *Beyond Engineering: How Society Shapes Technology*, Oxford University Press, 358pp.

Raiffa, H. (1982). *The Art and Science of Negotiation*, Harvard University Press, 373pp.

with J. Richardson and D. Metcalfe (2002). *Negotiation Analysis*, Harvard University Press, 548pp.

Rauch, J. "Seeing around Corners," *The Atlantic Monthly*, April 2002.

Robbins, S.P. (2003). *Organizational Behavior*, Prentice Hall, 675pp. (There are multiple editions of this textbook, the most recent versions of which are co-authored by T.A. Judge. I prefer the earlier editions.)

Rochlin, G.I. (1996). "Reliable Organization: Present Research and Future Directions," *Journal of Contingencies and Crisis Management*, 4(2), pp. 55–59.

Roethlisberger, F.J. and W.J. Dickson, with the assistance of H.A. Wright (1941). *Management and the Worker: An Account of a Research Program Conducted by the Western Electric Company, Hawthorne Works, Chicago*, Harvard University Press, 615pp.

Schelling, T.C. (1978, 2006). *Micromotives and Macro Behavior*, W.W. Norton and Co., 252pp. in 1978, 270pp. in 2006.

Shapira, Z. (ed.) (1997). *Organizational Decision Making*, Cambridge Series on Judgment and Decision Making, Cambridge University Press, 397pp.

Simon, H. (1945–1997). *Administrative Behavior: A Study of Decision-Making Processes in Administrative Organizations*, The Free Press, 368pp.

Taylor, F.W. (1911). *The Principles of Scientific Management*, W.W. Norton, 144pp.

van Wolferen, K. (1990). *The Enigma of Japanese Power*, Vintage Books, 504pp.

PART IV

THE POLICY PROCESS AND S&T POLICY (MAINLY) IN THE UNITED STATES

How is public policy formulated, implemented, and refined over time and what role (if any) does analysis play? These are questions addressed in Chapter 16. The chapter begins with a discussion of the factors that shape the identification of problems that command attention and the emergence of policies to address those problems. Of course, the world is forever changing, and it is rare that any policy solution will remain effective for all time, hence the need to think about policies that can evolve and adapt as conditions change and more is learned. The chapter also explains that formal policies promulgated by government or other organizations are not the only mechanisms that can promote desirable and avoid undesirable behaviors and outcomes.

Rarely is it possible to develop a detailed policy design and expect it to be sustained over time in evolving political, institutional, and technical environments. Hence in many situations it is inevitable that the policy processes will involve "muddling" – that is, making incremental adjustments to existing policies and strategies. Often this works well. Sometimes it can be an invitation to disaster. Closely related to these issues is the final topic discussed in Chapter 16: the many difficulties and complications that can arise in implementing and sustaining a policy once it has been developed.

Many readers of this book are likely to be concerned with policy processes in the United States. Those who are not may still find that some of the issues they address are framed or influenced by U.S. experiences. Chapters 17 and 18 provide a brief and highly selective history of the evolution of science and technology policy in the United States. World War II is a natural break point in the narrative. Before the war, government was often very reluctant to play a major role in issues of science and technology. During and after the war that situation changed dramatically.

Finally, Chapter 19 provides a summary of contemporary institutions and mechanisms for science and technology advice at different levels of government. While the focus is on the United States, the chapter concludes with brief, separately authored sections that discuss similar issues in the European Union (EU), Japan, China, and India.

16

Analysis and the Policy Process

People who are new to the field of policy analysis often think of policy making in terms of an analyst sitting at the elbow of a policy maker, performing analysis that helps them make decisions. Sometimes this happens, but more frequently the policy process is far more convoluted. Rather than leading to immediate results, analysis often starts a slow process of building consensus in an expert community so that in the future, when an opportunity arises to make a policy decision, insights from the analysis have become part of a shared framing and vision of the field. The first section of this chapter explores these ideas in greater detail.

The next several sections explore a variety of strategies that may be used to produce more effective policy designs when the opportunity does arise to design new policy and make a policy decision. The chapter closes with a discussion of the "the science of muddling through," the difficulties that can arise in implementing a policy, the value and importance of sometimes adopting a strategy of "intellectual playfulness," and a brief discussion of the issue of "implementation."

16.1 POLICY WINDOWS

In his book *Agendas, Alternatives and Public Policies*, John Kingdon (1984) provides the most useful description of the policy process that I have found. Anyone who is serious about working on issues of public policy should at least read the summary in chapter 9 of that book.

Kingdon argues that "agenda setting" and "alternative specifications" are key precursors to policy formulation. He draws a distinction between a condition and a problem. The world is full of conditions, but only a few become problems in the space of policy makers.[1] Conditions may transform into

[1] Writing about environmental and ecological issues, Downs (1972) observed that problems often move through an "issue-attention cycle" that he describes as consisting of: (1) "the pre-problem

problems if they become identified as violating important values, through comparison with other political units including other countries,[2] or when a condition is reclassified to fall in one category rather than another.[3] Kingdon also outlines a variety of reasons why problems fade from policy agendas.

Kingdon describes three separate streams that involve:

> problems, policies and politics each [of which] have lives of their own. Problems are recognized and defined according to processes that are different from the ways policies are developed or political events unfold. Policy proposals are developed according to their own incentives and selection criteria, whether or not they are solutions to problems or responsive to political considerations. Political events flow along on their own schedule and according to their own rules, whether or not they are related to problems or proposals.
>
> But there come times when the three streams are joined. A pressing problem demands attention, for instance, and a policy proposal is coupled to the problem as its solution. Or an event in the political stream, such as a change of administration, calls for different directions. At that point, proposals that fit with the political event, such as initiatives that fit with a new administration's philosophy, come to the fore and are coupled with the ripe political climate. Similarly, problems that fit are highlighted, and others are neglected.

I have illustrated this model approximately in graphical form in Figure 16.1. However, readers should read Kingdon's description to fully understand the model and its nuances.

In his book, Kingdon provides a number of examples of policy processes that illustrate this model at work. A more recent illustration of the model is provided by the introduction of cap and trade approaches to deal with sulfur air pollution in the United States.[4] For years, economists, and others in the world of environmental management, had been doing analysis and writing about the advantages of cap and trade strategies as compared with more conventional strategies of command and control. When in the late 1980s a policy window opened because of the legislative deadline to revise a portion of the U.S. Clean Air Act, there were economists serving in the White House Council

stage"; (2) a stage of "alarmed discovery and euphoric enthusiasm"; (3) "realization of the cost of significant progress"; (4) "gradual decline of intense public interest"; and (5) a post-problem stage during which entities that were created during the previous stages persist, continuing to address the problem.

[2] In the 1970s, a key factor in the United States deciding that energy consumption was not tightly coupled with the level of GDP, but could be modified through efficiency measures, resulted from comparisons of U.S. energy intensity with that of a number of European countries. However, foreign comparisons often do not play well in the American political environment given its penchant for "exceptionalism," witness issues such as gun control and passenger rail service.

[3] For example, it seems likely that a reason that conservative members of the U.S. Congress have worked to prevent DHS and CDC from funding research on gun violence is that they wish to avoid the issue of guns in America being reclassified as an issue of public health.

[4] Thanks to Prof. Robert Hahn for some of the details in this example.

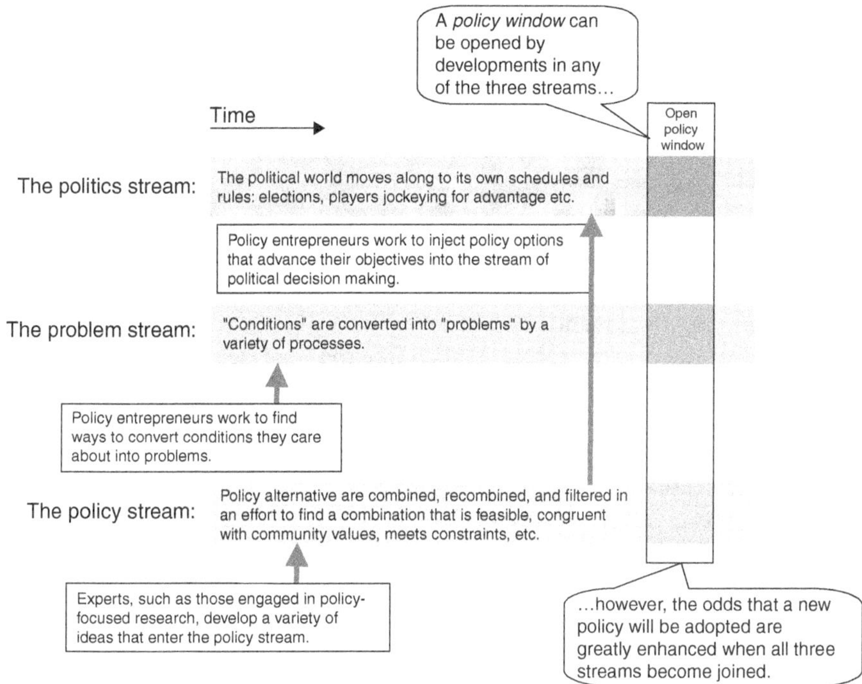

FIGURE 16.1. A diagrammatic representation of Kingdon's model of the policy process. Kingdon argues that there are three separate streams that he terms "policies, problems, and politics." Each of these streams has a life of its own. While a policy window leading to some policy action can be opened by events in any of the streams, the odds of a new policy emerging are greatly enhanced when all three streams become joined. Policy windows open and close – sometimes as a result of predictable events such as elections and sometimes as a result of random and often unpredicted external events. When that happens, if the policy stream contains good ideas, that are relevant to the problem at hand, they may be adopted.

on Economic Advisors who were well-versed in these ideas. At the same time, key players at EPA saw an opportunity for career advancement by supporting a new approach. With backing from President George H.W. Bush, largely achieved thanks to the work of White House Counsel C. Boyden Gray, and with strong support from the Environmental Defense Fund (EDF), an environmental NGO, they managed to inject the idea of trading into the Congressional discourse, buttressed by solid academic supporting literature, with the result that it was adopted. If there had not been more than a decade of previous research on this topic, or if the right people had not been present to serve as policy entrepreneurs, the change might not have occurred.[5]

[5] For another example that illustrates the Kingdon model, see the discussion of the development of the Office of Naval Research (ONR) in Section 18.3.

Kingdon argues that:

> The generation of policy alternatives is best seen as a selection process, analogous to biological natural selection. In what we have called the policy primeval soup, many ideas float around, bumping into one another, encountering new ideas, and forming combinations and recommendations. The origins of policy may seem a bit obscure, hard to predict and hard to understand or to structure.

This model of different, perhaps disparate, ideas and concepts being cut and pasted together does not sit very well with policy analysts who like to think of themselves as developing a coherent, integrated policy formulation that a decision maker subsequently implements. It is, however, an all too realistic description of the policy process – much like the "sausage making" characteristic of legislative development. Holding together a set of attributes for a policy prescription throughout the process of adoption and implementation requires constant attention and vigilance. Even a momentary loss of attention may result in other policy entrepreneurs adding modifications that serve very different objectives.[6] While processes of persuasion are typically used to achieve consensus in the problem stream, Kingdon argues that bargaining is the basic mode of reaching consensus in the political stream. This takes place through "trading provisions for support, adding elected officials to coalitions by giving them concessions that they demand, or compromising from ideal positions to positions that will gain wider acceptance."

READING 16.1

John W. Kingdon, "Chapter 9: Wrapping Things up," in *Agendas, Alternatives and Public Policies*, Little, Brown and Company, pp. 205–218, 1984.

DISCUSSION QUESTIONS FOR READING 16.1

- To the extent that the Kingdon model of the policy process is correct, what do you see as the roles that analysts might play in this process?
- Could analysts play a role in turning "conditions" into "problems" for which solutions might be developed?
- What, if any, do you see as the connection between the Kingdon model of the policy process and the garbage can model discussed in Section 15.3?

16.2 POLICY MAKING AS A PROCESS OF PUNCTURED EQUILIBRIUM

Baumgartner and Jones (1993) argue that when a general policy subsystem becomes well-established, a policy monopoly often arises in which specific

[6] See Sapolsky (1990) and the discussion of the origins of ONR in Section 18.3.

agencies and actors dominate the way issues are framed, and control who has standing to frame and take positions with respect to the topic.

While policy sometimes evolves gradually through incremental change, Baumgartner and Jones (1993) argue that "over the long run, open democratic political systems are characterized both by policy monopolies, as the political system struggles with its limited ability to process numerous issues simultaneously, and by turbulent disruptions, as attention is directed at the issue again. That is, democratic systems are composed of punctured partial equilibria." They write:

> When issues reach the public agenda on a wave of popular enthusiasm, conditions are at their best for the construction of a new policy sub-system ... [In contrast] when an issue emerges on the national agenda in an atmosphere of criticism ... conditions are ripe for the destruction or dilution of any policy subsystem that may have been created in the past. Criticism of experts encourages political leaders to pay more attention to the details of policy making within specialized policy communities, whereas enthusiasm leads political leaders to delegate power to experts.

Because there is a diversity of policy subsystems, each of which is able to consider important issues in their respective domains as they arise, during periods of quasi-equilibrium the overall policy process is able to engage in a form of "parallel processing." However, since humans are boundedly rational (see Chapter 12), once issues are elevated to the attention of political leadership they must of necessity be addressed in a serial manner (Simon, 1985). Baumgartner and Jones (1993) suggest that "the job of losers in a policy subsystem is to move the issue [they care about] from the realm of parallel processing to the realm of serial processing by reallocating attention."

Policy shifts through punctuated equilibrium may grow out of the gradual accumulation of public concerns and pressures. An example is the shift in U.S. public attitudes and regulatory approaches with respect to nuclear power that occurred during the 1960s and 1970s.[7] Such a shift through punctuated equilibrium may also arise as the result of some abrupt precipitating event that commands wide public attention. Examples include the Fukushima nuclear accident that gave rise to German Chancellor Merkel's decision to move away from nuclear power, or the terrorist attack of September 11, 2001, that led the Bush Administration to create the U.S. Department of Homeland Security and undertake a dramatic widening of surveillance and related activities.

Such shifts may also emerge as the result of actions by a few key policy actors. An example is provided by the history of the process by which the Reagan Administration chose to undertake its Strategic Defense Initiative for ballistic missile defense (BMD), commonly termed the "Star Wars" program.

[7] For a detailed discussion, see chapter 4 of Baumgartner and Jones (1993).

Writing for the Congressional Research Service (CRS), Hildreth (2007) notes that:

The United States has pursued research and development in anti-ballistic missile (ABM) systems since the late 1940s. In the mid-1960s, it developed the Nike-X system, which would have used ground-based, nuclear-armed interceptor missiles deployed around a number of major urban areas to protect against Soviet missile attack. Many analysts recognized that such protection would be limited, in part because the Soviet Union could probably saturate the system with offensive warheads and just a few warheads could achieve massive damage against a "soft" target like a city.

In his brief CRS history of BMD, Hildreth (2007) goes on to outline the evolution of research and the development and shifting missions of ABM systems such as Sentinel and Safeguard.

In the early 1980s, Edward Teller began to argue that space-based X-ray lasers, pumped with radiation from a nuclear detonation, could be used to destroy incoming ballistic missiles. Teller gained the ear of a few key players in President Reagan's National Security Council staff. While Reagan was vague about the technical details, the idea of providing an impenetrable shield against incoming missiles resonated with Reagan's long-standing and very legitimate concerns about the adequacy of a defense policy based solely on deterrence.

Hedrick Smith provides a remarkable inside account of how in a matter of weeks, working in secret, a small handful of NRC staff converted an agreement by the Joint Chiefs about the need to expand research in BMD into a Presidential speech announcing a program to develop and implement a program for a massive nationwide missile shield. As Smith recounts, the proposal was developed with almost no input from the technical community beyond the advice of Dr. Teller.[8] When, late in the process, Presidential Science Advisor George Keworth was consulted, he reportedly chose not to relay the cautionary advice he had recently received on the feasibility of comprehensive BMD from his technical advisors,[9] and instead chose to go along with the President's political judgment. Frantic last-minute efforts by other senior policy advisors, cabinet officials, and senior defense leaders to delay until further study could be conducted were unsuccessful. On March 23, the President presented the speech, arguing that:

if the Soviet Union will join with us in our effort to achieve major arms reduction, we will have succeeded in stabilizing the nuclear balance. Nevertheless, it will still be

[8] In an informal seminar in the Department of Engineering and Public Policy at Carnegie Mellon just a few weeks before the President's March 23 speech, Dr. Teller laid out many of the ideas that became the core of the SDI program, using phrases that were later echoed in the President's speech.

[9] I have been told by a senior staffer that Keworth had a document in his pocket from the White House Science Council that raised serious technical doubts about the feasibility of BMD but chose not to present it, deferring to what he saw as a political imperative. See Section 19.6 on the Office of Technology Assessment for a discussion of some of the subsequent fallout from analysis of the "Star Wars" proposal.

necessary to rely on the specter of retaliation, on mutual threat. And that's a sad commentary on the human condition. Wouldn't it be better to save lives than to avenge them? Are we not capable of demonstrating our peaceful intentions by applying all our abilities and our ingenuity to achieving a truly lasting stability? I think we are. Indeed, we must.

After careful consultation with my advisers, including the Joint Chiefs of Staff, I believe there is a way. Let me share with you a vision of the future, which offers hope. It is that we embark on a program to counter the awesome Soviet missile threat with measures that are defensive. Let us turn to the very strengths in technology that spawned our great industrial base and that have given us the quality of life we enjoy today.

What if free people could live secure in the knowledge that their security did not rest upon the threat of instant U.S. retaliation to deter a Soviet attack, that we could intercept and destroy strategic ballistic missiles before they reached our own soil or that of our allies?

I know this is a formidable, technical task, one that may not be accomplished before the end of this century.

Yet, current technology has attained a level of sophistication where it's reasonable for us to begin this effort. It will take years, probably decades of effort on many fronts. There will be failures and setbacks, just as there will be successes and breakthroughs. And as we proceed, we must remain constant in preserving the nuclear deterrent and maintaining a solid capability for flexible response. But isn't it worth every investment necessary to free the world from the threat of nuclear war? We know it is.

At the heart of the President's proposal lay the use of directed energy weapons (DEWs). In July 1987, a group of 17 leading physicists, convened by the American Physical Society, published a report that concluded:

Although substantial progress has been made in many technologies of DEWs over the last two decades, the Study Group finds significant gaps in the scientific and engineering understanding of many issues associated with the development of these technologies. Successful resolution of these issues is critical for the extrapolation to performance levels that would be required in an effective ballistic missile defense system. At present, there is insufficient information to decide whether the required extrapolations can or cannot be achieved. Most crucial elements required for DEW systems need improvements of several orders of magnitude. Because the elements are interrelated, the improvements must be achieved in a mutually consistent manner. We estimate that even in the best of circumstances, a decade or more of intensive research would be required to provide the technical knowledge needed for an informed decision about the potential effectiveness and survivability of directed energy weapons systems. In addition, the important issues of overall system integration and effectiveness depend critically upon information that, to our knowledge does not yet exist. (Bloembergen and Patel et al., 1987)

READING 16.2

Hedrick Smith, "SDI: Shortcutting the System" and "The Power Cocoon," pp. 603–616 in *The Power Game: How Washington Works*, Random House, 793pp., 1988.

DISCUSSION QUESTIONS FOR READING 16.2

- What thoughts about the role of policy analysis, and of science and technology advice to government, do you come away with after reading Smith's account?
- Many have argued that even though "Star Wars" as originally proposed would never have worked, President Reagan's commitment to build the system played a key role in persuading the Russians to change course, leading to the end of the Cold War. What is your view of this argument?

16.3 ADAPTIVE POLICY AND LEARNING

Often policy makers do not get things right the first time, or the circumstances change so that what once made sense no longer works very well. It is difficult to open another policy window to correct or fine-tune a policy – and, when a new window does get opened, one can never be sure what may happen (see the discussion of the garbage can model in Chapter 15).

In engineering, we differentiate between systems that run "open loop," that is, without corrective feedback, and those that run "closed loop," that is, with feedback to the system to provide corrective adjustment. Unfortunately, too much public policy runs open loop, in the sense that once it has been put in place it does not get revisited. Authorizing legislation often delegates a fair amount of discretion to regulatory agencies in how they implement rules. However, because the process of formulating a rule and getting it implemented requires enormous effort, agencies tend to want to get something fixed in place and not have to revisit it.

Cass Sunstein (2013) has been a strong proponent of "retrospective analysis" that is designed to learn how policies have performed with a view to improving them in the future. He argues that such analysis can facilitate "the repeal or streamlining of less effective rules and the strengthening or expansion of those that turn out to do more good than harm." Sunstein argues that regulations should be "written and implemented so as to facilitate reliable evaluation." He institutionalized these views by adding section 6 to Executive Order 13563 (EO, 2011) that reads:

> Sec. 6. *Retrospective Analysis of Existing Rules.* (a) To facilitate the periodic review of existing significant regulations, agencies shall consider how to promote retrospective analysis of rules that may be outmoded, ineffective, insufficient, or excessively burdensome, and to modify, streamline, expand or repeal them in accordance with what has been learned ...
>
> (b) Within 120 days of the date of this order, each agency shall develop and submit to the Office of Information and Regulatory Affairs a preliminary plan ... under which the agency will periodically review its existing significant regulations.

One powerful tool that legislators and agencies can use to assure that regulations and other policies do not become outmoded is to specify a "sunset" date at which a regulation or piece of enabling legislation ceases to exist unless it is revisited and renewed.

In a project to develop a regulatory framework for the geological sequestration of carbon dioxide, we proposed an adaptive framework under which at least once every seven years, an independent expert committee would consider all the experience that was accumulating around the world and advise the relevant regulatory entities on changes that should be considered (Morgan et al., 2012). While industry generally complains about the inflexibility of regulations, when we first briefed this idea to relevant industry people we received strong push back – "give us a stable regulation so we know the rules of the game." Once we explained that any individual project could continue to operate under the rules with which it was licensed (or switch to the revised rules if they preferred), the proposal was viewed as acceptable.

Kai N. Lee (1993) has been a vigorous proponent of learning and adaptive management as a policy strategy.[10] He argues for an approach to natural resource policy that adopts the simple imperative that "policies are experiments: *learn from them*." Building on his experience as a member of the Northwest Power Planning Council in helping to manage water, fish, and other resources in the U.S. Pacific Northwest, Lee argues that an experimental science-based approach to improve the shared knowledge on which resource management policies are developed can provide the "compass" for this process. Bounded conflict in political arenas, through which varying interests are balanced, can allow the management process "to detect errors and force corrections." This politically mediated correction provides the stabilizing "gyroscope" for the process. If they are applied together, with a recognition that the outcome will be noisy so that participants need to exercise patience, Lee argues that "civic science" mediated through appropriate political processes can lead to the "social learning" that is necessary to grope our way toward better management policies.[11]

16.4 DIVERSIFICATION AS A POLICY STRATEGY

Manski (2013) makes a case for adopting a diversity of policies (i.e., different plausibly good treatments for different populations) "when a society must treat a population of persons and does not know the best treatment." He writes: "Sequential treatment of new cohorts of persons strengthens that appeal of diversification. The reason is that society may now benefit from learning, with observation of the outcomes experienced by earlier cohorts informing treatment choice in later cohorts."

[10] Portions of discussion of Lee's book are derived from Morgan (1994).

[11] Lee is exceptionally well qualified to address this issue. After earning a Ph.D. in physics, he switched to political science and earned a tenured faculty position in that field at the University of Washington.

READING 16.3

Kai N. Lee, "Chapter 3: Compass: Adaptive Management," pp. 19–50, and "Chapter 4: Gyroscope: Negotiation and Conflict," pp. 51–86 in *Compass and Gyroscope: Integrating Science and Politics for the Environment*, Island Press, 243pp., 1993.

Lee explains that this chapter:

> describes a learning strategy that does not assume that adaptive policies in large ecosystems will be designed and executed by rational actors in an ideal world. This involves a two-way adjustment: on one side, to suggest institutional designs and practices that can compensate for the inevitable weaknesses and unavoidable failings of real institutions; and on the other, to temper and frame expectations of what is attainable in an imperfect world. The only world we have.

DISCUSSION QUESTIONS FOR READING 16.3

- What does Lee mean by "adaptive management"?
- Why does Lee argue that "human interactions with nature should be experimental?"
- What institutional, behavioral, and political factors can make it difficult to adopt a strategy of adaptive management?
- What assumptions about the sensitivity and linearity of environmental responses are implicit in Lee's argument?

Such diversification strategies are especially feasible in a federal system such as the United States in which 50 different states can serve as laboratories for policy assessment. While it does not do this as often as it probably should, Manski (2013) notes that:

> The federal government can provide incentives to the states to encourage them to enact desirable portfolios of policies. Thus, the federal government can encourage adaptive diversification across states, modifying the incentives as knowledge of treatment responses accumulates. The federal government played such an active role in welfare policy in the late 1980s, when it encouraged states to institute and evaluate variations on the then-existing program of Aid to Families and Dependent Children.

Of course, to maximize learning and achieve their effectiveness, diversification strategies must be well-instrumented so that assessment and learning are possible. Then, if they are to be effective someone must engage in careful impartial comparative analysis in order to extract correct lessons. Without such analysis, word-of-mouth "lessons" may bear very little relation to what has actually transpired.

Sometimes political factors, such as opposition by some in the U.S. Congress for support for various kinds of social science research, can make it difficult to perform such analysis. This is a space that has been too little explored by impartial public interest private philanthropy.[12]

16.5 SOCIAL CONTROL THROUGH NORMS, LEGAL PROHIBITIONS, COMMAND, AND MARKETS

Societies have always exercised constraints on the behaviors and activities of their members. While they overlap somewhat, and there are often hybrid models, Figure 16.2 provides a very simple taxonomy.

It is easy in today's complex society to forget the powerful role played by social norms. Norms govern many of our behaviors and can be especially important in the management of common pool resources. Elinor (Lin) Ostrom (1990)[13] conducted extensive studies of situations in which "institutions for collective action" have been developed that limit what Garrett Hardin (1968) has termed "the tragedy of the commons." Such institutions limit the demands placed on common-pool resources (CPR) (grazing lands, ocean fisheries, national parks, media receiving pollution, etc.), thus avoiding their becoming overexploited and ruined for all (see Table 16.1).

While many institutions for collective action are knowingly developed, there are also instances, especially in traditional cultures, in which such systems have evolved without the members of the affected society fully understanding their consequences. One especially notable example is the system of "water temples" that grew up to manage the allocation of irrigation waters for farms in traditional Bali. Anthropologist J. Stephen Lansing (2007) writes:

> I first became curious about the water temples in the mid-1970s, when I was gathering materials for a study of the historical evolution of temples in Bali. One of the peculiarities of Balinese temples is their anonymity: most temples look exactly alike, and except for a few days each year when festivals are held, they are generally left empty and abandoned. The functions of the temple, and the identities of the gods worshiped within, are often known only to the temple's congregation. In a landscape dotted with hundreds of nearly identical temples, it is not a simple matter to work out their histories and purposes. The existence of a separate class of "water temples" is not mentioned in the scholarly literature on Bali, and I doubt that I would have become aware of the existence of the water temples but for the fact that my period of fieldwork happen to coincide with the phenomenon that seemed at first to have nothing whatsoever to do with the temples: the onset of the "Green Revolution" in Balinese agriculture.

Farmers were being urged to plant new strains of high-yield rice, and to grow those strains continuously. At first yields went up, but then they fell due to

[12] I say "impartial public interest" because recent years have seen the rise of a class of "philanthropy" that, while masquerading as operating in the public interest, is in fact focused on advancing specific political agendas. See Mayer (2016).

[13] In 2009, Ostrom was the first woman to win the Nobel Prize in Economics for her work on the management of collective pool resources, i.e., "the commons."

TABLE 16.1. *A speculative list of design principles for institutions to successfully manage common-pool resources (CPR), as inferred by Elinor Ostrom from her studies of long-enduring CPR institutions (table reproduced from Ostrom, 1990).*

1. Clearly defined boundaries
   Individuals or households who have rights to withdrawal resource units from the CPR must be clearly defined, as must the boundaries of the CPR itself
2. Congruence between appropriation and provision rules and local conditions
   Appropriation rules restricting time, place, technology, and/or quantity of resource units are related to local conditions and to provision rules requiring labor, material, and/or money
3. Collective-choice arrangements
   Most individuals affected by the operational rules can participate in modifying the operational rules
4. Monitoring
   Monitors, who actively audit CPR conditions and appropriator behavior, are accountable to the appropriators or are appropriators
5. Graduated sanctions
   Appropriators who violate operational rules are likely to be assessed graduated sanctions (depending on the seriousness and context of the offense) by other appropriators, by officials accountable to those appropriators, or by both
6. Conflict-resolution mechanisms
   Appropriators and their officials have rapid access to low-cost local arenas to resolve conflicts among appropriators or between appropriators and officials
7. Minimal recognition of rights to organize
   The rights of appropriators to devise their own institutions are not challenged by external governmental authorities
   For CPRs that are part of larger systems:
8. Nested enterprises
   Appropriation, provision, enforcement, conflict resolution, and governance activities are organized in multiple layers of nested enterprises

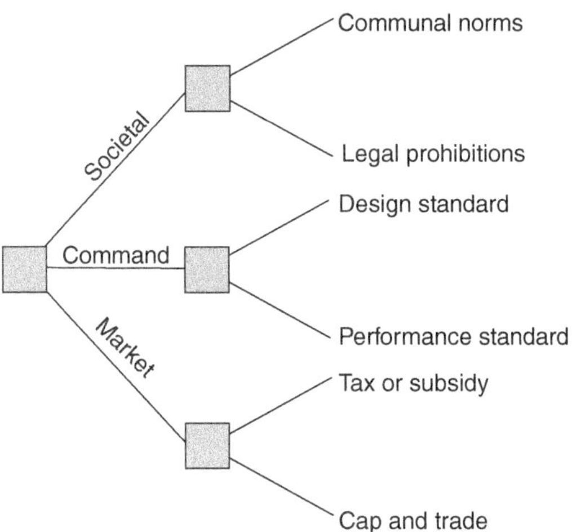

FIGURE 16.2. A rough taxonomy of strategies employed by society to avoid undesirable behaviors and activities by its members.

water stress and pest infestations. Lansing found that local Balinese agricultural engineers had begun to suspect that the problem was the result of abandoning the complex traditional system of water and cropping allocation that had been controlled by the rituals of the water temples. Lansing (2007) explains that his studies had persuaded him that "the primary role of water temples was in the maintenance of social relationships between productive units." He notes that:

> The Green Revolution approach assumed that agriculture was a purely technical process and that production would be optimized if everyone planted high-yield varieties of rice as often as they could. In contrast, Balinese temple priests and farmers argued that the water temples were necessary to coordinate cropping patterns so that there would be enough irrigation water for everyone and reduce pests by coordinating fallow periods.

Lansing collaborated with systems ecologist James Kremer to build a computer simulation model that demonstrated that this was in fact the case (Lansing and Kremer, 1993). A later agent-based model built with John Miller found that results similar to traditional norms emerge from the simulation (Lansing and Miller, 2005). They conclude:

> The cooperation that sustains the Balinese rice farming system is truly remarkable. Without centralized control, farmers have created a carefully coordinated system that allows productive farming in an ecosystem that is rife with water scarcity and the threat of disease and pests. The game-theoretic model we develop[ed] ... inspired by a generation of careful anthropological fieldwork, provides a compact explanation for many of the most salient features we observe in the system.
>
> While externalities caused by either water scarcity or pests would, in isolation, be expected to imply a serious market failure, the ecology of the rice farming system links these two externalities in such a way that cooperation, rather than catastrophe, is the result. Depending on the underlying ecological parameters in the system, there are regimes in which the farmers would like to carefully coordinate their cropping patterns (in particular have identical fallow periods) so as to control pest populations. There are other regimes in which coordination is not an equilibrium, even though coordinated farming would result in greater aggregate crop output. We identify at least two indirect mechanisms by which the system can escape from such a trap. The first is to have the up-stream farmers share their water with the downstream farmers, and we find that under many circumstances, both parties are willing to engage in such bargains. The second, a bit more counterintuitive, is that increases in pest damage can drive the system into a coordinated equilibrium enhancing aggregate output.

There are some things that society does not allow. Rather than depend only on social norms, many Western societies operate with legal prohibitions. In the United States, these are covered under "criminal law" (e.g., theft and murder) and "tort law" (e.g., nuisance, defamation, and some forms of negligence).

In addition, society needs to regulate or limit the nature and extent of many activities that are not banned outright. For example, it limits the amount of effluent that someone can emit to the air or water. For most of the first part of the twentieth century, command-and-control was the basic approach adopted for much regulation. The most common approach was to use design standards – regulation that specified specifically how a particular activity must be performed. Over time, people began to understand that mandating a specific design often limited the degree to which people could be inventive, sometimes resulting in much higher costs than necessary to meet a regulatory goal. This realization led to arguments in favor of "performance-based" regulation, that is, regulation that specifies what actors must achieve, without specifying the details of how they should achieve it.

Assigning property rights is another way to manage resources (e.g., quotas for fish catch) and externalities (emission permits). Economists have long argued that the most efficient way to deal with externalities such as noise or pollution is to "internalize" them, that is, find some way to place a price on them so that those who are causing them have to include the associated cost in their decision making. This can be done with emission or effluent taxes. One of the first applications of such taxes involved emission fees for facilities along the Rhine River (see Section 10.6). More recently, the EU and a number of individual nations have chosen to use taxes on emissions as their way of controlling atmospheric releases of carbon dioxide.

A closely related approach is called "cap and trade." Under this arrangement, a cap on total emissions is established, permits are allocated in some manner, and then those who need more can purchase them from those who do not need them as much. Parson and Kravitz (2013) explain that emissions taxes and cap and trade:

> are equivalent under certainty and perfect enforcement, but they differ if uncertainty, political economy of enactment or imperfect enforcement is present. With uncertainty, each form fixes one dimension of the outcome (price or quantity), but market response determines the pollution level; under [tradable] permits, market response determines the permit price, which should be equal to the marginal cost of control.

Cap and trade should really only be used in cases like carbon dioxide, where the resulting pollutant is well mixed. There have been proposals to apply this strategy to other problems such as mercury emissions from power plants. However, in that case, the approach makes far less sense since many of the impacts are local. The fact that it is cheaper to clean up mercury from a facility at one end of the state does nothing to help the people and local environment being exposed to mercury from another facility at the other end of the state.[14]

[14] In contrast to mercury, the situation for controlling lead pollution provides an intermediate example. When the primary source was lead emitted from the tailpipes of ubiquitous automobiles fueled by leaded gasoline, a cap and trade approach could be justified (Schmalensee and Stavins, 2015). Now that lead has been removed from gasoline, and the primary sources are point sources such as smelters and battery recycling plants, using cap and trade does not make sense.

16.6 THE SCIENCE OF "MUDDLING THROUGH"

Many policy analysts like to think in terms of developing and implementing coherent policies to address a problem. In a paper titled "The Science of 'Muddling Through,'" Lindblom (1959) terms this as the "rational-comprehensive" or "root" approach to policy formulation. He terms an alternative, much more incremental strategy a process of "successive limited comparisons" or "branch" method. Table 16.2 contrasts the two approaches.

Lindblom argues that for complex problems, the root method is simply impossible:

> Although such an approach can be described, it cannot be practiced except for relatively simple problems and even then only in a somewhat modified form. It assumes intellectual capacities and sources of information that men simply do not possess, and it is even more absurd as an approach to policy when the time and money that can be allocated to a policy problem is limited, as is always the case.

The situation is further complicated by the fact that, in almost all cases, participants in the process have somewhat different values and objectives. As a consequence, Lindblom (1959) argues that rather than ranking values, administrators must choose directly "among alternative policies that offer different marginal combinations of values." As noted by Raiffa (1982), while different parties may have very different values and objectives, they may nonetheless be able to reach agreement about which policy to choose from a set of alternative options.

Lindblom (1959) argues that:

> In the method of successive limited comparisons, simplification is systematically achieved in two principle ways. First ... through limitation of policy comparisons to those policies that differ in relatively small degrees from policies presently in effect ... [Second] public administrators ... largely limit their analysis to incremental or marginal differences ... [both] because they desperately need some way to simplify their problems ... [and] in order to be relevant. Democracies change their policies through incremental adjustments. Policies do not move in leaps and bounds.

He further argues that because key values in a society each have their "watchdog" over time, the process is self-correcting with the result that "In a society like that of the United States ... it can be argued that our system often can assure a more comprehensive regard of the values of the whole society than any attempt at intellectual comprehensiveness." Lindblom (1959) asserts that:

> For all the apparent shortcomings of the incremental approach to policy alternatives with its arbitrary exclusion coupled with fragmentation, when compared to the root method the branch method often looks far superior ...
>
> Policy is not made once and for all; it is made and re-made endlessly. Policy making is a process of successive approximations to some desired objective in which what is desired itself continues to change under reconsideration.

TABLE 16.2. *Attributes of the two methods for policy development that Lindblom (1959) discusses (table modified from Lindblom, 1959).*

Rational-comprehensive or "root" method	Successive limited comparisons or "branch" method
1. Clarification of values or objectives distinct from and usually prerequisite to empirical analysis of alternative policies 2. Policy-formulation is therefore approached through means–ends analysis: First the ends are isolated, then the means to achieve them are sought 3. The test of a "good" policy is that it can be shown to be the most appropriate means to desired ends 4. Analysis is comprehensive; every important relevant factor is taken into account 5. Theory is often heavily relied upon	1. Selection of value goals and empirical analysis of the needed action are not distinct from one another but are closely intertwined 2. Since means and ends are not distinct, means–ends analysis is often inappropriate or limited 3. The test of a "good" policy is typically that various analysts find themselves directly agreeing on a policy (without their agreeing that it is the most appropriate means to an agreed objective) 4. Analysis is drastically limited: i. Important possible outcomes are neglected ii. Important alternative potential policies are neglected iii. Important affected values are neglected 5. A succession of comparisons gradually reduces or eliminates reliance on theory

Given that he believes the root method is infeasible for addressing complex problems, Lindblom (1959) argues that to guard against some of its limitations, agency administrators should be sure that among their personnel they have two types of diversification:

> administrators whose thinking is organized by reference to policy chains other than those familiar to most members of the organization, and even more commonly, administrators whose professional or personal values or interests create diversity of views ... so that even within a single agency, decision making can be fragmented and parts of the agency can serve as watchdogs for other parts.

The fact that Lindblom's description of policy making is clearly correct for many policy processes suggests that society should be careful when it pursues technologies whose safe operation and management requires coherent and consistent oversight. John Kemeny (1980) succinctly illustrated this point in his report as the chair of the Presidential Commission to examine the Three-Mile

Island nuclear accident. Writing on the evolution of nuclear policy, he drew the following analogy. Suppose, he wrote, "that Congress designed an airplane, with each committee designing one component of it and an eleventh hour conference committee deciding how the various pieces should be put together?" Kemeny asks, would any sane person fly in such an airplane?

READING 16.4

Charles E. Lindblom, "The Science of 'Muddling Through,'" *Public Administration Review*, *19*(2), pp. 79–88, 1959.

While I find it much less useful, 20 years later Lindblom wrote a follow-up paper that a few readers might also wish to look at:

Charles E. Lindblom, "Still Muddling, Not Yet Through," *Public Administration Review*, *39*(6), pp. 517–526, 1979.

DISCUSSION QUESTIONS FOR READING 16.4

- Why does Lindblom argue that in all but the simplest cases, it is simply unrealistic to develop an overarching policy solution that will be implemented and sustained in a coherent way?
- To the extent that Lindblom's assessment is correct, what are the implications of his observation for the design of public policies?
- What do you think of the argument that one implication of Lindblom's argument is that "society should be careful when it pursues technologies whose safe operation and management requires coherent and consistent oversight"?

The process of developing budgets at virtually all levels of government provides a clear illustration of "muddling through." John (Pat) Crecine has studied the process of budgeting at the municipal level and developed computer simulations that emulate the interactions among the key players in the budgetary process. In agreement with Lindblom, Crecine (1969) observes that:

> normative theories of public resource allocation founded in public finance and welfare economics are concerned ... with maximizing net social welfare, a community utility function, and the like ...
>
> For two reasons ... welfare economics and public finance approaches are likely to be of little help in the search for a positive theory of budgeting. First the assumptions underlying these theories seem to require abilities no decision-maker possesses. Second, the series were constructed for different purposes and designed to explain different phenomena than those [involved in developing municipal budgets]. The economic branch of the literature [on budgeting] is largely concerned either with the way decisions *should* be made or with how they're made in a more global level.

Like the participants in the budget process Crecine studied, "Lindblom's administrator is a man with limited knowledge, limited information, and limited cognitive ability, making a policy choice in an uncertain world by 'drastically' simplifying the problem in making marginal adjustments in past 'successful' policies to formulate current policies."

16.7 WE CAN'T ALWAYS JUST MUDDLE THROUGH

I argued above that, in light of Lindblom's insights, it may be unwise to undertake activities that require sustained and coherent attention unless at the same time society can create stable institutions that can manage them in a coherent way for as long as is needed (see Section 16.6). However, situations arise in which we do not have a choice. The planning in the restructured power system, and policies to abate emissions of carbon dioxide and greenhouse gases, provide two examples.

When vertically integrated power companies ran the power system they routinely engaged in long-term resource planning, assessing where new generation was needed and what transmission upgrades and expansions needed to be undertaken in order to assure the continued provision of reliable electric services. For a while after "restructuring" we muddled along, coming up with strategies to keep the system operating. More recently, however, people have come to realize that market-based solutions, with their focus on short-term efficiency, are not sufficient. As a consequence a variety of new approaches are being developed in order to once again introduce some long-term planning into the system.

Climate change offers an even more compelling example of a situation in which simple muddling along will not lead to adequate outcomes. In an opinion piece in the *Proceedings of the National Academy of Science* I argued:

> After decades of talk the world is finally showing signs of muddling its way toward a range of policies to reduce emissions of carbon dioxide. The recent Paris accord will require nations to regularly report on their emissions and plans, and hence take more seriously the need for abatement. Incremental steps toward reducing emissions in the U.S. include the switch to natural gas, and the implementation of the Clean Power Plan for existing power plants. Outside the U.S. the ongoing efforts of the EU, the agreement between the U.S. and China, and efforts to limit emissions from aircraft and ocean shipping, are also promising incremental steps.
>
> Muddling through, however, has serious repercussions. Among them: investing in short-sighted technology and policy approaches that do not scale up. This could occur, in part, because most future emission reductions will proceed nation-by-nation and sector-by-sector. While such a bottom-up approach can be a good thing, without careful foresight it can also lead to solutions that actually impede rather than facilitate deeper emission cuts ... Once they become firmly established, complex regulatory systems, the bureaucracies that have been created to enforce them, and the emergence of interest groups with a stake in continuing their operation (think corn ethanol), can be extremely difficult to change.
>
> If climate policy is ultimately to be successful, "muddling" will need to be combined with some longer-term "visioning." Modest first steps that reduce emissions of greenhouse gases are wonderful, but to stabilize the climate the world must ultimately reduce

emissions of greenhouse gases by at least an order of magnitude ... It is not too soon to start thinking about how to avoid getting stuck with policies that do not scale up – how to avoid regulatory lock-in and move past early incremental steps to achieve much deeper reductions. (Morgan, 2016)[15]

In this piece I went on to identify a variety of actions that could be undertaken today in order to avoid muddling our way to a future in which achieving deep reductions in emissions could become difficult or perhaps even impossible. I concluded my piece by arguing that "without some longer-term 'visioning' of how to gracefully move past short-term strategies to address the longer-term need for major emission reductions, progress could stall. The success of today should not become the burden of tomorrow."

16.8 THE TECHNOLOGY OF FOOLISHNESS

When developing policy options, it is important not to seize upon the first idea that comes to mind, but to spend time brainstorming. Section 2.8 introduced and discussed James March's (1976) wonderful essay, "The Technology of Foolishness," in which he argues that a valuable strategy for assessing existing goals is to temporarily suspend the rules of rational behavior and engage in intellectual playfulness in order to identify new, possibly superior goals and behaviors. The same approach can also be very useful in inventing new policy designs.

March argues that after playing for a while and coming up with new insights, one should then reimpose the rules of rational thought, doing so in a way that is informed by the new insights obtained through having spent some time playing around with alternatives. Many serious organizations and policy analysis groups may be reluctant to encourage such "playfulness," but done in the right way and at the right time, it can sometimes lead to much more appropriate policy solutions.

Years ago, when I chaired a committee that included Herb Simon and John (Pat) Crecine we argued that promoting "intellectual playfulness" in a wide variety of different contexts should be one of the objectives of undergraduate education at Carnegie Mellon University. I am pleased to report that our Board of Trustees endorsed the idea!

READING 16.5

James G. March, "Chapter 5: The Technology of Foolishness," in J.G. March and J.P. Olsen (eds.), *Ambiguity and Choice in Organizations*, Universitetsforlaget, pp. 69–81, 1976.

[15] The original text contains a variety of citations to the literature that, for ease of reading, have not been included in this excerpt.

This book may be hard to find but the essay has been reproduced online in several forms.

DISCUSSION QUESTIONS FOR READING 16.5

- Why does March argue that intellectual playfulness can be a critical element of developing good goals, policies or strategies?
- Why and under what circumstances does March argue one should: treat goals as hypotheses; intuition as real; hypocrisy as a transition; memory as an enemy; and experience as theory?

16.9 IMPLEMENTATION

It is fine to develop wonderful policy ideas, but they are typically not worth much unless they can be implemented.

Pressman and Wildavsky (1973) performed an extensive assessment of the issues that arose in the process of implementing a set of programs developed by the U.S. Federal Economic Development Administration in Oakland, California – a city that had experienced a long history of social and economic problems. The two subtitles that Pressman and Wildavsky added to the cover page of their book summarize their story (Figure 16.3).

While the program set out to do all sorts of wonderful things to promote economic and social development in Oakland, clearly it was not as successful as its proponents had hoped.

Details of some of the difficulties the program encountered can be gotten by skimming chapters 5 and 6 of the book. A key insight from their assessment is the obstacles that can arise when a policy can only be implemented with the agreement and support of a number of existing parties. These difficulties can occur even if those parties "agree with the substantive end of the proposal and still oppose (or merely fail to facilitate) the means to effectuate it." Reasons Pressman and Wildavsky (1973) list for this include:

1. *Direct incompatibility with other commitments* – Participants may agree with the merits of a proposal but find that it is incompatible with other organizational goals ...
2. *No direct incompatibility, but preference for other programs* ...
3. *Simultaneous commitments to other programs* – participants may agree with the proposal, have no contradictory commitments, and not prefer any alternative programs, but they may have other projects of their own that demand time and attention ...
4. *Dependence on others who lack a sense of urgency in the project* ...
5. *Differences of opinion on leadership and proper organizational roles* ...
6. *Legal and procedural differences* ...
7. *Agreement coupled with lack of power* – Certain participants may agree enthusiastically with a proposal, but they may lack the resources to do much to help it.

TABLE 16.3. *The probability of successfully completing an implementation as the number of approvals from others that can prevent success increases.*

Probability of agreement on each clearance point (%)	Probability of success after 70 clearances	Number of agreements that reduce probability below 50%
80	0.00000013	4
90	0.00064	7
95	0.004	14
99	0.49	68

HOW GREAT EXPECTATIONS IN WASHINGTON
ARE DASHED IN OAKLAND
OR
WHY IT'S AMAZING THAT FEDERAL PROGRAMS WORK AT ALL
THIS BEING A SAGA OF THE
ECONOMIC DEVELOP ADMINISTRATION
AS TOLD BY
TWO SYMPATHETIC OBSERVERS WHO SEEK TO BUILD MORALS
ON A FOUNDATION OF
RUINED HOPES

FIGURE 16.3. Front piece from Pressman and Wildavsky (1973) which concisely summarizes their experience with a set of programs developed by the U.S. Federal Economic Development Administration in Oakland, California.

In the book, they provide examples of each of these in the context of the Oakland project.

Pressman and Wildavsky (1973) lay out a flow chart of the approvals or agreements (which they term "clearance points") that had to be achieved for various policies to be successfully implemented. They then note that it does not take many parties disagreeing, or not acting at a clearance point, before the odds of success drop to a very low level. Table 16.3 summarizes their argument.

An obvious insight from this work is that in designing a new policy it is highly desirable to minimize the number of clearance points that must be passed to achieve success. One way to do that is to create an entirely new organization that has full authority over all aspects of implementing a policy. However, legislatures and others are typically reluctant to do this in most circumstances. As noted above, one strategy to address legitimate concerns about creating ever more bureaucracy is to include a sunset rule that applies a fixed term to a new entity's existence.

Bardach (1977) sees implementation as entailing a "management game against the enthropic forces of social nature" against which he argues "there is no permanent solution." He goes on to note that "once this fact is recognized, the implication for policy designers is clear: design simple, straightforward programs that require as little management as possible." He further argues that:

> Other things [being] equal, policy designers should prefer to operate through manipulating prices and markets rather than through writing and enforcing regulations, through delivering cash rather than services, through communicating by means of smaller rather than large units of social organization, and through seeking clearances from fewer rather than more levels of consultation and review.

He argues that once a policy has been designed, it should be subjected to an implementation game in which players attempt to find weaknesses and break it. He advocates:

> the imaginative construction of future sequences of action→consequent conditions→actions→consequent conditions ... [Policy designers should work on] inventing a plausible story about "what will happen if ..." or, more precisely, inventing several such stories. Telling stories to oneself and to one's professional peers helps to illuminate some of the implementation paths that the designer does not want taken. He or she is then in a position to redesign some features or the implementation ... trial and error through successive iterations [should] produce better and better endings.

Essentially Bardach is calling for people to apply a "red team" approach before trying to implement a policy. This is great advice – which, while simple and inexpensive, is sadly almost never followed!

Building on the work of Bardach and several others, Sabatier and Mazmanian (1980) developed a general conceptual framework for the process of implementation, which they define as "the carrying out of a basic policy decision, usually made in a statute (although also possible through important executive orders or court decisions). Ideally that decision identifies the problem(s) to be addressed, stipulates the objective(s) to be pursued, and in a variety of ways 'structures' the implementation process." Sabatier and Mazmanian (1980) advance the framework shown in Figure 16.4, and discuss each element in some detail. Readers can probably infer the direction of influence of most of the factors that are listed. For example, an implementation problem is likely to be more easily solved if there is valid theory and technology and if there is little diversity in the target group. Similarly, an implementation problem is less likely to be easily solved if the target group constitutes a large fraction of a diverse total population and if success requires large behavioral change.

Summarizing Sabatier and Mazmanian's arguments, Kirst and Jung (1982) explain that "four variables most affect a program's first three to five years of implementation." These are summarized in Table 16.4.

Finally, Sabatier and Mazmanian (1980) provide two simple conceptual sketches to illustrate how a successful and somewhat less successful implementation might play out over a period of two decades. These sketches are reproduced in Figure 16.5.

TABLE 16.4. *Kirst and Jung's (1982) compact summary of four variables that Sabatier and Mazmanian (1980) argue most affect a program's first three to five years of implementation.*

1. The "strength" of the statutes and ensuing regulations	How precisely and consistently the objectives are specified and ranked, and (b) how clearly authority is delegated to organizational subunits
2. The presence of a "fixer"	A key legislator or administrator ideologically attuned to program requirements who controls resources important to crucial actors and who has the status, desire, and staff to monitor closely the implementation process
3. The resources of various constituency groups	The salience of an issue, the solidarity, the access to policy channels and information, and the availability of side payments for representatives from implementing agencies and intended target-group recipients
4. The commitment and leadership of agency officials	The direction and ranking of statutory objectives in officials' preference ordering; (b) the skills in realizing these preferences

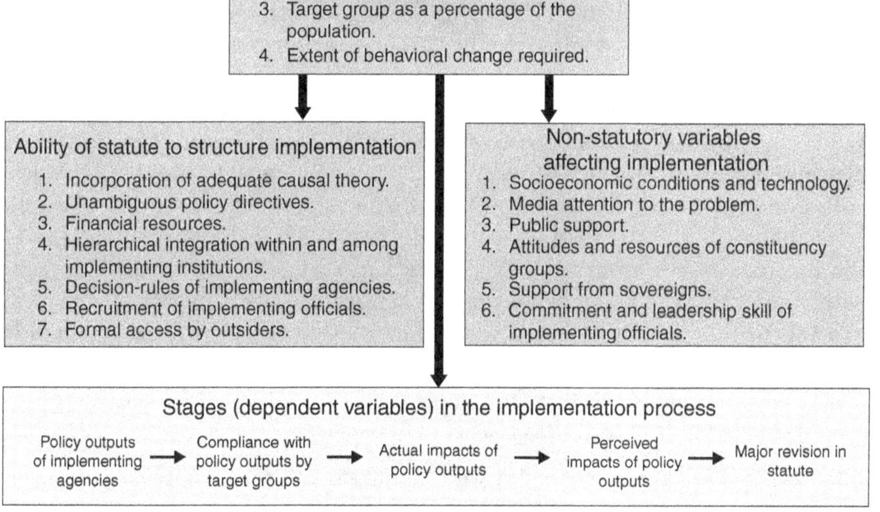

FIGURE 16.4. Conceptual framework of the implementation process. Figure redrawn from Sabatier and Mazmanian (1980).

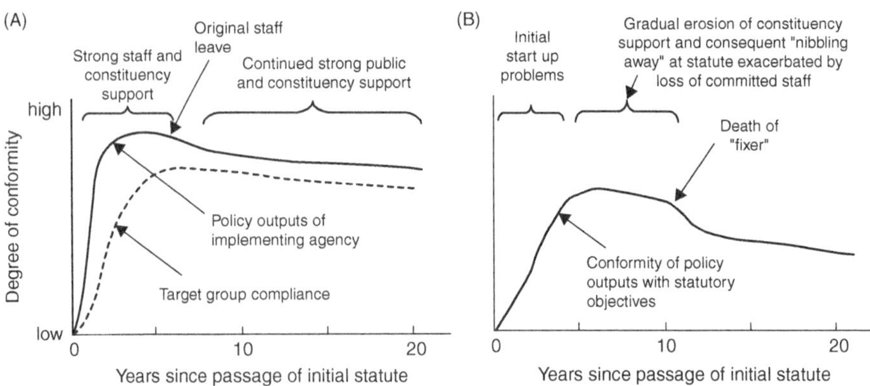

FIGURE 16.5. Conceptual sketches of **A.** how a successful implementation might play out over time and **B.** a less successful implementation scenario in which there are difficulties with initial start-up and then gradual erosion occurs. Figure redrawn from Sabatier and Mazmanian (1980).

Sabatier and others have applied their approach to analyze over twenty specific policy implementations (Sabatier, 1986) and found it to be generally useful. At the same time, he finds that too strong a focus on a "clear and consistent" policy objective is "a mistake." In most cases, there are a "multitude of partially-conflicting objectives." He notes that the failure to take a longer view of a policy (e.g., ten years rather than three or four) is important, because a longer view allows one to capture learning that takes place over time. He acknowledges that his approach has been "focused too much on the perspective of program proponents, thereby neglecting the strategies (and learning) by other actors which would provide the cornerstone for a more dynamic model" (Sabatier, 1986).

The perspective articulated by Sabatier and Mazmanian, by Pressman and Wildavsky, and by a number of others can be described as "top down," in the sense that it starts with some centrally enacted legislation or promulgated policy and then explores the issues that arise in the process of trying to implement that policy in the field. A second perspective has developed that can be characterized as "bottom up" (e.g., Hjern and Hull, 1982). Rather than begin with some centrally promulgated policy action, such as a piece of legislation, this approach is more concerned with addressing a policy problem and exploring the various factors (that may or may not include a specific piece of legislation or some similar central promulgated policy initiative). Sabatier (1986) has drawn the distinction as follows:

> Top-downers have been preoccupied with (a) the effectiveness of specific governmental programs and (b) the ability of elected officials to guide and constrain the behavior of civil servants and target groups. Addressing such concerns requires a careful analysis of the formally approved objectives of elected officials, an examination of relevant

performance indicators, and an analysis of the factors affecting such performance. Bottom-uppers, on the other hand, are far less preoccupied with the extent to which a formally enacted policy decision is carried out and much more concerned with accurately mapping the strategies of actors concerned with a policy problem. They are not primarily concerned with the implementation (carrying out) of a policy *per se* but rather with understanding actor interaction in a specific policy sector.

Sabatier (1986, 1988) has outlined a strategy by which the strengths of the top-down and bottom-up approaches can be combined.

REFERENCES

Bardach, E. (1977). *The Implementation Game: What Happens after a Bill Becomes a Law*, MIT Press, 322pp.

Baumgartner, F.B. and B.D. Jones (1993). *Agendas and Instability in American Politics*, University of Chicago Press, 298pp.

Bloembergen, N. and C.K.N. Patel (co-chairs) et al. (1987). "Report to the American Physical Society of the Study Group on Science and Technology of Directed Energy Weapons," *Reviews of Modern Physics*, *59*(3), pp. S1–S209.

Crecine, J.P. (1969). *Governmental Problem-solving: A Computer Simulation of Municipal Budgeting*, Rand McNally, 338pp.

Downs, A. (1972). "Up and down with Ecology: The 'Issue-Attention Cycle,'" *The Public Interest*, *28*, pp. 38–50.

EO 13563 (2011). *Improving Regulation and Regulatory Review*. Available at: www.gpo.gov/fdsys/pkg/FR-2011-01-21/pdf/2011-1385.pdf.

Hardin, G. (1968). "The Tragedy of the Commons," *Science*, *162*(3859), pp. 1243–1248.

Hildreth, S.A. (2007). "Ballistic Missile Defense: Historical Overview," Congressional Research Service Report RS22120, 6pp.

Hjern, B. and C. Hull (1982). "Implementation Research as Empirical Constitutionalism," *European Journal of Political Research*, *10*(2), pp. 105–115.

Kemeny, J.G. (1980). "Saving American Democracy: The Lessons of Three Mile Island," *Technology Review*, *83*(June–July), pp. 64–75.

Kingdon, J.W. (1984). *Agendas, Alternatives and Public Policies*, Little, Brown and Company, 240pp.

Kirst, M. and R. Jung (1982). "Chapter 6: The Utility of a Longitudinal Approach in Assessing Implementation: A Thirteen-Year View of Title I, ESEA," in W. Williams et al., *Studying Implementation: Methodological and Administrative Issues*, Chatham House Publishers, pp. 119–148.

Lansing, J.S. (2007). *Priests and Programmers: Technologies of Power in the Engineered Landscape of Bali*, Princeton Univesity Press, 216pp.

Lansing, J.S. and J.N. Kremer (1993). "Emergent Properties of Balinese Water Temple Networks: Coadaptation on a Rugged Fitness Landscape," *American Anthropologist*, *95*(1), pp. 97–114.

Lansing, J.S. and J.H. Miller (2005). "Cooperation, Games, and Ecological Feedback: Some Insights from Bali," *Current Anthropology*, *46*(2), pp. 328–334.

Lee, K.N. (1993). *Compass and Gyroscope: Integrating Science and Politics for the Environment*, Island Press, 243pp.

Lindblom, C.E. (1959). "The Science of 'Muddling Through,'" *Public Administration Review*, *19*(2), pp. 79–88.

(1979). "Still Muddling, Not Yet Through," *Public Administration Review*, *39*(6), pp. 517–526.

Manski, C.F. (2013). *Public Policy in an Uncertain World: Analysis and Decisions*, Harvard University Press, 199pp.

March, J.G. (1976). "Chapter 5: The Technology of Foolishness," in J.G. March and J.P. Olsen (eds.), *Ambiguity and Choice in Organizations*, Universitetsforlaget, pp. 69–81.

Mayer, J. (2016). *Dark Money: The Hidden History of the Billionaires behind the Rise of the Radical Right*, Doubleday, 449pp.

Morgan, M.G. (1994). "Review of *Compass and Gyroscope: Integrating Science and Politics for the Environment* by Kai N. Lee, Island Press, 1993," *American Scientist*, *82*, pp. 475–476.

(2016). "Muddling Through on Climate Policy Won't Be Enough," *Proceedings of the National Academy of Sciences*, *113*(9), pp. 2322–2324.

Morgan, M.G., S.T. McCoy, J. Apt et al. (2012). *Carbon Capture and Sequestration: Removing the Legal and Regulatory Barriers*, RFF Press/Routledge, 274pp.

Ostrom, E. (1990). *Governing the Commons: The Evolution of Institutions for Collective Action*, Cambridge University Press, 280pp.

Parson, E.T. and E.L. Kravitz (2013). "Market Instrument for the Sustainability Transition," *Annual Reviews of Environmental Resources*, *38*, pp. 415–440.

Pressman, J.L. and A. Wildavsky. (1973). *Implementation: How Great Expectations in Washington Are Dashed in Oakland, or, Why It's Amazing That Federal Programs Work at All, This Being a Saga of the Economic Development Administration as Told by Two Sympathetic Observers Who Seek to Build Morals on a Foundation of Ruined Hopes*, University of California Press, 182pp.

Raiffa, H. (1982). *The Art and Science of Negotiation*, Harvard University Press, 373pp.

Sabatier, P.A. (1986). "Top-down and Bottom-up Approaches to Implementation Research: A Critical Analysis and Suggested Synthesis," *Journal of Public Policy*, *6*(1), pp. 21–48.

(1988). "An Advocacy Coalition Framework of Policy Change and the Role of Policy-Oriented Learning Therein," *Policy Sciences*, *21*(2–3), pp. 129–168.

Sabatier, P. and D. Mazmanian (1980). "The Implementation of Public Policy: A Framework of Analysis," *Policy Studies Journal*, *8*(4), pp. 538–560.

Sapolsky, H.M. (1990). *Science and the Navy: A History of the Office of Naval Research*, Princeton University Press, 142pp.

Schmalensee, R. and R. Stavins (2015). *Lessons Learned from Three Decades of Experience with Cap-and-Trade*, No. w21742, National Bureau of Economic Research, 25pp.

Simon, H. (1985). "Human Nature in Politics," *American Political Science Review*, *79*, pp. 293–304.

Smith, H. (1988). *The Power Game: How Washington Works*, Random House, 793pp.

Sunstein, C.R. (2013). *Simpler: The Future of Government*, Simon & Schuster, 260pp.

17

The Period Prior to World War II

This chapter, and the one that follows, briefly sketch a number of strands in the evolution of the history of science and technology policy in the United States. Readers may ask, "Why include an historical discussion in a book on the theory and practice of policy analysis – an inherently forward-looking endeavor?" In a paper for the American Historical Association titled, "Why Study History," Peter Stearns (1998) argued:

> People live in the present. They plan for and worry about the future. History, however, is the study of the past. Given all the demands that press in from living in the present and anticipating what is yet to come, why bother with what has been? Given all the desirable and available branches of knowledge, why insist [on the study of history]?
>
> History helps us understand change and how the society we live in came to be … The past causes the present, and so the future. Any time we try to know why something happened … we have to look for factors that took shape earlier. Sometimes fairly recent history will suffice to explain a major development, but often we need to look further back to identify the causes of change. Only through studying history can we grasp how things change; only through history can we begin to comprehend the factors that cause change; and only through history can we understand what elements of an institution or a society persist despite change …
>
> Further, studying history helps us understand how recent, current, and prospective changes that affect the lives of citizens are emerging or may emerge and what causes are involved. More important, studying history encourages habits of mind that are vital for responsible public behavior, whether as a national or community leader, an informed voter, a petitioner, or a simple observer.

The deep connections between science, technology, and the national government, which we take for granted today in the United States, have not always existed. While many of the U.S. founding fathers had significant technical knowledge and an interest in science and technology, attempts to translate that interest into government involvement in the support of science or education during the late eighteenth and early nineteenth centuries failed in the face of a political desire to minimize the role and power of central government, especially in areas such as education.

This chapter focuses on a few selected aspects of the evolving relationship between natural science, technology, and the U.S. Government between the time of the Constitutional Convention and the lead-up to World War II in the late 1930s and early 1940s. My objective is twofold: to help readers gain some understanding of the nature of, and reasons for, the reluctance of most political leaders to involve the U.S. national government in direct support of science and technology, and to illustrate the rather random and stochastic nature of changes when they did occur (see the discussion of "policy windows" in Section 16.1). I am not an historian. Rather than pretend that I am, in both this and the next chapter I have quoted at length from a number of authors who have delved deeply into primary sources from the relevant eras.

The events discussed in this chapter are summarized in the timeline in Figure 17.1. Readers interested in a more comprehensive historical account, including developments in agricultural research, public health, transport, and patents, are advised to begin with:

- Hunter Dupree, *Science in the Federal Government: A History of Politics and Activities*, Johns Hopkins University Press, 460pp, 1986.

Dupree (1986) observes that:

> The idea that the federal government should become the patron of science was easily within the grasp of the framers of the Constitution. As educated men of the eighteenth century, they knew that European governments had often supported science and their set of fundamental values led them to hold all branches of philosophy in high regard. Hence as they went about their political task of reconciling the great interests of the new nation, they gave some consideration to the constitutional position of science in the government they envisaged.

During the debates in the Constitutional Convention, proposals were advanced to include authorization for the creation of a national university and to provide federal charters of incorporation for an organization that would promote learning in the arts and sciences. In the end, none of these proposals survived.

Portions of Article 1 Section 8 of the U.S. Constitution (Figure 17.2) provide what limited authority was initially granted to the federal government in the areas of science and technology. Clause 1, which refers to providing for the general welfare, was interpreted quite narrowly in subsequent years. Clauses 5, 7, and 8 provided some initial latitude for government involvement in science and technology – the development of weights and measures obviously requires technical expertise, as does roads. Benjamin Franklin had proposed the explicit mention of canals, but this was opposed by smaller states that feared they might end up being required to cross-subsidize the development of such infrastructure for the benefit of larger states. Over the next two-and-a-half centuries the interpretation of Clause 3, the "commerce clause," has been expanded

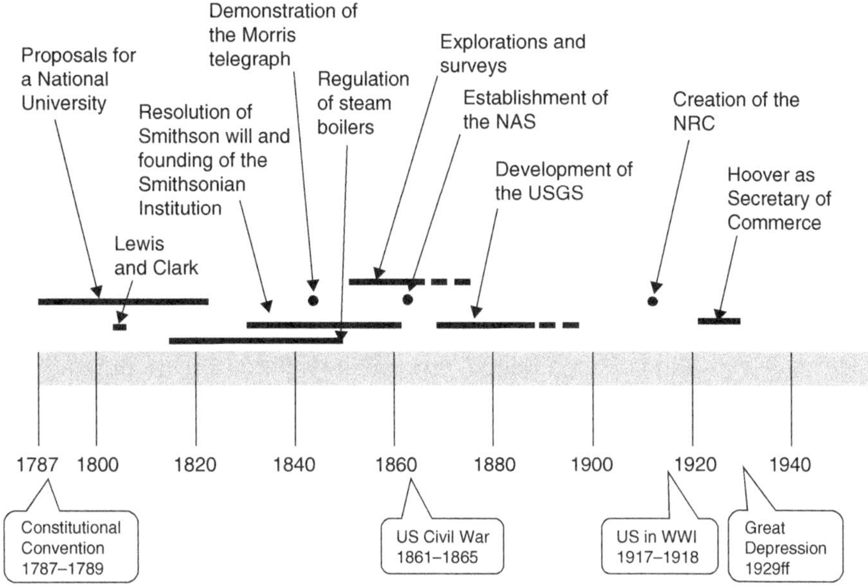

FIGURE 17.1. Timeline of the events discussed in this chapter.

Section 8

1: The Congress shall have Power To lay and collect Taxes, Duties, Imposts and Excises, to pay the Debts and provide for the common Defence and general Welfare of the United States; but all Duties, Imposts and Excises shall be uniform throughout the United States;

2: To borrow Money on the credit of the United States;

3: To regulate Commerce with foreign Nations, and among the several States, and with the Indian Tribes;

4: To establish an uniform Rule of Naturalization, and uniform Laws on the subject of Bankruptcies throughout the United States;

5: To coin Money, regulate the Value thereof, and of foreign Coin, and fix the Standard of Weights and Measures;

6: To Provide for the Punishment of counterfeiting the Securities and current Coin of the United States;

7: To establish Post Offices and post Roads;

8: To promote the Progress of Science and useful Arts, by securing for limited Times to Authors and Inventors the exclusive Right to their respective Writings and Discoveries;

FIGURE 17.2. Portions of Article 1 Section 8 of the U.S. Constitution that granted limited authority to the federal government in the area of science and technology. In later years the interpretation of Clause 3, the "commerce clause," was expanded to cover a wide range of activities. Clauses 5, 7, and 8 provided some initial latitude for government involvement in science and technology. Dupree (1986) notes that had Clause 8 stopped after the first nine words, the situation would have been very different.

to cover a wide range of activities, but its initial interpretation was narrow. Dupree (1986) notes that had Clause 8 stopped after the first nine words, the situation would have been very different!

Proposals for the creation of a national university continued to arise in the decades that followed. Near the end of his presidency, Washington proposed to donate 19 acres and some stock to support such an institution. Jefferson even learned that the University of Geneva was losing its state funding and proposed to move the entire institution to become the core of a national university (Dupree, 1986). However, these and subsequent proposals were always successfully opposed by those interested in limiting federal power.

The constitution did authorize the establishment of a system of patents and the creation of standards for weights and measure. Both of these responsibilities were assigned to the office of the Secretary of State. Dupree (1986) writes:

> There is something sublime and pathetic in the spectacle of the Secretary of State and a battery of professors from the University of Pennsylvania gathered around ... [a] distilling apparatus in the ... [Secretary of State's] office to test the efficiency of a mixture supposed to help make salt water fresh. By a series of well-turned experiments, Jefferson proved that the fresh water came from the distilling process, long known and even used at sea, and that the mixture added did not enhance its efficiency.

17.1 THOMAS JEFFERSON AND THE LEWIS AND CLARK EXPEDITION

The French explorers Louis Jolliet and Jacques Marquette were the first Europeans to pass the mouth of the Missouri in 1673. Subsequent French exploration in the region was slow. Near the end of the seventeenth century, the French founded a number of Christian missions along the lower Missouri; however, largely because of hostilities with some Native American tribes, they did not explore very far up-river. The region was transferred to Spain in 1762. For the next two decades Spain had very little knowledge of the upper reaches of the Missouri. Because there were not Spanish officials with appropriate frontier skills, exploration of the region for the Spanish in the late eighteenth century was conducted by James MacKay (who was Scottish) and John Evans (who was Welsh).[1] None of these explorations penetrated into the Rocky Mountains (Wood, 2003). The region was officially transferred to the United States during the presidency of Thomas Jefferson as a result of the Louisiana Purchase in 1803.

Jefferson assumed the presidency in 1801 after a particularly contentious campaign. Dupree (1986) writes:

[1] When they headed up the Missouri River from St. Louis, Lewis and Clark had with them copies of maps of the river as far upstream as the Mandan Villages in North Dakota. MacKay and Evans had prepared these maps a decade earlier (see chapter 4 in Wood, 2003), and Clark had met briefly with MacKay before the expedition departed.

> Jefferson's fame as an exponent of science was not entirely an asset. During the election of 1800 ... the opposition linked this interest with deistic religious ideas and his partiality for the French, even questioning the value of scientific attainments to a public man. [Dupree quotes one contemporary as remarking] "if one circumstance more than another could disqualify Mr. Jefferson from the presidency it would be the charge of his being a philosopher." ... [Indeed, Dupree reports that there was concern in some circles about] a sinister connection between science and dangerous ideas ... [and observes that the fact] that Federalist propagandists should devote space to the charge of dangerous knowledge ... shows their low esteem of the popular appeal of science and is perhaps the key to the long record of congressional reluctance to help it throughout this period.

A few days before becoming President in 1801, Jefferson appointed the young Captain Meriwether Lewis as his personal secretary (paid out of Jefferson's personal funds). In offering the position Jefferson explained that the job would involve more than dealing with private concerns, "but also to contribute to the mass of information which it is interesting for the administration to acquire. Your knowledge of the Western country, of the army and of all its interests & relations has rendered it desirable ... that you should be engaged in that office" (as quoted by Ambrose, 1996). The reference to "Western country" reflects Jefferson's decades-long interest in the American West.

After traveling up to the Arctic Ocean in 1789 on the river that now bears his name, Alexander Mackenzie spent 1791 in Great Britain learning modern methods to determine longitude (Sobel, 2005). In 1793, on his second attempt to cross Canada to reach the Pacific, Mackenzie successfully reached the mouth of the Bella Coola River in what is now British Columbia.

Eight years later Mackenzie's account was published in London. Ambrose (1996) writes that "Jefferson ordered a copy as soon as he heard of the book's existence, but did not have one in his hands until the summer of 1802." When the book finally arrived, he and Lewis "devoured it." Jefferson was deeply concerned about possible British dominance in the Pacific Northwest. The upshot was that even before the Louisiana Purchase, Jefferson was already planning to send Lewis on an expedition up the Missouri River and on across the Rockies to the mouth of the Columbia River. Lewis received a crash education from Jefferson on geography and botany in the President's outstanding library at Monticello, and on navigation, medical treatment, and related topics by experts in Philadelphia. Once the Louisiana Purchase was completed, Jefferson secured $2500 from Congress together with authorization to access Army supplies. Lewis recruited William Clark to co-direct the expedition, which set out down the Ohio River from Pittsburgh in a specially constructed 55-foot keelboat on August 31, 1803.

Bernard DeVoto (1952) writes that Clark was Lewis's complement:

> a native rather than a seeker of the wilderness, an extrovert, genial and outgoing ... a wilderness craftsman ... If Lewis had talent for geography, Clark had genius for it. He had a similar genius for handling Indians ... And Indians liked him ... They talked about him at council fires as a friend and their hope of justice and protection.

For readers interested in outdoor adventure, the *Journals* of the Lewis and Clark expedition make wonderful reading,[2] in my view only rivaled in the exploration of the western United States by John Wesley Powell's account of his expedition down the Colorado River through the Grand Canyon. The accounts of the many interactions with Native American peoples, descriptions of the wild and fascinating country, encounters with the grizzly bears that teemed around the great falls in the Yellowstone River, overland portages, wild rides down the rivers of the west to the Columbia, the rain- and fog-drenched winter spent at Fort Clatsop at the mouth of the Columbia, and the long slog back to St. Louis, are all breathtaking. Bernard DeVoto writes, "To read the *Journals* is to realize that no one who went up Missouri before them was anywhere near as intelligent, and that of the westering Canadians only Alexander Mackenzie and David Thompson had any of their intellectual distinction, and they in small measure." The journals, maps, and specimens the expedition brought back were of enormous value. While Jefferson reveled in the many specimens, Ambrose (1996) notes that:

> the political payoff of the expedition was not curious animals and plants but maps and solid information about the trans-Mississippi Indians. These were contained in Clark's map of the Missouri and Lewis's statistical report on the tribes ... Together, the map and report surpassed both in scope and reliability anything hitherto available to the American government on the American West.

Dupree (1986) explains that there was no government arrangement to house any of the materials brought back, or to publish the full journals, which did not appear in their entirety until 1904. He argues that despite the fact that the expedition was "a jewel in the history of exploration ... it found no supporting institutions in the government and created none."

17.2 CREATION OF THE COASTAL SURVEY

The early Republic suffered from a shortage of people with advanced scientific training. One important exception was Ferdinand Hassler, a Swiss-trained surveyor who emigrated to the United States in 1805. As the need grew for reliable topographical maps of coastal areas, the presence of Hassler (who had originally come to join an agricultural colony) presented an important opportunity.

NOAA's official history reports:

> The Office of Coast Survey is the oldest U.S. scientific organization, dating from 1807 when President Thomas Jefferson signed "AN ACT TO provide for surveying the coasts of the United States." While the bill's objective was specific – to produce nautical charts – it reflected larger issues of concern to the young nation: national boundaries, commerce, and defense.
>
> The new agency experienced some growing pains in the early years. Ferdinand Hassler, who was eventually to become the agency's first superintendent, went to

[2] Available at: www.americanjourneys.org/pdf/AJ-100e.pdf.

England to collect scientific instruments and was unable to return through the duration of the War of 1812. After Hassler returned, he started work on a survey of New York Harbor in 1817, but Congress stepped in to suspend the work because of tensions between civilian and military control of the agency. After several years under the control of the U.S. Army, the Survey of the Coast was reestablished in 1832, and President Andrew Jackson appointed Hassler as Superintendent.

In the ensuing years, the young agency tackled additional responsibilities. In addition to conducting hydrographic surveys and producing nautical charts, U.S. Coast Survey conducted the first systematic study of the Gulf Stream, designed tidal prediction machines, and established the geodetic connection between the Atlantic and Pacific coasts.[3]

As is often the case with official histories, this rather dry straightforward account masks considerable political and other turmoil. Dupree (1986) notes that while in England, Hassler overspent on his purchase of high-quality surveying equipment by $5000, which made Congress very unhappy. That he could even pursue such a mission during the War of 1812 is clearly an interesting commentary on the very different nature of warfare in the early nineteenth century. Once Hassler got the survey up and running, he was intent on doing the work his way, gradually working outwards from a baseline he had established in New York. The result was that states up and down the Eastern Seaboard grew impatient.

The Chaplain of the Navy successfully lobbied Congress to get a clause inserted in legislation that only military officers could be employed by the survey, with the result that Hassler was out of a job. However, because there was no one in the military who had comparable expertise, the survey languished.[4] It was not until 1832 that Hassler was finally reappointed director and serious surveying resumed. During the interregnum he had worked for the Department of the Treasury where he established a scientifically based program of weights and measures.

Once back in charge of the Coastal Survey, problems continued. A successful effort was made to move it to the Navy. Hassler bristled at the oversight and control. The only authority he agreed to submit to was a board of scientists. Jackson finally moved the survey back to the Department of the Treasury in 1836.

In recognition of the serious lack of people with technical expertise, in 1815, after his outstanding service in the War of 1812, Sylvanus Thayer was granted $5000 to study at École Polytechnique and travel elsewhere in Europe. Thayer had attended Dartmouth College and graduated from West Point.[5] While in

[3] From www.nauticalcharts.noaa.gov/staff/hist.html.

[4] Arguments were also advanced at that time that rather than accept the prime meridian through Greenwich, the new republic should create its own prime meridian.

[5] In 1867, Thayer made a gift of $40,000 to the Trustees of Dartmouth College to establish "a School or Department of Architecture and Civil Engineering." This laid the foundation for what is today Dartmouth's Thayer School of Engineering.

Europe he amassed a large collection of science and mathematics textbooks. Upon his return to the United States he was appointed Superintendent of West Point, which became the first U.S. engineering school, supplying the expertise needed by the Army Corps of Engineers and the many surveying and civil engineering projects the nation would pursue over the course of the coming decades.

Among the pieces of surveying equipment that Hassler had brought back from Europe was a transit telescope, a critical piece of equipment for measuring accurate time for use with naval chronometers. While the U.S. Congress had spent decades in adamant opposition to the establishment of an observatory, the Navy's need for accurate chronometers led to what Dupree (1986) describes as "the classic example of the surreptitious creation of a scientific institution by underlings in the executive branch of the government in the very shadow of congressional disapproval." The transit instrument was set up and operated on the Capitol grounds. As the need for astronomical observations continued to grow, in 1842 Congress authorized the construction of the Naval Observatory. Once authorized, Lieutenant James M. Gilliss traveled to Europe to visit leading observatories to secure the necessary instruments, books, and other materials.

17.3 THE SMITHSON WILL AND THE CREATION OF THE SMITHSONIAN INSTITUTION

An English chemist and mineralogist named James Smithson, who was the illegitimate son of Hugh Smithson, the first Duke of Northumberland, and Elizabeth Hungerford Keate Macie, a wealthy widow who was a cousin of the Duchess of Northumberland, died in 1829.[6] His will specified that "in the case of the death of my third nephew... I then bequeath the whole of my property ... to the United States of America to found in Washington, under the name of the Smithsonian Institution an establishment for the increase in diffusion of knowledge among men" (Dupree, 1986). The Smithsonian's official history reports:

> Smithson, the illegitimate child of a wealthy Englishman, had traveled much during his life, but had never once set foot on American soil. Why, then, would he decide to give the entirety of his sizable estate – which totaled half a million dollars, or 1/66 of the United States' entire federal budget at the time – to a country that was foreign to him?
>
> Some speculate it was because he was denied his father's legacy. Others argue that he was inspired by the United States' experiment with democracy. Some attribute his philanthropy to ideals inspired by such organizations as the Royal Institution, which was dedicated to using scientific knowledge to improve human conditions. Smithson

[6] Smithson died in Genoa, Italy, on June 27, 1829, and was interred nearby. In 1904, Smithsonian Regent Alexander Graham Bell brought Smithson's remains to the United States to rest at the Institution that his bequest created. For more historical details, see the Smithsonian archives, available online at: http://siarchives.si.edu/history/james-smithson.

never wrote about or discussed his bequest with friends or colleagues, so we are left to speculate on the ideals and motivations of a gift that has had such significant impact on the arts, humanities, and sciences in the United States.[7]

Nobody in America had heard of Smithson, and when it became apparent that a sum of $500,000 would come to the United States, there was heated discourse in the U.S. Congress about the appropriateness of accepting the bequest. Dupree (1986) explains:

> the old arguments about the constitutionality of the National University came up again. John C. Calhoun led the opposition in the Senate claiming that "acting under this legacy would be as much the establishment of a National University as if they appropriated the money for the purpose; and he would indeed much rather appropriate the money, for he thought it was beneath the dignity of the United States to receive presents of this kind from anyone." ... Calhoun's fellow South Carolinian W.C. Preston ... put the austere doctrine somewhat more racily when he claims that "every whippersnapper vagabond that has been traducing our country might think proper to have his name distinguished in the same way."

Dupree (1986) goes on to elaborate the various sides of the argument at some length. The several pages (pp. 66–70) he devotes to describing the debate make amusing reading for anyone interested in seeing that, while the preoccupations were different, much of the political debate in the U.S. Congress in the first third of the nineteenth century sounded much like it does today. Of course, being practical Americans, once all the political dust had settled, Congress accepted the bequest, without resolving how to deal with establishing the institution.

Eight years later in 1844, Congress returned to address the disposition of the Smithson bequest. The issue "had become something of a scandal both because of the years of delay and because of the depreciation of the state bonds in which the treasury department had had the bad judgment to invest the money" (Dupree, 1986). Debate began in June 1844. Again, readers should read Dupree's account (pp. 76–79), which provides a wonderful illustration of a "garbage can model" in action (see Section 15.3).

Options proposed and opposed, often expressed in most colorful language, included: an institution for useful science including agricultural experiments, natural history, chemistry geology, and astronomy; a university; a "grand and Noble public library"; a school for the education of children; an astronomical observatory; an institution for the direct low-cost diffusion of knowledge to the populace on a broader scale; as well as others. Once again, when all the political grandstanding subsided and the dust had settled, Congress proved incapable of reaching a decision. Instead, they opted to simply create an institutional structure governed by a board of regents. Dupree (1986) writes:

> The library provision had been softened to give the regents power to make an appropriation "Not exceeding an average of twenty-five thousand dollars annually, for the

[7] From www.si.edu/About/History.

gradual formation of a library composed of valuable works pertaining to all departments of human knowledge." ... [T]he museum function ... also had a loophole in that the regents were to take over government collections "in proportion as suitable arrangements can be made for their reception." Most of the other functions were implied only by the facilities of the building, which beside a library and natural history cabinets was to house a chemical laboratory, a gallery of art, and lecture rooms. The secretary would have charge of the buildings, record proceedings, serve as keeper of library and museums, and most importantly, employ assistants ...

As soon as the Congress had done its work, the Board of Regents found they could mold the Institution's very nature without leaving the law behind.

Many readers no doubt know the Smithsonian as a set of outstanding museums on the mall in Washington, DC. It is that, but it is also much more. The accomplished scientist, Joseph Henry, became the Institution's first secretary.[8] He initiated and supported a series of scientific studies, promoted high-quality publication of results, and was willing to spin off activities when others were prepared to take them over (as for example when the Institution's early work in meteorology was spun off to help start what is now the National Weather Service).

This tradition of serious scientific endeavor continues to this day. While rarely appreciated by the general public, in addition to its archives, libraries, and museums, the activities of the Smithsonian include: the Smithsonian Astrophysical Observatory in Arizona; the Conservation Biology Institute at the National Zoo; an Environmental Research Center in Edgewater, Maryland; a Marine Station in Fort Pierce, Florida; a Museum Conservation Institute in Suitland, Maryland; and a Tropical Research Institute in Panama.

17.4 APPROPRIATION OF FEDERAL FUNDS FOR TECHNOLOGY DEMONSTRATION

With few exceptions, during the first part of the nineteenth century Congress remained unwilling to use public money to support either scientific or technological undertakings. One early exception involved the telegraph. Four years after inventor Samuel F.B. Morse demonstrated the operation of his telegraph to the House Committee on Commerce in 1838, he was able to secure an appropriation of $30,000 to build a 61-km demonstration line from Baltimore to Washington. However, after that early success, Congress refused to appropriate any additional funds.

A second exception was a $20,000 appropriation to Charles G. Page to work on the development of an electric motor under the general supervision of the Secretary of the Navy. Unlike later rotating machines, Page's device was a reciprocating armature engine that he used to propel a locomotive at 19 miles per hour. As in the case of the telegraph, once the device

[8] The SI unit of induction is named the Henry.

had been demonstrated, Congress refused to appropriate any additional funds. After these two initial exceptions, for many years Congress remained unprepared to devote additional public resources to the development of new technologies.

17.5 THE EXTENDED SAGA OF REGULATIONS TO PREVENT STEAM BOILER EXPLOSIONS

Today we take it for granted that the U.S. Federal Government has the authority to pass regulations to protect health, safety, and the environment under the commerce clause of the Constitution. However, as noted in Section 10.6, this is a relatively modern development, in part brought about when, after 50 years of deaths and serious injuries resulting from explosions of steam boilers, Congress finally overcame its reluctance to do anything that might limit private enterprise and passed legislation that imposed regulation and testing on boilers.

This remarkable saga has been carefully documented by John Burke (1966), who observes:

> Though federal regulatory agencies may contribute to the general welfare, they are not expressly sanctioned by any provisions of the U.S. Constitution. In fact, their genesis was due to marked change in attitude of many early nineteenth-century Americans who insisted that the federal government exercise power in a positive way in an area that was non-existent when the Constitution was enacted. At the time, commercial, manufacturing, and business interests were willing to seek the aid of government in such matters as patent rights, land grants, or protective tariffs, but they opposed any action that might smack of government interference or control of their internal affairs. The government might act benevolently, but never restrictively ...
>
> Although the Constitution empowered Congress to regulate interstate commerce, there was still some disagreement about the extent of this power even after the decision in *Gibbons v. Ogden*,[9] which ruled that the only limitations on this power were those prescribed in the Constitution.

Steam boiler explosions began almost as soon as steam engines converted from earlier atmospheric pressure condensing systems to high-pressure systems. Fatalities and mayhem mounted, partly as a result of inferior designs and inadequate maintenance, and partly as a result of irresponsible behaviors such as wiring safety valves shut so as to run faster than competitors and establish a record as "the fastest boat on the river." As a result, both ordinary citizens and technical experts began to call for government intervention. Opponents' arguments that tort liability should be sufficient to limit the risks became increasingly less persuasive as fatalities, injuries, and property

[9] In *Gibbons v. Ogden*, the U.S. Supreme Court ruled that the commerce clause of the Constitution granted the federal government the right to regulate navigation. For details, see: http://en.wikipedia.org/wiki/Gibbons_v._Ogden.

losers mounted. Despite a number of fatal explosions, similar arguments held sway in the U.K. The situation was quite different in more traditionally statist France, where, once the hazard had been identified, regulations were issued in 1823.

Burke (1966) documents that after the explosion of the steamer *Aetna* in New York harbor in 1826 (which had an early cast iron boiler), the New York public became erroneously convinced that cast iron boilers were not as safe as copper boilers. In a development that is reminiscent of some modern consumer misconceptions, market pressures forced the continued use of copper in many steam ships in the east long after it had become abundantly clear that copper was inferior to cast iron. Burke quotes one owner who, having recognized the superiority of cast iron, said that he would continue to employ copper boilers because the public "have made up their minds that they have a perfect right to be scalded by copper boilers if they insist upon it." As a result of the *Aetna* explosion, a resolution was introduced in the House calling for an inquiry, but no action resulted.

Soon after the establishment of the Franklin Institute in Philadelphia in 1824, it began to direct attention to the problem of boiler explosions. Over the course of the subsequent decade the Institute undertook a series of wide-ranging experimental studies that resulted in a clear understanding of the problem of boiler explosions and a variety of recommendations for design specification and inspections that could be used to manage risks.

Burke (1966) reports that:

> Between 1825 and 1830 there had been forty-two explosions killing about 273 people, and in 1830 a particularly serious one aboard the "Helen McGregor" near Memphis killed 50 or 60 persons [see Figure 17.3], again disturbing the Congress. The House requested the Secretary of the Treasury ... to investigate the boiler accidents and submit a report ... The report prompted a bill proposed in the House in May 1832.

However, the House Committee's report was not especially supportive, and the bill died. Four years later, a detailed report prepared by the Franklin Institute was submitted to the House by the Secretary of the Treasury. After some delay, this report did finally prompt legislative action in 1838; however, the result was so watered down that it had very little impact on the ongoing epidemic of explosions. Burke (1966) writes:

> Experience proved that the 1838 law was not preventing explosions or loss of life. In December of 1848 the commissioner of patents, to whom Congress turned for data, estimated that in the period 1816–1848 a total of 233 steamboat explosions had occurred in which 2,563 persons had been killed, 2,097 injured with property losses of $3 million ...
>
> The toll of life in 1850 was 277 dead from explosions, and in 1851 it rose to 407.

Finally in 1852, after almost a half-century since the first explosions, the Congress acted, passing a law that set detailed requirements for the design,

FIGURE 17.3. Explosion of the *Helen McGregor* near Memphis, TN, in 1830, which killed between 50 and 60 people and prompted some ineffectual Congressional interest. Image from Wikimedia Commons.

operation, and testing of steam boilers. Burke (1966) concludes that the "belief that Congress should in no circumstances interfere with private enterprise was now supported by only a small minority." In addition to dramatically reducing deaths and injuries from boiler explosions, the far broader result was to lay the foundation for much of the federal health, safety, and environmental regulation of the twentieth century.

READING 17.1

John G. Burke, "Bursting Boilers and the Federal Power," *Technology and Culture*, 7, pp. 1–23, 1966.

DISCUSSION QUESTIONS FOR READING 17.1

- What did the Supreme Court rule in *Gibbons v. Ogden* and why is that case important in the interpretation of the commerce clause of the U.S. Constitution?
- What was entailed in the studies conducted by Alexander Dallas Bach organized at the Franklin Institute, what did those studies conclude, and what role did the findings play in the years that followed?

- Why did tort law prove inadequate to address the problem of steamboat boiler explosions?
- Burke writes that for most of the first half of the nineteenth century, "commercial, manufacturing, and business interests were willing to seek the aid of government in such matters as patent rights, land grants, or protective tariffs, but they opposed any action that might smack of government interference or control of their internal affairs. The government might act benevolently but never restrictively." Discuss this statement in light of political discourse in the United States today.

17.6 THE UNITED STATES EXPLORING EXPEDITION, 1838–1842

Motivated by factors such as the success of the Lewis and Clark expedition and the growing U.S. whaling industry, the sixth President of the United States, John Quincy Adams, proposed an exploring expedition to the northwest coast. While this proposal never took off, it was widely promoted by Capt. John Cleves, who had a bizarre theory that the earth was composed of a series of hollow concentric spheres. Cleves believed that an expedition to the North Pacific could validate this theory and made numerous public lectures around the country to promote this idea.[10] Cooler heads ultimately prevailed, informed in part by reports gathered by whalers who had ventured into the North Pacific.

The expedition was finally authorized in 1836 and $150,000 was appropriated together with an authorization for Naval support. This happened sufficiently long after the original John Quincy Adams proposal that President Andrew Jackson, a strong Adams political opponent, could treat the expedition as a new idea. Dupree (1986) and Philbrick (2003) provide detailed descriptions of the various machinations that ensued in organizing and getting the expedition launched before an odd collection of six ships set sail in 1838 under the overbearing and insecure leadership of Charles Wilkes. While Wilkes made the four-year undertaking extraordinarily trying for the officers and crew, the expedition did manage to definitively establish the existence of the Antarctic continent and perform extensive surveys of a number of Pacific islands and, more critically, Puget Sound and the mouth of the Columbia River. By the

[10] Bizarre theories about the Arctic persisted throughout the nineteenth century. In 1879, with support in part from the *New York Herald*, Captain G.W. De Long led an expedition to the high Arctic on the *Jeannette* in order to confirm a theory that once one passed through a ring of ice that surrounded the Arctic Ocean the polar region was ice free. The *Jeannette* became trapped in the ice and was ultimately crushed and sank. Many of the crew made a successful escape to northern Siberia by dragging their boats across the pack ice to reach open water and perform a perilous sea voyage to the mouth of the Lena River. Unfortunately, while De Long made it to land, he died before reaching a settlement. However, a number of the crew did survive (Sides, 2014). The *Jeannette* expedition largely put an end to the theory of the ice-free high Arctic.

time the expedition returned, the presidency had changed parties, and the new national leadership under President Tyler actively downplayed the accomplishments of an activity that had been promoted by their political opponents. Interested readers can find a very readable detailed account, focused especially on the performance of Charles Wilkes, in Philbrick (2003), and a compact description of the expedition at: https://en.wikipedia.org/wiki/United_States_Exploring_Expedition, as well as many details through the Smithsonian at: www.sil.si.edu/digitalcollections/usexex.

The Smithsonian's Jane Walsh reports that:

> the collections amassed between April 1838 and June 1842 by the United States Exploring Expedition, under the command of Charles Wilkes, weighed nearly 40 tons. The naval officers, crew, and nine civilian scientists, who sailed on six small ships for four years, gathered specimens of natural history at nearly every stop, including several thousand zoological specimens, 50,000 plant specimens,[11] thousands of shells, corals, fossils, and geological specimens, even jars of sea water from different localities ... They also collected 2,500 ethnological and archaeological specimens, which they generally referred to as "curiosities," to illustrate the varied cultures with whom they came in contact.
>
> The official collection was first catalogued and exhibited in the Great Hall of the Patent Office during the 1840s. In 1858 it was transferred by order of the United States Congress to the Smithsonian Institution. The result of the transfer of the government's collections was the establishment of the United States National Museum at the Smithsonian Institution, which until that time had been devoted almost exclusively to research. Today, the specimens constitute the core of nearly every collection in every scientific department in the National Museum of Natural History.[12]

Secretary of the Navy J.P. Kennedy authorized a second major expedition, the U.S. North Pacific Exploring Expedition that ran from 1853 to 1856. Again, readers can find a compact description of the expedition at: https://en.wikipedia.org/wiki/North_Pacific_Exploring_and_Surveying_Expedition. And details are available through the Smithsonian at: http://siarchives.si.edu/collections/siris_arc_217410.

17.7 THE ESTABLISHMENT OF THE U.S. NATIONAL ACADEMY OF SCIENCES

After decades of resisting the establishment of any bodies or facilities for basic science that were associated with the federal government, and without the presence of a number of the strong states' rights members from southern states, Congress approved the creation of the National Academy of Sciences (NAS)

[11] Most of the world's most accomplished botanists were in Europe. Harvard's Asa Gray arranged to travel there to work on the collection with a number of colleagues. However, because seeking European advice on an American collection was politically sensitive, the purpose of the trip was kept somewhat obscure.

[12] From www.sil.si.edu/digitalcollections/usexex/learn/Walsh-01.htm.

FIGURE 17.4. A painting of President Lincoln with the Act creating the NAS and a number of the luminaries of nineteenth-century U.S. science (left) hangs in the Academy's Board Room (right). Such an event never occurred. Left-hand figure reproduced with permission from National Academy of Sciences, photographed by Mark Finkenstaedt. Right-hand figure photographed by the author.

during the closing session of the lame duck Congress elected in 1860 before the war. The public lore at the NAS is that the Academy was established by President Lincoln to provide science advice to the federal government. Indeed, as illustrated in Figure 17.4, a painting that dominates the boardroom at the NAS celebrates this fact by showing President Lincoln with the Act, accompanied by a set of luminaries of science. However, no such event ever occurred.

Instead, as Hunter Dupree (1986) explains, the effort to establish the NAS was promoted by an informal group of leading scientists (most of whom were based in Cambridge, MA, Philadelphia, PA, and Washington, DC). The group called themselves the Scientific Lazzaroni, and had as their stated purpose to gather periodically to "eat an outrageously good dinner together." The anti-Darwinian Louis Agassiz was a key mover in this group (Dupree, 1986).

After unsuccessful attempts by the Lazzaroni to establish a private national university in Albany and later in New York, the group persuaded Senator Henry Wilson (R-MA) that the nation needed a National Academy of Sciences. Dupree (1986) writes that a decision was made to proceed with speed and secrecy. When Senator Wilson left a meeting with a subset of Lazzaroni members:

> he had with him the draft of a bill which named fifty scientists, incorporated them as individuals into a National Academy of Sciences, and gave them the power to perpetuate themselves by filling vacancies. Nothing in the law or in any public statement either at the time or later gave any clue to the identity of the authors of the list or the criteria of selection ...
>
> Senator Wilson gave notice in the Senate on February 20 [1863] of his intention to introduce the bill, and on February 21 he did so. It contained only three sections. The first listed the fifty incorporators. The second gave them power over their own rules and membership. The third provided for an annual meeting and stated that "the Academy shall, whenever called upon by any Department of the Government, investigate, examine, experiment and report upon any subject of science or art, the actual expenses ... to

be paid from appropriations which may be made for the purpose, but the Academy shall receive no compensation whatever for any services to the Government of the United States ..."

As the Senate rushed through matters large and small on that last day [before it adjourned for good], Wilson followed a long line of private petitions by asking "to take up a bill that will consume no time, and to which I hope there will be not opposition ... it will take but a moment I think and I would like to have it passed."

The first section of the bill, that listed the initial fifty members of the NAS, was not read out on the floor. Sections 2 and 3 were read and the Senate passed the bill. "The House took up the Senate's bill considerably after seven o'clock in the evening and passed it without comment. Lincoln signed it the same evening" (Dupree, 1986).

As word trickled out, and the science community discovered that the United States had acquired a National Academy of Sciences, and that a number of eminent scientists were not members, considerable turmoil ensued.

For the four years following its creation, the future of the NAS under its first President, Alexander Bach, remained precarious. Two other older institutions were already playing some of the roles that the NAS hoped to play. The American Academy of Arts and Sciences (founded in 1780) had been the locus of the most substantive scientific debates between Louis Agassiz and Asa Gray on the new Darwinian theory of evolution (Dupree, 1959). The much younger American Association for the Advancement of Science (AAAS; founded in 1848) had also become an important focus of national scientific discourse. Indeed, AAAS members were concerned that their organization might be eclipsed by the new NAS. However, Bruce (1987) explains that:

Far from claiming the life of the AAAS, the National Academy of Sciences hung for some time on the verge of losing its own. Eminent members resigned or were dropped for non-attendance. The Academy's twice yearly meetings rarely drew twenty, and some, like James Hall, did not come because so few came. With annual dues of five dollars, and no government support at all, the academy could afford to publish only four reports and one volume of memoirs during its first fifteen years. And the federal government remained disinclined to seek the Academy's counsel or even receive it when offered, thus negating the Academy's official reason for being.

Joseph Henry saved the National Academy by reluctantly taking on its presidency after the death of Alexander Dallas Bach in 1867, mainly out of loyalty to Bach's memory. He proposed to resign in 1873 but was prevailed on not to. So he bore the cross to the day of his own death in 1878. Had he not, the Academy would have gone under. The challenge, however, as he wrote in 1868, was not just to keep the academy alive but also to "render it useful."

As part of his effort to achieve that, he managed to change membership rules and to assure that new members would be elected based on clear accomplishment in original research.

Bruce (1987) observes that, "recalling World War II and developments since, one might suppose that government science flourished during the Civil War.

It did not." Rather, he explains that most of the exploring expeditions ceased work and some records were lost. In addition, he notes that "Far from expanding scientific research in the armed services, the war took some Army and Navy officers away from their scientific assignments." For example,

> Since his great United States exploring expedition of 1838–42, Capt. Charles Wilkes had been on special service in Washington superintending publication of the expedition's massive reports. By 1859 Congress had appropriated more than a quarter million dollars for the purpose, and more was needed. But the war suspended further publication, and Wilkes himself was ordered to sea duty in April 1861. That November he seized two Confederate diplomats from the British mail steamer *Trent*, precipitated an Anglo-American diplomatic crisis, and thereby won more celebrity than science had ever brought him. (Bruce, 1987)

17.8 THE GREAT WESTERN EXPLORING EXPEDITIONS

A number of exploring expeditions in the west were undertaken in the years after the Lewis and Clark expedition and before the Civil War. For example, Major Stephen H. Long was involved as a leader in five expeditions between 1817 and 1823 that explored the upper Mississippi and the Great Plains (Colorado's Longs Peak bears his name). Philbrick (2003) reports that "Between 1840 and 1860, the federal government would publish sixty works associated with the exploration of the West while subsidizing 15 Naval expeditions around the world. The expenditure for these expeditions and other scientific publications would be enormous, representing somewhere between one-quarter to one-third of the annual federal budget." The years following the end of the Civil War in 1865 saw a burst of interest in exploring the topography and geology of the lands of the west. Rabbitt (1989) explains:

> On March 2, 1869, Congress for the first time authorized western explorations in which geology would be the principal objective: a study of the geology and natural resources along the fortieth parallel route of the Intercontinental Railroad under the Corps of Engineers, and a geological survey of the natural resources of the new state of Nebraska, under the direction of the General Land office.

Clarence King directed the exploration of the 40th parallel. Frederick V. Hayden directed the Nebraska survey. Rabbitt (1989) reports that:

> Both the King and Hayden surveys were successful. In 1870, the King survey, without solicitation, received additional funds for another three years in the field. The Hayden survey received additional appropriations in 1868 and 1869 for exploration in Wyoming and Colorado, and in 1869 was placed directly under the Secretary of the Interior.

Beginning as a much smaller and informal effort, John Wesley Powell also began a series of western explorations. Powell, who was an instructor at Illinois State Normal University, had risen to the rank of major during the Civil War and had lost his right arm during the battle of Shiloh. In 1867, he took a first group of his students to the Colorado Rockies. While he received no direct government appropriation, through his army connections he managed to secure approval to draw on military stores during this first expedition. In 1869, he undertook a much more ambitious effort, going down the Colorado River through the Grand Canyon in wooden boats.

Powell's report, *Exploration of the Colorado River of the West and Its Tributaries*, has become a classic in expedition reporting (Powell, 1875). Among the most exciting sections is his account of their passage through the Cañyon of the Lodore. Readers who share my passion for outdoor activities should download the report from the Web and read the account of losing one of the expedition's wooden boats in a rapid and saving the crew, some vital equipment, and a keg of whiskey the crew had smuggled on board.[13]

On his return to Washington after this first trip down the Colorado in 1870, Powell secured $10,000 for a Geographical and Topographical Survey of the Colorado. An additional $20,000 was appropriated in 1872 to complete the survey. Not only was Powell interested in the physical geography of the region, but he also took a keen interest in Native American cultures, ultimately founding the Bureau of Ethnology (later the Bureau of American Ethnology) that was created by an Act of Congress in 1879.

With so many survey activities in the field, Rabbitt (1989) writes:

> Inevitably, conflicts developed between the Hayden survey, mapping the territories of the United States, and the Wheeler survey, mapping the areas west of the hundredth Meridian. In 1874, Congress was provoked to a thorough discussion of civilian versus military control of mapping. In the testimony heard by the Congressional committee, much of it on the purposes and efficiency of the mapping, Powell credited King's Fortieth parallel survey with the most advanced techniques which Hayden and he had later adopted. In the end Congress concluded each survey had been doing excellent work for the benefit of the people and there was sufficient work for both the Interior Department and the War Department for years to come.

Powell cut his Illinois connection and took up residence in Washington, DC, in 1874, where he extended his efforts to direct the "Geographical and Geological Survey of the Rocky Mountain Regions." Because of his interest in Native American cultures, in 1879 he arranged for an Act of Congress to create the Bureau of Ethnology.

Based on his extensive work in the west, in 1878 Powell published his *Report on the Arid Region of the United States*,[14] in which he argued that these lands would need to be viewed differently than lands in the more eastern parts of the United States, that establishing individual small farms would not be a viable strategy for settling them, and that only with large-scale civil engineering projects could water be provided to make portions of them useful for agriculture.

[13] See: http://pubs.usgs.gov/unnumbered/70039238/report.pdf. The account starts on p. 22.

[14] Available online at: http://pubs.usgs.gov/unnumbered/70039240/report.pdf.

Unfortunately, too few listened to these informed views, instead adopting the erroneous climatological theory that "rain follows the plow."[15] The unfortunate result was that over the course of subsequent decades, many small-holding farms were established across the arid west that proved to be unsustainable, giving rise to considerable hardship among many settlers.

17.9 THE CREATION OF THE U.S. GEOLOGICAL SURVEY

In 1878, Congress asked the NAS to conduct a review of the several ongoing western survey activities, some of which had begun to overlap. Dupree (1986) explains that:

> Powell gave the committee a full statement of his ideas on the nature of government science ... he demanded, first, one general management, and second "that the division of labor should have a scientific base." Geology should be one department and mensuration another. "If ecology, botany, and zoology are to be embraced in the general scientific survey, each subject should have but a single organization, with a single head subordinated to the general plan."

Bruce (1987) explains: "The Academy's acting president, Othniel Marsh, stacked the committee against the army, and so its report following Powell's suggestions, called for the replacement of all the surveys by the permanent agency, United States Geological Survey, under the interior department." The U.S. Geological Survey was created by an Act of Congress in March 1879, charged initially with the classification of public lands. Dupree (1986) explains that "Immediately the struggle between the former rival surveys shifted to the executive, revolving about the appointment of a director."

Rabbitt (1989) reports that:

> Hayden, who had been directing geological surveys in the Department of the Interior for a dozen years, was the obvious candidate to be director of the new national survey but a small group that considered Clarence King better qualified undertook to secure the appointment for him. On March 20, 1879, President Hayes sent to the Senate the nomination of Clarence King to be the first Director of the U.S. Geological Survey. The Senate confirmed the nomination on April 3, and King took the oath of office on May 24. The Fortieth Parallel Exploration under King's direction had led the way in converting western exploration to an exact science. His new position gave him a unique opportunity to influence the development of Federal geology.

King's tenure was troubled and he resigned in 1881, to be replaced by Powell. In the years that followed, Powell displayed a combination of scientific and political insight and leadership that clearly established him as one of the first great leaders of federal science. One early problem was that Congress had limited the domain of the survey to public lands. Dupree (1986) writes:

[15] For a concise discussion, see: https://en.wikipedia.org/wiki/Rain_follows_the_plow.

Perhaps his greatest stroke was in securing authority to nationalize the survey. After a bill to extend it into the states had met the fate of King's [earlier] effort, Powell asked his friends on the Appropriations Committee of the House ... to allow a minor change in the wording of the section of the sundry civil bill that served as an organic act. The phrase added was "and to continue the preparation of a geological map of the United States" ... To make a geologic map, he had to make a topographic map first. The little phrase gave him all he needed to embark on the program the National Academy had envisioned for the Coast and Interior Survey which Congress had killed in 1879.

Once this authorization was obtained, Rabbitt (1989) explains, Powell:

redirected all topographic work toward preparation of the geologic map and began topographic mapping to provide a base for the geologic map in Eastern as well as Western States. Topographic mapping became the largest part of the Geological Survey program. Paleontologic and stratigraphic studies to support the geologic mapping program were also begun throughout the country.

During his 13-year tenure as director of the U.S. Geological Survey, Powell laid the foundations to create what today remains one of the premier science agencies of the U.S. Government.

17.10 WORLD WAR I AND THE CREATION OF THE NATIONAL RESEARCH COUNCIL

Many other interesting science-related developments occurred during the latter part of the nineteenth century, including the Allison Commission that explored the possibility of creating a Department of Science; the passage in 1862 and 1890 of the Morrill Acts that led to the creation of Land Grant Colleges; the growth of the National Bureau of Standards; and the rise of agricultural, public health, and medical services and research.[16] However, in the interest of brevity I am now going to jump forward by several decades to World War I and discuss the creation of the National Research Council (NRC).

In 1915, as the war in Europe became increasingly serious, Secretary of the Navy Josephus Daniels established a Naval Consulting Board under the Chairmanship of Thomas Edison. Edison created a board consisting of "practical" men, by which he meant no academic scientists and no involvement by the National Academy of Science.

This gave rise to concern among members of the science establishment, especially on the part of George Ellery Hale, the founder and director of the Mt. Wilson Observatory and foreign secretary of the National Academy. Kevles (1978) explains:

Hale shared the members' traditional wariness of thrusting the Academy upon the government, but surely in a national emergency they could offer services to the administration without appearing like mere political supplicants. In June 1915, after the sinking

[16] See Dupree (1959) for good accounts of these and many other developments.

of the *Lusitania*, Hale ... supposed that President Woodrow Wilson might welcome an offer of assistance in the event of war. Conklin, a fellow academy activist who knew Wilson from his Princeton days, advised against the idea as premature. Hale agreed to drop it for the time being. Ten months later, April 19, 1916 the day after Wilson issued an ultimatum to Germany over the sinking of the *Sussex*, Hale rose in the Academy's annual meeting in Washington to offer a resolution: in the event of a break in diplomatic relations, the Academy would place itself at the disposal of the government ... Hale's resolution was endorsed unanimously.

A week later William Henry Welch, the Johns Hopkins president and president of the Academy, led a delegation ... to the White House. After Welch rehearsed the Academy's special relationship to the government, Hale went on to stress to Pres. Wilson the importance of research for defense and argue that the academy could plan an arsenal of science for the country.

President Wilson approved the undertaking with the understanding that the effort should be pursued quietly so as not to create political problems, given Wilson's continued stand of neutrality. In June 1916, the Academy formed a National Research Council (NRC). Hale approached the Naval Consulting Board about the possibility that the NRC might collaborate with them in the area of submarine detection, but was rebuffed and told that NRC might work in a subordinate capacity.

Through some political maneuvering, Hale and others managed to obtain public support from the White House and the NRC embarked on a series of studies to assist in defense preparedness. With the resumption of unrestricted submarine warfare, Admiral David W. Taylor, Chief of the Naval Bureau of Construction and Repair, asked NRC to address the problem of detecting submarines. The effort was given top priority under Robert Millikan (whom many readers will know for his experiment with the use of oil drops to measure the charge on the electron). The physicists went to work, devising what was essentially an acoustic phased array, which in field trials in New London considerably out-performed the devices being developed by the Naval Consulting Board. Nothing succeeds like success, and Edison came around to seeing the value of scientists in the war research effort. NRC investigators went on to make similarly important progress on problems such as sound-ranging to detect the location of enemy artillery batteries.

On the administrative front, Dupree (1986) explains:

The wartime NRC became a central scientific agency to an extent never dreamed of by the National Academy. It performed a real function as a clearinghouse of information in the focus of scientific personnel. Most of the great research efforts of the war fell at least nominally within its sphere. Yet it showed equally definite limitations. It never developed an adequate full-time administration to direct all phases of its program as a unit ...

It never became the dispenser of large funds, and much of what money it had was from the private foundations. The only effective way it had to get military research funds was to have its scientists commissioned in some particular branch of the army. As the war went on, more and more of the NRC's program went over to military control. It was a spawning ground of much-needed military scientific laboratories more than an independent agency supplementing the military programs. It became also less capable of initiating projects, depending increasingly on the assumption that the military knew what to ask for. In this respect, the Office of Scientific Research and Development of World War II started from a position immensely stronger than that held by the NRC in 1917–1918.

Because, once commissioned, scientists held lower-level ranks as officers, they did not have direct access to senior military leaders. As we will see in the next chapter, when Vannevar Bush created the system of government-supported science and technology research and development during World War II he was careful to assure that scientists did not receive military commissions so that they could interact with military leaders at the highest levels.

17.11 HERBERT HOOVER AS SECRETARY OF COMMERCE

Herbert Hoover had the misfortunate to be elected president just eight months before the stock market crashed in October 1929. Because today his presidency enjoys a largely negative reputation, it may seem strange to some readers that I have chosen to include a section on him in this chapter. However, before he became president, Hoover had a remarkably varied and accomplished career, and had shaped the evolution of U.S. science and technology policy in important ways.

Hoover was born in Iowa in 1874. He grew up in Oregon in a Quaker family. He entered the newly established Stanford University as a member of its first class and graduated in 1895 with a degree in geology. He became a successful mining engineer, working in Australia and later China (where he learned Chinese). As a mining engineer he made important process innovations. He became an independent consultant, grew a very successful global business, and became reasonably wealthy.

Hoover first rose to national prominence by organizing food relief in occupied Belgium during World War I, and then after the war, across Europe as head of the U.S. Food Administration.

As Secretary of Commerce from 1921 to 1928, Hoover believed that "enlightened businessmen would act voluntarily in the public interest once they were made fully aware of the value of cooperative individualism, associationalism, and the elimination of waste" (Wilson, 1975). He promoted these ideas through a wide variety of conferences and through vigorous reorganization of his own department, as well as through efforts to promote reorganization of other Cabinet agencies. He undertook his work with enormous vigor:

Within his first month in office, he met with the Directors of the U.S. Chamber of Commerce to explore ways to develop closer relations between the department and the

> business community, commenced monthly meetings with the editors of the major business newspapers, began to consider whether commercial aviation should come under civilian or military control, asked the Federal Trade Commission to investigate foreign monopolies over essential goods and foodstuffs, urged the reorganization of the railroad system and the adoption of pay scales for railroad workers, advocated development of a national waterway system, proposed to search for new foreign oil sources, recruited an academic Advisory Committee on statistics for the department, and began reorganizing the department's bureaus. And, in his spare time, he continued overseas American Relief Administration (ARA) relief work and the Federated American engineering society study of waste in the industry and promoted the organization of the Foreign Trade Financing Corporation. (Clements, 2010)

Hoover's program consisted of three legs: "organized waste reduction ... [The generation of] statistical information ... [including] statistically informed production planning ... [and a program to promote] trade-expansion" (Hawley, 1974). Hoover addressed these issues in the context of a number of specific industrial sectors including housing, the railroads, coal mining, and agriculture.

> Despite the danger of price malpractices, he believed that trade associations were beneficial because of their ability to undertake industrial research and effect standardization and efficiency within the industrial and commercial field. This latter – industrial standardization and efficiency – particularly appealed to a man with Hoover's engineering background, and he championed all moves in that direction. As a result, the Commerce Department sponsored over 900 Group conferences between 1921 and 1924 and had 229 committees at work on various phases of the problem. Hoover simultaneously promoted industrial and scientific economic research as a primary weapon against waste and inefficiency. The national Bureau of Standards, established originally to maintain standards of measurement, was transformed under Hoover into an agency that also handled much scientific and industrial research. (Murray, 1974)

Hawley (1974) explains that:

> Hoover's initiatives quickly ran into three major obstacles... strong resistance from established agencies ... the difficulty of fitting cooperative stabilization inside the framework of the antitrust laws ... [and s]harp criticism from business groups that were not being consulted or represented and who looked upon Hoover's schemes of public–private cooperation as amounting to an informal version of recognizing and using monopolistic chosen instruments.

In addition to being naive about the willingness of industrial and labor leaders to place collective social good above their private interest, Hoover was not a charismatic leader. He believed that "through the magic of education, volunteerism, and cooperativism, ... [it would be possible to] avoid the type of statist bureaucracies, make-work endeavors, and government backed cartelization that would later become significant features America's managerial state" (Wilson, 1975).

Without much legislative authorization Hoover also took steps to address the problems of allocation of radio frequencies as well as the regulation of the advertising content in broadcast radio. He also tackled the issue of regulating the growing field of aviation, creating an Aeronautic Branch in the Commerce Department.[17]

Concerned that industrial research was rapidly using up the stock of accumulated basic scientific knowledge and that inadequate investments were being made to replenish that stock, Hoover championed the creation of a National Research Fund. At the NAS:

> Hale first suggested such a possibility at a meeting of the [NAS] Council in March 1924. A year later he reported a plan to establish a research foundation under Academy auspices and through its funds to "increase and strengthen American contributions to the mathematical, physical, and biological sciences" by making sums available to the ablest and most productive investigators engaged in pure research. On May 8, 1925, at a meeting at the Metropolitan Club in Washington attended by Andrew W. Mellon, Herbert Hoover ... William Welch, Thomas H. Morgan, and Vernon Kellogg, Hale presented a modified plan, an Academy proposal for a National Research Endowment, its purpose to redress the imbalance between industrial research and its source, basic science. (Cochrane, 1978)

The effort was announced with great fanfare. The Academy announced a goal of raising $20 million, to be spent at the rate of $2 million/year. A 25-member Board of Trustees was set up under Hoover's chairmanship. Kevles (1978) notes that:

> Hoover knew ... that raising $20,000,000 for pure science would be quite difficult, not least because the trustees aimed to obtain a sizable fraction of the funds out of corporations chartered to make profits, not to engage in philanthropy ... to assure that the National Research Endowment qualified for corporate largess, the trustees changed its name to the National Research Fund and proposed to spend, rather than invest each contribution in the year it was made. That way, a corporate donation would be no mere philanthropy, but a current expense, a payment for new knowledge, and as such, both legal and tax deductible ...
>
> Industrial corporations generally preferred to make their investments in pure research in their own company laboratories, where technologically promising discoveries could be patented before they were published.

Corporate contributions to the National Research Fund ended up being modest, with support only coming from AT&T, U.S. Steel, the member companies of the National Electric Light Association, and the American Iron and Steel Institute.

Cochrane (1978) notes that:

> The Academy came to realize that so large a fund might not be collected and in any event probably could not, without trial experience, be expended effectively. With the assent of those who had pledged support to the undertaking, the Academy initiated a

[17] It was only after a number of mid-air collisions, including the collision of a United DC-7 and TWA L-1049 over the Grand Canyon in 1956 that killed all 128 on board the two aircraft, as well as several subsequent mid-air collisions, that Congress finally passed the Federal Aviation Act of 1958 that led to the creation of the FAA.

new campaign, for a National Research Fund, setting the more modest goal of $1 million a year for a five-year period. That goal, with just seven contributors, was reached in the spring of 1930; and the Academy, amid the reverberations of the Great Crash, made plans to launch the program that October. The eventual default of one contributor in providing his share forced the Academy to release the others from their pledges.

In 1934, most of the $379,660 that had been collected to initiate the effort was returned to donors (Dupree, 1986). Nevertheless, Dupree observes:

The National Research Fund stands as a pioneer effort to redress the imbalance between basic and applied science. It was also the only large, new effort in the 1920s to deal with the whole pattern of science in the United States as a single unit. Its scale was sufficiently ample that its full operation would have made a measurable impression on American science. It might even have become a central organization for basic research. Whether it would eventually have achieved this promise is futile to ask, for it did not possess the stamina for the storms of the 1930's.

Hoover was an unlikely candidate for president in the spring of 1927 when flooding began to take place in the Mississippi river basin. The situation quickly grew worse. As it became apparent that New Orleans might be flooded, on April 22, President Coolidge named Hoover to head the flood effort. This he did with great energy and with carefully orchestrated public relations. Barry (1997) notes that while Coolidge was not deeply engaged and did very little:

Hoover did everything. For months hardly a day passed without his name appearing in a heroic and effective posture, saving the lives of Americans. He was the focus of newsreels, of magazine feature stories, of Sunday supplements. The flood influenced the treatment of him on other questions as well. Almost like the president, everything he did was news. Not counting flood-related stories, references to him in the press tripled during the three months after the flood compared to the three months before the flood.

Barry (1997) provides a detailed account of Hoover's activities during and after the flood in which he set out to substantially transform the social and economic well-being of residents in the Mississippi basin and delta. In these efforts he was far from successful. He also made a number of promises to the African American community that enlisted their support but on which, Barry argues, he never delivered.

Nonetheless, because of the massive national publicity, once Coolidge indicated that he would not seek a second term, Hoover was catapulted to the position of front-runner. He became the 31st president of the United States in March 1929 – just seven months before the stock market crash that plunged the nation into years of economic depression.

Hoover's one-term presidency ended in March 1933 when Franklin D. Roosevelt became president. During the early years of the Roosevelt Administration, unsuccessful efforts to secure recovery funds for science were made by a presidentially appointed Science Advisory Board chaired by MIT President Carl Compton. Later, a National Resources Board and then a National Resources Committee were only somewhat more successful. In the latter stages of the New Deal, some funds from the Works Progress Administration (WPA) did find their way into science and engineering programs in state universities, and there was some recovery of budgets in federal science agencies, but it was not until the eve of U.S. involvement in World War II that federal funding for research and development began a rapid and unprecedented growth.

READING 17.2

For a compact, if occasionally acerbic, account of basic science in the United States prior to World War II, read:

- Daniel S. Greenberg, "Chapter 3: When Science Was an Orphan," in *The Politics of Pure Science*, Plume/Signet, 325pp., 1967.

DISCUSSION QUESTIONS FOR READING 17.2

- Greenberg writes that prior to World War II, "honor and financial reward were bestowed upon the tinkerer, the gadgeteer, the Yankee engineer, those, in short who could translate knowledge into utility ... Herbert Hoover estimated that from all sources, the nation was spending a total of 200 million a year in the application of science, but only 10 million in pure research." Why was this the situation, and was it unique to attitudes toward basic science?
- Describe the important difference between German and U.S. universities in the late nineteenth and early twentieth century.
- What was the role of major corporate laboratories in the 1920s and the period between the two world wars?
- Describe the impact of the Great Depression on science in leading U.S. universities such as the California Institute of Technology.

REFERENCES

Ambrose, S.E. (1996). *Undaunted Courage: Meriwether Lewis, Thomas Jefferson and the Opening of the American West*, Simon & Schuster, 511pp.

Barry, J.M. (1997). *Rising Tide: The Great Mississippi Flood of 1927 and How It Changed America*, Simon & Schuster, 524pp.

Bruce, R.V. (1987). *The Launching of Modern American Science: 1846–1876*, Knopf, 446pp.

Burke, J.G. (1966). "Bursting Boilers and the Federal Power," *Technology and Culture*, 7, pp. 1–23.

Clements, K.A. (2010). *The Life of Herbert Hoover: Imperfect Visionary 1918–1928*, Palgrave Macmillan, 607pp.

Cochrane, R.C. (1978). *The National Academy of Sciences: The First 100 Years, 1863–1963*, National Academy Press, 694pp.

DeVoto, B. (1952). *The Course of Empire*, Houghton Mifflin Co., 647pp.

Dupree, A.H. (1959). *Asa Gray: American Botanist, Friend of Darwin*, Johns Hopkins University Press, 503pp.

(1986). *Science in the Federal Government: A History of Politics and Activities*, Johns Hopkins University Press, 460pp.

Greenberg, D.S. (1967). *The Politics of Pure Science*, Plume/Signet, 325pp.

Hawley, E.W. (1981). "Herbert Hoover and Economic Stabilization, 1921–22," in E.W. Hawley (ed.), *Herbert Hoover as Secretary of Commerce: Studies in New Era Thought and Practice*, University of Iowa Press, pp. 43–77.

Kevles, D.J. (1978). *The Physicists: The History of a Scientific Community in Modern America*, Alfred A. Knopf, 489pp.

Murray, R.K. (1974). "Herbert Hoover in the Harding Cabinet," in E.W. Hawley (ed.), *Herbert Hoover as Secretary of Commerce: Studies in New Era Thought and Practice*, University of Iowa Press, pp. 19–42.

Philbrick, N. (2003). *Sea of Glory: America's Voyage of Discovery: The U.S. Exploring Expedition, 1838–1842*, Viking, 452pp.

Powell, J.W. (1875). Part 1 of *Exploration of the Colorado River of the West and Its Tributaries Explored in 1869, 1870, 1871, and 1872 under the Direction of the Smithsonian Institution*, U.S. Government Printing Office, 291pp.

Rabbitt, M.C. (1989). *The United States Geological Survey: 1879–1989*, USGS Circular 1050, 62pp.

Sides, H. (2014). *In the Kingdom of Ice*, Doubleday, 454pp.

Sobel, D. (2005). *Longitude: The True Story of a Lone Genius Who Solved the Greatest Scientific Problem of His Time*, Macmillan, 184pp.

Stearns, P.N. (1998). "Why Study History?," *The American Historical Association*. Available at: www.historians.org/about-aha-and-membership/aha-history-and-archives/archives/why-study-history-(1998).

Wilson, J.H. (1975). *Herbert Hoover: Forgotten Progressive*, Little Brown and Company, 307pp.

Wood, W.R. (2003). *Prologue to Lewis and Clark: The Mackay and Evans Expedition*, University of Oklahoma Press, 234pp.

18

U.S. Science and Technology Policy from World War II to 1960

Summarizing relations between science and the U.S. federal government over the course of the first 150 years of the Republic, Daniel Greenberg (1967) exaggerates only slightly when he writes:

> it may be difficult to realize that prior to 1940, not only was there a mutual aloofness between the federal government and the most influential and creative segments of the scientific community, but there were strong feelings on both sides that the separation was desirable. In maintaining a distance from science, the federal government was not out of harmony with the anti-intellectual strain that pervaded American life. And, in being distant from government, the scientific community was not bowing to the fact that it was not wanted, but was also pridefully responding to rebuffs and crude treatment it considered inimical to its integrity. Science was the first to recognize that it needed government's support and that government needed its skills, but the recognition came slowly, and on the eve of World War II, mutual aloofness remained the dominant theme.

World War II resulted in fundamental and irreversible changes in the relationship between science, technology, and government in the United States. As in the previous chapter, here I will focus on just a few of those developments: Vannevar Bush and the creation of, and role played by, the wartime Office of Scientific Research and Development (OSRD); the postwar efforts to create a National Science Foundation (NSF); the emergence of the Office of Naval Research, and the key role it played when creating the NSF took longer than expected; the debate over military versus civilian control of atomic and nuclear weapons and energy; and a few key developments in the 1950s and 1960s. Readers interested in a more comprehensive historical account are advised to begin with:

- David M. Hart, *Forged Consensus: Science, Technology and Economic Policy in the United States, 1921–1953*, Princeton, 267pp., 1998.

- Bruce L.R. Smith, *American Science Policy since World War II*, The Brookings Institution, 230pp., 1990.
- William A. Blanpied, *A History of Federal Science Policy: From the New Deal to the Present*, Rice University Press, 259pp., 2010.

18.1 VANNEVAR BUSH AND U.S. DEFENSE RESEARCH AND DEVELOPMENT DURING WORLD WAR II

Few individuals have had as profound an impact on the evolution of U.S. science and technology policy as Vannevar Bush, who led the civilian research effort during World War II that resulted in critical technological developments ranging from high-frequency radar, radar-controlled gunnery, and the proximity fuse, to amphibious vehicles, techniques for submarine detection, and a variety of important medical advances including the high-volume production of penicillin and the development of better drugs for use against malaria, and, of course, the atomic bomb. All of these developments made important contributions to winning the war. While the atomic bomb helped speed the end of the war, radar is probably the single technical innovation that did the most to win it. Further, Gertner (2012) notes that radar involved "a far larger investment on the part of the U.S. Government probably amounting to $3 billion as contrasted with $2 billion for the atomic bomb." Of course, there is no denying the fact that the development of atomic weapons had a profound effect on postwar geopolitics and science advice.

Kevles (1978) records that Bush's grandfather had been a whaling captain and that his father "had left his strict Cape Cod Methodist home to crew on a mackerel boat." By the time Vannevar was born in 1890, his father had returned from the sea to work as a Universalist minister in a town north of Boston. Bush biographer G. Pascal Zachary (1997) reports that Bush, a strong-willed young man, showed occasional sparks of belligerency and endured occasional bouts of illness.[1] As a youth he showed great promise in mathematics and science, and, perhaps just as important, proved adept with his hands. Zachary notes that in "tinkering in his basement, Bush shared an activity with many middle-class boys around the country. The romance of invention … was contagious … [and] Bush realized that the path of the inventor offered him perhaps the only means of achieving success without sacrificing his maverick leanings."

In 1909, when Bush graduated from Chelsea High School, he was an independent-minded, politically conservative New Englander. According to Zachary, "he was impatient with pomp, an outsider who resented the elite of society but hungered for recognition too." He went to Tufts University in Boston, where he earned a B.S. and M.S. in engineering, paying his way in part

[1] Portions of the text in the first several paragraphs of this section have been adapted with permission from a book review I wrote (Morgan, 1998) for *IEEE Spectrum* of G. Pascal Zachary (1997), *Vannevar Bush: Engineer of the American Century*.

Vannevar Bush in the early 1940s (photo from Wikipedia)

by tutoring other students. On one occasion, Zachary notes, Bush read the textbook for a course in advance and asked the professor if he could cut class and just take the final exam when it was given. Instead, the professor gave him the final exam on the spot, which Bush passed and was granted credit for the course.

After working briefly at General Electric Co., Bush entered a doctoral program at Clark University but then transferred to MIT, where, in less than a year, he completed a Ph.D. in the newly created department of electrical engineering. In 1916, he accepted an academic position at Tufts and in parallel became laboratory director for American Radio and Research Corporation (Amrad). Three years later he moved back to the department of electrical engineering at MIT as a professor of power transmission, where he expanded his program of research and industrial consulting.

Bush's work at Amrad eventually led to the creation of a new company, Raytheon Corporation, which grew rapidly, supplying vacuum tubes for the consumer radio market. Bush prospered along with it.

In 1932, Karl Compton, MIT's new president, appointed Bush vice-president and dean of engineering. While this position gave him wide administrative responsibilities and greater exposure on the national scene, it did not end his research activities or consulting. His research at MIT focused on applying advanced mathematical methods to power systems. Because these defied closed-form solutions, he developed an analogue computing machine called a "differential calculator," and later also worked to develop "rapid selectors" for searching large physical files such as banks of microfilm.

As the risk of war grew in the late 1930s, Bush became concerned about the need to build the research and development foundation that he believed would be needed to assure victory. He had already begun to expand his activities in Washington, DC, when in early 1939 he was named the president of the Carnegie Institution of Washington and to the chairmanship of the National

Advisory Committee for Aeronautics (NACA), positions that provided the springboard that soon vaulted him to the pinnacle of power.

Kevles (1978) explains that Bush's involvement with NACA:

drew him increasingly into the defense program and he frequently discussed the general state of American military preparedness with his friends Frank Jewett [Head of AT&T Bell Labs], Karl Compton [president of MIT], and James B. Conant [president of Harvard]. All of them emphatically pro-Ally they were drawn together, Bush recalled, by "one thing we deeply shared – worry."

Having learned from the NRC experience in World War I in which scientists served as lower-ranking commissioned officers who did not have access to senior military leaders, Bush concluded that there needed to be a defense research group, operated as part of the government by civilian scientists. Kevles (1978) explains that:

In May 1940 the influential governmental lawyer Oscar Cox arranged for Bush to discuss his proposal with Harry Hopkins. Now the Secretary of Commerce, Hopkins was considering the mobilization of the nation's technical genius through a new inventor's council ... Hopkins agreed to keep the administration of inventions separate from the organization of science and gave Bush the green light for what had now been named the National Defense Research Committee, or NDRC.

Hopkins biographer Robert Sherwood (1948) notes that Hopkins was "always receptive to new ideas that were both daring and big" and that:

Hopkins was immediately impressed with Bush's proposal and with Bush himself. There were certain points of resemblance between the two men. Bush was also thin, quick, sharp and untrammeled in his thinking. He knew what he was talking about and, like Hopkins, with a good sprinkling of salt. He had prepared a succinct memorandum outlining his proposals. Hopkins read it with approval and then arranged an appointment for Bush to talk with the President about it. When Bush went to the White House he was prepared to answer all kinds of questions and meet probable objections, but he found that Roosevelt had already studied the memorandum with Hopkins: after uttering a pleasantry or two he wrote on it, "O.K. -F.D.R" – and Bush was out of the President's office a few moments after he had entered it.

Subsequently Bush, in consultation with Hopkins, drafted a letter to himself for the President's signature. That letter, with a few additions which provided for close co-operation between N.D.R.C. and the military authorities, was signed by Roosevelt on June 15, the day after the fall of Paris.

Sherwood (1948) notes that in setting up both NDRC as well as several other organizations, Roosevelt "used antiquated and generally inadequate legislation as his authority because he did not want to risk possible conflict with the Congress on any issue other than the one he considered the main one – which was selective service."

Rather than create a physical entity and move people, Bush adopted the strategy of contracting with existing university research groups and other laboratories. In his 1970 book, *Pieces of the Action*, he notes that this:

decision proved to be important, not only for the war years but also for the post war period. In fact it set a pattern that meant a great deal eventually to advancing education in this country. We decided that we would make contracts for research directly with universities, not with individuals therein. And we decided that, in so doing we would pay the full costs of the program ... This does not sound like a very radical departure from previous practice, but it was ... we proposed to pay [a university's] overhead costs, the portion of its general expenses properly attributable to the added operation ... This sounds reasonable. It certainly did to the university executives. But not to old hands in the Washington bureaus. They did not pay much attention at first – probably didn't know it was going on. Later, when things began really rolling, I was visited by representatives of the Bureau of the Budget, the General Accounting Office, the Civil Service Commission, etc. They accused me of being in a plot to fatten up the universities at government expense. But by then there was not much they could do about it. I just told the Appropriations Committee of the House what I was doing and how I was doing it. They seemed to think it was alright so that was that. (Bush, 1970)

Bush appointed five senior colleagues to each head a separate general-purpose research division: "Compton on radar and allied matters, Conant on chemistry and explosives, Jewett on communications and transportation, Tolman on armor and ordnance, and Coe on patents and inventions" (Bush, 1970).

The British had made considerable progress on radar research. The set of meter-wave Chain Home Stations were providing early warning of German bombers but lacked sufficient resolution to precisely vector fighter aircraft for interception. Sir Henry Tizard and Eddie Bowen understood the importance of microwave radar for this purpose and were strong proponents of developing airborne microwave radar for fighter interceptors. In August 1940, Winston Churchill was reluctantly persuaded to give up on the British effort to secure access to the American Norden bombsight in a trade for military-related British scientific knowledge (Zimmerman, 1996; Phelps, 2010). A seven-man team, under the leadership of Tizard, was dispatched to brief the still neutral Americans on a number of Great Britain's most advanced technologies with no strings attached. Among the devices that the delegation brought with them was their best high-frequency resonant cavity magnetron tube that had been invented just a year previously by John Randall and Henry Boot.[2] The British magnetron, which outperformed the microwave amplifiers that the United States then had by a factor of a thousand (Phelps, 2010), produced 10-centimeter microwaves that held the potential to dramatically improve radar's resolution and sensitivity. While the British radar community clearly had the capability to develop the technologies, faced with the ongoing German blitz they needed America's industrial base to mass-produce radar systems.

Robert Buderi (1996) and Stephen Phelps (2010) have outlined how the arrival of the British mission, and the magnetron, served to nucleate U.S. radar

[2] Although it had rather little impact on the course of the war, the latest designs for the jet engine were also part of the collection brought by the British delegation. For an historical account of the development of the turbojet engine, see Constant (1980).

research. After a frantic round of meetings and technical demonstrations, Vannevar Bush authorized independent entrepreneur Alfred Loomis to organize the creation of a new centralized radar research laboratory.[3]

In a rapid-fire insider process that would drive today's government acquisition lawyers apoplectic, Bell Laboratory's Frank Jewett was deftly squeezed out and the new effort was created at the Massachusetts Institute of Technology (although Bell Labs did extensive work on developing magnetrons, which were then mass-produced by AT&T's Western Electric Company). Alfred Loomis (see box) and Ernest Lawrence recruited physicist Lee DeBridge to head the new Radiation Laboratory. The lab's name was chosen so as not to be overly specific about its true mission. In part because they were the only people with significant prior experience at microwave frequencies, DeBridge promptly set out to recruit some of the country's top atomic physicists to this effort.

Because NDRC was still operating at a modest scale, progress on microwave radar faced administrative obstacles at first. Indeed, for a while it looked like the Rad Lab might lose funding (either John D. Rockefeller, Jr. or Alfred Loomis anonymously underwrote salaries for a short while to keep things going). However, Kevles (1978) notes that by:

> August 1941 the Rad Lab ASV, for air to surface vessel radar, was detecting capital ships twenty to thirty miles away and surfaced submarines two to five miles distant. The equipment displayed the location of the vessels on a circular oscilloscope screen called the Plan Position Indicator, which allowed the pilot to determine at a glance their range and bearing relative to his plane.

Radar-based technologies developed at the Rad Lab and then rapidly moved out into industry production included both ship and airborne systems, systems to accurately aim anti-aircraft guns, and IFF technology to help differentiate friendly aircraft from those of attackers (Phelps, 2010).[4]

Before the United States entered the war, getting the new technology adopted by the U.S. military took some considerable persuasion, especially in the Navy where Admiral Ernest King took a dim view of civilian scientists becoming involved in defense matters. However, once the new radar was widely deployed it dramatically transformed anti-submarine operations from a defensive role (based on convoys) to an offensive role (submarines had to surface at night to get air and recharge batteries, at which time they could be seen with the new radars).

Another radar-based technology that had a large impact on the war effort, especially in the air battle of Britain, the Battle of the Bulge, and against

[3] Portions of the text in this section have been adapted with permission from a book review I wrote with my father, Millett G. Morgan (Morgan and Morgan, 1998) for *IEEE Spectrum* of Robert Buderi (1996), *The Invention that Changed the World*.

[4] Readers interested in a gripping blow-by-blow account of British–U.S. efforts in the development and deployment of radar, and a detailed description of the profound impacts that it had on the war effort, will find Phelps (2010) fascinating reading.

kamikaze attacks in the Pacific, was the proximity fuse – a compact radar system placed in shells that triggered the explosion when the shell got within a lethal distance of its target. This device, which was originally developed by the British and then considerably refined by American researchers, was one of the war's most closely held secrets and has been credited as among the most significant contributors to the military success of the Allies.

The need for funds grew rapidly. Bush (1970) explains:

> I remember that we discussed how much money we should ask for initially, and I suggested five million. It shows how rapidly things can change when there is a war. Frank Jewett thought we could not possibly spend such an amount promptly and effectively. It did not take us long to get over that idea. Soon we were talking hundreds of millions.

As the magnitude of the undertaking grew, it became apparent that a new organizational arrangement was needed that secured support directly from Congress, rather than through the White House. The result was an executive order on June 28, 1941, that established the Office of Scientific Research and Development (OSRD), which combined the NDRC and the Committee on Medical Research to become the primary vehicle for civilian defense research throughout the balance of the war. Bush was director and Conant was his deputy. The result was a "civilian-controlled preserve, reporting directly to the President, working toward military objectives, in close liaison with the military, but independent of the military" (Greenberg, 1967). By 1944, "OSRD was spending $3-million a week on 6000 researchers at more than 300 industrial and university labs" (Zachary, 1997).

Work on developing the atomic bomb experienced a slower start than work on radar. Bush was not a physicist and the Uranium Committee that he had established, under the chairmanship of Lyman Briggs, was dubious that uranium would prove to be useful in the current war. The committee moved very slowly, and focused as much on using atomic energy for power as for a bomb. The British committee on Military Application of Uranium Detonation (MAUD) had concluded that a bomb was indeed possible and this information was shared with Briggs. Phelps (2010) notes that Briggs locked the report in his safe and did not share it with the rest of his committee until Marcus Oliphant, who had been a member of the MAUD committee, traveled to the United States to try to get a serious development program launched. After his meetings in Washington failed to spark much interest, he traveled to Berkeley to meet with Ernest Lawrence, who became convinced of the urgency of starting a U.S. development program. Bush arranged a meeting in Chicago with Compton and Conant, after which Conant briefed Bush, and serious efforts began.

Minuscule amounts of plutonium were first created with the 60-inch cyclotron by investigators working at Lawrence's Berkeley lab (Hiltzik, 2015). It was clear that in addition to U_{235} plutonium would also make an excellent fissile material for a bomb if it could be produced in sufficient quantity in a reactor – a process Fermi set out to demonstrate in Chicago. Several strategies were pursued in parallel to separate U_{235} (which makes up 0.72 percent of natural uranium). Lawrence converted one of his older cyclotrons into a mass spectrometer and demonstrated that separation could be achieved, and on that basis developed the "calutron" system at Oak Ridge that produced the uranium used in the Hiroshima bomb. Both the Trinity test bomb and the bomb used at Nagasaki employed plutonium, which had been produced in reactors in Hanford, WA.

While the program to develop the atomic bomb began as part of OSRD, as it grew larger, Bush arranged to have it moved directly under Army control as a program termed the Manhattan District:

> By December 1941 the program had arrived at the point of engineering and actual construction of plants for producing material for the bomb. [The Manhattan District] was set up for two reasons. First it made no sense whatsoever for O.S.R.D. to try to create the enormous engineering and construction organization that would soon be needed. Second, we were rapidly running into the expenditure of really large amounts of money, and it was far easier to obtain these through War Department channels. (Bush, 1970)

While the Manhattan District operated under Army control, it had far less hierarchical bureaucracy than a typical military organization. Greenberg (1967) explains that:

> The Los Alamos Scientific Laboratory, which fabricated and tested the atomic bomb, was originally to be a military laboratory. But prospective recruits from academic science rebelled when they learned they were to work under the military ... their feelings were that "a military laboratory could accomplish nothing significant. Differences in rank between commissioned and civilian researchers would breed friction ... a military organization would introduce a dangerous rigidity ..." The civilians prevailed, and the Los Alamos laboratory was organized as an adjunct of the University of California.

The Rad Lab, and other OSRD organizations, enjoyed even greater intellectual freedom to innovate. In contrast, with the exception of aeronautics, German war research operated in a far more incremental mode under direct military controls and restrictions.[5]

Bush (1970) notes that:

> Part of the plan for the Manhattan District, as I worked it out with [Secretary of War] Stimson, was the creation of a Military Policy Committee. This consisted of myself as chairman, with Conant as my deputy, General Styer and Admiral Punell. It served as a board of directors for General Groves. It met frequently, had no staff or secretary present, kept no formal records, but provided a point at which every important move could be discussed and closely examined.

[5] Fears that the Nazis might develop an atomic bomb first fueled much of the urgency of the U.S. program, since much of the knowledge on which the bomb was based had originated in Europe. While there were also Japanese scientists who had understood the possibility of developing both atomic and hydrogen bombs, there was considerably less concern that the Japanese were actively developing such weapons.

From time to time Bush briefed President Roosevelt on developments, but he reports that the president largely trusted the judgments of the scientific community that was developing the bomb.[6]

While the atom bomb ended World War II, it was the many developments from OSRD, especially those involving high-frequency radar, the proximity fuse, high-volume production of penicillin, and more prosaic developments such as the amphibious tracked DUKS, that played a definitive role in leading to victory.

BOX 18.1 VANNEVAR BUSH ON THE SOCIAL STATUS OF ENGINEERS

The relationship between civilian and military personnel went through an evolution during the war ... At first scientists were received at least with tolerance ... but engineers were something else again. Among older military men the engineer was at first regarded as in all probability a thinly disguised salesman, and hence to be kept at arm's length.

Our military people were by no means alone in this mistaken view as may be suggested by this anecdote: Some time after the war, Prince Philip came over to this country and paid an unexpected visit to the National Academy of Science. Dr. Detlev Bronk who was then the president of the Academy, hastily tried to get a group together to greet him. I hustled over to the Academy, and as we waited for the others, the Prince and Bronk and I had a very congenial discussion ... [However,] there came a moment when congeniality chilled, gave way to courtesy with less warmth, and that moment occurred when the discussion brought out the fact that I was an engineer ... it was true of the British – and they have not quite recovered from it yet – the engineer was kind of a second-class citizen compared to the scientist.

This is the way things were at first in our relations with the military in our war effort. So all O.S.R.D. personnel promptly became scientists ... The business of elevating the scientist to a pedestal probably started with this move, and it has certainly persisted ... Even recently when we sent the first astronauts to the moon, the press hailed it as a great scientific achievement. Of course it was nothing of the sort; it was a marvelous skillful engineering job. (Bush, 1970)

[6] For detailed accounts of the development of the bomb, see Rhodes (1986) and Hiltzik (2015). Hiltzik and Thorpe (2006) provide detailed accounts of the successful postwar campaign to question the security status of J. Robert Oppenheimer, who had been the scientific director of the bomb development work at Los Alamos. This effort, which led to Oppenheimer losing his security clearance and being barred from advisory roles to the U.S. Government, was spearheaded by FBI Director J. Edgar Hoover, Senator Joseph McCarthy's House Un-American Activities Committee, and AEC Commissioner Lewis Strauss, who wanted Oppenheimer banned from government service because he opposed the development of the hydrogen bomb.

BOX 18.2 ALFRED LEE LOOMIS (1887–1975)

Working with Vannevar Bush and Ernest Lawrence, Alfred Loomis played a key role in facilitating the mobilization of the U.S. physics community before and during World War II.

Loomis studied math at Yale and then studied law at Harvard. During World War I, as an officer in the U.S. Army, he worked on improving artillery at the Aberdeen Proving Ground, where he invented a device to measure the muzzle velocity of shells.

After the war, with his brother-in-law, Landon Thorne, he acquired and ran Bonbright & Company, turning it into a large, highly successful, electric utility holding company. Unlike many other Wall Street investment bankers, Lewis and Thorne believed in holding most of their assets in cash. As they became more concerned about the high level of speculation in the 1920s, they liquidated most of their other holdings before the stock market cash. As a result, Loomis weathered the depression with his considerable wealth intact.

Alfred Lee Loomis.

While he developed a large fortune, Loomis's true passion was physics. He used his considerable wealth, and the assistance of Johns Hopkins physics professor Robert Wood, to learn physics and assemble one of the world's finest labs in a large house he had purchased for the purpose in the gated community of Tuxedo Park, north of New York City. There he pursued studies in a number of different fields including ultrasound and precision timekeeping. He and Wood made frequent trips to leading physics labs in Europe, both to meet with leading physicists and to purchase advanced equipment.

Physicists from all over the world spent time at the Tuxedo Park lab. Loomis sponsored, arranged funding for, and used his vast commercial and other contacts to secure material for many experimental studies and instruments, including copper and iron for one of Ernest Lawrence's large cyclotrons. Loomis did not like publicity, so virtually all these efforts were undertaken quietly, with little public notice.

Before World War II, on the advice of MIT president Karl Compton, Loomis became interested in microwaves. When the Tizard mission brought the best British cavity magnetron to the United States, meetings to discuss how to build on this dramatic new technology were held with Welsh radar expert Edward George "Taffy" Bowen and others at Loomis's lab at Tuxedo Park. Bush subsequently appointed Loomis to chair the microwave committee for OSRD, and together with Ernest Lawrence he recruited leading physicists from across the country to staff the vital Rad Lab at MIT. He used his many connections to get the lab up and running in remarkably short time. Among his many inventions, Loomis is credited with the invention of the Loran radio navigation system, which played a key role in air operations in both the European and Pacific theaters, and with driving the development of ground control approach (GCA) to support aircraft landing in bad weather.

Loomis's first cousin was Henry Stimpson, who served as Roosevelt's and Truman's Secretary of War. Stimpson often used Loomis (and vice versa) as a back channel to spur the more rapid adoption of radar and other promising new technology when the military did not proceed with sufficient speed.

Loomis also played a role, along with Lawrence, in establishing and staffing the Manhattan Project that led to the development of the atomic bomb.

After the war, Loomis returned to a quiet private life, declining, for example, William Golden's inquiry about perhaps becoming the first presidential science advisor.[7] He had purchased 17,000 acres on the island of Hilton Head and also had homes in New York, California, and on Long Island.

Loomis was elected to the National Academy of Science in 1940. President Truman awarded him the Presidential Medal of Merit. He received honorary degrees from Wesleyan, Yale, and Berkeley. He was a member of the MIT Corporation from 1931 until his death, and a founding member of the Board of the RAND Corporation.

For details on the life and work of Alfred Loomis, see:

- Jennet Conant, *Tuxedo Park: A Wall Street Tycoon and the Secret Palace of Science That Changed the Course of World War II*, Simon & Schuster, 330pp., 2002.
- Luis W. Alvarez, "A Biographical Memoir of Alfred Lee Loomis (1887–1975)," *U.S. National Academy of Science Biographical Memories*, *51*, pp. 309–342, 1980. Available at: www.nasonline.org/publications/biographical-memoirs/memoir-pdfs/loomis-alfred.pdf.
- Michael Hiltzik, *Big Science: Ernest Lawrence and the Invention That Launched the Military-Industrial Complex*, Simon & Schuster, 512pp., 2015.

[7] See the discussion of William Golden in the box in Section 19.1.

18.2 *SCIENCE THE ENDLESS FRONTIER* AND THE CREATION OF THE NATIONAL SCIENCE FOUNDATION

In 1944, a number of developments, including restlessness among the scientific staff at the Metallurgical Lab at the University of Chicago that saw their task to develop plutonium production coming to completion, "led Bush to realize that it was time to lay plans for nourishing science when peace returned" (Greenberg, 1967).

> While restlessness in the ranks provided Bush with an incentive to get on with postwar planning for science, an even greater motivation was provided by the events on Capitol Hill. There, Senator Harley M. Kilgore, a West Virginia new dealer, continually on the lookout for issues to mold to his populist vision, held the chairmanship of the Subcommittee on War Mobilization of the Committee on Military Affairs ... Seeing how well science was serving the war, layman Kilgore – to the horror of scientist-engineer Bush – proceeded to draw plans for a great postwar collaboration of science and government, a matter which the senator felt could be accomplished without any significant departures from the administrative procedures traditionally followed by government. There would, of course, have to be a new federal agency – a foundation of sorts – to support research, the Senator reasoned. (Greenberg, 1967)

Kilgore saw a major function of the proposed foundation as tackling a wide range of applied social problems under government supervision and direction. In contrast, Bush wanted to see a set of arrangements that would turn basic science loose to pursue a largely self-defined and self-directed agenda. As NSF historian George Mazuzan (1994) recounts:

> As early in the war as 1942 ... accelerating government–science community relationships interested some politicians about whether research support would be continued after the war.
>
> The situation prompted a New Deal senator from West Virginia, Harley Kilgore, to introduce in 1942, 1943, and 1945 successive pieces of legislation aimed ultimately at creating a National Science Foundation. Reflecting his populist New Dealer views, Kilgore envisioned a broad science organization (including the social sciences) that supported through grants and contracts both basic and applied research and incorporated geographic distribution of research funds. The agency would be responsible to political authority. The year-to-year Kilgore hearings and legislation quite naturally interested the scientific community, which had a major stake in the outcome.

Alarmed by these ongoing developments,[8] Bush obtained a letter (which he wrote) from President Roosevelt requesting that OSRD prepare a report

[8] Greenberg (1967) reports Bush as saying that the Kilgore approach held "grave danger to the full development of science" and would have "set up a gadgeteer's paradise." Similar reactions arose in some quarters when, during the 1970s, the NSF ran a program called "Research Applied to the Nation's Needs" or RANN. Criticism "came from segments of Congress, from other agencies, and particularly from the science community (including the Science Board and most Foundation staff), which feared that RANN would drain funding from the traditional aspects of basic science" (Mazuzan, 1994).

outlining how arrangements for the support of science should be organized in the postwar era. Bush assembled a series of panels to help develop the report. The result was a document titled *Science the Endless Frontier* (Bush, 1945).

READING 18.1

Vannevar Bush, *Science the Endless Frontier*, U.S. Government Printing Office, 183pp., 1945. This report is viewed by many as the founding document of modern federal support for basic science.

DISCUSSION QUESTIONS FOR READING 18.1

- How does the organization that is proposed in this document differ from the NSF that exists today?
- Why is this document widely held to have laid the foundation for postwar science and technology research in the United States?
- In the years after its publication this document is widely argued to have espoused a "linear model" of technical innovation (see Box 18.3). Given that Bush was a sophisticated observer of the process of moving research into practice, why do you suppose he might have framed the argument in this way?

Bush began *Science the Endless Frontier* by observing that:

> Progress in the war against disease depends upon the flow of new scientific knowledge. New products, new industries and more jobs require continuous additions to knowledge of the laws of nature, and the application of that knowledge to practical purposes. Similarly, our defense against aggression demands new knowledge so that we can develop new and improved weapons. This essential, new knowledge can be obtained only through basic scientific research.

Recognizing that much of the output of OSRD during the war had built on a store of basic scientific knowledge that had been built up over past decades, Bush believed that there was an urgent need to replenish that store.[9] In *Science the Endless Frontier* he wrote:

> The responsibility for the creation of new scientific knowledge – and for most of its applications – rests on that small body of men and women who understand the fundamental laws of nature and are skilled in the techniques of scientific research. We shall

[9] Much of that knowledge had come from Europe, but of course after the war European science, and especially the German universities that had produced so much of it, lay in shambles. Even today, German universities are still struggling to regain their former excellence, which was decimated by Nazi policies, especially the persecution of its many outstanding Jewish scientists, a large number of whom managed to flee to the United States.

have rapid or slow advance on any scientific frontier depending on the number of highly qualified and trained scientists exploring it.

In order to achieve new scientific understanding and educate the scientists who would produce it, Bush argued that:

> The Government should accept new responsibilities for promoting the flow of new scientific knowledge and the development of scientific talent in our youth ...
>
> The effective discharge of these new responsibilities will require the full attention of some overall agency devoted to that purpose ...
>
> I recommend that a new agency for these purposes be established. Such an agency should be composed of persons of broad interest and experience, having an understanding of the peculiarities of scientific research and scientific education. It should have stability of funds so that long-range programs may be undertaken. It should recognize that freedom of inquiry must be preserved and should leave internal control of policy, personnel, and the method and scope of research to the institutions in which it is carried out. It should be fully responsible to the president and through him to the Congress for its program.

Bush proposed that the National Research Foundation (NRF) be governed by nine Members "who should be persons not otherwise connected with the government and not representative of any special interest, who should be known as the National Research Foundation Members selected by the president on the basis of their interest in and capacity to promote the purposes of the foundation." These Members would then select and appoint a Director.

The proposed NRF would have had five divisions, each with its own set of members and an executive director: the division of medical research; the division of natural sciences; the division of national defense; the division of scientific personnel and education; and the division of publications and scientific collaboration. Clearly, this NRF would have had a much broader scope than today's NSF.

Senator Harley M. Kilgore (D-WVa) in office from 1941 to 1956. Photo from Wikipedia.

Released in July 1945, Bush's proposal immediately became controversial. President Truman found it unacceptable because the Director, who would be responsible for disbursing public funds, would be appointed by the Members of the Foundation and would not be a direct presidential appointment. Social scientists were dismayed that the foundation would only focus on natural science and medicine.[10] Senator Kilgore continued to promote his alternative approach that was focused on addressing identified social problems.

Greenberg (1967) notes that by mid-1946:

> a Kilgore–Magnuson compromise on the science foundation bill, weighted toward the Kilgore concept, passed the Senate but failed in the House. The following year, Senator H. Anderson Smith of New Jersey, introduced a compromise, reflecting the Bush position. President Truman swiftly responded to its passage with a veto message declaring that the Smith bill "contains provisions which represent such a marked departure from sound principles for the administration of public affairs that I cannot give it my approval. It would in effect, vest the determination of vital national policies, the expenditure of large public funds, and the administration of important governmental function in a group of individuals who would be essentially private citizens. The proposed National Science Foundation would be divorced from control by the people to an extent that implies a distinct lack of faith in the democratic process."

After President Truman's veto, it was several more years before an NSF bill was finally passed and the agency was established in 1950. In the meantime, things moved on. With OSRD shut down, the Office of Naval Research picked up support of much of the nation's basic research, other parts of the military picked up more defense-related research, and the NIH (originally created in 1930) grew to encompass most federally supported medical research. Much basic aeronautical research continued in the Air Force and under the National Advisory Committee for Aeronautics (NACA) that was later incorporated into NASA.

[10] Social science was not added to the mandate of the NSF until 1976 when the Directorate for Biological Sciences was expanded to become the Directorate for Biological, Behavioral, and Social Sciences. This was of course an odd combination. Greenberg (1991) writes: "Despairing of internal reform, social scientists took to the lobbying route. Individually and through their professional societies, they pitched their case to Congress on the theme of dangerous knowledge gaps that can be filled only by an expansion of social science research. In committee hearings and in special seminars for members of Congress and staff, social scientists ranged over intractable problems, from urban poverty to productivity, from the deficiencies of the census to drug control. Bills were introduced to elevate the social sciences at the science foundation ... NSF responded ... with a committee for a long study of a matter that few felt really required further study. The committee, as expected, concluded that a separate directorate should be established. On October 11, 1991 NSF announced the creation of its Directorate for Social, Behavioral, and Economic Sciences." NSF research in the social sciences continues to be controversial. Budgets have remained very modest, and conservative members of Congress, and others, have periodically mounted efforts to eliminate or dramatically reduce NSF's social science programs.

BOX 18.3 MODELS OF THE INNOVATION PROCESS

The view of how science and technology lead to useful products and services that is outlined in *Science the Endless Frontier* has often been characterized as a "linear model." That is, basic science leads to technology, which in turn leads to useful products and services.

Given his wide research and industrial experience it seems doubtful that Bush himself believed strictly in such a model, but the formulation was widely adopted in the decades that followed by those who have lobbied to increase government support for research in basic science. Figure 18.1 displays such a "linear model."[11]

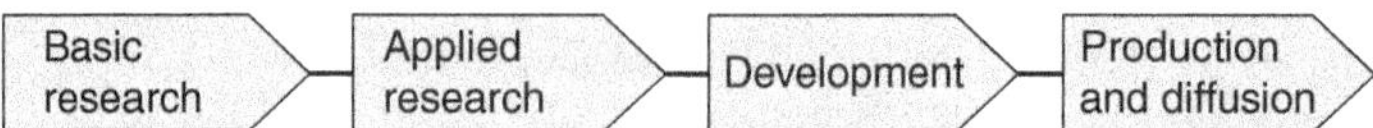

FIGURE 18.1. Illustration of the "linear model" of innovation. While different authors have labeled the elements slightly differently, the core idea is that basic research drives the process. Ideas feed forward to applied research (engineering) and then on to the development and production of new goods and services. While often cited in the past as justification for investment in basic research, virtually no serious student of innovation believes this is how the world works. For an historical discussion of the linear model, see Godin (2006).

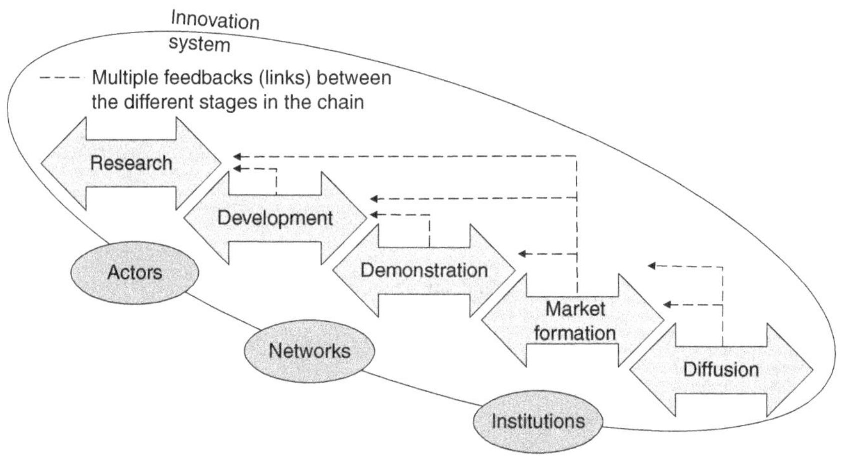

FIGURE 18.2. One example of the "chain-link model" of the process of innovation. This one is based on one presented by Gallagher et al. (2012).

[11] For an historical discussion of the linear model, see Godin (2006).

Today most discussions of the process of innovation adopt what is generally termed the "chain-link model" developed and promulgated by a variety of people including Stephen Kline of Stanford, Keith Pavitt of SPRU, and many others. These diagrams take a variety of different forms, but all share the basic characteristic that they contain a great deal of feedback between the various elements. Figure 18.2 shows one example of such a model.

Louis Branscomb (1997) has elaborated the idea of "basic," noting that while there is basic *scientific* research there is also basic *technological* research, and that frequently the results of basic technological research (i.e., the development of new measurement and fabrication methods) are what make progress possible in basic scientific research.

Donald Stokes (1997) added interesting insight to the issue of classifying different types of scientific and technical activity. Citing the work of Louis Pasteur that advanced the fundamental understanding of microbiology while simultaneously solving important practical problems in fermentation, Stokes argued that thinking in terms of a basic↔applied continuum is mistaken. He broke the axis in the middle to make a two-dimensional space (Figure 18.3) and then mapped various scientific and technical activities into four quadrants, terming the upper right quadrant Pasteur's Quadrant (Figure 18.4).

See Appendix 2 for a set of readings in the area of technology and innovation.

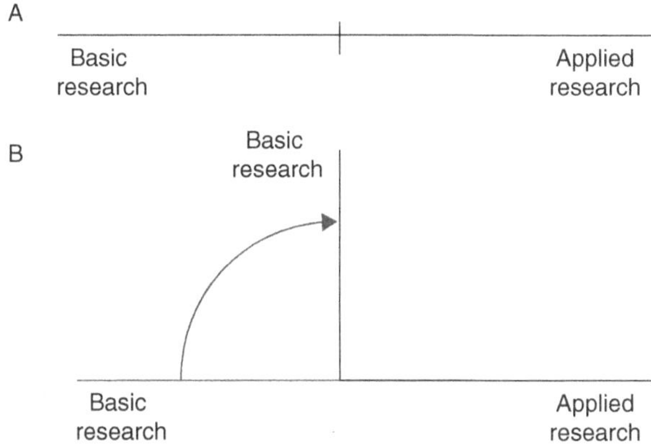

FIGURE 18.3. Donald Stokes argued that thinking in terms of a basic↔applied continuum (**A**) is a mistake. Instead, one should think in terms of a two dimensional space as shown in **B**.

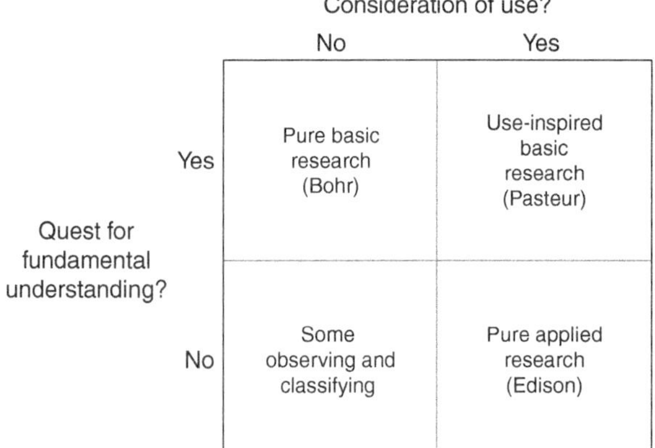

FIGURE 18.4. Having introduced the two-dimensional space shown in Figure 18.3, Stokes then labeled three of the quadrants after Louis Pasteur, Niels Bohr, and Thomas Edison. Stokes left the lower left quadrant blank. In my view, while it proved to be of great value a century or more later, much of the observational and classifying activities of nineteenth-century naturalists and astronomers might be placed there.

18.3 THE OFFICE OF NAVAL RESEARCH: FILLING THE GAP BETWEEN OSRD AND NSF[12]

Shortly before the war, Vice Admiral Harold G. Bowen recognized in atomic energy great promise not just for weaponry but also for ship propulsion. As chief of the service's Bureau of Engineering, Bowen set out to build an institutional base in the Navy through which he could direct the development of atomic ship propulsion. However, his brash style won him so many enemies, both inside and outside the service, that he lost his Bureau of Engineering assignment.

Instead, during the war, he was appointed technical assistant to the Secretary of the Navy, and built a close relationship with James Forrestal, then Undersecretary of the Navy. Hence, when Forrestal was promoted to Secretary in 1944, Bowen's star rose again. He received a major new post, Head of the Office of Research and Inventions (ORI), from which he once again began to maneuver to build a program to develop atomic propulsion.

The Navy's relations with civilian scientists were coordinated during the war by a group of young officers known as the "bird dogs," in the Office of the Coordinator of Research and Development headed by Admiral Julius A. Furer. These were a "group of bright, imaginative, resourceful young

[12] Most of the text in this section has been adapted, with permission, from a review I wrote (Morgan, 1991) for *IEEE Spectrum* of Harvey M. Sapolsky's book *Science and the Navy: The History of the Office of Naval Research* (Sapolsky, 1990).

naval officers, most of them PhD's in science, who acted ... as his cocky troubleshooting ambassadors to the naval operating arms" (Kevles, 1978). Near the end of the war, they developed a series of proposals for Navy support for basic civilian research, which they tried but failed to sell to the Secretary of the Navy.

With the creation of ORI, the bird dogs and their interest in civilian research were transferred to Admiral Bowen's jurisdiction. While Bowen had previously opposed civilian involvement in Navy research, he now worked hard to obtain new legislative authority for an Office of Naval Research (ONR) and, once he obtained it, to vigorously promote the bird dogs' ideas as vehicles to build an R&D program in atomic propulsion. Kevles (1978) explains:

> In the fall of 1945 Bowen and his staff traveled around the country with promises of research funds and promptly raised suspicions among academic scientists.[13] Would not military support involve irritating red tape, crippling security restrictions, and projects of primarily military, nonscientific interest? But Bowen's office minimized the red tape and allowed university scientists virtually complete freedom in the conduct and publication of their research. Equally important, Bowen's office funded not only militarily relevant but even purer research projects. It also left initiative for proposing projects up to the academics. The navy chose which projects to support with the help of a cadre of civilian scientific advisers ...
>
> In February 1946 Bowen's staff announced that they had negotiated contracts with forty-five schools and industrial firms; by August 1946, when the bill establishing ONR was signed into law, Bowen already had in force 177 contracts totaling $24,000,000 with eighty-one Universities or private and industrial laboratories.

Unfortunately for Bowen, at a crucial moment in the struggle to gain responsibility for atomic propulsion, Forrestal became preoccupied with other matters, and in a classic bureaucratic battle, Bowen lost atomic propulsion to the Bureau of Ships, where Captain Hyman G. Rickover took over the new program.

Having failed in his objective, Bowen went on terminal leave, leaving in place a strong ONR with a vigorous staff free to pursue their dream of supporting basic civilian research. Basic physical science research was supported through the "Science Branch," which presided over programs in physics, nuclear physics, mechanics and materials, electronics and communications, mathematics, and fluid mechanics. There was also a "Medical Science Branch," which supported research in physiology, biochemistry, bacteriology, psychology, psychophysiology, biophysics, and in enviro-physiology. A "Program Branch" supported work more directly relevant to the Navy's needs, but even then the research done in areas such as geophysics was in some cases rather fundamental in nature. A number of regional offices were opened around the

[13] Amazing as it may seem from the perspective of today's world, these delegations not only had to persuade reluctant investigators that accepting Navy money (as grants) for basic research would not jeopardize academic independence, but also had to persuade university administrators to accept full-cost recovery that included overheads.

country. The wartime OSRD London liaison group was converted into ONR-London, which continues to this day.

With the creation of the NSF bogged down in wrangling between the president, the Congress, and the senior leaders of the science establishment, ONR moved in and filled the gap.

This history provides a classic illustration of Kingdon's model of a policy window (see Section 16.1).

When NSF finally was created in 1950, Alan T. Waterman, who had previously served as deputy chief of ONR, moved over to become NSF's first director. Many of the contracting strategies first pioneered at ONR were adopted by the new NSF.

18.4 CIVILIAN CONTROL OF ATOMIC ENERGY AND WEAPONS

Unlike radar research, which remained under civilian control through OSRD and the Rad Lab at MIT throughout the war, the Manhattan Project, the U.S. program to develop atomic bombs, was managed by the military under the overall direction of General Leslie Groves. As the war came to an end, debate grew over how atomic weapons and energy should be governed. While there were some who briefly hoped that it might be possible to place weapons under some form of international control, Soviet moves to take over Eastern Europe, and the onset of the Cold War, rather quickly ended those hopes.

In May 1945, Secretary of War Henry Simpson created a secret high-level "Interim Committee" to advise on matters related to atomic weapons and energy. Two months later, OSRD's Conant submitted a legislative proposal to the Interim Committee to create a nine-member commission consisting of five civilian and four military members to oversee and manage all future atomic activities. This proposal became the basis of the "May–Johnson bill" that was submitted to Congress with support by President Truman, General Groves, as well as Bush and Conant.

Because this bill would have retained a substantial degree of military control over all things atomic and nuclear, many scientists and others mounted vigorous opposition,[14] President Truman quietly dropped his support, and the bill died. As the Department of Energy's (DOE) "History of the Manhattan Project" reports:

> Civilian versus military control had become the core issue in the legislative battle over atomic energy. On December 20, Brien McMahon, freshman Democratic senator from Connecticut who two months earlier had successfully created and became chair of the Senate's Special Committee on Atomic Energy, introduced a substitute to the May-Johnson bill. His bill, which called for five civilian commissioners and gave the

[14] The Federation of American Scientists grew out of opposition to military control of atomic issues, and specifically opposition to the May–Johnson bill by roughly 3000 scientists from various facilities associated with the Manhattan Project (Greenberg, 1967).

commission strict control over the production of fissionable material and the fabrication and stockpiling of weapons, essentially excluded the military. Hearings on the new McMahon bill began in late January 1946. Groves and Secretary of War Robert P. Patterson opposed McMahon's bill, citing weak security provisions and the low military presence. Groves also disliked the stipulation that commission members be full time (he thought that more eminent commissioners could be obtained if work was part-time), and he objected to the bill's provision that atomic weapons be held in civilian rather than military custody. These arguments were not without effect. Although few in Congress advocated military control, most did not want the military totally excluded from atomic energy matters. As a result, the McMahon bill, over the next several months, underwent considerable revision. The Senate approved the bill on June 1, and the House approved it on July 20, with a subsequent conference committee eliminating most substantive amendments added by the House. President Truman signed the McMahon Act, known officially as the Atomic Energy Act of 1946, on August 1.[15]

The Atomic Energy Act of 1946 resolved the controversies, decreeing that both the development of nuclear weapons and the development and regulation of nuclear power would be under civilian, rather than military, control. The former is now the responsibility of DOE. Reactor development is also overseen by DOE. Today the regulation of nuclear power falls under the jurisdiction of the Nuclear Regulatory Commission (NRC).[16]

18.5 IGY, SPUTNIK, THE SPACE RACE, AND THE (PHANTOM) MISSILE GAP

After years of Cold War isolation, scientific cooperation between the Soviet Union and the West began to expand in the years after Stalin's death in 1953. This culminated in 1957 in the establishment of the International Geophysical Year, or IGY, which was devoted to cooperative study by many countries, including both the United States and the Soviet Union, of 11 areas of earth science: aurora; air glow; cosmic rays; geomagnetism; gravity; ionospheric physics;[17] precision mapping of longitude and of latitude; meteorology; oceanography; seismology; and solar activities.

The IGY produced a wide range of valuable geophysical data and understanding. It also produced a major geopolitical shock. After a week-long

[15] From www.osti.gov/manhattan-project-history/Events/1945-present/civilian_control.htm.

[16] Originally reactor development and the promotion of nuclear power, as well as its regulatory oversight, were all managed by a single agency, the Atomic Energy Commission (AEC). Placing promotion, development, and regulation under one agency came to be understood as entailing a conflict of interest. Responsibility for development now lies with DOE. Regulatory responsibility lies with NRC, which was created in 1974.

[17] My father, Prof. Millett G. Morgan of Dartmouth College, chaired the U.S. Ionospheric Committee during the IGY. I was a high school junior at the time, and every night during the winter of 1957, on cross-country skis, I climbed to the top of our hill outside Hanover, New Hampshire, to change the 16 mm film in an aurora "all sky camera" and change the paper in a chart recorder for a magnetometer.

meeting on rocket and satellite research for the IGY held at the U.S. National Academy of Sciences in Washington, participants had gathered on the evening of October 4, 1957, for a reception at the Embassy of the Soviet Union. While there had been hints during the meetings, the assembled party learned at the reception that the Soviets had secretly developed and launched the first Earth-orbiting satellite. NASA chief historian Roger Launius writes:

> The party had gathered in the second floor ballroom at the embassy [of the Soviet Union] when a little before 6:00 p.m. Walter Sullivan, a reporter with the *New York Times* who was also attending the reception, received a frantic telephone call from his Washington bureau chief. Sullivan learned that the Soviet news agency Tass had just announced the launch of *Sputnik 1*, the world's first Earth-orbiting artificial satellite ... The news was quickly passed to Lloyd Berkner, the official American delegate to CSAGI.[18]
>
> When told the news, Berkner acted with the characteristic charm of his polished southern gentleman demeanor. Clapping his hands for attention, he asked for silence. "I wish to make an announcement," he declared. "I've just been informed by the *New York Times* that a Russian satellite is in orbit at an elevation of 900 kilometers. I wish to congratulate our Soviet colleagues on their achievement."[19]

The very public U.S. satellite program, Project Vanguard, was behind schedule and over budget. Its unsuccessful attempt to launch a small satellite two months later on December 6 failed on the launch pad. The United States did not successfully launch a small satellite (on an Army rocket) until January 31, 1958.

Given that launching an Earth-orbiting satellite was an IGY objective, Berkner's cordial congratulations were certainly in order, but the fact that the project had been pursued in secret was a source of considerable concern. Of even greater concern in national security circles was the fact that the Soviets had launched into orbit an 83.6-kg payload and a 7.5-tonne launch vehicle. Concern became even greater when on November 3, 1957, a yet larger and heavier Sputnik II was launched, carrying a live dog. The ability to launch such large masses carried clear implications for the development of strategic missiles, tipped with atomic warheads.

NASA historian Launius notes that "The launch of *Sputnik 1* had a 'Pearl Harbor' effect on American public opinion."[20] In the area of national security, concerns after Sputnik gave rise to expanded budgets and a wide range of other developments, including the creation of the Advanced Research Project Administration (ARPA), which in the years that followed played a key role in supporting the development of computers and computer science.

NSF historian George Mazuzan (1994) notes that:

[18] Comité Speciale de l'Année Geophysique Internationale.

[19] From http://history.nasa.gov/sputnik/sputorig.html.

[20] The "Pearl Harbor" reference was introduced by Edward Teller appearing on Edward R. Murrow's television show. President Eisenhower, struggling to control the public hysteria, "upbraided [AEC Chairman] Lewis Strauss for his protégé's loose talk" (Hiltzik, 2015).

Sputnik raised questions about the ability of the nation's education system to compete. Congress responded with the National Defense Education Act of 1958. It emphasized science education and became a significant part of the country's science policy. The act provided a student loan program, aid to elementary and secondary school instruction in science, mathematics and foreign languages, and graduate student fellowships. While it was directed mostly at students rather than institutions, and was administered out of the United States Office of Education, the law had an important impact on federal support of science education. Both its fellowships and its institutional benefits followed geographic distribution patterns rather than the competitive elitist format typical of Foundation programs. Of even greater significance, however, the act opened the way for future legislation that redefined many of the relationships between the federal government and the education community.

Fallout from Sputnik also played a role in John F. Kennedy's 1958 Senate campaign and his subsequent 1960 run for the presidency in which he charged that the Eisenhower Administration had allowed a "missile gap" to develop that placed the United States in grave danger. Whether he knew at the time that this was not the case, or only learned later, has been a subject of considerable controversy.

REFERENCES

Alvarez, L.W. (1980). "A Biographical Memoir of Alfred Lee Loomis (1887–1975)," *U.S. National Academy of Science Biographical Memories*, *51*, pp. 309–342. Available at: www.nasonline.org/publications/biographical-memoirs/memoir-pdfs/loomis-alfred.pdf.

Blanpied, W.A. (2010). *A History of Federal Science Policy: From the New Deal to the Present*, Rice University Press, 259pp.

Branscomb, L.M. (1997). "From Technology Politics to Technology Policy," *Issues in Science and Technology*, *13*(3), pp. 41–48.

Buderi, R. (1996). *The Invention That Changed the World: How a Small Group of Radar Pioneers Won the Second World War and Launched a Technical Revolution*, Simon & Schuster, 575pp.

Bush, V. (1945). *Science the Endless Frontier*, U.S. Government Printing Office, 183pp.
(1970). *Pieces of the Action*, William Morrow Co., 366pp.

Conant, J. (2002). *Tuxedo Park: A Wall Street Tycoon and the Secret Palace of Science That Changed the Course of World War II*, Simon & Schuster, 330pp.

Constant, E.W. (1980). *The Origins of the Turbojet Revolution*, Johns Hopkins University Press, 311pp.

Gallagher, K.S., A. Grübler, L. Kuhl, G. Nemet, and C. Wilson (2012). "The Energy Technology Innovation System," *Annual Review of Environment and Resources*, *37*, pp. 137–162.

Gertner, J. (2012). *The Idea Factory: Bell Labs and the Great Age of American Innovation*, Penguin Press, 422pp.

Godin, B. (2006). "The Linear Model of Innovation the Historical Construction of an Analytical Framework," *Science, Technology & Human Values*, *31*(6), pp. 639–667.

Greenberg, D.S. (1967). *The Politics of Pure Science*, Plume/Signet, 325pp.
(1991). "'Soft' Science Grows up," *Washington Post*, November 13.
Hart, D.H. (1998). *Forged Consensus: Science, Technology and Economic Policy in the United States, 1921–1953*, Princeton University Press, 267pp.
Hiltzik, M. (2015). *Big Science: Ernest Lawrence and the Invention That Launched the Military-Industrial Complex*, Simon & Schuster, 512pp.
Kevles, D.J. (1978). *The Physicists: The History of a Scientific Community in Modern America*, Alfred A. Knopf, 489pp.
Mazuzan, G.T. (1994). *NSF 88-16: A Brief History*. Available at: www.nsf.gov/about/history/nsf50/nsf8816.jsp.
Morgan, M.G. (1991). "Review of *Science and the Navy: A History of the Office of Naval Research* by H.M. Sapolsky," *IEEE Spectrum*, *28*(2), p. 11.
(1998). "An EE Who Swayed the World," review of G.P. Zachary, *Vannevar Bush Engineer of the American Century*, *IEEE Spectrum*, *35*(3), pp. 10–12.
Morgan, M.G. and M.G. Morgan (1998). "Bigger than 'the Bomb,'" review of Robert Buderi (1996), The Invention that Changed the World, *IEEE Spectrum*, *35*(8), pp. 8–9.
Phelps, P. (2010). *The Tizard Mission: The Top-Secret Operation That Changed the Course of World War II*, Westholme Publishing, 325pp.
Rhodes, R. (1986). *The Making of the Atomic Bomb*, Simon & Schuster, 886pp.
Sapolsky, H.M. (1990). *Science and the Navy: A History of the Office of Naval Research*, Princeton University Press, 142pp.
Sherwood, R.E. (1948). *Roosevelt and Hopkins: An Intimate History*, Harper, 979pp.
Smith, B.L.R. (1990). *American Science Policy since World War II*, The Brookings Institution, 230pp.
Stokes, D.E. (1997). *Pasteur's Quadrant: Basic Science and Technological Innovation*, Brookings, 280pp.
Thorpe, C. (2006). *Oppenheimer: The Tragic Intellect*, University of Chicago Press, 413pp.
Zachary, G.P. (1997). *Endless Frontier: Vannevar Bush, Engineer of the American Century*, The Free Press, 518pp.
Zimmerman, D. (1996). *Top Secret Exchange: The Tizard Mission and the Scientific War*, McGill-Queen's University Press, 252pp.

19

Science and Technology Advice to Government

Unlike many parliamentary systems, the federal government of the United States is organized as three separate branches. The Executive Branch operates under the direction of the President and consists of a number of "executive branch agencies." Some of these are "cabinet-level" agencies such as the Department of State, the Department of Defense, the Department of Energy, and the Department of Commerce. Others are independent regulatory bodies such as the Federal Communications Commission. The Environmental Protection Agency is not a cabinet-level agency, although the Administrator is normally given cabinet rank.

The Legislative Branch consists of the U.S. Senate and the U.S. House of Representatives. While much more limited in number and scope than Executive Branch agencies, the Legislative Branch also has a number of supporting organizations including the Library of Congress, the Government Accountability Office, the Congressional Budget Office, and the Congressional Research Service.

The Federal Judiciary is organized hieratically with 94 district courts, a number of other specialty courts, 11 courts of appeal, and the Supreme Court. Like the Legislative Branch, the Judiciary has a small number of supporting organizations including the Judicial Conference of the United States, the Federal Judicial Center, and a few others.

19.1 SCIENCE AND TECHNOLOGY ADVICE TO THE PRESIDENT

Does the president of the United States need a science advisor and a supporting staff based in the White House? To those of us who work in science, technology, and public policy, the answer to this question is an obvious and emphatic yes. However, before we turn to a brief review of presidential science advice, it is worth considering the words of Bruce Smith (1992), who argues:

Presidents and their immediate advisors have rarely felt quite the same need for science advisors as most heads of agencies, especially the technical agencies. [A reason for this is that] ... presidents deal with issues of value and value conflicts. The science they need to know can be explained by an intelligent and informed lay advisor in the context of the broad policy issue under review. [And,] ... the policy game is different at the presidential level. Senior agency officials view advisory committees as helping to persuade the next decision making echelon of the soundness of their plans ... The president has no need for this function. The buck stops with him.

Before providing a detailed assessment of past White House science advice, Smith also raises provocative questions about the need for a standing committee of outside experts in science and technology, raising the possibility that ad hoc panels might serve presidential needs as well or better. However, most modern presidents have tended to prefer to have a core group of experts who can bring a consistent perspective to bear on a wide range of topics, while recruiting others with specific expertise for special studies or reviews as the need arises.

As we saw in Section 18.1, during World War II Vannevar Bush effectively served as President Roosevelt's science advisor, able to secure access to the Oval Office when needed, and to draw upon a cadre of the nation's science and technology elite. OSRD was disassembled at the end of the war, and for a while there was no formal system in place to provide science and technology advice to President Truman.

In 1950 William T. Golden, a New York investment banker and aid to AEC Chairman Lewis Strauss, was charged by President Truman to study the overall effectiveness of the military's technical programs. Golden became concerned that there was a need for an effective science advisory apparatus at the White House level. In his report to the president, he recommended the creation of both a full-time science advisor post and a part-time advisory committee. (Smith, 1992)

Reflecting on this work, Golden observed:

The world was, or seemed to be, a simpler place in mid-1950, when, after the outbreak of the Korean War, President Truman, with strong encouragement from Congressional leaders, asked me to serve as a special consultant to advise him on the organization and utilization of the government's research activities. Emphasis was to be on the military aspects. The study involved discussion with some 150 scientists, government officials, academic leaders, and industrialists. My recommendation, dated December 18, 1950, "For the appointment of an outstanding scientific leader as Scientific Advisor to the President" was promptly approved by President Truman. (Golden, 1988)

The initial result was a committee specifically focused on defense-related research. It took a few years before Golden's arrangement was fully implemented under President Eisenhower in October 1957 with the appointment of James R. Killian, Jr.[1] as Presidential Science Advisor and the creation of the

[1] Killian served as the tenth president of MIT from 1948 to 1959. His highest earned degree was an S.B. in management from MIT. As the *New York Times* noted on the occasion of his death,

BOX 19.1 WILLIAM T. GOLDEN (1909–2007)

An investment banker and not a scientist, Bill Golden nevertheless played a key role in the development of twentieth-century U.S. science and technology policy. During World War II, Golden served in the U.S. Navy's Bureau of Ordnance. After the war he worked with Lewis Strauss, chair of the new Atomic Energy Commission. At the request of President Truman, he conducted a study that led to the creation of the first institution to provide science advice to the president. He served in many other advisory capacities related to science and technology. He served as the Treasurer of the American Association for the Advancement of Science (AAAS) from 1969 to 1999. In 1979, Golden earned a Masters degree in biology from Columbia University. In recognition of his many contributions to science and technology, he received five honorary doctorates. In his later years, Golden wrote and edited a number of books on science and technology, including:

- William T. Golden (ed.), *Science and Technology Advice to President, Congress, and Judiciary*, Transaction Publishers, 523pp., 1988.
- William T. Golden (ed.), *Science Advice to the President*, Pergamon Press, 256pp., 1980.

For details, see: http://en.wikipedia.org/wiki/William_T._Golden and www.aaas.org/page/william-t-golden.

William T. Golden. Image courtesy of NSF.

he was "a science administrator, not a scientist." See: www.nytimes.com/1988/01/31/obituaries/james-killian-83-science-adviser-dies.html.

Presidential Science Advisory Committee (PSAC). Smith (1992) writes, "the period from the creation of the science advisor post in the Eisenhower administration until President Kennedy's assassination [in] November 1963 is the period that most observers have deemed the golden age of presidential science advising."[2]

I must admit to becoming somewhat depressed when I read the historical accounts of the issues that presidential science advisors and the members of PSAC were dealing with over those years. While a handful of important non-defense issues were addressed (such as the work that led to implementation of on-board transponders on aircraft in the U.S. air traffic control system), this period was the depth of the Cold War, and most of the high-level technical attention was going to nuclear weapons, ICBMs, and other defense-related issues.

The Kennedy years, and even more the Johnson years, began to illuminate the tensions that can arise if a president's advisors are not closely aligned with administration policy or if the president does not have a strong interest in receiving science advice. Things grew worse as the Vietnam War was escalated during the later Johnson years. Smith (1992) reports "a small but telling sign of LBJ's attitude toward PSAC was his decision in 1968 to ban committee members from eating in the White House mess." Things went from bad to worse in the Nixon years. There were strong disagreements within the scientific community about proposals to build an anti-ballistic missile (ABM) defense system, and about a program to build a supersonic transport (SST). These and other disagreements resulted in a continued marginalization of the science advisor and PSAC. The final breaking point arrived when Richard Garwin (then an IBM Fellow at the Thomas J. Watson Research Center and a member of PSAC) agreed to testify to the Congress on the SST. While Garwin took care to focus on technical issues and not draw on materials from PSAC deliberations, the White House saw this as a direct attack by one of its own on a policy the Administration strongly endorsed: "One White House staffer declared, 'Who the hell do these science bastards think they are?' Another said, 'Who needs this bunch of vipers in our nest?' " (Smith, 1992). The result was that President Nixon abolished the office of science advisor as a position in the White House in 1973, disbanded PSAC, and appointed H. Guyford Stever, then Director of the National Science Foundation, to serve as presidential science advisor. A support office was created as part of NSF. Insulated from the growing Watergate scandal, this office was able to make useful contributions to the development of U.S. national energy policy.[3]

[2] For a full list of science advisors since 1939, see: http://en.wikipedia.org/wiki/Office_of_Science_and_Technology_Policy.

[3] I was a program officer in the Office of Computing Affairs at NSF at that time. In parallel with my responsibilities to build a research program on the social impacts of computing, I was drawn into many of the ongoing energy-related activities at the NSF, and on the side found time to edit a book of collected papers on energy (Morgan, 1975). My office looked right out at the Old

The arrangement with NSF continued until the latter years of the Ford Administration when, in 1976, an Act of Congress established the position of presidential science advisor and created the Office of Science and Technology Policy.[4] At that time Congress did not recreate PSAC. During the Reagan Administration, science advisor Jay Keyworth established a White House Science Council that reported directly to him. The current President's Council of Advisors on Science and Technology (PCAST) was established in 1989 near the beginning of the first Bush Administration.

The continued tension between a president's policy agenda and the advice of experts in science and technology is well illustrated by the decision by President Reagan to pursue the development of a major ABM system (dubbed the "Star Wars" program – see Section 16.2).

READINGS 19.1

Detlev W. Bronk, "Science Advice in the White House," *Science, 186*, pp. 116–121, October 11, 1974.

Bruce L.R. Smith, "Chapter 8: Science Advisers at the Presidential Level," pp. 155–188 in *The Advisers: Scientists in the Policy Process*, Brookings, 238pp., 1992.

DISCUSSION QUESTIONS FOR READINGS 19.1

- Why, according to Bronk, did members of the National Science Board initially oppose Golden's proposal to establish a science advisor to the president?
- What was the nature of the argument Bronk made to President Eisenhower that he should not cancel the satellite program that was part of U.S. participation in IGY?
- Smith argues: "The kind of advice the president most needs concerns the complex interplay of issue substance with politics and the relation of any set of policies to the larger goals of the administration. The best equipped to advise the president on such issues are political generalists who can integrate enough knowledge of policy substance with the intricacies of political timing, nuance, and aspiration." Do you agree with this argument? Why, or why not?
- Describe the events that Smith outlines in the section he titles "The Fall and Rise of the Presidential Science Advisory System."
- In your view, were Richard Garwin's actions with respect to congressional testimony on the SST appropriate? If yes, why? If no, how should he have proceeded differently?

Executive Office Building where senior Nixon Administration staff were burning the midnight oil increasingly consumed by the Watergate scandal.

[4] For current details, see: www.whitehouse.gov/administration/eop/ostp.

19.2 THE ADMINISTRATIVE PROCEDURE ACT

As we saw in Section 17.5, it was only with the greatest reluctance that after fifty years of ever more serious and catastrophic boiler explosions, the U.S. Congress became persuaded of the necessity of abandoning traditional tort-based approaches to managing the challenges of an increasingly complex and technological society. During the final decades of the nineteenth century and first decades of the twentieth century, it became increasingly clear that the Legislative Branch needed to delegate authority to various regulatory agencies if it was to address the challenges of a modern economy and an ever more complex technological society. Shepherd (1996) writes: "Before 1900, approximately one-third of present federal agencies already existed. For example, the Interstate Commerce Commission gained life in 1887. In the first three decades of the twentieth century, during which conservatives dominated national politics, the number of agencies doubled." Legislative efforts to limit the power of such agencies began before the Great Depression but were dramatically intensified by opposition to the Roosevelt Administration's New Deal programs. Republicans, Southern Democrats, business interests, and the American Bar Association (ABA) led the fight to block New Deal programs. In his 126-page historical retelling and analysis of the more than two decades of political fighting that finally culminated in the passage of the Administrative Procedure Act (APA), Shepherd (1996) explains that, as New Deal programs grew:

> Owners of large businesses, together with the big-firm lawyers who represented the businesses and whose livelihoods depended on the businesses' success, fought the new federal and state economic controls bitterly ... Businesses argued that biased agency officials exercised a lawless discretion against business interests, and ravaged businesses' freedom and profits ... The NLRB [National Labor Relations Board] and SEC [Securities and Exchange Commission] caused special irritation: businesses asserted that the NLRB favored unions and that securities regulation unfairly punished businesses and limited their ability to raise capital.

After repeated attempts in the Congress to implement strict limits on New Deal agencies, in 1939 Roosevelt "moved to deflect the new momentum for strict control of agencies that the introduction of the APA bill had sparked. On February 16, approximately one month after the APA bill's introduction in the Senate, Roosevelt asked his attorney general to form a committee to study administrative reform and propose legislation" (Shepherd, 1996). After a variety of further efforts by Republicans, Southern Democrats, business interests, and the ABA, in December 1940, Congress passed the Walter-Logan bill, which Roosevelt immediately vetoed. By a narrow margin the House failed to override the veto. Four weeks later, the Attorney General's report was released, which offered possible liberal and conservative bills. However, as the United States began to make serious preparations for, and then entered, World War II, Congress's attention moved elsewhere.

Once the war ended, and a slightly more receptive President Truman came to the presidency, serious efforts began to develop a compromise bill. By this time, conservatives and the ABA had concluded that some bill was better than no bill. Nevertheless, negotiations dragged on for many months. Shepherd (1996) explains that as it began to look like the bill would finally pass:

> each party to the negotiations over the bill attempted to create legislative history – to create a record that would cause future reviewing courts to interpret the new statute in a manner that would favor the party. The parties to the negotiations recognized that little official legislative history would accompany the bill. The bill had sprung not from public debate in Congress, as other bills had, but from months of private, off-the-record negotiations. Each party sought to create a favorable account of the negotiations ...
>
> The parties attempted to manufacture legislative history because the bill was ambiguous. The ambiguity was intentional. Months before the bill reached a vote in either house, each interest group had issued its interpretation of the bill's provisions. Although the interpretations differed markedly, the groups chose not to revise the bill to resolve the disagreements...
>
> Ambiguity was essential to reaching agreement. Without it, no agreement could have occurred.

The Administrative Procedure Act (PL 79–404) finally passed on June 11, 1946. In summarizing this saga of more than 20 years, Shepherd (1996) writes:

> The landmark Administrative Procedure Act of 1946 and its history are central to the United States' economic and political development. The APA was the bill of rights for the new regulatory state. In a new era of expanded government, it defined the relationship between government and governed. The APA's impact has been profound and durable and represents the country's decision to permit extensive government, but to avoid dictatorship and central planning. The APA permitted the continued growth of the regulatory state that exists today.

Shortly after the passage of the Federal Administrative Procedure Act, the Uniform Law Commission developed an analogous model law for U.S. states (which it has subsequently revised).[5] Today many U.S. states have adopted versions of this law.

Regulatory agencies engage in two types of decision making: the quasi-legislative function of rule making and the quasi-judicial function of adjudication. In both cases, the APA spells out how agencies are to proceed. Rule making can be conducted either as "informal rule making" or "formal rule making." Most of the regulatory activity conducted by agencies such as EPA, FAA, FCC, FERC, and many others is conducted as informal rule making.

After it has developed a draft regulation under informal rule making, the APA requires that an agency provide public notice (by publishing the draft in the Federal Register; see www.federalregister.gov). Time must then

[5] For details on the non-partisan Uniform Law Commission, see: www.uniformlawcommission.com.

be allowed for public comment. Sometimes members of the public (including individuals, companies, NGOs, etc.) simply submit their comments in writing to the relevant agency. Often, especially for major or controversial proposed rules, hearings will be held at which members of the public can appear and offer their views. It is not at all unusual for a proposed rule to accumulate many hundreds or even thousands of comments. In finalizing the rule, the APA requires that the agency consider the record of submitted comments. Failure to do so can be legal grounds for courts to subsequently overturn the rule.

Once an agency has finalized a rule, it is published in the Federal Register. At this point, the APA provides provisions for Judicial review. If any party affected by the rule believes that it is not justified, they can take the agency to court. Courts are typically prepared to consider procedural matters – does the rule fall within the scope of the enabling legislation that granted the agency authority to act? Did the agency collect the evidence it should have, and give due consideration to all relevant facts? Courts have typically been reluctant to get into the substantive details – that is, to second-guess the agency on how it interpreted the facts and performed its analysis.

While less widely used, as the name implies, formal rule making operates almost like a court trial, with an administrative law judge hearing testimony from relevant parties. Similarly, adjudication (as, for example, in a decision by the NRC to grant an operating license to a specific nuclear plant) adopts a more formal procedure. Here, too, there must be prior notification, but then the procedure involves formal cross-examination before an Administrative Law Judge with parties represented by lawyers. As with informal rule making, the final decision under formal rule making and under adjudication must be clearly based on substantial evidence in the record.

Three more recent laws are also relevant to the operation of federal agencies that need science and technology expertise and advice. These are:

- The Freedom of Information Act (FOIA), PL 89–487, passed in 1966.
- The Federal Advisory Committee Act (FACA), PL 92–463, passed in 1972.
- The Government in the Sunshine Act PL 94–409, passed in 1976.

READING 19.2

The Administrative Procedure Act; The Freedom of Information Act; The Federal Advisory Committee Act; The Government in the Sunshine Act.

DISCUSSION QUESTIONS FOR READING 19.2

- These four Acts are full of legal "boiler plate" that can make them a bit hard to read. What do you see as the two or three key elements of each?

- Describe the steps that the Administrative Procedure Act requires an agency to go through when it wants to develop and promulgate a new regulation.
- If an agency wants to create an advisory committee, and the OMB gives it approval to do so, what steps must it go through to create the committee and to hold a meeting?
- What types of information are *not* accessible for a request made to an agency under the Freedom of Information Act?

19.3 EXAMPLES OF SCIENCE AND TECHNOLOGY ADVICE TO EXECUTIVE BRANCH AGENCIES

Most agencies of the U.S. Government need technical advice and assistance. Indeed, this advisory apparatus has become so important in the United States that Sheila Jasanoff has termed it the "fifth branch."[6] Two books that between them do a good job of describing and assessing these science advisory systems are:

- Bruce L.R. Smith, *The Advisers: Scientists in the Policy Process*, Brookings, 238pp., 1992.
- Sheila Jasanoff, *The Fifth Branch: Science Advisers as Policy Makers*, Harvard University Press, 302pp., 1990.

Probably the two most accomplished and successful science advisory boards are the Defense Science Board (DSB), created in 1956 to provide high-level technical advice to the Secretary of Defense and other senior leadership across the Department of Defense,[7] and the EPA Science Advisory Board (SAB), created in 1978.

The charter of the DSB specifies that:

> The Board is not established to advise on individual DoD procurements, but instead shall be concerned with the pressing and complex technology problems facing the Department of Defense in such areas as research, engineering, and manufacturing, and will ensure the identification of new technologies and new applications of technology in those areas to strengthen national security. (DSB, 2012)

The DSB performs studies by organizing panels made up of DSB members as well as other outside experts. Smith (1992) notes that "The scope and parameters of a study are often the focus of considerable maneuvering and jockeying for position. The military services as well as the defense R&D bureaucracy

[6] The first three branches of the U.S. federal government are, of course, the executive, legislative, and judicial. The press (and sometimes various interest and other groups) are sometimes referred to as the fourth branch or the fourth estate.

[7] There are a number of other advisory boards across DoD serving the needs of each of the uniformed services as well as providing advice on other specific issues.

seek to define the parameters in a way that limits the scope of possible outcomes." Smith (1992) has provided a concise history of the DSB that outlines how its role has evolved. As with other advisory boards, the DSB has worked best when it has enjoyed strong support from the Secretary of Defense and the Director of Defense Research and Engineering (DDRE). Smith characterizes the DSB as "one of the federal government's most hardworking and prestigious technical advisory boards."

In 1958, just two years after the establishment of the DSB, a second, rather different advisory system called the Jasons was established under the auspices of the Institute for Defense Analysis.[8] The Jasons grew out of Project 137, a 1958 summer study commissioned by ARPA and conducted under the auspices of the Institute for Defense Analysis.[9] The original idea had been to lay the foundations for a separate small, elite laboratory to address advanced concepts in defense. However, that idea was abandoned and in its place a program of summer studies that performed in-depth analysis of specific defense-related problems was created (Finkbeiner, 2006). Most of the original members of the Jasons were outstanding mid-career physicists. Over the years, the membership of the group has aged. Political discord in the United States during the Vietnam War led to tensions among the Jasons over studies of topics such as the electronic barrier designed to limit the movement of Việt Cộng troops from the north to the south.[10] While defense and security remain a central focus, in more recent years Jason studies have addressed a number of non-defense issues including climate change and risks to the power system posed by solar mass ejection. DARPA support for the Jasons ended in 2002.[11] Primary support now comes from the Office of the Assistant Secretary of Defense for Research and Engineering. For additional discussion of the Jasons, see Finkbeiner (2006).

As with the DoD, various scientific boards provide different types of advice across the U.S. Environmental Protection Agency (EPA). Analogous to the DSB, the most important of these is the EPA Science Advisory Board, or SAB. The SAB was created in 1978 by Public Law 42 U.S. Code § 4365 that stipulates:

> The Administrator of the Environmental Protection Agency shall establish a Science Advisory Board which shall provide such scientific advice as may be requested by the Administrator, the Committee on Environment and Public Works of the United States Senate, or the Committee on Science, Space, and Technology, on Energy and Commerce, or on Public Works and Transportation of the House of Representatives.

[8] Today the Jasons are managed by the Mitre Corporation.

[9] The Project 137 report, "Identification of Certain Current Defense Problems and Possible Means of Solution," has now been declassified and can be found at: www.dtic.mil/dtic/tr/fulltext/u2/323409.pdf. The name 137 refers to the value of the reciprocal of the fine structure constant.

[10] See: https://en.wikipedia.org/wiki/McNamara_Line.

[11] The change came because DARPA wanted to appoint three new members. However, the Jasons had always selected and appointed their own members and were not willing to allow DARPA to choose members (Finkbeiner, 2002).

In practice, with the exception of occasional testimony to the House Science Committee by the SAB chair on the EPA's budget, interactions by the SAB with the Congress have been quite limited. However, on some occasions, when the House Science Committee has not been particularly supportive of the EPA mission, this provision of dual reporting has become a source of contention.

The primary mission of the EPA SAB is to:[12]

- review the quality and relevance of the scientific and technical information being used by the EPA or proposed as the basis for Agency regulations;
- review EPA research programs and plans;
- provide science advice as requested by the EPA Administrator; and
- advise the agency on broad scientific matters.

The nature and function of the SAB has evolved over time. According to Jasanoff (1990), "After the political debacles of the early 1980s, the reinstatement of a credible scientific advisory system became a high priority for the agency and such gestures as opening up the appointment process publicly reaffirmed the agency's commitment to securing advice in a politically untainted manner." When the Republicans took control of the House of Representatives in 2010, the new leadership of the House Science Committee adopted a very critical perspective on the SAB and on the role of science at the EPA. That committee also adopted a very critical perspective on the peer review of research at the NSF, especially in relation to social science.[13] This sort of activity is not new, and has gone on from time to time whenever congressional leadership has adopted a more conservative political perspective and when members have wished to avoid scientific findings that are at odds with their political preferences.

As noted in Chapter 1, Arthur Kantrowitz (1975, 1995) proposed the idea of a science court that would assess the state of science and then pass on that assessment so that the policy process could make its judgments. In contrast, Jasanoff's assessment of the role of the SAB is that:

> The notion that science advisers can or do limit themselves to addressing purely scientific issues … seems fundamentally misconceived. Other common myths – for example, that scientists are always conservative in assessing risks or that advice is merely a pretext for delaying action – also seems exaggerated. Rather, the advisory process seems increasingly important as a locus for negotiating scientific differences that carry political weight. Scientific advice may not be a panacea for regulatory conflict or a fail-safe procedure for generating what technocrats would view as good science. It is, however,

[12] See: http://yosemite.epa.gov/sab/sabpeople.nsf/webcommittees/board.

[13] See, for example: http://science.house.gov/press-release/committee-republicans-introduce-bill-reform-epa's-scientific-advisory-process; www.insidehighered.com/news/2014/06/02/house-passes-nsf-funding-bill-takes-slap-social-sciences; http://news.sciencemag.org/policy/2014/10/battle-between-nsf-and-house-science-committee-escalates-how-did-it-get-badwww.slate.com/blogs/weigel/2014/06/04/house_appropriations_for_2015_include_specific_cuts_for_political_science.html.

part of a necessary process of political accommodation among science, society and the state and it serves as an invaluable function in a regulatory system that is otherwise singularly deficient in procedures for informal bargaining. (Jasanoff, 1990)

READINGS 19.3

Bruce L.R. Smith, "Chapter 3: The Effective Use of Science Advisors: The Defense Science Board," pp. 48–67, and "Chapter 4: Science, Law and Regulation: The EPA Science Advisory Board," pp. 68–100, in *The Advisers: Scientists in the Policy Process*, Brookings, 238pp., 1992.

While Smith's historical accounts are over 20 years old, they remain the most concise and straightforward descriptions of the development and operation of the DSB and SAB.

DISCUSSION QUESTIONS FOR READINGS 19.3

- In the case of both the DSB and the SAB it took some years to figure out an effective mode of operation. How did that process play out and what resolutions were reached?
- Describe the political flap that resulted when the Reagan Administration's transition team created the EPA SAB "hit list." In the end, why did it not have much of a long-term consequence for the agency?

Note: Both my colleague Lester Lave and I were on the "hit list." Indeed, I still include an entry in my resume under the section on "Awards and Recognition." Prof. Sol Michaelson of the University of Rochester, who had a reputation among some as being pro-industry, was also on the list with the citation "rumored to be pro-environmental." He told me that the citation did wonders for his reputation with his graduate students!

19.4 THE NRC AND THE NATIONAL ACADEMIES

As noted in Chapter 17, the NAS was created by an Act of Congress in 1863 during the Civil War. In order to better support analysis for the government, the National Research Council (NRC) was created in 1916. During World War I, NRC scientists received military commissions. This arrangement proved awkward, limiting the level at which scientific advice could be provided to the U.S. military, and has not been adopted since.

Today, the National Academies consist of three academies – the original NAS, the much newer National Academy of Engineering (NAE, created 1964) and the National Academy of Medicine (previously the Institute of Medicine or IOM, created 1970), as well as the NRC. The NAS, NAE, and NAM are

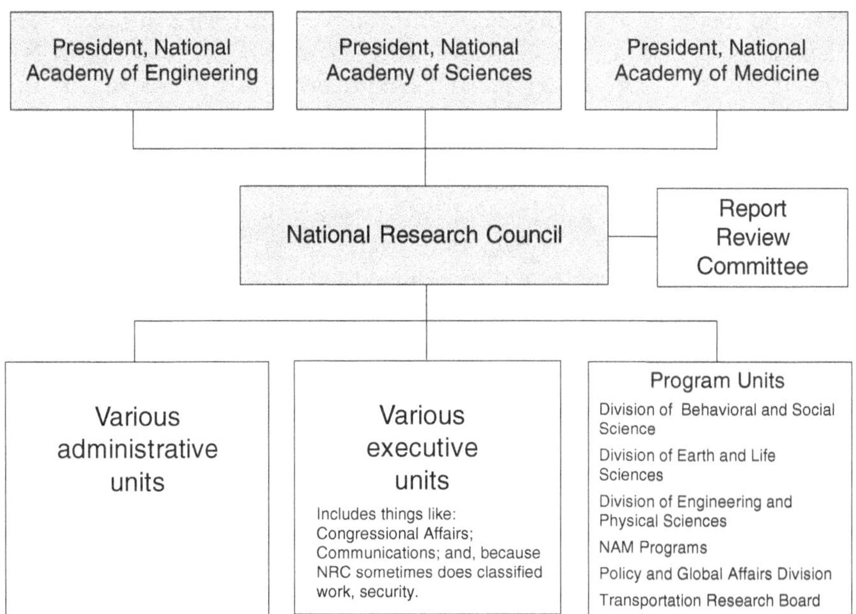

FIGURE 19.1. Structure of the National Research Council (NRC). Details, together with the names of current office holders, can be found at www.nationalacademies.org/directories.

honorific organizations, whose members are elected and are among the leading experts in their respective domains. The three academies do have small executive staffs, but when someone refers to a "National Academies Study" they are almost always referring to a study conducted by the NRC. The NRC is subdivided into various areas of specialization and conducts consensus studies and runs other activities such as roundtables, workshops, and similar functions for government and other clients.[14] Figure 19.1 shows the structure of the NRC.

One or two NRC Ph.D.-level staff and one or two clerical staff support a typical NRC consensus panel study. Staff will often be shared among several ongoing studies. The panel itself consists of a group of experts selected to cover the range of topics addressed in the study. While travel and other expenses are covered, members of study panels serve without compensation.

The NRC has always been scrupulous about issues such as balance in the make-up of its panels, and in addressing and dealing with issues such as conflict of interest. Of course, its panels sometimes reach conclusions that some parties do not like. In the late 1990s, two organizations (the Animal Legal Defense

[14] For general information and a list of ongoing projects being conducted by each NRC division, go to: www.nationalacademies.org/nrc.

Fund and the Natural Resources Defense Council) that were not happy with the findings of specific NRC panels filed suit in an effort to force all the NRC committees to operate under the full requirements of the Federal Advisory Committee Act (FACA). Opening up the deliberations of NRC consensus panels to full public scrutiny would have fundamentally undermined their ability to provide independent and balanced advice.[15] In the event, a compromise was struck, and, while NRC panels now must comply with some elements of FACA, after gathering evidence in presentations from experts in public sessions, panels continue to be able to perform their deliberations in private.[16]

Once an NRC study panel has been created, one of its first tasks is to be briefed on issues of conflict of interest. Then in a closed session, each member is expected to verbally outline their present activities and explain any that might constitute a conflict. Because experts who are most knowledgeable about a topic may have conflicts, NRC does not preclude them from participating in a study, but it is important to assure that a panel has balance, and that all members are aware of the perspectives and interests that their fellow panel members bring to a study.

Studies operate within a "statement of task" that has been approved by the commissioning organization (most typically one or more parts of the federal government) and by the NRC's Governing Board. A typical study will run for a year or two and hold a series of meetings. The first one or two meetings typically focus on gathering information and further framing the problem. Later meetings are then devoted to developing and writing the report. While the option exists for a panel member to file a dissenting view on some aspects of a study, considerable effort is made to make reports the unanimous product of the study panel. The amount of writing and editorial assistance provided by the staff is a strong function of the specific individuals involved. In most cases, panel members do most of the writing as well as the analysis.

Once a report has been completed in final draft form, it is submitted to the Report Review Committee (RRC). One or more members of that committee supervise the review process. They, along with RRC staff, select reviewers (numbers range from 10 to 20 or more), prepare a summary of the issues raised by reviewers that it is most important for the committee to address, and review and assess the adequacy of the committee's responses and revisions. These reviews can be quite time-consuming, but because they are so careful and exhaustive, they are what assures the quality of the overall NRC report process.

The NRC review process runs "closed loop" in the sense that, once a year, the full RRC and senior staff from across the Academy complex (including the

[15] For an opinion piece on this issue that I published in *IEEE Spectrum* at the time these efforts were being made to apply FACA to the NRC, see Morgan (1997).

[16] For details on the modification that was made to the Federal Advisory Committee Act, see: www.nationalacademies.org/nrc/na_053088.html.

presidents of the NAS, NAE, and NAM) meet for two days to revisit issues that have arisen during reviews that have been conducted during the past year, and identify procedural and other things that need to be changed or improved.

While the preparation of conventional NRC consensus reports is a slow and expensive process (often requiring more than a year and costing between half a million and a million dollars or more), NRC reports are the "gold standard" for this type of analysis, and the envy of many governments and analysts all around the world. However, because they are expensive and take time, there has been growing pressure on the NRC in recent years to develop other kinds of products. Often a panel will issue a letter report as an interim product. Sometimes it, or one of the standing parts of the NRC, will organize a workshop. In that case, a summary of the proceedings may be produced but no formal recommendations from the participants will be reported. Round tables are also increasingly popular. Members of a round table do not have to be approved through the NRC's conventional vetting methods, and can include agency staff. While they cannot produce shared recommendations or conclusions, agency people find them a useful way to quickly hear opinions from, and listen to interactions among, a wide range of individual experts and stakeholders. Finally, the NRC continues to explore strategies by which it might accelerate a fraction of its consensus panel reports. Two obstacles to doing this are: (1) the fact that unpaid expert volunteers who make up a panel have "day jobs" so there is a limit to how much time they can devote to a brief rapid study, and (2) on more challenging topics it typically takes two or three face-to-face meetings before the members of a multi-disciplinary panel have come to understand each other and begun to form shared ideas of how they should proceed.

In recent years, the NRC has developed procedures to make all of its reports available online. For details, visit www.nap.edu.

19.5 THINK TANKS AND CONSULTING FIRMS

A wide range of non-profit and for-profit organizations offer policy analytic services to both government and the private sector. Most of the for-profit firms such as the Analysis Group, the Brattle Group, CH2MHILL, ICF International, McKinsey, and many others, perform management consulting or execute specific analytical or management tasks under government contracts that are awarded on a competitive basis.

Some parts of government laboratories, including parts of several of the labs operated under contract for the U.S. Department of Energy (DOE), perform policy-focused analysis and research. In addition, a number of other organizations have been created as Federally Funded Research and Development Centers or FFRDCs. These entities operate under special legal arrangements that, on the one hand, make it much easier for government agencies to pass funds to them, but on the other hand place significant limits on where they can seek or compete for funds.

Outside of the DOE labs, among the best-known examples of FFRDCs that work on issues in science and technology policy are those run by IDA, MITRE, and RAND. Several of these organizations such as RAND (Project Air Force) began life strictly as FFRDCs but have now evolved other legal units that can perform other kinds of contract work for both government and private parties.

In the domain of science and technology policy, a number of private non-profit entities such as the Brookings Institution and Resources for the Future (RFF) also play important roles. Both Brookings and RFF operate in a quasi-academic mode, performing research and publishing reports, books, and papers in the refereed literature. While a number of these organizations obtain core funding from endowments, virtually all seek contracts from federal sources to support much of the work they do. Recent decades have also witnessed the development of a number of think tanks that adopt specific ideological perspectives on the work that they undertake. As detailed by Mayer (2016), this has been especially true of those promoting a conservative ideology.

19.6 THE CONGRESSIONAL OFFICE OF TECHNOLOGY ASSESSMENT

There has long been controversy about whether and to what extent the U.S. Congress needs expert advice. The classic legislative model for acquiring the information a Member needs to make legislative judgments is to hold hearings, during which various parties provide testimony, sometimes in an adversarial environment similar to that of expert witnesses testifying in a legal trial. Schneier and Gross (1993) argue that hearings provide:

> a context that forces the confrontation of opposing viewpoints without doing violence to collegial relations [among members]. Through clever questioning of a witness, a legislator can challenge a colleague's perspectives without challenging the person. Meanwhile he or she can learn what he needs to know through interpersonal communications, a type of exchange particularly congenial to the personality type of the politician.

Of course, hearings are not the only way in which a member acquires information; a constant stream of individuals and organizations troop through Congressional offices to brief and lobby staff and members.

This classic model may have worked well before Congress found itself dealing with a wide variety of complex technical issues. But as Morgan and Peha (2003) argue:

> Information and facts are not the same thing as knowledge, understanding and insight. Whereas some early commentators in science, technology and public policy adopted a two-step model in which the technical community produces facts and the political community then uses them to make decisions (Kantrowitz, 1975; Weinberg, 1972), most serious contemporary students of science and technology policy analysis argue that when the problems are complex, raw facts are rarely of much use. An intervening step

is needed, a step of balanced analysis and synthesis that sorts, integrates, and analyzes information to frame the issues and extract knowledge and insights. [See Figure 1.3.]

In this context, Kingdon (1973) argues, "Congressman need not just information, but information that is usable. It must be predigested, explicitly evaluative information which takes into account the political as well as the policy implications of voting decisions." In short, before it can reasonably address complex issues in science and technology policy, Congress needs balanced, high-quality policy analysis.

Of course, such analysis is sometimes available from the Executive Branch, or from various private parties. However, beginning in the late 1950s, and culminating during the early Nixon Administration, many members of Congress came to believe that they needed their own independent source of technical advice.[17] To address this need, Congress passed the Technology Assessment Act of 1972, creating the Congressional Office of Technology Assessment or OTA.[18]

OTA was created as a small bipartisan agency of the Congress. Its activities were overseen by a Technology Assessment Board (TAB). The Act specifies:

The Board shall consist of thirteen members as follows:

1. six Members of the Senate, appointed by the President pro tempore of the Senate, three from the majority party and three from the minority party.
2. six Members of the House of Representatives, appointed by the Speaker of the House of Representatives, three from the majority party and three from the minority party.
3. the Director, who shall not be a voting member.

A major responsibility of the Board was to select and approve the topics to be studied by OTA. Blair (2013) argues that it also played an important role in screening requests for studies and deflecting those that were not appropriate.

For the first several years of its operation, OTA struggled to find its way. However, once physicist Jack Gibbons became director in 1979, the agency settled into a stable mode of operation. Margolis and Guston (2003) report that:

In 1995, the year of its closure, OTA's budget represented 1% of the legislative appropriations bill. The number of staff hovered around 200 ... Most employees were analysts with advanced degrees, working in a relatively flat organizational structure ... 25% of the staff held a master's degree, 37% a Ph.D. and 10% a J.D. or M.D.

While officially the TAB chose the studies to be performed, the reality was rather more complex. Typically, OTA staff would hold conversations with staff and chairs and members of committees in order to determine needs. Then, after some iteration, a formal request was developed and sent to OTA, which

[17] For an account of this "pre-history," see chapter 2 of Blair (2013).

[18] Note that while OTA lost its funding in 1995, the Technology Assessment Act is still in force, with the result that, at least in principle, OTA could be re-established through the simple act of appropriating funds.

transmitted it to the TAB for approval. Frequently requests from different committees were combined so that more than one committee would be the requester for a study.

Unlike the NRC, in which outside experts perform most studies, OTA studies were performed by staff. This assured that reports would be responsive to the needs of Congress. An external advisory committee was formed at the beginning of each study. Membership was carefully chosen to represent not just all relevant areas of technical expertise, but also all relevant interests so that the OTA could consider and reflect all of those perspectives in its reports.

Because it worked in an often partisan environment in which there was considerable controversy, OTA rarely provided definitive recommendations but rather, in much the same manner as "discovery" in legal proceedings, it framed problems and laid out constraints and options that Congress should consider. Figure 19.2, drawn from a summary report on the future of U.S. Space Launch, displays one such strategy.[19] Blair (2013) explains that:

> by the late 1980's OTA had begun to more frequently deliver other types of reports in addition to full assessment reports, such as summaries, interim reports, focused special reports, background papers, and other shorter term deliverables. The efforts to produce a variety of report formats were intended to provide more timely and useful advice as requested by congressional committees. Preparation of a one or two page "report brief," on occasion affectionately referred to as the "senator-sized version," was a routine part of the OTA report release process, but its credibility relied on the existence of the major assessment report.

Over the course of its operation, OTA produced approximately 750 assessments and other kinds of products. Figure 19.3 is a plot of OTA report production. While OTA's reports were intended for the Congress, many others also found them extremely useful.

> [OTA] reports were widely used by interest groups, academics and the general public. By laying out problems, and a range of possible solutions, the reports helped to inform a wide range of national debate. Many ... in and outside the Congress with whom we have discussed these issues have argued that sometimes the most important impacts of OTA studies did not come from direct inputs provided to Committees and Members. They came, instead, through informed feedback from constituents who used OTA reports to frame and support their arguments on all sides of an issue. Sometimes OTA performed studies of issues well before they got onto the active political agenda. When this happened their reports helped to provide structure to the political discourse when the issue later became "hot." (Morgan and Peha, 2003)

[19] I served as chair of the Advisory Committee for the series of OTA reports on space launch. When Peter Blair first asked me to do this, I told him I was not an expert on the subject, to which he replied, "That's OK, there will be plenty of technical experts who have strong and conflicting views. We need a chair who is technically knowledgeable, knows how to run a meeting, and can help us extract, assess and compare all those different views."

A catalog and full copies of OTA's reports can be found online at www.princeton.edu/~ota.

In 1994, when the control of both the House and Senate passed to the Republicans after the mid-term election, House Speaker Newt Gingrich set out to have Congress reduce taxes and trim government expenditure as had been promised under the "Contract with America" during the preceding political campaign. Blair (2013) notes that in:

> the weeks following the election and before the 104th Congress convened, the new leaders translated the contract into a list of 95 major federal programs targeted for elimination. The "contract" also included a pledge to trim the scale of Congress significantly, with reduction in the size of Members' and Committee staffs by a third and substantial reductions in the size of all the congressional support agencies – GAO, CRS, CBO, and OTA.
>
> The new congressional majority singled out OTA, by far the smallest of the support agencies, for elimination since its elimination was conveniently symbolic. That is, while OTA's budget was less than 1 percent of the Legislative Branch Appropriations Budget, its elimination allowed the House Leadership to claim credit for abolishing an entire federal agency – the only such elimination that was ultimately sustained as part of the Contract with America proposals.

While Blair is correct that OTA was defunded for symbolic reasons, I believe there were also other factors at work. OTA worked for committees, not individual members, and with new Republican majorities in both chambers, most of the new committee chairs had not had previous experience in using OTA and so did not provide a constituency in support of its continued operation. There were also a number of key members who had other, more fundamental reasons for wanting to terminate the OTA. Most OTA reports were not especially controversial, and indeed were sometimes cited by proponents on both sides of the aisle in Congressional debates. However, a few reports turned out to be highly controversial. Most notable among these was a series of reports on missile defense (ABM or what was colloquially referred to as the Reagan Administration's "Star Wars" proposals). These deeply annoyed a number of powerful members. While neutral in tone, the technical assessments in these reports made it very clear that the proposed system was most unlikely to work. This finding was fundamentally at odds with the political objectives of Administration supporters.[20]

Given that, for any high-visibility controversy, a wide variety of organizations perform assessments (e.g., in the case of missile defense, the American

[20] While OTA produced several formal reports (OTA, 1985a, b), prior to that, working as a consultant, Ashton B. Carter at MIT prepared a critical technical critique in the form of a OTA Background Paper (Carter, 1984). Carter concluded that the prognosis for developing a perfect impenetrable missile shield was "extremely pessimistic" so that even with the system in place, "mutual assured destruction ... is likely to persist for the foreseeable future." The Pentagon tried to discredit Carter personally, and stopped only after OTA Director Jack Gibbons contacted the Secretary of Defense and told him to instruct his people to stop.

Congressional Alternatives

Congress could choose to support the development of many different types of space transportation vehicles. To determine which of these alternatives is most appropriate and most cost-effective, Congress must first make some broad decisions about the future of the United States in space. A commitment to key space program goals will entail a similar commitment to one or more launch vehicle systems. Although highly accurate cost estimates do not exist, the analysis in this study suggests that some launch systems are more economical than others to accomplish specific missions.

If Congress wishes to:	*Then it should:*
Limit the future growth of NASA and DoD space programs:	*Maintain existing launch systems and limit expenditures on future development options.* **Current capabilities are adequate to supply both NASA and DoD if the present level of U.S. space activities is maintained or reduced.**
Deploy the Space Station by the mid-90s while maintaining an aggressive NASA science program:	*Continue funding improvements to the Space Shuttle (e.g., ASRM and/or LRB)* and/or begin *developing Shuttle-C:* **The current Space Shuttle can launch the Space Station, but will do so more effectively with improvements or the assistance of a Shuttle-C. Although Shuttle-C may not be as economical as other new cargo vehicles at high launch rates, it is competitive if only a few heavy-lift missions are required each year.**
Send humans to Mars or establish a base on the moon:	*Commit to the development of a new unpiloted cargo vehicle (Shuttle-C or Transition launch vehicle or ALS) and continue research and funding for Shuttle II and the National Aerospace Plane.* **A commitment to piloted spaceflight will require a Shuttle replacement shortly after the turn of the century. Large planetary missions will also need a new, more economical, cargo vehicle.**
Continue trend of launching heavier communications, navigation, and reconnaissance satellites and/or pursue an aggressive SDI test program to prepare for eventual deployment:	*Commit to the development of a new unpiloted cargo vehicle (Transition launch vehicle) by the mid-to-late 1990s.* **In theory, current launch systems could be expanded to meet future needs; however, new systems are likely to be more reliable and more cost-effective.**
Deploy SDI and/or dramatically increase the number and kind of other military space activities:	*Commit to the development of a new unpiloted cargo vehicle (Transition Vehicle or Advanced Launch System).* **Current launch systems are neither sufficiently economical to support SDI deployment nor reliable enough to support a dramatically increased military space program.**

Meeting the space transportation needs of specific programs is only part of the reason for making changes to the current launch systems. Congress may wish to fund the development of critical new capabilities or improvements to the "quality" of space transportation, or Congress may wish to ensure that funding serves broader national objectives.

If Congress wishes to:	*Then it should:*
Maintain U.S. leadership in launch system technology:	*Increase funding for space transportation basic research, technology development, and applications.* **Maintaining leadership will require an integrated NASA/DoD technology development program across a range of technologies. Focused technology efforts (ALS, Shuttle II, NASP) must be balanced with basic research.**
Improve resilience (ability to recover quickly from failure) of U.S. launch systems:	*Fund the development of a new high capacity, high reliability launch vehicle (Transition launch vehicle or ALS) or expand current ground facilities or reduce downtime after failures or improve the reliability of current launch vehicles.* **At high launch rates, developing a new vehicle is probably most economical.**
Increase launch vehicle reliability and safety:	*Aggressively fund technologies to provide: 1) improved subsystem reliability; 2) "engine-out" capability for new launch vehicles; 3) on-pad abort and in-flight engine shutdown for escape from piloted vehicles; and 4) redundancy and fault tolerance for critical systems.*
Reduce environmental impact of high launch rates:	*Limit the use of highly toxic liquid fuels and replace Shuttle and Titan solid rocket boosters with new liquid rocket boosters or clean-burning solid boosters.* **The United States will be relying on Shuttle and Titan vehicles through the turn of the century. As launch rates increase, the environmental impact of the Shuttle solid rocket motors and the solid and liquid Titan motors will become more important.**

FIGURE 19.2. Example of the "If Congress wants to…, then it should…" strategy that OTA sometimes used to frame issues without telling members of Congress what they should do. Reproduced from: http://ota-cdn.fas.org/reports/8826.pdf.

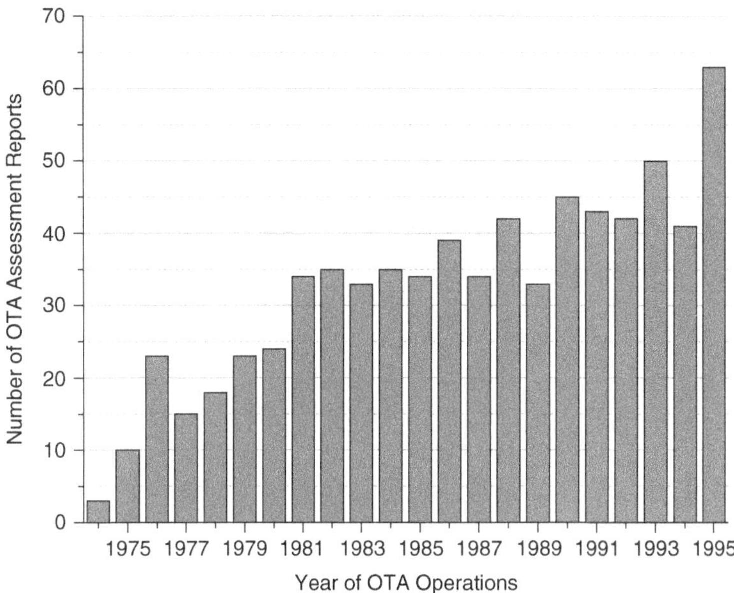

FIGURE 19.3. Annual number of OTA reports over the life of the agency. Figure courtesy of Peter Blair.

Physical Society had performed a series of analyses), one lesson from the OTA experience may be that an organization charged with performing analysis for highly partisan legislative bodies should seek to avoid working on high-visibility politically charged topics, and focus on the many other issues that require balanced technical analysis and assessment. Indeed, before taking on any study, the U.S. Government Accountability Office (GAO) performs a "risk assessment" – an assessment of the risks that may arise to the GAO itself if it agrees to pursue the requested study.

The defunding of OTA left an institutional gap that has yet to be adequately filled. In 2001, Jon Peha and I organized a workshop to explore and assess a range of institutional arrangements that might be adopted to fill the gap (Figure 19.4). With a number of colleagues we subsequently produced a book that explores the general problem of providing science and technology advice to the Congress and outlined six possible alternative institutional arrangements that might be used to fill the gap. In a final chapter, we argued that:

> The current sources of independent balanced analytical support which the Congress can routinely command do not span the full range of response times. There is a gap for studies that require more than a few weeks but less than 18 months. The CRS does an excellent job of providing short-term assistance. The National Research Council is often used for longer-term studies which, except in special circumstances, usually require a year or more. In between, there is a gap – Congress has no reliable balanced impartial sources of analysis

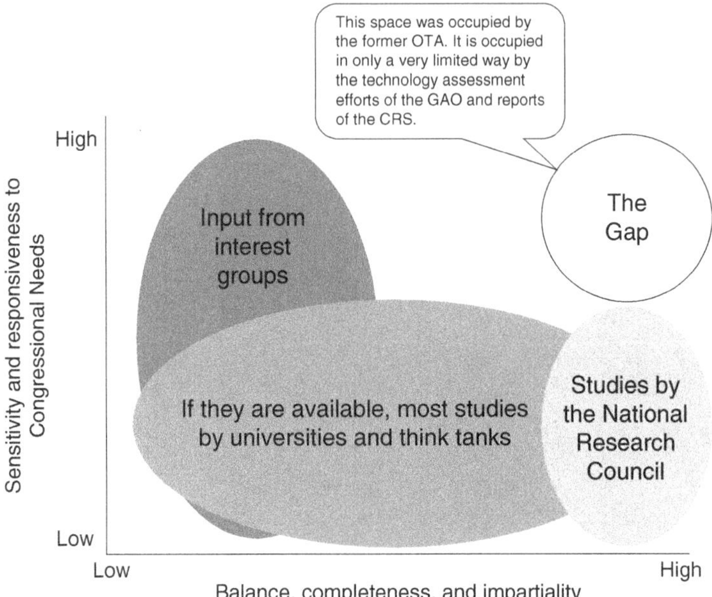

FIGURE 19.4. Illustration of the gap in analytical capabilities available to Congress. Figure redrawn and modified from Morgan and Peha (2003).

and synthesis on policy problems involving issues of science and technology to which it can routinely turn for help on these intermediate time scales. (Morgan and Peha, 2003)

To date no adequate substitute has been found for the services once provided by OTA. Beginning in 2002 Senator Bingaman's office began to explore using the GAO for technology assessment.[21] A small number of such studies have been produced.[22] Over time, CRS has also begun to build more in-depth technical analytical capability and perform assessments that are quite substantive. While CRS works for members, and does not release its reports and other work products directly to the public, members and staff and others do routinely make them available.[23] CRS employs about 400 policy analysts who work in one of five divisions: American law; domestic social policy; foreign affairs, defense and trade; government and finance; and resources, science, and industry. Details can be found at: www.loc.gov/crsinfo/research.

There have been several other efforts both to re-fund the OTA, or to create other institutional arrangements to fill the gap (Figure 19.4) in analytical

[21] For a discussion of the GAO effort, see chapter 8 in Blair (2013).

[22] See, for example, GAO (2002, 2011). For a full list, see: www.gao.gov/technology_assessment/key_reports. For an assessment of GAO's first effort in technology assessment, see appendix 3 in Morgan and Peha (2003).

[23] See, for example: http://fas.org/sgp/crs and http://fpc.state.gov/c18185.htm.

capability for the Congress (Morgan and Peha, 2003; Knezo, 2005), but to date none has succeeded. As Peha and I observed:

> Congress is a representative body that responds to its constituents. Most Members do not have technical or policy analytic backgrounds. Several of those who do have argued to us that if the Congress is going to create institutional arrangements to fill the gaps ... outside constituents will have to mobilize to persuade the Congress that this capability is sorely needed, and that its addition will lead to more informed decisions that better serve the public interest. Absent such external encouragement, it is unlikely that the majority of Members and Congressional Staff will take action to make such institutional changes. (Morgan and Peha, 2003)

During its existence many parliaments and governments around the world looked at the OTA model, liked what they saw, and created their own similar institutions. In chapter 5 of Morgan and Peha (2003), Norman Vig provided a summary of many of the institutions that were created and continue to function in Europe.

SUGGESTED RESOURCES TO LEARN MORE ABOUT THE HISTORY, PERFORMANCE, AND DEMISE OF THE OTA

Peter D. Blair, *Congress's Own Think Tank: Learning from the Legacy of the Office of Technology Assessment (1972–1995)*, Palgrave Macmillan, 128pp., 2013.

M. Granger Morgan and Jon M. Peha, *Science and Technology Advice for Congress*, Resources for the Future Press, 236pp., 2003.

19.7 SCIENCE AND TECHNOLOGY ADVICE TO THE JUDICIARY

The judicial community is large and complex. The report of the Carnegie Commission on Science, Technology, and Government observed that it consists of "53 independent systems, one federal, one for each state, and one each for the District of Columbia and Puerto Rico" (Carnegie Commission, 1993). It went on to note that:

> In the federal system, there are 94 independent district courts and 13 appellate courts that comprise more than 700 trial judges and 150 appellate judges; all of these judges are appointed for life by the president with the advice and consent of the Senate. There are also tens of thousands of judges in state judiciaries. State judges are generally either elected or appointed for fixed terms of service.

In addition to these courts of general jurisdiction, there are also a number of specialty courts.

Unlike the iterative refinement of empirical evidence and testing of hypotheses that constitutes the process by which science is done, the judiciary is about making decisions at a specific moment on the basis of the evidence presented in an adversarial setting. As Supreme Court Associate Justice Stephen Breyer (2000) has explained, in the case of court decisions involving matters of science and technology:

> The search is not a search for scientific precision. We cannot hope to investigate all the subtleties that characterize good scientific work. A judge is not a scientist, and a courtroom is not a scientific laboratory. But the law must seek decisions that fall within the boundaries of scientifically sound knowledge.
>
> Even this more modest objective is sometimes difficult to achieve in practice. The most obvious reason why is that most judges lack the scientific training that might facilitate the evaluation of scientific claims or the evaluation of expert witnesses who make such claims. Judges typically are generalists, dealing with cases that can vary widely in subject matter. Our primary objective is usually process-related: seeing that a decision is reached fairly and in a timely way. And the decision in a court of law typically (though not always) focuses on a particular event and specific individualized evidence.

As the Carnegie Commission (1993) notes, unlike the process of science, "in the legal system ... all the players are forced to make decisions at a particular moment in time, while ... [the] scientific process is going on."

Federal Appeals Court Judge Danny Boggs (1988) explains that:

> Many of the most noted science-related cases have come out of review of federal regulations. Perhaps maddeningly to scientists, such cases are generally not supposed to turn on the ultimate "truth" of the scientific judgment reached by the regulatory agency. That is a judgment for the agency itself to make. The judicial function is primarily to assure that prescribed procedures have been followed, though such procedures generally include a requirement that this decision be a "reasoned" one.

Of course, not all trials that involve matters of science and technology derive from the review of federal regulations. Not infrequently toxic tort and other such cases involve "dueling expert witnesses":

> In theory, at least, the federal trial judge's ability to obtain information and judgment is almost unlimited (and most states follow the federal rules). He may appoint his own expert witnesses ... allow reports and tests of many types to be admitted as evidence, and otherwise overcome any obstacles to placing before him (or a jury...) any evidence needed. (Boggs, 1988)

Judges can also appoint their own independent expert(s) to advise them on understanding and interpreting the evidence. However, it is the rare judge who feels the need and is willing to do this.

> Early in the 1960s, the judiciary in several jurisdictions tried to remedy the difficulties caused by partisan experts' testimony in personal injury lawsuits by creating "impartial medical panels." In Pittsburgh and New York, for example, the courts appointed well-known doctors from various medical specialties as neutral advisers to the judge and jury. Their function was to diagnose, evaluate and explain the medical evidence whenever the parties' doctors disagreed about what the evidence showed. After a flurry

of interest lasting a few years, the impartial panel idea fell into disuse. Many members of the bar were against the panel plan, apparently because they believed the judge's and panel's influence over the disputed issues frustrated the working of the adversary process. (Rosenberg, 1988)

Rosenberg notes that while the use of "technical advisors" who have both technical and legal expertise is

firmly established and well accepted in the Court of Appeals for the Federal Circuit ... the major reason the technical advisor model has not been accepted for other courts is that the legal profession is generally wary of allowing in-court experts to speak inaudibly and anonymously to the judges in ways that may determine the results of sharply contested cases. (Rosenberg, 1988).

Many of us who come from technical backgrounds are less than fully persuaded that an adversarial strategy is the best route to determining "truth" in complex issues of science and technology. Boggs (1988) reminds us that scientific truth is only one of the factors, along with equity and similar social considerations, that courts must consider. He argues that "Bad scientific decisions by individual courts aren't fatal to scientific advance, or the social good; they just may slow things down a bit. The legislative branch can always step in and make sweeping decisions to avoid difficulties raised by courts."

19.8 SCIENCE AND TECHNOLOGY ADVICE IN THE U.S. STATES AND REGIONAL GOVERNMENTS

It is tempting to think of U.S. science and technology advice to government solely in terms of the federal level. That would be a mistake. As Dupree (1986) documents, during the nation's first 150 years, states were often well ahead of the federal government in their willingness to support developments in science and technology and in seeking technical advice. While concerns about states' rights often limited federal involvements, many states saw scientific and technical development in fields such as geology (mining), aquatic biology (fishing), agriculture, and transportation as translating directly into economic development for the benefit of their citizens. State university systems, many supported after the Civil War by the Land Grant program, along with specialized agencies within state government, became the locus of expertise upon which economic development depended.

In recent decades, many states have come to see the development and promotion of high technology as especially appealing. The Pew Center on the States (Pew, 2007) has observed:

The pressure on the 50 states to attract jobs, money and a talented workforce has been building for decades. It's now singularly intense. Huge new overseas competitors like China and India are competing for the same pools of cash and people as California, Indiana and the rest. Moreover, some international players like Singapore, Finland and

Ireland are demonstrating remarkable prowess at strategically planning for economic growth. Meanwhile, the speed with which innovation spreads makes no competitive lead secure.

As a result, today states must accelerate their efforts or risk becoming economic backwaters. Specifically, they must become places where new ideas are discovered, invented or given their first big break.

A meeting summary from the NRC (2008) explains:

States have funded these efforts in a variety of ways. Sometimes they have earmarked increased tax revenues approved by popular votes or by state legislatures ... some states have set aside funds from general appropriations ... many of these initiatives seek to take advantage of the physical proximity of researchers, businesses and policymakers.

In addition to drawing upon expertise that resides among staff in state government and universities, many state agencies have external scientific and technical advisory boards. While arrangements vary by state and over time, some governors, and even some city mayors, appoint science advisors.

State academies of science or similar organizations exist in over 80 percent of the states. Some like the New York Academy of Science or the California Council on Science and Technology are of extremely high quality, with members who are international leaders in their fields.

While individual governors and mayors undertake their own initiatives, there are also a variety of cooperative activities that take place through the National Governors Association and the United States Conference of Mayors.

The National Governors Association maintains standing committees on topics that involve substantial technical content such as natural resources, homeland security and public safety, and economic development. The Association also runs sessions at its annual meetings as well as workshops on topics such as "Emerging Energy Technologies," and "Science, Technology and Economic Growth."

In a similar way, the United States Conference of Mayors maintains standing committees in such technical areas as energy and environment. In 2012 it created a Technology and Innovation Task Force whose objectives include:[24]

- Creating a vision for the future of cities as engines of innovation and technology;
- Serving as a convener bringing the necessary public and private sector participants – the technology drivers, the business leaders and the mayors – together to discuss the applications of promising technologies and innovative systems to improve our cities;
- Designing, launching, and participating in projects and endeavors that demonstrate how innovation and technology can create economic and social value for our cities and residents.

[24] http://usmayors.org/innovation.

Finally, there are several national organizations of regulators and others who operate at the state level. One of the more technical-focused of these is the National Association of Regulatory Utility Commissioners (NARUC). Most commissioners come from legal backgrounds. Through sessions at annual meetings and its many standing and special committees, NARUC undertakes a wide variety of activities to help commissioners become knowledgeable about the technical aspects of electric power and communication technologies and track new technical developments.

19.9 SCIENCE AND TECHNOLOGY ADVICE TO EUROPEAN GOVERNMENTS AND TO THE EUROPEAN UNION

With Inês Azevedo, Carnegie Mellon University, Pittsburgh, PA

Unlike the United States, European governments are organized as parliamentary systems. The party, or coalition of parties, that secures a majority in the parliament then forms the government. The head of government is typically the prime minister. There is generally also a head of state who is separately elected, or in the case of constitutional monarchies, such as Britain or Sweden, assumes that position through inheritance.

The head of state, whose discretionary authority varies somewhat across different nations, typically appoints the prime minister. For example, in the U.K. the monarch appoints the leader of the largest party (or largest coalition) in the House of Commons to form a government and serve as prime minister. In Germany, the Bundestag elects the federal chancellor, who forms the cabinet. In theory, the elected French president has somewhat greater discretionary authority, but in practice the president appoints the head of the largest party in the National Assembly to serve as prime minister, who then forms the government.

Norman Vig and Herbert Paschen (2000) compiled an extensive history and description of the varying roles and functions of the organizations that provide science and technology advice to European parliaments, most of which were modeled in varying degrees on the now disbanded U.S. OTA. Vig (2003) reports that as of 2003, 15 Parliamentary Assessment offices had been created by European nations. He notes:

> The British parliamentary office of science and technology [established in 1989] is now a permanent unit of the U.K. Parliament and it carries on a variety of advisory functions under the direction of a nonpartisan oversight panel made up of members of both Houses of Parliament and outside experts ... [In contrast] the German technology assessment board [TAB, established in 1990] is in many ways modeled after OTA but is operated under contract by a major outside research institute [part of the Helmholtz Association].

A number of other advisory arrangements exist beyond these parliamentary offices. For example, since 1964 the U.K. has had a Chief Scientific Adviser who, with a staff of roughly 50 experts, provides advice to the prime minister and the cabinet. In addition, each department has a Chief Science Officer who reports both to their respective departments as well as to the Chief Scientific Adviser. As of 2016, this entire group was holding a regular weekly breakfast meeting.

While it lacks the equivalence of a large executive arm like the National Academies' NRC, from time-to-time the Royal Society provides advice to government in the form of reports. In addition, the U.K. enjoys a strong tradition of policy-focused consultancies and university analysis groups. Most notable among the latter are Cambridge, Cardiff, Kings College London, the London School of Economics, and University College London. One of the oldest programs, now somewhat eclipsed by newer efforts, is the Science Policy Research Unit (SPRU) at the University of Sussex. Created in 1966, for many years SPRU focused broadly on issues of science, technology, and innovation policy, often providing advice to various organs of the European Union.

In Germany the National Academy of Natural Sciences,[25] the Academy of Engineering, and the Berlin Brandenburg Academy of Science (Social Science and Humanities) have created a joint Academy Research and Consultancy Initiative that has been constituted to organize and provide science and technology advice to the government and its ministries on topics like the ongoing energy transition (Energiewende). When a request is received it is assessed in terms of the expertise that is needed, and assigned to the relevant Academy to coordinate the study.

As noted above, unlike other parliamentary advisory groups, the parliamentary Technology Assessment Board (TAB) is associated with the Karlsruhe Institute of Technology, one of the laboratories of the Helmholtz Association. Its small office is located in Berlin. The TAB's mission is to:[26]

- analyze the potentials of new scientific and technological developments and explore the associated opportunities;
- examine the framework conditions for implementing scientific and technological developments; and
- analyze their potential impacts in a comprehensive forecast, pinpoint the opportunities of a certain technology, and indicate the possibilities for avoiding or reducing any associated risks, to provide policy makers alternative options in the policy-making process.

Beyond these arrangements several formal committees such as SRU, the German Advisory Council on the Environment, and WBGU, the German Advisory Council on Global Change, provide advice on specific topics. Finally, government officials often turn for advice to senior experts including the leaders of

[25] Known as the Leopoldina, the German National Academy of Natural Science was founded in 1652 and is believed to be the oldest continuously existing learned society in the world.

[26] See: www.itas.kit.edu/english/tab.php.

national institutes such as the Potsdam Institute for Climate Impact Research (PIK) and the Institute for Advanced Sustainability Studies (IASS), both of which are located near Berlin in the city of Potsdam.

In France, scientific and technical advice is provided to the Parliament by the OPECST (Office Parlementaire d'Évaluation des Choix Scientifiques et Technologiques)[27]. This organization was created in 1983 with a mission "to inform Parliament of the consequences of the choice of scientific and technological options, in particular, so as to enable it to make enlightened decisions" (OPECST, 2015). It does this by collecting information, undertaking study programs and performing a variety of assessments. In a structure reminiscent of the U.S. OTA, the members of OPECST:

> are appointed so as to ensure proportional representation of the political groups, belonging both to the National Assembly and to the Senate. It is composed of 18 M.P.s and 18 Senators; each member may be appointed as a "rapporteur" ... [that is] an M.P. or senator in charge of writing a report on a given subject.
>
> The OPECST is chaired alternately for a period of three years by a member of either assembly. Internal rules stipulate that the First Vice-President shall belong to the other Assembly. (OPECST, 2015)

French science and technology research policy has undergone a variety of changes since World War II.[28] In 1954, a Conseil Supérieur de la Recherche Scientifique et du Progress Technique was created, but it lasted only four years. It was dismantled by Charles de Gaulle, who replaced it with three different organizations. Pierre Mendès-France organized the Colloque de Caen, which established the vision for the current system of research in France. By 1959, the design of a mechanism for specific funds for R&D had been established. The 1960s saw a move toward supporting the development and growth of industrial R&D as a way to boost France's economic competitiveness. To that same end, in the 1970s, the Délégation Générale à la Recherche Scientifique et Technique was created under the Minister for Industry, with responsibility for coordinating research. It was moved under the prime minister in 1977, and then terminated in 1981 with the creation of the Ministère de la Recherche et de la Technologie. Since then, France has created and dismantled several groups with the mission of providing insight on issues of science and technology:

1. The Conseil Supérieur de la Recherche et de la Technologie (1981–2013) was created to provide information to the ministry responsible for research and graduate education. The minister served as the Conseil's president, which included scientists and representatives of the private sector. The group was consulted on all key decisions related to science

[27] For details see: www2.assemblee-nationale.fr/14/les-delegations-comite-et-office-parlementaire/office-parlementaire-d-evaluation-des-choix-scientifiques-et-technologiques.

[28] For a detailed review of the science and technology policy in France, see: http://media.enseignementsuprecherche.gouv.fr/file/Mission_des_archives/52/5/Etat_general_des_fonds_Recherche_06_version_GB_141525.pdf.

and technology policy pursued by the Government, such as the decisions about the distribution of the public R&D budget.

2. The Comité d'Orientation Stratégique (1995–1998) was created to advise the president. It was succeeded by the Conseil National de la Science (1998–2005), which in turn was replaced by the Haut Conseil de la Science et de la Technologie (2006–2013). In 2006, at its inception, the Haut Conseil was placed under the French president, who selected its participants (mostly renowned scientists). By 2009, a new decree established that the Haut Conseil should instead be under the auspice of the prime minister. The composition of the Conseil was also changed to include both scientists and industry leaders.

In 2013, both the Conseil Supérieur de la Recherche et de la Technologie and the Haut Conseil de la Science et de la Technologie were abolished and a new Conseil Stratégique de la Recherche was created. This new entity was placed under the umbrella of the office of the prime minister.

Turning now to non-governmental organizations, across Europe there are a number that play a role in science, technology, and policy. Two unusual examples are IRGC and MISTRA. IRGC, the International Risk Governance Council, was created in 2003 as an independent foundation supported by the Swiss Government and various others, including SwissRe. IRGC has addressed a wide range of topics in science, technology, and policy, most involving some issue of risk governance. Over time, its institutional arrangements have evolved. Today IRGC is affiliated with EPFL, the École Polytechnique Fédérale de Lausanne.

MISTRA, the Swedish Foundation for Strategic Environmental Research, was created in 1993 when a more conservative Swedish government transferred a large block of funds that had been accumulated for labor into an endowment to establish a foundation that conducts a wide range of policy-relevant research on environmental topics. Two other interesting policy-focused Swedish organizations are the Stockholm Environmental Institute and the Stockholm International Peace Research Institute.

In Italy, the Fondazione Eni Enrico Mattei (FEEM) is a non-profit, non-partisan research institution devoted to the study of sustainable development and global governance. In recent years, much of its work has focused on issues of climate change.

Finally, no list of European organizations focused on science, technology, and policy would be complete without a mention of IIASA, the International Institute for Applied Systems Analysis, located in Laxenburg, Austria, near Vienna. IIASA was established in 1972 as the result of an initiative by President Lyndon Johnson of the United States and Premier Alexei Kosygin of the Soviet Union, in order to create a neutral place for research collaboration on applied and theoretical issues in systems science between scholars from the East and West. Howard Raiffa served as its first director. IIASA is supported by national foundations and governments. With the end of the Cold War, its mission was broadened to apply interdisciplinary analytical approaches to a wide range of global environmental, economic, and technological problems and to issues in social change.

As noted in Chapter 6, the Dutch have had a long tradition of analysis and civic engagement in public policy decision making. Hence, it is not surprising that there are more university programs in technology-policy research and education in the Netherlands than in all the rest of Europe combined (e.g., at Delft, Eindhoven, Utrecht, and others). More recently, two graduate programs in Engineering and Public Policy have also been established in Portugal (at IST in Lisbon and at Porto).

Finally, before turning to a discussion of the European Union, it is important to note that Europe is the home of a number of international organizations with major roles in science, technology, and policy, including the Organization of Economic Cooperation and Development, the International Energy Agency, and a number of UN-affiliated international regulatory bodies.

The European Union: Many science and technology activities and policies across Europe are tightly intertwined with the European Union (EU). Today the EU consists of seven major units. The EU's executive arm is called the *Commission*, which proposes and drafts legislation and ensures the application of EU law. As of 2016 there were 23,000 staff members working in the Commission in departments, known as Directorates-General (DGs) or services, each responsible for a particular policy area and headed by a Director-General.[29] The *EU Council* comprises the heads of EU member states. It meets four times a year and provides broad policy direction to set the organization's policy agenda. The *Parliament* is the EU's legislative arm. Its members are elected directly by voters across the member states. The legislative acts of the EU take the form of *directives*, which require member states to achieve a set of outcomes *without* dictating the means of achieving that result. Under a system known as "subsidiarity," member countries define how to implement the objectives of the directive through national legislation as a way to meet the overarching goals from the EU directive. Since 1987 the EU Parliament has had a technology assessment unit called STOA (Scientific and Technological Options Assessment) that is composed of 24 members. At the request of any member or parliamentary body STOA conducts a variety of "Scientific Foresight Projects" and organizes forums and other events.

The organization and structure of the EU as they exist today are the result of a long process initiated in the aftermath of World War II. In the immediate postwar period there was a pressing need to speed social and economic recovery and minimize the risk of future conflict (Judt, 2005).

As early as 1945, Winston Churchill proposed the creation of a United States of Europe: "to promote harmonious relations between nations, economic

[29] See: http://ec.europa.eu/about/index_en.htm#directorates.

cooperation, and a sense of European identity" (Mauter, 1998). In 1948, Robert Schuman called for the creation of an *Assembly for Europe,* a supra-national democracy. In 1949, Schuman argued:

> We are carrying out a great experiment, the fulfillment of the same recurrent dream that for ten centuries has revisited the peoples of Europe: creating between them an organization putting an end to war and guaranteeing an eternal peace ...
>
> Audacious minds, such as Dante, Erasmus, Abbé de St-Pierre, Rousseau, Kant and Proudhon, had created in the abstract the framework for systems that were both ingenious and generous. The title of one of these systems became the synonym of all that is impractical: Utopia, itself a work of genius, written by Thomas More, the Chancellor of Henry VIII, King of England ...
>
> Our century, that has witnessed the catastrophes resulting in the unending clash of nationalities and nationalisms, must attempt and succeed in reconciling nations in a supranational association. This would safeguard the diversities and aspirations of each nation while coordinating them in the same manner as the regions are coordinated within the unity of the nation.[30]

Energy and resources policy, and in particular the productions of coal and steel, provided the glue to realize Schuman's vision. In 1950, in the *Schuman Declaration,* Schuman (with input from Jean Monnet) proposed that Franco-German production of coal and steel should be put under a supra-national authority, one that would be open to the participation of other European nations. Shortly thereafter, France, West Germany, Italy, and the Benelux countries signed the Treaty of Paris establishing the European Coal and Steel Community, as well promulgating the *Europe Declaration*, which established the supra-national principle as the foundation of the new democratic organization in Europe.

Not surprisingly (indeed, as still happens today), events in Europe were being heavily shaped by American policy – in particular, nuclear policy. Guzzetti (1995) explains that:

> after the Soviet nuclear tests in 1949, a policy based on absolute secrecy in all areas of atomic research had lost much of its meaning and the possibility arose that scientific collaboration with Western Europe could have valuable results both technologically and politically. The new American position was put forward in Europe by Isidior I. Rabi, the American representative at the UNESCO General Assembly in Florence in June 1950, when he declared that after economic aid and military cooperation, the time had now come for the United States to make its contribution to the scientific renaissance of Europe.

By 1953, several European countries had joined CERN, the European Organization for Nuclear Research, due to a spurt of enthusiasm generated by President Eisenhower's program of "Atoms for Peace." The ratification of the convention nevertheless encountered difficulties as other European integration processes were pushed in parallel.

[30] See: www.schuman.info/Strasbourg549.htm.

These activities led to the agreements under the *Treaty of Rome* on January 1, 1958, and the founding of the European Economic Community (EEC). Initially signed by the Benelux countries, France, Italy, and West Germany, the Treaty proposed the progressive reduction of customs duties and the establishment of a customs union, the creation of a common market for goods, workers, services and capital within the EEC member states, and the creation of common transport and agriculture policies and of a European Social Fund. The Treaty also established the European Commission (the executive arm of the Communities) and EURATOM. The term "European Communities" emerged, referring collectively to the European Coal and Steel Community, the European Economic Community (which initially had a focus on the agriculture policy), and the European Atomic Energy Community.

Article 4 of the EURATOM treaty also gave the Commission the task of promoting and facilitating nuclear research of member states and implementing the Communities' research and training programs. This effort led to the creation of today's Joint Research Centers (JRCs), which have the missions of informing EU policy design (and specifically to supporting the DGs) by providing independent scientific evidence.

Today, the JRCs are organized as different Institutes that are located in Belgium (Institute for Reference Materials and Measurements), Germany (Institute for Transuranium Elements), Italy (Institute for Environment and Sustainability; Institute for Energy and Transport; Institute for Health and Consumer Protection; Institute for the Protection and Security of the Citizen), the Netherlands (Institute for Energy and Transport; Nuclear Security Unit), and Spain (Institute for Prospective Technological Studies). The JRCs (as well as several academic and other institutions) also play an important role in "supporting successful investment in knowledge and innovation foreseen by the Horizon 2020 Work Program, the EU's program for research and innovation."[31]

In the late 1960s and early 1970s, Europe was increasingly caught up in debate over the technology gap: the difference between technological advances in the United States and Europe was widening. In a high-profile book,[32] *Le Défi Americain*, Jean-Jacques Servan-Schreiber (1967) argued that the United States and Europe were engaged in a new type of economic war in which technological advances would determine the winners. European countries reacted to this argument in widely different ways, with some encouraging U.S. firms to create European subsidiaries, some suggesting they should abandon R&D altogether and focus on industrial production, some calling for the implementation of protectionist policies, and still others suggesting joining forces ("a technological Marshall Plan") (Guzzetti, 1995).

[31] https://ec.europa.eu/jrc/en/about/jrc-in-brief.

[32] The French-language version sold an unprecedented 600,000 copies in Europe and the English translation was also very widely read.

In *L'Europe et les Investissements Américains,* Christopher Layton et al. (1968) proposed that the Communities ought to collaborate with the U.K. He also suggested that the Communities would need to continue to strengthen areas of success (such as CERN and the research on fast reactors). In the field of aviation, he suggested that cooperation was needed (this became bilateral for Concorde and trilateral for Airbus). He called for the creation of consortia in information technology, and for an integrated transport system for the European territory and emphasized the need of the Channel Tunnel. To strengthen Europe's basic research he proposed the creation of a European Science Foundation, which would start by launching an oceanography program and also create centers of excellence in molecular biology under the protection of the European Molecular Biology Organization (EMBO). Finally, he highlighted the importance of improving student mobility. In March 1965, a working group (the Maréchal group) was formed to understand how member countries could coordinate their policies for science and technology. Its resulting report suggested several areas of possible cooperation: computers, transportation, oceanography, metallurgy, pollution, and meteorology. However, two years later in 1967 France vetoed the participation of the U.K., Denmark, Ireland, and Norway in the Communities, leading to increased tensions among parties and a reversal of these ideas (though they re-emerged a few years later and provided the backbone of COST's program). Finally in 1974, 24 years after the creation of the U.S. National Science Foundation, the European Science Foundation was created.

The seminal Single European Act of 1987 (SEA) – the major revision of the 1957 Treaty of Rome – established the goal of a single European market by 1992 and codified Europe's political cooperation. The SEA includes a chapter on Research and Technological Development (Article 24, Title VI).[33] In the 1980s the Commission came to understand the importance of innovation, and that innovation does not follow a linear model from research, to development, to design, to engineering, and finally to production. The commission embraced concepts of the "Chain-Link Model" (see Box 18.3) in which the interactions between knowledge and innovation are much more fluid with complex feedback loops at each stage. The commission organized science and technology efforts around a "Framework Programme for Research and Technological Development," which remains in use today. The first Framework Programme (FP) ran between 1984 and 1988, the second ran from 1987 to 1991, and so on, up to the Seventh Framework Programme, which ran from 2007 to 2013. In the meantime, the Amsterdam Treaty of 1997 changed the rules so that instead of requiring a unanimous decision for the Framework Programmes to be adopted, decisions are now made by a qualified majority vote by the Council of Ministers (the overall decision needs to be made in agreement by the Council and the EU Parliament). The budget levels for the Framework

[33] http://eur-lex.europa.eu/legal-content/EN/TXT/PDF/?uri=OJ:L:1987:169:FULL&from=EN.

Programmes increased substantially and constantly over this time period, from 3.75 billion euros in the first program to over 53 billion euros in the seventh program. Plans for the eighth FP (2014–2020), called Horizon 2020, were to allocate 80 billion euros.

In 2000, the Commission proposed the idea of a European Research Area (ERA) to better integrate, coordinate, support, and supplement the national research efforts, which the Commissions deemed to be lacking:

> It cannot be said that there is today a European policy on research. National research policies and Union policy overlap without forming a coherent whole. If more progress is to be made a broader approach is needed than the one adopted to date. The forthcoming enlargement of the Union will only increase this need. It opens the prospect of a Europe of 25 or 30 countries that will not be able to operate with the methods used so far.[34]

FPs six and seven were designed to support this goal, and were organized through a series of specific funding instruments: *Integrating Projects*; *Networks of Excellence*; and *Specific Targeted Research Projects*.[35] In 2002, the European Council established a target for EU R&D investment intensity to approach 3 percent of GDP[36] (still the goal that the EU would like to achieve by 2020).[37]

Horizon 2020 departed from the previous FPs in several ways. First, the program's name changed to "Framework Programme for Research and Innovation." It was designed to support other higher-level policy efforts of the EU such as Europe 2020 and Innovation Union. It foresaw a >20 percent increase in support over the previous FP and was organized around three pillars:

- Excellent Research (which focuses on basic sciences), which is managed by the European Research Council (ERC) and funds future and emerging technologies' research, researcher mobility efforts, and also large European research infrastructures;
- Industrial Leadership, managed by DG Enterprise;
- Societal challenges.

Efforts to create a more formal institution to provide science and technology advice to the EU leadership began in 2012 with the creation of the position of Chief Scientific Adviser to the President of the European Commission. Anne Glover, the first Chief Scientific Adviser, served in that capacity from 2012 to 2014. Largely because she publicly supported GMOs, a view not consistent

[34] http://eur-lex.europa.eu/LexUriServ/LexUriServ.do?uri=COM:2000:0006:FIN:EN:PDF.

[35] Also at that time enormous attention was devoted to developing and using indicators and metrics for goals and performance. Most researchers found the resulting process to be excruciating!

[36] www.consilium.europa.eu/ueDocs/cms_Data/docs/pressData/en/ec/71025.pdf.

[37] http://eur-lex.europa.eu/resource.html?uri=cellar:21493022-a617-11e3-8438-01aa75ed71a1.0003.05/DOC_1&format=PDF.

with EU policy, the position of Chief Science Advisor was not extended when the presidency of José Manuel Barroso ended. Jean-Claude Juncker decided to formally restructure the Bureau of European Policy Advisers, which included the Chief Scientific Adviser. The new group is called the European Political Strategy Centre (EPSC).

EU Commissioner for Research, Science and Innovation Carlos Moedas has suggested that a European Innovation Council should be created. In 2015, he appointed seven top scientists to fill the gap in policy advice.[38] These advisors are part of a larger scientific group called the "Scientific Advice Mechanism" that has been established to provide independent scientific advice to the Commission.[39]

In summary, over the course of more than six decades, the European science and technology organizational structure has slowly and tortuously taken shape. Science and technology advice exists at a national level, but progress is still needed in how science and technology can better support the overarching goals of the EU.

19.10 SCIENCE AND TECHNOLOGY ADVICE TO GOVERNMENT IN JAPAN

Jun Suzuki, National Graduate Institute for Policy Studies, Tokyo, Japan

The supreme executive power in the Japanese Government is the cabinet, headed by the prime minister. The cabinet is collectively responsible to the Diet, Japan's bicameral legislature. In the current Japanese system, the Council for Science, Technology and Innovation (CSTI) and its predecessors has played a pivotal role in shaping science and technology (S&T) policy. There are also many *shingikai* (deliberation councils) in ministries related to S&T. *Shingikai* are a unique part of the Japanese system for consensus building and are stipulated by law. In addition, some independent organizations have provided advice on forming S&T policy voluntarily or in response to requests from the government. Finally, in the aftermath of the 2011 Tōhoku earthquake, there has been a move to create positions for chief science advisors, whose function is to counsel ministers.

Council for Science, Technology and Innovation: The Council for Science and Technology (CST) was established in 1959. It was chaired by the prime minister, and included relevant ministers as well as a number of S&T experts. CST engaged in regular deliberations under the guidance of the Science and Technology Agency. Its major objectives included long-range policy planning and identifying and analyzing important research and development (R&D)

[38] www.sciencemag.org/news/2015/11/european-commission-appoints-top-scientists-fill-policy-advice-gap.

[39] https://ec.europa.eu/research/sam/index.cfm?pg=faq.

programs. CST did not have its own R&D budget to allocate to projects, but influenced other ministries' policies through coordination and evaluation.

In 2001, as part of a broader administrative reform, four "Important Councils" were set up to support the cabinet. The CST was transformed to become one of these, with the new name of the Council for Science and Technology Policy (CSTP). The fact that CSTP meets once a month illustrates the strong commitment that the cabinet has to S&T policy. CSTP's role is to investigate and discuss basic S&T policies, including the Science and Technology Basic Plan that is issued every five years, investigate and discuss budget allocation, and assess Japan's key R&D projects, especially big ones.

CSTP was renamed the Council on Science, Technology and Innovation (CSTI) in 2014 to underscore the importance that Japan places on innovation policy. It also started to distribute its own R&D budget (about $500 million) to a few targeted projects, which are called the Strategic Innovation Program. Between 2001 and 2014, CSTI chartered 14 subcommittees, with more than 60 subordinate ad hoc groups (i.e., working groups, task forces, and project teams). As of 2015, five subcommittees remained active, with 11 subordinate bodies. Over 120 secretariat staff members work for CSTI. As with the U.S. White House Science Office, many are seconded from other ministries and the private sector for limited terms (typically, two years).

Shingikai and private councils: In addition to CSTI, there are many *shingikai* and private councils in Japan's central and local governments regarding the country's S&T policy.[40] A private council forms upon request from the minister or a high-level government official and plays a major role in shaping policy (see, for example, Abe et al., 1994). There are some criticisms of *shingikai,* including an argument that they are under too strong control of the government, that they are used as means of avoiding accusations, or that they conceal bureaucratic responsibility. However, as Japanese society becomes more and more diverse, and as S&T information grows increasingly complex, the role of *shingikai* in consensus building and consolidating experts' knowledge is becoming crucial. Many observers credit *shingikai* with enhancing the fairness and rationality of administrative decision making, and in some cases, even implementing policies. Schwartz (1993) pointed out that consultative councils perform these functions by:

1. Including representatives with opposing interests and helping them to agree on mutually acceptable policies;
2. Serving government as useful listening posts (Japanese ministries typically sound out concerned parties and lay the groundwork for new initiatives);

[40] Legally CSTI is not a *shingikai*, but it shares common objectives and functions with *shingikais* and private councils.

3. Offering councilors' parent organizations a valuable means for learning the views and plans of the government and other interest groups; and
4. Having interest groups share some measure of responsibility for the success of the policies they help create.

Ministries and *shingikai* that are directly relevant to S&T policy include the Cabinet Office, which hosts the Committee on the National Space Policy, the Atomic Energy Commission, and the Committee of the Japan Agency for Medical Research and Development. The Ministry of Education, Culture, Sports, Science and Technology (MEXT) hosts the Council for Science and Technology and the National University Corporation Evaluation Committee. The Ministry of Economy, Trade and Industry (METI) hosts the Industry Structure Council, the Council for Small and Medium Enterprise Policy, and the Industrial Property Council. The Ministry of Health, Labor and Welfare (MHLW) hosts the Health Sciences Council. The Ministry of Internal Affairs and Communications (MIAC) hosts the Information and Communications Council. The Ministry of the Environment (ME) hosts the Central Environment Council, and the Nuclear Regulation Authority. Also, since these ministries have national research laboratories and/or R&D funding agencies as the Incorporated Administrative Agency (IAA), each of them hosts the Evaluation Committee for IAA.

Independent organizations: The Science Council of Japan (SCJ), established in 1949, represents the community of Japanese scientists and engineers. It consists of 210 council members and some 2000 general members elected by academic societies. The Council's activities include conducting exchanges with international academic bodies, interacting with government S&T agencies, making recommendations to the government, lobbying to improve conditions for researchers, and providing safety advice in terms of nuclear energy (NSF, 1997). However, the SCJ does not contribute as much to the process of creating policies as its U.S. counterpart, the National Academies.

The National Institute of Science and Technology Policy (NISTEP) is attached to MEXT, and the Research Institute of Economy, Trade and Industry (RIETI) is attached to METI. NISTEP and RIETI are two major public think tanks that focus on S&T policy. NISTEP gathers data on scientific activities, observes and analyzes S&T trends, and conducts commissioned research (for example, from CSTI) on S&T policies. RIETI conducts policy analysis, mostly from economic viewpoints, and maintains close communication with METI officials. Some private-sector think tanks such as the Mitsubishi Research Institute also conduct research commissioned by government agencies on S&T policies.

Chief science advisors: The Great East Japan Earthquake and the Fukushima nuclear disaster brought the defects of Japan's advisory system into sharp relief. Before the disaster, the Atomic Energy Commission and the Nuclear Regulation Authority did not provide effective recommendations to prepare for a big tsunami and severe nuclear plant accident, despite warnings from some scientists. This largely resulted from councilors having a close relationship with the nuclear power industry. Furthermore, in the midst of the catastrophe, the prime minister appointed several scientists as advisors. However, without enough expertise and experience, they could not actively participate in decision making. All this pointed to the need for strong and independent scientific advisors for the government (Nature, 2011). Based on these experiences, in 2011 the private council to the Minister of State for Science and Technology Policy recommended that a chief science advisor be appointed for every minister.[41] As of 2015, however, only the Minister of Foreign Affairs has appointed a chief science advisor, and it is not likely that this trend will continue.

19.11 SCIENCE AND TECHNOLOGY ADVICE TO GOVERNMENT IN CHINA

Xue Lan, Tsinghua University, Beijing, China

In analyzing S&T policy advice in China, it is important to start with a consideration of the process by which S&T policy is made. In general, national S&T policy in China is made at two levels. At the strategic level the Central Committee of the Communist Party of China (CPC), headed by the Politburo and the General Secretary, is in charge of defining overall vision and strategic directions, while the State Council, headed by the premier, is the highest official body making S&T-related policies. At the administrative level China has a dedicated national government agency, the Ministry of Science and Technology (MOST), which is responsible for designing and implementing various S&T policies.

Many ministerial-level government agencies are also involved in developing and implementing S&T policies. These include the Ministry of Finance, the National Development and Reform Commission (NDRC), the National Natural Science Foundation, and several others. Nominally, MOST is the agency responsible for the design of overall national S&T policies and for coordinating national R&D spending. Until recently, different ministries had their own R&D programs and spending obligations outside the rubric of MOST. The general public perceived these as repetitive and wasteful. The 2015 S&T management reform was aimed at addressing this lack of coordination.

There is also a "leading group" that falls between the two levels and plays a coordinating function among various government agencies and MOST. The group was originally established in the 1980s as the "Leading Group on Science and Technology." Education was added to its mandate in the 1990s. This leading group is usually headed by the premier or a vice premier, with ministers of relevant government ministries as its members (Serger et al., 2015). In 2012, this

[41] See: "The Report of the Study Group on the Course of Action to Pursue Science, Technology and Innovation Policy" (in Japanese), Japanese Cabinet Office, 2011. Available at: www8.cao.go.jp/cstp/stsonota/kenkyukai/houkokusho.pdf.

group was reconstituted as the Leading Group for National S&T Reform and Innovation System Development, with the State Councilor (equivalent to vice premier) Liu Yandong serving as its chairwoman, and representatives from 26 different government agencies and other public institutions as its core members.[42]

Science and technology policy advice in China can also be discussed at two levels, one involving advice to the top leadership, such as to the Politburo, the president, or premier; and the other at the level of advice to administrative bodies, especially MOST. While there is only one formal mechanism at the national level on S&T policy advice,[43] there are many public research institutes and university research centers that are focused on S&T policy issues.

S&T policy advice at the top leadership level: The only formal S&T policy advice mechanism is the Special Committee on Strategic Advice and Comprehensive Evaluation (SCSACE), created in June 2015 at the special invitation of the Leading Group for National S&T Reform and Innovation System Development of the Central Government. The Committee, chaired by the former President of the Chinese Academy of Engineering, Xu Kuangdi, was composed of 14 people, mostly representatives from national S&T establishments such as Chinese Academy of Sciences (CAS), Chinese Academy of Engineering (CAE), Chinese Association of S&T (CAST), former presidents of Tsinghua University and Peking University, and former CEOs of leading high-tech companies.[44] It was part of the institutional innovation designed in the most recent S&T system reform. It would provide strategic advice and reviews to the national S&T strategic planning process, including goals, programs, and implementation. This special committee would also nominate a larger committee to be formally established later.[45]

In addition to SCSACE, there are several ways that the top leadership can receive and request advice on S&T policy issues.

The first way is to get advice from CAS, CAE, CAST, and leading research universities, which are depositories of S&T expertise and representative of the interests of S&T communities. They are perceived as institutions with both expertise and impartiality. They can submit their research reports and recommendations to the top leadership. Their advice is also sought when major national strategies are designed. In recent years, it has become customary that formal review and feedback from CAS, CAE, and other institutions will be sought before major strategic policies related to S&T are published.

Another way is to get advice from individuals in S&T communities. Scientists, particularly senior members in S&T communities, often write and

[42] See www.most.gov.cn/yw/201208/t20120801_95997.htm.

[43] In 2003 at a collective study session of the Politburo of CPC on the issue of S&T development, the author proposed the establishment of a National S&T Advisory Committee, which was later reported in the media.

[44] At the time of this writing the author was the only member of the committee from the S&T research community.

[45] See: www.most.gov.cn/ztzl/shzyczkjjhglgg/dtxw/kjb/201506/t20150617_120097.htm.

send recommendations based on their individual observations to the top leadership, who sometimes will make remarks on those recommendations. These "remarks" will later be translated into actions by relevant government agencies such as MOST. A famous example is the start of China's high-tech program (the "863" program). In March 1986, four senior Chinese scientists, Wang Daheng, Wang Ganchang, Yang Jiachi, and Chen Fangyun (all members of the Chinese Academy of Sciences), wrote to then senior leader Deng Xiaoping, suggesting that China should initiate an R&D program to follow foreign high-tech development. Deng Xiaoping read the suggestions and remarked, "This needs to be decided quickly without delay," which led to the creation of China's 863 high-tech development program.

There are also organized ways for the top leadership to solicit advice on specific topics through consultation meetings and collective study sessions. Consultation meetings, organized by senior leaders such as the president or premier, allow the top leadership to get advice directly from experts on various topics. The process is somewhat similar to the testimony process in other countries. Invited experts will often prepare written statements and be invited to make some initial remarks, followed by discussions between top leaders and the invited experts.

A "collective study session" is a more formal way for the top leadership to learn about the current domestic and international state of the art on a particular topic, the major policy challenges, and the recommendations of the invited speakers, usually two. After Hu Jintao assumed the position of the General Secretary of CPC in 2002, he made such collective study sessions a regular feature of the Politburo activities, which were attended by not only Politburo members, but also ministers in the Party system and the State Council, and major leaders in People's Congress and Political Consultation Conferences (China's parliament system). As of this writing, over 100 sessions have been organized on various topics, including economic, social, political, legal, and historical issues. Several of these sessions were related to S&T issues, in two of which the author was one of the invited speakers. President Xi Jinping has diversified the style of the study sessions by also bringing the Politburo members outside the Zhongnaihai Compound (the central headquarters for the CPC and the State Council).

S&T policy advice at the administrative level: Almost all the ways of providing S&T policy advice to the top leadership level are also used at the administrative level. There are also institutionalized mechanisms that provide more formal policy advice at this level.

Similar to many other Chinese government ministries, there is an in-house research institution affiliated with MOST called the Chinese Academy of S&T Development Strategy (CASTD),[46] which is responsible for serving

[46] http://2015.casted.org.cn/cn.

MOST's policy needs. CASTD has 100 employees, more than two-thirds of whom are professional staff. MOST may also commission studies from outside public research institutions or universities when the required policy expertise lies outside that of CASTD, or the neutrality of the study is a major concern.

Another common approach for MOST, when seeking S&T policy advice in a particular domain or for a specific activity, is to establish a formal advisory body. For example, beginning in 2015 MOST was in charge of drafting the thirteenth Five Year Plan for Science, Technology, and Innovation. It established a formal advisory committee inviting CEOs of major companies, university leaders, scholars, and retired senior officials from the relevant agencies. The function of such an advisory body is to provide external ideas and suggestions on the specific issues at stake. Such bodies can also be created for major S&T programs, such as Mega-projects. The most common way these bodies work is for members to meet together to review major policy documents in preparation. Sometimes, they also play the role of an external review body.

19.12 SCIENCE AND TECHNOLOGY ADVICE TO GOVERNMENT IN INDIA

Anshu Bharadwaj and V.S. Arunachalam of the Center for Science Technology and Policy, Bangalore, India

Like the United States, the federal government in India also has three branches: Legislature, Executive, and Judiciary. The main institutions responsible for providing science advice to the Executive are: Department of Science and Technology (DST), Department of Scientific and Industrial Research (DSIR), and the Department of Biotechnology (DBT). These three departments support a large number of research laboratories all across the country. These cover areas such as: aeronautics, chemicals, drug research, electronics, mining and fuel research, etc. The DBT has emerged as an important department for supporting research programs in biology, food and nutrition, bioinformatics, etc.

The prime minister almost always heads the two important Departments of Atomic Energy and Department of Space. This is because of the strategic importance of these sectors. The prime minister also heads the Ministry of Planning; in particular he is the Chairman of the NITI Aayog (erstwhile Planning Commission), which functions like the nation's policy think tank. The NITI Aayog also networks with research organizations to leverage their expertise for policy advice to the prime minister.

In addition, the Defense Research and Development Organization (DRDO) has a large network of research laboratories. The Director of DRDO is also the Scientific Advisor to the Defense Minister and provides crucial advice on all defense-related matters. The DRDO also generates a large number of spin-off technologies, which are of use for civilian applications.

The Office of Principal Scientific Adviser (PSA) to Government was created in 1999 to provide crucial science advice to the government and the cabinet. The PSA also chairs the Scientific Advisory Committee to the cabinet, which is the apex body to render advice on S&T policies. The Committee has a wide representation of people from scientists, technologists, universities, and industries. The Committee's main tasks include: preparing for a knowledge-based economy, promoting medical- and agricultural-oriented S&T, technological cooperation with foreign countries, and use of scientific tools for disaster management.

The above-mentioned institutions are formal structures for providing science advice to the government. In addition, several line ministries have their own mechanisms for sector specific inputs. For instance, Ministries of Agriculture, Telecommunications, and Petroleum and Natural Gas have dedicated research laboratories, advisory committees, and institutions, which provide science advice relevant to the ministry. For instance, the Indian Council of Agriculture Research (ICAR) is the apex body for coordinating and guiding research in agriculture, including fisheries, horticulture, and animal sciences. In recent times, the ministries have increased their reliance on think tanks and academic institutions to provide such policy advice.

At the state level, these arrangements are not so well structured. The process for factoring science-based inputs into policy is rather loosely defined in most states. In most cases, the states rely on expert committees set up from time to time to examine specific issues. The states also rely on the federal government for overall guidance on science policy.

In addition, there are several interesting instances in which the judiciary has taken important executive decisions involving the use of science-based inputs. This is especially true in the case of environmental issues. For instance, the Supreme Court directed the Delhi government to deploy Compressed Natural Gas (CNG) instead of diesel in cabs and autos. Before doing this the Supreme Court had set up a committee consisting of environmental experts, which advised the court on this matter. Similarly, the Supreme Court is monitoring the cleaning of the river Ganges.

In recent years, research institutions and think tanks have been playing an increasingly important role in national policy. This is perhaps because governments are faced with an increasingly aspirational electorate and have ambitious plans and targets for development. Therefore, central and state governments are actively engaging with think tanks to solicit high-quality advice in the design and implementation of government policies and flagship programs. This is especially true in subjects where science and technology are key enablers such as energy, climate mitigation and adaptation, water, transport, urban infrastructure, and also in social sectors such as education and health. For instance, NITI Aayog (the Government of India's policy think tank called the National Institution for Transforming India) has worked with several non-governmental think tanks to develop a national energy model, which is used for long-term energy projections. NITI Aayog has also worked with non-governmental think tanks to develop a roadmap for low-carbon inclusive growth. The government has also actively engaged with think tanks in developing policies for electric vehicles and in energy storage. The government makes an effort to reach out to expertise resident in the research institutions and think tanks for high-quality policy advice.

The government of Prime Minister Narendra Modi has also relied significantly on the power of technology to improve service delivery to citizens and reduce corruption and transaction costs. The objective is to use mobile telephony to facilitate citizens' interface with government machinery by delivering government services such as pensions, insurance, subsidies for electricity and cooking gas, etc. Since this is an ambitious program, the government is relying on inputs and advice from a large number of players, including telecom operators, industry, and civil society.

REFERENCES

Abe, H., M. Shindo, and S. Kawato (1994). "Chapter 5: Advisory Councils," in *The Government and Politics of Japan*, University of Tokyo Press, 244pp.

Blair, P.D. (2013). *Congress's Own Think Tank: Learning from the Legacy of the Office of Technology Assessment (1972–1995)*, Palgrave Macmillan, 128pp.

Boggs, D.J. (1988). "Science and Technology Advice in the Judiciary," *Technology in Society*, *10*, pp. 317–321.

Breyer, S. (2000). "Science in the Courtroom," *Issues in Science and Technology*, *16*(4).

Bronk, D.W. (1974). "Science Advice in the White House," *Science*, *186*, pp. 116–121.

Carnegie Commission (1993). "Science and Technology in Judicial Decision-Making," a report of the Carnegie Commission on Science, Technology, and Government, 92pp.

Carter, A.B. (1984). *Directed Energy Missile Defense in Space*, Background Paper, U.S. Congressional Office of Technology Assessment, 97pp.

DSB (2012). *Charter of the Defense Science Board*. Available at: www.acq.osd.mil/dsb/charter.htm.

Dupree, A.H. (1986). *Science in the Federal Government: A History of Politics and Activities*, Johns Hopkins University Press, 460pp.

Finkbeiner, A. (2002). "DARPA and Jason Divorce in Spat over Membership," *Science*, *295*, p. 2340.

(2006). *The Jasons: The Secret History of Science's Postwar Elite*, Viking Press, 336pp.

GAO (2002). *Technology Assessment: Using Biometrics for Border Security*, GAO-03-174, Government Accountability Office, 242pp.

(2011). *Technology Assessment: Climate Engineering – Technical Status, Future Directions, and Potential Responses*, GAO-11-71, Government Accountability Office, 135pp.

Golden, W.T. (ed.) (1980). *Science Advice to the President*, Pergamon Press, 256pp.

(ed.) (1988). *Science and Technology Advice to the President, Congress, and Judiciary*, Transaction Publishers, 523pp.

Guzzetti, L. (1995). *A Brief History of European Union Research Policy*, Office for Official Publications of the European Communities, 238pp.

Jasanoff, S. (1990). *The Fifth Branch: Science Advisers as Policy Makers*, Harvard University Press, 302pp.

Judt, T. (2005). *Postwar: A History of Europe since 1945*, Penguin Press, 878pp.

Kantrowitz, A. (1975). "Controlling Technology Democratically," *American Scientist*, *63* (Sep.–Oct.), pp. 505–509.

(1995). "The Separation of Facts and Values," *Risk*, *6*, pp. 105–110.

Knezo, G.J. (2005). "Technology Assessment in Congress: History and Legislative Options," CRS report for Congress, RS21586, May 20. Available at: http://fas.org/sgp/crs/misc/RS21586.pdf.

Kingdon, J.W. (1973). *Congressmen's Voting Decisions*, Harper & Row, 313pp.

Layton, C., P. Uri, and W. Dowling (1968). *L'Europe et les Investissements Américains*, Gallimard, 255pp.

Margolis, R.M. and D.H. Guston (2003). "Chapter 3: The Origins, Accomplishments, and Demise of the Office of Technology Assessment," in M.G. Morgan and J.M. Peha (eds.), *Science and Technology Advice for Congress*, Resources for the Future Press, 236pp.

Mauter, W.R. (1998). "Churchill and the Unification of Europe," *The Historian*, *61*(1), pp. 67–84.

Mayer, J. (2016). *Dark Money: The Hidden History of the Billionaires behind the Rise of the Radical Right*, Doubleday, 449pp.

Ministère de l'Enseignement Supérieur et de la Recherché (2010). *Les Mémoires de la Recherche: Etat des versements*, Mission des archives, 302pp.

Morgan, M.G. (1975). *Energy and Man: Technical and Social Aspects of Energy*, IEEE Press, 536pp.

(1997). "Why Congress Should Preserve the NRC's Independent Technical Advice," *IEEE Spectrum*, *34*(12), pp. 59–60.

Morgan, M.G. and J.M. Peha (2003). *Science and Technology Advice for Congress*, Resources for the Future Press, 236pp.

Nature (2011). "Critical Mass," editorial, *Nature*, *480*, p. 291.

NRC (2008). *State Science and Technology Policy Advice: Issues, Opportunities and Challenges*, National Academy Press, 100pp.

NSF (1997). "Japanese Government Organization for Science and Technology," U.S. National Science Foundation Report 97-11. Available at: www.nsf.gov/od/oise/tokyo/reports/trm/rm97-11.html.

OPECST (2015). "The Parliamentary Office for Scientific and Technological Assessment: A Presentation," 4pp. Available at: www2.assemblee-nationale.fr/content/download/31593/288206/file/plaquette_opecst_anglais.pdf.

OTA (1985a). *Ballistic Missile Defense Technologies*, U.S. Congressional Office of Technology Assessment, 325pp.

(1985b). *Anti-Satellite Weapons, Counter Measures and Arms Control*, U.S. Congressional Office of Technology Assessment, 146pp.

Pew (2007). "Investing in Innovation," a report of the Pew Center on the States, 75pp.

Rosenberg, M. (1988). "Improving the Courts' Ability to Absorb Scientific Information," in W.T. Golden (ed.), *Science and Technology Advice to the President, Congress, and Judiciary*, Pergamon, pp. 480–483.

Schneier, E.V. and B. Gross (1993). *Legislative Strategy: Shaping Public Policy*, St. Martins Press, 289pp.

Schwartz, F. (1993). "Chapter 9: Of Fairy Cloaks and Familiar Talks: The Politics of Consultation," in G.D. Allison and Y. Sone (eds.), *Political Dynamics in Contemporary Japan*, Cornell University Press, 311pp.

Serger, S., E. Wise, and E. Arnold (2015). *National Research and Innovation Councils as an Instrument of Innovation Governance*, Swedish Governmental Agency for Innovation Systems, VINNOVA Analysis VA, 72pp.

Servan-Schreiber, J.-J. (1967). *Le Défi Americain*, Denoël, 343pp.

Shepherd, G.B. (1996). "Fierce Compromise: The Administrative Procedures Act Emerges from New Deal Politics," *Northwestern University Law Review*, *90*(4), pp. 1557–1683.

Smith, B.L.R. (1992). *The Advisers: Scientists in the Policy Process*, Brookings, 238pp.

Vig, N.J. (2003). "Chapter 5: The European Experience," in M.G. Morgan and J. Peha (eds.), *Science and Technology Advice to Congress*, RFF Press, pp. 90–98.

Vig, N.J. and H. Paschen (eds.) (2000). *Parliaments and Technology: The Development of Technology Assessment in Europe*, State University of New York Press, 399pp.

Weinberg, A. (1972). "Science and Trans-Science," *Minerva*, *10*(April), pp. 209–222.

Appendix 1

A Few Key Ideas from the History and Philosophy of Science

Some readers may wonder why a book on the theory and methods of policy analysis includes an appendix that summarizes a number of key ideas from the literature in the history and philosophy of science. Because these ideas are part of the core knowledge of most people working in science, technology, and public policy, a basic familiarity is important for those planning to join the field. References to concepts such as "paradigms" and "gestalts" are common, and practitioners who do not understand where the concepts originated are at a disadvantage. Especially important is the ability to understand the concept of a "falsifiable proposition" and be able to differentiate between propositions that are, and are not, falsifiable.

In grade school or junior high school science classes, many of us encountered a description of the scientific method that looked something like the left-hand side of Figure A1.1. Much of the discourse in the philosophy of science has revolved around questions such as where and how do hypotheses originate, how are observations made and interpreted, when and how are general models of how the world works (or "gestalts") updated, and what differentiates "science" from other forms of thinking and reasoning?

The somewhat more sophisticated diagram to the right in Figure A1.1 captures a number of the topics that are discussed in the sections that follow.

A1.1 Francis Bacon and the Empirical or Scientific Method

While it had precursors in the Greek, Roman, and Arabic worlds, modern empirical science (that is, science based on observation and measurement) had its origins with people such as Nicolas Copernicus (1473–1543), who made the case for a heliocentric planetary system; Tycho Brahe (1546–1501), who built an amazing naked eye observatory on the island of Hven off the coast of Denmark and made extensive measurements of the location and motions of

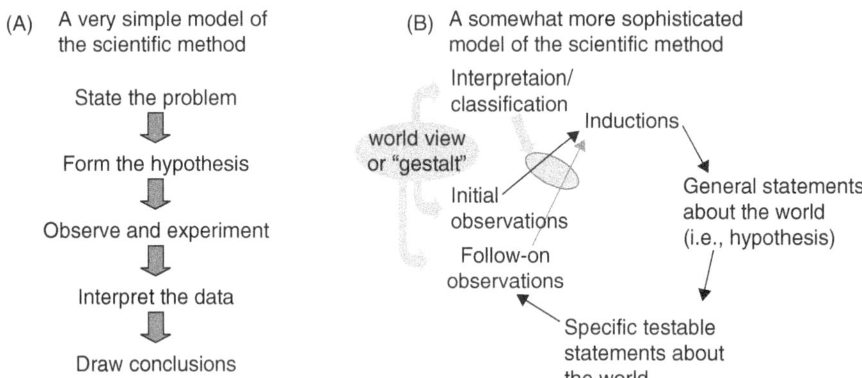

FIGURE A1.1. **A** is the sort of description of the scientific process that many of us encountered when we first took science courses in junior high school. **B** begins to add some of the complications that are discussed in this appendix.

stars and planets;[1] Johannes Kepler (1571–1630), who used Brahe's planetary data to develop mathematical laws that describe planetary motion; and Galileo Galilei (1564–1642), whose early telescopes helped to cement a new world view of Earth's place in the heavens.

Francis Bacon (1561–1626) is generally credited as among the first to formally articulate a basis for empirical science. Bacon argued that before one could engage in serious scientific study, it was essential to purge one's thinking of four erroneous thought processes that he called "idols." He labeled these:

1. Idols of the Tribe (*Idola tribus*): a tendency to equate perception with reality and to see more order and connection in the world than truly exists.
2. Idols of the Cave (*Idola specus*): a tendency to judge on the basis of one's own education, experience, taste, etc.
3. Idols of the Marketplace (*Idola fori*): a recognition that words are not precise and can lead to confusion in common usage.
4. Idols of the Theatre (*Idola theatri*): impacts from academic dogma and earlier philosophies and laws (which he said were the inventions of imagination without intellectual value).

Bacon argued that a method based on inductive logic could lead to truth. He argued that one should:

- list all cases in which a known phenomenon occurs;
- list all cases in which it does not occur;
- list those in which it occurs to different degrees;

and then,

[1] For an excellent account, see Christianson (2000), *On Tycho's Island*.

- examine the three lists and use them to determine the element(s) present that produce the phenomena.

While Bacon supported experimentation, he believed such experimentation should be guided by prior hypothesis. However, he never really examined the nature of hypothesis. Bacon's ideas about empirical methods were subsequently elaborated by Thomas Browne (1605–1682) and then, two hundred years later, by John Stuart Mill (1806–1873).

A1.2 Karl Popper: "Falsifiability," and Deduction versus Induction

We move next to Vienna in the first part of the last century. Karl Popper (1902–1994) was troubled by several theoretical frameworks that commanded much attention in the intellectual life of the city at that time.[2] He writes, "among the theories that interested me Einstein's theory of relativity was no doubt by far the most important. Three others were Marx's theory of history, Freud's psycho-analysis, and Adler's so-called 'individual psychology' " (Popper, 1980). He notes that:

> We all – the small circle of students to which I belonged – were thrilled with the results of Eddington's eclipse observations [see Figure A1.2] which in 1919 brought the first important confirmation of Einstein's theory of gravitation ...
>
> The three other theories ... were also widely discussed among students at the time ...
>
> It was during the summer of 1919 that I began to feel more and more dissatisfied with these three theories ... and I began to feel dubious about their claims to scientific status ... I felt these other theories, though passing as science, had more in common with primitive myths than with science; that they resembled astrology more than astronomy.

Popper concluded that focusing on "verifying" or "confirming" theories was a misguided approach. Especially if the theory was not very precisely and completely stated, it was simply too easy to interpret evidence as providing support. He quotes a telling interaction he had with Adler:

> Once in 1919 I reported to him a case which to me did not seem particularly Adlerian, but which he found no difficulty analyzing in terms of his theory of inferiority feelings, although he had not seen the child. Slightly shocked, I asked him how he could be so sure. "Because of my thousandfold experience," he replied; where upon I could not help saying "And with this new case, I suppose your experience has become thousand-and-one-fold."

Popper argued that "A theory which is not refutable by any conceivable event is non-scientific." In his view, the line of demarcation between science and non-science arises from the fact that scientific theories are falsifiable – that is, they make a claim about the world that can be subjected to empirical test.

While his focus on the idea of falsifiability was an important contribution, Popper ended up taking the concept too far. Experiments and observations often yield results that are at odds with underlying theory. Scientist do not

[2] While not a part of the "Vienna Circle," the group of philosophers who gathered around Moritz Schlick to explore new philosophical ideas in logical positivisim, Popper had a number of interactions with them and was clearly influenced by their work.

READING A1.1

Karl Popper, "Science: Conjectures and Refutations," in E.D. Klemke, R. Hollinger, and D.W. Rudge (eds.), *Introductory Readings in the Philosophy of Science*, Prometheus Books, pp. 19–24, 1980.

For some perspective on this reading, also read or skim:

Deborah A. Redman, *Economics and the Philosophy of Science*, Oxford University Press, pp. 27–35, 1991.

This reading talks about "positivists." A positivist believes that what cannot be measured or observed has no place in a physical theory.

EXERCISE A1.1

Write three statements about the world that are falsifiable. Describe the experiment that would allow you to determine if the statement is false. Now write three statements about the world that are *not* falsifiable. Why is it not possible to describe an experiment that would allow you to determine if the statement is false?

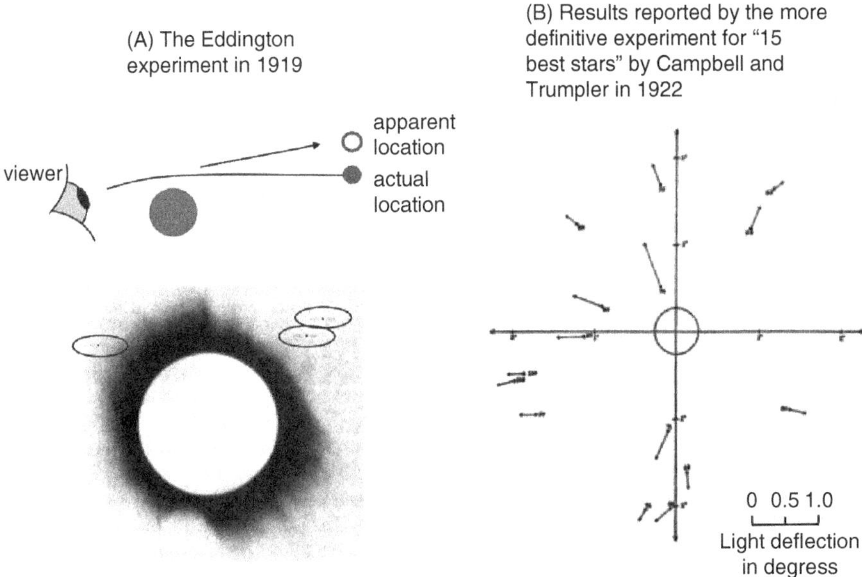

FIGURE A1.2. **A** shows results from Eddington's observation of the apparent displacement of stars as a result of the influence of the gravitational field on their passing light measured during a total eclipse on May 29, 1919 observed on the island of Principe off the west coast of Africa. Figure from Dyson et al. (1920). **B** shows results from a more definitive observation conducted by Campbell and Trumpler (1928) in Western Australia on September 21, 1922. Results are the mean of measurements made with two separate instruments for the best 15 measured stars.

throw out a promising theory just because results from a single experiment do not seem to fit. Rather, they work to try to understand why they are not getting the results they anticipated. The more firmly established the underlying theory, the more likely they are to persist and ultimately find an explanation for the observation. Okasha (2002) offers a classic astronomical example:

> Newton's gravitational theory ... made predictions about the paths planets should follow as they orbit the sun. For the most part these predictions were borne out by observation. However, the observed orbit of Uranus consistently differed from what Newton's theory predicted. This puzzle was solved in 1846 by two scientists, Adams in England and Leverrier in France, working independently. They suggested that there was another planet, as yet undiscovered, exerting an additional gravitational force on Uranus. Adams and Leverrier were able to calculate the mass and position that this planet would have to have ... shortly afterwards the planet Neptune was discovered almost exactly where Adams and Leverrier had predicted.

Adams and Leverrier did not view the inconsistent results as a falsification of Newtonian mechanics. Rather, they used *induction* to infer that there must be another planet.

Popper spent much of his career arguing that science did not use induction, only deduction. However, case after case in the history of actual discoveries has shown this view to be incorrect. For those working in policy analysis, to which a Bayesian interpretation of probability is second nature, Popper's absolutist position seems silly. While it is nice when we can make definitive statements from which a conclusion can be reached through deduction, it is far more common that one can only make statements based on "inference to the best explanation," an idea that harks back to Bacon's arguments about constructing three lists.

A1.3 Hypothesis

A hypothesis is a statement about what may be. It offers a proposed explanation of a phenomenon or about how the world or some system of interest works.

Where and how do scientists develop hypotheses that warrant testing? On the one hand, as Popper argued, a good hypothesis should advance an idea that, when tested, presents a significant risk in the prediction it makes – as in the case of the Einstein/Eddington example. On the other hand, scientists do not want to waste their time testing implausible hypotheses. Accordingly, most scientific hypotheses are developed to provide explanations about observations that are not adequately or fully explained by existing theory.

Quine and Ullian (1980) have provided a thoughtful discussion of five virtues of a good hypothesis. They are: conservatism; modesty; simplicity; generality; and refutability.

A number of the issues raised by Popper, Quine, and Ullian are alive and well in physics today on topics such as string theory (see, for example, Cartwright and Frigg, 2007).

READING A1.2

W.V. Quine and J.S. Ullian, "Hypothesis," in E.D. Klemke, R. Hollinger, and D.W. Rudge (eds.), *Introductory Readings in the Philosophy of Science*, Prometheus Books, pp. 196–206, 1980.

A1.4 Thomas Kuhn: Paradigms and Scientific Revolutions

How does science change its understanding and view of the world over time? In his book *The Structure of Scientific Revolutions*, Thomas Kuhn (1922–1996) argued that change does not come in a gradual, incremental way but rather through a sudden shift in world view or "paradigm." Kuhn (1962) argued that such "scientific revolutions are inaugurated by a growing sense ... that an existing paradigm has ceased to function adequately in the exploration of an aspect of nature to which that paradigm itself had previously led the way."

Examples of such paradigm shifts include the shift from a geocentric to a heliocentric model of the universe; from the phlogiston model of combustion to Lavoisier's oxygen-based explanation of combustion; from a creationist to Darwin's evolutionary perspective on the origin of species; the switch from classical Newtonian physics to modern relativistic and quantum physics; and the transition from cellular biology to molecular biology.

Because Kuhn had earned a Ph.D. in physics (he participated in radar research during World War II), many of the examples he drew upon were from natural science. He argued that these revolutions or changes in paradigm were not incremental but entailed a sudden shift in how the relevant field viewed the world, and that they occur when there is wide adoption among peers. Kuhn (1962) writes, "Like the choice between competing political institutions, that between competing paradigms proves to be a choice between incompatible modes of community life." He argues that "As in political revolutions, so in paradigm choice – there is no standard higher than the assent of the relevant community."

Kuhn describes the process of doing science as involving periods of "normal science," during which investigators work to refine and fill in details within an existing paradigm, punctuated by occasional revolutions, in which a field undergoes a fundamental "paradigm shift." After the new paradigm is accepted, he argues that scientists cannot go back to the previous mode of thinking about the world. During the period of "normal science," evidence accumulates that the present paradigm is not able to adequately explain all aspects of the world, but for the most part, that evidence is ignored until a shift occurs.[3]

[3] Physicist Max Planck offered a rather simpler model when he said "Science progresses one funeral at a time." He elaborated that "A new scientific truth does not triumph by convincing its opponents and making them see the light, but rather because its opponents eventually die, and a new generation grows up that is familiar with it." See: www.goodreads.com/author/quotes/107032.Max_Planck.

BOX A1.1 DEFINITIONS FROM THE UNABRIDGED AMERICAN COLLEGE DICTIONARY

induction: any form of reasoning in which the conclusion, though supported by the premises, does not follow from them necessarily; the process of estimating the validity of observations of part of a class of facts as evidence for a proposition about the whole class.

deduction: a process of reasoning in which a conclusion follows necessarily from the premises presented, so that the conclusion cannot be false if the premises are true; a conclusion reached by this process.

gestalt: a unified whole; a configuration, pattern or organized field having specific properties that cannot be derived from the summation of its component parts.

schema: (in Kantian epistemology) a concept, similar to a universal but limited to a phenomenal knowledge, by which an object of knowledge or an idea of pure reason may be apprehended.

I was completing my Ph.D. in applied physics when I first read Kuhn and remember very distinctly thinking, "no, that is not the way science works today ... today the best scientists are forever on the lookout for evidence that does not conform to existing theory because they know that is how basic contributions get made." Nevertheless, just as Popper overdid his arguments about falsification while at the same time contributing an important insight, so, too, Kuhn's arguments about paradigms provide some important insights.

READINGS A1.3

T.S. Kuhn, *The Structure of Scientific Revolutions*, University of Chicago Press, 1962.

Pages 91–109 lay out his basic argument about science undergoing occasional paradigm shifts. You may choose to skim the details and focus on his central idea. Pages 110–117 discuss "gestalts" or world views. This is worth more careful reading. Finally, pp. 143–147 discuss Kuhn's view of "normal science" versus paradigm-testing science and should be read with care.

Again, for some perspective on this reading, also read or skim:
Deborah A. Redman, *Economics and the Philosophy of Science*, Oxford University Press, pp. 16–22, 1991.

A key idea in Kuhn is that the paradigm or mental model one adopts of how the world works shapes what one actually observes when looking at the world. In a paper titled "Why a Diagram Is (Sometimes) Worth Ten Thousand Words," Larkin and Simon (1987) argue that:

human abilities to recognize information are highly sensitive to the exact form (representation) in which the information is presented to the sense (or to memory). For example, consider a set of points represented either in a table or x and y coordinates or as geometric points on a graph. Visual entities such as smooth curves, maxima and discontinuities are readily recognized in the latter representation, but not in the former.

Of course, while readers of this book are experienced in looking at and interpreting such plots, many people are not. Larkin and Simon argue that for a graphical representation to be valuable, the viewer must already possess a mental model of what is being represented. They write:

Consider, for example a physical chess board which we would represent as a set of squares, each with an (x,y) location and connections to adjacent squares. Any person can "see" on what squares the pieces lie and locate adjacent or nearby squares ... But a chess expert may "see" things on the board not evident to the non-expert observer. For example, an important feature of a chess position is an open file: a sequence of squares that are vacant running from the player's side of the board to the opponent's side ... [However, for the non-expert] only the individual unoccupied squares may be visible. (Larkin and Simon, 1987)

Some years ago, I did work related to the possible biological effects of AC electric and magnetic fields. When I first started going to conference talks on the cellular effects of such fields, I found the images of cells that investigators showed to be completely incomprehensible. It was only after I spent a couple of months reading intensively in modern biology that I began to recognize the different organelles that were being displayed in those slides.

Grinnell (1987) offers a very nice discussion of this same issue. He writes, "Gestalts are unified wholes with the characteristic that the arrangement of component features provides information not apparent in the features alone" (Figure A1.3). He continues, "observing a particular type of object presupposes that the concept of the object is already in the observer's mind; in addition the presence of the concept prevents the observer from seeing things in other ways ... *seeing things one way means not seeing them another way*." This is, of course, the essence of Kuhn's argument about paradigms.

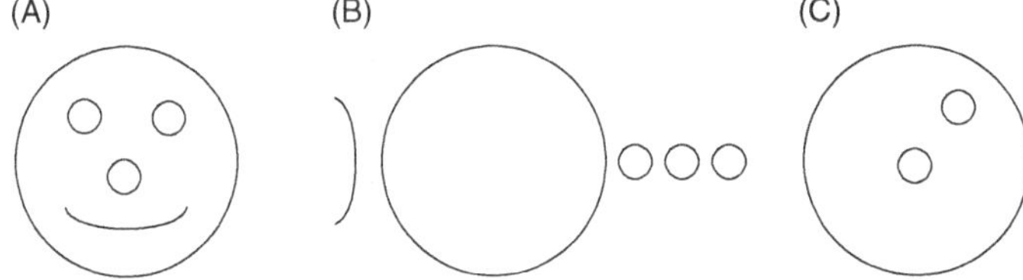

FIGURE A1.3. Illustration, after Grinnell (1987), showing that a gestalt depends on the arrangement of components, not just the features alone. We see **A** as clearly a face; **B** has the same features, but we do not see anything more than the components. A biologist might see **C** as a simple cell with a nucleus and a second organelle such as a mitochondria.

FIGURE A1.4. Two classic examples of switching perspectives. The image on the left can be seen either as a drinking goblet or as two faces. The image on the right can be seen either as a duck or as a rabbit. Both images are from Wikipedia.

The classic vase/face or rabbit/duck examples from the psychology of perception is often used to illustrate this point (see Figure A1.4). The analogy is only partly adequate because we can switch back and forth between the two perceptions, while Kuhn argues the scientist cannot switch back after a change in paradigm.

SUGGESTIONS FOR ADDITIONAL READING

For a very readable and compact summary of many of the key ideas in the philosophy of science, see:

- Samie Okasha, *Philosophy of Science: A Very Short Introduction*, Oxford University Press, 144pp., 2002.

Drawing most of his examples from biology, a second very nice treatment is provided by:

- Frederick Grinnell, *The Scientific Attitude*, Westview Press, 141pp., 1987, and 2nd ed., Guilford Press, 180pp., 1992.

Grinnell explains that for graduate students the book provides "an introduction to the collective thought process and politics of science that should make it easier to survive in graduate school and beyond; and for professionals it is an invitation to reflect on the conduct and direction of modern science." Early chapters provide nice discussions of the idea of "gestalts"; the assertion that "an observer's previous knowledge and experience determine what aspects of a scene will be interesting to the observer"; a discussion of the importance of intersubjectivity; and a much richer concept of hypothesis and hypothesis testing than that advanced by Popper.

The back half of this book (chapters 4–7) addresses some more macro issues about graduate education (the process of acculturating new scientists into the field); issues in career development including the role of publication and journals; the academic system, etc.

Finally, on the issue of what is and is not science, readers may enjoy:

- Andrew Fraknoi, "Your Astrology Defense Kit," *Sky and Telescope*, pp. 146–150, August 1989.

REFERENCES

Campbell, W.W. and R.J. Trumpler (1928). "Observations Made with a Pair of Five-Foot Cameras on the Light-Deflections in the Sun's Gravitational Field at the Total Eclipse of September 21, 1922," *Lick Observatory Bulletin*, *397*, pp. 130–160.

Cartwright, N. and R. Frigg (2007). "String Theory under Scrutiny," *Physics World*, pp. 14–15.

Christianson, J.R. (2000). *On Tycho's Island: Tycho Brahe and His Assistants, 1570–1601*, Cambridge University Press, 451pp.

Dyson, F.W., A.S. Eddington, and C. Davidson (1920). "A Determination of the Deflection of Light by the Sun's Gravitational Field, from Observations Made at the Total Eclipse of May 29, 1919," *Philosophical Transactions of the Royal Society A*, *1920*, pp. 291–333.

Fraknoi, A. (1989). "Your Astrology Defense Kit," *Sky and Telescope*, August, pp. 146–150.

Grinnell, F. (1987). *The Scientific Attitude*, Westview Press, 141pp.; 2nd ed. (1992) Guilford Press, 180pp.

Kuhn, T.S. (1962). *The Structure of Scientific Revolutions*, University of Chicago Press, 172pp.

Larkin, J.H. and H.A. Simon (1987). "Why a Diagram Is (Sometimes) Worth Ten Thousand Words," *Cognitive Science*, *11*(1), pp. 65–100.

Okasha, S. (2002). *Philosophy of Science: A Very Short Introduction*, Oxford University Press, 144pp.

Popper, K. (1980). "Science: Conjectures and Refutations," in E.D. Klemke, R. Hollinger, and D.W. Rudge (eds.), *Introductory Readings in the Philosophy of Science*, Prometheus Books, pp. 19–24.

Quine, W.V. and J.S. Ullian (1980). "Hypothesis," in E.D. Klemke, R. Hollinger, and D.W. Rudge (eds.), *Introductory Readings in the Philosophy of Science*, Prometheus Books, pp. 196–206.

Redman, D.A. (1991). *Economics and the Philosophy of Science*, Oxford University Press, pp. 27–35.

Appendix 2

Some Readings in Technology and Innovation

An important literature, not covered in this book, addresses issues in technology, innovation, and economic development. In order to partly remedy this omission, my colleagues Daniel Armanios, Erica Fuchs, and Francisco Veloso, each of whom approaches these issues from a somewhat different perspective, have kindly suggested a number of key references (which I have organized alphabetically in categories) to help readers get started in exploring these topics.

National Innovation Systems

Acemoglu, D. and J.A. Robinson (2012). *Why Nations Fail*, Crown Publishers, 529pp.

Evans, P.B. (1995). *Embedded Autonomy: States and Industrial Transformation*, Princeton University Press, 323pp.

Nelson, R. (1993). *National Innovation Systems: A Comparative Analysis*, Oxford University Press, 541pp.

Steil, B., D.G. Victor, and R.R. Nelson (2002). *Technological Innovation and Economic Performance*, Princeton University Press, 476pp.

Innovation Policy

Godin, B. (2004). *Measurement and Statistics on Science and Technology: 1920 to the Present*, Routledge, 360pp.

Graham, O.L. (1994). *Losing Time: The Industrial Policy Debate*, Harvard University Press, 370pp.

Hart, D.M. (1998). *Forged Consensus: Science, Technology, and Economic Policy in the United States, 1921–1953*, Princeton University Press, 297pp.

Lane, J., K. Fealing, H.J. Marburger, III, and S.S. Shipp (eds.) (2011). *Science of Science Policy: A Handbook*, Stanford University Press, 386pp.

Lerner, J. (2012). *Boulevard of Broken Dreams: Why Public Efforts to Boost Entrepreneurship and Venture Capital Have Failed – And What to Do about It*, Princeton University Press, 240pp.

National Research Council (1999). *Funding a Revolution: Government Support for Computing Research*, report of the Committee on Innovations in Computing, Communications, and Lessons from History, U.S. National Academies Press, 273pp.

Pielke, R.A. (2007). *The Honest Broker: Making Sense of Science in Policy and Politics*, Cambridge University Press, 188pp.

Theory on Technology Change

Lerner, J. and S. Stern (eds.) (2012). *The Rate and Direction of Innovative Activity Revisited*, National Bureau of Economic Research Conference Report, University of Chicago Press, 632pp.

Lin, J.Y. (2012). *New Structural Economics: A Framework for Rethinking Development*, World Bank, 3710pp.

NBER (1962). *The Rate and Direction of Inventive Activity: Economic and Social Factors*, a Conference of the Universities–National Bureau Committee for Economic Research and the Committee on Economic Growth of the Social Science Research Council, Princeton University Press, 635pp.

Padgett, J.F. and W.W. Powell (2012). *The Emergence of Organizations and Markets*, Princeton University Press, 583pp.

Shapiro, C. and H. Varian (2013). *Information Rules: A Strategic Guide to the Network Economy*, Harvard Business Press, 352pp.

A Few Other Classics

Fagerberg, J., D. Mowery, and R. Nelson (eds.) (2005). *The Oxford Handbook of Innovation*, Oxford University Press, 680pp.

Merton, R.K. (1968). "The Matthew Effect in Science," *Science*, *159*(3810), pp. 56–63.

(1973). *The Sociology of Science: Theoretical and Empirical Investigations*, University of Chicago Press, 605pp.

Nelson, R.R. and S.G. Winter (1982). *An Evolutionary Theory of Economic Change*, Belknap Press of Harvard University Press, 454pp.

Schumpeter, J.A. (1934). *The Theory of Economic Development: An Inquiry into Profits, Capital, Credit, Interest, and the Business Cycle*, Harvard University Press, 255pp.

Solow, R. (1957). "Technical Change and the Aggregate Production Function," *The Review of Economics and Statistics*, *39*(3), pp. 312–320.

Appendix 3

Some Readings in Science and Technology Studies

The field of Science and Technology Studies concerns itself with issues of how society shapes and is shaped by science and technology. One starting place for readers with technical backgrounds is:

- R. Pool, *Beyond Engineering: How Society Shapes Technology*, Oxford University Press, 1997, 358pp.

Readers with science and engineering backgrounds who are unfamiliar with the idea of "social construction" will find Pool's description on pp. 12–15 a very congenial introduction. Readers who have not thought about the issue of "lock in" will find the discussion of the QWERTY typewriter keyboard and other examples in chapter 5 especially interesting. Pool's chapter 8, "Managing the Faustian Bargain," is one of the best discussions available of the work by Todd LaPorte and his colleagues on high-reliability organizations (see Section 15.6 of this book).

Moving a bit more deeply into the STS literature, Langdon Winner has produced two classic books, the second of which is:

- L. Winner, *The Whale and the Reactor*, University of Chicago Press, 1986, 200pp.

If you are only going to read one chapter of this book, my advice would be to read chapter 2, "Do Artifacts Have Politics?." This chapter includes accounts of how Robert Moses built the overpasses too low for buses on a parkway leading to the beaches on Long Island so that poorer and minority city residents could not easily make it to the beaches,[1] and how Cyrus McCormick II used pneumatic molding machines to break the power of skilled mechanics.

[1] Winner recently assured me that this account is basically correct. However, for a different perspective, see B. Joerges (1999). "Do Politics Have Artefacts?" *Social Studies of Science*, *29*(3), pp. 411–431.

Next are two papers by Sheila Jasanoff, the first for people not familiar with the field, the second a more theoretical treatment of much of the modern literature:

- S. Jasanoff, "What Judges Should Know about the Sociology of Science," *Judicature*, 77(2), 1993, pp. 77–82.
- S. Jasanoff, "Chapter 2: Ordering Knowledge, Ordering Society," in S. Jasanoff (ed.), *States of Knowledge: The Co-Production of Science and Social Order*, Routledge, 2004, pp. 13–45.

Finally, here are two handbooks that provide a much wider and deeper introduction and pointers into the field:

- S. Jasanoff, G.E. Markle, J.C. Peterson, and T. Pinch (eds.), *Handbook of Science and Technology Studies, Sage Publications*, 2001, 832pp.
- E.J. Hackett, O. Amsterdamska, M.E. Lynch, and J. Wajcman (eds.), *The Handbook of Science and Technology Studies*, MIT Press, 2008, 1065pp.

For an interesting literary discussion of the tension between the American pastoral ideal and spreading industrialization, see:

- L. Marx, *The Machine in the Garden: Technology and the Pastoral Ideal in America*, Oxford University Press, 1964, 414pp.

Index